Ludovic Kennedy was born
and educated at Eton and Christ Church,
Oxford. Since 1955 he has been well known
on British television – first as a newscaster,
then as presenter and interviewer on
programmes such as *This Week, Panorama,
Tonight, 24 Hours, Midweek* and *Did
you See?* The maker of many successful
documentaries, including *Battleship
Bismarck* and *Great Railway Journeys of the
World*, he has also written a great number of
naval books and travel anthologies as well as
four books on miscarriages of justice and his
autobiography, *On My Way to the Club.*

Portrait by Aubrey Davidson-Houston

TRUTH TO TELL

The Collected Writings of

Ludovic Kennedy

BLACK SWAN

TRUTH TO TELL
A BLACK SWAN BOOK 0 552 99505 3

Originally published in Great Britain by Bantam Press,
a division of Transworld Publishers Ltd

PRINTING HISTORY
Bantam Press edition published 1991
Black Swan edition published 1992

Extracts taken from:
Pursuit: The Chase and Sinking of the Bismarck (Collins 1974)
10 Rillington Place (Panther 1971)
Euthanasia: The Good Death (Counterblast Series, Chatto & Windus 1990)

This book was set in 10pt Melior by
Phoenix Typesetting, Burley-in-Wharfedale, West Yorkshire.

Black Swan Books are published by Transworld Publishers Ltd.,
61–63 Uxbridge Road, Ealing, London W5 5SA, in Australia by Transworld
Publishers (Australia) Pty. Ltd., 15–23 Helles Avenue, Moorebank,
NSW 2170, and in New Zealand by Transworld Publishers (N.Z.) Ltd.,
3 William Pickering Drive, Albany, Auckland.

Made and printed in Great Britain by
Cox & Wyman Ltd, Reading, Berks.

For Robert Kee
BBC
TRI
NCR

CONTENTS

FOREWORD

As I HAVE recounted in my autobiography, *On My Way to the Club*, I first knew that I wanted to become a writer at the age of about fifteen. Having no clear idea then of what I wanted to write about (as my father kept pointing out) I saw myself in a general way as the new white hope of the novel and the stage, though in the end had to settle, as most do, for something rather less. I might have become a better and a better-known writer had I given myself to it full-time, but the call of broadcasting had always been there too, and eventually that occupied at least half my time and energy for some thirty-five years.

I have always seen these two careers as complementary, satisfying two sides of my temperament. While writing is a solitary affair, television has provided the excitement and fun of working with others to meet a deadline and with it the heightened sense of occasion that precedes a public performance. I also think that the indecent exposure element of television presentation ('See what a good boy am I!') was, at least in the early days, a means of finally overcoming the sense of personal inadequacy which had clouded much of my youth, and of thus gaining public acceptance. On the other hand I have never felt able to ascribe to television the influence and importance that politicians like Lord Wilson and Lady Thatcher did and do. Certainly what is said or done on it, especially if controversial, makes an initial impact, but because the flickering images die as they are born, it is always an ephemeral impact. I never heard of anyone whose views were fundamentally changed by anything they saw or heard on television, but I have seen many instances of it confirming existing prejudices. Education, information and entertainment are what television is supposed to foster and what in fact it does best; and I am glad to have played some part in helping to promote them.

But writing is my first and last love; and the days spent alone with my typewriter (I abandoned the word processor after three weeks), chiselling out an article or a chapter of the current book, having total control over my own material, have been the most rewarding of my life. In the early days it was never easy and I would sometimes spend an hour or more in the construction of one small paragraph. But as I gained the confidence to develop a style, it became progressively easier so that today an article which would have kept me occupied all day is now completed between breakfast and lunch. Even so I am never satisfied with less than two drafts, sometimes more, in order to make my meaning as clear as words will allow, and also, so as not to lose forward momentum, to try and ensure that the last line of any paragraph and the last word of any line leads naturally to the next. I also attach importance to euphony, the *sound* of words as assembled in a certain order on the page.

Every writer of worth believes he has truths to tell so I hope I will not be thought presumptuous in bestowing that title on this collection. But in those books and articles about miscarriages of justice which may be judged to have been the mainstream of my writing life, truth, actual factual truth, takes on a terrible importance. Because truth was suppressed, both at the time and long afterwards, Timothy Evans, James Hanratty and Richard Hauptmann were executed for murders committed by others, Stephen Ward was driven to suicide as the result of the lies of prostitutes, Patrick Meehan, David Cooper, Michael McMahon, the Guildford Four and the Birmingham Six (and many, many others) spent some of the best years of their lives in prison as a consequence of police corruption and judicial incompetence; and some, if not all, would have been hanged had capital punishment still been in force. As a boy of a romantic turn of mind who had been brought up to believe that the British system of justice was the best in the world, I was all the more shocked when after the war I found that the assumption was often far from true. I think that my first book on this theme, *10 Rillington Place*, was also the first to challenge head-on the accepted wisdom of the courts, and for a young man venturing for the first time into a field that was not his, it was not a wholly comfortable experience. And yet when it came to it, in that and other cases, there was not the legal comeback I had anticipated. For when the truth is pointed out to those who have suppressed it, they are generally too taken aback and, I suspect, ashamed, to mount any sort of counter-attack. I am only too aware that living in a democracy such as ours has enabled me to do this.

I am again grateful to my wife for much sound advice and for supplying the title. I wish to express my thanks to HarperCollins for granting me permission to print an edited version of *Pursuit* which Fontana republished for the fiftieth anniversary of the *Bismarck* battle in May 1991, to Gollancz for permission to include an edited version of *10 Rillington Place* which is still in print in Grafton paperback, and to Chatto & Windus for permission to use material from *Euthanasia: The Good Death* in their Counterblast series. Robert Kee has, once again, been kind enough to vet the entire manuscript. I am also more than grateful to Ursula Mackenzie, my editor at Bantam Press, and to my literary agent, Gill Coleridge, for the happiest of working relationships and much good advice.

NAVAL

NELSON'S BAND OF BROTHERS

MY FAMILY HAS had many naval connections. First there was Captain Archibald Kennedy, RN, who after retirement at the end of the eighteenth century lived at No. 1 Broadway, New York City, but returned to the family home of Culzean Castle in Ayrshire on succeeding to the earldom of Cassillis: his son Robert was my twice great grandfather. Later came my father's bearded Uncle Will, Commander-in-Chief at the Nore, a lifelong destroyer of fur, feather and fin, outwardly a Puritan, in practice a bit of a lecher. And lastly my own father who rarely spoke of his naval days, though I knew that he had loved them more than any other. In his dressing-room at home were photographs of his ships and shipmates, his naval sword and a fragment of the Victory's flag at Trafalgar, left by a forebear whose husband had been a midshipman at Nelson's funeral. On the walls of the garage he had hung plaques bearing the names and mottoes of some of his ships.

When I was at prep school my Scottish grandfather took a house on the Moray Firth at Nairn every summer; and every year we waited for the arrival of the Atlantic fleet. With my father I would sit on the parapet at the end of the lawn and watch transfixed as the great grey flotillas, battleships and battlecruisers, cruisers and carriers and destroyers crept slowly along the northern shore and into the anchorage of Invergordon. One magical day we motored round there and had tea with a cousin who was navigating officer of the battle-ship Nelson; and I was so bowled over by the experience that on the way home I told my father that I too wanted to join the Navy. For various reasons (health was one, my incompetence with maths another) this was not possible in peacetime; but when in 1939 war broke out, I lost no time in writing to the Admiralty to offer my services. Their reply reached me six months later when I was sub-lieutenant of a fleet destroyer at Scapa Flow, regretting that there were no vacancies then but advising me to try again in another six months. It was during the war that I wrote my first book, Sub-Lieutenant, a light-hearted account of my early life and of the two years I spent in the fleet destroyer. Because it was the first of its kind and there was a shortage of other new books, it did very well, selling 20,000 copies.

It brought a long-term reward too. Having had only one year at Oxford before the war, and being aware of my ignorance of almost everything after it, I returned there in 1946 for another two years. During my last term in the summer of 1948, when I was uncertain what to do when I came down, I received a message from the historian A. L. Rowse at All Souls saying that he had a proposition he would like to put to me. He had been asked by a firm of publishers to commission a series of books on historical subjects. He had read Sub-Lieutenant and was also aware that I had been Literary Editor of the undergraduate magazine Isis and founder chairman of the OU Writers Club: I was therefore well qualified to write the book he had in mind, a study of Nelson's captains. He could not have suggested a more attractive proposition. Three years later the book was published under the title of Nelson's Band of Brothers (Nelson's name for them), and then republished some twenty years later by Collins with the simpler title of Nelson's Captains. Here is my account of the events leading up to the battle of Trafalgar.

To the casual reader the years 1803–5 are singularly devoid of naval interest. No fleet actions took place: no grand expeditions were launched. And yet these were two of the most important years in England's history; for her seamen the most arduous.

For Napoleon was surrounded. When Nelson took his station in the Victory off Toulon he completed the last link in a chain which stretched from the Texel to the north coast of Italy. Inside this chain Napoleon was impotent. He had the greatest army in the world and he was powerless to use it. Without sea-power his grandiose schemes for foreign aggression were set at nothing.

There remained, as he saw it, but one thing to do – to disregard the perimeter and strike at the centre, to attack England itself: once the centre had fallen, the perimeter would collapse with it. It was true that half his fleet were still making their way back from the West Indies to Rochefort, Ferrol and other Atlantic ports, but he did not intend to use them. He had accepted the supremacy of British sea-power and he proposed to ignore it.

This time invasion was to be no threat. Napoleon was in deadly earnest. He mobilized the resources of all France. Men were sent into the forests to hew down trees, and orders went out to all seaport and river towns of northern France to hasten the construction of flat-bottomed boats. The Grand Army began assembling in the areas of the Channel ports. Nor was France to undertake the enterprise alone: the Dutch were to provide 200 barges and 16,000 troops, the Swiss 30,000 troops. Napoleon intended that by the autumn 150,000 men would be ready to embark in 2,000 barges. They would sail on a foggy night in three groups and land in southern England: he would lead the expedition in the aptly named *Prince de Galle*. The impotence of his own ships would be to his advantage; for they would keep the British fleet immobilized off Brest. By the time Cornwallis arrived in the Channel, London would be sacked and among the ruins he would be accepting the country's surrender. The Grand Army was to destroy British sea-power.

In England the news of the project was at first received sceptically: there had been scares of this sort before and they had come to nothing. But as the great armament grew and rumours, magnified a hundredfold, filtered into London, the seriousness of the danger was appreciated. 'I begin to be half alarmed at the attempt to invade this country,' wrote Betsey Fremantle,[1] 'these horrid French are such desperate wretches.' Another correspondent wrote that the topic of invasion had superseded every other from conversation. Yet the mood of the country was more anger than fear: Napoleon was beginning to be hated as never before: and

[1] Wife of Thomas Fremantle, Nelson's friend and captain of the *Ganges*.

no-one doubted that if he came he and his hordes would be driven into the sea. 'I trust, my dear Fremantle, in God and English valour,' wrote Nelson from Toulon, 'we are enough in England if true to ourselves.'

This Shakespearian cry summed up the feeling everywhere. When preparations for resistance were made, the whole country answered to the call. 'Everybody here is a soldier,' wrote Eugenia Wynne, Betsey's sister at Burton, 'whether they like it or not.' On the whole they did. In answer to a request for volunteers 300,000 men came forward, among them Cabinet Ministers, poets and peers. There were no weapons to give them except pikes, and with these they drilled enthusiastically all over the countryside. As far north as the Lake District and the lowlands of Scotland, Wordsworth and Scott sweated on route marches over their native hills. Even the children became infected: from her bedroom at Swanbourne, Betsey watched seventeen Winslow boys, wearing paper caps and armed with sticks, march down the village street. All over the country great beacons were built to give warnings of the first landings: along the Channel coast a chain of Martello towers was erected as a first line of defence.

But as those who wielded British sea-power knew, England's defence lay elsewhere. They knew – although they could not convince their countrymen – that the navigational difficulties of Napoleon's schemes were impossible to overcome and that without a supporting battle-fleet his project must fail. When Admiral Montagu captured two invasion craft in the Downs he thought them so contemptible that they must be a feint for a different attack elsewhere. To a group of nervous fellow peers St Vincent replied caustically: 'I do not say they cannot come, my Lords. I only say they cannot come by sea.' The safety of the realm lay where it had always lain, not in pikes or beacons or Martello towers, but in the wooden walls; in the tested hands of the victors of St Vincent, the Nile and Copenhagen; in Keith and Louis off the Texel, Saumarez and Blackwood in the Channel, Cornwallis and Collingwood off Brest, Fremantle at Ferrol, Nelson, Hardy, Murray and Keats in the Mediterranean. It was those storm-tossed, weather-beaten ships, on which the

Grand Army never looked, that stood between it and the dominion of the world.

Although by the New Year of 1804 Napoleon's naval advisers had reached the same conclusions, it was a long time before the Emperor would admit it; and he never gave up hope or relaxed his preparations. As late as the autumn of 1804 Foley wrote to Nelson: 'We are more than ever threatened with invasion.' During these long months the chain that surrounded France was never broken. '*Les Anglais*,' wrote the Naval Prefect at Brest despairingly, '*sont constamment sur nos côtes.*' The strain on ships and crews, aggravated by St Vincent's economies, was terrific; and it needed men of the calibre of Nelson and Cornwallis to withstand them.

Their object – to keep their fleets at sea – was the same, but their problems were different. Cornwallis was within a day's sailing of England and had some of his wants supplied. Such visits were few and brief, for he was determined never to relax the watch. Against the merciless buffeting of the seas, bitter weather and lack of fresh food there were no remedies. 'Our ships are so worn down,' wrote the second Secretary of the Admiralty, 'that they are like post-horses during a general election.' When Collingwood arrived in harbour after a spell off Brest, he found the *Venerable* rotten to the core. 'We have been sailing for the last six months with only a sheet of copper between us and eternity.' The crews, in one captain's words, were 'worked to death'; and with salt beef, maggoty biscuits and stagnant water as their diet, it was impossible to check disease. Sir Robert Calder's crew became so infected with ulcers that he landed the worst on an island in Berehaven Bay to be cured by milk, vegetables, 'and the smell of earth'. The ship's company of the *Ganges* went down with a raging inflammation of the eyes; Fremantle stayed in his cabin for four days, his head swathed in bandages and a night-cap. Such outbreaks were the rule rather than the exception.

Nelson's chief problem was to keep his 'crazy' ships seaworthy: refitting was impossible, as his slender force of ten sail never exceeded that of the French in Toulon, and the nearest dockyards at Malta and Gibraltar were over seven hundred miles away. Nor, St Vincent told him, could he expect reinforcements. The health of the Fleet, although constantly on his mind, presented fewer difficulties, for the Mediterranean climate afforded an abundance of fruit and vegetables. More important was to keep the men contented, for being so far from home and with no prospect of returning to it, they felt in danger of being forgotten. It was a very real danger, as Nelson knew. When the City of London voted its thanks to the blockading fleets, they mentioned Cornwallis's flag-officers by name but omitted Nelson's. In reply to Nelson's protest the Lord Mayor said that he did not know who Nelson's flag-officers were. In order to combat the terrible effects of stagnation, of what Nelson called 'allowing the sameness of prospect to satiate the mind,' he kept the Fleet constantly on the move. Sometimes they visited the Maddalena Islands between Sardinia and Corsica, sometimes they looked in at Villefranche, Barcelona or Rosas. The results were all that Nelson hoped. In December 1804, eighteen months after taking the command, he wrote to the Admiralty: 'The Fleet is in perfect good health and good humour, unequalled by anything which has ever come within my knowledge, and equal to the most active service which the times may call for.'

The strain of the blockade fell most heavily on the captains. Such small luxuries as they enjoyed were small compensation for the responsibilities for their ships and health of their men. Often in rough weather they remained on deck all night, and days went by without their taking off their clothes. Nor, because tradition demanded they live mostly in seclusion, could they find relaxation in social intercourse. 'What is the use,' complained Fremantle, 'of large apartments and neat without society?' They snatched at any trivial pastime to occupy their minds. One captain grew mustard and cress on the quarter-deck, another kept a small aviary. Fremantle took to brewing spruce beer and smoking 'segars': in desperation for reading material he embarked on *Family Secrets*, a book of unnatural occurrences, thrust upon him by the purser: this sufficed until a parcel of Shakespeare and Cobbett arrived from Betsey. Their thoughts were divided equally between their ships and their homes; and no two worlds could have been more different. 'On the quarter-deck I am the captain,' wrote Codrington, 'in my cabin I am the husband and father with a full sense of the blessing of being so.' Nelson told Lady Hamilton that his only thoughts were of her and the French Fleet.

Their greatest comfort was letters from home. 'Pray tell me all you can think about our family,' wrote Collingwood, 'and about the beauties of your domain – the oaks, the woodland and the verdant meads.' Codrington told his wife that all her little chit-chat, however ridiculous in other eyes, was entertaining to him. For their part the captains found letter-writing difficult for, as Fremantle put it, the 'very sad sameness' made all days like one. 'It would be little to tell you,' said Codrington, 'that yesterday we wore ship and the day before we tacked ship, although any difficulties attending those simple acts might require all our skill and exertion.' Their letters, like their wives', were full of trivialities. Fremantle spoke of his need for toothpaste, of the goat that fell down the hatchway and deprived him of milk for his tea, of the dishonesty of his servant David, of his cook who knew nothing but roast and boiled.

Any deviation from routine was an opportunity for a long letter. When the *Ganges* visited Gibraltar for a refit, Fremantle drew up a journal of where he had dined, how he had spent the evening and his observations on the company; at Ferrol he described a dinner-party ashore where among his fellow guests were the captains of the French ships he was blockading. But such visits were rare and for the most part the captains suffered what Collingwood called 'unremitting hard service, giving up everything that is pleasurable to the soul or soothing to the mind, and engaging in a constant contest with the elements.'

Apart from his flag-captain Thomas Hardy and his First Captain or Fleet Administrator, Rear-Admiral Murray, who, Nelson said, were everything he could wish or desire, his captains were unknown to him. 'I am with perfect strangers,' he wrote soon after joining, 'although I believe very good men.' Except for Keats he did not attain the same intimacy with them as his comrades of the Nile. But on all he exercised the same healing influence, making them feel they belonged to an envied and exclusive brotherhood. He abhorred formal councils of war, preferring to take them into his confidence by walks on the quarter-deck or in the easy conversation of the dinner-table. His trust, as always, was implicit. 'I can assure you, Sir,' he wrote to a Spanish nobleman, 'that the word of every captain of a British man-of-war is equal, not only to mine, but to that of any person in Europe, however elevated his rank.'

There are many instances of his extraordinary tact and consideration. Keats complained that Murray was deliberately withholding a supply of hammocks of which his men were in need. Any other admiral would have sent Keats a sharp rebuke. But Nelson explained in the gentlest terms that there were not the hammocks to spare. 'The situation of the First Captain is certainly a very unthankful office, for if there is a deficiency of stores he must displease the whole fleet . . . I wish, my dear Keats, you would turn this in your mind and relieve Admiral Murray of the uneasiness your conversation has given him.' When Captain Layman was placed at the bottom of the list of commanders for running the *Raven* brig on the rocks, Nelson pleaded with the First Lord to rescind the sentence. 'I own myself one of those who do not fear the shore, for hardly any great things are done in a small ship by a man that is; therefore I make very great allowances for him. Nor do I regret the loss of the *Raven* compared to the value of Captain Layman's services which are a national loss.' This was the Nelson touch and its effect was magic. 'The admirals and captains,' wrote his secretary, 'are all wonderfully attached to him and as contented as men can be. Those that had been a long time in the country before we arrived and were anxious to get home have forgot that entirely.'

By the summer of 1804 Napoleon at last realized what his advisers had been pressing all along, that only with the support of his fleet could an invasion of England succeed. As the months passed, his ambitions grew. To reinforce his own ships he proposed to add the fleet of Spain. Secret negotiations with his old ally bore fruit when Pitt, hearing that French troops were on their way to take over the ships at Ferrol, decided to force Spain's hand. A squadron of frigates was ordered to intercept a Spanish treasure-fleet returning from South America. The Spanish flagship blew up, carrying to the bottom the Captain General of Peru and his wife and family. On 12 December 1804 Spain declared war.

Napoleon's final grand design was that the squadrons at Brest, Toulon and Rochefort, commanded by Admirals Ganteaume, Villeneuve and Missiessy, together with what Spanish ships were available at Cadiz and Cartagena, should break their blockades simultaneously and sail for the West Indies. While waiting for each other there they were to destroy as much British trade as possible, then having formed a junction of fifty sail of the line, to double back to Europe, enter the unguarded Channel and rendezvous with Napoleon off Boulogne.

From the start the scheme misfired. The only squadron to break out was Missiessy's who, having reached the West Indies and waited in vain for Ganteaume and Villeneuve, sailed for home. An angry Napoleon, not knowing of Missiessy's return, ordered Villeneuve to try again. This time he succeeded in getting clear, picked up one French and five Spanish ships under Admiral Gravina off Cadiz and with a total of seventeen ships of the line headed for Martinique. Nelson wasted a week in the Mediterranean looking for him, then from intelligence picked up at Gibraltar went in pursuit. In the West Indies he missed Villeneuve by a whisker; who having heard of Nelson's arrival lost no time in turning for home. Again Nelson made after him, but fearful that Villeneuve might fall on British shipping in the Bay of Biscay, dispatched the fast brig Curieux under Captain Bettesworth to England with the news. Eighteen days later the new First Lord of the Admiralty, the eighty-year-old Lord Barham, made his dispositions: the blockading squadrons off Rochefort and Ferrol to unite under Rear-Admiral Sir Robert Calder and take station to meet Villeneuve a hundred miles west of Cape Finisterre. The timing could not have been better. On 22 July (the same day that Nelson arrived at Gibraltar and stepped ashore for the first time in two years), Villeneuve with his seventeen sail and Calder with his fifteen met. But Calder was *not of the stuff of Nelson, and having captured two Spanish ships made no attempt to re-engage. 'I had no friendly port to go to, and had the Ferrol and Rochefort squadrons come out, I must have fallen an easy prey.' Villeneuve, thankful for such a speedy release, made for Cadiz. Three weeks later Nelson and the* Victory *reached Spithead; and the day after he set out in the rain, for the last time, for Merton and London.*

The ignorance of Englishmen as to sea affairs had been reflected during the past three months in the country's changing moods. First it was one of anger: people were shocked at the apparent ease with which the enemy moved in and out of port. 'Their idea is', wrote Collingwood, 'that we are like sentinels standing at a door who must see and may interrupt all who attempt to go into it.' As the weeks passed without news of Nelson or the combined fleets they became afraid. In their fear they blamed Nelson just as they had done at his failure to find Brueys.[1] 'The cry is stirring up fast against him,' wrote Admiral Lord Radstock to his son in the *Victory*, 'and the loss of Jamaica would sink all his past services into oblivion.' Then came the news of the pursuit across the Atlantic, Nelson's saving of the West Indies, and the return of the combined Franco–Spanish fleets to harbour.

The relief was enormous. Nelson's enterprise captured the public imagination like nothing before. Everywhere people's hearts flowed with thankfulness, and their welcome exceeded that of his greatest victories. At Portsmouth crowds thronged the ramparts and greeted his barge with prolonged huzzas. In London he was welcomed 'almost as a conqueror'. He could not venture into the street without being surrounded by a mob. 'It is really quite affecting,' wrote Lord Minto, 'to see the wonder and admiration and love and respect of the whole world.'

Nelson took a more sober view. 'I am now set up as a conjuror,' he told Keats, 'and God knows they will soon find out I am far from one.' His mind was already on the future. On his first morning in London he called on the

[1] The French admiral he had defeated at the battle of the Nile in August 1798.

First Lord who, he confessed, was almost an entire stranger. Barham had always been sceptical of Nelson's reputation, but a half-hour's interview altered his opinion; and it was arranged that Nelson should return to the Mediterranean as soon as he and the *Victory* were ready.

Nelson divided the last ten days of August between his home at Merton and London. It was a time of bustle rather than repose, for he had many engagements to fill, his house was full of relations and there was a constant stream of visitors. But all the time he was thinking of when he would be called and of the tactics he would adopt when finally he fell in with the French Fleet. Captain Keats stopped at Merton after paying off the *Superb*, and to him, pacing the strip of grass he called the quarter-deck, Nelson outlined his tentative plan of attack.

The established system of conducting a sea-fight was for both fleets to converge from parallel lines, and for each ship to grapple with her opposite in the line. The disadvantage of this method, said Nelson, was that no day was long enough to obtain a decisive result. He would therefore form his fleet into three divisions. One would be kept in reserve to be employed by the admiral commanding it as circumstances required. With the other two divisions in line abreast, he would launch his attack at right angles to the enemy's line. He hoped to break the line at about a third of the way from the van-ship: the van and rear would be immobilized, the centre crushed: it was the embodiment of his favourite dictum: 'Only numbers can annihilate.' 'What do you think of it?' he asked Keats, and then before Keats could reply, he exclaimed: 'I'll tell you what I think of it. I think it will surprise and confound the enemy. They won't know what I am about. It will bring forward a pell-mell battle, and that is what I want.'

The call came sooner than Nelson expected. When Napoleon heard of Villeneuve's return to Ferrol he was waiting with his army at Boulogne. Furious at his failure, he ordered him to sail again. On 13 August Villeneuve left Ferrol with an augmented fleet of twenty-nine sail of the line. News of his departure reached England soon after Nelson's arrival and people again became uneasy. But Villeneuve did not get far. His ships were rotten, the crews seasick and mutinous, and he knew that he could not reach the Channel without fighting Cornwallis. On 15 August he abandoned the enterprise and fled for Cadiz. Collingwood guarding the approaches with three sail retired southwards; then having sent for Admirals Calder and Bickerton and dispatched the *Euryalus* to England, he resumed his watch.

The *Euryalus* made a five-day passage to Lymington, and on the evening of 1 September Captain Blackwood set out in a post-chaise for London. At five the next morning he called at Merton and found Nelson already up and dressed. There was no need to explain his arrival. 'I am sure you bring me news of the French and Spanish Fleets,' said Nelson, 'and I think I shall yet have to beat them.' Blackwood went on to London where the news soon spread. 'Thank God, thank God, a thousand and a thousand times,' wrote Lord Radstock to Nelson, 'that these Jack O'Lanterns are once more safely housed without having done that mischief which was so justly to be dreaded.' From the Channel greater news followed. Disgusted by the timidity of his admirals, Napoleon had given up all plans for invasion, broken his camp, and marched southwards to face a new Russo–Austrian alliance which Pitt had once more brought into being. The Grand Army had bowed to British sea-power.

England was now ready to take the offensive. On the morning of Blackwood's arrival Nelson followed him to the Admiralty and saw the First Lord. He agreed to join the Fleet as soon as the *Victory* was ready. His command was to include the whole of the Mediterranean, Gibraltar, and the approaches to Cadiz.

At the end of the interview Barham picked up a copy of the Navy List and asked Nelson to choose his captains. 'Choose yourself, my Lord,' replied Nelson, 'the same spirit actuates the whole profession. You cannot choose wrong.' But Barham insisted. With his vast experience he knew, as St Vincent had known in 1798, and Nelson himself knew, the importance of dependable subordinates. 'Have no scruples, Lord Nelson, there is my secretary. Give your orders to him and rely on it that they shall be implicitly obeyed.'

Most of the captains of Nelson's choice were already with the Fleet. But there was one he could help. Two days before he had received another letter from Captain Berry[1] with the postmark Edinburgh. Two changes at the Admiralty had led Berry to hope for employment, but all his requests had been turned down. The consequence, he said, was disgust on his part and a resolve to apply no more; and he had taken his wife on a tour of the Lake District and Highlands. 'A man's standing in the Service,' he wrote bitterly, 'and his reputation – and who has not that reputation that served with you – all goes for nought. I know Your Lordship will do what you can.' Such an appeal was not to be resisted.

There was some doubt as to Hardy's ability to serve. The long months at sea had brought on severe rheumatism, and on arrival at Portsmouth he was very ill. Nelson had asked the Admiralty to appoint Captain Conn (late of the *Canopus*) temporarily, so that in case of emergency 'I may not have a perfect stranger with me.' However, a week's convalescence in Dorset (during which he had a long audience with the King on his last visit to Weymouth) restored Hardy to health; and on the day after Blackwood's arrival he returned to Portsmouth.

Nelson's last ten days in England are among the most romantic of his life. In his own time it was not Trafalgar that stamped his fame but the years of endurance which led to it. The chase to the West Indies had established the country's faith in him as never before; and when people heard that he was going out once more, nothing could restrain them. Messages of goodwill poured in from all over England. Sam Sutton called in person at Merton, Admiral Murray waited for him at Portsmouth. In London, Lords Hood and Radstock sent messages they would shake his hand at any place, day and hour that he cared to name. The Prince of Wales, just back from Stowe where he had been a fellow guest with Betsey, summoned him to Carlton House to say goodbye. Pitt, at his last interview, accompanied him to the door of Downing Street. 'I do not think,' said Nelson proudly, 'he would have done so much for a prince of the blood.'

Lord Minto said that Nelson's reception on his arrival was beyond anything in a play or a poem. So, too, was

---

[1] Sir Edward Berry, Nelson's flag-captain at the battle of the Nile.

his departure. It is impossible to read the story of the last weeks of his life without feeling that it was part of a predestined pattern.

Nelson's genius was composed of many parts. There was his devotion to duty, his singleness of mind, his courage, his humanity, his pride; but greater than all of these was his absolute surrender to his destiny. What makes his story one of the greatest of historical tragedies is his certainty of approaching death and conquest of the spirit over it. During these last days the thought of return hardly entered his head. Before leaving London he called on the upholsterers who were storing Hallowell's coffin[1] and told them, light-heartedly enough, that he might soon need it. On the night of his departure from Merton he prayed by the bedside of his daughter; then, before entering the coach, he wrote in his private diary:

'*Friday night.* At half past ten, drove from dear, dear Merton where I left all which I hold dear in this world to go to serve my King and Country. May the great God whom I adore, enable me to fulfil the expectations of my country; and if it is His good pleasure that I should return, my thanks will never cease being offered up to the throne of His mercy. If it is His good Providence to cut short my days upon earth, I bow with the greatest submission, relying that He will protect those so dear to me, that I may leave behind. Amen. Amen. Amen.'

He arrived at Portsmouth early the next morning and was met by Hardy. He dispatched his business by noon and in the afternoon made his way to the bathing-machines where the *Victory*'s barge was awaiting him. The story of his final departure is told in Southey's famous words:

'A crowd collected in his train, pressing forward to obtain a sight of his face – many were in tears and many knelt down before him and blessed him as he passed. All men knew that his heart was as humane as it was fearless; that there was not in his nature the slightest alloy of selfishness or cupidity; but

[1] Made by Captain Hallowell's carpenters from the mainmast of Admiral Brueys's flagship *L'Orient* after the battle of the Nile, and given to Nelson as a present.

that with perfect and entire devotion he served his country with all his heart and with all his soul and with all his strength: and therefore they loved him as truly and fervently as he loved England.'

He embarked in the barge with Hardy, and the crowds thronged upon the parapet waved after him. He turned to Hardy and murmured: 'I had their huzzas before. Now I have their hearts.' It was what he had always wanted.

Next morning the *Victory* and the *Euryalus* made sail out of harbour and set course for Cape Trafalgar.

During the past month Collingwood had been keeping watch off Cadiz. On 22 August he was joined by Bickerton and four sail from the Mediterranean, and a week later by eighteen sail under Calder, including the remnant of Nelson's Mediterranean Fleet. With this force he waited for Nelson's arrival.

Collingwood was not a popular officer. It is odd that he should have been a friend of Nelson, for no two men could have been less alike. 'In the life of Lord Collingwood,' wrote George Elliot many years later, 'he is represented as the kindest-hearted and most considerate old man possible. I was many years in company with him and always considered him a selfish old bear. That he was a brave, stubborn, persevering and determined officer everyone acknowledged, but he had few, if any, friends and no admirers. In body and mind he was iron, and very cold iron.'

Collingwood's conduct of the Fleet was the very opposite to that of Nelson. He seldom entertained, he discouraged intercourse between his captains, he allowed no neutral provision boats to enter the Fleet. His officers did not take to this kindly. They did not want society so much for its own sake as for what Captain Codrington called 'that harmony so essential to a fleet destined to act well together; *of binding the captains to their admiral*.' Calder, said Codrington, had no opportunity of entertaining his captains except by chance. 'A court martial on board his ship yesterday admitted us to as social a dinner as I was ever at. It was really a most animating sight; an admiral surrounded by twenty of his captains in social intercourse, showing a strong desire to support each other cordially and manfully in the event of battle.'

But such occasions were rare. The captains became disgruntled and their only consolation, said Fremantle, lay in the arrival of Nelson. 'I expect very soon to see your Lordship's handwriting at the bottom of my order,' Admiral Louis wrote, 'believe me it would be one of the first comforts I could name.' Codrington exclaimed in despair: 'For charity's sake, send us Lord Nelson, oh, ye men of power!'

He came at last on 28 September, and his coming was more wonderful than he or they had dreamed. 'Lord Nelson is arrived,' wrote Codrington, 'and a sort of general joy has been the consequence.' On his first two evenings all the admirals and captains dined in the *Victory*. 'The reception I met with on joining the Fleet,' he wrote, 'caused the sweetest sensation of my life. The officers who came on board to welcome my return forgot my rank as Commander-in-Chief in the enthusiasm with which they greeted me.' Fremantle told Betsey: 'The whole system here is so completely changed that it wears quite a different aspect.' Captain Duff of the *Mars*, an officer unknown to Nelson, wrote: 'He is so good and pleasant a man that we all like to do what he likes without any kind of orders. He is the pleasantest admiral I ever served under.'

For his Mediterranean captains Nelson had a special word. 'I was truly glad to see my old friends again,' he wrote to Louis, 'I have much to tell you.' Fremantle dined in the *Victory* with only Collingwood as his fellow guest; and Nelson gave him a letter from Harriet that Betsey had been safely delivered of her third daughter. Fremantle thought Hardy very ill – 'twenty years older than when I last saw him,' but well suited to his job: Nelson had 'grown fatter' and looked better than ever. 'I staid with him until eight at night – he would not let me leave him before. He desired me to come to him whenever I chose and to dine with him as often as convenient.'

Greetings over, Nelson made preparations for battle; for he knew that the presence of so many ships in Cadiz would strain its resources to breaking-point and that soon Villeneuve must put to sea. He removed the Fleet from within sight of Cadiz to about fifty miles to the westward, so as to lure Villeneuve out and prevent his own ships from being driven into the Mediterranean by a westerly gale. He posted Blackwood in the *Euryalus* off the harbour approaches and kept communication with him by a chain of battleships. 'Let me know every movement,' he told him, 'I rely on you that we can't miss getting hold of them. Watch all points and all winds and weathers.'

Stocks of food and water were very low and Nelson ordered his ships to proceed to Gibraltar in rotation to re-provision. The first to go were Rear-Admiral Louis's squadron consisting of the *Canopus*, *Queen*, *Spencer*, *Tigre* and *Zealous*. Louis and Hallowell were heartbroken. 'You are sending us away, my Lord,' complained Louis, 'the enemy will come out and we shall have no share in the battle.' Nelson comforted him. 'The enemy *will* come out and we shall fight them; and I send you first to insure your being here to help beat them.' But Louis had spoken to Nelson for the last time.

On 9 October Nelson circulated his famous memorandum of attack – the final version of the plan he had outlined to Keats in the garden of Merton. He had already described it to the admirals and captains on the two nights after his arrival, and its effect had been magical. 'When I came to explain to them the Nelson touch,' he told Lady Hamilton, 'it was like an electric shock. Some shed tears, all approved. "It was new – it was singular – it was simple!" and from admirals downwards it was repeated, "It must succeed if ever they will allow us to get at them." '

The memorandum opened with the celebrated phrase: 'The order of sailing is to be the order of battle.' This was to save time, for every moment was precious. Then followed the plan of attack: two divisions to break the enemy's line at the centre, the third to support one of the other two. But it was not to be adhered to rigidly. 'Nothing is sure in a sea-fight beyond all others . . . In case signals can neither be seen nor perfectly understood, no captain can do very wrong if he places his ship alongside that of an enemy.' Here, summed up in a few words, was what Nelson had practised all his life – liberty for subordinates within a framework of law. It was what made him turn out of the line at St Vincent, it was what won him the Battle of the Nile; it was the great quality which stamped his conduct of the Fleet in peace and war.

31

And during these last days Nelson worked for that other great ideal which had served him so well in the past – perfect cohesion of the Fleet, the 'binding of captains to their admiral'. 'I am not come forth to find difficulties,' he wrote to Ball,[1] 'but to remove them.' Collingwood complained of his new flag-captain, Rotherham. 'We can, my dear Coll, have no little jealousies,' Nelson reminded him. 'In the presence of the enemy, all Englishmen should be as brothers.' Louis, on his way to Gibraltar, informed Nelson that Blackwood was not keeping his proper station. Blackwood wrote testily to Nelson refuting it. 'Do not, my dear Blackwood,' replied Nelson, 'be angry with anyone. It was only a laudable anxiety in Admiral Louis and nothing like complaining.' To Admiral Knight he wrote: 'In our several stations, my dear Admiral, we must all put our shoulders together, and make the great machine of the Fleet intrusted to our charge go on smoothly.'

In keeping with this attitude was his treatment of Rear-Admiral Sir Robert Calder. Public opinion in England against Calder had been stirring up fast: Nelson's brilliant pursuit to the West Indies had made Calder's failure seem all the more lamentable. ('We are all raving mad at Sir Robert Calder,' wrote one lady. 'I could have done better myself.') On joining the Fleet, Nelson had the unpleasant duty of informing Calder of the Admiralty's disapprobation and that a court of inquiry had been ordered. Calder had been at sea ever since his action, and had little idea of the stir against him. 'Sir Robert has an ordeal to pass through,' Nelson told Collingwood, 'which he little expects.' Calder begged Nelson to be allowed to return home in his flag-ship, the *Prince of Wales*; and subject to the arrival of reinforcements, Nelson agreed. But with Louis's squadron at Gibraltar, Nelson could hardly deprive the Fleet of a ninety-gun ship. When Calder heard that he was to go home in a frigate, he wrote to Nelson: 'The contents of your Lordship's letter have cut me to the soul. If I am to be turned out of my ship, after all that has passed, I have only to request I may be allowed to take my captain and such officers as I find necessary for the justification of my conduct as an officer,

[1] Captain of the *Alexander* at the battle of the Nile.

and that I may be permitted to go without a moment's loss of time. My heart is broken.' Nelson's humanity could not resist this appeal; and though Calder was no friend, he gave him permission to return in the *Prince of Wales*, thus depriving himself on the eve of battle of one of his most powerful ships. 'I may be thought wrong as an officer to disobey the orders of the Admiralty,' he wrote to Barham, 'but I trust that I shall be considered to have done right as a man, and to a brother officer in affliction – my heart could not stand it and so the thing must rest.'

Calder's departure reduced Nelson's force to twenty-eight sail, but the balance was partly restored by the arrival of Berry in the *Agamemnon*. Berry had had an exciting passage, having fallen foul of the Rochefort squadron the night before; and only superb seamanship had enabled him to escape. The *Agamemnon* was the ship in which, ten years earlier on the Riviera, Nelson had assumed command of his first detached squadron. It was a happy circumstance that she should arrive to take part in his last battle, commanded by her old first lieutenant and one of his most devoted admirers.

Berry's reputation as a fighter was proverbial and his arrival caused a wave of optimism. 'Sir E. Berry is such a bearer of good fortune,' Blackwood wrote to Nelson, 'that I feel the enemy will make a bolt.' Nelson was more laconic. 'Here comes that fool Berry. Now we shall have a fight.' Six days later, at seven in the morning, the *Euryalus* was observed flying the long-awaited signal: 'The Enemy is coming out of port.'

When Nelson received Blackwood's signal he was fifty miles out in the Atlantic. He hoisted the signals 'General Chase' and 'Prepare for Battle' and stood with the Fleet towards the Straits. They continued under a press of canvas all day, but by one o'clock the next morning when they reached the entrance to the Straits there was no sign of the enemy. Nor, as Nelson had hoped, was there any news of Louis.

Unknown to him the combined fleets had had great difficulty in leaving harbour and were only now clearing the coast: they were steering to the north-westwards so as to get a clear run through the Straits. Nelson heard this news at 7 a.m.

and wore his fleet on to a parallel course. Visibility was poor and Blackwood did not have another opportunity of speaking to Nelson until the afternoon. 'The enemy', he telegraphed, 'appears determined to push to the westwards.' 'That they shall not do,' wrote Nelson in his diary, 'if in the power of Nelson and Bronte to prevent them.'[1] And he signalled to Blackwood: 'I rely on your keeping sight of the enemy.'

By 2 p.m. the combined fleets were well clear of the coast, and stood southwards for the Straits. Nelson continued on his northerly course, for he was afraid that if he showed himself too soon Villeneuve might bolt for Cadiz. Collingwood had come on board the day before, and urged him to attack at once. But Nelson was not the hot-blooded fighter he is sometimes represented: before every action he weighed the chances and made his dispositions accordingly. What he wanted was a full day's fighting, for only this could assure him the annihilating victory he had planned. To begin an action which might be broken off by darkness or by Villeneuve bolting for Cadiz would be worse than no action at all. Not until 8 p.m., when the combined fleets were to the eastwards of him, did he too turn south.

There was nothing to do now but maintain his distance and bearing from the enemy and alter the course of his Fleet as they altered theirs. He signalled his night instructions to Blackwood: 'If the enemy are standing to the southwards or towards the Straits burn two blue lights together every hour in order to make the greater blaze. If the enemy are standing to the westwards, three guns quick, every hour.' That evening he entertained a party of midshipmen to dinner. 'Tomorrow,' he said to them, 'I will do that which will give you younger gentlemen something to talk and think about for the rest of your lives. But I shall not live to know about it myself.'

The two fleets steered southwards all night. At four in the morning the British Fleet again wore to the northwards. This was a preliminary to the attack and to cut off Villeneuve's line of retreat from Cadiz. Then at 6.30 Nelson hoisted the signal for his twenty-seven ships to form order of sailing in two columns (the third he discarded owing to lack of

[1] Nelson had been created Duke of Bronte by the King of Naples.

34

numbers), to steer eastwards towards the enemy fleet, and to prepare for battle.

Slowly the great ships took up their stations. In the weather column the *Victory* was followed by the *Téméraire*, *Neptune*, *Leviathan*, *Conqueror*, *Britannia*, *Agamemnon*, *Ajax*, *Orion*, *Minotaur* and *Spartiate*: a mile to the southward Collingwood's lee column formed up in the order *Royal Sovereign*, *Belleisle*, *Mars*, *Tonnant*, *Bellerophon*, *Colossus*, *Achilles*, *Revenge*, *Polyphemus*, *Swiftsure*, *Defence*, *Thunderer*, *Prince* and *Defiance*. Ten miles away on the eastern horizon, Villeneuve was standing to the southward with his thirty-three ships strung out in one single column. He watched Nelson's approach for about half an hour: then his nerve failed and he turned to the northward to bring Cadiz under his lee. By this manoeuvre Admiral Dumanoir Le Pelley in the *Formidable* led the van, Villeneuve in the *Bucentaure* and Admiral Cisneros in the *Santissima Trinidad* were in the centre, and Gravina in the *Principe de Asturias* commanded the rear. But Villeneuve was now too far to the southward to have any hopes of reaching Cadiz. Nelson swung his column a point or two to the northwards and signalled to Collingwood: 'I mean to attack the enemy's van and centre.'

Never did British sailors prepare to go into action with more confidence in their cause nor more certain hopes of success. An officer in the *Belleisle* wrote that he was woken by the cheering of the crew, and that the delight on their faces exceeded anything he had ever witnessed. The first lieutenant of the *Ajax* found some of his men polishing the guns 'as if for an inspection', and others dancing a hornpipe. 'All seemed deeply anxious to come to close quarters with the enemy.' During the morning the ships' companies were piped to dinner. The crew of the *Tonnant* sat down to bread and cheese and ale. 'Believe me,' said one of them, 'we ate and drank and were as cheerful as ever we were over a pot of beer.' The composure of the officers was also remarked on. An officer who spoke to Collingwood several times during the day was amazed that 'he did not show the slightest change from his ordinary manner.' His flag-captain, Rotherham, was asked to remove his cocked hat as it would make a mark for enemy sharpshooters. He replied that he had always fought in a cocked hat and always would.

Yet no-one doubted the gravity of what lay ahead. Many officers and men made their wills. A sailor in the *Revenge* heard several of his shipmates say: 'If one of Johnny Crapeau's shots knocks my head off, you will take all my effects; and if you are killed and I am not, why I will have all yours.' Nelson sent a last line to Lady Hamilton; Captains Blackwood and Duff wrote to their wives that they hoped to prove themselves worthy of them. Midshipman Aikenhead expressed his feelings to his family much as Midshipman Thorp had done before Santa Cruz: 'Should I, my dear parents, fall in defence of my King, let that thought console you. I feel not the least dread of my spirits. Accept, perhaps for the last time, your son's love.' Of these officers, only Blackwood was to survive the day.

In the *Victory* Nelson was making his own final preparations. He had sent for Blackwood early in the day and told him that he meant to keep him on board until the last minute, as he was going to 'bleed' the captains of the frigates. Blackwood asked if he might have the command of one of the two battleships whose captains had gone home as witnesses for Sir Robert Calder. Nelson refused him, saying it was their first lieutenants' 'birthrights'; but the mention of his unfortunate admiral struck a sympathetic chord. 'Hardy,' he said, 'what would poor Sir Robert Calder give to be with us now?'

Soon after Blackwood arrived Nelson took him and Hardy to his cabin to witness a last codicil to his will, in which he left Lady Hamilton and his daughter Horatia 'as a legacy to my King and country'. Then the two captains accompanied Nelson on an inspection of the mess-decks where the men of a dozen nations were waiting by their guns. Several times Nelson asked Blackwood how many prizes he thought they would take. Blackwood suggested fourteen would be 'a glorious result'. Nelson replied: 'I shall not be satisfied with anything less than twenty.'

Many of Nelson's officers were concerned about his safety, for which he showed his usual disregard. Hardy pointed out that his medals and orders would make him a conspicuous target for enemy riflemen. Nelson agreed, but said it was now too late to be shifting a coat. Blackwood urged him to move his flag to the *Euryalus* where it would be easier to conduct the battle. Nelson said that he would not hear of it and gave as his reason, 'the force of example'. The two captains then persuaded him to let the *Victory* drop back to third in the line, as it was essential that he should keep out of fire as long as possible. Blackwood went over to the *Téméraire* and *Neptune* to order them ahead. But Nelson made no attempt to shorten sail, and when the *Téméraire* crept up on his quarter he shouted over: 'I'll thank you, Captain Harvey, to keep in your proper station.' A few minutes later Fremantle received the same curt order.

A little after eleven o'clock Nelson retired to his cabin to compose his famous farewell prayer. With the opening lines he sketched in, simply and fittingly, the background picture, the fulfilment of his life's work. 'At daylight saw the enemy's combined fleet from East to E.S.E. Bore away. Made the signal for order of sailing and to prepare for battle.' This was the overture; then, with a humility matched only by his transcendent courage, he gave himself up to his destiny. 'May the Great God whom I worship grant to my country and for the benefit of Europe in general, a great and glorious victory; and may no misconduct in anyone tarnish it; and may humanity after victory be the predominant feature in the British Fleet. For myself individually I commit my life to Him who made me, and may His blessing light upon my endeavours for serving my country faithfully. To Him I resign myself and the just cause which is entrusted to me to defend. Amen. Amen. Amen.'

Lieutenant Pasco, the flag-lieutenant, now entered the cabin on some personal request. He found the admiral kneeling at his desk in prayer, and withdrew. ('I could not at such a moment disturb him with any grievances of mine.') Nelson followed him to the poop. The wind had dropped almost entirely, but a heavy swell was setting from the westward, which heralded the approach of a storm. Fearful that after the battle the Fleet would be driven on a lee shore, Nelson signalled to prepare to anchor at the close of day.

It was at this moment, all preparations having been made, that he asked Blackwood whether he did not think that one more signal was wanting. After consultation with him and Hardy he called to his flag-lieutenant: 'Mr Pasco, I wish to say to the Fleet, "England confides that every man will do his duty." You must be quick for I have one more signal to make which is for close action.' Pasco asked if he might substitute 'expects' for 'confides' as the former was in the signal book and the latter not. 'That will do,' replied Nelson, 'make it directly.' Throughout the Fleet the signal was received with bursts of cheering: on some the effect was described as 'truly sublime'; others, who missed the emotional content ('Do our duty!' cried one man. 'Why, of course we'll do our duty.'), were happy that their beloved admiral had remembered them.

The distance between the two fleets was now less than a mile. The scene, as one captain described it, was 'beautiful' and one which few ever forgot. The clouds had disappeared and the pale blue of the sky contrasted with the richer colour of the sea. The combined fleets, still standing to the northward with the wind on their larboard beam, were strung out in one long crescent, the bulge towards the coast. Some of their ships were painted black, others black with red and yellow streaks. In the centre, shining in scarlet and white and with a huge, white figurehead of the Holy Trinity, towered the four-decked *Santissima Trinidad*. The British Fleet had kept their formation of two columns, about a mile apart, with Collingwood's slightly in the lead: the figurehead of his ship was a full-length carving of George III, wearing the battle-dress of a Roman emperor and with the twin emblems of Fame and Fortune blowing golden trumpets on either side. As the great ships, with their black-and-yellow chequered hulls and carrying a full spread of canvas, glided through the water, they looked like a flock of great, white birds. On board many of the bands were playing 'Britons, strike home', and 'Rule, Britannia!'

The last twenty minutes were the most exacting of all. There is nothing more awful for a fighting man than to remain static under fire, having the means but not the sanction to reply to it. The enemy, being beam on to the British columns, were able to open fire first, and before long had begun to inflict casualties. The anxiety to return fire was very great, if only as a means of covering the ships in smoke; but the captains' orders were explicit and no-one disobeyed them. Villeneuve, watching this slow relentless approach, animal-like in its stealth, was quite unnerved. 'Nothing but victory', he murmured to his officers, 'can attend such gallant conduct.'

A little after noon Nelson watched Collingwood break the enemy's line between the *Santa Ana* and the *Fougeux*. 'See how that noble fellow Collingwood carries his ship into action,' he cried. His own turn was about to come, and now it was time to say goodbye to the faithful Blackwood. 'I can do no more,' he said to him. 'We must trust to the Great Disposer of all events, and to the justice of our cause. I thank God for this great opportunity of doing my duty.' They shook hands at the front of the poop. 'I trust, my Lord,' said Blackwood, 'that on my return to the *Victory* I shall find your Lordship well and in the possession of twenty prizes.' Nelson's reply remained with him for the rest of his life: 'God bless you, Blackwood. I shall never speak to you again.'

During the last few hundred yards of her approach the *Victory* ran through a curtain of fire. Her steering-wheel was smashed, her sails and rigging cut to pieces: there were many casualties on the upper deck, including Nelson's secretary Mr Scott. As Nelson and Hardy were pacing the deck a splinter tore off the buckle of Hardy's shoe. 'This is too warm work to last long,' said Nelson. Then the moment came for breaking the enemy's line. Their ships were so close together that Hardy called out that he could not get through without running on board the *Bucentaure* or *Redoutable*. 'I cannot help it,' replied Nelson. 'Go on board which you please.' The *Victory* crossed the wake of the *Bucentaure* and poured the whole of her larboard broadside into her stern, killing and wounding 400 men; then she ranged up alongside the *Redoutable*. One by one the other ships followed her into action.

For the next three hours the battle raged with a ferocity that equalled the victory at Copenhagen. 'When the game began,' said a sailor of the *Royal Sovereign*, 'I wished myself at Warnborough with the plough; but when they had given us one duster, I bid Fear kiss my bottom and set to in good

39

earnest.' Midshipman Castle of the same ship told his family: 'It was glorious work. I think you would have liked to see me thump it into her quarters.' Many ships fought so closely that their guns touched the enemy hulls. After each salvo the crew of the *Victory* poured water on the sides of the *Redoutable*, so as to prevent both ships from catching fire. Soon the smoke in the gun-decks became so thick that the crews could not see their neighbours. 'All that they knew', said one seaman, 'was the crash of the shot smashing through the rending timbers, and then followed the hoarse bellowings of the captains of the guns as men were missed at the posts, calling out to the survivors, "Close up there, close up."' The slaughter was terrible. With her first broadside the *Royal Sovereign* killed and wounded more than half the crew of the *Fougeux*. Of the *Redoutable*'s ship's company of 600, 490 were killed and 81 wounded. Dr Scott, the chaplain of the *Victory*, described the cockpit as a butcher's shambles.

Stories of individual bravery were legion. Under the terrible fire of the British guns, the enemy ships began to drop out of action one by one, and orders were given for boarders. Captain Durham of the *Defiance* ordered Midshipman Jack Spratt to take possession of *L'Aigle*. All the *Defiance*'s boats were smashed, so Spratt placed a sword in his teeth and an axe in his belt and calling to the others to follow him, plunged into the sea. But the noise of the guns drowned his orders and he reached *L'Aigle*'s stern alone. He fought his way single-handed from the gunroom to the poop, killing and wounding several men, and although badly wounded himself, succeeded in holding the poop until the two ships touched and his comrades were able to jump over and relieve him. A seaman of the *Conqueror*, whose leg was amputated, said to the surgeon: 'Ah, Mr Beattie, I shall live now half as cheap as before: one pair of stockings will serve me twice as long.' In the *Tonnant* a splinter almost severed a gunner's toe from his foot. An officer urged him to go to the cockpit and have it dressed. 'No, sir, I am not the fellow to go below for a scratch'; and taking out his knife he calmly cut off his toe. Captain Cooke of the *Bellerophon* was killed at almost the same moment as his lifelong friend, Captain Duff of the *Mars*. As he fell to the deck his quartermaster ran up to carry him below. 'No, let me lie quietly a moment,' said Cooke; a moment later he uttered his last words: 'Tell Cumby never to strike.'

At about the same moment Nelson fell, struck by a bullet from a sharpshooter in the *Redoutable*'s rigging. Hardy ran up to help him. 'Hardy, I believe they have done for me at last,' he heard him say. 'I hope not, my Lord.' 'Yes,' came the sure reply, 'my backbone is shot through.'

Three marines raised him gently in their arms to carry him to the cockpit. He placed a handkerchief over his face so that the crew might not know what had happened. Although suffering greatly, his mind remained alert. Observing that the tiller's ropes which had been shot away had not yet been replaced, he called to a midshipman to tell Hardy of it.

At the entrance to the cockpit, Dr Beatty, the surgeon, and Mr Burke, the purser, lifted Nelson from the arms of the marines. They stumbled, and Nelson asked who was carrying him. When told, he said: 'Ah, Mr Beatty, you can do nothing for me. I have but a short time to live. My backbone is shot through.'

Dr Beatty laid him against the ship's side, stripped him of his clothes and covered him with a white sheet. He examined the wound but could find no injury to the backbone. He asked Nelson what were his symptoms. Nelson replied that he felt a gush of blood in his breast every minute, and that he had no feeling in the lower part of his body. Beatty knew then that there could be no hope, but he kept the news from all except Hardy, Burke and Dr Scott.

For the next hour, surrounded by his wounded officers and men, and attended by the chaplain and purser, Nelson lay quietly in the *Victory*'s cockpit. From time to time sounds of cheering came to him from above. He asked what it signified and was told by Pasco who, also wounded, lay a little way from him, that another ship had struck. He began to get very hot and repeatedly asked to be fanned and for a drink of lemonade. Dr Scott and Mr Burke comforted him, saying that he would still live to bring home the news of a glorious victory. 'It is nonsense, Mr Burke, to suppose I can live,' he replied. 'My sufferings are great but they will soon be over.'

During this time Nelson called out frequently for Hardy. When he did not come his anxiety became very great. 'Will no-one bring Hardy to me? He must be killed.' At length Mr Bulkeley, Hardy's assistant, arrived to say the captain could not leave the deck but would come down as soon as possible. He came at about half past two, and they shook hands. 'Well, Hardy,' said Nelson, 'how goes the battle? How goes the day with us?'

'Very well, my Lord. We have got twelve or fourteen of the enemy's ships in our possession.'

'I hope,' said Nelson, 'none of *our* ships have struck.'

'No, my Lord, there is no fear of that.'

Nelson then said: 'I am a dead man, Hardy. I am going fast. It will all be over with me soon. Come nearer to me.' Hardy bent down and Nelson whispered: 'Pray let my dear Lady Hamilton have my hair and all other things belonging to me.' After a few more minutes' conversation, Hardy again shook hands and returned to the deck.

Nelson now instructed Dr Beatty to attend to the other wounded as nothing further could be done for him. A few moments later he recalled Beatty to say that all power of motion and feeling below his breast had gone, 'and *you*', he said emphatically, 'very well know I can live but a short time.' While Beatty re-examined him Nelson again exclaimed: 'You *know* I am gone.' In the face of such courage Beatty could hide the truth no longer. 'My Lord, unhappily for our country, nothing can be done for you.' Overcome with emotion he turned aside. 'I know it,' said Nelson, 'I feel something rising in my breast which tells me I am gone.' Then he was heard to murmur several times: 'God be praised. I have done my duty.'

Hardy now made his second appearance, this time to congratulate Nelson on certain victory. Fourteen enemy ships had struck, possibly fifteen. 'That is well,' said Nelson, 'but I bargained for twenty.' Then, his mind still on his duty, he exclaimed emphatically: 'Anchor, Hardy, anchor!' Hardy said that he supposed that Collingwood would take it on himself to direct affairs. 'Not while I live, I hope, Hardy,' cried Nelson, raising himself from the bed. 'No, do *you* anchor. For if I live I'll anchor.' Exhausted, he fell back. In calmer tones he told Hardy that he felt the end was now near. 'Don't throw me overboard, Hardy.' 'Oh, no,' replied Hardy, 'certainly not.' 'Then,' said Nelson, 'you know what to do.'

The moment had now come for Nelson to take farewell of Hardy. This famous scene is familiar to most Englishmen, although in the course of years it has lost all its meaning. Nelson's request to Hardy to kiss him has become, like other catch-phrases of history, a subject more for laughter than tears. Some Englishmen indeed, not liking to believe their greatest admiral asked anything so effeminate, and ignorant both of Nelson's character and the written testimonies of Dr Scott and Dr Beatty, have created a legend that he said 'Kismet'.

And yet it was one of the most moving moments of Nelson's life. For of all his captains it was Hardy, in the last analysis, whom he loved most. His relationships with Troubridge and Ball had been more intimate, but because of that less sure; for although they praised him freely, they were not slow to criticize. What raised Hardy, in Nelson's eyes, above all others was his self-sufficiency. He had offered Nelson neither praise nor criticism, but had served him with a faithful and silent devotion; nor had Nelson ever dared to speak to him in the extravagant way he did to the others. He knew in his heart that Hardy loved him, but because it had never been said, he did not know.

It would be foolish to attach too much importance to the words of a dying man; but Nelson was in full possession of his faculties to within a few minutes of the end. Is it too fanciful to suggest he wanted a final proof of what he had believed all along? To have asked Berry or Ball to kiss him would have been not only ridiculous but unnecessary; to ask Hardy was to demand something wholly alien to his nature. The captain knelt down and lightly kissed his forehead. 'Now I am satisfied,' said Nelson. 'Thank God, I have done my duty.'

And now came the final act of this strange drama. Hardy stood a moment in silence looking down at the admiral. In that moment it may have occurred to him that Nelson was thinking that he had kissed him, not because he wanted to but because he could not refuse a dying man's request.

Quietly he knelt down again and of his own accord brushed his lips on the admiral's forehead. 'Who is that?' asked Nelson. 'It is Hardy,' replied the captain. 'God bless you, Hardy,' said Nelson.

Hardy left the cockpit and returned to where the battle was raging on deck. Nelson's breathing now became very difficult. He asked his steward to turn him on his right side, and when this was done he said: 'I wish I had not left the deck, for I shall soon be gone.' To Dr Scott he said: 'Doctor, I have not been a *great* sinner,' and reminded him that he was leaving Lady Hamilton as a legacy to his King and country. His thirst increased and he asked repeatedly for drinks and to be fanned. His speech became more and more inarticulate. The last words he was heard to utter were: 'God and my country.' At thirty minutes past four he died.

Nelson's great and glorious victory had been granted. Of the thirty-three ships of the combined fleet, eighteen were captured, including Villeneuve's flagship, the *Bucentaure*, and the huge *Santissima Trinidad*, which struck to Fremantle. The four French van-ships under Dumanoir le Pelley escaped to the northwards; but a fortnight later they were brought to action off Cape Ortegal by Sir Richard Strachan, and all surrendered. The eleven remaining ships reached Cadiz, but never put to sea again. The British casualties of 1,700 killed and wounded were less than a third of the enemy's; and they took some 20,000 prisoners. 'There never was', Collingwood wrote, 'so complete an annihilation of a fleet.'

The two enemy commanders-in-chief did not long survive Nelson. Villeneuve was taken prisoner on board the *Neptune* where Fremantle found him 'very low'; then, when Blackwood was ordered home, he was shifted to the *Euryalus*. Villeneuve's conduct had earned him respect and sympathy, and when he went to live at Bishop's Waltham on parole, Pitt and Barham ordered that he was to be treated with every consideration. Blackwood, who had formed a high admiration for him, was shocked to find that he had been restricted 'the same as the lowest officers to whom country paroles are given, that is to a mile or so about the town on the turnpike road, and a fine of a guinea if out after five o'clock.' A word in the proper quarter put things to rights, but soon after Villeneuve was released on exchange. He never reached Paris. On the morning of 22 April 1806, he was found murdered in a hotel bedroom at Rennes. The criminal was not identified, but it was whispered that he was a secret agent of Napoleon.

Gravina's end was more noble. In the action he had been badly wounded in the arm. He refused to have it amputated and blood-poisoning set in. 'I am a dying man,' he said in March 1806, 'but I hope and trust that I am going to join the greatest hero the world almost ever produced.' A few days later he was dead.

If Nelson had lived long enough to bring the Fleet to anchor, victory would have been complete. But Collingwood admitted that the thought had never occurred to him. He did not give the order until later in the evening when the gale was on them, by which time it was too late. The next four days were a nightmare for the Fleet. The storm raged unceasingly, they had no sight of sun, moon or stars, they were, in the words of one captain, 'fatigued beyond measure,' and the death of Nelson lay heavy upon them. Collingwood gave orders one moment and cancelled them the next. 'What he is doing, God knows!' commented Codrington, and Fremantle wrote: 'The poor man does not know his own mind five minutes together.' Many of the prizes were driven ashore and wrecked, others became unmanageable and were burnt. When the main body of the Fleet came to anchor south of Cadiz on 28 October, only four were left afloat.

The *Pickle* schooner, Lieutenant Laponetiere, left the Fleet on the 26th with Collingwood's dispatches. Off the Scilly Isles she spoke the *Superb*, outward bound to join the Fleet; her news was a cruel blow to Keats, who was hoping to arrive in time for the action, and was carrying letters from Lady Hamilton. The *Pickle* reached Falmouth on 4 November: Lieutenant Laponetiere set out in a post-chaise and arrived at the Admiralty at one o'clock on the morning of the 6th. He was shown up to the First Secretary, who was preparing for bed, and greeted him with the dramatic words: 'Sir, we have gained a great victory, but we have lost Lord Nelson.'

Everywhere the magnitude and significance of the victory was overshadowed by the death of Nelson. Lord Malmesbury wrote that he had never seen so little public joy. Even the mob were silent. 'What!' they cried, 'light up because our Nelson is killed!' Pitt, accustomed to being woken at all hours, was unable to get to sleep again, and rose at 3 a.m. for the day's work. Betsey learnt the news of the greatest naval victory since the Armada by the maid Nelly's 'ghastly appearance after breakfast'. The King was so upset he was unable to speak. 'I had not upon any occasion,' said his secretary, 'seen His Majesty more affected.' In many places people wept openly. At Naples the poet Coleridge wrote that passers-by stopped to shake his hand because they had seen the tears on his cheek and guessed that he must be English. At Castellamare George Elliot half-masted the *Aurora*'s colours and fired minute-guns. Until receiving a 'very proper rebuke for not saluting for the victory,' he had not thought to do otherwise.

Yet it was among Nelson's Fleet that his death was felt most deeply. 'All seemed to feel,' wrote one officer, 'not only that some great national calamity had befallen the land, but as if each individual had lost a friend and a leader.' A sailor in the *Royal Sovereign* wrote home: 'All the men in our ship are such soft toads, they have done nothing but blast their eyes and cry. Bless you! – chaps that fought like the devil sit down and cry like a wench.' Blackwood told his wife that he had never been so shocked or upset in his life and even the aloof Collingwood was moved to tears. Codrington wrote that Hallowell could hardly support himself. Keats and Louis wrote highly emotional letters to Lady Hamilton. Louis asked for some personal memento. 'I never made such a request before and never shall again, for no man can ever have the warmth of my heart and soul so strong and sincere.' Dr Scott summed up the feelings of them all: 'When I think, setting aside his heroism, what an affectionate fascinating little fellow he was, how dignified and pure his mind, how kind and condescending his manners, I become stupid with grief for what I have lost.'

The *Victory*, with Nelson's body preserved in a cask of spirits, was towed by the *Neptune* to Gibraltar. After a short refit she and the *Euryalus* sailed for England. At Portsmouth, Hardy and Blackwood discussed the codicil to Nelson's will which they had witnessed, and agreed that it should be put before the Government as soon as possible. They were both too busy to visit Merton, but assured Lady Hamilton of their good intentions. 'Hardy may have spoken his mind on former occasions more freely than you could have wished,' wrote Blackwood; 'but depend on it, the last words of our lamented friend will influence his conduct.' And Hardy told her: 'It was ever our dear Lord's last request to be kind to you, which I trust I shall never forget.'

But despite Hardy's and Blackwood's efforts, Nelson's dying request was never answered; and after Trafalgar, Lady Hamilton quickly fades from the scene. Ball, Louis and Hardy wrote frequently, offering their help in any way; but she seldom answered their letters. Never a woman with a sense of money, she was soon in debt; and in 1815 she died in poverty at Calais.

Hardy remained at Portsmouth a week and then sailed for the Nore. At Chatham, Nelson's body was transferred to Hallowell's coffin, which had been sent down from London. It was placed on board the Commissioner's yacht, which proceeded slowly up river past ships with flags half-masted and to the sound of minute-guns from batteries ashore. At Greenwich the coffin was received by Lord Hood and taken to a private apartment, preparatory to the lying-in-state.

The funeral was fixed for 9 January, and on the three days preceding, Nelson's body lay on view to the public in the Painted Hall. Hallowell's coffin had been enclosed in another made by Mr France of Pall Mall, emblazoned with emblems of his victories and described as 'the most superb ever seen in Europe'. It was covered with a black velvet pall lined with white satin, and erected on a platform six feet high. Above was a great black canopy festooned with gold and surmounted with a golden wreath bearing the word TRAFALGAR. The chamber was lighted by candles placed on silver trays beside the coffin and by double rows of sconces round the walls. Ten banners on staves, bearing the quarterings of Nelson's arms, hung pendant towards the coffin. Ten mourners from the Lord Chamberlain's office, two on either side of the coffin, three on either side of the canopy, attended the body by day and night. Volunteers of the Greenwich and Deptford Associations kept the huge crowd continually on the move. During the three days' lying-in-state over 30,000 people passed through the chamber.

On 8 January the coffin was conveyed in a procession of State barges to the Admiralty. It lay overnight in the Captains' Room, watched by Dr Scott. Between three and four the next morning when it was still dark, crowds began assembling in the streets between the Admiralty and St Paul's, where Nelson was to be buried. At eight-thirty they heard the great bell of the cathedral tolling mournfully. With the coming of light – a clear crisp January day – troops took up their positions along the route. The principal mourners – the princes of the blood, representatives of the Lords and Commons, senior naval and military officers, officials of the College of Heralds and Nelson's relatives – assembled in Hyde Park, and then made their way by St James's Park and Constitution Hill to the Admiralty.

Here the coffin was brought out of the Admiralty Yard and placed in the funeral car, which had been modelled after the hull of the *Victory*. The figurehead represented Fame: above the stern was a poop lantern with the word VICTORY emblazoned in yellow letters. The sides were decorated with escutcheons; between them were scrolls bearing the names of enemy ships Nelson had destroyed or captured, SAN JOSEF, L'ORIENT, TRINIDAD and BUCENTAURE. An ensign fluttered at half-mast.

At noon the huge procession formed up and started off. It was led by a body of cavalry, artillery and infantry from regiments quartered within a hundred miles of London, under the command of General Sir David Dundas. After them came forty-eight seamen of the *Victory* and forty-eight pensioners of Greenwich Hospital; officials of the College of Heralds; representatives of the City companies; two knights of the Bath (Sir Samuel Hood and Sir Thomas Trigge); members of the House of Commons; barons, viscounts, earls, marquises, dukes and princes. Then came the funeral car, closely followed by the Chief Mourner, Admiral Sir Peter Parker (senior admiral in the Fleet), supported by Admirals Lord Hood and

Radstock, and with Captain Blackwood as train-bearer. He was followed by six Assistant Mourners, Admirals Curtis, Pole, Hamilton, Caldwell, Bligh and Nugent, and by Captain Hardy bearing the Banner of Emblems. After them came Nelson's relatives, and several hundred naval and military officers brought up the rear. The procession was so long that these officers did not leave the Admiralty until after the troops under Dundas had reached St Paul's.

What impressed most onlookers was 'the awful silence', broken only by the distant strains of the Dead March in *Saul* and the occasional sounding of minute-guns. 'It seemed,' wrote Lady Bessborough, 'one general impulse of respect beyond anything that could have been said or contrived.' As the funeral car passed along the Strand the rustle of people uncovering their heads could clearly be heard. Many people thought the numbers of soldiers excessive, and rested their eyes on Hardy and the 'dear forty-eight *Victory* men'. 'We had rather see them,' they said, 'than all the rest.'

At St Paul's, twelve seamen of the *Victory* lifted the coffin from the car and carried it inside the western door. Here they were relieved by the principal pall-bearers, Admirals Orde, Whitshed, Harvey and Taylor. The procession moved slowly up the aisle, through shafts of golden sunlight streaming down from the high windows, past pews thronged with people who had been waiting patiently since seven in the morning, past the opening to the crypt under the dome and into the choir. The organ broke into the opening strains of 'I Know that My Redeemer Liveth'.

The service had begun at two o'clock. By the time it was over darkness had fallen, and the cathedral was lit by rows of torches along the walls and by a huge octagonal lantern suspended under the dome. The bier, covered in black velvet and fringed with golden tassels, was placed in the choir to receive the coffin. The four admirals took their places alongside it. Six others – Domett, Drury, Douglas, Wells, Coffin and Aylmer – held a canopy above it: this was made of black velvet, supported by six small pillars and crowned with six plumes of black ostrich feathers; the valance was embroidered with emblems of Nelson's victories and his coat-of-arms, coronet and crest in gold.

The procession moved in inverse order from the choir to the opening to the crypt under the dome. Here the canopy was withdrawn and the pall removed. Clarenceux King of Arms placed Nelson's coronet on the coffin, and the Chief Mourner and relatives gathered round the opening. At thirty-three minutes past five o'clock Nelson's last remains were lowered slowly into the crypt. Softly the choir began the last verse of the concluding anthem: 'His body is buried in peace.' Louder the chorus answered: 'But his name liveth for evermore.'

PURSUIT

THE CHASE AND SINKING OF THE *BISMARCK*

THE FLEET DESTROYER I joined early in 1940 was the Tartar, one of sixteen 'Tribal' destroyers completed just before the war and organized in two flotillas: they were then among the handsomest ships in the Navy, powerfully armed, lavishly fitted out and with elegant, flowing lines. Sadly only four survived the war.

During my two years in the Tartar we were part of the Home Fleet, based at Scapa Flow in the Orkney Islands, an ideal anchorage for covering the waters between Norway and the north of Scotland across which German warships would have to pass on sorties to or from the Atlantic. As I have described in my autobiography we took part in many exciting operations which included the 1940 Norwegian campaign, the 1941 raid on the Lofoten Islands, escorting the convoy which brought Winston Churchill in the Prince of Wales back from his Atlantic Charter meeting with President Roosevelt, and a 1942 Arctic convoy to Murmansk in which our sister ship Matabele was sunk with the loss of all but two of her crew.

The high point though was the part we played in escorting the battleships Rodney and King George V in the pursuit of the German battleship Bismarck in May 1941, and which resulted in her destruction in the Atlantic a week later. After the war I made a documentary film on the operation and had the benefit of contributions from the actor Esmond Knight who was serving on board Prince of Wales and Baron Burkard von Müllenheim-Rechberg, then a lieutenant-commander and senior officer of the Bismarck's hundred survivors. But a fifty-minute documentary film can only sustain some 7,000 words of commentary and our researches had thrown up enough for a book. With the film out of the way I wrote the book which I called Pursuit. *It was published by Collins in 1974.[1] What follows is a pared-down version of it.*

It was a May evening of 1941, a time when most of Europe had yielded to Hitler, and across the narrow moat that had made and saved her, a truculent Britain faced Germany alone. To the west, across the steep Atlantic, and to the east, beyond the Vistula, the two giants marked time: their turn would come, but now they were spectators, uneasily neutral, also alone.

In the daytime, in the country, you hardly knew a war was on. Dusk was for remembrance, in cities especially, Coventry, Hamm, Hamburg, Devonport, Genoa, Brest: then the black-out curtains were drawn and the street lights doused, and the streets became like long tunnels and men and women rabbits, diving in and out of bright warrens, shutting away until morning the perils and peradventures of the night. It was like that always, even when the bombers didn't come, and when they did come, it was another story.

In a few places in Europe the lights still shone. In Stockholm, for instance, considered by some to be a dull, clean city servicing dull, progressive people, but then, like its partners in neutrality at the other end of Europe, Madrid and Lisbon, a buzzing beehive of espionage and intrigue. Here the Germans and the British had embassies and other front organizations, spied on each other, bribed Swedes and others to spy for them, touted for hot tips like how much iron ore was coming down from Narvik and the wavebands of British radar, coded dark secrets for London and Berlin, and sent them by radio or aeroplane, in the trouser-legs of sea-cooks and the incredible memories of agents.

An unlikely man to find mixed up in all this was Captain Henry Denham, Royal Navy, who liked nothing better than sailing and racing small boats. He'd been naval attaché in Copenhagen in 1940 when the Germans overran Denmark, and getting out, had been asked to go to Sweden to do the same. Why, he never knew: he understood no Swedish, it

[1] Fontana published a paperback of *Pursuit* in May 1991 to coincide with the fiftieth anniversary of the battle. It is still in print.

was the only European country where he hadn't been.

He reached Stockholm in June 1940 via Narvik and the North Cape, crossing the frontier to Finland with the Wehrmacht half a day behind. At first, lacking the language and contacts, it had been uphill work. But he had persevered, called on the right people, been congenial at parties, and now, a year later, had several useful informants, in the Swedish armed forces and without. He lived in a comfortable, small flat in the Riddargatan, but he met informants elsewhere, at the embassy or in the woods. He knew his flat was watched from the building opposite, and that his telephone was tapped, and he suspected bugging too.

On this evening in May, Captain Denham was in his flat when the telephone rang. It was the British embassy in the Strandvägen. Colonel Roscher Lund had arrived to see him. It was urgent.

Colonel Roscher Lund was the military attaché of the exiled Norwegian government in London, a friend and colleague of Denham and the most reliable of his informants: he knew many Swedish officers, having done liaison work with their interception and cryptography service before the war. One man he knew well was Major Törnberg, himself half-Norwegian and Chief of Staff to Colonel Petersén, head of the Swedish secret service. Törnberg hated the Germans for what they had done to Norway, felt no disloyalty to his own country in passing on to Roscher Lund information that might be useful to Britain in the prosecution of the war. Twice a week, in the evenings, Roscher Lund brought papers to Denham at the embassy: Denham made abstracts of what he thought important and Roscher Lund returned the papers to Törnberg's office before it opened in the morning. Denham and Roscher Lund referred to Petersén as 'P' to preserve his security.

Denham got out his bicycle and set off for the embassy, five minutes away on the waterfront. Never before had Roscher Lund asked for a special meeting, so he guessed something unusual was up.

At the embassy they went to Denham's office. Roscher Lund's message was brief and undramatic. It was a report from 'P''s office that two big German warships with sea and air escort had been sighted that afternoon off the south coast of Sweden. There was no indication of the source, which was in fact the Swedish cruiser *Gotland*: so delicate was the matter that not even Roscher Lund knew of it. As a result Denham doubted its reliability, and it wasn't until long afterwards that he realized that someone in 'P''s office, Törnberg probably, knowing this intelligence to be vital to Britain, had taken special, cautious steps to see that he was informed.

Roscher Lund left, and Denham drafted a telegram to the Admiralty, classified Most Immediate, graded B.3. Within an hour it had been put into cipher and was zinging its way from the Gothenburg radio masts across the North Sea to London.

'Kattegat today 20th May. At 1500 two large warships, escorted by three destroyers, five escort vessels, ten or twelve aircraft, passed Marstrand course north-west. 2058/20.'

The secret was out. *Bismarck* and *Prinz Eugen* were on their way. Operation *Rheinübung* had begun.

The *Bismarck* was built by Blohm and Voss of Hamburg and went down the slipway there on St Valentine's day, 1939, the anniversary of Nelson's great coup at the battle of Cape St Vincent. The German government declared the ceremony a state occasion. Hitler, Raeder, Keitel, Göring, Goebbels, Hess, Ribbentrop, Himmler, Bormann, von Schirach were all present on the podium, and Hitler in a speech hoped her future crew would be imbued with Bismarck's iron spirit. The bands played, the Nazi flags curled in the air, Hitler and Raeder beamed happily and a vast crowd cheered to see Bismarck's granddaughter, Dorothea von Loewenfeld, christen their greatest ship with the name of their greatest Chancellor. She was a sixth of a mile long, 120 feet wide, designed to carry eight 15-inch guns and six aircraft, with 13-inch armour made of specially hardened Wotan steel on her turrets and sides. Listed as 35,000 tons to comply with the London Treaty, she would in fact be 42,000 tons standard displacement and over 50,000 tons fully laden. There had never been a warship like her: she symbolized not only a resurgent Navy but the whole resurgent German nation.

During the next eighteen months, in peace and war, she lay alongside the quay fitting out, an iron antheap swarming with dockyard workmen. There were welders and fitters to fashion her superstructure plate by plate, men with cranes to step her masts, lower her twelve boilers, swing on board her four gun turrets each of a thousand tons, Anton and Bruno forward, Caesar and Dora aft,[1] electricians to make light and power circuits, fire-control and telephone systems, fix radio panels, suction fans, compasses, radar; shipwrights to stow anchors and cables; plumbers to install wash-basins and wastepipes; carpenters to fit cabins, messes, operations rooms, charthouse. That summer, while the Wehrmacht sketched in the boundaries of a new German Empire from the Pyrenees to the North Cape, the Atlantic to the Oder, the ship took shape. Key officers joined, like Adalbert Schneider, gunnery commander, Gerhard Junack, engineer officer in charge of damage control. Later came others, Walter Lehmann, chief engineer, Wolf Neuendorff, navigating officer, Hans Oels, executive officer. Third gunnery officer was Burkard, Baron von Müllenheim-Rechberg, of an old Alsatian family, father killed in the Army in the First World War, brother Wendelin killed in the Luftwaffe at the beginning of this one. Before the war he'd been assistant naval attaché under Ribbentrop at the embassy in London, had a flat off Grosvenor Square and many English friends, had already seen action twice, in *Scharnhorst* when she sank the *Rawalpindi*,[2] later as second in command of the destroyer *Erich Giese* when she sailed to Narvik.

Last came the captain, Ernst Lindemann from the Rhineland, aged forty-five, clever and cool, top of his term as a cadet, specialist in gunnery, chain-smoker and coffee-drinker, blond hair sleeked back. Junack admired him, respected his knowledge of engineering, called him the right

[1] The Germans called their turrets A and B forward and C and D aft, the British A and B forward, X and Y aft.

[2] Commanded by the author's father.

55

man in the right job. With him came his steward, ex-waiter of his favourite Hamburg restaurant, a man nervous about military service but happy to be taken to sea in something so large and safe. By 24 August the ship was ready to be handed over: the band played on the quarter-deck, the Nazi naval ensign was run up, *Bismarck* was commissioned into the German navy.

During the next month *Bismarck* continued fitting out and completing her complement: signalmen, store-keepers, sick-berth attendants; cooks, coders, clerks; seamen, stokers, stewards. Like the rest of the German navy they were all volunteers and regulars and had to pass a strict examination to be accepted; most of those who applied failed. They signed for four years initially with an option at the end of a further twelve. Their average age was twenty-one: few had seen action of any kind, and for most this was their first ship: they worked on board in the daytime, lived in accommodation ships like the *Oceania* and *General Artigas* at night. Later, as the ship prepared for sea, they moved into messes, like the British navy had hammocks to sleep in, lockers for clothes: each mess peeled its own potatoes but the cooked food was fetched in containers from central galleys: unlike the British navy beer was available instead of rum, and there was a weekly free issue of cigarettes. As the sailing date neared, the ship filled with stores: flags, flour, duffel coats, typewriters; bandages, carcasses, signal pads, paint; sausages, crockery, charts, binoculars; soap, blankets, cipher books, cigarettes; hammocks, potatoes, light bulbs, lavatory paper; everything to meet the wants of this floating town and the 2,000 men who were to make their home in her.

On 15 September 1940 *Bismarck* was weaned, left the crèche of Hamburg, slipped the cords that tied her to the shore, glided down the lazy Elbe towards salt water and the open sea. And those who saw her pass on the long journey from Hamburg to the river's mouth and through the Kaiser Wilhelm Canal to Germany's other side, housewives in Altona, sailors and dockers in Brunsbüttel, farmers and soldiers on guard in Schleswig-Holstein, marvelled at what they saw. Warships combine uniquely grace and power, and *Bismarck*, massive and elegant, with the high flare of her bows and majestic sweep of her lines, the symmetry of her turrets, the rakish cowling of her funnel, her ease and arrogance in the water, was then the most graceful, most powerful warship yet built. No German saw her without pride, no neutral or enemy without admiration.

The fleet commander for the operation was to be Admiral Günther Lütjens who had already conducted two sorties with the battlecruisers *Scharnhorst* and *Gneisenau*. During the German Navy's capture of Narvik in 1940 the ships had covered the landings from seaward and briefly engaged the British battlecruiser *Renown*. Then in January 1941 Lütjens with the two ships had broken out into the Atlantic and in a two-month cruise sank over 100,000 tons of Allied shipping before turning for Brest. It was the German naval staff's intention that the battlecruisers should join *Bismarck* and *Prinz Eugen* in the Atlantic, but *Scharnhorst* needed repairs to her boilers and *Gneisenau* was hit by a torpedo in an air attack which was to put her out of action for six months.

Günther Lütjens was then fifty-one, a long, lean lamp-post of a man, with cropped hair like most German officers, and a dour, tight expression which some said concealed a dry sense of humour. He was born in Wiesbaden, son of a merchant, entered for the naval college at Kiel in 1908, passed out twentieth from a class of 160, had a reputation for mastering whatever he studied. He'd fought in torpedo-boats in the first war, off Flanders and in the Channel, in the thirties commanded the cruiser *Karlsrühe* on a trip to the Americas while Dönitz was commanding the *Emden* on a voyage to the Far East. On return the cruisers rendezvoused in Vigo, Spain, then steamed back to Germany together. Later Lütjens became Chief of Personnel and Admiral commanding torpedo-boats. In the Norwegian Campaign of 1940 he'd deputized for Admiral Marschall in *Gneisenau* as Fleet Commander, being awarded the Knight's Cross.

Lütjens was a man wholly dedicated to the service, courageous, single-minded, stoical, austere, taciturn as a Cistercian monk. He was not a Nazi, gave Hitler the naval not the party salute, always wore an admiral's dirk of the old Imperial Navy, not one with a swastika. His friend Admiral Conrad Patzig who succeeded him as Chief of Personnel called him 'one of the ablest officers in the Navy, very logical and shrewd, incorruptible in his opinions and an engaging personality when you got to know him.' Few did. To those who admired him, he was shy and withdrawn, to others aloof and remote. He believed that young officers should wed themselves to the Navy, and when Chief of Personnel was inflexible about the rule that no officer should marry until earning a certain level of pay. He practised what he preached, didn't marry until forty and then very happily, two children now and a third on the way. His sister had married his friend Captain Backenköhler, Marschall's former Chief of Staff.

At the beginning of May Lütjens flew to Gotenhafen and embarked with the officers of his staff. The operation was given its code-name, Rheinübung (Rhine Exercise), and a starting date of 18 May. On 5 May, Hitler and his staff travelled to Gotenhafen by special train to inspect *Bismarck* and *Tirpitz*. Raeder did not accompany him, the first time in eight years on such a visit he had not done so. He gives no reason in his memoirs, as though it were something to be hushed up, but elsewhere he speaks of Hitler's malign influence and the ease of succumbing to his wishes. Aware of Hitler's lack of enthusiasm for surface ship operations, fears of sinkings and loss of prestige, he had not given him the squadron's exact sailing date: he may have felt that Hitler would have wormed it out of him, panicked at realizing there was less than two weeks to go, ordered its cancellation. All Lütjens had to do if asked was say he didn't know.

Instead of Raeder, there went with Hitler General Keitel, Chief of the General Staff, later to be hanged at Nuremberg. Captain von Puttkamer, Hitler's naval aide, was also present and Walther Hewel, Ribbentrop's liaison officer at the Führer's headquarters.

At Gotenhafen ('the very hideous Gotenhafen' Hewel called it) the party embarked in the yacht *Hela* in the inner harbour, and steamed out to where *Bismarck*, massive and graceful, was lying at anchor in the roads: perhaps even Hitler caught his breath at the sight of her. The crew were lined up on deck with Admiral Lütjens, Captain Lindemann, Commander Oels and the officers of the watch waiting at the gangway to receive him. Hitler was piped over the side, the officers presented to him. He then inspected the crew and the ship. In the fore gunnery transmitting station he stayed nearly half an hour listening to Sub-Lieutenant Cardinal explaining how speed, course, wind-direction, temperature were fed into the machine, how the machine came up with the right angles of deflection and elevation for the guns. It was this sort of technical talk that Hitler liked, much better than old Raeder gassing about sea-power. Keitel, a gunner himself, found it absorbing too.

Then Lütjens took Hitler to his cabin, with von Puttkamer but without Keitel. Lütjens gave an account of his earlier cruise with *Scharnhorst* and *Gneisenau*, then told Hitler that this time because of *Bismarck*'s superiority, he would be able to take on any convoy escort while *Prinz Eugen* attacked the merchant ships. Was there then nothing to worry about, asked the cautious Hitler, what about torpedo-carrying aircraft? Yes, agreed Lütjens, that was a worry, his biggest worry, though he thought the ship's tremendous fire-power could cope with it – on another occasion he told a friend that with *Bismarck*'s armour, torpedo hits would be felt as bee stings that hurt but didn't damage. He might have added what all senior officers felt, that had the intriguing Göring not denied the Navy its air arm, had the aircraft carrier *Graf Zeppelin*, lying even now in the yards at Gotenhafen, half-completed and abandoned, been accompanying him, his worries would have been considerably less. Hitler, said von Puttkamer, was pleased to find that the experienced Lütjens shared his concerns. He then went ashore in the *Hela* and inspected the *Tirpitz* in the harbour. Captain Topp begged him to allow his ship to accompany *Bismarck* on her first operation. Hitler listened but said nothing. The party then returned to the train. 'Visit unbelievably impressive,' Hewel wrote in his diary that night. 'Concentration of force and the highest technical development.'

On 16 May Lütjens reported the squadron ready to proceed from midnight on the 18th–19th, and during the next two days six tankers and their supply ships sailed from French Atlantic and Norwegian ports to take up waiting positions. These ships would keep *Bismarck* and *Prinz Eugen* supplied with oil, ammunition, food and water for at least three months. In addition four weather ships were sailed and the tanker *Wollin* was ordered to stand by in Bergen harbour.

On the morning of Sunday 18 May Admiral Lütjens held a final conference in his cabin, attended by his staff officers and Captains Lindemann and Brinkmann. Group North had recommended the Iceland/Faeroes passage as the shortest route into the Atlantic saving time and fuel, but it was here that Lütjens had run into the cruiser *Naiad* in January and been obliged to turn back. The Denmark Strait route between Iceland and Greenland had been used successfully by *Scheer*, *Hipper*, and other raiders, and as he had subsequently negotiated it himself with *Scharnhorst* and *Gneisenau*, he had cause to think it the safest.

After the conference Lütjens went in his barge to the harbour to inspect *Prinz Eugen* and her crew, but neither to them nor her officers did he say a word about the impending operation. Various last-minute supernumeraries joined the two ships: a hundred officers and men from the merchant service as prize crews for all the merchant vessels they hoped to capture, a batch of midshipmen from *Tirpitz* for war training, reporters and cameramen from Dr Goebbels's Propaganda Ministry, hungry for pictures of sinking British ships. Dr Menke, of the Navy's legal department, came on board to discuss with Dr Langer and Commander Oels disposal of men under arrest. Two of these were a sickbay petty officer who had been caught stealing from his messmates, and a cadet charged with drunkenness. The sickbay petty officer was sent ashore for disrating and punishment, and so missed the ship's sailing. The cadet asked and was given permission to have his punishment ashore postponed until after the operation, and so remained on board.

In the afternoon *Prinz Eugen* left the harbour and proceeded into the bay for degaussing trials against magnetic mines, and then *Bismarck* weighed. As the anchor came up from the Baltic seabed and the crew on the fo'c'sle hosed down the cables, the band on the quarter-deck a sixth of a mile away played '*Muss 'i denn?*' ('Must I leave?'), a ballad of grief and parting. It was the first time they had played it and later it was to be criticized as a possible breach of security. People on shore watched the two ships exercising until evening when they disappeared into the dusk.

They proceeded independently through the night and at eleven the next morning rendezvoused off Arkona, the northernmost cape of Prussia, with a flotilla of minesweepers and the destroyers *Friedrich Eckholdt* and *Z.23*. At noon Captain Lindemann addressed *Bismarck*'s crew on the loudspeaker system and told them officially what they had already guessed, that they were going on a three-month cruise in the Atlantic to destroy British shipping. He finished: 'I give you the hunter's toast, good hunting and a good bag!' The news was welcomed, for it dispelled mystery, cleared the air, challenged the spirit: *Bismarck* was the most powerful warship in the world, Führer, admiral, captain had said so, they could see it too, there was nothing in the world she and they could not do. One or two perhaps, those who had read of the British Navy's strength and traditions, looked over the side at the grey Baltic slipping astern, wondering uneasily what the future might bring.

All that day and night the squadron sailed in formation westwards and northwards, the escorts leading, then *Bismarck* with the admiral's flag, white with a black cross fluttering at the fore, then *Prinz Eugen*. They passed through the Fehmarn Belt, skirted the eastern edge of Kiel Bay where they were joined by the destroyer *Hans Lody*, sailed through the Great Belt which divides two parts of Denmark, and on through the waters that Nelson had taken on his way to victory at Copenhagen 140 years before. At 4 a.m. a signal was received saying air reconnaissance of the British fleet at Scapa Flow had not been possible the day before because of cloud. Dawn broke to reveal a calm and empty sea, for as a security measure Group North had frozen all shipping movements in the Kattegat and Skagerrak during the squadron's passage. They had not reckoned with the *Gotland*, though, which showed up soon after, grey in the sunlight against the green of the Swedish coast, steaming on a parallel course. She kept company with the German ships for several hours: then off Marstrand they swung away to port, shaping a north-westerly course across the Skagerrak for a landfall at Kristiansand in southern Norway.

Gotland sent a routine signal to Stockholm, and Lütjens wirelessed to Group North that he believed his presence had been betrayed.

At Scapa Flow in the Orkney Islands, ten miles from the north coast of Scotland across the racing waters of the Pentland Firth, lay the British Home Fleet. Scapa was ideal for guarding the approaches from the North Sea to the Atlantic, a sweep of water ten miles by eight ringed almost entirely by islands, a natural refuge for war-weary ships. Once on a time the Vikings had come here to plunder and settle, gave to the islands their old Norse names, Pomona on the north, Hoy to the west, Flotta and Hoxa to the south, Burray and South Ronaldsay in the east. Here a generation earlier Admiral Jellicoe had commanded the Grand Fleet, steamed out that May evening of 1916 with his squadrons of battleships to meet the High Seas Fleet off Jutland. Here at war's end the High Seas Fleet were brought in like lambs, lay rotting at anchor for months while the politicians argued their disposal, until on Midsummer's Day 1919 at a signal from their admiral, the crews opened their sea-cocks and they all guggle-guggled to the bottom; some were raised and broken up, others still littered the sandy floor between Bring Deeps and Cava. And here one October night at the beginning of this war the bold Günther Prien had cocked a snook at British sea-power, taken his U-boat into the Flow through a narrow, unguarded eastern channel, torpedoed and sank the battleship *Royal Oak* with huge loss of life, crept out on the ebb as unobtrusively as he had come, returned to a hero's welcome in Germany.

Admiral Beatty called Scapa the most damnable place on earth, most of the lads agreed. The islands were heather and grass, seabirds and sheep, and across the bare face of the Flow tempests blew, often for days on end. There were no shops, restaurants, girls, just a couple of canteens to dispense warm beer, a hall for film-shows and the occasional concert-party, football fields that too often fathered the signal, 'All grounds unfit for play'. And yet now in the summertime when the Flow sparkled blue in the morning sun and the hills of Hoy were touched with purple and green, at night-time too when the Northern Lights wove pale patterns over the sleeping ships, the place had a rare beauty.

It was here, while Admiral Lütjens was steaming up the Norwegian coast in his new flagship *Bismarck*, that the British Admiral, Tovey, lay moored off Flotta in his new flagship *King George V.* Tovey was fifty-six now, a small, blue-eyed, twinkly man, last of a family of eleven. He entered the Navy at fifteen, won his spurs at Jutland commanding the destroyer *Onslow*, helped sink the German light cruiser *Wiesbaden*, at one moment in the battle was quite close to Raeder. Like Raeder he was deeply religious, prayed night and morning, once asked publicly why people were so shy of talking about faith, not realizing others were different from himself. He was a natural leader, radiated confidence, could be quite fierce sometimes but it soon passed. A jokey admiral wrote of him when captain of the *Rodney*, 'Captain Tovey shares one characteristic with me. In myself I would call it tenacity of purpose. In Tovey I can only call it sheer bloody obstinacy.' Churchill found the same, called him stubborn, tried to get rid of him. Tovey did what he thought right, refused to kow-tow to titular superiors, hated 'Yes-men' in others. He was a civilized man, dressed well, liked good food and wine and company, had a golf handicap of 4, played for the Navy. Like many naval officers he would address foreigners loudly and slowly, was often astonished to find they spoke English too. He liked Poles and Americans especially, and he adored King George VI.

On board the flagship was a green telephone which, when the Fleet was in Scapa, was connected to a special shore line to the Admiralty in London. It was the same line on which Jellicoe had spoken to Churchill when he was First Lord of the Admiralty twenty-six years earlier. On this telephone, in the early morning of 21 May, Tovey's secretary, Captain Paffard, and his Chief of Staff, Commodore Brind, learnt from the Admiralty of Denham's signal, received during the night. To them, as to Tovey, it came as no surprise. It was known from intelligence that both *Bismarck* and *Prinz Eugen* had completed training, and one agent's report that new charts were being delivered to *Bismarck* and another's from France that battleship moorings were being prepared at

Brest, made it clear her time in the Baltic was coming to an end. Further, during the past ten days there had been an unusual increase in German air activity, daily reconnaissance flights over the Flow, additional flights over the Denmark Strait and between Greenland and Jan Mayen, so that on 18 May, at the moment Lütjens was leaving Gotenhafen, Tovey ordered the cruiser *Suffolk* on patrol in the Denmark Strait to keep a sharp look-out, especially near the ice-edge, and her sister ship *Norfolk* to sail from Iceland to relieve her, that in case of emergency both ships might have full tanks.

Through the night the German squadron steamed northwards up the Norwegian coast, steering a zigzag course to avoid British submarines. To those newly joined the weather was kind: a calm sea with a gentle wind from the north-east. A signal from Group North reported photographic reconnaissance of Scapa Flow the day before as showing (correctly) three heavy ships (*King George V*, *Prince of Wales*, *Hood*), a carrier (*Victorious*) and several cruisers and destroyers. A further signal reported the decoding of a British message to all coastal aircraft to look out for the German squadron, reported on a northerly course, but a note in the *Prinz Eugen*'s log reveals that this didn't come to Captain Brinkmann's attention until evening. At breakfast on the messdecks there was cheering news on the wireless: the day before German paratroops had made a massive descent on Crete.

Just before 9 a.m. Admiral Lütjens signalled the squadron to enter the Norwegian fjords. Off the island of Marstein the two ships turned to starboard and entered the quiet waters of Korsfjord, the tongue of water that leads to Bergen. Pilots came aboard, took *Bismarck* to Grimstad fjord, just south of Bergen, *Prince Eugen* to Kalvanes Bay, north-west of it, the three destroyers to Bergen. *Bismarck* anchored close inshore, a stone's throw from the grey rocks and trim red and yellow wooden houses and sheep grazing on the young grasses. Farmers and fishermen stared with astonishment at what they saw, the sailors stared back, conquerors and conquered, neither comprehending, so near together, worlds apart. Four merchant ships were ordered alongside each of the big ships, one on each beam and quarter, as anti-torpedo protection for the engine-rooms, propellers and rudders. Admiral Lütjens signalled *Prinz Eugen* to oil from the tanker *Wollin* and to be ready to sail in the evening.

What reasons caused Lütjens to enter Korsfjord we shall never know, for typically he left none. Possibly he felt that by topping up *Prinz Eugen*'s tanks he could defer the decision whether to break out by the Denmark Strait or the Iceland–Faeroes passage or even the Faeroes–Orkney passage until the last moment. Whatever the reason it was as foolish a decision as that of allowing the ships to leave home waters by the Baltic rather than the North Sea. Had they gone through the Kiel Canal, left Brunsbüttel in the afternoon, oiled at Trondheim or Narvik or even steamed straight to the tanker *Weissenburg* in the Arctic, they would have stood a good chance of getting out unobserved. To send them by daylight through the narrow waters of the Kattegat and Skagerrak was to invite the attention of neutrals and agents, which was exactly what had happened. Further, Admiral Raeder knew it; for a signal sent that very morning from Admiral Canaris, head of the *Abwehr* or Counter Intelligence Service, stated that he had proof positive of British agents' reports of the squadron's outward movements. For the squadron, in the light of this knowledge, to be permitted to enter Bergen, the nearest Norwegian harbour to British air bases, was asking for trouble, like a burglar loitering outside his local police station.

And trouble came. At about 1.15 p.m. Flying Officer Suckling in an RAF Spitfire, almost at the end of his search, spotted two warships 25,000 feet below. They looked like cruisers: he turned, made a run over the fjords, opened the shutter. At the time no-one in *Bismarck* or *Prinz Eugen* saw him: it wasn't until fifteen minutes later that the alarm bells sounded, by which time Suckling and his happy snaps were quarter-way back to Wick.

In *King George V* Tovey waited anxiously for further news. But now came a change in the weather, a mist settled over the sea, it began to rain. The hours went by and a creeping fear started to gnaw at Tovey's heart, that the German ships had sailed, were even now heading towards the Atlantic where no less than eleven allied convoys were at sea. If so, there were no heavy ships to stop them. It was nine in the evening and growing dark when he made up his mind. To Vice-Admiral Holland in the *Hood* he made a signal to take the *Prince of Wales* under his orders together with the destroyers *Electra*, *Anthony*, *Echo*, *Icarus*, *Achates*, *Antelope*, proceed to Iceland to refuel and then take up a position south-west of the island so as to cover both the Iceland–Greenland and Iceland–Faeroes gaps.

Just before midnight the destroyers slipped their moorings in Gutter Sound, formed line ahead to pass through the Switha gate. Outside the Flow, at the edge of the Pentland Firth, they waited for *Hood* and *Prince of Wales*. On the quarter-deck of the *King George V*, which for exercise he paced so often, Admiral Tovey watched the old battlecruiser and the new battleship weigh, swing round on their engines, glide southwards through the mist and darkness towards the Hoxa gate. *Hood* led the way, proud and elegant, Admiral Holland's flag fluttering at the fore. The crew of the gate-vessel drew aside the huge underwater anti-submarine netting, the two ships passed through, the destroyers took station ahead. Twenty-one years before *Hood* had sailed this way to Scandinavia, on the first mission of her long and wonderful career. She had been here many times since. Now she was leaving for the last time. No landsman would ever see her again.

At Kalvanes during the afternoon *Prinz Eugen* oiled from the *Wollin*, the destroyers from a tanker in Bergen harbour. *Bismarck*, incredibly, didn't oil at all, despite having sailed short and burned over a thousand tons since leaving Gotenhafen. It was an astonishing omission, in sharp contrast to the British Navy's wartime rules that on reaching harbour oiling took priority over everything else. Admittedly the tanker *Weissenburg* in the Arctic was only a day's steaming away, and there was little likelihood of meeting the enemy *en route*. Yet the decision allowed no margin for error or change, it showed an amateurishness in planning, a lack of experience of ocean warfare for which in the end Lütjens would have to pay.

Also in the afternoon crews of both ships painted out camouflage markings, substituted battleship grey to confuse them with British ships; and Lütjens and his staff closely examined the previous days' aerial photographs of Scapa sent down by special car from Bergen. Fighter planes circled the two ships continuously, 'buzzing' Norwegian boats that got too near; patrol craft moved to and fro across the entrance to the fjords, Norwegians ashore noticed their crews peering over the sides. Later, when painting over the camouflage was finished, the men of both ships were allowed to laze about, sleep, read, play games on deck. Many wrote last letters home, taking care not to say where they were: Lindemann gave his to a Luftwaffe officer who went ashore just before the squadron sailed.

At about 7.30 the German squadron weighed anchor and headed north towards the Denmark Strait. During the next two days they painted out the huge swastikas on forecastle and quarter-deck to mislead British aircraft. On the night of 23 May they were approaching the most dangerous part of the break-out, the narrow passage, at this time of year not more than thirty to forty miles wide, separating the edge of the Greenland ice-pack from the north coast of Iceland. Presently the pack-ice came into sight to starboard, the ships turned to steer parallel to it, went on again to 27 knots. Soon they were among the big, flat ice floes that had broken off from the pack-ice and were drifting southwards. There were frequent alarms as look-outs mistook floes for ships and at times swift avoiding action had to be taken; but Lütjens maintained the speed of the fleet, knowing the next few hours were critical.

It was late afternoon when the worst fears of the chief meteorologist, Dr Externbrink, were realized: the weather began to clear. The fog melted away, the pack-ice, broad, dense, blue-white and green, unravelled itself ahead and to starboard: beyond and far away against an azure sky rose the tops of Greenland's icy mountains, sharp and clear in the gunnery range-finder lenses. Ahead, for the first time in nearly thirty-six hours, there was a clear path of water between three and ten miles wide. Only to port in the direction of Iceland did a thick wall of fog still lie, yellow-grey in colour, mottled with shifting patterns of white, what sailors call the ice-blink, the fierce reflection of the glare from the pack-ice.

Word of the change soon spread, and young Germans who until a week or two before had never been outside home waters peered through the slits of turrets and round the corners of doors, silent with wonder at what they saw. This was the edge of the world, the land beyond the rainbow, out there in those empty wastes were to be found polar bears like in the Berlin zoo, real, live Eskimos and the road to the North Pole. How strange to be here, the young ones thought, if only the family could see me now.

On the bridge of the *Prinz Eugen* too the officers, cold in their leather trousers and winter woollies, gazed through binoculars at the transformation of this twilight world: Captain Brinkmann, tall and heavy, leaning on the port side of the bridge, naval cap perched on top of balaclava, gloved hand holding a smouldering cigar; Commander Beck, the navigator, Lieutenant Reckhoff, officer of the watch and like Ascher in *Bismarck* a fugitive from the Argentine after the death of the *Graf Spee*, Commander Busch, a popular naval writer, married to an English wife and sent on board by Berlin to describe the operation. Captain Brinkmann trained his binoculars on the thick wall of fog to port and said: 'If they're anywhere in these parts, they're in there.'

He was right, they were; their names were *Norfolk* and *Suffolk* and a little later, while Commander Busch and other officers were finishing a quick meal in the dimly lit wardroom aft, the ship's alarm bells rang.

For the men of the *Norfolk* and *Suffolk*, the three-funnelled eight-inch-gun cruisers that were part of the First Cruiser Squadron, patrolling the Denmark Strait was not a popular job. They had been doing it for days, weeks, though it seemed like months, years. To and fro, up and down they went, nothing but the division of watches to mark the passing time. Today the weather was tolerable, mostly it was vile. Seas the size of houses would come from every side, so that on duty or off one could rarely rest, was always bracing the body, bending body and knees like some frozen skier to meet the motion of the ship. The bows dug deep into the dark sides of the travelling water-hills, flung the spray upwards where the Polar wind caught it, hurled it over the ship, on deck and superstructure and the faces of crouching men, froze it on steel and skin. One saw nothing but an agony of water, grey-green or blue-black, spume-tossed, marble-streaked, heard nothing but the thunder of the seas against the sides, the yell of the wind above. Off duty men ate and slept like automatons, browsed in magazines or comics. The wireless was popular, it required no effort: Tommy Handley with his 'Itma' show and the spy Funf, Vera Lynn, the Forces' Sweetheart, the singer with the catch in her voice, these made you forget where you were, made you think of London or home. Churchill too was good value, talking of *Herr* Hitler and the *Narzies*, Churchill was good for morale.

The captain of the *Suffolk*, Robert Ellis, was very tired. When on 18 May he got Admiral Tovey's order to oil, his ship had already been ten days on patrol in the vilest weather. He made a fast night passage to Hvalfjord on the west of Iceland, remaining on the bridge most of the time, snatched a few hours' sleep while oiling was in progress, returned to the bridge for another night passage back. It wasn't too bad a trip, for during the ship's last refit the bridge had been 'arcticized', that is closed in and steam-heated: this was luxury compared to the open bridge of the *Norfolk*, though it made for a tendency to sleep.

While Captain Ellis was on his way back to the Strait, his admiral, Frederick Wake-Walker in the *Norfolk*, was steaming to Isafjordur, a deep cleft on Iceland's north-west peninsula of Vestfirdir, to look at a new radar station: *Suffolk* was to join him there to receive final instructions. Wake-Walker was a torpedo specialist who in 1940 had superbly organized the evacuation of the British Army from the beaches of Dunkirk, a tall impressive-looking man, very technically minded, not much humour or imagination, a friend of Tovey. His hobbies were shooting, sketching and looking for wild flowers. He took the shooting on a farm at Scapa, and in Iceland, said David Kelburn, his flag-lieutenant, 'he'd go thundering off in search of saxifrage and that sort of thing.'

At ten on the foggy morning of 23 May the *Suffolk* edged in to the entrance to Isafjordur, the bleak cliffs of Vestfirdir towering above, and soon a signal lamp was winking from *Norfolk*'s bridge. *Suffolk* was to proceed within radar distance of the pack-ice opposite Vestfirdir, there patrol parallel to it in a south-west/north-east direction, each leg of the patrol to last for three hours. *Norfolk* would station herself some fifteen miles to the south of her, in case the Germans risked skirting the edge of the minefield. If nothing had been sighted by the following morning the two ships would rendezvous to check positions.

Ellis swung his ship round and made off through the fog towards the pack-ice. He was in buoyant mood, for it looked as though he might be using a new toy in which he had taken a great interest, a radar set of an improved kind which had been fitted on the last refit. Radar then was in its infancy: this set had a range of thirteen miles and covered all sectors except either side of the stern.

On reaching his patrol area Ellis found, as Lütjens was soon to find, clear water along the ice-edge, good visibility over Greenland, but on the Icelandic side the fog stretching a long way in either direction. When, therefore, he was on his north-easterly run, i.e. facing the direction in which the enemy might come, he kept in the open water near the ice-edge, knowing his radar would pick them up a long way ahead. But on the south-westerly leg when the bridge superstructure and funn ¹ smoke obscured the view astern and the radar was blind, ne steered down the edge of the wall of fog, ready to slip into it if an emergency arose. It was not his business to fight the *Bismarck*, but keep in touch with her until bigger ships arrived.

The afternoon passed without incident. Look-outs and radar operators in the *Suffolk* and *Norfolk* – and farther south too, in the cruisers *Manchester*, *Birmingham*, *Arethusa*, in trawlers like *Northern Sky* and *Northern Isles*, in the *Hood* and *Prince of Wales*, *King George V* and *Repulse* now steaming with their cruisers and destroyers to positions south of Iceland, pilots and observers of Coastal Command seeking gaps in the overcast between Iceland and Orkney – all these were sweeping the seas with instruments and binoculars in search of the German ships. There hadn't been a whisper of them since Suckling had seen them in the Bergen fjords two days before: in that time they could have steamed over a thousand miles: they could be just over the horizon, already at the edge of the Atlantic, on their way back to Germany, at anchor in a Norwegian fjord. Everyone had his own theory, no-one had a clue to work on.

It was Able Seaman Newell in the *Suffolk* who brought suspense to an end. The ship was on her south-westerly leg when at 6 p.m. he took over the position on the bridge of starboard after look-out. An hour and a quarter later, when sweeping his sector between the beam and the stern for perhaps the fiftieth time, he saw something which for the rest of his life he would never forget – the *Bismarck*, black and massive, emerging from a patch of mist on the starboard quarter, not more than seven miles away. 'Ship bearing Green One Four Oh,' he shouted, as though his life depended on it, which it did, and then as the *Prinz Eugen* swam into his lenses, '*Two* ships bearing Green One Four Oh.'

The *Suffolk* sprang to life. Captain Ellis ordered hard a-port and full speed ahead to get into the fog. Another officer pressed the alarm bells, all over the ship men leapt from mess-bench or hammock, slid into sea-boots, snatched coats and scarves, lifebelts and tin hats, raced down passageways and up and down ladders to reach their action stations: others, luckier, went thinly dressed to the warmth of engine-room or wireless office. Swiftly the ship answered the helm, leaned heavily to starboard: in the wardroom where dinner had started, crockery and cutlery went crashing to the deck. On the quarter-deck Ludovic Porter, the ship's commander, took off for the bridge, 'as though airborne'. A midshipman, surfacing from a deep sleep, caught a glimpse of the German ships as he tottered to his action station, thought they were *Hood* and *Prince of Wales*.

It was going to take a couple of minutes for *Suffolk* to reach the fog, and everyone on the bridge watched *Bismarck* coming on at them, noted the high V of her bow-wave, waited fearfully for the crash of her first salvoes. Miraculously they never came. *Suffolk* breached the fog wall unharmed. Safe inside she waited, sending out a string of enemy reports, watching the two blips on the radar scan that represented the German ships pass from right to left. When the enemy was some thirteen miles ahead – at the limit of *Suffolk*'s radar range but well within scope of *Bismarck*'s guns, she ran out of the fog and took up position in *Prinz Eugen*'s wake.

Norfolk, meanwhile, fifteen miles away inside the fog, had picked up the first of *Suffolk*'s signals: her captain Alfred Phillips was in his sea-cabin eating cheese on toast when the Yeoman of Signals burst in with the news. Phillips at once increased speed and steered for the open water, but in his eagerness not to lose touch, he misjudged the direction, emerged from the fog to find *Bismarck* only six miles ahead, coming straight at him. This time there was no doubting her readiness. As *Norfolk* swung to starboard to get back to the safety of the fog, *Bismarck*'s guns roared in anger for the first time. On the *Norfolk*'s bridge they saw the ripple of the orange flashes and brown puffs of cordite smoke, heard the scream of the shells – a sound which some have likened to the tearing of linen and others to the approach of an express train. Admiral Wake-Walker saw the sea to starboard pocked with shell splinters, observed one complete burnished shell bounce off the water fifty yards away, ricochet over the bridge. Great columns of milk-white water rose in the air, 200 feet high. Five salvoes in all *Bismarck* fired before *Norfolk* regained the mist: some straddled, and splinters came on board; but there were no casualties or hits.

Now *Norfolk* waited for *Bismarck* and *Prinz Eugen* to pass, as *Suffolk* had done, and when they were decently ahead, took station on the enemy's port quarter in case he suddenly altered course to port. *Suffolk* remained more or less astern of the enemy, knowing that he couldn't make an alteration to starboard because of the ice. Sometimes the German ships could be seen far ahead. When they disappeared in mists and snow flurries, Wake-Walker relied entirely on *Suffolk*'s radar, for *Norfolk*'s set, with its fixed aerials, was to all intents and purposes useless.

Ever since *Suffolk*'s contact with *Bismarck*, she had been sending out a stream of wireless reports of the enemy's position, course and speed. But none had reached base because of icing to her aerials and it was *Norfolk*'s sighting report that was first picked up by ships and shore establishments of the Atlantic command; by Admiral Tovey in *King George V*, then

600 miles to the south-east, as relieved as Churchill and the Admiralty in London that his dispositions had been correct; by the battleship *Rodney* which with four destroyers and the troopship *Britannic* had left the Clyde the day before for a refit in Boston, and was now 800 miles to the south; by the ships of the troop convoy WS8B which had also left the Clyde the day before, bound for Suez via the Cape and now feeling somewhat naked without *Victorious* and *Repulse*; by Vice-Admiral Sir James Somerville of Force H in Gibraltar harbour, to whom the news was then only of academic interest but whose turn would come later. But the man to whom the news was of greatest moment was Vice-Admiral Holland in the *Hood*, which with *Prince of Wales* and their destroyers were now only 300 miles away and steering on a converging course.

If any one ship could be said to have been the embodiment of British sea-power and the British Empire between the wars, it was 'the mighty *Hood*', as Britain and the Navy called her, and for later generations it is hard to convey the blend of affection, admiration and awe in which she was held, not only at home but by hundreds of thousands throughout the world.

She was an old lady now, one of the oldest in the Navy, laid down in 1916 in the Clydebank yards of John Brown, who later built the great Queens, named after a family who had given the Navy four famous admirals, Lord Hood who helped Rodney defeat the French in the West Indies in the eighteenth century, his brother Lord Bridport who was with Howe at the Glorious First of June, Sam Hood who helped Nelson win the battle of the Nile, Horace Hood killed at Jutland when his flagship *Invincible* blew up. She was launched by his widow, Lady Hood, in August 1918, just three months before the Armistice, the biggest warship ever built, longer even than *Bismarck* (860 feet as compared to 828) though narrower in the beam, with – like *Bismarck* – eight fifteen-inch guns mounted in pairs in four turrets. Her maximum speed of 32 knots made her the fastest warship of her size in the world, going flat out it took a ton of oil to drive her half a mile. She was a beautiful ship, elegant and symmetrical like *Bismarck*, yet dignified and restrained, without the aggressive sweep of *Bismarck*'s lines or the massiveness that spoke of held-back power. But she had one great defect, a lack of armour on her upper decks. *Hood* had been laid down before Jutland where three British battle-cruisers were destroyed by German shells which, fired at long range, had plunged vertically through the lightly protected decks, exploded inside. All big ships built after Jutland had strengthened armour. *Hood*'s armour was strengthened on her sides but not on her decks: they were to be her Achilles' heel.

Between the wars, when a quarter of the globe was still coloured red for Britain, the *Hood* showed the flag, as they used to say, to the Empire and the world. She went on cruises to Scandinavia and South America, to the Mediterranean and the Pacific, to the old world and the new. Her 1923–4 world tour, in company with *Repulse* and five cruisers, was described as 'the most successful cruise by a squadron of warships in the history of sea-power'. They visited South Africa, Zanzibar, Ceylon, Singapore, Australia, New Zealand, the Pacific Islands, San Francisco, the Panama Canal, Jamaica, Canada, Newfoundland. Their arrival anywhere caused huge crowds to gather, filled the pages of the local press. A girl in Melbourne noted: 'Every road and pathway was thick, and many families were making a day of it, taking out all the children and hampers of food and bottles of beer. The Bay was dotted with sailing boats.' The mist lifted to reveal *Hood* and her consorts coming in. 'It was a wonderful sight – something I shall never forget, everyone cheering and the kids running up and down and the sirens of all the ships in the harbour going off.' In *Hood*'s eleven-month voyage millions of people saw her, hundreds of thousands came aboard. She was a unique blend of strength and beauty, the outward and visible manifestation of sea-power: looking at her one understood what 'Rule Britannia' meant. Her visitors fingered the brasswork and fondled the guns, walked the long decks and climbed the superstructure, took snapshots galore, stunned by the scale and wonder of it all. Her public relations too were immaculate. Finding in Honolulu that a Boy Scout chosen to represent Hawaii at an assembly in Copenhagen had missed the steamer to the United States, *Hood*'s admiral gave him free passage on the boys' mess-deck and won a garland from the American press. When she arrived in San Francisco, the mayor, bowled over by her size and beauty, said: 'We surrender our city unto you. We capitulate.'

The days were filled with parades, receptions, sport, the nights when the squadron lay shining and still in the harbour like golden scarabs, with more receptions, dinners, dances, so that it was a relief to get to sea, catch up with letters and paperwork, slip back into the comfortable, familiar routine, time parcelled out in watches. Then there would be nights of leisurely steaming between tropical islands, phosphorescence in the wake and a skyful of stars above, young men on fo'c'sle and quarter-deck remembering hospitality received and given, girls kissed or laid, wondering how it might be next time. They left goodwill where they went, for the British sailor, insular but gregarious, had a knack of being congenial to those he met, Imperial cousins or foreigners with funny ways. When they got home, says *Hood*'s biographer, 'they had strengthened friendships and revived alliances. They had become a fireside story, and one ship – her photograph in thousands of homes – had become a legend.'

People in Britain saw her too, in spring and summer when she visited the Forth and Clyde and Invergordon, Plymouth and Portsmouth and Liverpool; on open days the locals swarmed aboard, the children were given rides on the capstan, sent whizzing down special chutes, fed sticky buns and ginger pop and ship's ice-cream. One moment the ship would be there, at the town's edge riding gracefully at anchor, the next she would be gone and people would hear the rumble of her guns far out at sea, like summer thunder echoing in the hills, and be comforted, for that was her real business, and yet be concerned, for her business was war.

In the thirties, war and talk of war was increasingly in the air. This was when *Hood* was supposed to go into dock for a long refit, have her main deck armoured as it always should have been, but by now Hitler and Mussolini were in power, crisis followed crisis and to have allowed *Hood* to go out of commission for the months needed for the alterations was unthinkable. She had a brief refit just before the war, mainly to put anti-aircraft guns on her upper deck: these and other additions increased her deep load by 3,000 tons, made her aft an even wetter ship than usual, so that in heavy seas her quarter-deck often went under, she lay down and wallowed like a dog.

And now on this May evening of 1941 *Hood* was on her way to do what she had been designed to do twenty-six years before, engage on the high seas her country's enemies in battle. The wind, from the north, was rising, and she pushed her long nose into the oncoming swell, threw great gouts of water aside, rose and fell, wet but marvellously steady. Astern and a little on the quarter was *Prince of Wales*, ahead the screening destroyers. Two had gone to Iceland to refuel, four were left: the gunner of the *Electra*, Mr Cain, looking at the flagship across the darkling sea, thought her never so impressive. 'With *Hood* to support us we felt we could tackle anything . . . there was no beating her . . . it was inconceivable to think that anything could happen to her.'

On *Hood*'s bridge stood Vice-Admiral Lancelot Holland who had come on board only ten days before. Holland was fifty-four, a gunnery specialist, a short slim man with almost white hair. He was shy at first but companionable when you got to know him, had a wry sense of humour, was well read, very able, intensely ambitious: one evening in his cuddy he thumbed through the Navy List with his flag-lieutenant, said it was either him or Bruce Fraser for First Sea Lord. In 1936, his only child, a gifted youth of eighteen who wrote poems and painted, died of polio, he and his wife had never got over it. As an admiral he'd already seen action in the Mediterranean in November when on Somerville's orders he'd taken five cruisers to attack the Italian battlefleet off Cape Spartivento, a bold, brave thrust that might have paid dividends if the Italians had not turned and run.

From the wing of *Hood*'s bridge Holland looked astern at where *Prince of Wales*'s great bulk lifted and fell, felt reassured, despite her deficiencies, to have her with him. Since leaving Scapa he had exercised the two ships in range and inclination practice and signalled tactical intentions: if *Hood* and *Prince of Wales* were together when the enemy was met, fire would be concentrated; if apart, they would fire independently and report each other's fall of shot; radar was not to be used unless action was imminent for fear the enemy might pick up its transmissions and alter course away. Preparations had been made and now there was nothing more to do but leave things, as Nelson once said, to the Great Disposer of Events. For the first few hours of the voyage tension in the squadron had been high, for it seemed as though battle was imminent: Lieutenant Esmond Knight, once and future actor, reflected it when he wrote of a feeling of unrest and excitement, 'I lay on my bunk and tried to read but the lines refused to register. I sat at the desk and tried to draw a funny picture for the ship's magazine, but the idea just would not come.' But now nearly two days had gone by without further news: tension had eased and it began to seem as though this trip, like so many others in the past, was just one more false alarm.

The bubble was pricked at four minutes past eight on the evening of the 23rd when *Hood* picked up the first of *Suffolk*'s reports. With his staff officers Admiral Holland studied the chart closely, plotted *Bismarck*'s position and course relative to his. Then he signalled the squadron to increase speed to 27 knots on a course of 295°, and for the destroyers to follow at best speed if they could not keep up. Over the loudspeakers the ship's companies were told that action was expected within a matter of hours.

Now *Prinz Eugen* was in the lead, *Bismarck* astern of her, *Norfolk* and *Suffolk* ten to fourteen miles astern of *Bismarck*, all going at nearly 30 knots, for the weather was calm, all creaking and groaning at the strains being put upon them. Four bows churned white furrows out of the leaden sea, the water slapped against the sides with quick, sharp blows like those from a wet towel, then fell back, hissing and frothing like detergent on the troubled swiftly passing surface, white on peppermint green. Aft, beneath each stern, a great plume of water was thrown up like a burst water-main by the thrashing screws, collapsed and disappeared in the bubbling champagne wake. In all the ships was heard the sucking, hollow drone of the ventilation fans drawing the air into the interior, the insistent, high-pitched whine of the turbines turning at maximum speed. The vibration was terrific, especially aft in the tiller-flats and engine-rooms where the plates shuddered and juddered and cried out, and things left unsecured in cabins and messes went tumbling to the deck, despite an even keel. Even in *Suffolk*'s charthouse, high up near the bridge, the plotting officer David Paton found his hand shaking as if with Parkinson's disease, could barely keep pencil and ruler steady.

As the chase settled down, some of the German crews were puzzled why the world's greatest battleship should be running away from two British cruisers; so Lindemann and Brinkmann broadcast that their orders were to avoid action with enemy warships in order to reach the Atlantic undamaged and destroy merchant shipping. These same orders had given Lütjens discretion to turn back on meeting *Norfolk* and *Suffolk*, but thinking the British fleet was still at Scapa, he saw no reason to: when darkness came, he and his staff hoped, they would give the cruisers the slip. This optimism was shared by those in *Prinz Eugen*. In the vacant staff medical officer's cabin that had been allocated to him, Commander Busch sat up late with Commander Jasper, the gunnery officer, and Lieutenant Albrecht, a first world war U-boat officer but now a civilian from Siemens, an expert on naval guns, drinking out of tooth-glasses beer they'd got from *Wollin*. They were cheerful and confident. 'The feeling of absolute security', wrote Busch (echoing what Cain in *Electra* was feeling as he looked across at *Hood*), 'was shared by every man in the ship's company. In our beautiful ship and in *Bismarck* too, the men felt safe,' adding that if things got bad, they could always rely on superior speed to get away.

But in this quiet sea they had no superior speed and could not get away. Often *Norfolk* and *Suffolk* were blotted from sight in snow flurries and fog patches, but when the visibility cleared, there they still were; and their situation reports to the Admiralty when decoded by the German cryptographic teams showed them aware of Lütjens's every alteration of course or speed. At first the Germans believed the British must have some sensitive, underwater, hydrophonic detection gear similar to their own, then, that they were picking up German radar transmissions. It was some time before they realized that at least one enemy ship was equipped with a radar set far superior to theirs. The question of British naval radar had not been discussed in the operation orders because the German naval staff believed they had none. The discovery of it at this time and place was for Lütjens and his staff a shock.

The hours passed, the four ships continued thundering south. In *Prinz Eugen* they went to second degree of readiness, four hours on watch, four hours off, but in *Bismarck*, *Norfolk* and *Suffolk*, they remained at action stations, allowing men to doze off, go and relieve themselves, fetch chocolate or cigarettes, in ones and twos at a time. Night came on, a bosky half-light in which sky and sea merged. Blackout curtains were drawn across passageways, smoking forbidden on exposed positions on deck. On the bridges of the four ships, where the only light came from the upward glow of the compass rose, shadowy figures moved about: the two admirals, Lütjens and Wake-Walker, the four captains, Lindemann and Brinkmann, Phillips and Ellis, officers of the watch, navigating and torpedo officers, signalmen, communications ratings, bridge messengers, look-outs, officers from other positions snatching a few minutes to get the latest news. German or British, these men were doing the same sort of thing, wearing the same kind of uniforms, using the same sort of instruments, giving the same commands, differing only in the causes they were fighting for, the countries where they came from, the patterns of their speech. On *Suffolk*'s bridge cold stomachs were warmed by bully-beef and cocoa, in *Prinz Eugen* by soup and coffee. Once the chase had settled down, there was little to disturb its monotony save, in the British ships, the fear of losing contact, in the German ones the hope of getting away. Near *Suffolk* a snow goose detached itself from a passing flock, kept the ship company, flying above the fo'c'sle. Some officers wanted to shoot it down, have wardroom goose for next day's dinner, but Captain Ellis, remembering the Ancient Mariner, said no.

The men of *Hood*, *Prince of Wales* and their destroyers, told that action was expected before the night was out, felt the chill of fear in their bowels, a heightening of sensation, a quickening of the blood. They were about to undergo a novel

79

experience, do what the ship had been built for and what they had been trained for: fight. For most, so far, war had been what for most participants it always is, boredom and discomfort, long patrols in winter weather, seeing nothing, meeting nobody, dog days in harbour when you had to listen to the radio to know a war was on. And now the moment which had lived only as an embryo in the wombs of their minds had gestated, was at the point of birth, there was absolutely no avoiding it.

By 9 p.m. the squadron had worked up to 27 knots, which in the rising sea was as much as they could manage. It was rougher here than where the *Bismarck* was, and the destroyers were finding it increasingly uncomfortable. Their bows lunged at each oncoming wave like a steeplechaser at Becher's, breasted the crest, rose on and up until they were pointing at the sky and it seemed the ship must become airborne, hung there a moment, then as the wave passed astern, fell like a roller coaster towards the trough, hit the water with a crack like a cannon so that keel plates shuddered and it felt as if the ship must come apart with the shock.

To Cain in the *Electra* the water parted on either side in green-white walls, and the spray cascaded over the ship like sheets of heavy rain. Sometimes from *Hood* and *Prince of Wales* the destroyers were lost to sight in spray, ghost ships sailing in a cocoon of ectoplasm. The big ships were taking it green too: Cain, watching them rise and fall from the juddering bridge of the *Electra*, the water streaming from the nostrils of the hawse-holes in their bows, saw them as two angry dragons.

At ten the British squadron began preparations for battle. In the wardroom of the *Prince of Wales*, before it was turned into an emergency casualty station, Esmond Knight attended a briefing by the ship's gunnery officer. Then he went to the cinema flat, where only a few days before he had been watching Bing Crosby, to join a queue waiting for anti-flash gear, white gloves and strange white hoods like those of the Ku Klux Klan, to protect hands and faces from burns. In all the ships, officers and men went to cabins and messes and put on clean underwear and socks, a ritual the British Navy has always observed before battle to protect wounds from infection. While there, they sat down, many of them, wrote farewell notes to parents, wives, sweethearts, for no-one doubted the gravity of what lay ahead.

In his cabin Esmond Knight wrote two letters, then took down pictures, photographs and other breakables and wrapped them in the bedclothes, for the blast from *Prince of Wales*'s own guns would soon smash them, let alone anything *Bismarck* could do. He dressed carefully, tucked trouser-legs into seaboots, put on several sweaters and a warm scarf – for his action station was in the exposed Air Defence Position above the bridge – tied a lifebelt around his chest, saw that tin hat and binoculars – a German Zeiss pair he had bought in Austria before the war – were handy, then sat down in a chair to try and compose himself. He thought of the birds he loved to watch, remembered with pleasure the sight of two fulmar petrels which had kept company with the ship all day, skimming the water one on either side, travelling at over 25 knots, yet hardly ever seeming to move their slender wings. He recalled too the mountain caps of Iceland which he had seen away on the starboard beam just before coming down, and how strangely pink they looked.

But try as he would he could not keep his mind off the coming battle. 'All the time there was a persistent little voice crying out from every nook and cranny in the ship that we were to be in action before many hours, and that nothing could avoid it.' The unaccustomed creaking and groaning and vibration as the ship raced through the water seemed somehow doom-laden. He thought of Hamlet, as any actor would. 'To die – to sleep no more.' Was this how it would end? A fellow officer looked in, said he found it impossible to sit still, was going forward to see what was happening. Esmond dozed, saw as others did in their troubled minds weird shapes and fancies dance before his eyes.

Presently the squadron went to action stations, and every-where men closed up, in the wind and spray of the upper deck, in the fug of the engine-room, in the cool and claustro-phobia of shell-room and magazine. Water-tight doors were closed, ammunition hoists tested, communications checked, guns elevated and trained: in each of *Prince of Wales*'s tur-rets the civilian technicians from Vickers-Armstrong, never dreaming they would be required to fight a sea-battle and wishing they were snug at home in bed, stood by to keep their guns in action. Down below, men looked more carefully than usual at temperature and pressure gauges, listened more acutely to orders from the bridge, to wireless messages coming in from the ether. Cooks damped down the fires of galleys, and in sickbay and wardroom doctors and sickberth attendants sterilized instruments, prepared anaesthetics and morphine. On his way to the bridge superstructure Esmond Knight passed his ornithologist friend who shouted at him and pointed excitedly to starboard. Esmond turned, expecting to see *Bismarck* on the horizon at least, saw instead what he and his friend had longed to see for years: bobbing contentedly on the water not a hundred yards from the ship, a Great Northern Diver.

During the night *Norfolk* and *Suffolk* lost contact with the enemy, regained it later. By 4 a.m. they were only 20 miles north-west of Admiral Holland, an hour later 15 miles. At 5.10 Holland signalled instant readiness for action, and in *Prince of Wales* Captain Leach broadcast to the ship's company that they expected to be in action within a quarter of an hour. He was followed by the ship's chaplain's flat, metallic voice: 'O Lord, thou knowest how busy we must be today. If we forget thee, do not thou forget us.'

Esmond Knight sat in his Air Defence Position above *Prince of Wales*'s bridge, wearing, like others round him, a tin hat perched on top of an anti-flash hood, a combination that seemed to him somewhat comic. Ahead, fine on the *Prince of Wales*'s bow, the *Hood* was bucketing along into battle, her screws churning up a tremendous wake, her huge white battle ensign curling and flapping in the wind. Astern, and still out of sight beyond the funnel haze, were the four destroyers, left behind by the turn to the south and now vainly trying to catch up. Down below on the bridge, captain, officers and look-outs kept binoculars fixed on the clear but still empty horizon.

Captain Leach gave an order, and a lad of eighteen, Knocker White by name, was given a pair of glasses and a spare coat, told to go aloft at once, up the swaying mast to the crow's nest, keep his eyes glued to the starboard beam, sing out loud and clear when the enemy's topmasts came into sight.

The minutes passed, agonizingly slowly: any moment now, thought Esmond Knight, they would see the great ship which until this moment had been to all of them only a name. No-one on the bridge said anything, every eye, every pair of binoculars was trained to starboard: there was no sound but the bows slicing the water and the wind tearing and snatching at the halyards. Then, from above, came the voice, a thin, reedy cry, but no doubting its urgency: '*Enemy in sight!*' Everyone looked up and there was Knocker White, leaning out of the crow's nest and pointing excitedly to starboard. '*Enemy in sight!*' he cried again, so there should be no mistake. On the bridge they trained binoculars in the direction of the boy's arm, the 14-inch guns in their huge turrets and the director tower and rangefinder began swinging round too. For a few moments there was nothing to see, the bridge being so much lower than the crow's nest; then from below the rim of the horizon the tops of two masts appeared, the superstructures, the ships themselves. Black they seemed to Esmond Knight in the dawn light, black and sinister and powerful. This was the enemy, come out of its lair, and to those in the British ships who had never seen a German warship before, there was something evil in the silent, purposeful way they raced southwards, hell-bent on their mission of destruction, as if the Atlantic was suddenly theirs.

And so the two admirals, Lütjens and Holland, riding on their great chargers, came at each other like knights of old, with guns for lances and armoured bridges for visors and pennants streaming in the wind. And beneath their feet, on the airy decks and in the warm bellies of their mounts, were their 6,000 young seconds, half on either side, who felt no personal ill will towards each other at all, who in different circumstances might have played and laughed and sung together, kissed each other's sisters, visited each other's homes, but now, because of this time and place, were at each other's throats, concentrating as never before to ensure that they killed first, that their knights' lances toppled the other in the tourney.

For a few moments then, as the two squadrons converged in that cold, pale dawn, with the eastern sky pink and violet on the low cirrus and a hazy blue above, there was in all the ships a silence made more striking by the knowledge of the thunder that was to come. Men's voices and hands had done all they could by way of preparation: the only sounds now were sea sounds, bows slicing the water, whistling wind and spray.

On *Hood*'s bridge a man with headphones on his ears began singing out softly the closing ranges as given from the gunnery control position, like the conductor of a Dutch auction. And at about the same time as Admiral Holland's Chief Yeoman of Signals was hoisting the preparatory signal to open fire to *Prince of Wales*, Admiral Lütjens was ordering his Chief Yeoman to hoist the signal to open fire to *Prinz Eugen*. When the range was down to 13 miles, Admiral Holland said, 'Execute.' The Chief Yeoman shouted to the flag deck, 'Down Flag 5,' Captain Kerr said, 'Open fire' and in the control tower the gunnery officer said 'Shoot!'

There came the tiny, tinkly, ridiculous ding-ding of the fire gong, like an overture scored for triangle, for a moment the world stood still, then the guns spoke with their terrible great roar, the blast knocked one almost senseless, thick clouds of cordite smoke, black and bitter smelling, clutched at the throat, blinded the vision, and four shells weighing a ton apiece went rocketing out of the muzzles at over 1,600 miles an hour. To Busch in the *Prinz Eugen*, *Hood*'s gun flashes appeared as 'great, fiery rings like suns'. Then it was *Prince of Wales*'s turn, Esmond Knight in his air defence position was deafened by the crash of the forward turrets, felt the breath squeezed from his body, was unable to see for the smoke. As it cleared, he saw an orange ripple of fire run down the length, first of *Bismarck*, then *Prinz Eugen*.

In the tightly shut armoured control position on *Bismarck*'s bridge Lütjens and his staff rocked to the roar of *Bismarck*'s opening salvo. This battle was not of his choosing, for his instructions were to shun any engagement with enemy forces not escorting a convoy, and he had delayed permission to open fire so long that there were some in *Bismarck* and *Prince Eugen* who thought he was hoping to avoid it. But with the ice to the west of him, the two cruisers to the north,

84

and Holland's force to the east, there was no escape; and in that situation his orders were to fight all out.

Now the shells were in the air, like flights of arrows, and men on either side, counting the seconds until their arrival, asked themselves anxiously where they would fall. Some believed they were directed to them personally, had their name on them as the saying went, felt the first stirrings of panic. 'He's fired,' came the agitated voice of a petty officer on *Prinz Eugen*'s bridge, and Captain Brinkmann said quietly, 'Keep calm, man. Of course he's fired. Now let's see what comes of it.' With a shriek and a roar the shells fell, great geysers of water leapt in the air, high as houses, white as shrouds. *Hood*'s shells landed in the vicinity of *Prinz Eugen*, but not dangerously so, *Prince of Wales*'s were a thousand yards short of *Bismarck*; but the shells of *Bismarck* and *Prinz Eugen* were deadly accurate, they enveloped *Hood* in a curtain of splashes, the men of *Prince of Wales* saw it with horror and relief.

The shells went to and fro, east and west. One from *Hood* landed just ahead of *Prinz Eugen*, the water rose in a tall, white column and, falling, drenched fo'c'sle and upperworks, smeared the lenses of periscopes and telescopes that jutted out from the armoured control position on the bridge. Other splashes rose on the port bow, and Captain Brinkmann ordered the helmsman to steer towards them, knowing that salvoes never land in the same place twice. Then he opened the heavy door, went outside to see through dry binoculars. *Prinz Eugen*'s first salvo had been a little short, now she was firing her second. Twenty seconds went by, Brinkmann saw the white fountains shoot up, some short, some over – a straddle – and then a flame leapt up on *Hood*'s boatdeck amidships. 'It's a hit,' shouted one of Jasper's crew excitedly, 'the enemy's on fire.' Busch saw the fire as 'a glaring blood-red rectangle which began to emit thick fumes', Captain Leach in *Prince of Wales* as 'a vast blow-lamp', Captain Phillips in *Norfolk* as 'a glow that pulsated like the appearance of a setting, tropical sun.'

On *Hood*'s bridge the fire was reported by the torpedo officer as being caused by a shell-burst among the 4-inch anti-aircraft ammunition. Able Seaman Tilburn, one of the

4-inch guns' crews, was ordered with others to put the fire out, was about to do so when ammunition in the ready-use locker started exploding, so they all lay flat on the deck. Then another shell, or perhaps two, hit *Hood*, killing many of the gun crews now sheltering in the aircraft hangar; and part of a body, falling from aloft, struck Able Seaman Tilburn on the legs.

Then the incredible happened. When Schneider in *Bismarck* saw the fire on *Hood*'s boat-deck, he ordered an immediate broadside, and presently, and for the fifth time in four minutes, *Hood* was hidden by a curtain of shell splashes. But at least one shell of that broadside made no splash: it came plunging down like a rocket, hit the old ship fair and square between centre and stern, sliced its way through steel and wood, pierced the deck that should have been strengthened and never was, penetrated to the ship's vitals deep below the water-line, exploded, touched off the 4-inch magazine which in turn touched off the after 15-inch magazine. Before the eyes of the horrified British and incredulous Germans a huge column of flame leapt up from *Hood*'s centre. One witness in *Norfolk* said it was four times the height of the mainmast, another that it 'nearly touched the sky'. Busch saw it as a red and white funnel-shaped glow, Esmond Knight as a long, pale red tongue, Lieutenant-Commander Havers in *Suffolk* as a stick of red rhubarb, Lieutenant Schmitz, the war artist in *Prinz Eugen*, as in the shape of a sinister fir-tree. It was followed by a thick mushroom-shaped cloud of smoke which to Lieutenant-Commander Towell in *Prince of Wales* had the appearance of steam, but which Esmond Knight described as 'dark yellow, like the smoke from a gorse fire'. One of the oddest things about the explosion was that it made no noise. On *Hood*'s bridge Midshipman Dundas and Signalman Briggs heard nothing unusual, and Esmond Knight said, 'I remember listening for it and thinking it would be a most tremendous explosion, but I don't remember hearing an explosion at all.' As the smoke welled upwards and outwards bits and pieces of *Hood* could be seen flying through the air – part of a 15-inch gun turret, the mainmast, the main derrick. Captain Brinkmann noticed the ship's shells exploding high up in the smoke, bursting like white stars. To Esmond Knight it seemed the most famous warship in the world was blowing up like a huge Chinese Christmas cracker.

In all disasters, however unexpected and dramatic, there is often a moment, maybe no longer than a fraction of a second, when those about to die comprehend dimly that something unusual has happened, that things are not as they should be. On *Hood*'s bridge, after the great flame had shot up, there was time for Signalman Briggs to hear the officer of the watch report the compass had gone, the quartermaster to report the steering had gone, the captain to order a switch to emergency steering: then the ship fell sideways like a collapsing house. On the boat-deck Able Seaman Tilburn was conscious of a most extraordinary vibration. He saw a man beside him killed, another's side ripped open by a splinter and the guts coming out, went over to the side to be sick, found the deck level with the water. And elsewhere in the ship there were others calmly watching dials or adjusting levers who suddenly were aware that something very strange was happening to them, who, as they were lifted off their feet, and plates and bulkheads collapsed around them, sensed for one terrible, brief moment, no longer than it takes a flash of lightning, that death had come to fetch them.

In *Prince of Wales*, *Bismarck* and *Prinz Eugen* only a handful of men saw *Hood*'s end with their own eyes: the vast majority were below decks and to them the incredible news came on inter-com and by telephone, second hand. Some simply did not believe it. *Prinz Eugen*'s executive officer, Commander Stoos, on duty in the lower command post, hearing his captain's voice announcing the news, said quietly, 'Some poor fellow up there has gone off his head.' In *Bismarck*'s after transmitting station Leading Seaman Eich heard Commander Schneider's joyous shout, 'She's blowing *up*,' and would remember the long drawn out '*uuup*' for the rest of his life. In the after director tower Müllenheim-Rechberg heard it too, and despite orders to stick to the two cruisers, couldn't resist swinging round to see for himself. The smoke was clearing to show *Hood* with a broken back, in two pieces, bow and stern pointing towards the sky. As he watched, he saw the two forward turrets of *Hood* suddenly spit out a final salvo: it was an accident, the circuits must have been closed at the moment she was struck, but to her enemies it seemed a last defiant and courageous gesture.

Now *Prince of Wales* had to go hard a-starboard to avoid the wreckage ahead, and Jasper, through *Prinz Eugen*'s main rangefinder, saw on the far side of *Prince of Wales* a weird thing – the whole forward section of *Hood*, rearing up from the water like the spire of a cathedral, towering above the upper deck of *Prince of Wales*, as she steamed by. Inside this foresection were several hundred men, trapped topsy-turvey in the darkness of shell room and magazine. Then *Prince of Wales* passed, both parts of *Hood* slid quickly beneath the waves, taking with them more than 1,400 men, leaving only a wreath of smoke on the surface. 'Poor devils, poor devils!' said Jasper aloud, echoing the thoughts of those around him; for as sailors they had just proved what sailors do not care to prove, that no ship, not even *Hood*, is unsinkable, and that went for *Bismarck* and *Prinz Eugen* too.

But joy and awe were both short-lived, for the battle was not yet over. Before the blowing up of *Hood*, *Prinz Eugen* had already been ordered to shift her fire to *Prince of Wales* and now *Bismarck* had to make only the smallest of adjustments to find the range too. On *Prince of Wales*'s bridge they saw the burst of black smoke from *Bismarck*'s cordite and the long ripple of orange flashes from her guns, knew this time without a doubt where they were aimed, what they were capable of doing. Yet Captain Leach was not despondent. His own guns had found *Bismarck* with the sixth salvo, straddled and hit. If everyone kept a cool head, they might win a victory yet.

The salvo fell and then there was chaos. A 15-inch shell went clean through the bridge, exploded as it went out the other side, killing everyone except the captain and Chief Yeoman of Signals, and the navigating officer who was wounded. Young Midshipman Ince was among the dead, aged eighteen and full of promise, at his prep school voted the boy with the best influence. On the deck below, the plotting officer, unable to distinguish between hits from *Bismarck* and the firing of *Prince of Wales*'s own guns, was unaware anything had happened until blood trickled down the bridge voicepipe, dripped on to his chart.

This same shell did for Esmond Knight too. He remembered hearing the salvo, 'like a great rushing cyclone', then everything went hazy and he was having a dream about the band playing in Hyde Park, there was a high, ringing noise in his head and he came to, thinking he was dying, feeling a little sad about it, nothing more. He heard the crash of another salvo and cries of 'Stretcher-bearer!' and 'Make way there!' He was conscious of a weight of dead men on him and screams and the smell of blood, and the dreadful thin noise some men make when dying. 'Get me out of here,' he shouted weakly, and strong hands pulled him to his feet. 'What the hell's happened to you?' a voice said, and Esmond turned and looked at him and saw nothing. The man whose delight in life was visual things, painting pictures, watching birds, was already among the ranks of the war-blinded, would now never see the Harlequin Duck or Icelandic Falcon, or anything but dim shapes again.

For most Englishmen the news of *Hood*'s death was traumatic, as though Buckingham Palace had been laid flat or the Prime Minister assassinated, so integral a part was she of the fabric of Britain and her Empire. Admiral Wake-Walker, announcing the tragedy to the Admiralty and the world with his laconic signal '*Hood* has blown up', felt compelled to classify it 'Secret', as though somehow this might prevent the dreadful news reaching Hitler. Many people simply did not believe it. Cain on watch in the *Electra* thirty miles to the north thought the Yeoman of Signals was trying to be funny, rounded on him fiercely. 'My God, but it's true, sir,' the man replied, his eyes filling with tears. Farther south Commander Baker-Creswell in his destroyer *Bulldog*, which only fifteen days before had captured the U-boat *U.110* and her secret cipher machine, thought there had been a mistake in the name. He had known *Hood* all his naval life, dined in her wardroom in Hvalfjord only two or three weeks before. Beyond him Herbert Wohlfarth in *U.556*, bound for the coast of France, also thought there'd been a mistake, asked U-boat Command for a repeat. In the same area the famous Captain Vian, hero of the *Altmark* affair, whose 4th destroyer flotilla was soon to play its own part in the *Bismarck* operation, said later that he had felt no stronger emotion at any time in the war – and this from a man who many thought had no emotions. Captain Phillips of the *Norfolk*, who had once been her gunnery officer, was utterly shattered, so was Admiral Somerville, whose flag she had so recently flown. Lofty Earl, who had served in her as a boy and was now quartermaster of the *Glenroy* fighting the battle of Crete, unashamedly broke down and cried.

Abroad too, all over the Empire and in South America and the United States, those who remembered her gliding gracefully into their harbours or lying like a golden jewel there at night, who had entertained or been entertained by her young men, danced beneath white awnings on her quarter-deck to the music of her band, strolled on her decks and seen her power and majesty for themselves, were incredulous and aghast. They remembered, many of them, where they were when they heard the news, just as people today can tell you where they were when they heard of the death of President Kennedy. Señor Gomez, of the London Bar, Gibraltar, who had collected laundry from her many times between the wars, was in a pub in London's Fulham Road, heard it on BBC radio. 'I think the world has come to an end. I truly think we are finished, señor. If the Germans can sink *Hood*, I say to myself, then there is no more hope.' Others, all over Britain, felt the same. If *Hood* could not stop *Bismarck*, what could? What now lay between her and the destruction of the Atlantic convoys? Later, resolution set in, an urge to avenge *Hood*'s death at all costs, but now before the shock wore off, a question-mark arose in the minds of many, as it had at the time of Dunkirk.

And what of *Hood*'s survivors? Admiral Wake-Walker could not spare *Norfolk* or *Suffolk* to look for them, but *Hood*'s own destroyers were not far off and they were ordered to the spot. A Hudson aircraft piloted by Flying Officer Pinhorn, one of two Coastal Command planes from Iceland that had watched the battle, contacted one of the destroyers, gave her a course to steer. In all four destroyers, preparations went ahead for the reception of shell-shocked and exhausted men: blankets and warm clothing were drawn from stores, hot soup brewed in the galleys, sick-bays made ready for the wounded.

The ships set course southwards in line abreast, several miles apart. After two hours hard steaming it was clear to those in *Electra* that they had reached the edge of the scene. There were patches of oil on the water, a floating drawer full of ratings' documents, odd bits of wood, little else. They steamed on at slow speed, saw three Carley rafts not far apart, one man on each: Midshipman Dundas, Able Seaman Tilburn, Signalman Briggs. Was this all then, all that had survived of the great ship's company? Mr Cain remembered how the ship looked at Sunday divisions, line upon line of men mustered on her upper decks 'like a small army'. 'There *must* be more,' said the Engineer Officer, 'there can't be only *three* of them.' But no, that was all. They searched a long time, found other small pieces of wreckage, a marine's hat with the number RMB X738 on it, but nothing human, not even bodies. The rest of the small army, Admiral Holland, Captain Kerr, ninety other officers, more than 1,400 men lay a thousand fathoms down, their ship their tomb, there they would lie for ever.

For the rest of that day Bismarck *and* Prinz Eugen *continued south, closely followed by* Norfolk *and* Suffolk *and the wounded* Prince of Wales. *Because of damage done to* Bismarck*'s forward oil tanks by a shell from* Prince of Wales, *Lütjens now had to abandon his plan for commerce raiding and three hours after sinking* Hood *he signalled naval headquarters in Paris that he was making for Brest. But there was no reason why* Prinz Eugen *should not be detached to attack convoys and that evening* Bismarck *turned briefly towards her pursuers to enable her consort to get away.*

Then in the early hours of the following morning, when it seemed as though the zig-zagging British ships were at their furthest distance from Bismarck, *Lütjens ordered Lindemann to put the wheel hard over to starboard to try and shake them off.* Bismarck *slowly described a huge loop, through west to north and east, crossed her own wake and that of her pursuers, then resumed her southerly course. The ruse succeeded. When dawn came the seas astern of her were empty. For the next twenty-four hours the* Bismarck *pushed on south, heavy seas and the damage reducing her speed to*

20 knots. Yet the joy of the Germans in thinking they had got clean away and the despair of the British that they had lost her were both short-lived. At 10.30 the next morning one of several Catalina aircraft sent out to locate her sighted her through a gap in the clouds bucketing along some 700 miles from Brest.

But the only British ships still in the chase, the modern King George V and the ancient Rodney were 150 miles astern, and at their maximum speed of 22 knots there could be no possibility of them catching up. There remained one last hope, Admiral Somerville's Force H, the aircraft carrier Ark Royal with the battle-cruiser Renown and the cruiser Sheffield coming north from Gibraltar. If the Ark Royal could send off a torpedo striking force that might slow down Bismarck further, there was just a chance of Tovey and his two battleships reaching her. In mid-afternoon an attack by nine Swordfish torpedo planes was launched, but the pilots mistook Sheffield for Bismarck, luckily without obtaining any hits. On return to Ark Royal the planes were rearmed, and around eight o'clock, as the light was beginning to fade from the sky, a second striking force flew off.

On the admiral's bridge of the *King George V* and in the plotting-room just off it, Tovey and his officers once more waited for news. This time they did not have the approach of *Rodney* to distract them, nor were any more calculations to be made about the enemy's position and theirs: questions of fuel and endurance had long been decided, they knew that in less than three hours, barring a miracle, they would have to turn for home. Everyone was very tired, physically and emotionally, the movement of the ship did nothing to ease it. In the long, following sea the bows yawed sideways like a car in a skid, the spray-drenched quarter-deck which Tovey and Brind so often paced at Scapa rose and fell like a Big Dipper, the ship leant heavily to starboard, stayed there like a determined drunk until the quartermaster, with the wheel hard a-port, eased her slowly back to the given course. Astern, in a light that was now beginning to fade, *Rodney* with her long snout like a giant dachshund's reached towards them, sniffing the air, as though fearful of getting left behind.

In Tovey's plotting-room the officers stood quietly round the plot, holding on to voice-pipes or table edges for support, bracing stomach muscles and knees to meet the motion of the ship. The plot itself was bare, ruler and dividers and rubber tucked away until it was necessary to pencil in the enemy's position for perhaps the hundredth time. But despite the tiredness and the difficulty of keeping upright, people were too restless to stay still: they moved up to the compass platform to chat to the captain or officer of the watch, lit cigarettes and stubbed them out, puffed at cold pipes, started conversations that petered out. Only the admiral seemed wholly cool, in command of the situation and himself, radiating confidence and serenity. It was a confidence that Lütjens, for all his courage, did not have, for it was an outgoing thing, it permeated through the ship to the humblest able seaman, so that those who waited at their action station for news, young men who had never spoken to him, barely seen him, believed that under this man things would be all right, that whatever path he asked them to take would be the right path, that whatever the outcome there would be no regrets. It had been the same with their forebears and Nelson a century and a half before.

And now the buzzer from the wireless office sounded, another signal had arrived. The Fleet Signal Officer unwrapped it, read, 'From the leader of the striking force. Estimate no hits.' It was the final blow, though no less than what they were expecting, miracles were things of the past. And yet to have come so far, to have been robbed like this at the last moment, was a bitter thing. Tovey said nothing, smiled as though his partner had just lost him the match on the last green, which in a way he had.

In *Rodney* too the disappointment was intense, for the men were keyed up, hopeful that after all their great efforts, the enemy would be delivered to them at last. Captain Dalrymple-Hamilton, who believed in keeping his men abreast of developments, addressed the ship's company over the loudspeakers. 'I am very sorry to tell you that we have just received a signal that the second Swordfish attack on the *Bismarck* has been completed, and that there have been no hits. As a result we have lost our last chance of slowing down the enemy and bringing him to action.' The commander asked permission to go from Action to Defence Stations and it was granted. Those who fell out felt intensely weary, like a long-distance runner about to breast the tape, who sees his nearest rival shoot past him.

Although all hope had gone, the squadron steamed on, there was nothing else for it to do. Presently another signal arrived on the admiral's bridge, this time from *Sheffield*. 'Enemy's course 340°,' it said. Tovey looked at it, baffled: 340° was north-north-west or directly towards them. Then he understood. 'I fear Larcom has joined the reciprocal club,' he said bitingly. What he meant was that Larcom had mistakenly judged *Bismarck* to be moving from right to left instead of left to right. It was a not uncommon mistake, especially at long range and in poor visibility, though hardly to be expected from so senior an officer. Poor old Larcom, everyone thought, to make such a balls-up at this time.

But a few minutes later another signal arrived, this time from a shadowing Swordfish. 'Enemy steering due north,' it said. This was even more baffling: the general opinion was that *Bismarck* must have turned a complete circle to avoid torpedoes, was now swinging to starboard to get back on her original course. A few more minutes passed, in which no-one knew quite what to think, then a further Swordfish report confirmed *Sheffield*'s estimate of a course of north-north-west. And then *Sheffield* reported again, this time a course of north.

Now there was no doubt about it, something very serious had happened to *Bismarck*, very serious indeed. Tovey and his officers looked at each other with incredulity and joy.

The *Bismarck* was turning to port at high speed when the torpedo struck. On the bridge Lindemann ordered the wheel to be centred. She refused to answer to it, went on swinging to port, began to heel sharply to starboard. In the after transmitting station Ordinary Seaman Alfred Eich saw on the engine-room indicator the ship was doing 28 knots, while the compass repeater showed she was steaming in a circle. In the after control tower Müllenheim-Rechberg looked at the rudder repeater, saw the wheel was jammed at 15° to port. Farther and farther *Bismarck* heeled to starboard, farther than ever before, so some thought she would capsize: they looked at one another with disbelief and fear, and one man voiced their thoughts, 'She's sinking'.

But Lindemann ordered a reduction of speed and though the ship still went on circling, she presently eased to a more or less even keel, headed into the wind. Presently a report reached the bridge of the torpedo damage. The torpedo had struck right aft at least twenty feet down, breached the steering gear compartments, flooded them: the three propellers were unharmed, but the rudders were jammed at 15° port. Water was also coming into the ship from where the after hydrophones had been destroyed and into the port engine-room up the shaft tunnel that led to the propellers. Ordinary Seaman Blum, on damage control duty, remembered the time in the Baltic when they'd practised damage to the steering gear compartment, how he'd had to feign dead. He remembered too his lieutenant saying then, 'The chances of such a hit are a hundred thousand to one against.'

The first thing to do was try and free the jammed rudders, which meant getting men into the flooded steering compartments, so the ship was put at slow speed into the wind, on a course of between north and north-west, which in the tumultuous seas gave her the least motion; and on the loudspeakers came the pipe, 'All divers report aft'. It was going to be a long and difficult business, for it meant first entering the flooded main steering compartment to unclutch the motor, then going into the flooded hand-steering compartment and coupling that up.

Before the work was begun, however, Admiral Lütjens did a strange thing. Believing the rudders were beyond repair and the ship doomed, anxious to secure his own passport to Valhalla, he signalled Berlin with typical brevity: 'Ship unmanoeuvrable. We fight to the last shell. Long live the Führer.' Such heroic exultation at such a time cannot have done much to help the morale of the admiral's staff officers nor of the wireless room operators who, because of frequency problems, took nearly two hours to pass it to Group West. Elsewhere in the ship morale was high. 'We had great trust in our captain and what he could do for us,' said one man, 'and so remained full of hope.'

Presently two engineer officers, Lieutenants Giese and Richter, came aft with the carpenter's party. They shored up the bulkhead above the steering compartments, stopped the leak from the broken hydrophonic gear and got the water out of the port engine-room. Commander Lehmann with two stokers in diving suits meanwhile had reached the armoured hatch leading to the main steering compartment. They opened it. At once the sea-water came surging and gushing into the passageway, then as the stern rose the level in the compartment dropped dramatically, the water was sucked back into the sea. The stern fell again like a lift out of control, banged against the trough, the water came surging upwards and quickly the armoured hatch was secured and battened down. No diver could possibly get down there, let alone move about and work.

The little group came up on the quarter-deck, Herzog watched them from his station at the 37 mm flak, saw them joined by the captain and two midshipmen. The captain didn't stay long, then the others began arguing. Herzog said Lehmann seemed the only calm man among them. Someone suggested a diver going over the stern, reaching the rudders that way, but they were positioned right under the stern counter, there was nothing for a diver to cling to, in that seaway he would be sucked right down or smashed to pieces against the side. Others volunteered to blow off the rudders with explosives – give their lives in the process – but even if a man could get near them, he would almost certainly damage the propellers as well; and once they were out of action, the ship would be completely impotent.

So all that remained was to see if the ship could be steered south-east by propellers alone. Back on the bridge where it was almost dark Lindemann tried every combination of telegraph orders he could imagine, but whatever he tried, the result was the same; for a while the ship's head pointed more or less in the direction he wanted, then the 15° of port rudder brought the bows slowly back into the wind, towards the north-west and danger, away from safety and home. There was not a thing wrong with the engines or main armament; but this absurd 15° of port rudder made the ship helpless as a babe.

On *Bismarck*'s course of north being trebly confirmed, Tovey at once altered south towards her. The two flagships were closing at a mean rate of over 30 knots, he thought there might be a chance of action before the light went. But when Somerville's signal reported the critical torpedo hit on the starboard quarter, he told his staff he would postpone attack until morning. 'I shall never forget', said his secretary, Captain Paffard, 'the horrified look on Daddy Brind's face.' Brind who was Chief of Staff feared, as all the staff did, that *Bismarck* would repair her damage, slip away in the night. But Tovey knew what he was doing: with rain squalls bringing visibility down to under a mile and a forecast of a pitch-black night, it was impossible to say where anyone was and the conditions gave him no advantage. All the same, said Paffard, 'It was a decision that must have taken tremendous moral courage.'

Tovey radioed Somerville to take Force H twenty miles south of *Bismarck* so as to be clear of his approach, while he hauled off to the north-eastwards so as to remain between the enemy and Brest: before dawn he would run down to the south-westwards to engage *Bismarck* against the sunrise with the advantages of sea and wind. Then he went to his sea-cabin, wrote a message for the ship's company and handed it to Captain Patterson.

To K.G.V.

The sinking of the *Bismarck* may have an effect on the war as a whole out of all proportion to the loss to the enemy of one battleship.

May God be with you and grant you victory.

J.T. 26/5/41

In *Rodney* they had fallen out action stations after thinking the Swordfish attack had failed, now General Quarters was sounded on the bugle, and men who had gratefully turned in to warm hammocks, scrambled out again, pulled on sea-boots and duffel coats, grabbed tin hats and lifebelts, stumbled in the darkness and went towards their action stations. All over the ship there was the sound of running feet on deck and ladders, the clanging of hatches, the dull thud of the closing of watertight doors. When the news came they were not going to be in action that night, the men were allowed to doze at their stations, the communications ratings took it in turns to stay awake. The captain came on the loudspeakers again, told them *Bismarck* was damaged, that they and *King George V* would engage her at dawn. All over the ship men cheered to know that they would be avenging the *Hood* after all. Then the chaplain came on: 'Almighty God, most merciful Father, we make our address to thy Divine Majesty that Thou wouldst take the cause into Thine own hand, and judge between us and our enemies', echoing the thoughts of Christian soldiers down the years, what Raeder in Berlin and many in *Bismarck* must have been praying for too.

The events of that long night in *Bismarck* are difficult to record with any certainty; for by now most of the crew were near exhaustion and later when some came to recall them, their memories were confused by subsequent events, horrors that were yet to come.

In big ships news travels slowly, unless there is an announcement from the bridge; this is especially so at action stations when men are immobile at their posts, cut off from one another. The whine of the turbines may take on a higher or lower pitch indicating an increase or decrease in speed, course may be altered this way or that, but the general assumption is that the captain on the bridge knows his business, and if there is something to tell them, they will be told. In *Bismarck* it had been broadcast there had been a hit affecting the rudders; but it was known that men were working on it, they had faith in each other and their ship, and with many hours of darkness still ahead there was every reason to suppose the damage would be made good and they could then continue home. Meanwhile there were instruments to be watched and tended, shells to be brought up from below, guns to be trained and fired: there was no time to speculate or brood, energies were needed elsewhere.

On the bridge though, as the night went on, the seriousness of the situation became increasingly apparent. Reports from aft indicated that all attempts to free the jammed rudder had failed, that nothing more could be done: in the wireless room the growing strength of enemy signals (and whatever of their contents the cryptographic team were still able to obtain) made it clear the final reckoning could not long be delayed. It was what Lütjens had been expecting all along. 'To the Führer of the German Reich, Adolf Hitler,' he signalled just before midnight, 'We fight to the last in our belief in you, my Führer, and in the firm faith in Germany's victory.' Hitler replied from the Berghof two hours later, 'I thank you in the name of the German people,' and he also sent a message, perhaps at Raeder's prompting, to the *Bismarck*'s crew. 'The whole of Germany is with you. What can still be done will be done. The performance of your duty will strengthen our people in the struggle for their existence.' There were other messages of encouragement and farewell. Raeder signalled, 'Our thoughts are with you and your ship. We wish you success in your hard fight.' Later, to strengthen resolve for the battle ahead, Lütjens signalled Raeder, 'Propose award of Knight's Cross to Commander Schneider for sinking of *Hood*'. Hitler was in his study when his adjutant brought him the message, nodded approval. Two hours later *Bismarck*'s crew heard on the loudspeaker Lindemann's voice read out Raeder's personal signal to Schneider: 'The Führer has awarded you the Knight's Cross for sinking the battle-cruiser *Hood*. Hearty congratulations.'

These messages were double-edged: they were designed to help morale but they underlined a situation in which help for morale was needed. From Group West came signals of more practical encouragement. All available U-boats were steering for *Bismarck*, the ship should transmit beacon signals for them on 852 metres and 443 kc's. Three tugs were on their way to take *Bismarck* in tow, the *Ermland* had sailed with supplies of fuel, and squadrons of bombers – eighty-one aircraft, some remember being said – would be reaching the ship by dawn.

And yet as time went on and the course and speed of the ship remained the same, there was a smell of death in the air and some began to talk openly about what few dared to think:

that with every hour that passed, the gap between themselves and *Rodney* and other enemy battleships was slowly but inevitably closing. In one engine room a man went berserk, wanted to stop the ship: Junack had to telephone for a guard to take him to the doctor for sedation. In another, Werner Lust found some former *Karlsruhe* artificers very nervous, they had been sunk before. He himself dozed, on and off, despite threats of court-martial. Up top some of the flak crews, with nothing to do, gathered round Chief Petty Officer Wienand. They liked Wienand, he was always patient, never shouted at them. He talked of his home in Hamburg, and his wife and their plans for the future. He pulled out a wallet and showed his companions his wife's photograph. 'Isn't she pretty?' he said, and then: 'If I don't survive, I want one of you to go and see her and tell her my last thoughts were of her.' Most of his audience were unmarried and one said, things weren't so bad, U-boats and bombers were on the way to rescue them. 'Yes, I know all that,' said Wienand, putting the picture back in the wallet, 'but I don't really believe it any more. It all sounds too good to be true.' It could be said of Wienand, as it was of Lütjens, that he wanted his men to face reality: that way they would cope better when the time came.

There were others who, with little to occupy them, increasingly felt the same, officers especially, those who had knowledge of the signals going backwards and forwards, knew the reality of the situation more than most; Müllenheim-Rechberg, sitting in the after control tower with one or two officers of the prize crews, said he felt 'like meat on the slab waiting for the butcher's chopper'. It was bad too for those whose work was over, who had no part to play in the coming battle: the flak crews, most of whose ammunition was now expended, Dr Externbrink and his fellow meteorologists, the merchant navy captains and the prize crews, the pilots and observers of the Arado aircraft, cooks and cobblers, tailors and stewards, the bandsmen whose instruments lay unwanted in their lockers. From exhaustion these and others, all over the ship, slept: the guns' crews in their huge turrets, the supply teams at the ammunition hoists, stokers and engine-room staff below, doctors and sickberth attendants in the sickbay. Lying in cots there were the stokers who had been scalded when one of *Prince of Wales*'s shells burst, the airmen whose legs had been broken by the explosion of an earlier torpedo, a man recovering from an emergency operation for appendix. On the tables near them saws and scalpels, rubber gloves and syringes, cotton wool and bandages and ampoules of morphia hinted at the frightfulness to come.

Some, as they dozed, had nightmares, as Esmond Knight had had before the battle of the Denmark Strait, saw weird shapes, heard screams and cries, imagined the battle had already begun, woke sobbing; others dreamed of home and those they loved, saw them with a fierce intensity, believed they were close to them, at home in Germany in May; waking, they remembered, felt fear again in the gut.

But because they were so young and weren't ready to die, didn't even want to contemplate the idea of their own deaths it was so horrible, they thought of things to give them hope. They had sunk the *Hood* in six minutes, hadn't they, the biggest warship in the world, and what they had done once, they could do again: bombers and U-boats were arriving in the morning, they would soon sink the British ships or at least prevent them from attacking; and any moment now it might be announced that the rudders had been repaired and they could slip quietly away, by nightfall be safe in France. With such thoughts young minds comforted themselves as they waited hopefully for a sea-change. But there was no change nor news of any: the turbines kept their plaintive, low-pitched whine, the water slopped against the sides, the plates groaned and creaked as the bows rose and fell, and with each hour that passed hopes got progressively fainter.

At the Berghof that evening, Hitler was entertaining guests in the big hall, watching the latest newsreels. Since the sinking of the *Hood*, Raeder had been in touch by telephone, keeping him abreast of events. Now the telephone rang once more. It was Raeder to tell him about the hit on the rudder. He took the news calmly, said his Luftwaffe adjutant, Colonel von Below, though when told that the ship was unmanoeuvrable, he remarked with some bitterness, 'Why is our Air Force not able to do that sort of thing to the British?' Later a teletype message came from Raeder saying that gale force winds were preventing the dispatch of light forces and tugs and adding that if a press notice was thought desirable, it should read: 'The battleship *Bismarck* on entering the Bay of Biscay had another brush with enemy forces and was hit by a torpedo aft' – a clear indication that Raeder believed that nothing more could be done, wanted to prepare the nation for the blow that was to come.

The guests left by side doors, Hitler took von Below to his study. He became increasingly depressed, says von Below, fretting about the effect of the loss of the ship on German prestige. Perhaps his mind went back to the happy day of the launching three years before when he had stood on the podium with the old Chancellor's granddaughter, and the crowds cheered and the sun shone and Europe was at peace. When Lütjens's signal about fighting to the last shell arrived, he dictated his replies to von Below, perhaps at Raeder's prompting. At 3 a.m. Luftwaffe headquarters rang to say the first planes had taken off to search for the ship and attack the British forces, though at the extreme limit of their range. Hitler dismissed von Below and went to bed.

She lay there wallowing in the unrelenting seas, like a great, wounded, sullen bull. The *picadors* had done their work, thrust their darts deep into flank and shoulders, taken half her power from her. Now she waited for the arrival of the *torero*, for the last trial of strength whose result was a foregone conclusion. But if she had to die, as bulls did, then she would die bravely and with dignity, that too was determined.

With the coming of the light a partial stand-down was piped to allow men to stretch cramped limbs, get some refreshment, walk about. Most stayed put: some, deep in sleep, never heard the pipe, others were too worn out to move. 'Look out for friendly aircraft, look out for friendly submarines,' chanted the loudspeaker hopefully, but this too went ignored, nobody believed it any more. Records were played to stop people brooding. One man remembered hearing '*Warum ist es am Rhein so schön?*' – 'Why is it so lovely by the Rhine?'

Müllenheim-Rechberg left the after control, made his way to the wardroom where soup was being served, took a little to warm him, exchanged a few desultory remarks with others as unshaven and bleary-eyed as himself. Then he went to the bridge, entered the armoured conning tower. Eich had been there a little earlier, seen the captain congratulating Schneider on his Knight's Cross: Lindemann was smoking as usual, but otherwise seemed relaxed, Eich was impressed by his composure.

But things had changed when Müllenheim-Rechberg arrived. There was very little activity going on. Dr Externbrink, Commander Neuendorff and others of the admiral's staff and bridge watch were stretched out asleep. Müllenheim-Rechberg observed Lindemann's steward pouring out his coffee – the steward whom Lindemann had recruited from his favourite Hamburg restaurant, who had been happy to join *Bismarck* because she seemed so large and safe. He noticed Lindemann was wearing an inflated lifebelt, went over and saluted: Lindemann looked at him dully, didn't return the salute, which Müllenheim-Rechberg thought strange as he had once been his aide. 'He looked like a man doomed to destruction,' Müllenheim-Rechberg wrote afterwards, 'dead tired, waiting patiently for the end.' He moved to the chart table, saw the drunken course the ship had been steering through the night, a picture that was self-explanatory. Then he went aft, back to his post, and on the superstructure passed Lütjens and Commander Ascher, the staff operations officer, returning to the bridge; Müllenheim-Rechberg saluted, the admiral saluted back.

At a little after eight o'clock an enemy cruiser was reported on the port bow. Lütjens and Ascher raised their glasses, recognized an old friend, the cruiser *Norfolk*, which they had first seen in the Denmark Strait three and a half days before. Now, after thirty-six hours' solitary high-speed steaming she had arrived on the scene in the nick of time, as the final curtain was about to go up. She flashed her light at *Bismarck*, then veered away. A rain squall swept over *Bismarck*, and when it had cleared, her officers on the bridge saw with tired eyes two battleships dead ahead. One was *King George V* class, the other, as expected, *Rodney*.

Lütjens and Netzbandt had seen *Rodney* from the bridge of *Gneisenau* only ten weeks earlier, when one night after they had sunk several ships from a convoy her long silhouette had suddenly become visible against the light of the blazing *Chilean Reefer*. Then Netzbandt had put *Gneisenau*'s wheel over, gone on to full speed, they had melted into the night. There was no use trying that today: now *Rodney*'s turn had come and she and her consort stood relentlessly towards them. Schneider took up his position in the gunnery control tower, non-duty officers were piped to the big charthouse, throughout the ship the alarm bells were sounded for the last time.

On the bridge of *King George V* and *Rodney* officers and lookouts strained through binoculars to catch a first glimpse of the ship that for days now – it seemed like weeks – had been in the very marrow of their lives. Did she really exist? She had the same sort of grim reality as the giant in the boy's story-book. And what did she look like, this monster that had sunk their beloved *Hood*?

And then, suddenly, there she was; 'veiled in distant rainfall,' wrote Lieutenant-Commander Guernsey, 'a thick, squat ghost of a ship, very broad in the beam, coming straight towards us.' 'Enemy in sight' came over the *Rodney*'s loud-speakers and telephones, and all over the ship men cheered. The time was 8.43 a.m., the range twelve and a half miles, and Captain Dalrymple-Hamilton gave the order to open fire.

Before *Rodney*'s first salvo had landed, the fire-gong sounded in *King George V*. On the upper bridge Captain Patterson and his officers, on the lower the admiral and his officers, waited in tin hats and with cotton wool stuffed in their ears to deaden the sound, for the flagship's opening roar. Within seconds it came, like a small earthquake, the bitter cordite fumes catching at their throats, the explosion of the charges stunning them. The compass bounded out of its binnacle, a pile of signals was sucked upwards like a tornado, scattered to the winds.

The salvoes fell as *Bismarck* was turning to starboard to bring all her guns to bear: great, white clumps rose all round her, higher than her foremast. Then it was her turn. In the British ships they saw a ripple of orange fire down the length of her, followed by a pall of cordite smoke, far blacker and thicker than their own. 'Time of flight fifty-five seconds,' announced a keen officer of the admiral's staff, and started counting off the time that was left. 'For heaven's sake,' said Tovey, not wanting to know the moment a shell might strike him, 'shut up!' Even so they waited anxiously on the bridges of the two battleships for the salvo to arrive, the men of each hoping it was aimed at the other. They felt an instinct to duck, then the thunderbolt fell off *Rodney*'s bow, short, in a pattern of huge splashes and Guernsey and others on the bridge of *King George V* breathed a sigh of relief.

At ten miles' range *Norfolk*, to the east of Tovey, joined battle with her 8-inch guns. *King George V* and *Rodney* continued firing with their foremost turrets and were soon claiming straddles and hits. But *Bismarck* was finding the range too, her third salvo straddled *Rodney*, a few splinters came aboard. One passed through the starboard side of the anti-aircraft director, smashed the cease-fire bell, passed through a tin hat on a hook, severed the trainer's telescope, hit the fire gong and grazed the trainer's wrist, after which the director was evacuated and the crew took shelter below. Captain Dalrymple-Hamilton turned to port to avoid the next salvo and bring the after turret into action. 'I watched *Rodney*,' said Guernsey, 'to see if she was being hit, but she just sat there like a great slab of rock blocking the northern horizon, and then suddenly belched a full salvo.' With his own eyes he saw some of the one-ton shells come whizzing out of the barrels at 1,600 mph, watched them 'like little diminishing footballs curving into the sky'.

At a minute before nine, when the range was down to eight miles, Tovey ordered *Rodney* and *King George V* to turn from south-east to south to bring the full weight of their guns to bear. Just before *Rodney* turned, Captain Coppinger, who was beside Captain Dalrymple-Hamilton on the bridge, taking notes of the battle, saw the burst of a heavy shell on *Bismarck*'s fo'c'sle, while another sent a sheet of flame up the superstructure. After the turn, *Bismarck* was seen to be altering to starboard too, to keep all her guns bearing, so that both forces were steaming on opposite courses, almost parallel.

Now a fourth British ship arrived to join the battle. It was the cruiser *Dorsetshire*, cutting things even finer than *Norfolk*. After 600 miles steaming at speeds that varied between 20 and 32 knots she opened fire on the enemy from the south. She appeared at a useful moment, for the battleships were now steaming downwind, the funnel gases and cordite smoke hung about the bridge and round the gunnery control tower, making aiming at *Bismarck* difficult.

And now *Bismarck* shifted her fire from *Rodney* to *King George V*, spat out a salvo. Guernsey heard the whine of its approach, saw four tall fountains rise near the fo'c'sle, one short, three over. He wondered if the next would hit, found himself edging into the doorway at the back of the bridge, then remembering it was only splash-proof plating, stepped boldly forward. On the scan in the radar office they tracked some of *Bismarck*'s shells coming towards them, held them from about three miles out to half a mile in. The radar officer said it was no more alarming than seeing enemy gun flashes, and the period of suspense was much less. They also tracked the flight of their own shells, lost them at five miles out.

Only a quarter of an hour after the two ships had turned south, Dalrymple-Hamilton found *Bismarck* beginning to draw past him: if he continued on this course he would be masking the fire of *King George V* on his other side, so interpreting in the widest sense Tovey's permission for him to manoeuvre independently, he did what no captain of a British warship had done since the Battle of Cape St Vincent 144 years earlier – took his ship out of the line, and while the enemy was engaging *King George V*, turned *Rodney* right round to a course of north. Tovey, following a few minutes later, called up to Patterson: 'Get closer, get closer, I can't see enough hits!'

In the big ships they were too occupied with fighting to take an objective view of the battle. It was different in their escorting destroyers, *Tartar* and *Mashona*: these last two

Tovey had detached at the start of the action to return to Londonderry to fuel, but having come so far they weren't going to miss the battle for anything.

They were *aficionados* at the bull-fight, come to see how *torero* Tovey killed his first bull, spectators at a public execution. They saw things the combatants were unaware of, the sun for the first time in days shining from between white, racing clouds, and the wind, still strong, marbling and stippling the green water, whipping the tops from the short, high seas. One officer in *Tartar* was struck by the colour contrasts; bits of blue in the sky, a blue they hadn't seen for days, the blackness of *Bismarck* and the grey of the British ships, the brown pall of cordite smoke and the orange flashes of the guns, shell-splashes white as shrouds.

It was a lovely sight to begin with, a pageant, another officer called it, wild, majestic, almost too bright and clean for the matter in hand. It seemed strange to think that within those three Leviathans were 5,000 men, it was irrelevant somehow, this was a contest between ships, not men. That was how it always was in a sea-fight, you killed people whom you did not know and could not see, whom you had little cause to think even existed.

Bismarck was a menace that had to be destroyed, they knew that, a creature that would have cut the arteries that kept their country alive. And yet to see her now, surrounded by enemies on all sides, hopelessly outgunned and outnumbered, was not a pretty sight. She was a ship after all, perhaps the finest they had seen, and ships were their livelihood and life. As they watched the shells from the battleships and cruisers tearing into her, they thought of her crew, seamen like themselves. 'What that ship was like inside,' said George Whalley, 'did not bear thinking of; her guns smashed, the ship full of fire, her people hurt; and surely all men are much the same when hurt.'

By 10 a.m. the *Bismarck* was a battered burning wreck, her guns twisted and silent, full of huge holes in her sides and superstructure through which fires glowed and flickered, grey smoke issuing from a hundred cracks and crevices and drifting away on the wind, listing heavily to port, but at the foremast her admiral's flag and at the mainmast the German naval ensign still bravely flying. In the British ships they looked at her with awe and admiration, awe that such a magnificent ship should have to be reduced to this, admiration that her crew had fought so gallantly to the end.

As they watched, the lifeless ship took life – the enemy in person, a little trickle of figures running aft along *Bismarck*'s quarter-deck, climbing the guard-rails and jumping into the sea, unable to stand any more the inferno aboard, welcoming like lemmings death in the cool, kind sea. And presently in the British ships fire was checked, for the *Bismarck* no longer menaced anyone, her life was almost at an end.

There was nothing more now for Tovey to do. Whether *Bismarck* sank sooner or later was immaterial: what was certain was she would never get back to port. He had already stayed ten hours longer than he had said his fuel would allow, and U-boats would soon be on the scene, if they had not reached it already. He signalled *Rodney* to form up astern, gave orders to Patterson to take the flagship home. And as he left he made a general signal to ships in company: 'Any ship with torpedoes to close *Bismarck* and torpedo her.' Only one ship, *Dorsetshire*, still had torpedoes, and when Tovey's signal reached her, Captain Martin had already anticipated it. Closing in to a mile and a half on *Bismarck*'s starboard beam, she fired two torpedoes, both of which hit. She then went round the other side, at just over a mile fired another which also hit.

Far off now in *King George V*, halfway to the horizon, Tovey saw through his glasses the great ship slowly keel over to port until her funnel was level with the water, go on turning until she was completely upside down. He remembered Jutland and the sinking *Wiesbaden*, was already forming in his mind the words of his official dispatch: 'She put up a most gallant fight against impossible odds, worthy of the old days of the Imperial German navy.' The stern dipped below the surface of the water, then the main keel: the great flared bows were last to go, and then all that was left to show where *Bismarck* had been were hundreds of men in life-belts, swimming in oil and water.

When the survivors were clear of the ship, she slowly rolled over away from them until she was bottom up.

Müllenheim-Rechberg and Junack looked for signs of torpedo damage, couldn't see any. Heinz Staat noticed two men sitting on the upturned keel, making no effort to save themselves. The stern went under and then the rest of her, taking all their personal belongings and hundreds of dead and wounded.

The *Dorsetshire* came round from the port side where she had fired her last torpedo, lay stopped in the sea a little way off; and survivors who had wondered if they were not escaping death by shellfire for death by drowning felt a new surge of hope: even if it meant being taken prisoner, they were going to be rescued, they were going to live.

They struck out as well as they could towards the cruiser, though with the high seas and the oil from *Bismarck*'s tanks and the wounds of many, it wasn't easy. Müllenheim-Rechberg, swimming along, passed a man who said, 'I've no left leg any more.' Staat remembered being told that when you died of cold, you first felt it in the testicles, but it was his feet and fingers that were getting numb. After more than an hour's swimming the first of them reached the *Dorsetshire*'s side, where rafts, ropes, scrambling nets, fenders, lifelines of all kinds had been let down. Müllenheim-Rechberg noticed that many men, not seamen, didn't know how to grip a straight rope, urged them to get into ropes with bowlines. Staat's fingers were so frozen that he couldn't grip the rope at all, seized it with his teeth, was hauled on board that way. Müllenheim-Rechberg put his foot in a bowline rope, was pulled up by two sailors: when he reached deck level he tried to grab the guardrail, was too exhausted and fell back into the sea: he got into the same rope again, was hauled up by the same two sailors, this time took no risks, said in immaculate English, 'Please help me on board' which they did. Midshipman Joe Brooks of the *Dorsetshire* went down one of the lifelines, tried to get a bowline round a German who had lost both arms and was gripping the lifeline with his teeth: the ship rolled heavily, they both went under, Brooks never saw him again. Herbert Blum reached the *Dorsetshire*'s bow, was sucked under by a sea, felt himself under the keel, then came up the other side. The waves carried him away from *Dorsetshire*, but *Maori* was lying stopped a little way off, he managed to reach her and was hauled safely up.

The *Dorsetshire* had picked up some eighty men and the *Maori* some twenty, many more were in the process of being hauled up and hundreds more were waiting in the water when an unexpected thing happened. *Dorsetshire's* navigating officer, Lieutenant-Commander Durant, sighted on the starboard bow two miles away a smoky discharge in the water. He pointed it out to Captain Martin and others on the bridge. No-one knew what it was but the most likely explanation was a U-boat: the Admiralty had sent a warning that U-boats were on the way, and they were lucky not to have encountered any already. And if it was a U-boat, *Dorsetshire*, laying stopped in the water, was a sitting target. In the circumstances Captain Martin had no choice but to ring down for full speed, and in *Maori* Commander Armstrong did the same.

The water round *Dorsetshire's* stern foamed and bubbled with the sudden exertion of the screws. Slowly, then faster, the ship moved ahead. *Bismarck* survivors who were almost on board were bundled over the guardrails on to the deck; those halfway up the ropes found themselves trailing astern, hung on as long as they could against the forward movement of the ship, dropped off one by one, others in the water clawed frantically at the paintwork as the side slipped by. In *Dorsetshire* they heard the thin cries of hundreds of Germans who had come within an inch of rescue, had believed that their long ordeal was at last over, cries that the British sailors, no less than survivors already on board, would always remember. From the water *Bismarck's* men watched appalled as the cruiser's grey side swept past them, believed then that tales they'd heard about the British not caring much about survivors were true after all, presently found themselves alone in the sunshine on the empty, tossing sea. And during the day, as they floated about the Atlantic with only life-belts between them and eternity, the cold came to their testicles and hands and feet and heads, and one by one they lost consciousness, and one by one they died. Of the 2,000 men who had sailed from Gotenhafen ten days before, only 107 survived.

MENACE

THE LIFE AND DEATH OF THE *TIRPITZ*

HAVING TAKEN PART *in the pursuit and destruction of the* Bismarck, *I had every hope of repeating the experience with her sister ship* Tirpitz *(named after the founder of the German navy) nine months later. By late 1941* Tirpitz *had completed her trials in the Baltic and in accordance with Hitler's orders that every German warship that was not in Norway was in the wrong place, sailed for Trondheim in January 1942; here a special berth had been prepared for her at the head of Foettenfjord, near Trondheim, some forty miles from the open sea. Her purpose in being there was threefold: as a springboard for attacking the Arctic convoys sailing to and from Murmansk and Archangel; to act as a fleet in being to tie down British battleships in Scapa Flow; and as a powerful unit in defence of Norway against a seaborne landing which Hitler was convinced would eventually take place.*

Having learnt of Tirpitz's *arrival Winston Churchill at once realized the menace she posed to allied shipping. 'The destruction or even crippling of this ship is the greatest event at sea at the present time. No other target is comparable to it. I regard the matter as of the highest urgency and importance.'*

His warning was timely, for six weeks later Tirpitz *and her destroyers under the command of Vice-Admiral Otto Ciliax (fresh from bringing* Scharnhort, Gneisenau *and* Prinz Eugen *from Brest through the English Channel to Wilhelmshaven) sailed to attack the Arctic convoy PQ12, then approaching the North Cape en route to Murmansk. Their departure was observed by the submarine* Seawolf *whose report was soon in the hands of Admiral Tovey, who with the battleships*

111

King George V, Duke of York, *the carrier* Victorious *and a destroyer screen that included* Tartar *was cruising to the westward of PQ12 and ready for any eventuality. But for the next two days the weather was atrocious, preventing Ciliax from finding the convoy and Tovey from finding Ciliax. Indeed Tovey had more or less abandoned his search when an intercepted Ultra signal (that is one enciphered on the German most secret Enigma machine) reached him, in which two of Ciliax's destroyers which had gone to Narvik to refuel were informed of the exact time and position for joining* Tirpitz *the next morning. On receipt of this Tovey sailed the fleet towards* Tirpitz's *estimated position and ordered the* Victorious *to fly off torpedo-carrying aircraft to attack her. They found her where they expected to and launched an attack. Unfortunately it was poorly carried out,* Tirpitz *avoided all the torpedoes and escaped up Vest Fjord to the shelter of Narvik.*

A second opportunity came a few days later, after Tovey had taken the fleet back to Scapa Flow. Another Ultra intercept gave advance warning of the night chosen for Tirpitz *to sail from Narvik to Trondheim; and a flotilla of destroyers, of which* Tartar *was one, were ordered to close the Norwegian coast and then sail up it in line abreast and two miles apart, in order to intercept* Tirpitz *on her way south. I was then the* Tartar's *torpedo officer, and I have described my recollection of the events of that night in my autobiography.*

Back in her berth at Foettenfjord Tirpitz *was unsuccessfully attacked in April by a force of British bombers and then in June she sailed to join other warships in Altenfjord to attack the Arctic convoy PQ17. In the event they did not need to attack it, for thinking that they had already left harbour (despite assurances from his intelligence officers that they hadn't) the British First Sea Lord, Dudley Pound, panicked and ordered the convoy to scatter and its escorts to withdraw. As a result twenty-four of the thirty-five ships that comprised the convoy were sunk by aircraft and U-boats; and* Tirpitz *returned to Foettenfjord to undergo a refit.*

This news was now the signal for the British naval authorities to go ahead with a new form of attack which they had been preparing; the penetration of Tirpitz's *anchorage*

by two 'chariots' or human torpedoes which the Italians had
already employed with much success against the British fleet
in Alexandria. The chariot was the same size as a 21-inch tor-
pedo with a 600-pound detachable warhead. Two men rode
it, the one in front operating the rudder and hydroplanes,
his companion navigating, negotiating the protective nets,
and fixing the warhead to the enemy's hull. Submerged,
the chariot had a speed of 3 knots with a range of eighteen
miles.

A base for the chariots was established at Fort Blockhouse,
Portsmouth, in April, and soon after the first of the charioteers
or, as the Admiralty called them, 'Volunteers for Hazardous
Operations', arrived for training. Among the thirty-one volunteers were Sub-Lieutenant Jock Brewster, a Scot, Sergeant
Craig of the Royal Engineers, Able Seaman Brown and
Able Seaman Bob Evans. They underwent escapes in the
90-foot diving tank, practised riding dummy chariots in
an experimental tank, then, when the operational chariots
arrived, carried out exercises on them in a deserted part of
Portsmouth harbour.

But in Portsmouth they could be seen, and as secrecy was
essential a new base was established as far from habitation
as possible – in the desolate Loch Erisort near Stornoway in
the Hebrides. Here further prolonged exercises were carried
out in conditions similar to those of the Norwegian fjords,
and here Brewster, Craig, Brown and Evans learned that they
had been chosen for an attack on the *Tirpitz*. Two other men,
Able Seamen Billy Tebb and Malcolm Causer, were detailed
to act as their dressers.

Now came the question as to how to transport the chariots
to as near the target as possible. Obviously no warship or
other large vessel would be able to penetrate far into German-
controlled Norwegian waters; indeed the only vessel that
stood any chance of bluffing its way past the shore batteries
and guard-vessels was a local fishing-boat or trawler, of
the kind that frequented these waters. But where to find
one?

The only harbour in Britain in which such vessels were
to be found was at Lunna Voe in the Shetland Islands,

the headquarters of an extraordinary clandestine organization nicknamed the 'Shetland bus'. Here were based several Norwegian fishing-boats which had escaped from Norway since the occupation; their crews, under British supervision, were now running a two-way service to the Norwegian fjords, taking over agents, saboteurs, radio equipment and weapons, and bringing back returning agents, volunteers and refugees. One of these boats, the *Arthur*, skippered by Leif Larsen, had already taken agents to and from Trondheim. Now Larsen was asked if he would take two chariots and their crews over to attack the *Tirpitz*. He at once agreed.

But there was much to be done first. Once inside Norwegian waters the *Arthur* had to pass as a genuine local fishing-boat. What papers would she need to be cleared by the guard-boat that lay close to Agdenes, at the mouth of Trondheimsfjord? A Norwegian agent, Arne Christiansen, was sent from Sweden to Trondheim to find out. He contacted various resistance workers from whom he learned that the *Arthur* would require a cargo manifest, a certified crew list, ship's registration papers, identity cards for each of the crew, special permits to enter the Trondheim military zone, and a certificate signed by the various German harbourmasters of all the ports the *Arthur* had visited during the past three months. The resistance people promised to obtain sets of all these, as well as details of the nets surrounding the *Tirpitz* which had been made in a local factory.

A month later another Norwegian agent, Odd Sörli, went to Trondheim from Sweden, collected the necessary papers and, disguised as a Norwegian pastor, brought them first to Stockholm, then to London. Here rubber stamps were made similar to those used on the stolen papers, signatures were copied, and a complete set of forged documents was prepared for the *Arthur* and her crew. On their arrival in Shetland they were smudged with dirt and oil and handled by Larsen and others to give the impression of age.

While all this was going on, the *Arthur* was being converted. On deck special cradles were constructed to carry the 2-ton chariots for the twenty-four-hour journey across the North Sea, and the ship's derrick was strengthened to lift them in and out of the water. Then, as it was essential to hide the chariot crews and dressers during the dangerous run past the guard-boat and up the inner reaches of the fjord, a secret compartment was built between the engine-room and the hold to keep them out of sight, and two eyebolts were fitted to the *Arthur*'s keel for towing the chariots deep underwater. The hold itself would contain a cargo of peat, a commodity common to both Shetland and Norway.

Finally preparations had to be made for the crews of *Arthur* and the chariots to escape after the attack, as without Trondheim-stamped papers there could be no question of them attempting a return passage past the guard-boat. After the attack the chariot crews would make their way to the south shore of the fjord where cars would be waiting to take them to the Swedish frontier. The *Arthur*'s crew and the two dressers would then scuttle the *Arthur* and make their way to another part of the fjord where a lorry filled with hay in which they could hide would also be waiting. If either or both of these arrangements failed, there would be a rendezvous on top of a certain hill the following day; and if that failed, both crews would be equipped with maps and rations to find their own way to Sweden.

Now everything was ready for a full-scale exercise of the operation, as near to the real thing as could be devised. One evening the *Arthur*, with chariots and crews on board, sailed from Lunna Voe and set course south-west. She passed Cape Wrath on the north-eastern tip of Scotland, and entered the remote Loch Cairbawn. At the far end of the loch, the hills behind her and protected by a row of nets, lay the old battleship *Nelson*: it was as similar a target to *Tirpitz* as they could get. They made fast alongside the depot-ship *Alecto*, and next day Admiral Sir Max Horton, who was staying on board *Nelson*, came over to meet them.

That evening the two dressers helped Brewster, Craig, Brown and Evans into the diving gear. The chariots were lowered and mounted, and the four men sped away towards the darkened battleship, their heads like four black balls skating along the surface of the water, then sliding silently beneath the waves. Then, and on subsequent evenings, they cut their way through the nets, laid dummy charges on the

Nelson's keel, and stole away unobserved. Was this how it would be on the night?

On a crisp, bright October morning, they set out at last on their great adventure. There were ten of them on board, Larsen and his three Norwegian crew – Björnöy in charge of the engine, Kalve and Strand – the four charioteers and the two dressers. Not far from the coast a gale sprang up, and soon they were steaming into a rough easterly sea. Many were seasick, but they celebrated Brewster's twenty-fifth birthday with a tot of gin. Next day the weather abated, and in the evening they sighted mountains ahead. Next morning, very early, they nosed their way into the shelter of the islands, and Larsen dropped anchor in a small desolate bay.

Now it was time to lower the chariots into the water and fix them to the eyebolts in the hull for the 100-mile journey through the fjords. But no sooner had the tarpaulins and nets covering them been removed than there was a cry of 'Air-craft!' from the look-out in the bows. They had just about time to replace the coverings before the plane zoomed overhead.

This plane and others remained uncomfortably close all morning, so Larsen decided to move elsewhere. In another, even remoter anchorage, the chariots were lowered over the side, and Brewster and Evans, having changed into diving gear, soon had them positioned beneath the keel.

Since leaving Shetland the *Arthur* had been receiving regular radio messages, based on Spitfire reconnaissance flights, that the *Tirpitz* was still at Trondheim. Now, with less than forty-eight hours to go before the attack (they were a day late on schedule but an extra day had been allowed for), and in waters where they might be searched at any time, they decided to throw the radio receiver overboard, together with the chariot's cradles, and any other gear not usually to be found in a local fishing-boat. The machine-gun they had been given for emergencies was stowed in the secret compartment along with the rucksacks and provisions for the escape.

The *Arthur*'s last stop was to be the village of Hestvik, on the east coast of an island only some fifteen miles from the Agdenes fortress. Here it had been arranged for Larsen to obtain from a local contact the latest information on Ger-man minefields and shipping control. But on the way, going up the Trondheimsleden, the engine began knocking badly. Björnöy thought it was the piston, and that water had got into the cylinder. It became worse and worse, and by the time they reached Hestvik at 11 p.m. the engine was about to die on them.

'You strip the engine,' said Larsen to Björnöy, 'while I go and see my contact.'

The contact's name was Nils Ström, a local storekeeper, and in his shop Larsen said, 'Do you need any peat?'

This was the cue for Ström to say, 'No, thank you. Did Odd Sörli send you?', but instead he said, 'Yes, we could do with all you've got.'

Christ, Larsen thought, have I come to the wrong man? He said, 'I can't let you have more than a little. Those were Odd Sörli's instructions.' For a moment Ström looked blank, then the truth dawned on him. He told Larsen about the control system in the fjord, and the papers the Germans most wanted to see. Then the two of them went back to the *Arthur* to see what had happened to the engine.

Björnöy, covered in oil, showed them the piston. 'Look,' he said, 'it's badly cracked. You can see. We can't sail with that.'

Ström took Björnöy to the house of the village blacksmith, and woke him up; he was a friend of Ström's and very reliable. For two hours Björnöy worked in his forge on the damaged piston, then as it was growing light he returned with it to the *Arthur*. After reassembling the engine and testing it, he said to Larsen, 'It should get us to Trondheim, but that's about all.'

It wasn't the happiest augury for the last part of their trip, but there was nothing to be done except hope. It was now 7 a.m.: Larsen and Björnöy had been up most of the night. 'We'll have a couple of hours' sleep,' said Larsen, 'and then we'll go. We must all be fresh for tonight.' Bluffing their way past the guard-boat at Agdenes would, as everyone knew, be by far the most hazardous part of the voyage. When Larsen first sighted her below the Agdenes fortress close to the northern shore, everyone went to their stations: Larsen and Björnöy in the wheelhouse, Strand at the engine, Kalve in the bows, the six Britishers in the secret compartment, with the electric switchboard in the engine-room covering the entrance to it.

So far that morning there had been a light breeze on the water, but as they neared the guard-boat Larsen observed to his horror that the sea was a flat calm. Looking over the side he could see the chariots clearly in the water. How could the Germans in the guard-boat fail to observe them too?

A hundred feet from the guard-boat Larsen gave the order to stop engines, and the familiar tonk-tonk of the motor abruptly ceased. A group of German sailors in the bows watched the *Arthur* approach, and as she eased alongside Larsen saw one of them staring at the water around the stern. Had he seen the chariots? Kalve, in the *Arthur*'s bows, threw a heaving line across to the German boat, and by lucky chance it landed on the sailor's shoulders. His attention distracted, he hauled in the line to secure the *Arthur* alongside. The captain of the guard-boat, a lieutenant, stepped on board.

'Papers!' he said.

Larsen gave him the forged documents, hoping that a glance would be sufficient, and they would soon be on their way. But the lieutenant went down the hatch to the cabin, sat down at the mess-table, and spread the papers before him.

'I see you come from Kristiansund,' he said, 'do you know my friend the harbourmaster, Lieutenant Ormann?'

Larsen wondered if this was a trap.

'Yes,' he said vaguely.

'He is an old friend of mine,' said the lieutenant, 'we went to school together.'

The lieutenant continued his leisurely scrutiny of the papers so long that in the darkness of the secret compartment the Britishers wondered if there had been a hitch. If so, they had the machine-gun and revolvers with them, and were prepared to fight.

'What is your cargo?' asked the lieutenant.

'*Torö*,' said Larsen (the Norwegian for peat).

'What is that?'

Larsen resisted an impulse to use the English word.

'Stuff for burning,' said Larsen, 'you dig it from the ground.'

'How do you spell it?' Larsen told him, and he carefully wrote it down.

'Any radio on board?'

'No.'

'Cameras?'

'No.'

'Passengers?'

Larsen thought of the six men below.

'No.'

The lieutenant said, *'Hier ist Ihr Ausweis,'* and handed him the permit. 'You will give this to the harbourmaster at Trondheim on arrival.'

They went on deck. The lieutenant peered into the wheelhouse, and down into the engine-room, then with a wave indicated to Larsen that he could go.

The lines were cast off, Larsen put the engine slow ahead. The water frothed at the stern, hiding the chariots from view. Slowly the guard-boat dropped astern.

In the *Arthur* the relief was tremendous. The chariot crews and dressers were released from their compartment and came on deck. Everyone wanted to shout and sing. Now there was nothing but forty miles of clear water between them and their target, between the little St George and the huge dragon, lying unsuspecting in its lair at the head of the fjord.

All afternoon the *Arthur* chugged slowly along the northern side of the fjord. The sea remained calm and the weather fine. There was a lot of shipping going in either direction. When a destroyer, outward bound, passed them, they had to slow right down to prevent its wash rocking the chariots.

At dusk they reached the end of the south-eastern leg of the fjord, and turned north. Here there was a slight change in the weather; a wind had risen and clouds were gathering ahead. The dimmed lights of Trondheim came abeam, and they could see against the night sky the twin spires of its cathedral. There were fifteen miles to go.

'Better get ready,' said Larsen.

Craig and Evans went below, and the dressers helped them into their diving suits. Brewster and Brown followed. The moment for which they had all been waiting was now at hand; the long months of training, the perilous and successful journey through the fjords – all were now about to come to fruition. They were about to try to sink the *Tirpitz*:

somehow the idea seemed too fantastic to be true. Brewster was putting on the lower half of his diving dress when there was a sudden jolt, and he was thrown sideways.

'The weather's worsening,' somebody said.

For Larsen in the wheelhouse, it was worsening more than he dared believe. In the last half hour the wind had freshened considerably. The ship was steaming into a nasty head sea, at one moment her bows riding the crest of the waves, at the next plunging into the trough. With every rise and fall of the ship there would be a similar rise and fall for the chariots. How long could the towing wires stand the strain?

There was a loud thud, heard by everyone, as one of the chariots, rising sharply upwards, hit the propeller. Then, suddenly, the *Arthur*'s motion eased.

'I think the chariots have gone,' said Larsen. 'We'll have to inspect them and see.'

They made their way towards the shore, and in a sheltered bay Evans in his diving suit went over the side. He surfaced a moment later with the news that everyone had feared: both chariots were gone.

In the little wheelhouse British and Norwegians looked at each other in anguish and dismay. To have come as far as this, to have brought themselves and their weapons to within striking distance of their target, then at the eleventh hour to be robbed of it, was something that did not bear thinking about. Nobody said anything; there was nothing to say.

There could no question of going back down the fjord: their papers had not been stamped at Trondheim, and anyway the engine was on its last legs. All that was left to them was to scuttle the *Arthur* and make their way ashore. They were nowhere near where the Trondheim resistance people were waiting, so, with emergency provisions and maps, they would have to walk the sixty miles to Sweden on their own.

At two in the morning, having thrown the peat overboard, five of them went ashore in the dinghy. One returned to the *Arthur,* and when they had opened the seacocks and bored holes below the water-line, the rest went ashore too. The ten men set off together towards the east, and after reaching a wood they lay down to sleep. Then, because such a large party might arouse suspicion, they decided to split: Larsen, Kalve, Craig, Evans and Tebb in one party, Brewster, Brown, Causer, Björnöy and Strand in the other.

After a variety of adventures and some hardship in the snows and bitter cold, both parties reached the Swedish frontier. Brewster's party, keeping to the high ground, all crossed over safely, but Larsen's group, coming lower down because of exhaustion to Evans, was challenged by Norwegian frontier guards. There was an exchange of shots; one of the guards and Evans was hit. The rest of the group found their way across the border.

Next day the Germans found Evans in a deserted hut to which he had crawled, took him to hospital and nursed him back to health. Under interrogation by the Gestapo he told them everything he knew about the chariots and their functions; then, his usefulness over, and on Hitler's orders, he was shot.

A week later the rest of the party were flown to England. In Trondheim the *Arthur* was raised (her masts were showing above the water), and as a result of the information supplied by Evans her various secrets were uncovered.

And at the end of Foettenfjord, hardly aware of all the fuss that had so concerned her, the *Tirpitz* quietly went on with her refit.

By January 1943 Tirpitz's refit was completed, and she sailed again for Altenfjord as the best advance post to attack the Russian convoys, should the always reluctant Hitler give permission. In London, Churchill wrote to the Chief of Combined Operations, the First Sea Lord, the Chiefs of the Air Staff and Bomber Command one of his celebrated memoranda:

> Have you given up all plans of doing anything to *Tirpitz*? We heard a lot of talk about it five months ago which all petered out . . . It is a terrible thing that this prize should be waiting and no one able to think of a way of winning it.

In fact another weapon to destroy the menace had been fully tried and exercised and was now ready for action.

This was the midget submarine or X-craft, 51 feet long, 6 feet in diameter and with a diving depth of 300 feet. Instead of torpedoes it carried side charges containing two tons of amatex explosive which would be released on the bottom under the Tirpitz's *hull.*

During 1942 the building of the X-craft and the training of their crews went on apace. On 26 August the first of them, X-3, after successful trials in Portland harbour, was loaded on to a railway truck and taken to Faslane on the Clyde, from where she made her way downstream to a base at Port Bannatyne in the Kyle of Bute. Her captain designate was Lieutenant Donald Cameron, RNR, and his first lieutenant John Lorimer; an engine-room artificer completed the crew of three.

X-4 was the next to arrive, under the command of Lieutenant Godfrey Place, DSC (an amiable officer with a habit of losing his own clothing and borrowing other people's). X-5 reached Faslane soon after, X-6 in January 1943, and the remaining four in February and March. All had been built with the object of attacking *Tirpitz* and other large enemy units. During early exercises there was a nasty moment when X-3, under Lorimer, sank, and he and two trainees only just managed to escape from the bottom. On another occasion a sub-lieutenant was washed overboard from the casing of X-4 and never seen again.

In the early summer the boats transferred to Loch Cairnbawn, just as the chariots had done, and carried out intensive exercises, cutting their way through nets and laying dummy charges beneath the keels of the battleship *Malaya*. Another sub-lieutenant was lost while net-cutting, so it was decided to add a qualified diver to each X-craft's crew. On off-duty days the crews visited the villages of Kylesku and Drumbeg for scones and fresh eggs, fought mock battles in the heather, and supported local *ceilidhs* with their own highly original interpretations of Highland dancing.

It had been originally planned to attack the *Tirpitz* in Trondheim, a journey that the X-craft could have made under their own power. But with *Tirpitz*'s move to Altenfjord they would have to be towed. How? Fishing-boats like the *Arthur* did not have the pulling power, and in any case were the wrong boats for that area. They could be carried on board their depot-ship and released off the coast, but a sighting by enemy aircraft would jeopardize the whole operation. In the end it was decided they would make the 1,000-mile journey in tow of parent submarines.

Next, as with the chariots, it was essential to have the latest intelligence on *Tirpitz*'s whereabouts. One source for this was a courageous Norwegian named Torstein Raaby; earlier in the war he had been operating a secret transmitter at Tromsö, but had had to flee to Sweden and thence to England. He was returned to Norway with a radio set in the Norwegian submarine *Ula,* made his way to Altenfjord, and managed to obtain a job as a roadman at Alta. Here he set up his radio and, using the receiving aerial of his neighbour, a German officer, as a transmitter, sent daily intelligence reports to London on the dispositions of the German fleet. He also made a detailed sketch map of the fleet anchorages and the nets guarding them and took them over the border to Sweden, where they found their way first to Captain Denham in Stockholm, thence to the Admiralty in London.

Air reconnaissance was harder to arrange, as Altenfjord was beyond the range of British bases. Approaches were made to the Russians, and after some initial reluctance they gave permission for half a dozen Spitfires to be temporarily based at Vaenga, within easy flying distance of Altenfjord.

By mid-August training was complete, and a date for attacking the German ships fixed for the period 20–25 September. This meant leaving Cairnbawn not later than 11 September. Because of the appallingly cramped living conditions in the X-craft (vertical clearance was no more than 4½ feet) it was decided that passage crews should man the boats for the eight days it would take to reach the release zone, with the operational crews resting in the parent submarines.

On 30 August the submarine depot-ship *Titania* sailed into Cairnbawn in the company of the submarines *Thrasher, Turbulent, Seanymph, Sceptre, Syrtis* and *Stubborn.* For three days parents and midgets exercised in towing and transferring crews, and on 6 September the midgets were hoisted on board their depot-ship *Bonaventure* for the fitting of the

2-ton side-charges of amatex explosive. All that was left now was the briefing of the crews.

At 4 p.m. on 11 September, the six parent submarines, with their brood in tow, left Cairnbawn at two-hourly intervals and headed north. In daylight hours both parents and midgets would remain submerged, the midgets surfacing for fifteen minutes every six hours to ventilate the boat; at night the parents would travel on the surface to recharge their batteries. Communication would be by telephone wires threaded through the towing ropes.

The first three days of the passage, with each pair of submarines spread twenty miles apart, were uneventful. On the 14th, as a result of further Spitfire reconnaissance, they received a signal giving up-to-date news of the enemy ships. *Tirpitz* was anchored off a spit of land at the end of Kaafjord, a finger of Altenfjord; *Scharnhorst* was at the head of Kaafjord, near the entrance; *Lützow* was in Lange Fjord, ten miles to the north. All were surrounded by nets. In addition there was a double row of nets stretching across the entrance to Kaafjord. The targets were to be: *Tirpitz,* X-5, X-6 and X-7; *Lützow,* X-8; and *Scharnhorst,* X-9 and X-10. The attacks were to be made between 1 a.m. and 8 a.m. on 22 September.

The next three days were less happy. In the early hours of the 15th the tow between *Seanymph* and X-8 parted. X-8 surfaced, was unable to find *Seanymph,* but by chance came across *Stubborn* and X-7. She lost them soon after by steering the wrong course, and it wasn't until the evening of the 16th that *Seanymph* at last found her. After thirty-six hours on their own, the passage crew were exhausted, and the operational crew were transferred by rubber dinghy to relieve them.

Meanwhile a greater misfortune had occurred to X-9. In the early morning of the 16th, she dived after fifteen minutes on the surface. Six hours later her parent *Syrtis* dropped hand-grenades for her to surface, but she did not appear. It was found the tow had parted. *Syrtis* retraced her steps along the line of advance but there was no sign of X-9. She continued searching all day and most of the night, but X-9 was never seen again. Probably, when the tow rope parted, the boat had taken a downward dive and been crushed by the pressure before the crew had time to correct it. Now there were only five boats to make the attack.

On the morning of the 17th misfortune struck again. The wayward X-8, once more in tow of *Seanymph,* was having increasing difficulties with her trim. Air could be heard escaping from the buoyancy chamber in the starboard side-charge, and with the boat listing further and further to starboard there was no alternative but to jettison the charge. This inevitably meant a list to port, and when it was reported that the port side-charge was flooding the captain had to jettison this too. With all her explosives gone X-8 was now out of the operation; she was therefore scuttled and her passage crew transferred to *Seanymph.* Now there were four.

Between the 17th and the 19th *Truculent, Thrasher, Sceptre* and *Syrtis* made their landfalls on the Norwegian coast. On the 19th, a Sunday, Lieutenant Alexander, captain of *Truculent,* held divine service for those not on duty, forty feet below the surface. He read the familiar, traditional prayer for those at sea: 'Oh, Eternal Lord God, who alone spreadest out the heavens and ruleth the raging of the sea . . .', and there was a special prayer 'for our comrades in arms about to embark on their hazardous operation'.

By dawn on the 20th all four operational and passage crews had been safely exchanged. Even so events were not without incident. On the evening of the 19th and again on the 20th Lieutenant Jupp in *Syrtis* sighted a U-boat on the surface. Both were sitting targets, but his orders were not to make any enemy attacks for fear of jeopardizing the operation, and he let them go by.

A more unpleasant incident happened to Godfrey Place in X-7. A floating mine had become entangled in the tow rope to *Stubborn*; it drifted down it and became wedged on X-7's bow. With great presence of mind Place made his way along the casing, and spent seven minutes trying to push it clear with his foot – 'the first time in my life', he said afterwards, 'that I ever shoved a mine clear by its horns.'

Between 6.30 p.m. and 8 p.m. on the 20th Lieutenant Henty-Creer in X-5, Lieutenant Cameron in X-6, Lieutenant

Place in X-7, and Lieutenant Hudspeth in X-10 (whose target, since the mishaps to X-8 and X-9, had been shifted from *Scharnhorst* to *Tirpitz*) slipped the tow ropes from their parent submarines and pointed their small craft east, towards the German minefields that guarded the approaches to Altenfjord. They were all unaware of each other's whereabouts, but in twenty-four hours' time they were scheduled to reach Tommelholm, one of a group of small islands near the entrance to Kaafjord, just four miles from the *Tirpitz*. At dawn the day after they would attack. Under a bright moon and with the northern lights shimmering in the sky, all four X-craft crossed the minefield safely and entered the inner leads.

X-10 dived at dawn on the 21st, intending to travel submerged all day up Söröy Sound and Stjern Sound. But first the motor of the periscope failed, so it was impossible to hoist it, then the gyro compass went off the board. So Lieutenant Hudspeth bottomed in a small fjord north of Sternöy to make repairs. The crew worked all day, but it soon became evident that water had seeped into the electrical equipment, and little could be done. Underwater the boat was almost blind.

At dusk Hudspeth surfaced, and steering by magnetic compass set course up Stjern Sound, keeping to the north shore. By midnight he was into Altenfjord, and hoping to be at the entrance to Kaafjord by dawn. A vessel appeared ahead and X-10 dived. When Hudspeth tried to raise the periscope, there was a crackling noise and a smell of burnt rubber: the motor, partially repaired, had burnt out again. The gyro compass was still out of action, and now the light in the magnetic compass failed.

So Hudspeth again surfaced, and steered for Tommelholm, two miles from the Kaafjord entrance. There he took X-10 to the bottom, and once more set about repairs. It was now 2 a.m. on the 22nd, the morning of the attack. They had just six hours in which to make good the damage, find a way through the Kaafjord nets, and lay their mines under *Tirpitz*. On the face of it, the chances seemed slim.

X-6's troubles were of a different nature. She had developed a list of 10 degrees to starboard during the passage, due to flooding of the starboard side-charge, and this now increased to 15 degrees. Cameron tried to correct it by ditching excess stores and shifting others to port. In addition the periscope was leaking and badly misted over.

After crossing Söröy Sound, X-6 dived at 1.25 a.m. on the 21st, when it was growing light, and for the rest of the day continued submerged up Stjern Sound and Altenfjord. At dusk she was near Tommelholm and surfaced close inshore to charge her batteries. Cameron climbed on to the casing and saw the floodlights on the Kaafjord nets two miles away: there was no sign of any other X-craft. He observed the headlights of a car going along the coast road, and wrote in his log: 'Wondered if it might be carrying the German admiral, and speculated on his reactions tomorrow if all went well.'

There were one or two scares during the night, such as the door of a hut close to the water opening and spilling out men, whose voices could clearly be heard. Later a German torpedo-boat appeared from nowhere and there was an emergency dive. Just before 1.45 a.m. on the 22nd Cameron set course, submerged, for the Kaafjord nets.

But he hadn't gone far when the periscope again began clouding over. Twice Cameron stopped to repair it, but with little success. Without an effective periscope, how would he find his way through the nets?

By 4.45 a.m. he had reached the nets, and was considering how best to negotiate them when he sighted first a ferryboat coming up Kaafjord outward bound and then a coaster about to pass into the fjord. Knowing the entrance gate would be open only for a few minutes longer, knowing too that his craft was too blind to follow submerged, he made an instant decision: 'Stand by to surface. Stand by engine.'

His crew could hardly believe their ears. To sail into a heavily guarded enemy anchorage *on the surface.* Surely the men on the gate control-boat *must* see them. But Cameron knew what he was doing. With the periscope housed and the boat well trimmed down and partly hidden in the coaster's wake, X-6 passed unmolested into Kaafjord. At the other end, 4,000 yards away, lay *Tirpitz.*

'Dive, dive, dive!'

They slid down again into the black, friendly depths. Here the periscope was found to be in worse shape than ever, and for the third time X-6 was stopped to repair it. Little could be done, but now Cameron could delay no longer, as they were only two hours from the deadline for the attack. Slowly Cameron felt his way down the fjord, once in his blindness scraping the cable that moored a destroyer to her buoy, once fouling the bottom section of a floating pontoon.

A little before 7 a.m. Cameron, looking through his fogged periscope, saw some dark blobs which he took to be the flotation buoys of *Tirpitz*'s nets, and noticed a space between them. Hoping that this was the entrance for boats, for which he had been aiming, he steered straight for it. Seconds later he raised the periscope again. The blobs had disappeared; only a great, grey, indistinct mass showed through the fogged lens. It was the *Tirpitz*, 100 yards away. They were through.

Godfrey Place in X-7 had the most trouble-free early passage of the lot. On passage through the Söröy minefield on the evening of the 20th he sighted Henty-Creer and X-5 (whom he had last seen in Loch Cairnbawn ten days before) and they exchanged greetings of 'Good hunting' and 'Good luck'. He made the passage up Stjern Sound and Altenfjord without incident, and at 4.30 p.m. sighted the *Scharnhorst* steaming north (she was *en route* to gunnery exercises).

At dusk Place arrived at Tommelholm. He spent the night charging batteries and diving to avoid numerous small craft, but without sighting any of the others. He let the crew come on deck in turns for fresh air. 'It was a calm, peaceful evening,' he wrote later, 'we could hear the broadcasts from the tankers and supply ships down in the anchorage. It was hard to believe our target was only four miles away.'

Just before 1 a.m., a little earlier than Cameron, he set off for the Kaafjord nets. Like Cameron he was lucky in finding the gate open to let in a minesweeper, and was able to follow her through submerged. So far his journey had been according to the book. Now his difficulties began.

First he ran X-7 straight into nets reserved for *Lützow*, now empty. He took an hour to free himself, then, threading his way between the shipping at anchor, proceeded towards

Tirpitz's nets at seventy feet – it was unlikely, he thought, that they stretched that deep. But he was wrong; he went straight into them.

'Full astern. Empty the tanks.'

X-7 came up a few feet but only succeeded in pulling the meshes after her. Place thought how the buoys holding the nets on the surface must be jigging up and down, and that it could be only a matter of time before a look-out in *Tirpitz* spotted them. He went slow ahead, full astern, hard a starboard, hard a port, all to no avail. Just when he was thinking he might have to send his diver up to cut the meshes, the boat unexpectedly broke free.

'Ninety-five feet!'

Surely the nets would not stretch as deep as this; sixty feet was as low as British nets went.

'Slow ahead.'

But once again the boat came to a stop, and everyone could hear and feel the meshes scraping on the bow. Place could not understand it: the depth of water was only 120 feet; surely the nets did not stretch to the bottom. What he was not to know was that there were two sets of nets surrounding the *Tirpitz*; one that stretched downwards from the surface, and another, nearer the ship, that went upwards from the bottom. Without knowing it, he had passed under the net that stretched from the surface, and was now enmeshed in the one laid on the bottom.

Gently he eased X-7 out, and rose to the surface to see where he was.

'Up periscope!'

He grasped the periscope handles and put his head to the eyepiece. A hundred yards away, across clear water, rode the *Tirpitz*.

'Half ahead. Sixty feet.'

X-7 moved inexorably towards her target. Now nothing could stop her from accomplishing the mission on which she had set out, for which her crew had been preparing for more than two years; time and place had coincided.

At thirty feet there was a slight bump as X-7's bows grazed the battleship's side.

'Stop.'

X-7 dropped below the huge hull, the shadow of the ship clearly visible through the glass scuttles. The time fuses on the explosives had already been set to one hour.

'Release port side-charge.'

The boat lifted slightly as the charge fell away to the bottom.

'Slow ahead.'

With marvellous calm Place manoeuvred his craft down the length of the ship until he reckoned he was beneath the after turrets.

'Release starboard side-charge.'

Once again the boat rose a little with the added buoyancy. The four members of the crew felt a sense of tremendous exhilaration. They had done what they had been asked to do; whatever happened now, nothing could ever take that away from them.

'Starboard twenty. Half ahead.'

Carefully Place pointed the bows of X-7 towards the nets. They had found a way through them with difficulty. Could they now find a way out?

On board the *Tirpitz* the day had started with the calling of the hands at 5 a.m. (7 a.m. German time). At the same time (and fortunately for Cameron and Place) the hydrophone listening watch was secured for routine maintenance. At 7 a.m. (9 a.m. German time) Captain Meyer sat down to breakfast in his cabin.

Seven minutes later, Cameron in X-6, working his way blindly along the western shore of the fjord, hit a rock and, with the boat momentarily out of control, surfaced. Before disappearing she was observed briefly by a petty officer in *Tirpitz*, but thought to be a porpoise. Five minutes later she surfaced again, off *Tirpitz*'s port beam. This time there was no doubt about it. A burst of small arms fire was directed at her (she was too near for the heavier armament to bear), the officer of the watch made the signal for close watertight doors, and Captain Meyer hurried to the bridge.

Seeing roughly his position through the blurred periscope, Cameron ordered full astern, and the half-alerted crew of *Tirpitz* (the bridge *should* have made the signal for action stations) watched fascinated as X-6 moved inevitably towards them. Sub-Lieutenant Leine went away in the ship's motor-boat, armed with hand-grenades and a grappling-hook, and reached X-6 as she bumped into the ship abreast of B turret.

Cameron, hearing the bump, ordered: 'Release side-charges.'

Four more tons of amatex slid to join those of X-7 at the bottom under *Tirpitz*'s bow. The boat, lightened, came further out of the water.

'Open all main vents and No. 2 Kingston. Slow astern.'

In a few minutes the boat would sink beneath them. Cameron opened the hatch, and with raised hands he and his crew came up on the casing and stepped into the launch. Leine had already secured his grappling rope to X-6, but with the boat going astern and sinking he had to cut it free to avoid the launch being pulled under. Leine went alongside the gangway, the crew of X-6 climbed to the quarter-deck, saluted, and were made prisoner.

Meyer's immediate concern was to move his ship as far out of harm's way as possible, so orders were given for the instant raising of steam. It would take at least an hour to get under way, so divers were piped to go down and examine the hull for limpet mines, and a big wire was prepared for scraping along the ship's bottom. The duty Arado seaplane crew were piped to stand by for launching, and destroyers in the fleet anchorage were ordered to carry out an anti-submarine patrol.

Only four minutes later a second submarine was seen to surface 100 yards away. This was X-7 trying to free herself from the nets in which she had again become entangled. Fire was immediately opened, hits were observed, and soon after the craft disappeared. Not knowing whether the midgets carried torpedoes or mines, and appreciating that he might be in greater danger outside the nets than inside, Meyer decided not to put to sea, and instead gave instructions for the ship's bow to be moved to starboard (both submarines having been sighted to port) by veering and shortening the cables.

From all accounts there seems to have been some panic in *Tirpitz* at this time, with men running aimlessly to and fro, aware that disaster was about to strike them – a view confirmed by the actions of the four prisoners who were seen looking frequently at their watches – yet powerless to prevent it. Slowly the minutes ticked by as Cameron, Lorimer, Kendall and Goddard waited anxiously for the explosion they all hoped would sink the *Tirpitz*, yet spare them their own lives.

At twelve minutes past eight the charges went off with tremendous force, creating a whip effect that lifted the ship upwards and was felt from stem to stern. 'There was the most God Almighty bang,' said Lorimer. 'All the lights went out and I was thrown off my chair.' Kendall said, 'There was complete darkness. Fire sprinklers showered foam on us. The ship started to list to port. Seamen ran in all directions. Bursts of machine-gun fire were interspersed with the loud crashes of the secondary armament firing wildly. It was impossible to take it all in.' And one of the German sailors, Schimanski, said, 'Everybody was running around, nobody really knew what had happened to us.'

Because of the move of the ship's bows to starboard, the three charges originally placed under the forward keel plates had exploded some sixty yards away and were not as lethal as had been hoped; to the intense disappointment of the prisoners the *Tirpitz* remained afloat. Yet she had been severely, even critically, damaged. Many of the decks and passageways were buckled and twisted; A and C 15-inch turrets had been lifted off their turntables; many tons of water had entered the bottom compartments, one generator room and the after steering compartment being flooded. Range-finders, fire-control instruments, radio and radar equipment were all put out of action, and two Arado aircraft were severely damaged. As a result of Place's second charge placed aft, none of the three propeller shafts could be turned, and the port rudder was smashed. One man had been killed and fifty wounded, several with broken legs.

Half an hour later a third submarine was sighted off the starboard bow, some 250 yards beyond the nets. This was Henty-Creer's X-5, which had not been sighted since he and Place had exchanged greetings on their way in. She was hit repeatedly before disappearing, and then the destroyer

Z-27 dropped depth-charges over the area where she had submerged. No trace of her or her crew was ever found.

The prisoners were taken below to be interrogated by the staff officer, Commander Emden. But it soon became clear that they were prepared to give no information beyond their names, ranks and numbers. Captain Meyer therefore, being a humane man and admiring the gallantry of their attack, ordered that they should be given coffee and schnapps and somewhere to sleep. Soon after, the door opened, and in came a dripping Godfrey Place, wearing a sweater, boots and long underpants.

After several fruitless attempts to find a way through the nets he had finally cleared them by surfacing at speed and at an angle and sliding over them. Then he had run into another net. The explosion of the charges had freed him from this, but had caused extensive damage to X-7. Her compass and diving gauges were out of action, so she could stay either on the surface or on the bottom, but lacked all manoeuvrability underwater. Place decided to escape on the surface, but as soon as he reached it he was met by a fusillade of fire which holed the boat in several places and destroyed his periscope.

There was nothing left but to abandon ship. The craft surfaced again near a gunnery-target raft and Place opened the hatch and waved his white sweater in surrender. The others were about to follow when the boat, already awash, sank beneath him. Place swam to the raft and was picked up by a boat from *Tirpitz*.

Later that morning, a sixth survivor joined the others: Bob Aitken, another of Place's crew. His was a nightmare story. As the boat began to sink under the rush of water into the forward compartment, he, Bill Whittam and Willie Whitley descended slowly the 120 feet to the bottom. Their only chance of survival now was by Davis Escape Apparatus. This meant putting on water-tight oxygen masks, then flooding the craft slowly so that when the water reached their necks and the pressure outside was almost equal to that inside they could open the hatches and rise to the surface. It was agreed that Whittam should go up by the forward hatch, Whitley aft, and Aitken by whichever of the two was clear first.

Three of the vents letting in the water were blocked, so it rose very slowly. It took half an hour to reach their thighs and the cold was intense. When the water met the electrical circuits, the fuses exploded, the lights went out and the boat was filled with smoke and chlorine gas from the batteries. Crouching in the icy cold and darkness on the bottom of the sea, and breathing carefully through their masks, they waited for the water to reach their necks. It was another half-hour before it was level with their chests, and all the time the precious oxygen was giving out.

Now Aitken groped his way forward to see if he could help Whittam open the forward hatch. He couldn't see Whittam because of the dark, and he couldn't call to him because of his mask. He felt for him with his hands but there was nothing where Whittam should have been. Then his foot touched Whittam's body underwater. His oxygen had run out. Whittam was dead.

Aitken felt his way back aft. His own oxygen had almost given out. He switched on the two small emergency bottles, but he knew they would give him only a few breaths apiece. In the after compartment he groped for Whitley, but found that Whitley was dead too. With the last of his oxygen almost gone, and feeling he was about to faint, he raised his hand to the hatch with a last despairing effort. It opened. He sped upwards to the surface, yet managed to remember to spread his escape apron in front of him to slow his speed and so avoid getting the bends. On the surface he drew great gulps of air into his starved lungs. A boat picked him up.

Next day Captain Meyer, anxious that his prisoners should not share the same fate as Able Seaman Evans of the chariots, had his prisoners transferred to Tromsö hospital and thereafter to Germany for internment as prisoners of war. There, a year later, Place and Cameron learned they had been awarded the Victoria Cross.

Tirpitz had been severely damaged and ideally should have been sent to Kiel or Wilhelmshaven for repairs in dry-dock. But that would have meant a thousand-mile journey under tow with the ever present risk of attack by submarine or aircraft. So a repair ship, the Monte Rosa and 800 dockyard workmen were sent to Altenfjord and with most of Tirpitz's crew in billets ashore, worked all through the winter of 1943–4 to make her seaworthy.

And now a different form of attack on her was being prepared – by aircraft of the Fleet Air Arm flying from carriers positioned off the Norwegian coast. Decrypted German naval signals in March 1944 showed that Tirpitz *was once again ready for sea and that full speed trials had been arranged for her on the early morning of 3 April. Admiral Sir Bruce Fraser in his flagship* Duke of York *(which had recently sunk the* Scharnhorst*) ordered aircraft from four carriers to make two attacks, the first to coincide with her leaving her berth in Kaafjord at around 5.30 a.m., when without the benefits of her smoke screen and flak posts ashore she would be at her most vulnerable, the second an hour later. Both attacks – bombs and machine-gun fire to rake the decks – were highly successful, causing widespread structural damage, killing 122 of the crew and wounding 316 others, and putting the ship out of service for several months.*

But she was still afloat and still a menace, and now other means had to be found to destroy her. And this time they were to be Dr Barnes Wallis and his huge Tallboy bombs.

Dr Barnes Wallis was fifty-three when war broke out, an aircraft designer by trade, and described as 'having the air of a diffident and gentle cleric'. He had been designing since the end of the First World War, and was responsible for the airships R-100 and R-101, later the Wellington bomber. From the beginning of the war he became convinced that the standard 500 lb bomb then in use was far too small and ineffective; what he wanted was a bomb weighing several tons, a plane specially adapted to carry it, and a precision bomb-sight.

It took Dr Wallis nearly three years and several treatises before his ideas were accepted. His first big bomb, a 3-tonner, was designed to breach German dams. Successful experiments led to the formation of the famous No. 617 'Dambuster' squadron which in 1944, under Wing-Commander Guy Gibson, burst the walls of the Moehne and Eder dams, releasing millions of tons of water into the countryside.

Air Marshal Sir Arthur Harris, Chief of Bomber Command, was so impressed that he persuaded Wallis to design a 6-ton bomb, to be fitted in converted Lancasters, for attacking the German secret weapons sites. Thus was born the famous 21-foot-long Tallboy or 'earthquake' bomb, so constructed that it would gain speed as it fell and penetrate the earth to some eighty feet before exploding. It was deployed with shattering effect on various targets in northern France and Germany, and now it was decided to use it against the *Tirpitz*.

Thirty-six Lancaster bombers from Nos 617 and 9 squadrons under the command of Wing-Commander J. B. Tait, a much decorated officer, were detailed for the attack. But as the planes, with their heavy loads, did not have the range to reach Altenfjord and return, it was agreed with the Russians that they would fly first to an airfield on an island at Yagodnik near Archangel, deliver the attack from there, return to Yagodnik for refuelling, and thence fly to the United Kingdom. An attack from the east would have the added advantage of surprise.

The planes left Lossiemouth in Scotland on 10 September. Thirty eventually reached Yagodnik next day, but six lost themselves over unfamiliar territory, force-landed and had to be abandoned. The British aircrews were accommodated in a houseboat, draped with a banner which read: 'Welcome to the glorious flyers of the Royal Air Force.' For three rainy days they were entertained with vodka, Russian war films and a football match, which the Russian aircrews won 7–0; they also suffered from mosquitoes and bedbugs.

On 15 September, on receipt of a favourable weather report, twenty-seven of the Lancasters, led by Tait, took off for the attack, approaching from the south-east. At first they flew low, not more than 1,000 feet, then for the sixty miles run-in to the target they climbed to over 12,000 feet. Thirty miles away the leading planes sighted *Tirpitz*, 'sitting under its cliff,' said one pilot, 'just as we'd been shown on the model'. They saw the flash of the battleship's big guns opening up on them and the smokescreen forming round the fjord. By the time they were over the target three minutes later the smoke screen had almost obliterated it. But not quite: for a brief last moment the tip of her foremast came into the sights of Tait's bomb-aimer, Daniels.

'Bomb sights on,' he shouted.

Away went Tait's bomb, and seconds later the bombs of most of the rest of the squadron, aimed at random into the centre of the thick blanket of smoke. Some of the last planes did not release their bombs, having no aiming point at all. When they returned to Yagodnik they claimed no hits, though all hoped that a lucky one had found its mark.

In fact they had been luckier than they knew, for Tait's Tallboy bomb had struck *Tirpitz* on the bows with devastating effect, passing through the ship's side and exploding beneath the keel. A great hole had been blown in the fo'c'sle, 30 feet deep by 50 feet long, letting in some 1,000 tons of water. There had also been two near misses. The armoured deck had been wrecked, the main engines put out of action, and many of the fire-control instruments again destroyed.

Tirpitz had now been crippled for life, and Captain Wolfe Junge (who had been Meyer's second-in-command and succeeded him in May) proposed to Admiral Dönitz, now Commander-in-Chief of the German navy, that she be taken out of service. But Dönitz still believed she had a role to play as a floating battery, no longer in the north where Russian troops were threatening Finmark, but at Tromsö, 200 miles to the south, where, despite the Normandy invasion in June, Hitler still believed a secondary attack might come.

On 15 October, with her bows temporarily patched up, *Tirpitz* left Kaafjord for the last time. Steaming at 7 knots, and escorted by every available warship in northern waters, she made her way south through the leads, arriving at Tromsö next day. A special berth had been prepared for her in the lee of Haaköy Island, three miles from Tromsö. Here the water was so shallow that it was considered that even if she was sunk in another air attack she would still be able to fire her guns to seawards while resting on the bottom. She brought her anti-torpedo nets and smoke canisters with her, and a squadron of fighters – for which every previous captain had pressed in vain – was posted to nearby Bardufoss airfield to protect her.

Her arrival at Tromsö was first reported by Egil Lindberg, a Norwegian agent operating from an attic in the town's mortuary, and confirmed soon after by a Mosquito reconnaissance plane. For the British this was a stroke of luck, for it meant that with suitable modifications to the Lancaster they would now have sufficient fuel to attack the ship from British bases and return. Accordingly the two squadrons that had made the attack from Russia had their mid-upper gun turrets and cockpit armour removed, extra fuel tanks installed, and the existing engines replaced with more powerful ones.

In the early hours of 29 October, thirty-two Lancasters, again under Tait, took off from Lossiemouth to make a further attack. They concentrated over a lake in Sweden, then formed up for their run-in to the target. But the weather was against them, with drifting clouds below the 13,000 feet at which they were scheduled to attack. Nevertheless they made several runs over the target and dropped their bombs. There was no sign of German fighters. All the planes returned except one which, damaged by flak, force-landed in Sweden.

One of the Tallboys, a near miss, had in fact caused considerable further damage, distorting the port propeller shaft and rudder and resulting in flooding along more than 100 feet of the port side aft. This meant the ship could no longer steam under her own power, and on Junge's recommendations her complement of 2,000 was reduced by some 400 men – mostly engine-room staff, as the engines were now required only to make steam for the generators and domestic services. The craters made by the Tallboys in the sea-bed had also revealed that the bottom consisted of mud, not, as had been thought, rock, and to prevent the ship capsizing in another air attack it was arranged for tons of rubble to be dumped by dredgers below her keel.

The once proud *Tirpitz* was now a partial wreck, flooded fore and aft, powerless to move, no longer functioning as a weapon either of offence or defence. Her crew, listening to the daily radio bulletins from Germany, with reports of continued advances by the Russians in the east and the Allies in the west, knew the war was as good as lost, and wondered what possible service was left to them to perform. They knew that sooner or later the big four-engine bombers would return, and go on returning until they had completed their task. 'God help us,' said Captain Junge, 'if one of those block-busters hits us.'

Junge himself was under orders to relinquish his command for an appointment in Berlin. He asked for the order to be countermanded for the sake of the crew. His request was refused and he left the ship on 4 November 1944. His successor was Captain Robert Weber, the ship's former gunnery officer, who had delighted the wardroom with his imitations of Hitler at the 1942 New Year's Eve party in Foettenfjord.

In Britain, meanwhile, it had been decided that any further attacks against *Tirpitz* would have to be made before the end of November; after that, in the high latitude of Tromsö, there would not be enough light, even at midday, for high-level precision bombing. Bad weather over Norway prevailed throughout late October and early November, but on 11 November Wing-Commander Tait was playing a game of football with his aircrews when he was summoned to the office of his chief, Air Vice-Marshal Ralph Cochrane. He appeared as he was, in striped jersey and studded boots.

'The weather forecast is good for Tromsö,' said Cochrane, 'we want you to go.'

'When, sir?'

'Now.'

That night the Lancasters and their Tallboys assembled again at Lossiemouth. It was a cold, clear, frosty night. At 2.30 a.m. on the 12th the engines of thirty-nine Lancasters were started up, and soon the darkened airfield was reverberating to their deafening roar. At 3 a.m. the first plane became airborne. Thirty-one others followed. Seven had icing problems and were unable to take off.

Through the night the Lancasters flew independently across the North Sea. The crews were in optimistic mood, believing that this would be third time lucky – though a few had nagging doubts about the German fighters, knowing that if they did appear they must expect heavy casualties. At dawn they were over Norway. 'It was the most beautiful morning,' said one pilot, 'mountains and snow and frozen lakes as far as you could see.' Once again the assembly area was the lake in Sweden, and one by one the big, black bombers arrived there, formed up into their allotted groups and, with Tait leading, set course for Tromsö.

On board the *Tirpitz* the day had started much as usual. The hands were called, colours hoisted and working parties detailed for cleaning and maintenance. Lieutenant-Commander Kühnen and Sub-Lieutenant Brunner went across to Haaköy in a boat to supervise the building of a landing stage. Lieutenant Schmitz, who had just returned from surveying a new berth for *Tirpitz* that might give her natural protection (the anchorage off Haaköy was quite exposed), was having breakfast in the wardroom before reporting to the captain. Ashore the engineer officer, Lieutenant-Commander Sommer, was waiting for a boat to take him to the ship.

It was about 7.30 a.m. when Captain Weber received the first reports of enemy aircraft, a long way south, and apparently heading in the direction of Sweden. The anti-aircraft officer, Lieutenant-Commander Fassbender, was informed, and alerted his own officers. At 8.15 a further report was received of three Lancasters over Mosjoen, still a long way away, but coming in *Tirpitz*'s direction. Captain Weber ordered action stations and the hoisting of the blue and yellow aircraft alarm flag – the signal for the few batteries on Haaköy and around Tromsö to prepare for aircraft attack.

Weber and other officers, among them his executive officer, Commander Muller, Lieutenant Schmitz, the signals officer, and the chaplain, Pastor Seeberg, went to the bridge. It was a clear, calm, cloudless day, the water smooth as glass, not a breath of wind anywhere, perfect conditions for attack. There were no high hills to hide *Tirpitz,* as there had been in Foettenfjord and Kaafjord, and the smoke canisters, though positioned, had not yet been primed. *Tirpitz* was as naked as if she had been at sea.

Time went by without further news. The ship was quite silent. Everyone waited quietly at their action stations, at the guns large and small, in the wireless room and communications centre amidships, at the range finders and radar post in the foretop, in the switchboard rooms and magazines far below. Then at long last, through the forward rangefinders, the planes were sighted, seventy kilometres away to the south-east, tiny, black insects, more than thirty of them, flying in tiered formation in groups of three and four, relentless in their approach.

At 9.38 a.m., when the Lancasters were some fifteen miles away, Captain Weber gave orders for the main armament to open fire. A and B turrets opened up first, then C and D turrets in barrage fire, their blast shaking the whole ship, deafening in their concerted roar. Then the high-angle anti-aircraft guns joined in; and puffs of brown smoke could be seen as the shells burst high up in the clear sky. But they made no difference to the bombers, which came resolutely on. Captain Weber and the bridge party entered the armoured conning-tower. Before they closed the overhead hatch they saw the first of the Tallboys leave the planes and, gathering speed, begin their descent towards them.

Others, too, saw the bombs fall – Kühnen and Brunner ashore at the landing stage, Sommer waiting for his boat, farmers on Haaköy, people in Tromsö who had been fore-warned of the attack by the increasing drone of the Lancasters' approach. With a roar that shook the town and broke windows in houses half a mile away the bombs landed, enveloping *Tirpitz* in a curtain of splashes that rose as high as her mainmast, a blend of water and mud. One bomb hit B turret, another struck amidships, penetrating the armoured deck before exploding, two others landed on the port side, opened up the ship's side as though with a can-opener, tore a great hole in her that let in thousands of tons of water.

The attack lasted just three minutes. Then there was near silence, the only sound the diminishing drone of the Lancasters as they headed seawards for home. As the smoke cleared, the watchers on shore saw that the ship had taken on a list to port. At about 20 degrees it seemed to be checked. Then, without warning, the after 15-inch magazine blew up, lifting C turret and her crew, weighing over 1,000 tons, bodily into the air, hurling it into the water forty yards away and sending up a huge column of smoke. Among her dead was Sub-Lieutenant Leine who, a year before, had tried to capture X-6 in *Tirpitz*'s launch.

Now, as the attention of those on shore returned to the ship, it was noticed that the list to port which had seemed to be checked was increasing. Slowly, very slowly, it seemed, the ship leaned further and further over, until the starboard keel plates began to show one side and the upperworks were level with the water on the other. For a moment she lay motionless on her side, then as more and more water poured into her torn compartments she turned right over until her upperworks touched the bottom and all that could be seen on the surface was her long, shiny keel, like a stranded whale. At long last *Tirpitz*'s life, along with those of 900 of her crew, had ended.

Such was the story of the battleship *Tirpitz*. Her career, unlike that of her sister *Bismarck,* which was brief and glorious, was long and pitiful. It was true that she had fulfilled a useful role as a fleet-in-being, tying down enemy forces that might have been used elsewhere. But in the last analysis wars are won by aggressive, not passive, action.

Neither in calibre of ships nor morale of men was the German Navy inferior to that of the British – only in the lack of resolution with which Hitler constrained the High Command. *Tirpitz* arrived too late on the scene to influence the Battle of the Atlantic; but had her flag officers been encouraged to attack the Arctic convoys with the same skill and initiative as the U-boat captains, even at the risk of loss, then the war in the Arctic might have been transformed. The destruction by surface forces of only one convoy and its escorts would not only have done wonders for the morale in the fleet and at home; it would have gone far towards persuading the British Admiralty that such convoys were no longer an acceptable risk, and so directly helped their comrades on the eastern front. As it was, a great ship built for the destruction of her enemies lived an invalid's life and died a cripple's death.

For a long time afterwards the ugly hulk remained where it lay. After the war the Norwegian government sold her to a salvage company, and over the years they picked her carcass clean. Today, thirty-five years later, all that remains of the last of Hitler's battleships are a few pieces of rusty iron lying on a quiet beach.

A VISIT TO ADMIRAL KARL DÖNITZ[1]

IF THERE WAS one wartime leader whose face was as familiar to me as that of Churchill or Montgomery, it was that of Admiral Karl Dönitz, at first the head of the German U-boat arm, later Commander-in-Chief of Hitler's navy and then at war's end his brief-lived successor as Chancellor. It was Dönitz who planned the brilliant operation in October 1939 when one of his U-boats penetrated the British fleet anchorage of Scapa Flow and sank the battleship Royal Oak *with the loss of more than 800 men. He was an outstanding leader, loved and respected by his captains and crews, whose morale – despite the loss of two out of every three boats – remained high until the end.*

Although not a member of the Nazi party he had a great admiration for Hitler, with whom he maintained a polite but formal relationship. Both his sons, serving in the German navy, were killed in the war, and after it he was tried for war crimes at Nuremberg and sentenced to ten years' imprisonment. He served the full term in Spandau prison in Berlin, along with his former chief, Admiral Raeder, von Schirach, Funk, Schacht and others, and was released in 1956.

When I was preparing a television documentary on the U-boat war in the Atlantic (in which I had taken part) he agreed to contribute.

It was winter when I first visited him, in the small ground-floor flat of the big, white house in Aumühle, south of Hamburg, where he had lived alone since the death of his wife. Among the bare trees, the sagging white fence that bordered the property and its peeling paint, stuck out

[1] A shorter version of this will be found in my autobiography, *On My Way to the Club.*

sharply: one knew instinctively it was not in his care.

At the side of the house a sign said, 'Eingang Dönitz', and an arrow pointed the way. Seeing the familiar name like that, proof that he was still alive, was quite a shock, almost as if the sign had said, 'Eingang Ribbentrop' or 'Eingang Göring' for this was a journey into the past. Of the old Hitler crowd only he, Speer and poor mad Hess imprisoned in Spandau still survived.

We rang the bell and heard a musical chime, which was surprising, and presently he opened the door, which was surprising, too, for he was once head of Germany, second Führer of the Third Reich. At eighty-one he looked much older than the famous wartime photographs, a little wrinkled nut of a man; but there was no mistaking the ferret-like head, the money-box slit of a mouth, the blue, commanding eyes. 'So!' he said, and put out a hand, as to a junior officer. 'Dönitz!' he said, lest we be in doubt, and I took his hand and said, 'Kennedy!' and thought, how incredible after all this time and everything I have heard or read that he should now be greeting me in his own home. He stood erect in the small, dark hall, shaking hands with each member of the BBC team, helping them to hang their coats, wonderfully polite.

'So!' he said again and gestured towards the living-room. It was a small, modestly furnished affair, like that of many a retired naval officer, whether at Hamburg or Havant: a bookcase with mainly naval titles, a tallboy with the bust of a young man on top, presumably one of his sons, another bookcase full of files, a row of plants by the window, a sofa and long table, a telephone, a desk. On the desk, photographs of his dead family: his wife, who died a year or two after he came out of prison, their two sons, one killed in U-boats, the other in E-boats; their only daughter and her husband, also in U-boats, who died of a coronary three years ago. And in the centre a crucifix, another surprise.

It was lighter in here than the hall, and I noticed how dapperly the admiral was dressed, clean, white shirt with spotless cuffs, tie neatly in place, a newly pressed charcoal-grey suit, shining shoes. He pointed to his ear-piece and said something in German. Christine, our interpreter, said: 'He says he's sorry about his deafness, it's because he's so old.'

Dönitz turned to me and said in good English: 'When I was a young man, people lived to be fifty-five or sixty. Later they lived to be sixty-five or seventy. I am eighty-one.' He took my arm in a fatherly way and laughed and said, 'A man like you will live to be ninety or one hundred.' He had an old man's quavering voice. Later Christine said: 'He's using "Du" to address us, as though he's known us all a long time.'

The admiral gestured towards the sofa and the table on which stood a bottle of Sandeman's sherry and glasses and a plate of biscuits. We sat down round the table, the admiral at the head, and I thought, this is how it must have been at briefing sessions at Wilhelmshaven and Kerneval, when he was giving his captains instructions for sinking British ships. He poured sherry for us, though it was three in the afternoon, and we sipped at it self-consciously and nibbled at the biscuits.

Now he picked up a sheaf of papers, covered with writing in his own firm hand. 'I have prepared,' he said, 'the answers to the questions you have sent.' (So in other times he might have spoken to Raeder or Hitler.) I felt stunned. He had insisted on seeing the questions in advance, and we had sent two, to fill three or four minutes at the end of our programme about the U-boat war. He had written, in English, what looked like the equivalent of twenty minutes.

He began reading his answers in silence, and so as not to disturb him, we remained silent too. He looked up, saw a reference book he wanted at the end of the table and said to our producer, who was sitting there: 'Ze book zere! Pass ze book!'

In others this might have seemed rude, but he said it with the ease and authority of one used to command. I remembered what the most successful of his U-boat aces, Admiral Kretschmer, had said to me in Emden the day before: 'He was the greatest military leader I ever met.' And what Jennisch, another of his captains, had said to me in Kiel: 'He was like a father to us all.' If authority over, and affection for, those subordinate to him are two criteria of leadership, we had already been shown them. Nelson, I recalled, possessed these qualities almost more than any other admiral.

The interview was as disastrous as I had feared. The admiral's prose was not for speaking, and he addressed the microphone as though trying to reach the farthest sailor on the longest parade ground in the Third Reich. I doubted if any of it would be usable, and afterwards we took pictures of him in the garden over which I hoped to distil the essence of what he had said.

Back in the flat the admiral got into his head that he had given us a false fact, and became almost demented in his efforts to verify it, darting from bookcase to filing cabinet, rummaging among his papers like a spaniel trying to flush a rabbit from a bush. 'I am looking for a single piece of paper,' he said, 'which my son-in-law Hessler brought back from London.' And, later, 'Age does terrible things to the memory. Five years ago I had a fact like this clear in my mind.'

He was unable to find it and, later, back in London, the producer and I each received several letters from him in his own hand, urging us to omit the passage in question. As by now we had decided to omit the entire interview (for the admiral's sake as much as our own) it was not hard to oblige.

It was summer when I went back to Aumühle, to repair television's omissions, put the questions I had not been able to put about Hitler, the U-boat war, Nuremberg and Spandau. This time I had with me only a *Telegraph Magazine* photographer and our interpreter, a German journalist from the *Daily Telegraph*'s office in Bonn. We had quite a job finding the house, for the trees were in leaf and the sagging white fence had been taken away. ('The landlord decided,' said Dönitz, 'that it had had its day.')

He looked older, frailer, the voice seemed even higher-pitched. There were no jokes this time, and though the sherry and biscuits were again on the table, he did not offer them. Perhaps he realized that, unlike television, where you can spend two hours setting up for two questions, this would be a longer, more taxing business.

I began with some personal questions. Why had he chosen to live at Aumühle? It had not been his choice, his wife had found the place when he was still in Spandau: it was nice being near the forest and in summer you could see the deer.

Was it not also convenient for naval reunions at northern ports? Yes, he said, not quite answering the question, there were naval reunions, though not so often as formerly.

Did he have private means or did the government give him a pension? He got a pension, according to the law. A Grand Admiral's pension? No, an Admiral's pension, *according to the law*. He seemed defensive about the pension, as though I was suggesting (and I suppose others had suggested) that a convicted war criminal should not be getting a pension at all.

Who looked after him? A woman whom his wife had found when they first came to live here, but she was away on holiday just now, and friends came in to help. I had seen this woman on the last visit, but noticed she had left in the afternoon. I had wondered then whether the Grand Admiral was left to forage in the fridge in the evenings, but could not bring myself to ask. He also had a secretary, he said, who used to be full-time, but now came once a week: that was why he wrote so many letters in his own hand.

Why, I asked, in the evening of his life, at an age when most men wished to be alone with their memories and thoughts, was he so ready to receive people like myself? 'Because so long as I am alive, I feel an obligation to tell historians the exact facts of history. Sometimes I think I'm too careful about the facts, but the truth must always be followed.' I began to understand his frantic search on my last visit for his son-in-law's slip of paper. For him the facts were sacred: they and they alone could explain and justify his life. 'More and more historians come to visit me. It is a good thing to have a task like this at my age. Then I don't think about myself.'

I asked about the U-boat war, and what single aspect of it he regretted most. I had expected him to say the lack of a German naval air arm, or the early torpedo defects or the failure to develop satisfactory radar. His answer was surprising. 'Not getting the 300 U-boats I asked for in 1939. If that had been approved, the result of the Battle of the Atlantic might have been very different.'

I said, 'But in 1943 you had more than 300 U-boats, and you couldn't do much with them.'

The admiral said, 'By that time you had excellent radar, airplanes covering the whole Atlantic, and H/F D/F (High Frequency Direction Finding) which could pinpoint a U-boat's position. By then the battle was lost.' I said, 'But if you had had the 300 U-boats earlier, say in 1941, there would have been greater pressure on us to introduce these counter-measures earlier.' 'No, no!' he said, quite agitated, as though I was questioning an article of faith. 'It would have been impossible for you to have introduced them so quickly.'

'Well, then,' I said, 'if the 300 U-boats would have won the Battle of the Atlantic, why were they not approved?'

'The C-in-C of the Navy, Admiral Raeder, did approve,' he said, 'but Hitler turned the request down. Other people wanted steel for other things. Hitler was continental-minded. He did not understand that you can never beat a sea power with a land victory, that in the end you have to have vic-tory at sea.'

Was he aware, I asked, that when the *U.110*, commanded by Lemp (the man who sank the *Athenia* on the first day of the war), sank in the Atlantic in May 1941, it stayed afloat long enough for us to capture its secret cipher machine? Yes, he said, he had learned of this, but it was only of limited impor-tance at the time, as the code was changed every four weeks. I remembered then what Captain Roskill, the official naval his-torian, had told me, that in 1959, after publication of his book on *U.110, The Secret Capture,* Dönitz had written to him saying, 'I still don't know whether the British broke our naval cipher.' Did not the Grand Admiral now realize, I asked, that, as the result of the capture of a weathership in the Arctic and intelligence gained elsewhere, we had been able to *continue* to break the German naval codes for the rest of the war?

He was vague in his reply, he had heard things but could not say for certain, there was no treachery, of that he was positive. I could not decide whether his vagueness was be-cause I was telling him something he was learning for the first time and he was discomfited, or that he knew what had happened and pride prevented him from admitting it – but I think it was the former.

He was vague, too, when I questioned him about some-thing that had puzzled me until a few years ago, the strange behaviour of U-boat crews in walking about in stockinged feet and talking in whispers when surface ships were attacking them. Did they do this, I asked, because it was thought that the British Navy was equipped with the same incredibly sensitive underwater listening devices as the German Navy (those in *Prinz Eugen* had picked up the propellers of *Hood* and *Prince of Wales* when they were still over the horizon)? Yes, he said. And when did he find out that our anti-submarine craft did not have these devices? There was a pause after the interpreter had spoken, then he said he could not say, he was not sure, so that again I was left wondering whether he had in fact ever found out.

He was much more definite when I asked how it was that despite terrible losses (two out of every three U-boat men never returned) the morale of his crews remained high to the very end. 'Because of the leadership we gave them. They understood that the orders were necessary and ones we would give our own relations – don't forget my two sons fell in the war. They understood that, although the Atlantic battle had been lost, every time they put to sea they were tying down planes that would otherwise have been bombing the Fatherland.'

Was he surprised when he learnt that Hitler had nominated him as his successor? Completely, he said. At first he thought it was because Hitler wanted him to go through the motions of capitulation, then Speer told him that Hitler had mentioned him as a possible successor in case of accident much earlier. And what did he see as his task? To give shelter and food to the population, and to stave off final capitulation until as many refugees as possible had been brought back from the East.

Heinrich Böll, the German novelist, had said to me a few weeks earlier that at this time in Germany Dönitz had had hundreds of deserters shot. Was it true? No, it was not. There was a naval officer called Jepsen who, in bringing back refugees from the East, had given his men permission to loot and then disbanded them. He, and two mutineers who had smashed the compasses of a destroyer, were court-martialled and in due course shot. 'I do not recall any other cases. In

1965 the West Germany judiciary reviewed all the courts martial of this time and found there had been no injustice.'

When had he first known of the Jewish death camps? 'When they were liberated. I was horrified. I couldn't believe such a thing was possible.' As if reading my thoughts, he said: 'Even today people say, "But you *must* have known about them earlier." I assure you I didn't, I was wholly occupied with naval matters, and in any case what happened there was kept very secret.'

I said, 'If you had known about them earlier, what would you have done?' He thought a long time before replying and said: 'I would not have accepted them. That is obvious. But who can say exactly what he would have done in the light of what he learns afterwards? I don't want to be a pretender.'

It was time to break for lunch. We asked the admiral to join us, but he declined as he had to have a special soup ordered by his doctor. We went to a lakeside restaurant and ate fresh trout and slept a little under the trees, and agreed how impressive was the admiral's memory and stamina. After lunch I read to him a message he had sent to various naval authorities on 4 March 1945 – just two months before the end of the war:

> Let us trust the leadership of Adolf Hitler unreservedly. Believe me, in my two years' activity as Commander-in-Chief of the Navy, I have experienced only that in his strategic and operational views the Führer was invariably right. Very often he alone held these views . . .

He did not like listening to this, it was obvious. 'I don't remember saying that, but I must have done. Yet is it surprising? Here was our country on the verge of defeat, everything collapsing round us. Now was the time to ask for absolute loyalty to the head of state, to prevent any further deterioration in morale.' He added, 'Don't forget the Casablanca conference had already decided Germany's future. We knew what lay in store for us.'

How did he see Hitler now, thirty years later? 'He was a demon. He had a demonic character. The nature of a demon is that he succeeds in disguising the demonic side of himself and gives an impression of acting for the general good, so that you do not question his qualities. Like many of my generation I had great faith in Hitler, and what he did to give Germany back its self-respect. I only fully realized the evil side of Hitler afterwards.'

We moved on to Nuremberg. What did he feel now about his conviction and sentence? He had no doubts. 'To condemn a soldier for doing what his oath has pledged him to is totally unjust and contrary to established practice. One of the fundamental canons of justice is "No punishment without a law". The legislation introduced at Nuremberg was retroactive. It had not been used before and has never been used since – not at Suez or in Korea or in Vietnam.

'I was acquitted of conspiracy to start a war of aggression. I was acquitted in regard to my conduct of the U-boat war. I was found guilty of *taking part* in a war of aggression, mainly because my U-boats had been deployed in the invasion of Norway – yet it is well known that the British were on the point of invading Norway themselves. Do you know that I was the *only* serving German officer to be convicted simply for taking part in the war? What was I supposed to do at the time of Norway? Say to Admiral Raeder, "No, no, I can't take part in this. It's a war of aggression." '

What about Hitler and Himmler then? If they had lived, should they have been tried? 'Most certainly. I myself wanted to have Himmler indicted for crimes against the German people, and he would have been tried in a German court had not events overtaken us.'

And what of the long years in Spandau prison? Did he feel very bitter about them? 'I cannot say I felt bitter. In a way I felt above it all. It is well known that the American judge Biddle was for my acquittal, and there were others – General Weygand, General Fuller, Professor Smith, many British and American naval officers – who said publicly I should never have been condemned. This gave me strength.' And how did he pass the time? 'By reading history. History teaches you to see the events of your own life in perspective. In this way I achieved tranquillity.'

And how did he think history would regard him? 'I have no idea. It is a question I have not thought of or worried about. I have done what I thought was right, according to my conscience. I couldn't have done anything else.'

The photographer took some more pictures, and then the admiral rose abruptly from his chair and said 'So!' I knew what it meant, a signal that he had had enough, that it was time for us to go. He said he would like to give me inscribed copies of two of his books. 'Write your name clearly on this piece of paper. So many people in Germany have names that are impossible to read.'

He showed us to the door, shook hands all round, still punctiliously polite. We went down the steps, past the 'Eingang Dönitz' sign and into the car.

On the way to Hamburg our German interpreter said to me: 'You were pleased with the interview? It went well?' I said I thought so. 'It is interesting to me,' he said, 'that you should be doing this interview. In Germany today, you know, we are not talking about these people any more. They are quite forgotten.'

FOUR NAVAL ATROCITIES

WHILE RESEARCHING AND writing Pursuit *and* Menace, *my books on the* Bismarck *and* Tirpitz, *I had been given much assistance from my friend the official naval historian, Captain Stephen Roskill. One day, while visiting him in Cambridge, I asked whether there was any event in the war at sea which he had not written about yet which he felt should be. He said there was: the episode in the summer of 1941 when the captain of a British submarine, Lieutenant-Commander Anthony Miers, had ordered the machine-gunning of seven Bavarian mountain troops in a rubber boat, survivors of an attack which he had mounted on the vessel that was taking them from German-occupied Crete to Athens. He described this as an atrocity of which the Royal Navy should be ashamed and as bad as that of the German U-boat captain Heinz Eck, who had also machine-gunned survivors of a ship he had sunk. Knowing of two other similar incidents, one German, the other British, which had occurred during the First World War, I thought it might be interesting to write an article contrasting the four incidents and the different fates that befell the chief participants; and the resulting article, 'Four Naval Atrocities' appeared in the* Daily Telegraph Magazine *in the early summer of 1991.*

War crimes are back in the news. Nearly half a century after the Nazi hierarchy, big and small, were brought to book at Nuremberg, the British government has announced its intention of bringing charges against a handful of old men resident here and against whom allegations of multiple murders during the Second World War have been made. I make no comment on this except to say that the problems of establishing convincing proof after so long a gap in time are likely to be insuperable.

What do we understand by the phrase 'war crimes'? Those who sat in judgement at Nuremberg interpreted it to include (for the first time in history) the actions of members of a sovereign government in initiating war; a decision which satisfied the then desire for retribution but, as was pointed out at the time, of dubious legal propriety: Lord Hankey called it 'victor legislation'.

Nor do I think that the air bombardments which each side inflicted on the other can properly be considered war crimes. Firstly they were instruments of policy and also because, however frightful the scale of destruction, the execution of them was entirely impersonal. The worst war crimes to my mind were those in which the perpetrators came face to face with their defenceless victims: the operators of the gas-chambers, SS men who shot prisoners of war and hostages, Japanese soldiers who raped and bayoneted women.

Because of its nature, there was one field of operations in both world wars in which those kind of crimes were rare, and that was the sea. Here were no lines of demarcation, no Jews or women and children to confuse the issue. Of all forms of modern warfare a sea battle is the most impersonal, for the face of the enemy at whom you lob shells or propel torpedoes or drop depth charges is rarely seen. And yet in the course of the two world wars, there were four cases of what I would call minor war crimes. Two of the four were German and two British; all four concerned submarines.

When the submarine came into being as a weapon of war at the turn of the century, the British viewed it with horror; not only because for the first time in history it made civilians, in the shape of the crews of merchant and passenger ships, direct targets, but because of the realization that in any war with Germany their submarines, loose on the Atlantic trade routes, might (and in 1917 and again in 1943 very nearly did) bring this country to its knees. This deep-rooted fear of it coupled with the failure of the British government to have it internationally outlawed led, during the First World War, to waves of quite unsubstantiated U-boat atrocity stories. It was war-stimulated hatred, wrote Admiral William Sims of the US Navy, that created the absurd yet powerful belief that German submarine commanders were devils in human form, intent not only on torpedoing enemy merchant ships but on murdering their crews as well. All the evidence, says Sims, shows that the vast majority were decent seamen; and in parenthesis, one notes that neither the German government nor press preached or encouraged a similar war hatred against America or England.

There was however one major exception, and that was the torpedoing at night in June 1918 of the hospital ship *Llandovery Castle*, bound from Canada to England, by the submarine *U.86*. Although attacks on clearly marked hospital ships were in contravention of the Hague Convention to which Germany was a signatory, there was a strong but unfounded belief in the German fleet that the British were using their hospital ships as carriers of troops and munitions. It was in the erroneous belief that the *Llandovery Castle* was carrying American airmen and shells that Commander Patzig of the *U.86* gave the order to attack.

The *Llandovery Castle* sank within ten minutes. Three lifeboats only got away. Patzig surfaced, took his boat among the survivors and from them learned that the ship had neither combatants nor munitions on board. Realizing the enormity of what he had done and that one day he might have to answer for it, he resolved to remove all evidence of the sinking by destroying the lifeboats and their occupants and by falsifying his log. Unfortunately for him one of the lifeboats, carrying twenty-four people (the only ones to survive from a ship's company and medical staff of 258), got away in the darkness, but on Patzig's orders his gunnery officer Dithmar and another officer Boldt directed fire at the other two lifeboats, sinking them and killing the occupants. During the return voyage the crew experienced acute depression, which Patzig tried to alleviate by a speech in which he said he would be answerable for what he had done to God and his own conscience.

Five months later the war ended and, under pressure from the British government, the German government ordered an inquiry into the affair; and as a result of affidavits made by the survivors of the lifeboat that had escaped and by members of the crew of the *U.86* and two British prisoners held on board, Patzig, Dithmar and Boldt were indicted on charges of killing shipwrecked people contrary to international law. Patzig, knowing there could be no defence for what he had done and that he faced severe punishment, disappeared before the date set for the trial. In July 1921 Dithmar and Boldt were charged before the German Supreme Court at Leipzig. In defence they pleaded obedience to superior orders, not accepted by the court on the grounds that they knew such orders to be illegal. Both officers were sentenced to four years' imprisonment, Dithmar was dismissed from the service and Boldt reduced to the ranks. But in the changed climate of the post-war years, both men were released after serving no more than a few months. Had the *U.86* been sunk by British forces after the incident and the three officers been among the survivors, it is probable, as happened on a similar occasion during the Second World War, that, after a court martial, all three would have been shot.

The British atrocity, the notorious affair of the Q-ship *Baralong,* was no less shocking. The idea of the Q-ship arose early in the war as a result of a practice among U-boat commanders to stop merchant ships encountered in order to examine them, then, if enemy, to allow their crews to disembark in lifeboats before sinking them by gunfire. In a memo of 3 February 1915 Winston Churchill as First Lord of the Admiralty explained the Q-ship's role.

I attach the greatest importance to the use of merchant ships with a concealed gun to entrap the commerce destroying submarines ... They should cruise in the area of the raiding submarine, stop when they are challenged, allow a boat to come alongside from the submarine, and then sink the submarine by gunfire, taking the boat's crew prisoners *or firing on them as convenient.* [author's italics]

It would be difficult to interpret the meaning of the last five words as other than an incitement to a war crime; but it was a reflection of the fear and loathing felt towards German submarine crews at the time; a reflection also embodied in a letter of 16 September 1915 from the Vice-Admiral, Coast of Ireland (where most of the sinkings were taking place) to the captains of the anti-submarine vessels under his command: 'I have got a barograph for the first sloop that sinks a submarine *with no survivors*' [author's italics].

The first fruits of the Q-ship policy came about in August 1915 with the arrival in the shipping lanes off southern Ireland of the warship *Baralong,* disguised as an American merchantman with huge stars and stripes painted on either side, carrying two concealed guns and a platoon of Royal Marines, and under the command of Lieutenant-Commander Godfrey Herbert. On 19 August the *Baralong* sighted the steamer *Nicosian,* bound from America to England with a cargo of mules, muleteers and fodder, being shelled by the German submarine *U.27.* Her crew had already taken to the boats. As the *Baralong* approached, the *U.27* disappeared behind the *Nicosian*'s stern which enabled Herbert to hoist the white ensign and run out his two guns unobserved. When the *U.27* reappeared from behind the *Nicosian*'s bows, she was met by a hail of fire from the *Baralong* and sank within a few minutes. Eleven or twelve of her crew jumped into the water and swam towards the *Nicosian* where ropes and a rope ladder had been let down for the lowering of the boats. On the flimsy excuse that if these survivors reached the *Nicosian,* they might scuttle or set fire to her, Herbert ordered the marines to open rifle fire, and half the Germans were shot either in the water or while trying to climb the ropes hanging from the ship's sides. Six however succeeded in boarding her.

Herbert now took the *Baralong* alongside the *Nicosian* and ordered the marines to seek out and deal with the U-boat men. This they did, and according to Herbert's official report, all six 'shortly after succumbed to the injuries they had received from the shelling of the submarine' – a ludicrous explanation of the deaths of men who had just swum a fair distance and then hauled themselves up hanging ropes; as wretched a lie as Patzig's falsification of the *U.86*'s log. Having hunted down each of the six, some of whom had taken refuge in the engine-room, others of whom, realizing their probable fate, had put on *Nicosian* crew members' clothing, Herbert's marines, on his orders and ignoring pleas of surrender, shot them in cold blood. When this news reached the Admiralty via outraged members of the *Nicosian*'s crew who had returned on board and seen what had happened, Herbert was asked for clarification. In a further statement he said that 'it may well be that certain things were done in hot blood which a calmer judgement might regret.' He maintained however that the marines 'could not afford to take risks'.

The Admiralty were only too happy to accept this, and in a letter to the Vice-Admiral, Coast of Ireland, they said that 'great credit is due to Lieutenant-Commander Godfrey Herbert and his officers and men for the skill and discretion shown in this encounter, and their application is to be conveyed to them accordingly'. The King had approved the award of the Distinguished Service Order to Herbert and his name had been noted for early promotion. Winston Churchill expressed his entire approval. The killing of the survivors could be forgotten.

But as with Patzig and the *U.86,* the stone that had been cast produced ever widening ripples. When a month later the *Nicosian* docked in New Orleans, four American members of her crew gave affidavits to the German consul there, telling in detail what they had seen. What particularly enraged the Americans was that the disguised *Baralong* had been flying the American flag, an act which the veterinary surgeon in charge of the mules called 'this monstrous contempt for the Stars and Stripes'. The affidavits came to the notice of the American government and led Robert Lansing, about to become Secretary of State, to write to President Wilson on 30 August:

> To me the conduct of the British naval authorities is shocking, and I sincerely hope that this matter may not become public, as it would seriously affect public opinion in Germany and might result in retaliatory measures of a most vigorous character.

But Lansing's hopes were not to be realized, and on 7 October the story broke in the American press. Their almost unanimous views were the same as his, and epitomized by the proprietor of the *New York State News*: 'The shocking manner in which the English murdered the German seamen after their ship was destroyed has confirmed my worst fears in regard to the behaviour of the English.'

Up to this time British merchant ships armed with a single gun had been allowed to depart unhindered from American ports, but now by direction of the President they were not to be given clearance until their captains had given assurances in writing that the guns would be used only for defensive purposes. 'It is no exaggeration to say,' wrote Captain Stephen Roskill, Britain's official naval historian, 'that the *Baralong* incident contributed to President Wilson and his Secretary of State Lansing executing almost a 16-point turn in their attitude towards us in 1916.'

In Germany too, and particularly in the light of false British stories of numerous U-boat atrocities, there was a similar expression of outrage. Protests (all ignored) were made to the British government through neutral channels, and after the war the German government demanded that Herbert should be brought to trial, just as the British government had demanded for the officers of the *U.86*. The British government refused. And yet, as Stephen Roskill wrote, 'If ever there was a case where a British naval officer could have been justifiably brought to trial on an issue of war crimes, it was surely Godfrey Herbert.'

So ashamed was the British government of what had happened that no account of it was allowed to be published in the press during the war and by the time that it did surface long afterwards, interest had faded. The cover-up was approved by the First Lord of the Admiralty, A. J. Balfour, whose view, according to his secretary, was that 'whatever happened on board the *Nicosian* was done in hot blood, without authority, in fair fight against an armed enemy in possession of the ship.' It was a travesty of the truth but it achieved its purpose: to sustain public belief in the honour of the navy, and preserve the fiction that its officers were incapable of such misconduct; foreigners might indulge in that sort of thing but not the heirs of Nelson. It was an attitude that was most elegantly expressed by Mr Colville Barclay of the British embassy staff in Washington. In a dispatch written for his ambassador to the Foreign Office in London, he described being summoned to the Secretary of State's office and shown by Mr Lansing the *Nicosian* crew members' affidavit. 'I expressed considerable surprise', he wrote, 'that he should believe such stories of cold-blooded murder by British sailors, stating that I had seen the story in the papers but had attached no importance to it, putting it down as merely another instance of those calumnious accusations so frequently made against us by the Germans. I also told him I had seen a denial of the story in the papers and sent him the cutting, copy of which is enclosed.'

A quarter of a century later Britain and Germany were at war again, and again, and for both sides, the submarine was to play a prominent part. Again, too, the vast majority of submarine commanders acquitted themselves honourably, observing the rules of maritime war as laid down in the Hague Conventions. Because of a submarine's cramped living conditions it was not obligatory on them to rescue survivors of ships they had sunk (though sometimes a token prisoner might be taken for interrogation or as proof of a sinking); but it was obligatory on them not to harm survivors. It was an obligation which one German and one British submarine captain flagrantly ignored.

The name of the German captain was Lieutenant-Commander Heinz Eck and early in 1944 he took the newly commissioned *U.852,* his first command, out of Kiel harbour for operations in the Indian Ocean. By mid-March he had reached a position some 300 miles west of Freetown, Sierra Leone and commenced a patrol. At this time the crew were under some strain, both from the rigours of the voyage – they had not stepped ashore for almost two months – the intense heat, and the knowledge that four of the last five U-boats on patrol in this area, two of them commanded by the much decorated aces Kuppisch and Schultz, had been sunk.

In the early evening of 13 March a steamer was sighted, and the crew went to action stations. She was the Greek *Peleus* of some 9,000 tons, outward bound from Freetown for the River Plate. Eck manoeuvred the *U.852* until he was ahead of her and fired two torpedoes. Both hit and within a few minutes the *Peleus* had sunk. Some twelve survivors managed to scramble on to rafts. Eck ordered his engineer officer, Hans Lenz, who spoke English, to call two of them on board to interrogate them about shipping movements in the area. They were then put back on their raft.

It was now dark, and Eck's wisest course would have been to put as much distance as possible between himself and the scene of the action before dawn. Had he done so, he could, at 18 knots on the surface, have been 150 miles away before reconnaissance planes sighted the wreckage. But, remembering what had been the fate of his predecessors on the station, he seems to have become panic stricken and, as a result, obsessed with the idea of destroying all evidence of the sinking. To this end he ordered small arms in the shape of machine-guns, grenades and pistols to be brought to the bridge and, while this was being done, he withdrew the *U.852* to a distance of a thousand metres from the wreckage. Here two officers, Lenz and the first lieutenant, Kolditz, approached Eck and said that they were not in agreement with what he proposed to do. 'Eck', said Lenz, 'replied that nevertheless he intended to eliminate all traces of the sinking.'

When the small arms were ready, Eck took the *U.852* back to the area of the wreckage, ordered a signal lamp to be shone on the scene and fire to be opened indiscriminately. Those who took part in the firing were mostly officers: Walter Weisspfennig, the boat's doctor who, as a member of the medical profession, was forbidden to bear arms; August Hoffmann, aged twenty-one, the second lieutenant; and Leading Seaman Schwender. When Lenz saw Schwender firing, and despite his earlier protestations, he seized Schwender's gun and joined in the fracas himself. Nor was it just a question of a few bursts here and there. For more than four hours the *U.852* cruised to and fro among the ever widening wreckage, bent on murder and destruction.

They were not as successful as they had hoped. Antonios Liossis, the *Peleus*'s chief officer, later wrote:

> . . . the submarine suddenly opened fire with a machine-gun. We all ducked and I could hear cries of pain from Kostantidinis who was hit by the bullets in several

places. The rafts became riddled with bullet holes but they did not sink because the tanks were filled with buoyant materials. The Germans also threw hand grenades at us, one of which wounded me in my right shoulder and back. The Germans were shining their signal lamp to see that everyone was finished off, but I lay very quiet, and as my back was covered in blood, I think they decided I was dead . . . Just before dawn Kostantidinis died.

It was not until one in the morning that Eck left the scene of his crime and set course southwards to round the Cape of Good Hope. After the excitement of the night's events (for many of the young crew it was their first sinking) what Eck called 'a bad mood' set in, similar, it would seem, to that experienced by the crew of Patzig's *U.86* after the murders of the survivors of the *Llandovery Castle.* It was a mood of guilt and shame which, Eck admitted, he shared himself. So he addressed the crew, just as Patzig had done, told them he had acted as he had with a heavy heart and asked them to remember German wives and children who had died in allied air attacks.

The world might never have heard of Heinz Eck and the *U.852* had not two things happened. The first was that although Eck was under the impression that he had killed all the survivors, four men managed to get away. They were Liossis the first officer, Agis Kefalas the third officer, a Greek seaman and a British greaser. They stayed together on one of the rafts until twenty-five days after the sinking when Kefalas, whose arms had been broken by grenade splinters, died of gangrene. There were sufficient provisions and water on the raft for the remaining three to survive until picked up by a passing steamer on 19 April and taken first to Lobito in Portuguese West Africa and then to London where they made statements.

The *U.852* meanwhile continued south. On 1 April she sank a transport off Cape Town, then proceeded up the east coast of Africa to operate in the Indian Ocean. On 2 May she was attacked on the surface by an RAF bomber and, having suffered many casualties and much damage, she ran aground on the coast of what was then Italian Somaliland. The British sloop *Falmouth* was detached to capture her but when she arrived on the scene it was to find half the U-boat destroyed by explosives and the crew standing on the beach. The U-boat's log, which had been slung over the side in a waterproof bag and attached to the conning-tower by a heaving line, was recovered.

The *Falmouth* took the *U.852*'s crew prisoner, and during the ensuing days her boarding officer, Kennedy Gordon, saw much of Eck and his fellow officers. He described Eck as 'a man of considerable charm, tall and handsome: the *U.852*'s crew obviously idolized him, though he was quite unlike the popular conception of a typical German officer.' The doctor, Weisspfennig, was 'blondish, heavily built with a sabre duelling scar on his cheek', and Gordon (not knowing of Weisspfennig's part in the massacre of the *Peleus*'s survivors) was impressed by his attentions to the *U.852*'s wounded. 'The engineer officer, Lenz, was at considerable loss to understand why the British entered the war on the part of Poland, describing the Poles as rubbishy peasants and certainly not worth fighting for.'

When the *U.852*'s log was inspected, a record of the sinking of the *Peleus* was found. In London this was compared with the statements of the ship's survivors, and after the taking of affidavits from the crew of the *U.852* it was decided to bring Eck, Hoffmann, Weisspfennig, Lenz and Schwender to trial for the murder of shipwrecked survivors contrary to the rules of war.

The trial took place in Hamburg in October 1945. The President of the Court was a British Brigadier called Jones and the other members were another Brigadier, an RN Commodore, an RNR Captain, two Greek naval captains (the *Peleus* being a Greek ship), and an English lieutenant-colonel: they were the jury. Counsel for the prosecution was a colonel from the Judge Advocate General's office. Counsel for the defence were a German professor of law, a German lawyer and a British major. The judge advocate or judge was Major A. Melford Stevenson, KC, a formidable barrister and later to win fame as an outspoken and controversial English High Court judge. It was his job to explain to the court the law and to sum up the evidence at the end. The five accused, all in naval uniform, took their places in the dock, Hoffman with the aid of a stick because of wounds to his legs during the air attack.

Although Melford Stevenson was doing the job he had been ordered to do, he personally was against the whole concept of war crimes which, like Lord Hankey's 'victor legislation', he saw as 'the only example in history of purely retributive justice, and as any sort of deterrent for the future, a total loss.' Nor did he pull any punches in his views of the other members of the court. He described the president, Brigadier Jones, as 'a splendid professional soldier' who, fed up with the wordy and irrelevant meanderings of the German professor, kept saying to Melford Stevenson, 'For God's sake, shut the old bugger up.' But, like Kennedy Gordon, he was struck by Eck. 'He really made the court feel low-class which many of them were. His courage and dignity were very impressive. Of all those in that court it is his personality that survives in my memory. It was clear he'd lost his head.'

Eck's defence was that of 'operational necessity', i.e. he had given orders to destroy all traces of the sinking to preserve the security of his own boat. But this was nonsense, as he could have put more than a hundred miles between himself and the scene of the sinking while it was still dark; and the court refused to accept it. The other four pleaded obedience to superior orders, but that had never been recognized as a legitimate defence in any of the countries that had signed the Hague Convention, and so it failed too. The final nail in the coffins of the defendants was the evidence of a former U-boat ace, Commander Adalbert Schnee, a veteran of sixteen war patrols and thirty sinkings and who, as a staff officer of U-boat command, had briefed Eck on his mission preparatory to his sailing. Asked whether he, in a similar situation to Eck, would have done what Eck did, he said categorically that he wouldn't. Asked if he had given Eck specific orders not to harm survivors, he replied that there was no need to as that had been promulgated in general naval orders at the beginning of the war. The court were also made aware of Article 11 of the Hague Convention which laid down that 'after every engagement the two belligerents, so far as military interests permit, shall take steps to look for the sick, wounded and shipwrecked, and to protect them against improper treatment.'

The guilty verdicts were inevitable. Eck, Hoffmann and Weisspfennig were sentenced to death, Lenz to life imprisonment, Schwender to fifteen years. Before Eck's sentence was carried out, he made a deposition for use in the defence of the forthcoming trial of Grand Admiral Karl Dönitz, the former U-boat chief, that at no time had Dönitz issued any orders that shipwrecked men should be killed. Then he, Hoffmann and Weisspfennig were taken from Altona prison, Hamburg, to Luneberg Heath, tied to posts and shot by firing squad.

The last of these four stories of naval atrocities concerns the third war patrol of the British submarine *Torbay* in the Mediterranean in the summer of 1941. *Torbay*'s captain was Lieutenant-Commander Anthony Miers, an outstandingly brave and offensively minded officer who was later awarded the VC for taking the *Torbay* into the enemy-occupied harbour of Corfu Roads and there torpedoing two merchant ships. 'I know of no other officer,' said one of his crew, 'who would sooner get you into a scrape, but whom you could rely on absolutely to get you out of it.' The Navy's view of Miers was mixed. Earlier in his career he had been court-martialled for striking a stoker and many found him brusque, even rude. Captain Roskill called him a Nazi-type officer, but those who served under him, like Commander Richard Compton-Hall, speak of his intense loyalty to his subordinates. On any reading he was a volatile personality with the shortest of fuses. Even his own son has called him 'a colourful and passionate character'.

On 28 June 1941 the *Torbay* sailed from Alexandria on a war patrol in the south-western Aegean, one of her objects being to disrupt enemy shipping between the Greek mainland and the German-occupied island of Crete. She had also been ordered to take part in an operation involving a shore landing and for this purpose had embarked two commandos, Corporal George Bremner and Corporal Jim Sherwood. The first part of the patrol was highly successful, the submarine accounting for several enemy schooners and caiques as well as an Italian U-boat. An inkling of what was to come is

165

to be found in the log for the early afternoon of 4 July where it was recorded that a schooner filled with troops was sunk by gunfire, 'using both Lewis guns *to destroy the boats and personnel*' (author's italics). Five nights later the *Torbay* caught up with three L-class caiques, the *LVI, LV* and *LI,* proceeding from German-occupied Crete to Athens with a cargo of bay leaves and raisins, as well as Wehrmacht mountain troops travelling home on leave. Having disposed of the *LVI, Torbay* came up with *LV.*

0357: Opened fire on second caique whose crew took to the water while those remaining on board made signals of surrender, shouting 'Captain is Greek'. The submarine was put alongside, the berthing party on the casing being accompanied and covered by one of the embarked soldiers with a tommy-gun with which to shoot an obviously German soldier as he was about to hurl a grenade.

After a brief pretence at being Greek, the whole party when addressed in German by the navigating officer replied in German saying, 'I am German.' They were all forced to launch and jump into a large rubber float and the demolition charge was then laid and fired.

After recording that the caique was of about 100 tons, wore the Nazi flag and had LV painted on her side, the log says this:

0427: Submarine cast off and with the Lewis gun accounted for the soldiers in the rubber raft to prevent them regaining their ship and then set off in search of Number Three [this was the *LI*].

The soldier who shot at the German who was about to throw a grenade (but according to the Germans missed) was Corporal Bremner. Miers ordered the other soldier, Corporal Sherwood, to shoot another German, but as he was unarmed Sherwood refused, and Miers ordered him below. Bremner said that while the demolition charge was being prepared, 'I captured and disarmed seven Bavarian Alpine troops whom

166

I shepherded aboard the casing of the *Torbay*. During the time I was on the casing I removed some of their headgear, insignia and badges of rank for identification purposes in Alexandria.' Bremner added that subsequently Miers took these from him. He asked Miers's permission to take the seven Germans below but Miers 'furiously refused, shouting that submarines never took prisoners,' and then he himself went below.

On the casing meanwhile the seven men, now disarmed, were forced into the rubber float. Miers then told his first lieutenant, Paul Chapman, to shoot them, but he refused. 'They were sitting ducks,' he said, 'I simply felt unable to do it.' Miers then called on a leading signalman to shoot them, saying, 'If you don't shoot them, I'll shoot you.' Miers was in the habit of making empty threats to shoot people (including Bremner on a later occasion). But the signalman, terrified that he meant it, and not daring to challenge his captain, obeyed.

Those on the *LV* who had called out 'Captain is Greek' were lying. He was in fact a twenty-two-year-old German sailor, Fritz Ehlebracht, and after the *Torbay* had opened fire he gave the order to abandon ship. Some, including himself, did so, but others remained on board. In the water he was a witness to the shooting of those on the rubber float in which, he said, Kurt Lux and Josef Pritzbilla were killed and Heinrich Reicheng and another man seriously wounded. The *Torbay*, he said, then circled round the men in the water and machine-gunned them too before setting off in the direction of the *LI* which was also sunk. Despite the demolition charge the *LV* did not sink and Ehlebracht and one or two others clung to the wreckage until morning. They were then sighted by a German reconnaissance plane which had been sent out to see why the caiques had not arrived, and soon after a Dornier flying-boat landed and picked up the survivors. In Athens, Ehlebracht wrote an account of what had happened for the German naval authorities, and this was given much prominence in German newspapers. Like the *Baralong* affair the ripples began to widen.

There can be no doubt that Miers's action was in every way as cold-blooded as what Eck was to do in the *U.852*.

Apologists for him have pointed out that there was this difference in that Miers had killed members of a fighting service who, if rescued, would live to fight another day. But the Hague Convention makes no distinction between classes of those shipwrecked. Indeed, Article 11 specifically includes 'soldiers on board' as among those to be respected. Furthermore, if Miers was convinced that his order to fire was a legal one, he would have had Sherwood and Chapman court-martialled for disobeying it; and he did not do so.

In his patrol report Miers did not attempt to disguise what he had done; but he could hardly have foreseen the consternation that would ensue when his superiors came to study it. What Admiral Cunningham, the Commander-in-Chief Mediterranean, and the Board of Admiralty were most concerned about were reprisals; for they had been informed of the publicity given to Ehlebracht's report in German and foreign newspapers.

'I feel sure that if the enemy discovers who was responsible,' minuted one of the naval staff, 'anyone from *Torbay* would be shot out of hand if they fell into enemy hands.' He urged that circulation of Miers's report be restricted on the grounds that it would otherwise be 'a mark of official approval of the machine-gunning of prisoners and survivors'. This was the aspect that most concerned the Flag Officer Submarines, Admiral Max Horton, who wrote to the Board of Admiralty,

> As far as I am aware, the enemy has not made a habit of firing on personnel in the water or on rafts even when such personnel were members of the fighting services: since the incidents referred to in *Torbay*'s report, he may feel justified in doing so.

And he urged the Admiralty to issue a policy statement. This they refused to do on the understandable grounds that if they were to emphasize that survivors should not be fired on, it might give the impression that this sort of thing was commonplace: they trusted captains, they said, 'to follow the dictates of humanity and the traditions of the service'.

Although others of the naval staff had minuted their disapproval of the shooting of survivors, it was not until after the end of the war that a senior officer condemned Miers in unequivocal terms. Rear-Admiral Clarence Howard-Johnston was asked by the Prime Minister, Winston Churchill, to let him have a list of any known war crimes committed by enemy submarines. He studied numerous incidents but could only find what he called 'one blatant case' (Eck and *Peleus*). Had he known about Miers, he said later, he would have told Winston of that too, 'to put him in the clear'. 'Miers,' he said, 'left a blot on the Royal Navy's record which can never be erased, but it was worse to try to hide it.'

Should it in fact have been hidden? Should he have been brought to trial by court martial for the second time in his career? On strictly legal grounds, yes. But to have removed from his command one of the most courageous and successful of British submarine captains at a time when our fortunes in the Mediterranean were at a low ebb was to ask of the Admiralty too much. Instead the Admiralty sent a letter instructing him in the strongest terms not to indulge in such practices again.

Even then the ripples did not cease. In 1943 Miers, now a Commander, was appointed British liaison officer to the submarine arm of the American Pacific Fleet, and the question arose as to whether his third war patrol report should be included among others then about to be sent to the US Navy. The general view was that it should not. 'Apart from the harm that it might do,' ran an Admiralty minute, 'it would very possibly involve Miers in personal opprobrium and might seriously jeopardize his mission.' It never went. But Miers did, and in May 1943 came on board the cruiser *Leander,* then commanded by Captain Roskill, to give a pep talk. 'At the end of it,' wrote Roskill, 'he produced a Wehrmacht cap [presumably one taken from Bremner] and waved it in the air as a trophy of war. It amused the men but left a nasty taste in my mouth.'

Worse, there was later reason to suppose that the reprisals that the Admiralty and Admiral Cunningham feared eventually took place; that it was the killing of the survivors of the *LV* that first led the Germans in this theatre to change their attitude towards British prisoners; and that Miers must bear some responsibility for the murder of British commandos captured in the Aegean in 1942.

Miers was subsequently promoted to Captain and Rear-Admiral, became Admiral President of the Royal Naval College at Greenwich and lived in honourable retirement at Roehampton. A few years ago I wrote to ask if I might discuss with him the events under review and sent him a copy of my book on the *Bismarck* action, *Pursuit,* to show an example of my writing. His secretary replied. She not only declined my offer, which didn't altogether surprise me, but added that the admiral was too busy to read my book and had sent it to a friend in hospital.

These four stories of naval atrocities are as good an example as one could find of Lord Hankey's 'victor legislation'. Had the Germans won the war, it is highly improbable that Patzig would have been indicted or that Dithmar, Boldt or Eck would have been brought to trial; and one can take it as read that both Herbert and Miers would have been shot, with or without court martial. Nations, like individuals, do not like admitting to actions of which they are ashamed, which is why no accounts of what Herbert and Miers did are to be found in the British naval histories of the two wars. And yet both were to have far-reaching effects: the former in effecting an unfavourable change in American public opinion concerning our conduct of the war, the second in giving to the then enemy a gratuitous piece of anti-British propaganda of which he made full use. In an ideal world justice is or should be indivisible. Between combatants in time of war it never can be. Yet those who brought Eck to trial at the end of the war might, remembering Miers, have tempered justice with mercy; for while their crimes were as near as makes no matter identical, their respective fates were altogether too disparate for comfort.

JUSTICE

JUSTICE

As I HAVE explained in my autobiography and elsewhere, the genesis of my interest in matters of justice was the library of my grandfather, Sir Ludovic Grant, one-time Professor of Public and International Law at the University of Edinburgh. On the top shelf lay a set of William Hodge's famous series, Notable British Trials; and on holidays in Edinburgh between the ages of fourteen and sixteen, I would mount the step-ladder and sit there for hours, utterly absorbed. Guy Fawkes, Burke and Hare, Charles Peace, Oscar Wilde, Madeleine Smith, Dr Crippen, Roger Casement, Bywaters and Thompson, Dr Buck Ruxton were some of those whose trials had been recorded verbatim. What fascinated me about them was on the one hand the wickedness, the depravity of those accused and on the other the majesty, the mystique, the immaculacy of the law. I never doubted then (who did?) the integrity of those taking part nor the correctness of verdict and sentence; that policemen could be corrupt, that witnesses could perjure themselves, that judges could be biased were thoughts that never even remotely occurred to me. Here was wickedness punished, virtue applauded, justice done.

Having thus initially looked at our criminal justice system with starry eyes, the shock later on of finding that things were not always what they purported to be was inevitably the greater. I never set out to make a career of writing books and articles about miscarriages of criminal justice but, as things turned out, one case was succeeded by another.

One or two critics who reviewed my autobiography suggested that there could have been another reason for my lifelong obsession, that is, one over and above a writer's occupational motivation of discovering the truth. When I was a boy I was told by my mother that my father had been court-martialled and reprimanded after the first war *for not taking strong enough measures to suppress a mutiny of naval reservists who were under his command. She said that the verdict had been disgraceful and that the Navy as a whole thought my father had been shabbily treated. At the time I suspected that my mother took this line out of loyalty to my father and I did not enquire further for fear of finding that my father had been truly guilty. Indeed it was not until I was preparing my autobiography in my mid-sixties that I felt the time had come to seek the truth of the matter. Having researched the papers on the case and studied my father's diaries, I found to my surprise and delight that my mother had been right in her opinion and the naval authorities wrong; that the press and scores of sympathetic letters from naval colleagues (many unknown to my father) were unanimous in declaring not only that the verdict was incorrect but that the proceedings should never have been brought. Did I not realize, the critics said, that in rehabilitating so many victims of miscarriages of justice I was, as it were, also rehabilitating my father? They may have been right; for although I did not know until a few years ago that the verdict against my father needed correction, there could well have been simmering in my unconscious for years the belief that the man whom I loved more than any other had been wrongly and cruelly treated.*

The first of many cases to arouse my disquiet, indeed disgust, was the infamous Craig–Bentley affair of 1949. Craig, the dominant partner, was sixteen and Bentley, an epileptic with a mental age of ten, nineteen. One night they broke into a warehouse in Croydon and were apprehended by police on the rooftop. Craig opened fire with a gun, killed one policeman and wounded another before they were taken into custody. At their trial both were found guilty of murder. Bentley was sentenced to death but Craig, too young to hang, was ordered to be detained during the Sovereign's pleasure: the law considered Craig capable of redemption, Bentley not. Few people thought that Bentley would be called on to pay the full penalty but the Home Secretary of the day, name of Maxwell Fyfe, thought otherwise and Bentley was duly hanged. Many of us were shocked by this decision which seemed contrary to all natural justice. I wrote a play based on the case called Murder Story, and it was put on at the Cambridge Theatre. It seemed to me that those who most vociferously backed the retention of hanging had no idea what it meant in human terms to those who had to carry it out. The theme of the play was how an illiterate youth like Bentley finds in the condemned cell and for the first time a meaning and purpose to his life; and as he finds it, his life is ended.

If some of the colloquialisms seem a little dated, it was written forty years ago.

MURDER STORY

ACT II

Scene 1

WE ARE IN the condemned cell of one of Her Majesty's
prisons. It is a bleak-looking room with high, bare walls,
and the only furniture is a bed in one corner and a table
and chairs in the middle. Above the table hangs an unshaded
electric-light bulb. In one of the side walls is a door leading
to a lavatory and wash-place, in the other, opposite, a bigger
door which gives the impression of being nailed up and out
of use: this leads to the execution shed. In the middle of
the back wall is the main door to the passageway; there is a
sliding panel in this at eye-level, protected by a small grille.
High up above this door is a barred window, looking out on
to the prison yard.

It is late afternoon, and Prison Officers GRAVES and
BARTHOLOMEW are sitting at the table, reading the evening
paper. BARTHOLOMEW is about forty, a tall, robust, severe-
looking man of rather military build. GRAVES is a year
or two older, a rounded little man with a mild, amiable
expression. There is the sound of a key turning in the main
door, and both officers put away their papers and stand
up. An officer pushes open the main door (which opens
inward) and lets in the GOVERNOR of the prison, followed
by Chief Officer BRIGGS. The GOVERNOR is a fine-looking
man of about fifty-five, with greying hair; his face denotes
strong character.

BRIGGS

Governor's visit!

[BARTHOLOMEW and GRAVES stand to attention.

GOVERNOR

All right, stand easy. (*He begins inspecting the cell.*) Tanner's
to come in here, is that right, and Clift's going next door?

BRIGGS

That's right, sir. And they share the wash-place between.

GOVERNOR

Yes. And of course you'll take the usual precautions they're
never in there together.

BRIGGS

Of course, sir.

GOVERNOR

Well, this cell's in pretty good shape.

BRIGGS

Cleaned out this morning, sir.

GOVERNOR (*by the bed*)

Yes. (*He fingers the bedclothes.*) Sheets and blankets been
cleaned?

BRIGGS

Just come from the laundry, sir.

GOVERNOR

Good. Let's have a look next door. Bartholomew, you've done
this job before?

BARTHOLOMEW

Yes, sir.

GOVERNOR

But you haven't, Graves.

GRAVES

No, sir.

GOVERNOR

Feel all right about it?

GRAVES

I think so, sir.

GOVERNOR

Well, there's not much to it. After the first day or two you'll find it's more monotonous than anything else. Bartholomew will keep you on the right track. The prisoners are at reception now. They'll be along presently. All right, Chief.

[*The* GOVERNOR *and* BRIGGS *go out.*

GRAVES

Gov's a decent sort, isn't he?

BARTHOLOMEW

Don't make 'em no better. Well, I'm glad we've got Tanner in here and not that other one.

GRAVES

Yes, he sounds a nasty piece of work.

BARTHOLOMEW

He *is*. Didn't you see him when he was in before?

GRAVES

No.

BARTHOLOMEW

Did three months for house-breaking last year. Must have been when you was sick!

GRAVES

Well, I never!

BARTHOLOMEW

Was I glad to see the last of him! You know how you can learn to deal with most chaps . . . get to know their ways and that sort of thing. Well, you couldn't with him. Wouldn't let you get within a mile of him. Something slimy about him. Like those creepy-crawlies you find under stones.

GRAVES

I wonder what Tanner's like?

BARTHOLOMEW

We'll see soon enough.

GRAVES

I didn't think they'd convict him, did you?

BARTHOLOMEW

No, I—can't say as though I thought they would.

GRAVES

Jury recommended him to mercy, too.

BARTHOLOMEW

Yes, but that don't make no difference to the verdict. That's for the Home Secretary.

GRAVES

Do you think he'll swing?

BARTHOLOMEW

Blimey, Bert, don't ask me. I don't know no more than you.

GRAVES

It don't seem quite right, do it?

BARTHOLOMEW

Well, he was found guilty, wasn't he?

GRAVES

Yes. But, after all, it wasn't him who fired the shot.

BARTHOLOMEW

Maybe not. But if he hadn't been there, there mightn't have been no shot fired. Sounds as though you was getting soft, Bert?

GRAVES

You ain't married, are you?

BARTHOLOMEW

What's that got to do with it?

GRAVES

Well, I am. And I got a kid just about the same age as this Tanner.

BARTHOLOMEW

So what?

GRAVES

Nothing, Barty, nothing. Just makes you think, that's all.

BARTHOLOMEW

You haven't done this lot before, have you?

GRAVES

No.

BARTHOLOMEW

Mind if I ask why?

GRAVES

I just haven't had a fancy to it. I suppose I've got too much imagination.

BARTHOLOMEW

Why you doing it now, then?

GRAVES

Well, I'm going through for promotion, see. Governor thinks I ought to have the experience.

BARTHOLOMEW

Imagination's a useful thing, Bert. I ain't got much of it myself, and there's times I envy those who have. But not in this job. As far as this job's concerned you don't want no imagination.

GRAVES

Yes, I can see that.

BARTHOLOMEW

When you read in the papers of a bloke doing some filthy crime it makes you pretty sore against him. You feel you wouldn't mind doing him in yourself. Then when he's been tried and sentenced and comes in here you feel quite different about him. You forget about what he's done. You see him for the first time as a human being—who's going to die. And so you feel sorry for him. Well, that's all right. It's only natural. The only thing is, you don't want to feel *too* sorry for him. You want to keep yourself detached like.

GRAVES

That's a bit difficult, ain't it?

BARTHOLOMEW

Depends on who the bloke is. Now with that Clift, for instance, I don't imagine much of a problem would arise. But with others it's different. Do you remember the Devlin case?

GRAVES

Rings a bell somewhere.

BARTHOLOMEW

Well, I did watch with him. About five years ago it was—in this very cell. One of the nicest blokes I've met anywhere. Nice manners, well educated, considerate to everybody. Gentle as a lamb, and spent most of his time reading Shakespeare. Well, do you know what he'd done?

GRAVES

What?

BARTHOLOMEW

He persuaded an old lady to come to his flat to give him her savings for investment. When he'd got the savings he killed her. Then he cut her body up into small pieces, put them in a trunk, and took it to the left-luggage office at St Pancras.

GRAVES

Jesus!

BARTHOLOMEW

That was one of the first cases I ever did. In those days I couldn't help thinking about what was going to happen to the bloke and feeling pretty sorry for him. But whenever I caught myself doing that then I started remembering about what he'd done to get in there. And that made things kind of even. Now I don't think about either. I just get along from day to day—and I advise you, Bert, to do the same.

GRAVES

You make it sound all very easy.

BARTHOLOMEW

It's a question of making up your mind, see—seeing certain things and shutting out others. Once you've done that you'll be all right. But if you *do* start worrying about Tanner and what's going to happen in there (*he indicates the door on the right*), then just remember what I told you. Think about that dead copper. And his missus. And the child he ain't never going to see.

[*Slight pause, then the sound of a key being turned in the main door.*
Here he is now.

[*The main door opens and an officer lets* JIM *in. The door closes behind him.* JIM *stands there looking very lost. He is dressed in prison clothes.*
All right, son, come on in. We ain't going to eat you.

JIM

I'm Jim Tanner.

BARTHOLOMEW

Yes, we know that. We been expecting you. My name's Bartholomew—they call me Barty for short, and this is Bert Graves.

GRAVES

Hullo, boy.
[JIM *looks suspiciously from one to the other.*

BARTHOLOMEW

Why don't you have a look round?
[JIM *starts looking round the cell with intense curiosity.*

JIM

Where's that door go to?

BARTHOLOMEW

That's your wash-place.

JIM

Can I have a look?

BARTHOLOMEW

Sure you can.
 [BARTHOLOMEW *unlocks the door, and* JIM *goes through. After a moment he re-enters.*
Everything all right?

JIM

Yes, thanks. (*He wanders round the cell and sees the door in the opposite wall. (To* GRAVES) Where's that go to?
 [GRAVES *hesitates, being at a loss for an answer.*

BARTHOLOMEW (*quickly*)

That don't go nowhere, son. That's out of use.

JIM

Oh!

BARTHOLOMEW

Well, that's about all there is to it. Why don't you come and sit down now and relax?

JIM

You going to stay here?

BARTHOLOMEW

Oh yes.

JIM

How long?

BARTHOLOMEW

About another four hours. Till we gets relieved.

JIM

I want to be by myself.

BARTHOLOMEW

Not in here, son.

JIM

Someone here all the time?

BARTHOLOMEW

That's right.

JIM

Night-time, too?

BARTHOLOMEW

Night-time, too.

JIM

But I don't want nobody. I want to be by myself.

BARTHOLOMEW

I don't think you'd like it in here by yourself. All those long
hours can be awful lonely, you know. I think you'll be glad
of a bit of company. Anyway, you don't have to talk to us if
you don't want. We won't make ourselves a nuisance—will
we, Bert? Now then, why don't you come and sit down?
    [JIM *slowly walks over to the table and sits down.*
Cigarette?

JIM

Oh, thanks.

BARTHOLOMEW

Light?

JIM

You going to have one?

BARTHOLOMEW

No, son, we're not allowed to.

JIM

Oh! Thanks.

BARTHOLOMEW

Anything particular you'd like to do? Play a game? Read a magazine?

JIM

I can't read. I don't know how.

BARTHOLOMEW

Oh!

JIM

You think that's funny, don't you?

BARTHOLOMEW

No, I don't see nothing funny in it.

JIM

My boss thought it funny. He laughed at me. In front of the other two.

BARTHOLOMEW

Well, I hope you gave him what for?

JIM

Why don't you think it funny?

BARTHOLOMEW

Look, son, you ever been inside before?

JIM

In prison?

BARTHOLOMEW

Yes.

JIM

No.

BARTHOLOMEW

Well, more than half the blokes in here can't read—or write either.

JIM

Go on!

BARTHOLOMEW

It's the truth, I'm telling you. Ain't it, Bert?

GRAVES

Certainly is.

BARTHOLOMEW

And no-one thinks anything funny about it.

JIM

No?

BARTHOLOMEW

No. It's quite a normal thing. So don't go getting ideas in your head that you're peculiar. Now then, how about a game of draughts?

JIM

I don't know how to play.

BARTHOLOMEW

We'll soon teach you. It's easy. Come on, Bert, help me set up the board.

[BARTHOLOMEW *and* GRAVES *take the draught-board and counters from the edge of the table and begin arranging them.*

I think you'll like this game. Get a move on, Bert—what's the matter?

GRAVES

I was just thinking.

BARTHOLOMEW

And what were you thinking?

GRAVES

Oh, nothing much. (*He goes on arranging the pieces, then stops again.*)

BARTHOLOMEW

Come on, Bert, come on.

GRAVES

Look, boy, this is just an idea, and you needn't pay heed to it if you don't want to, but—how would you like to learn to read?

JIM

Learn to read?

GRAVES

Yes.

JIM

How could I?

GRAVES

I could teach you.

BARTHOLOMEW

Here, steady on, Bert.

GRAVES

I've got a big box of letters at home. Made of wood, they are.
My kids used to have them. I could bring them in tomorrow,
if you liked. Then we could put them together and spell out
different words. Would you like that?

JIM

Yes.

GRAVES

Sure?

JIM

Yes, but . . .

GRAVES

What?

JIM

Well, there don't seem much point. Me being in here and all.

GRAVES

For all you or I know, boy, you may get out of here.

JIM

Yes, I'd like that. I'd like it very much.

GRAVES

Good!

JIM

My dad once promised he'd teach me to read. But he never did.

GRAVES

We'll make up for lost time, eh?

JIM

I wish we could start now.

BARTHOLOMEW

Well, you can't, son, so come and play a game of draughts.

[GRAVES *gets up and* JIM *takes his place. As* GRAVES *passes* BARTHOLOMEW, BARTHOLOMEW *says:*

You shouldn't put those crazy ideas into the kid's head. (*To* JIM) Now then, son. You're white and I'm black, see. You have to get your men over here, and I get mine over there—but we only move in the white squares. When one of my men is in front of yours, and there's a space behind him, then you can take him. Like this, see. Now single men can only move forward—but when you get a man through to my back line here, you crown him—make him a king, see—and kings can move either way. That's all there is to it. All right?

JIM

Think so.

BARTHOLOMEW

Here we go then.

JIM

Like that?

BARTHOLOMEW

That's right.
    [*They play for a few seconds.*
No, not that square, son. This one or that one. That's it. Now you've taken one of my men. Ah, but now I've taken one of yours.

JIM (*to Graves*)

I can spell a few words.

GRAVES

I'm sure you can.

JIM

But not long ones. I always have diffitulcy—diffitulcy——

GRAVES

Diffi*culty*.

JIM

Yes. I always have diffitulcy with long ones. (*He moves a man.*)

BARTHOLOMEW

Ah, that was a bad move. Look! One, two, three, and a king!

[JIM *makes another move.*

No, son. Only forwards, remember.

[JIM *moves again.*

Oo, that was another bad one. Look! One, two!

JIM

But you moved it back. You just said I couldn't move back.

BARTHOLOMEW

Ah, but mine's a king.

[JIM *moves again.*

Oo, not that way, not that way. Well, it breaks my heart to have to do it, but here we go. One, two, three, four. I'm afraid you aren't going to win this one, son. Never mind, it's only the first go.

[JIM *suddenly sweeps the board and counters on to the floor.*

JIM

I don't want to play this game. I don't like it. It's a silly game. And you're a silly man. I hate you. I want to have my soldiers.

[*The door opens and the* GOVERNOR, CHAPLAIN *and Chief Officer* BRIGGS *come in. The* CHAPLAIN *is a man of about thirty-five.*

BRIGGS

Governor's visit!

[BARTHOLOMEW *and* GRAVES *stand up.*

GOVERNOR

All right, stand easy. Hullo, what's happened to the draught-board?

BARTHOLOMEW

Had a little accident, sir.

GOVERNOR

Oh!
  [BARTHOLOMEW *starts picking up the pieces.*
Well, Tanner, you settling in all right?

JIM

Yes.

GOVERNOR

Quite satisfied with everything?

JIM

Yes.

GOVERNOR

Got everything you want?

JIM

Yes.

GOVERNOR

Anything special you'd like? Something from home perhaps?

JIM

Yes, I'd like my soldiers.

GOVERNOR

Your what?

JIM

My toy soldiers. They're in the dresser. In a big white card-
board box.

GOVERNOR

Well, that's rather an unusual request. But I don't see why
you shouldn't have them. Perhaps you'd arrange it, Padre.

CHAPLAIN

Certainly.

GOVERNOR

The chaplain's going to stay and talk with you for a little
while, Tanner. I'll be in tomorrow morning. All right?

[*The* GOVERNOR *goes out. The* CHIEF OFFICER *nods to*
BARTHOLOMEW *and* GRAVES. *They all go out, too.*

CHAPLAIN

May I sit down?

JIM

OK.

CHAPLAIN

What happened to the draught-board?

JIM

I threw it on the floor.

CHAPLAIN

Why?

JIM

It's a silly game. I don't like it.

CHAPLAIN

I see.

JIM

Why've the officers gone?

CHAPLAIN

They always go when I come in.

JIM

They said they had to be here all the time. Night-time, too.

CHAPLAIN

Yes, but it's different with me.

JIM

Why?

CHAPLAIN

Well, you and I have things to discuss privately—things we don't want anyone else to hear.

JIM

What things?

CHAPLAIN

Oh, I don't know. It's up to you really. Anything you feel you'd like to tell me.

JIM

Why should I tell you things?

CHAPLAIN

No reason at all. Except that my position here is a little different to the rest of the staff. In fact I don't really belong here at all.

JIM

No?

CHAPLAIN

No. You see, the resident chaplain is looking after your—
looking after Clift. So I've come from another prison so as to
be with you.

JIM

Oh.

CHAPLAIN

So we've got something in common to start with, haven't
we?
(*Pause.*) Tell me about your soldiers.

JIM

My soldiers?

CHAPLAIN

Yes. The ones you asked the Governor if you could have.

JIM

They're my soldiers. They're in a box in the dresser at my
home.

CHAPLAIN

Yes, I know. What do you do with them? Do you line them
up in rows or march them up and down, or what?

JIM

I fight battles.

CHAPLAIN

Oh, do you?

JIM

Yes. They're two sides, see, and I'm the general of one side.

CHAPLAIN

And who's the general of the other?

JIM

I don't know.

CHAPLAIN

And sometimes your side wins, and sometimes the other? Is that it?

JIM

No, I always win.

CHAPLAIN

What, every time?

JIM

Yes. My side knocks all the other side down. Like that. (*He bangs the table violently.*) And then they're dead.

CHAPLAIN

I see.

JIM

You think it's silly, don't you?

CHAPLAIN

Silly? No. Why should I?

JIM

My mum thinks it silly. She says only kids have soldiers.

CHAPLAIN

Oh well, you know what mothers are. No, I don't think it's silly at all. Matter of fact, I had an uncle who collected soldiers. He had hundreds of them.

JIM

Did he? What kind were they?

CHAPLAIN

Oh, all sorts. All different regiments in the Army. Some of them were on horseback. And he had guns and gun-carriages and ammunition wagons and—oh, yes, a wonderful great coach for the general.

JIM

I wish I could have seen them.

CHAPLAIN

Yes, I think you'd have liked them.

JIM

What did he do, your uncle?

CHAPLAIN

He was a bishop.

JIM

Go on.

CHAPLAIN

Yes, he was.

JIM

And he had toy soldiers?

CHAPLAIN

Yes.

JIM

Did he fight battles with them?

CHAPLAIN

Not exactly. He used to put them in a big glass case so that everyone could see. People used to come and look from miles round. They were very beautiful.

JIM

Well, I never.

CHAPLAIN

Look, Jim—you don't mind me calling you Jim, do you?

JIM

No.

CHAPLAIN

And you can call me Padre, if you like—that's what most of them call me. Is there anything you'd like to tell me—about why you're in here, and what happened, and that sort of thing?

JIM

Yes. Yes, there is something.

CHAPLAIN

What is it?

JIM

I never thought he'd use the gun. He said he wouldn't.

CHAPLAIN

Clift, you mean?

JIM

Yes. I'd never have gone with him if I thought he'd use the gun.

CHAPLAIN

But you knew he had it?

JIM

Yes, he showed it me. But he said it was just to frighten people.

CHAPLAIN

You had some sort of weapon yourself, didn't you? A cosh, or something?

JIM

Yes.

CHAPLAIN

Why?

JIM

Ted told me to take it. But I wouldn't have used it. I wouldn't have known how. You do believe me, don't you?

CHAPLAIN

Look, Jim, whether I believe you or not doesn't much matter.

JIM

It does matter.

CHAPLAIN

Why?

JIM

'Cos I'm telling the truth.

CHAPLAIN

You may be telling the truth, Jim, but, don't you see, I can't help you there. That's something you want to see your lawyer about. I can only help you in other ways.

JIM

What ways?

CHAPLAIN

As a friend.

JIM (*contemptuously*)

A friend? I had a friend once.

CHAPLAIN

Clift, you mean.

JIM

Yes. And I don't want no more.

CHAPLAIN

All right.

JIM

Anyway, how can you be a friend if you don't believe what I say?

CHAPLAIN

I never said I didn't believe you, Jim.

JIM

No, but you don't. I can see it in your face. You think I'm telling lies, don't you? Just like the others. Why do you come in here? I didn't ask for you. Why can't you let me be alone? All that talk about wanting to help me. You're a swine, you are—a bloody, stinking, dirty swine.

[JIM *gets up and seizes the* CHAPLAIN *by the throat.* BARTHOLOMEW *and* GRAVES *come in quickly. The* CHAPLAIN *releases himself.*

CHAPLAIN

All right, I can manage.

BARTHOLOMEW (*stopping*)

Sure, sir?

CHAPLAIN

Yes, I'll call if I want you.

BARTHOLOMEW

OK, sir.

[BARTHOLOMEW *and* GRAVES *go out.*

JIM

I might have killed you.

CHAPLAIN

I don't think so, Jim.

JIM

Why not?

CHAPLAIN

You're not the—killing type.

[JIM *breaks down and cries.*

JIM

I'm no good. I'm a failure. I ain't got no guts. That's what
Ted said. And he's right.

CHAPLAIN

Take it easy, Jim.

JIM

Why don't you clear out?

CHAPLAIN

I will if you want me to.

JIM

I do.

CHAPLAIN

Very well. (*He gets up slowly and moves towards the door.*)

JIM

I say——

CHAPLAIN

Well——?

JIM

Are they going to kill me?

CHAPLAIN

I don't know, Jim. You've put in an appeal, haven't you?

JIM

Yes.

CHAPLAIN

Well, that may be successful—though I wouldn't put too much hope in it, because they can only alter the verdict on a point of law. But even if it fails, you've still got the chance of a reprieve. The jury recommended you to mercy, didn't they?

JIM

Yes.

CHAPLAIN

Then I should say you've got a very good chance. You've got a lot to hope for.

JIM

What happens if I don't get what you said?

CHAPLAIN

Then, Jim, the law takes its course. Are you very afraid of what may happen?

[*A pause, during which the prison clock can be heard distantly striking four o'clock.*

JIM

Yes.

CHAPLAIN

Don't you think it might help if you had someone to share your fears? That's what I'm here for.

JIM

I don't know.

CHAPLAIN

Well, you might think about it. I'll come back in the morning and you can tell me what you've decided. How's that? (*He nods towards the grille.*)

JIM

All right.

CHAPLAIN

Good night, Jim.

JIM

Good night.
   [*The main door is opened and the* CHAPLAIN *goes out.* BARTHOLOMEW *and* GRAVES *come in,* BARTHOLOMEW *carrying a tray.*

BARTHOLOMEW

Four o'clock, son. Here's your tea.

THE CURTAIN FALLS

Scene 2

The cell about ten days later. GRAVES, JIM *and* BARTHOLOMEW *are seated at the table,* BARTHOLOMEW *a little apart from the others.* GRAVES *has his wooden letters in front of him and is giving* JIM *a reading lesson.*

GRAVES

Now then, we'll make out a little sentence, shall we? What's that?

JIM

M-o-t-h. Moth.

GRAVES

Right. And what's a moth do?

JIM

Flies round the light.

GRAVES

Right. How about this?

JIM

Moth—er. Mother.

GRAVES

And this?

JIM

Cat.

GRAVES

Now then, here's a long one for you.

JIM

Cat. Cayter . . . Cayter—pillar.

GRAVES

Don't spoil it. You were right the first time. What did you say this was?

JIM

Cat.

GRAVES

Well, then?

JIM

Catt—er—pillar. Oh, I see—caterpillar!

GRAVES

That's it.

JIM

Oh, that is funny! I never knew caterpillar looked like that.

GRAVES

Now here's the sentence for you.

JIM

Mother. Ate. The. Big—caterpillar. Mother ate the big caterpillar.

GRAVES

There you are.

JIM

I say, that's good! Did you hear that, Barty? Mother ate the big caterpillar!

BARTHOLOMEW

I bet it gave her indigestion.

JIM

Oh, that's funny! (*He laughs*) Did you hear what Barty said? He said he bet it gave her indigestion! (*He laughs again loudly.*) Let's do another!

GRAVES

I think that's about enough for now.

JIM

Oh, please, let's do another!

GRAVES

No. You'll get tired if you go on too long. Why don't you get out your soldiers? You haven't played with them for ages.

JIM

I don't want my soldiers. I want to do spelling.

GRAVES

Quite taken to it, haven't you?

JIM

Yes. It makes things kind of different. I can't explain, really. But when you see a word—written down, I mean—which you've only *talked* about, it makes it—well, sort of different. It makes you think of things like you didn't think of them before. It gives you—well, something to hold on to. I don't know how to say it really.

GRAVES

Think I know what you mean, boy.

JIM

It's something I feel. It's very nice.

BARTHOLOMEW

Well, son, the Governor will be in soon. We'd better tidy up the cell.

JIM

OK. Can I go to the wash-place?

BARTHOLOMEW

Half a mo'. (*He goes into the wash-place, locks the communicating door to the other cell, and returns.*) All right. Leave the door open.

[JIM *goes into the wash-place.* BARTHOLOMEW *starts tidying up the cell.* GRAVES *remains seated at the table, occasionally glancing through the door to see that all is well.*

GRAVES

Do you think the Governor will know about his appeal?

BARTHOLOMEW

I don't know, Bert, I'm sure.

GRAVES

They were hearing it this morning, weren't they?

BARTHOLOMEW

Yes, I believe so.

GRAVES

Barty——

BARTHOLOMEW

Yes?

GRAVES

Do you remember what you said to me the first day we was in here? How that when you found yourself worrying about if a fellow was going to swing, then you started thinking about what he'd done to get in here . . . and that made things sort of even? Do you remember that?

BARTHOLOMEW

Yes.

GRAVES

Well, I've been trying that.

BARTHOLOMEW

Oh yes.

GRAVES

Yes. And I don't find it works.

BARTHOLOMEW

No?

GRAVES

No. Do you?

BARTHOLOMEW

I don't know, Bert, I'm sure.

GRAVES

And I'll tell you another thing. Remember me telling you I had a kid about the same age as him? (*He gestures towards the wash-place.*)

BARTHOLOMEW

Yes, I think I do.

GRAVES

Well, he's courting. Got a nice girl, too. And last night he came to me and asked if I'd give him my permission to marry her.

BARTHOLOMEW

Oh yes?

GRAVES

Yes, and do you know why he had to do that? Because the law of this country reckons that until you're twenty-one you're not old enough to decide whether it's right to get married or not. It reckons a few other things, too. That you're not old enough to have a vote. Or sit on a jury. But you're old enough to go through there one fine morning and be hanged.

BARTHOLOMEW

Oh, leave it alone, Bert, can't you?

GRAVES

No, I won't leave it alone. I've got fond of that kid.

BARTHOLOMEW

You've got a damned sight too fond of him, if you ask me.

GRAVES

Well, haven't you?

BARTHOLOMEW

Look, I warned you about this, didn't I? I told you there was a danger of getting to feel sorry for the blokes who come in here. And have you paid any heed to it? No. In fact you've done just the opposite. Cosseted the kid like a bloody nursemaid. Given him spelling lessons. Made him feel he's not such a bad chap after all. And—what's worse —made yourself think so, too.

GRAVES

But not you?

BARTHOLOMEW

Bert, do I have to remind you again? That boy is in here because he's been found guilty of murder.

GRAVES

Murder! Don't make me laugh! Do you think he'd have been near the place if it weren't for that bastard next door? Murder indeed! He's not capable of killing a dog. But *this* is murder, if you like. Nothing hot-blooded about it either. Oh no! We put the bloke in here for a minimum of three weeks, and we don't even tell him whether he's going to die or not. We give

211

him a special hospital diet and let the doctor see him every day, so as to keep him in good physical trim. You and I have to stay here so he don't come to no harm. The padre sets about putting his soul in order. And then, when everything's nicely tidied up, we get two strong men to truss him up like a chicken, take him in there, and launch him into eternity. If that's not murder, then I'd like to know what the hell is!

BARTHOLOMEW

Oh, shut up, will you? Shut up!

GRAVES

No, I will not shut up. I've a right to speak my mind as much as any man.

BARTHOLOMEW

Not in here you haven't. You've got no bloody right at all. You took this job on with your eyes open. Now you find you don't like it. Well, that's all right, only don't tell me about it, see? Go and tell the Governor and say you want to be relieved.

GRAVES

I'm sorry.

[An officer opens the main door. The GOVERNOR comes in, followed by Chief Officer BRIGGS and the CHAPLAIN.

BRIGGS

Governor's visit!

[BARTHOLOMEW and GRAVES stand to attention.

GOVERNOR

All right. Where is he? In the wash-place?

BARTHOLOMEW

Yes, sir.

[BRIGGS nods to GRAVES, who goes into the wash-place briefly, then returns.

BRIGGS

Inspect the cell, sir?

212

GOVERNOR

No, not today.

[*There is rather an awkward pause. The* GOVERNOR *walks about the cell, seemingly preoccupied. The others remain standing.*

All right, stand at ease, stand at ease!

[BARTHOLOMEW *and* GRAVES *relax a little. The* GOVERNOR *comes up to the table and catches sight of the wooden letters.*

How are the lessons going?

GRAVES

Very well, sir.

[JIM *appears from the wash-place.*

GOVERNOR

Hullo, Tanner.

JIM

Hullo. You looking at my letters?

GOVERNOR

Yes. I hear your lessons are coming along nicely.

JIM

Yes, I did a big sentence today. Look! 'Mother ate the big caterpillar.' I showed it to Barty, and do you know what he said? He said he bet it gave her indigestion! Wasn't that good?

GOVERNOR

Look, Tanner, I'm afraid I've got some bad news for you.

JIM

Oh.

GOVERNOR

I'd better read it to you. (*He puts on his spectacles and takes a paper from his pocket.*) 'Court of Criminal Appeal. Regina and Tanner, J. This is to give you notice that the Court of Criminal Appeal, as duly constituted for the Hearing of

Appeals under the Act, has this day considered the Application of the above-named Appellant for Leave to appeal against conviction and sentence. And has determined the Same and has refused them.' (*He takes off his spectacles.*) That means your appeal has failed.

JIM

Oh!

GOVERNOR

I warned you not to put too much hope in it, didn't I?

JIM

Does that mean—— ?

GOVERNOR

You've still got a chance of a reprieve. And a very good chance, I should say.

JIM

Oh!

GOVERNOR

I hope you get it. Meanwhile, try and keep your chin up.
    [*The* GOVERNOR *nods to* BRIGGS, *who nods to* GRAVES *and* BARTHOLOMEW. *They all go out, except for the* CHAPLAIN. JIM *sits down at the table and the* CHAPLAIN *joins him.*

CHAPLAIN

You weren't expecting much from the appeal, were you?

JIM

No. Not after what you said. Still——

CHAPLAIN

It comes as a bit of a shock, doesn't it?

JIM

Yes.

CHAPLAIN

The reprieve's the thing you've got to hope for now.

JIM

Do you think I'll get it? The Governor said I might.

CHAPLAIN

I think you've got a very good chance. Better than average.
Your parents have started a petition for you, you know.
They've got several thousand names already.

JIM

Do they know? About my appeal? Mum and Dad, I mean.

CHAPLAIN

Your mother knows. I was speaking to her a little while
ago.

JIM

Is she here?

CHAPLAIN

Yes. She's coming to see you shortly.

JIM

And Dad?

CHAPLAIN

He's not here today.

JIM

He and Mum always come together.

CHAPLAIN

Look, Jim, you've probably heard the old phrase about bad
news coming together. Your father's not too well.

JIM

Oh!

CHAPLAIN

He's had a slight relapse. Nothing serious. But the doctor
doesn't want him to leave the house. Not for the present,
anyway.

JIM

Poor old Dad. Is Daisy coming?

CHAPLAIN

I'm afraid not. You see, she's had to go out to work.

JIM

But she's having a kid.

CHAPLAIN

I know. But things aren't too easy at home, Jim. There's not much money coming in.

JIM

Oh!

CHAPLAIN

So your mother's got a lot to worry about. Your father. Your sister. And you. She'll need a bit of cheering up.

JIM

Yes.

CHAPLAIN

I think she's going to find seeing you this afternoon a little difficult. And you're the only person who can help make it easier. Do you think you can do that?

JIM

Yes. Yes, I will. I'll try.

CHAPLAIN

Good boy. I hoped you'd say that.

JIM

It's all my fault, isn't it? What's happened to Mum and Dad. If I hadn't gone that night they'd be all right. Wouldn't they?

CHAPLAIN

Yes, but you weren't to know that. You mustn't take too much of the blame. (*Pause.*) You know, Jim, you've changed a lot since you've been here.

JIM

How do you mean?

CHAPLAIN

Well, before, you were all shut up in your shell. Didn't like anybody, didn't trust anybody. Now you've opened up, come out of your shell. You're like a different person. Don't you feel it yourself?

JIM

Yes.

CHAPLAIN

I wonder why?

JIM

Everyone's been very good to me. No-one's ever been so good to me. They've treated me—well, as though I mattered. Made me feel I was someone.

CHAPLAIN

And so you are.

JIM

Yes, but I'm scared, though. I'm ever so scared.

CHAPLAIN

About what may happen?

JIM

Yes. I wish I knew. It wouldn't be so bad if I knew.

CHAPLAIN

Have you thought about what we've been talking about these last few days?

JIM

You mean God and all that.

CHAPLAIN

Yes.

JIM

Yes, I've thought about it a bit. But I don't think I quite understand.

CHAPLAIN

Well, let me put it this way. Do you think you'd be less frightened if you knew—knew for an absolute certainty—that someone was waiting for you?

JIM

Yes, I suppose so. But there couldn't be——

CHAPLAIN

Why not?

JIM

Well, there just couldn't be. Not if you was dead.

CHAPLAIN

But there is.

JIM

How do you know?

CHAPLAIN

I don't *know*, Jim—that is, I can't prove it to you. It's just something I feel. And hundreds of thousands of people feel it, too. And if you feel a thing long enough and strongly enough, then in the end it becomes true—and you *know* it's true.

JIM

I'm sorry, I don't understand.

CHAPLAIN

Do you remember the bit I read you from the Bible about how God made the world?

JIM

About Adam and Eve and all that?

CHAPLAIN

Yes.

JIM

Yes. It was a nice story, that. I liked that story.

CHAPLAIN

And you believed it, didn't you? I mean, you believed it really happened?

JIM

Yes.

CHAPLAIN

Well then, doesn't it strike you as reasonable that if God put people into the world He's waiting to see them when they come out of it again?

JIM

Yes, I suppose so. I'm still scared, though.

CHAPLAIN

Everybody's got to die some time, Jim. Every single one of us.

JIM

Most people don't know when.

CHAPLAIN

Oh, but a great many do. Sick people. Old people. I've seen them.

JIM

Ain't they scared?

CHAPLAIN

Some of them are. But not those who—put their trust in God. I've never met anyone who was frightened of death who really believed in God. They're almost—glad. You see, they know they're going to a happier place.

JIM

What's God like? What's He look like?

CHAPLAIN

Different people see Him in different ways. Nobody really
knows, because nobody's ever seen Him. Many people think
of Him as a very old man, a very kindly old man with a long
white beard — rather like Father Christmas.

JIM

Father Christmas! I like that. Do you see Him like that?

CHAPLAIN

Yes, Jim, I think I do.

JIM

And He's waiting for me?

CHAPLAIN

Yes, He's waiting for you.

JIM

You wouldn't kid me?

CHAPLAIN

No, Jim, I wouldn't kid you.

JIM

How can I be sure He's waiting for me?

CHAPLAIN

You must try and get near Him. The nearer you can get to
Him, the easier it'll be.

JIM

What do I do?

CHAPLAIN

Talk to Him. Tell Him your thoughts. He won't answer you
—at least, you won't hear anything—but He'll be listening to

you all the time. And, Jim, you must pray to Him. Have you ever prayed?

JIM

No.

CHAPLAIN

Would you like to?

JIM

All right.

CHAPLAIN

Well, kneel down with me (*They kneel.*) That's right. And cross your hands. Like this. Now say this after me.
  [*The* CHAPLAIN *says, and* JIM *repeats, line by line, the following:*
God be in my head, and in my understanding.
God be in mine eyes and in my looking.
God be in my mouth, and in my speaking.
God be in my heart, and in my thinking.
God be at mine end, and at my departing.

JIM

That was lovely.
  [*They get up.*

CHAPLAIN

I thought you might like it. I've typed it out on a piece of paper so you can say it when I'm not here. (*He gives* JIM *the paper.*)

JIM

Thanks ever so. I could spell it out with my letters, couldn't I?

CHAPLAIN

Yes, of course. And I'll bring you another one later.

JIM

Oh thanks.

221

CHAPLAIN
I'm going to leave you now, Jim. Think you'll be all right?

JIM
Yes, thanks.

CHAPLAIN
Your mother'll be along shortly. Don't forget what I said. (*He nods towards the grille.*)

JIM
No.

CHAPLAIN (*moving towards the door*)
So long, Jim.
[*The door is opened, and the* CHAPLAIN *goes out.* JIM *takes the piece of paper over to his letters and starts spelling out the prayer.* GRAVES *and* BARTHOLOMEW *come in. When they see what* JIM *is doing they stop suddenly.*

JIM (*reading*)
God. Be. In. My. Head.
And. In. My. Understanding.
[*There is an eager, happy expression on his face. He reaches forward for the first letter.* BARTHOLOMEW *and* GRAVES *watch him as*

THE CURTAIN FALLS

Scene 3

The cell, about a fortnight later. It is the middle of the night and the only light comes from a dim blue lamp which has replaced the ordinary bulb.

JIM *is asleep in bed.* BARTHOLOMEW *and* GRAVES *are seated at the table playing cards. The clock goes 'ding-dong-ding-dong' four times and then strikes three.* JIM *stirs in his sleep. He is dreaming. He mutters a few incomprehensible sounds.* BARTHOLOMEW *and* GRAVES *look up.*

JIM (*asleep*)

No, don't. (*Hysterically*) Please don't! Don't. Don't. Oh no. No. No! (*He stirs and wakes up.*) Oh! Oh! Oh! Mum, I had such a horrible dream! I dreamt they was going to kill me. Oh, it was awful, Mum. (*Relieved*) It was only a dream, though. (*He raised himself up.*) Mum, where are you, Mum? Mum! Mum! (*He realizes where he is.*) Oh! Oh!

BARTHOLOMEW (*coming over*)

Take it easy, son.

JIM

Oh, Barty, I had such a horrible dream!

BARTHOLOMEW

Well, it's all over now. You just lie back and take it easy. Cigarette?

JIM

No, thanks. What time is it?

BARTHOLOMEW

Just gone three.

JIM

Oh! Barty——

BARTHOLOMEW

Yes?

JIM

When do you think I'll hear about the reprieve?

BARTHOLOMEW

Don't know, son. Any day now.

JIM

I don't think I'm going to get it. Do you?

BARTHOLOMEW

Well, let's hope you are.

JIM

Barty, what's it like? When they come for you, I mean?

BARTHOLOMEW

You don't want to think about that, boy. Won't do no good.

JIM

Yes, but if I know what it's like it won't be so bad. Not if I know. Please tell me.

BARTHOLOMEW

It's quick. Very quick. You hardly know a thing about it.

JIM

They come in the morning, don't they? Just before nine o'clock. Do they tie you up?

BARTHOLOMEW

I don't know, son.

JIM

Yes, they do. I know they do. And then what happens? Do they carry you, or do you have to walk?

BARTHOLOMEW

Why don't you leave it alone, Jim?

JIM

And then when it's over and I'm dead, what happens then? What do they do with me then?

BARTHOLOMEW (*losing control*)

Oh, shut up, boy, can't you? Shut up!

JIM

I'm sorry.

BARTHOLOMEW

No, it's not your fault. I'm afraid I forgot myself. Now, why don't you turn over and get to sleep?

JIM

Barty——

BARTHOLOMEW

Well?

JIM

The padre said I was allowed to ask you or Bert to be with me. If it happens, I mean.

BARTHOLOMEW

Oh, did he?

JIM

Yes. Have you been there before?

BARTHOLOMEW

Yes.

JIM

Often?

BARTHOLOMEW

Once or twice.

JIM

Would you do it again? For me?

BARTHOLOMEW

Why pick on me? Why not Bert or one of the others?

JIM

Well, you're kind of—strong. It wouldn't be so bad if I knew you was there.

BARTHOLOMEW

Strong, eh? Don't you think Bert's strong?

JIM

No. Not like you. Will you?

BARTHOLOMEW

I'd rather not, if you don't mind.

JIM

Why not? You done it before.

BARTHOLOMEW

I'd just rather not, that's all.

JIM

Please!

BARTHOLOMEW (*slightly hysterical*)

No, boy, I can't do it, I tell you. Now don't ask me no more.

JIM

Would Bert, do you think?

BARTHOLOMEW

I don't know what Bert would do. Why don't you ask him yourself? (*To* GRAVES) Here, Bert, the kid wants a word with you.

[GRAVES *comes over to the bed.* BARTHOLOMEW *moves away to the table.*

JIM

Bert——?

GRAVES

It's all right, Jim. I heard what you said. Do you think it would help?

JIM

Yes. 'Cos you're a friend, see? You and Barty're the best friends I ever had.

GRAVES

Thank you, boy. I appreciate that.

JIM

Will you, then—if it happens?

GRAVES (*after a slight pause*)

Yes, Jim, 'course I will.

JIM

You wouldn't mind?

GRAVES

Not if it would help, I wouldn't.

JIM

Oh, thank you, Bert! Thanks ever so!

GRAVES

Now you want to lie down and get some sleep.

[JIM *lies down and* GRAVES *tucks in the bedclothes. At the table* BARTHOLOMEW *puts his head in his hands and turns away.*

JIM

Bert——

GRAVES

Yes?

JIM

Will you read my book?

[GRAVES *nods, and goes over to the table to fetch it. He sees the emotional state* BARTHOLOMEW *is in, gives him a friendly, rather embarrassed pat on the shoulder and returns to* JIM's *bedside with the book.*

227

GRAVES (*reading*)

'There was a table set out under a tree in front of the house, and the March Hare and the Hatter were having tea at it. A Dormouse was sitting between them, fast asleep . . .'

THE CURTAIN FALLS

ACT III

Scene 2

The cell, two days later. It's mid-morning. GRAVES *is tidying up the cell and humming to himself as he does so. The door opens and the* CHAPLAIN *comes in. He is carrying a book.*

GRAVES

Morning, sir.

CHAPLAIN

Morning, Graves. Where's Tanner? Next door?

GRAVES

No, sir. Out at exercise.

CHAPLAIN

Oh, of course. I brought him a new book—*The Wind in the Willows.*

GRAVES

He ought to like that. We've finished that other one you gave him.

CHAPLAIN

Already?

GRAVES

Yes, we fairly race through them now.

CHAPLAIN

You've done a lot for that boy, Graves.

GRAVES

Done quite a bit for himself, sir. No news, I suppose.

CHAPLAIN

Not yet. The Governor's expecting to hear later this morning.

GRAVES

Leaving it a bit late, aren't they? Only two days to go.

CHAPLAIN

Yes, I suppose so.

GRAVES

Any views, sir?

CHAPLAIN

I think he'll get it. Anyway, let's hope so.

GRAVES

That's what we're all hoping. Atmosphere in the prison's something terrible.

CHAPLAIN

Yes.

GRAVES

Officers snapping at the prisoners, prisoners snapping at each other. Everyone's talking in whispers. People jumping when a door's slammed. 'Course, being a double execution makes it worse. We haven't had one of those for years.

CHAPLAIN

No.

GRAVES

Strange, isn't it, sir? Whenever we have a man in here—no matter what he's done—and his time's drawing to a close,

229

there isn't a man in the prison—you nor me nor the toughest crook among them—who isn't praying like hell he's going to get off.

CHAPLAIN

It's even stranger, Graves, that there's practically no-one in the world outside who realizes that.

GRAVES

No.

CHAPLAIN

I often wonder how long all this (*indicating cell*) would last if people could be called on to death-watch or witness executions like they do jury-service.

GRAVES

It wouldn't last five minutes, sir.

CHAPLAIN

No. Yet how shocked people would be if you were to suggest it to them. How we love getting others to do our dirty work for us. (*He makes as if to leave.*) Well, I'll be in later. See the boy gets the book, will you?

GRAVES

Excuse me, sir.

CHAPLAIN

Yes.

GRAVES

Well, if there *is* no reprieve, I promised the lad I'd be with him when his time came.

CHAPLAIN

Yes, I heard about that, Graves. It's very good of you.

GRAVES

I reckon it's the least one can do. But—well, I've never done it before.

230

CHAPLAIN

You know about it though.

GRAVES

Well, not really. I've always rather shut my eyes to that side of things.

CHAPLAIN

I see.

GRAVES

So I was wondering if you'd give me the gen, like. 'Course I'll get a proper briefing from the Chief later on. But I'd rather hear it from you.

CHAPLAIN

Yes, of course. (*He walks over to the nailed-up door and taps it.*) Well, you know where that goes to. Lucas—that's the hangman—gets here tomorrow afternoon. He goes straight in there and tests the machinery. The boy will be out exercising, so he won't hear anything. When he gets back Lucas takes a look at him through this peep-hole. That's for assessing the weight to allow for the right drop. Of course the boy won't know anything about it. (*He pauses.*) That's all for tomorrow. The next day the boy gets up at the usual time —I'll be here from five o'clock, by the way—and dresses in his own clothes.

GRAVES

His own clothes?

CHAPLAIN

Yes, didn't you know? It's always done in their own clothes.

GRAVES

Why?

CHAPLAIN

I'm not sure, really. It's a sort of tradition. I think it's because technically the boy isn't a prisoner. That is, he doesn't come

231

to prison *for* punishment but to *wait* for punishment. Something like that. Does it shock you?

CHAPLAIN

GRAVES

Well, yes, it does a bit.

CHAPLAIN

Yes, it did me, too, when I first heard of it. But one gets used to these things as one does everything else—or—almost everything else. Where was I? Oh, yes. Well, during those last few hours we do all we can for the boy. Keep his mind occupied and that sort of thing. But they're usually quite calm by then. They're ready. Then——

GRAVES

Does he get a drug or anything?

CHAPLAIN

No. He gets a tot of brandy just beforehand. That's the regulation. Then just before nine o'clock Lucas and his assistants come through there with the halters. You and I go into the shed. Lucas pinions the boy, then goes through there (*he points to the wash-house door*) and pinions Clift. They start moving towards the scaffold together. You and I can see them coming . . . (*His voice falters.*)

GRAVES

Yes.

CHAPLAIN

Well, I always find that the worst moment. When you see them walking like that towards the scaffold—*under their own power*— it seems, well, almost as though they'd consented to the idea of their own deaths. And in a way, of course, they have. It's the bravery of it that gets you—and the dignity. Sometimes I wonder if I could go to my death like that. I don't think I could.

GRAVES

What happens then?

232

CHAPLAIN

They get on the trap. There's always a second or two's delay while their legs are being pinioned. We tell the men to keep their eyes fixed on one of us. It's a tremendous help to them. Generally they look at me. But—well, you've meant such a lot to the boy, he may look at you. If he does, don't look away. Don't let him think you're embarrassed or ashamed at what's happening to him. Look him straight in the eyes. And—if you can—smile.

GRAVES

Christ!

CHAPLAIN

It's very quick, you know. Not more than twenty seconds from the time Lucas comes in here till it's all over. (*He rises to go.*)

GRAVES

How can you do it, Padre?

CHAPLAIN (*turning on his way to the door*)
Someone's got to help them. Haven't they?
[*Chief Officer* BRIGGS *comes in followed by* JIM *and* BARTHOLOMEW.

BRIGGS

All right, son, in you go. (*He goes out.*)

JIM

Hullo, Padre.

CHAPLAIN

Hullo, Jim. Had a nice walk?

JIM

Yes, thanks. I walked five hundred and twenty-two steps. I counted.

CHAPLAIN

Did you?

JIM

Yes. Barty tried to count his steps, too, but he couldn't remember. Could you, Barty?

BARTHOLOMEW

No, that's right.

CHAPLAIN

I've brought you another book. (*He shows it to him.*)

JIM

Can I see it?

CHAPLAIN

Yes, of course.

JIM

The Wind. In the. Willows. What a funny name. Oh, look at these pictures. That's a frog, ain't it?

CHAPLAIN

It's a toad actually. Same sort of thing.

JIM

But it's got glasses on. Ain't that funny. Barty, look at this. A frog with glasses on. And look at this one. He's driving a motor. Oh, Bert, you must come and look. There, see. A frog driving a motor. (*He turns the pages.*) I'm going to like this book. Thanks ever so, Padre.

[*The main door is unlocked. Chief Officer* BRIGGS *comes in, followed by the* GOVERNOR *holding a sheet of paper.*

BRIGGS

Governor's visit!

[*Everyone stands to attention except* JIM, *who remains seated at the table. Slight pause before the* GOVERNOR *speaks.*

GOVERNOR

Morning, Tanner.

JIM

Morning, sir.
  [*Another pause. The* GOVERNOR *clears his throat.*

GOVERNOR

Look, boy, I want you to be very brave.
  [JIM *gets slowly to his feet and faces the* GOVERNOR.

JIM (*breathlessly, in order not to show his terrible fear*)
OK, sir. OK. OK.

THE CURTAIN FALLS

10 RILLINGTON PLACE

How often are our destinies shaped by accident. It was as a result of Murder Story *that the case for which I am probably best known came my way. An Oxford friend, George Scott, had recently become editor of the now defunct literary magazine* Truth, *and among the books sent to him for review was* The Man on Your Conscience *by a retired solicitor called Michael Eddowes. The man in question was Timothy Evans, hanged in 1950 for a murder which, said Eddowes, had been committed by his fellow lodger John Christie who was himself hanged for other murders four years later. Eddowes's book was quite short and, because he was not a professional writer, poorly assembled. Yet, by the time I had read it three times, I had no doubts about his conclusions. 'I believe,' I ended my review, 'and unless fresh evidence is produced to the contrary, will continue to believe until I die, that on 9 March 1950 we hanged an innocent man.' In order that this truth be more widely known I resolved then to write a definitive book on the case, and after four years of research and writing,* 10 Rillington Place *was published in 1961.*

The venue was the last in a mean shabby cul-de-sac of ten tiny houses on either side of a street in the Notting Hill area of west London. Since then all the houses have been demolished for area development, and the street itself no longer exists. It was in 1938 that John Christie, bald and bespectacled, and his wife Ethel, both from Yorkshire, took over the lease of the ground-floor flat.

When Christie moved into Rillington Place, he had just turned forty. This is a depressing age for many men, one at which they are apt to look over their shoulders at the past and assess whether they have achieved what they wanted to achieve; an age, as Harold Nicolson says, at which most men go through a change of life no less disturbing than that of women. At this age many men find that ambition and desire have gone out of the window, that a need for security and a slower tempo of life have taken their place, that they are putting their children ahead of themselves. Christie had no children, which he said he always regretted, yet which was hardly surprising in view of the limited occasions when he was able to have intercourse. Looking over his own shoulder Christie had little to be proud of. He had come from a decent home, and had been given a good education; and he himself knew that he was of more than average intelligence. Yet he had seldom been able to hold down any job for more than a year or two, and all of these had been of the most menial clerical kind. He had had no less than six convictions for stealing, false pretences and violence; and however much he might excuse himself of these crimes, there was no denying he had been a failure. Looking around him he could not fail to observe that other men of his age and talents had now become chief clerks and assistant bank managers, and in so doing had achieved status and power. The price of status and power was hard work and drudgery, and these Christie had never been prepared to pay. Yet status and power were what he had always wanted, and now, in the early afternoon of his life, he wanted them more than ever.

It was not chance then that at this time Christie was casting about in his mind for some means to express his personality more fully: and it was not chance either that the means were ready at hand. After the political events of the autumn of 1938 the London Police Force had called for volunteers for their Emergency Reserve. Christie had noted this at the time, and now in the summer of 1939 he made formal application for his name to be put forward. For a man with his record, this was an astonishing piece of impudence, and it is hard to imagine how he could have thought he would get away with it. But as he was able to delude himself about his own integrity, he presumably thought it would be equally easy to delude others. He was quite right. Incredible to relate, the police made no enquiries about his past (they say now that the influx of new recruits was so great that it would have been impossible – yet one would have thought that a telephone call to Scotland Yard to find out if any candidates had a Criminal Record number would have been a fairly quick and simple matter), and in September 1939 Christie was enrolled as a full-time Special Constable in the War Reserve Police. 'I, John Reginald Halliday Christie,' he wrote on the enrolment form, 'do solemnly and sincerely declare and affirm that I will well and truly serve our Sovereign Lord the King in the office of Special Constable for the Metropolitan Police District without favour or affection, malice or ill-will; and that I will, to the best of my power, cause the peace to be kept and preserved, and prevent all offences against the persons and properties of His Majesty's subjects; and that, while I continue to hold the said office, I will, to the best of my skill and knowledge, discharge all the duties thereof faithfully according to the law.'

Christie was assigned to Harrow Road Police Station where he remained for four years. They were probably the happiest years of his life. It is somewhat ironic that it was false pretences in the past that had brought him up against the law, and now it was false pretences that had brought him on the side of the law. But then his whole life was a long series of false pretences. The authority he had always wanted he had now been given beyond the dreams of avarice. Nor was he slow to respond. He carried out his duties efficiently and conscientiously: with all that suppressed morality inside him he could hardly have done otherwise. He earned a first-aid certificate and two recommendations 'for ability relating to criminal offences'. He became known to some people in the district as 'the persecuting counsel'.

The more one looks at Christie's years in the police force, the more one sees how perfect a medium of expression it was for him. War is a time when people are expected to go into uniform, preferably military uniform. For Christie military uniform meant a return to the firing-line and the horrors of twenty years before (the possibility was remote, but the fear of it may have influenced him strongly). Police uniform was almost as good as military uniform, and a good deal safer. Moreover, uniform of *any* kind gave him, as his Boy Scout's uniform had given him in his youth, a *persona*, a cloak to disguise the shabbiness of his true self. It set him up in his own and his neighbours' eyes. His duties not only allowed him to go on leading the shadow life he had always loved, but specifically encouraged him to: dark alleyways and squalid cafés were his rightful province, and who knows what favours he was not able to obtain from prostitutes and petty criminals anxious to keep clear of the law? As a boy the sight of his dead grandfather had aroused in him fascination and pleasure: now the blitz gave him the opportunity of seeing bodies innumerable. As a boy he had always been bossed about: now he was bossing other people about. As a young man he had often been in prison: now he was in a position to send other people to prison. He had almost everything the heart could desire; and in 1943 what he desired was the body of Ruth Fuerst.

Ruth Fuerst was an Austrian girl who had come to England just before the war as a student nurse. She was seventeen years old, having been born at Voeslau near Vienna on 29 March 1922. She did not return to Austria when war broke out, thinking no doubt that it would be safer in England. She gave up her nursing and took a job in a munitions factory, the Grosvenor Works, in Davies Street. She lived in a single furnished room at 41 Oxford Gardens, which is only a few minutes' walk from Rillington Place. She was a tall girl, with dark brown hair and brown eyes. She was also a lonely girl, having no friends in this country when she arrived. She did not earn much as a munitions worker and she cannot have failed to notice the number of prostitutes that frequented the area round the factory. There is evidence that she took to part-time prostitution herself which, being young and pretty, she would have had little difficulty in doing. One writer says she was 'an amateur of some experience', and Christie himself said that she had friends who were prostitutes and that she had had a baby by an American soldier.

We do not know exactly in what circumstances Christie first met Fuerst. In one of the accounts which he subsequently gave, he said he met her on the beat, in another that it was in a snack-bar in Ladbroke Grove where he had gone to look for a man suspected of theft. Both accounts agree that the relationship between them developed gradually, the one saying that they had long talks on the beat, the other that she visited him several times in Rillington Place while his wife was at her part-time job at Osram's factory.

These facts are in dispute. What is not in dispute is that on a fateful day in the middle of August, when Ethel was on holiday with her relations in Sheffield, Ruth Fuerst went to Rillington Place to visit Christie, and never came out alive. In all his accounts of his affairs with women Christie said that it was they who pressed their attentions on him, and he was the shy, the bashful one. The old puritan could never admit to starting little naughtinesses himself. His account of Ruth Fuerst was no exception. 'She undressed,' he said, 'and wanted me to have intercourse with her.' It is much more likely that Christie had made a straight deal with her, that she was giving her favours either for a fee or as the price of Christie's silence in not reporting her soliciting on his beat. They went into the bedroom overlooking the backyard, and Christie's account of what happened then is quite brief. 'I got on the bed and had intercourse with her. While I was having intercourse with her, I strangled her with a piece of rope. I remember urine and excreta coming away from her. She was completely naked. I tried to put some of her clothes back on her. She had a leopard-skin coat and I wrapped this round her.' It was either just after the murder or just before it (Christie's accounts vary) that a telegraph-boy arrived at the house with a telegram from Mrs Christie to say she was arriving home that evening: so the disposal of the body became a matter of urgency. 'I took her from the bedroom into the front room and put her under the floorboards. I had to do that because of my wife coming back. I put the remainder of her clothing under the floorboards too.'

Christie cannot have had overmuch time to seal up the floorboards and clean up the mess in the bedroom before Ethel arrived. She was accompanied, no doubt to Christie's surprise, by her brother Henry Waddington. That night all three of them slept in the house, Christie and Ethel on the bed where a few hours earlier he had ravished and strangled Fuerst, Mr Waddington in the front room a few feet away from her still warm body. In the morning Mr Waddington took a train back to Sheffield, and in the afternoon Ethel went along to Osram's. When she had gone Christie got out his hammer and chisel, dug up the body and clothes from beneath the floorboards, and put them in the wash-house. He then went into the garden and began digging Fuerst's grave 'on the right-hand side of the garden, about halfway along towards the rockery. Neighbours watched me digging. They nodded "cheerios" to me.' At about ten o'clock that night, when it was quite dark, Christie told Ethel that he was going to the lavatory. He went to the wash-house and carried Fuerst's body into the garden. 'I put the body down the hole and covered it up quickly with earth.' He also buried the clothes. 'The next day I straightened the garden and raked it over. There was an old dustbin in the garden with holes in it which I used for burning garden refuse. When I was burning rubbish I got the idea into my head to burn the clothing, and what I could pull out I put into the dustbin and burnt it. Months later I was digging in the garden and I probably misjudged where it was or something like that. I found the skull and put it in the dustbin and covered it up. I dug a hole in the corner of the garden and put the dustbin in the hole about eighteen inches down. The top of the dustbin was open, and I still used it to burn rubbish.'

Why did Christie commit this horrible crime? Why did he become a necrophile? Why did he pick on Ruth Fuerst, a young and pretty girl who had certainly done him no harm? Because a lifetime of repressed masculine aggression had, at this time and place, come to its climacteric. There is no suggestion here of conscious reasoning, for Christie never was conscious of his own motivations. But it would seem that at this particular junction his various psychological defects, his fear of men, his fear of women, his sexual inadequacy, his sense of humiliation, his thwarted desires to dominate, all synthesized to determine the final act. Although Christie said that he had intercourse with Fuerst before he strangled her, it is more likely that he did it at the time of strangling her or just afterwards: for it seems that from about this time he was unable to obtain an orgasm with women until they were helpless and he no longer afraid of them. 'He hated those who tempted him and whom he could not satisfy.' It was not a poor Austrian girl called Ruth Fuerst that Christie was murdering, but his mother and sisters, prostitutes past and present, all of womankind. There is evidence too that he had unconscious hopes that the act would bring release. 'I remember,' he wrote in his memoirs, 'as I gazed down at the still form of my first victim, experiencing a strange, peaceful thrill.' Yet even this dreadful experience was of no value to him. On a conscious level he knew he had done something unspeakable, on an unconscious level he knew he must forget about it. 'After it was over,' he said later, 'I never gave it a thought.' Amnesia came, as to many murderers, to cloud the memory and wash away the guilt and fear. Because the act had no significance, the release had no permanence. Sooner or later the need for it would come again.

It came sooner rather than later. At the end of the year Christie applied for release from the police force. Why, we do not know, but even his conscience may not have been able to reconcile the events of August with the behaviour expected of a policeman; and the strain on an undiscovered murderer of working among men whose job was to discover murderers must have been well nigh unbearable. His application was granted and early in the New Year of 1944 he took up civilian employment at the Ultra Radio Works, Park Royal, Acton. He says that for a time he was engaged in the electrical department, but was later transferred to the dispatch department. He used to lunch in the canteen each day, and here he met a girl from the assembly department called Muriel Amelia Eady. Unlike Ruth Fuerst, Muriel Eady was highly respectable. She was a thirty-one-year-old spinster who lived with her aunt at 12 Roskell Road, Putney. Her father was in the Merchant Navy and away at sea. She was short and stout, with dark brown hair and brown eyes. Christie often ate his lunch beside her in the canteen, and learnt that she had a man friend with whom she was 'going steady'. One day he invited her to bring this friend round to Rillington Place to meet his wife and have tea. The meeting took place and on one or two later occasions was repeated. One evening all four of them went to the pictures.

By this time Christie was very attracted to Muriel Eady, and had already decided to do to her what he had done to Ruth Fuerst. She was one of the few victims he got to know for any length of time beforehand, and so he was able to write subsequently: 'I planned it all out very carefully.' There were two stumbling-blocks to his getting Eady to Rillington Place alone and undisturbed. One was the presence of Ethel who was always waiting for him when he returned from work; the other was that Eady, unlike Fuerst, would be certain to resist any sexual advances. The first problem solved itself when in the early autumn of 1944 Ethel announced that she was again going up to Sheffield for a holiday with her brother. The second problem was more difficult, and Christie tackled it in a most ingenious way. Some time previously he had learnt from Eady that she suffered from chronic catarrh. He had, he told her, just the thing to cure this, a special sort of inhalation device which he had used successfully on other people. He spoke casually of his time in the police force and the medical knowledge he had acquired there, knowledge which he himself admitted 'made it possible for me to talk convincingly about sickness and disease'. It was with gratitude that Muriel Eady accepted. The inhalation device which Christie had spoken of really existed: but it did not exist to cure Muriel Eady's catarrh. Christie admitted that in murdering Ruth Fuerst there had been a bit of a struggle; not much of a struggle, it is true, but violence of any degree was, as we know, something he abhorred. He hated the memory of Ruth Fuerst struggling and he did not want it to happen again.

One day early in October 1944, when Ethel was away in Sheffield, there was a knock at Christie's front door. It was Muriel Eady. He took her into the kitchen and gave her a cup of tea. Tea was always part of the ritual of Christie's murders. He then showed her part, but not all, of his inhalation device. This consisted of a square glass jar with a metal screw-top lid, containing a mixture of Friar's Balsam 'and other inhalants'. There were two holes in the lid and into one of these Christie had inserted a rubber tube some two feet long. He told Eady to sit down in a chair with her back to the window, handed her the tube and asked her to inhale. Soon she was breathing in the wholesome aroma of Friar's Balsam. What Christie did not tell Eady was what the other hole was for. It was for another length

243

of tube, one end of which Christie had previously fixed to a gas point situated between the window and the door. He now put the free end of this tube into the hole. Eady, with her back to the window, saw nothing. Christie released a bull-dog clip on the tube and soon Eady was inhaling gas as well as Balsam. When she was almost unconscious, Christie put back the bull-dog clip, lifted the girl out of the chair and carried her across the passage into the bedroom. He laid her on the bed, removed her drawers, and then did to her what he had done to Ruth Fuerst. 'I had intercourse with her at the time I strangled her.' Looking at the body afterwards, 'once again I experienced that quiet, peaceful thrill. I had no regrets.' Mrs Christie was not expected home that day, so there was no need for a hasty burial under the floorboards. Instead he took the body out to the wash-house, as he had also done with Fuerst, and left it there temporarily. Later in the evening, when he had time to collect himself, he removed the body to the garden and buried it 'on the right-hand side nearest the yard', that is a little higher up than the grave of Fuerst. This burial was somewhat easier than the previous one, as Eady had all her clothes on and there was therefore no problem of their separate disposal.

For the second time in just over a year Christie had literally got away with murder. He must have been astonished at how easy it was. The reader may be mildly astonished too, especially when one considers that both girls were reported missing to the police within a short time of their disappearance. But Ruth Fuerst, poor, friendless, a foreigner and a semi-prostitute, came from that shadow world where girls are always disappearing, leaving one place one day and bobbing up somewhere else the next. Eady was rather different. She had an aunt and a man friend, both of whom must have been deeply concerned about her, and she was known to have been on friendly terms with Christie. But the trouble here was that there was no body and no motive; and without either or both of these there could be no suspicion of murder. Also this was the time of the flying-bombs, a time when many people away from home were blasted into anonymity. This, eventually, was what was presumed to have happened to her.

The war over, Christie looked around for employment more congenial than that offered by the Ultra Radio Works. He decided to give the Post Office another try. This was where he had worked immediately after the First World War, and it was abuse of his position there that had led to his first conviction for stealing. Christie knew as well as anyone that Post Office officials convicted of stealing are never employed again. He must have reckoned that Post Office memory was short and that anyone who had successfully bluffed the police, and moreover could produce evidence that he had just served four years in the police, would have little difficulty in bluffing the Post Office. He was quite right. The Post Office welcomed him with open arms, and it was not until he had given them four years of his services as a clerk in the Savings Bank that they discovered their mistake and dismissed him.

Timothy John Evans was born in the mining village of Merthyr Vale in South Wales on 20 November 1924 – the same year that Christie, then aged twenty-six, began a nine months' sentence imposed on him at Uxbridge for stealing. Merthyr Vale lies in the valley of the River Taff, from which the ground rises steeply on either side to brown, bracken-covered hills. Evans's father, Daniel Evans, was a coal haulier and his mother, formerly Thomasina Lynch, was one of a large family of some ten or eleven brothers and sisters. Like many of the people in the district they were Roman Catholics, and were married at Aberfan Roman Catholic Church in 1920. Their eldest child, Eleanor Veronica, or Eileen, as she was called, was born in 1921. Three years later, when Timothy was already expected, Daniel Evans walked out of the house and never came back. Several years later Mrs Evans was granted a certificate from the local magistrate that her husband was presumed to be dead, and in 1929 she married a Mr Penry Probert, also in the coal industry. That same year she gave birth to her second daughter, Mary Josephine, or, as she was called, Maureen.

From the start Timothy Evans seems to have been a very backward boy. His mother says that he could not speak properly until he was five, and even then his attempts to pronounce his own name resulted in the sound of the single consonant 'T'. Between the ages of five and seven he went to the local school, but without learning much. At the age of eight such education as he had had was brought abruptly to a halt by a nasty accident. Bathing one day in the Taff he cut his right foot badly on a piece of broken glass. A dirty cloth was used to bandage it with the result that the wound developed a tubercular verucca or sore which never completely healed. For the next ten years the boy was in and out of hospitals – at times his leg swelled so badly that he had to go to bed – and he could only attend school infrequently. When he did, the simplest curriculum was beyond him.

The early thirties were a period of depression in the South Wales coal-fields, and in 1935 Mr Probert, who had been out of work for some time, decided to try his luck in London. He managed to get a job as a painter and decorator, and six weeks later the family followed him there. At first Timothy was able to attend St Francis Roman Catholic School in Portland Road, but then his foot grew worse and he had to enter the Princess Louise Hospital. He was there nine months. At the end of this time there was an outbreak of measles in the children's ward, and Mrs Probert was asked to remove him rather earlier than had been agreed upon. She tried to do this, but he gave way to such a fit of screaming and crying that she was obliged to leave him. He came quietly enough a week later and his mother wheeled him home in an old pram. For the next year he was a regular outpatient. Sometimes his foot remained quiescent, at other times he couldn't put on a shoe and the swelling ran up to his groin. In 1937 the boy expressed a wish to go back to live in Merthyr Vale with his grandmother, and as it was felt that the change of air might do him good, this was arranged. There was enough improvement at first for him to attend school again, but the headmaster complained that he wouldn't listen. According to his uncle, Mr Lynch, who also lived in Mount Pleasant, he was only really happy when hunting rats or 'down a stokehold'. On leaving school he got a job at the mines, but soon his foot began playing him up again and he entered the Merthyr Tydfil General Hospital. There was little improvement after two or three months, so in 1939 his mother brought him back to London. He was seen by Dr

Robertson of Barlby Road and sent first to St Charles Hospital and then to the Moorland Clinic for Tubercular Children at Alton, in Hampshire. He stayed there a year, and although his foot remained permanently deformed and he always walked with a slight limp, it never gave him quite the same trouble afterwards.

When he came out of the Moorland the war was in full swing. Naturally he was rejected for military service, and spent the next two or three years drifting from job to job. Sometimes, when he was unemployed, he would stay away from home two or three nights at a time. When his mother asked him where he had been, he would say that he couldn't remember. In 1946, when he and his mother were both working at a toy factory, the family moved from Cornwall Road, where they had been since 1938, to No. 11 St Mark's Road, which is just over two minutes' walk from 10 Rillington Place.

In 1946 Evans was twenty-two years old. He was a tiny little fellow, only five feet five and a half inches high, and he weighed just under ten stone. He had black eyes and shiny black hair which he kept plastered back. His face was long and rather thin. He has been described variously as 'a funny little chap', 'an ordinary working-class boy' and 'a little runt of a man'.

Yet if he was a poor specimen physically, he was even more so intellectually. Because of his foot he had had virtually no education at all, and he grew up unable to read or write anything beyond his own name. His backwardness had persisted all through his childhood, and when he was medically examined in 1949 he was found to have an intelligence quotient equivalent to that of a boy between ten and a half and eleven, and a vocabulary of a boy of fourteen. He was, therefore, in the literal if not the generally accepted sense of the word, half-witted. This is the most important single thing to remember about Evans, that he had the body of a man and the mind of a child: more than anything else it explains the shape of things to come.

Yet although he lacked conventional education, he was not without a certain instinctive intelligence or 'know-how'. Dr Curran has described him as 'primitive, shrewd', and several other people have called him 'worldly'. He had had experience of prostitutes and liked his beer. His two favourite public houses were the Kensington Park Hotel (or KPH as he called it) and the Elgin, both in Ladbroke Grove. On a Saturday night he would visit one or both of these and put down several pints of beer. He used to boast that he could drink any man under the table, but there is no evidence that this was put to the test. Mr Sid Carthey, the licensee of the Elgin, says that he was a nice boy when alone, but inclined to get rather silly when with a gang. He never saw him drunk. Evans's demeanour has been described as 'cocky and cheerful'. He seems to have had no enemies and most people who knew him liked him. He had a rather quick temper which would show itself when he was crossed or confused by things he didn't understand. Emotionally he was shallow and immature, and he had little sense of personal responsibility or the value of money. Although a Roman Catholic he had not practised his faith for years.

Sometime in 1947 a friend of Evans was going out with a girl called Connie who worked as a telephone operator at Grosvenor House. One of Connie's friends at the switchboard was Beryl Thorley, an extremely pretty girl of eighteen. Beryl lived in Cambridge Gardens, only a few hundred yards from St Mark's Road: her mother was dead and her father, who was employed as a general hand at Victoria Station, lived at Brighton. One evening Evans's friend arranged a blind date, and he, Evans, Connie and Beryl all went to the cinema. Evans found himself attracted to Beryl and on later occasions took her out alone. Within a few weeks they were engaged. Evans was a dutiful son and every evening took Beryl round to St Mark's to see his mother. They were married on 20 September 1947, at Kensington Registry Office, and after the marriage the pair moved into St Mark's Road. It was quite a large house and Mrs Probert was able to fit the family in satisfactorily.

Early in 1948 Beryl found she was pregnant; and notwithstanding Mrs Probert's generosity, it was clear that the limited accommodation at St Mark's Road could not cope with a baby as well. So they began looking for a place of their own; and it was Eileen who found it. She was returning from work one day in the train to Ladbroke Grove. Now all eastbound trains to Ladbroke Grove pass above the north side of Rillington Place, and as the train was slowing down to enter the station, her eye caught a 'FLAT TO LET' sign on the top-floor window of No. 10. On her way home she went to Rillington Place and took a note of the agents. They were Messrs Martin East, of 19 Gerrard Street, Soho. She told her brother what she had seen, and after he and Beryl had looked over the flat, which consisted of only two rooms, a kitchen at the back and a bedroom at the front, they decided to take it.

So it was that the families of Evans and Christie came together for the first time, with results that were to echo long after the deaths of all of them. There were few women who on meeting Christie for the first time did not loathe him, and Eileen was no exception. She spent a lot of her spare time helping her brother to decorate the flat and so bumped into Christie and his wife quite often. One of the worst things about Christie, she said, was that you could never hear him coming. This was Christie's intention: this was why he padded about the place in his plimsolls. One evening she was alone in the flat, painting; Tim had gone back to St Mark's Road to get some more brushes. Suddenly she was aware that Christie was beside her. She had not heard him come up the narrow, uncarpeted stairs, nor enter the room. He had a cup of tea in his hand and he said: 'I thought you might like this.' Eileen thanked him but said that she always drank tea without milk or sugar. Christie made no effort to go, and eventually Eileen said: 'Tim's coming back soon. He's gone to get some paint-brushes.' Christie seemed surprised. 'Oh, he's coming back, is he?' he said, and then he left as suddenly and silently as he came. Both Eileen and Maureen saw rather less of Mrs Christie, but what they did see they liked. 'She seemed to be terrified of Christie,' said Eileen, 'like a rabbit with a weasel. We all felt very sorry for her.'

Yet although Eileen and Maureen disliked Christie, Evans and Beryl did not share their dislike. It must be remembered that at this time Evans was twenty-three and Beryl nineteen, an age at which most people are happy enough to accept others as they find them, especially people as uncritical and happy-go-lucky as these two: moreover, the Christies were old enough to be their parents. By Easter the decorating of the two rooms was finished, and when the furniture, bought on a hire-purchase agreement for which Mrs Probert stood surety, had been moved in, Timothy and Beryl took possession. Evans was now working overtime for his firm and earning between seven and eight pounds a week, of which he gave Beryl £5 10s. for housekeeping. Despite the smallness of their two little rooms, the couple seem to have found their early days in Rillington Place very happy ones. When Mrs Probert found a better place for them to live in, a ground-floor flat with its own garden and lavatory, Beryl did not want to move. 'We've got everything nice up here now, and the Christies are all right.' This decision was to cost her her life.

In October 1948 Beryl went into Queen Charlotte's Hospital and gave birth to a baby daughter. She was called Geraldine. This was Mrs Probert's first granddaughter, and all the family received the news with joy. They had taken a great interest in Beryl's condition before the birth, helping her in various ways, and Mrs Probert herself had paid for the cost of the layette. Evans was delighted with his daughter, and continued to adore her for the length of her short life.

In due course Beryl returned to Rillington Place with the baby, and the couple endeavoured to pick up the threads of their old life. Evans worked a long day, leaving the house soon after 6.30 and often not returning until the early evening. Often he was required to make deliveries outside London, to places as far away as Bristol and Cardiff, and it says much for him that, without being able to read the signposts, he always managed to find his way. Like many illiterates he had a good memory and a sort of knack, which the blind have, of 'feeling' his way from one place to another. Most evenings the couple spent at home, although on Wednesdays it was their custom to leave Geraldine at Mrs Probert's while they went to the pictures, picking her up again on the way home. On Saturday Evans went to the Elgin or KPH for a drinking session. On Sunday mornings he called round at his mother's to help with the coal and any other rough work. On other days when he was out

Eileen or Maureen would call at Rillington Place to see Beryl and the baby.

But in the late summer of 1949 a new consideration entered their lives. Beryl once again found herself pregnant, a situation that neither she nor her husband had intended. The prospect of another child filled Beryl with dismay. Three people living in those two small rooms was bad enough, four would be insupportable. She would have to give up her part-time job in Ladbroke Grove; there would be another mouth to feed and even less money to feed it on. She was twenty years old, young and desirable, and she saw herself being tied to nappies and safety pins for the rest of her life. She started douching and syringing herself, but as she had only the haziest idea of what to do, she was unsuccessful. But she was determined not to have the child, and one day she told her husband that if all else failed she would have it aborted. Naturally enough he tried to dissuade her, for apart from anything else, few men can accept the idea of the destruction of their own seed. However she was adamant, and Evans asked his mother if she knew of anything that might help. She said she didn't and in any case didn't approve of interfering. Having tried various pills without success Beryl decided on an abortion. She told various people about this. She told Eileen, asking her not to tell Mrs Probert. She told Maureen, mentioning that she had heard that there was a man in the Edgware Road who would do it for £1. But the biggest mistake she made was to tell the Christies.

During the nine months that had elapsed since Beryl had returned to Rillington Place from Queen Charlotte's Hospital, the Christies and the Evanses had naturally seen quite a lot of each other. In that tiny match-box of a house they could hardly have avoided it. Mrs Christie seems to have been genuinely fond of Mrs Evans and the baby, and there is evidence that on several occasions she 'kept an ear open' for Geraldine when Beryl went out shopping. It would seem that Christie also took a liking to Beryl, though for rather different reasons: he himself as good as admitted it when he wrote later ' . . . without realizing it I could have been attracted to her . . . ' Certainly he had every opportunity to be. The occupants of a house like 10 Rillington Place live very much on top of one another. Whenever Beryl entered or left the house she had to pass the door of Christie's front room, and within a few feet of his kitchen; whenever she went to or from the lavatory in the yard, which she must have done two or three times a day on her own behalf and considerably more for the baby's slops, she had to pass between the Christies' bedroom and kitchen. If Christie was attracted towards her, as he says, one can see how tempted he must have been. In the past his sex life had been conducted largely in the shadows with women of the shadows. Yet here was a young, pretty and attractive girl of twenty living, almost literally, in his cwn backyard. It may well be that, more than any other woman he had known, she created in his mind the sort of conflict that he had always avoided by refusing to face it: the fact that she was both highly desirable and totally unobtainable. But there was no refusing to face it this time; for as long as the husband was in the house the desire could not be gratified, and as long as the girl was in the house, the desire would continue to be fanned. Christie was in a dilemma.

It is unlikely that the news that Beryl was trying to miscarry gave Christie any encouragement by itself; but with the further news that she was looking for someone to abort her, he may well have sensed, with a sudden wave of excitement, the part in the proceedings that he might play. What was it he had said about Eady? 'My knowledge of medicine made it possible for me to talk convincingly about sickness and disease and she readily believed I might cure her.' Could he not persuade Beryl that he could do for her as he had for Eady's catarrh? The fact that he knew as little about abortions as cures for catarrh was utterly beside the point. Here was a priceless, heaven-sent opportunity of achieving what he had desired for so long; of seeing Beryl naked, of touching her parts with his hands, and doing so moreover with her willing consent. Other, darker thoughts may have been at the back of his mind, but as he always acted compulsively rather than consciously, it is unlikely that he would have been fully aware of them. But that he was in a state of emotional tension at this time, we know for certain; for not having been near his GP, Dr Odess, for seven months (for Christie almost a record) he started going to the surgery again at the end of October to complain of nervous diarrhoea.

The first news that Evans had that Christie was prepared to abort Beryl was when he returned from work one evening during the first or second day in November. Christie met him in the passage and said that he would like to have a chat with him about the pills Beryl was taking to get rid of the baby. Together they went into Christie's front room where Evans could not have avoided seeing, as no doubt Christie intended him to, the framed photograph of Christie standing in police uniform and his first-aid certificates hanging on the wall. If only, Christie went on, Evans or Beryl had come to him in the first place, he could have done the job without any trouble at all. Evans said he was not interested. Christie then said that he had done several abortions on other women and they had all been successful. Obviously impressed by this lie, Evans said: 'I didn't think you knew anything about medical stuff.' Christie picked up the cue immediately. Not only did he know about medical stuff, but before the war he had been training to be a doctor and had to give it up because of an accident. This was just the sort of lie, based on the half-truths of the medical titbits picked up during his life and the accident he had had when he first came down to London, that one would expect from Christie. To press home the point he handed Evans what he called 'one of my medical books'. This was an ordinary St John's Ambulance first-aid book which Christie had acquired during his time in the police force, and do-it-yourself abortions are not, let it be said, one of the subjects on which instruction is given. Christie however knew that as Evans could not read, he would not understand the text, but might be suitably impressed by the pictures. Evans looked hopefully at these and then asked Christie how he actually did an abortion: to which Christie, not having the faintest idea, artfully replied that only he and the doctors would know about that sort of thing. He added (and this perhaps shows that he had already decided what he was going to do and wanted to safeguard himself) that with the stuff he used, one out of every ten would die of it. Evans repeated that he wasn't interested, said good night to Christie and went upstairs.

Beryl was awaiting Evans's return with some anxiety; for Christie had already told her – poor, gullible little creature – that he would have a word with Evans on the subject as soon as he came in. Beryl asked her husband whether Christie had had a word. Evans said yes, and told her what had taken place. He added that he had told Christie that he wanted nothing to do with it and she was to have nothing to do with it either. 'She turned round and told me to mind my own business and that she intended to get rid of it and she trusted Mr Christie. She said he could do the job without any trouble at all.'

This conversation took place on or about Tuesday, 1 November, the same day as Christie again went (as indeed in the circumstances he might have done) to Dr Odess to complain of nervous diarrhoea and to obtain a certificate to excuse him from work. Relations between Evans and Beryl continued to be strained, not only because of the disagreement about the proposed abortion but also because Evans had discovered that money he had given to Beryl for paying the rent and hire-purchase payments had been spent on other things. They had what Evans calls a 'terrific row' about this on the morning of Sunday, 6 November. He threatened to walk out on her for good and according to him she said: 'You can leave any time you like.' Rather than get involved in more arguments he spent the rest of the day at the pictures and the pub.

Monday, 7 November, broke grey and stormy. Evans got up at about 6 a.m. and soon afterwards Beryl started nagging at him. This constant nagging of Beryl's is hardly surprising in view of the anxiety she must have been suffering over her pregnancy and hopes and fears as regards terminating it: in the first stages of pregnancy many women are in a slightly unbalanced state anyway. 'I took no notice of her and went into the bedroom to see my baby before going to work. My wife told me that she was going to pack up and go down to her father in Brighton. I asked her what she was going to do with the baby so she said she was going to take the baby down to Brighton with her, so I said it would be a good job

254

and a load of worry off my mind.' Evans went off to work and during the day Beryl and Christie made arrangements for the proposed abortion to take place in Evans's flat the next morning. When Evans came back that evening he found Beryl still there. 'I said, "I thought you was going to Brighton?" She said, "What, for you to have a good time?" ' Beryl then said that she had made all arrangements with Christie for 'first thing Tuesday morning'. Evans did not make any comment on this because, he says, he didn't believe it was true: in fact he probably realized that it was true but that there was nothing he could do to prevent it.

Next morning, Evans got up as usual soon after 6 a.m. 'My wife got up with me. I had a cup of tea and a smoke and she told me: "On your way down tell Mr Christie that everything is all right. If you don't tell him I'll go down and tell him myself." So as I went down the stairs he came out to meet me and I said, "Everything is all right". Then I went to work.'

At this point the reader must proceed with caution. What exactly happened that morning in Rillington Place, no-one knows for certain and no-one now ever will know. Christie's own versions (three in all) of how he murdered Beryl are as contradictory as those of the murders of all his other victims. For some little time perhaps Beryl and Christie stayed in their respective flats, the one waiting hopefully to be aborted, the other waiting to do what he had already done to Fuerst and Eady. It is improbable that Christie made any move until Ethel had gone out, but it is also improbable that he kept her entirely in the dark, for he could not be certain that Beryl would not discuss the matter with her direct. In any case Ethel presented little danger; she was gullible enough to believe anything that anyone told her, and if this included her husband's ability and willingness to perform an abortion, she would accept it uncritically. It was probably towards the end of the morning – Christie himself said 'about lunch time' – that he mounted the stairs to the little kitchen where Beryl was waiting. She was dressed in a spotted cotton blouse, a light blue woollen jacket and a black skirt. She had probably removed her knickers in preparation before his arrival. According to Christie, 'she brought the quilt from the front room and put it down in front of the fireplace. I am not sure whether there was a fire in the grate. She lay on the quilt. She was fully dressed.' It seems almost certain that Christie, remembering the success he had had in gassing Eady, had brought with him his piece of rubber tubing, hoping to persuade Beryl that if she took a sniff or two of gas, the abortion would be a great deal less painful. He himself admits that a piece of rubber tubing was there: 'When she laid down there was a piece of gas tubing that I put to her face, a piece of gas piping going down the side of the fireplace with a tap that had been used, I think, for a gas stove at one time, and I attached this piece of tube and then brought it down near her face.' Whatever happened next must have happened very quickly. The most likely sequence of events is that Christie inserted either his finger or, for the sake of greater conviction, some blunt instrument like a spoon into Beryl's vagina, that almost simultaneously Beryl got into a wild panic, thrust aside the rubber tubing and began struggling, that Christie, now in a state of frenzied sexual excitement and seeing his victim about to slip away, began hitting her savagely in the face and when she was semi-conscious whipped out what he called 'my strangling rope' and strangled her. All this must have taken a matter of seconds. Christie himself said that he thought he strangled Beryl with a stocking, and although this is possible, it is not likely. When he had strangled her, there was time enough to turn off the gas, undo his buttons and attempt intercourse.

During the afternoon Christie moved Beryl's body from the kitchen into the bedroom and laid it on the bed. He covered the body with the eiderdown, or quilt, and then drew the curtains against prying eyes from the house opposite. At about 5.30 in the evening Evans returned and was met by Christie at the bottom of the stairs. Christie said, 'Go on upstairs, I'll come up behind you,' presumably so that Mrs Christie should not hear what he had to say. They climbed to the top flat and entered the kitchen. Evans lit the gas and then Christie said to him: 'It's bad news. It didn't work.' Evans asked where Beryl was and Christie said she was lying on the bed. 'So I went in the bedroom. I lit the gas, then I saw the curtains had been drawn. I looked at my wife and saw that she was covered with the eiderdown. I pulled the eiderdown back to have a look at her. I could see that she was dead and that she had been bleeding from the mouth and nose and that she had been bleeding from the bottom part.'

Bleeding from the mouth and nose are hardly what one would expect from an unsuccessful abortion, and just what one would expect from blows on the face followed by a successful strangulation. But in a situation like this no-one, and especially no-one of Evans's mental calibre, is likely to attach significance to something he is not looking for, and in any case Christie may well have explained away the marks by saying that Beryl had struggled during the operation and hit her head on a piece of furniture. Whatever the reason he gave, we have his own word for it that at this time 'Evans did not know his wife had been strangled'. The 'bleeding from the bottom part' is rather more puzzling, for there is no post mortem evidence that bleeding took place. It is not impossible that Christie, to whom nothing was too horrible, smeared blood from the face on to the bottom part to give greater verisimilitude.

Next, Evans went over to the cot, picked up the baby, wrapped it in a blanket and took it into the kitchen to feed it. Christie said, 'I'll speak to you after you've fed the baby,' and then left the room. When Christie returned Evans asked him how long his wife had been dead. Christie said, 'Since about three o'clock,' which was probably a good deal later than true. Christie then volunteered the further information that Beryl's stomach was 'septic-poisoned' and 'another day and she'd have gone to hospital'. This lie, based on the half-truth of Beryl's unsuccessful douchings, was again just what one would expect from Christie. It partially explained Beryl's death, it shifted much of the blame from himself on to her, and it would impress Evans by its medical know-how. Evans then asked Christie exactly what it was he had done, but Christie 'refused to tell me'.

Christie had now successfully surmounted the first danger to himself, that Evans might light on the true cause of Beryl's death. The second danger was even more acute, that Evans would lose no time in going to the police and get the whole matter cleared up. Some people have expressed surprise that he did not do this, but in the circumstances it would have been surprising if he had. Firstly, Evans knew (because Christie would have told him) that if he did go to the police Christie would face a criminal charge of manslaughter which would almost certainly put him in prison: this would be poor repayment, when all was said and done, to a man who had tried to help his wife out of a difficulty. Secondly, as again Christie must have been quick to point out, Evans was almost as much involved in Beryl's death as Christie, for by telling Christie that morning that everything was 'all right', he had made himself an accomplice to the act. (Christie himself admitted he went even further than this. 'I told Evans,' he wrote years later, 'that no doubt he would be suspected of having done it because of the rows and fights he had had with his wife. He seemed to think the same.') Thirdly, Evans was half Christie's age, a quarter of his intelligence, and in any case too stunned by what had happened to make a coherent plan about anything. And lastly and most important of all Christie was an ex-police officer of four years' standing whose word had all the authority of the law. When therefore Christie said that he proposed 'disposing' of the body, Evans had little choice but to accept. Christie said, 'I'll dispose of it down one of the drains.'

There remained the question of little Geraldine, who now had no-one to look after her. Evans suggested taking her round to his mother's that evening, but Christie, sensing immediate danger, said that this would cause suspicion right away (as indeed it would). He himself would think out some plan for the baby and tell Evans about it in the morning. The two men then went their separate ways to bed.

Christie and his wife say they were both asleep about midnight when they were woken by a loud thud, which seemed to come from upstairs, followed by a noise as of someone moving furniture about. This story was either an invention on their part or it was true. If it were true, and it may well have been true, then it was probably Evans stumbling about in the dark in order to have a last look at his wife. And if so, then Christie must have lain awake in terror, wondering whether Evans was going to discover for himself the true cause of Beryl's death. Presently however the noises ceased and the household slept. Evans, after putting the bloodstained eiderdown and blanket on which Beryl had lain into a cupboard, lay down beside the cot of his baby daughter. Christie and Ethel snuggled into the warmth of their double bed; and outside in the garden the remains of Fuerst and Eady rotted a little further.

Next morning from the sweet unconsciousness of sleep both Evans and Christie woke to face the hideousness and horror of what had happened. For Evans there must have come the realization that his actions of the night before had compromised him; but he had chosen his route and there could be no turning back now. Christie's problems were even more acute: he had to decide not only what to do with Beryl's body but, of greater urgency, what to do about the baby. He had told Evans the night before that he would look after the baby during the day. But he could not do so indefinitely. Nor could Evans. Nor could anyone without sooner or later inviting questions as to the whereabouts of its mother. But if mother *and* baby were to disappear altogether, then it might be safely said that they had gone away. It is likely that the idea of murdering the baby had by this time already entered Christie's mind. In one way his nature must have genuinely recoiled from so terrible an act. But it was a question literally of self-preservation, a question of the baby's life or his; and taken at that level there could be no choice. Christie met Evans on the stairs as he came down to go to work. He repeated to Evans that he would look after the baby during the day. 'He also,' in Evans's words, 'told me that he knew a young couple over in East Acton who would look after the baby, and he'd go over and see them.' Here of course Christie was stalling for time, though as with other things he may well have convinced himself that he could find a couple to adopt the baby. But he knew no one in East Acton, and he probably chose this place in preference to any other simply because the two words were familiar to him from the back of the No. 7 bus. Evans then went to work.

Between half past five and six Evans came home. He was met by Christie who told him that he had seen the young people from East Acton who were going to look after the baby and they would be in to fetch it the following morning. 'I fed the baby that night, and was playing with her by the fire when Christie came in. He said, "In the morning when you get up, feed the baby and dress her and then put her back in the cot, the people will be here just after nine in the morning to fetch her." He said, "I've told them to knock three times and I'll let them in." He also told me to pack some clothes for the baby.'

The next day Evans got up as usual, packed a case containing the baby's clothes, and after feeding and dressing it, left it in its cot. On the way out at about half past six he told Christie what he had done, and Christie confirmed that the people from East Acton were coming at nine o'clock. Since they were wholly a figment of Christie's imagination, it is almost needless to add that they never came. But this was the last day on which anyone claims to have seen Geraldine alive. Sometime during that day Christie murdered her in exactly the same way as he murdered all his other victims – by strangling her with a ligature, in this case a tie belonging either to him or Evans, with extreme force. Of all the murders he committed, it is likely that this one horrified Christie most; for there could be no possible excuse for the killing of a helpless child. He said of his state of mind after every murder: 'It didn't mean a thing to me. I never gave it a further thought.' The mechanism of his brain probably ensured that he forgot about this one even quicker than the others.

It must have been about this time that Christie decided that the continued presence of Evans at Rillington Place was going to be a source of embarrassment for both of them. He could hardly hope to do away with Evans as he had done with his wife and daughter, but he could persuade him to sell up his furniture and clear out of London for the time being. Anyone who doubts Christie's power over Evans should remember the pride with which he told a psychiatrist three years later: 'I could make Evans do or say anything I wanted.' And a prison officer who looked after Evans before his death wrote: 'I knew Evans in some of the most critical moments of his life and I think it quite easy for anybody to have moulded him to their plans.' To this end Christie visited, either this day or the next, his friend Mr

Hookway, the furniture dealer, of Portobello Road. There was a young chap in his house, a Mr Evans, who wanted to sell his furniture as he was moving out: would it be all right if he sent him along? Mr Hookway said it would be quite all right, and Christie said he would send him the following day. Evans meanwhile had run into trouble with his employers, the Lancaster Food Products. During the past few weeks it had been the custom for Beryl to go there every Friday to draw his basic wage of about £5 10s. This had come about because he had always been asking for advances in his salary. This particular Thursday, knowing that Beryl could not be coming in to collect his wages the following day, he again asked for an advance: Beryl had gone down to Brighton for a holiday, he said, and he wanted to send the money to her by registered post. For his employers this was the last straw. During the past fortnight they had found him increasingly slack in his work and even more prone to lying than usual. They therefore gave him the wages due to him, but they also gave him the sack.

At about half past five Evans returned to 10 Rillington Place. He went upstairs, and 'as I got into the kitchen Christie came up behind me. He told me that the people had called and took the baby with them and to pack the rest of her things, and he had a case and would take them over to East Acton with the pram and her chair later in the week.' Evans then told Christie about losing his job, and if Christie had been wondering how he was going to persuade Evans to get out of London nothing could have suited his purpose better; for the most cogent reason why Evans should stay in London, his job, had now gone. This was just another of the almost miraculous coincidences that were favouring Christie at this time. Christie made his proposal and Evans, by his own account, said 'All right'. He must have been thankful that there was someone about to take a decision for him. Christie then told Evans about his visit to Mr Hookway, and that Mr Hookway was expecting him the next day. Later in the evening Evans went down to Christie's flat and told Christie in Mrs Christie's hearing that he had packed up his job and was going to Bristol (where he had previously told Mrs Christie that Beryl had gone) to get a new job. It seems probable that this little incident was arranged at Christie's suggestion for Mrs Christie's benefit. One other matter Evans asked Christie that night, a matter on which he had obviously been brooding. How had he disposed of Beryl's body? Christie replied that he had disposed of it as he said he would dispose of it on the night of her death: down one of the drains. This phrase remained fixed in Evans's mind.

A few days later Evans sold his furniture to Mr Hookway for £40, and then took a train to Merthyr Tydfil and the house of his uncle and aunt, Mr and Mrs Lynch. They were surprised to see him. Evans said that he and his boss were touring the West Country looking for new branches and that their car had broken down at Cardiff: Beryl and Geraldine were staying with her father at Brighton. Evans asked if he could stay with them until the car was repaired and they agreed.

After ten days, and with no further news of Evans's boss and the car, or of Beryl and Geraldine, Mr Lynch suspected that something was amiss. So he wrote to his sister Mrs Probert to say that Tim was staying with them, and she replied that she hadn't seen Beryl or the baby for a month and that Tim had sold the furniture and vacated the flat. Taxed with this by Mr Lynch, Evans said his mother was lying.

Now Evans realized that it was time to do what he should have done all along – go to the police. But what should he tell them? He knew that if he incriminated Christie in any way, said that Christie had performed an abortion that had killed Beryl and then put her body down a drain, then Christie would be sure to deny it and incriminate him. So he invented a cock and bull story about a man giving him pills for an abortion which he had given Beryl and which had resulted in her death; after which he had put her body down the drain. The Merthyr Tydfil police telephoned the Notting Hill police who examined the drain in the manhole outside 10 Rillington Place and found nothing. Realizing that Christie had lied in saying that he would put Beryl's body in the drain, and that there was therefore no further need to try and protect him, he made a second statement in which he told everything that had happened. The Notting Hill police then made a search of the premises but found nothing incriminating: they missed

Muriel Eady's right thigh-bone which was propping up the garden fence. It was about this time too that Christie's dog Judy dug up Eady's skull, and after dark Christie dropped it through the window frame of a nearby bombed-out house.

Next, in view of Evans's allegations against Christie in his second statement, the police summoned Christie to Notting Hill Police station. By his own account he was there from 11 p.m. to 5 a.m.

At this time the case was wide open. For Christie it was the moment of truth, the moment when the Notting Hill police had to decide whether suspicion should be attached to him or Evans; and if to Evans and not him whether he could throw any light as to why Evans might have done it. As regards himself, not even the police could have foreseen the tremendous trump card he had up his sleeve. For he was, so to speak, one of them. He knew their jargon, their organization, their methods, the way their minds worked, the names of many of their colleagues: he may even have known, or known of, one or two of the officers attached to the station. We can be sure that he lost no time in speaking of his own experience in the force (including his two commendations) and doing everything in his power to gain their confidence; and the police would have been less than human if their suspicions had not been disarmed at the outset. He dismissed Evans's accusations as ridiculous. 'At no time have I assisted or attempted to abort Mrs Evans or any other woman . . . I cannot understand why Evans should make any accusations against me, as I have really been very good to him in lots of ways.'

The psychological effect on the Notting Hill police that night of Christie having been in the police force himself cannot be overemphasized; for right at the outset, before any bodies had been discovered, he succeeded in putting himself among the hunters instead of the hunted. It was a position from which the police, once they had accepted it, would, for their own prestige, be loath to remove him. And having accepted it, they could now talk to him as an equal, almost as a comrade in arms. What were relations like between Evans and Mrs Evans? they asked. Very bad, said Christie, they got on very badly, they were always rowing. Slowly he drew the noose round Evans's neck. 'Mrs Evans,' he said, 'has told my wife and I on more than one occasion that he has assaulted her and grabbed hold of her throat. She said he has a violent temper and one time would do her in.' The pens scratched across the page and the damning words were taken down. What else could Christie tell them? Well, he said, he knew all about Beryl's pregnancy and her trying to end it by syringing and douching herself. 'I said to her, in my wife's presence, that she was looking a physical wreck and advised her to stop it. We warned her of the consequences and she promised both of us that she would stop taking the stuff.' When had he last seen Mrs Evans? About 8 November, said Christie, when she was going out into the street. 'Later that day when Mr Evans came in at about 7 p.m. he told my wife and I that his wife and child had gone to Bristol with friends for a short holiday and that he was going down later in the week to visit them.' And when had Evans himself left? On the 14th, said Christie, after the van had come for the furniture; earlier in the week Evans had told him he had given up his job and was moving out. He concluded: 'It is very well known locally that he is a liar, and my wife and I have expressed the opinion that he is a bit mental.' Christie's statement was read back to him and he signed it. By it he had determined the pattern of events to come. Whatever doubts there may have been in the police's mind earlier in the evening as to which of the two men they wanted, there were none now.

By the following morning, the Notting Hill police had confirmed that Beryl and the baby were neither at Brighton nor Bristol. Although they had made one search of 10 Rillington Place, they now decided to make another. Accordingly Chief Detective Inspector George Jennings, who had been put in charge of the case, together with Detective Chief Superintendent Barratt and a biologist from Scotland Yard, made their way there and were let in by Christie. They searched the house from top to bottom and found nothing. They then went out into the backyard and garden. They observed, as the officers had observed the previous day, that there was no freshly dug earth. They also observed a broken dustbin, and they may even have poked about inside it. Had they been a little more curious and removed the rubbish from it, they would have found Ruth Fuerst's skull. It must have been a tight moment for Christie who with his wife was standing in the backyard, and one can imagine his relief when they moved away from the border. They looked into the lavatory and then they came to the wash-house door. One of the officers tried to open it but it would not budge. Mrs Christie said that the door sometimes got jammed and she would fetch a piece of metal to loosen it. When she had brought it, one of the officers inserted it into the door and it opened quite easily. Christie, all this time, 'was walking up and down the yard apparently in great pain, with his hands on the small of his back'. Illness, as usual, in time of stress, was coming to his rescue.

What happened next is best described in the words of Miss Tennyson Jesse:

'It was dark in the little wash-house, so dark that the officers had to shine a torch in. There was a copper in the left-hand corner and just next to it in the right-hand corner was a sink with the tap Mrs Christie had mentioned over it. Propped up against the sink was a stack of wood. There was nothing more to be seen but one of the officers reached down behind the wood and felt something there. They pulled out the wood and saw a package, tied up with sashcord, in what appeared to be a green tablecloth. They called Mrs Christie and asked her if she knew what was in it. They asked her to touch it, which she did. She said she did not know what was in it and had never seen it there before.

'The package was pulled out on to the cement just outside the wash-house. When the end of the cord was loosened a pair of feet slipped out.' At the same time the body of little Geraldine was found hidden under some wood behind the door with the tie that had strangled her still tightly knotted round her neck.

The Notting Hill police now telephoned through to Merthyr Tydfil where they had sent Detective Inspector Black and Detective Sergeant Corfield to bring Evans back. Black was told that 'bodies had been found' and that the evening papers would probably be full of it. All newspapers were to be kept away from Evans and he was to be brought to

London immediately. Black was not to discuss anything with Evans at all.

Black, Corfield and Evans left Merthyr Tydfil that afternoon. The journey to London was made mostly in silence, though occasionally words were exchanged on such neutral topics as the Queen's Park Rangers football club. Black describes Evans's frame of mind as 'sullen' but it would probably be more accurate to call it totally confused. His whole purpose in going to the police was to rid himself of his anxiety and fear and get the matter cleared up. The news that Beryl's body was not in the drain was a body-blow. If not there, where was it? He had been kept in confinement at the police station for over forty-eight hours, and for the last twenty-four hours, ever since he made his statement telling the truth, nobody had spoken to him. Why? Now two officers were taking him back to London on a charge of stealing a brief-case which he had not stolen, and they would hardly speak to him either. Why? Clearly they knew something that he didn't. But what? And what was going to happen to him when they got to London?

At about the time that Evans's train was passing through Didcot, a police car arrived at Notting Hill police station. Beryl's and Geraldine's clothing had arrived at the police station from the mortuary during the afternoon and Mr Jennings wanted the Christies to identify it. The clothing was lying on the floor when they arrived, and Christie of course was able to identify it only too easily. All the same it must have been a nasty moment for him, for the last time he had seen it was when he put the bodies in the wash-house three weeks earlier. He was then shown the tie with which he had strangled Geraldine: the knot was still in it, but it had been slit at the back. Did he recognize it? No, he said, he didn't. It certainly wasn't his tie, but come to think of it he had seen Evans wearing a tie *very like* that one. The police thanked the Christies for their trouble, and the police car took them back to Rillington Place.

At about 9.30 p.m. Evans's train drew into Paddington station, and his fears as to the future were in no way lightened by something that happened almost as soon as he stepped on to the platform. A flash-bulb exploded and a press photographer took a picture of him. Now this was a very significant incident. A press photographer would not have been there unless he had been tipped off by the police; and he would not have been tipped off by the police unless Evans was about to make the news as a man charged with murder. For the police to have gone as far as this shows the degree of certainty about Evans forming in their minds. The photograph, too, is revealing: the haggard, hag-ridden expression, like that of a hunted animal, gives some idea of the strain and anxiety he was suffering.

The party were met by Chief Inspector Jennings and driven in a police car to Notting Hill station. The ten-minute journey was made in silence. At the station Evans was taken into the charge room. There on the floor, side by side, lay the two piles of clothing. On top of Beryl's pile were the blanket, tablecloth and cord in which her body had been parcelled up. On top of Geraldine's pile was the tie, with the knot still in it, with which she had been strangled. While Evans was looking at these things, appalled, he heard the voice of Mr Jennings say: 'At 11.50 today I found the dead body of your wife, Beryl Evans, concealed in a wash-house at 10 Rillington Place, Notting Hill; also the body of your baby daughter Geraldine, concealed behind some timber in the same outbuilding, and this clothing was found on them.' Up to this point Evans had been too stunned to show any reaction, but now the tears came into his eyes and he bent down and picked up the tie, quite unable to believe what he had just heard and seen. The voice of Mr Jennings droned on: 'Later today I was at Kensington Mortuary, when it was established that the cause of death was strangulation in both cases.' Then came the final body-blow. 'I have reason to believe that you were responsible for their deaths.'

In that moment it must have seemed to Evans that the whole world was conspiring against him, that he himself was going off his head. Who? Why? Where? Why on earth should anyone want to strangle Beryl and Geraldine? The only person who *could* have strangled them was Christie, but why should he *want to*? It did not make sense. For nearly two years Evans had thought of Christie as a respectable ex-police officer, and for the last three weeks as a man who had tried to help his wife in a difficulty but who had failed. Now he was being asked to throw out this image in exchange for a madman who pointlessly strangled people. Yet it was not Christie who was being charged with murder but himself – and not only charged with the murder of his wife but of his baby daughter whom he loved more than anyone in the world. In a flash Evans must have realized the madness of his actions of the past three weeks – the running away from home, the selling of the furniture, the tearing up of Beryl's clothes, the lies to his mother, to his sisters, to Mrs Christie, to the police. Looking into the eyes of Mr Jennings he must have seen the absolute certainty of an officer who knows that he has found his man. Evans's world had tumbled about his head: the needle had gone off the board. 'Yes,' was all he could manage to say. 'Yes.' It could have meant anything or nothing.

In many murder cases it is the practice of the police, when they feel certain (though often wrongly) that the suspect they have arrested is guilty, to prise a confession out of him so as to be able to present a watertight case. They usually do this by a blend of threats and blandishments, one of the interrogating officers blowing hot and the other cold and then, to confuse the suspect, reversing the roles. That something of this kind occurred during the course of Evans's night-long interrogation at Notting Hill police station there can be little doubt. He himself said that if he didn't agree to what the police proposed, he was afraid that he would be taken downstairs and beaten up (which he would hardly have said if it had not been put to him). He was suggestible by nature and in the trauma in which he found himself as a result of learning that his wife had been strangled and his daughter, whom he thought was alive, had been strangled too, he didn't then, as he admitted at his trial, care much what happened to him. Because he was illiterate the two officers wrote the 'confession' for him. It was a document found afterwards to be false both in substance and detail, but that was not something that was noticed at the time. Evans signed his mark at the end of it and with it his own death-warrant.

Evans's trial took place at the Old Bailey in January 1950, a case (it was thought) of a squalid domestic drama and which did not rate a mention in the national press. The prosecuting counsel was Christmas Humphreys, QC, whose sarcastic and patronizing cross-examination of Evans does not make pretty reading. Christie was the chief prosecution witness and Mr Justice Lewis leant his weight to the prosecution too. The defence counsel was Malcolm Morris, QC, who made the best of an impossible job. The jury was out for only forty minutes and brought in an unanimous verdict of guilty.

The day after the trial ended Christie and his wife left London for a short holiday with her relations in Sheffield. A week later he was back in Dr Odess's consulting-room. Although the break had taken sufficient tension off him for Dr Odess to write in his notes: 'Improvement', the relief was only temporary. The strain of being back in London, and living again in the house where he had committed four murders, was too much. Two days later he went back to Dr Odess and when he was alone with him burst into tears. 'Very depressed,' wrote Dr Odess. 'Unable to work. Recommended holiday', although Christie had just had one. Christie's health was deteriorating rapidly, as it was bound to do while he was living with the knowledge that another man was going to die for his murders. As usual in this sort of situation he tried to convince himself that it was not his responsibility, that he had nothing to blame himself for. As he put it to Dr Hobson three years later: 'When the judge passed certain remarks, it just came to me that I was being responsible. It upset me a lot. I can't believe I was almost responsible for his death.' It upset him so much that he could hardly eat, and he began losing weight rapidly. When Dr Odess examined him in May of that year he found that he had lost two stone since the previous August. At the end of January Dr Odess had to increase the strength of the pheno-barbitone he was prescribing.

Evans meanwhile was settling into the routine of life in the condemned cell at Pentonville. He came into contact with many prison officers and officials, and to most of them he quietly and steadfastly maintained his innocence. All agreed that he was a model prisoner, not given to temper or depression: as Major Marriott, the Governor, put it: 'He doesn't seem to need special tact to handle.' Others spoke of his cheerfulness and resignation. Nearly everybody liked him, though his mental limitations made it difficult to communicate. Officer Bartholomew noted that he didn't understand figures over 100 and Major Haywood, the Deputy Governor, called him 'simple'. Dr Quinn, the Assistant Medical Officer, concluded after certain tests that he was 'feeble-minded', and Dr Coates, the Principal Medical Officer, thought him a 'dullard'. The Governor found him 'childish' and added, 'I don't think he is dull, but he is the type often met with in the Army – fool enough to forge his leave-pass, short-sighted.' It was this short-sightedness, the inability ever to relate his actions to their consequences, that had brought him where he was; and it was this same short-sightedness or lack of correlation that led one or two officers who attended on him to remark that he didn't fully understand what was going to happen. Officers Stevens and Lovegrove both agreed that he 'doesn't realize his position', and Officer Dyson who did many relief watches with him between 6 p.m. and 8 p.m. said: 'Two or three times he spoke of his release as a foregone conclusion, and of his subsequent return to his former life as a truck-driver.'

He spent much of his time playing cards, including Chinese patience which Officer Dyson taught him. His other interests were talking about boxing and football and looking at the pictures in magazines. Officer Gibson noted that he 'takes his fair share of conversation'. He ate and slept well, and during his two months in prison put on ten pounds in weight. Prison officers always note how much a condemned man boasts, lies and cheats, and the general opinion was that Evans practised these minor vices very little. Officer Gibson said of him, 'Quite a good loser – does not cheat,' and his boastfulness was only average. Most of his boasting was concerned with dogs and motorbikes, and the old one about his capacity for drink. To Officer Stevens, Evans talked about his wife and child 'almost as if he had forgotton the crime', and Officer Bartholomew noted: 'He speaks of his wife with respect.' His mother, step-father and sisters visited him regularly, and Officer Stevens observed: 'He keeps the conversation going when his visitors have failed to do so.' Often it was a case of 'Evans managing to comfort his mother rather than she him'. The Roman Catholic priest, Father Joseph Francis, visited Evans three times a week and found him 'an easy man to contact and attentive to spiritual advice'. Under his guidance, Evans, never a practising believer, attended Mass and Benediction on Sundays, and he told Father Francis that he would like to receive the Sacraments before the end. Nearly all the officers who attended on Evans noted that he 'shows no remorse'. As he was going to be hanged for a crime which he hadn't committed, it would have been odd if he had.

On 20 February Evans was taken by Officer Stevens to the Court of Criminal Appeal to listen to the hearing of his appeal before the Lord Chief Justice (Lord Goddard), Mr Justice Humphreys (the father of Mr Christmas Humphreys) and Mr Justice Sellers. According to Officer Stevens, Evans listened intently to all that went on. When he heard that the appeal had been dismissed he showed no distress and his only comments were that Lord Goddard and Mr Justice Humphreys were 'bloody old sods'. But Officer Bartholomew noted that when he got back to Pentonville he 'paced up and down the cell a bit uneasy like', and the next day Officer Davey observed that 'he appeared depressed'.

Yet Evans was wonderfully resilient, and although he must have realized that only the thin possibility of a reprieve now stood between him and the gallows, he managed to regain something of his cheerfulness and composure. The Deputy Governor, Major Haywood, noted that he 'was never seen brooding', although he did add: 'He is perhaps less jovial as the day approaches – perhaps more serious would be the word.'

As time passes condemned men gradually become resigned to their fate: they do not waste their time in trying to convince prison officers that they are innocent. Some of them say frankly that they are going to get what they deserve, and a few even manage to make jokes about being 'topped'. Evans was the classic exception. In Major Marriott's experience he was the only condemned man to maintain his innocence, quietly, definitely, and persistently, right up to the end.

Father Francis noted of him: 'He says he hasn't done it,' adding with a touching belief in the infallibility of British justice, 'Seems to have convinced himself it was another man.' But he also had the perception to note: 'He has always seemed to me a meek and mild person whom I cannot imagine doing anything violent.' This was the view of many other officers. Officer Stevens said of him: 'He doesn't act like a chap who has done two murders,' and Officer Dyson wrote: 'He appeared so harmless and the sort of man who would have run rather than fight. I don't mean he was cowardly but his attitude in the condemned cell was totally foreign to killing a baby.' Officer Lovegrove noted that 'he has not admitted doing it', and Dr Coates said: 'He sticks to the story of Mr Christie,' adding with the same blind faith in the law as Father Francis: 'Does not tell clumsy lies otherwise.' To Dr Quinn Evans he also maintained his innocence. 'He denies the murder and blames Christie.'

The date for the execution was fixed for 9 March, and on 4 and 5 March the usual statutory medical inquiry was held in the prison to see if Evans was fit to hang. It consisted of Dr Desmond Curran, a distinguished Harley Street psychiatrist, who had already been a member of the inquiries on Heath, Haigh, Riven, Rivett and many other post-war murderers, Sir Norwood East, the famous penal reformer, and Dr J.S. Hopwood, Medical Superintendent of Broadmoor. A statutory inquiry has at its disposal all the documents in the case, the depositions at the magistrates' court, a transcript of the trial, police and medical reports, and the evidence of the prison staff who have attended on the prisoner since conviction. Evans was interviewed on both days. Most of the preliminary questioning was devoted to Evans's childhood and past life, and he did not tell the inquiry anything they did not know already. They then came to the events of November, and the death of Mrs Evans. Once more Evans said exactly what he had said in his second Merthyr statement and at his trial. 'I had nothing to do with it. My wife was dead when I got home.' Why, he was asked, did he tell the police in his first Merthyr statement that he had put Beryl's body down a drain? 'I told them that,' he said, 'because that's where Christie said he had put it.' He went on: 'As far as I knew, my baby was in Acton. I didn't know she was dead until the police told me.' In that case, he was asked, why had he confessed at Notting Hill to murdering both of them? Because, he said, of the shock at hearing that his daughter was dead. 'I didn't care what happened then, so I made the statement.' He went on: 'Christie made arrangements to feed her till I came home on the 9th. That night my daughter was all right. The last time I saw her alive was Thursday morning. The people from Acton were supposed to be collecting my daughter on the Thursday.' He was asked how his health had been since he was at Pentonville and he said that he ate well and had 'a good night's sleep every night with no dreams'. He got on well with everybody in the prison, he said, and as far as he knew he had no enemies.

The next day the Board again questioned him about his various statements to the police. He said that he had not felt any easier after making his first statement at Merthyr but he definitely did feel easier after making his second statement at Notting Hill. Asked why, he said: 'Well, I broke down at Notting Hill. I had nothing else to worry about when I knew my daughter was dead. I didn't care.' He was more upset, he said, by the death of his daughter than his wife. With some emphasis he said, 'I *didn't* strangle my child.' Asked why Christie should have strangled her, he said, with penetrating truth: 'To be out of the way.'

He was asked if he was worried by what had happened, and he said, 'No, it doesn't come into my mind at all.' He admitted that when he did have to talk about it he found it very painful. He was asked if there was anything else he wanted to say and he said there was. 'The police caught me for a statement when I was upset,' he said, and then, with a kind of terrible pathos: *'The one thing that sticks in my mind is that I am in for something I haven't done.'* He was given permission to leave, and his last words, said with emotion and anger, were: 'I say Christie done it.'

However convincingly or otherwise these words may have sounded to the Board, it was no part of their duties to judge them. They were a medical, not a legal, tribunal; and their terms of reference were to ascertain what medical considerations there were, if any, to justify recommending to the Home

Secretary a reprieve. There were none. The prison officers were unanimous in describing Evans as 'of low mentality but no need for thinking mentally deficient'. Nothing that Evans had done or said gave the Board any grounds for challenging this verdict: and they reported to the Home Secretary accordingly.

The Home Secretary at the time was Mr Chuter Ede and he received the report in his office in Whitehall the next morning. Also on his desk was a petition for a reprieve signed by some eighteen hundred people, and a letter from Mrs Probert saying that her son must have had a brainstorm. With the Permanent Secretary, Sir Frank Newsam, Mr Chuter Ede studied all the documents with that care that Home Secretaries traditionally give to this appalling task. There was only one decision. Across the papers Mr Chuter Ede wrote: 'The law must take its course.'

Officer Dyson was on watch the evening when the news came. 'I remember we were playing Chinese patience when the key rattled in the lock. We immediately prepared to stand up. It was the Governor, the Principal Officer on duty, and the doctor, I believe. The Governor had a piece of paper in his hand. He asked Evans the usual questions about his health, comfort, etc. Then he waved the piece of paper he was holding slightly, and said that the reprieve had failed and the Home Secretary could see no reason to stay sentence. I looked at Evans. There was no change in his features. He just stood and stared at the Governor. Suddenly he remembered he was playing a game of cards. He sat down and said, "Let's get on with the game", or words to that effect. I was really amazed at the manner in which he took the Governor's words. On looking back I realize he was not mentally bright enough to know or gather what was being said. Personally I didn't feel like playing cards any more that session. It wasn't my life that was being taken. I was just a watcher, a spectator, and the proceedings had a sickening effect on me.'

Perhaps Evans might have protested more. Perhaps. But he was little more than a backward boy, and against him was marshalled in its glory the full weight and panoply of the law. As well try to change the stars in their courses. Perhaps too he dimly realized that a price had to be paid for all his lies and foolishness, that in a sense he bore some responsibility for what had happened; realized it in the way that primitive peoples who are chosen by their witch-doctors for human sacrifice realize and accept their fate.

His mother and sisters paid him their last visit. They were far more upset than he was. His mother said to him: 'Son, for my own peace of mind, did you do it? Make your peace with God now.' Evans looked her in the eyes and said, 'Mam, I didn't do it. Christie done it.' When it was time for the family to go, his sister Eileen stayed behind a moment after the others had gone. 'Look, Tim,' she said, 'you've got nothing to lose now. Tell me the truth so that I can know. Did you do it?' To her he said what he had already said to his solicitor, to Mr Morris, to Mr Humphreys, to the judge, to Officer Stevens, to Officer Dyson, to Dr Coates, to Dr Quinn, to Dr Curran, to Father Francis and to his mother. 'No, Eileen, I didn't do it. Christie done it.' Until this moment Mrs Ashby had not known whether he had done it or not: now, for the first time, she knew with absolute certainty he was innocent.

At 3 p.m. on the afternoon of 8 March Officer Dyson was on duty at the prison wicket-gate. The bell rang and he opened the door. It was the hangman Pierrepoint. He was taken to the corridor outside the condemned cell, and peered at Evans through the peephole to assess his build for the drop. Later in the afternoon, when Evans was out for exercise, he went to the gallows and tested the machinery. When this had been done Evans was brought back to his cell.

And so the shadows of that winter day closed in and Evans prepared to spend his last night on earth. Outside the thick walls of the prison people came home from work, some by bus and tube, some on foot, some together, some alone, some laughing and happy, some preoccupied and tired, but all unmindful of the man who a few hundred yards away was in their name about to be put to death. One might suppose that Evans spent his last night tormenting himself for the mistakes he had made and the fundamental injustice of his fate. But it is not likely. He did not think about the past: as he himself said, it was too painful. He slept well that last night, and they had to wake him in the morning. Father Francis was there, and to him Evans made his last confession – a confession not of guilt but of innocence. Then he took the Absolution and the Holy Sacraments.

The end, when it comes, is very quick. A few seconds before nine o'clock the Governor and Pierrepoint entered by the main door of the cell. Evans was seized and pinioned, hustled through the open door of the execution shed and placed on the trap. Pierrepoint put the hood on his head and the rope round his neck. Then he pulled the lever; and Timothy John Evans, twenty-five years old and innocent of any crime save that of having a ten-and-a-half-year-old brain, went to join his wife and child in Paradise.

Next morning, in a state of almost total collapse, Christie called on Dr Odess; and Dr Odess wrote in his notes: 'Certificate off work four weeks. Proceeding convalescent.'

Three years went by, then Christie found the old desires rising up in him again. The stumbling block to any further adventures was Mrs Christie who was now almost always at home. So just before Christmas 1953 he strangled her and put her body beneath the front-room floorboards where he had temporarily put the body of Ruth Fuerst. Then in fairly quick succession in the New Year he strangled and had intercourse with three prostitutes whose bodies he stacked in an alcove off the kitchen. He then walked out of the house.

A week later he was spotted by an observant policeman on Putney Bridge; and in due course sent for trial, found guilty of murder and hanged where Evans had been hanged in Pentonville prison in July 1953. Before his execution he admitted to the murders of all the women, including Beryl Evans. The nearest he came to admitting to the murder of Geraldine was that if there were proof that he had killed her, he would admit it: knowing that it was on the charge of murdering his daughter that Evans had been hanged, he was not going to admit to it voluntarily.

There being considerable public disquiet that Evans had suffered an appalling miscarriage of justice, the Home Secretary (the same Maxwell Fyfe who had once declared that there was no possibility of an innocent man being hanged and anyone who thought there was, was moving in the realms of fantasy) appointed a QC, Mr John Scott Henderson, to conduct an inquiry. This dim man, no doubt hoping to allay the disquiet, concluded in his report that justice had not miscarried; that it was entirely coincidence that the only two male occupants of this tiny house were both strangling women in just the same way without either knowing what the other was doing; and entirely chance that had led Evans to accuse of killing his wife a man who, unknown to him, had already killed two other women and buried them in the garden.

Although when 10 Rillington Place *was published, no critic disagreed with my findings, the government was reluctant to act, and it wasn't until another four years had gone by and we had formed the Timothy Evans Committee, supported by the former Home Secretary who had authorized Evans's execution, and lobbied extensively ministers and MPs, that a fresh inquiry was ordered.

This was another one-man show, conducted by a High Court judge, Sir Daniel Brabin, who, unwilling to admit to a total cock-up, concluded that while Evans had probably not murdered his baby, for which he had been hanged, he probably had murdered his wife, on which charge he had never been tried and for which there was virtually no evidence. This was enough for the then Home Secretary, Roy Jenkins, to recommend to the Queen the granting of what is quaintly called a posthumous free pardon; and so, sixteen years after his execution, Evans's name was finally and officially cleared.

In the longer term I have been told that 10 Rillington Place *was influential in the abolition of capital punishment.

THE TRIAL OF STEPHEN WARD

DR STEPHEN WARD was a lover both of high and low life. A successful osteopath whose clients included many rich and well-known people, he was also a talented artist who enjoyed the company of call girls. His two worlds met at a cottage he rented on the Cliveden estate of the late Lord Astor, one of his clients. There one night in July 1963 one of Lord Astor's guests, John Profumo, MP, Minister for War, met one of Ward's guests, the Murray's Club dancer and call girl Christine Keeler, as well as another of Ward's guests, the Soviet naval attaché, Captain Ivanov.

Subsequently Profumo and Keeler went to bed together, and because it was believed that she was also sleeping with Ivanov, the intelligence services were concerned that the Minister for War might be a security risk. After the Secretary of the Cabinet had spoken to him, Profumo ended his brief affair with Keeler and made a statement to the House of Commons denying that he had ever had an affair with her. Five days later the Home Secretary asked the Metropolitan Police Commissioner whether there was a police interest in Ward. There was none, but relying on some extremely dubious evidence from prostitutes, the police managed to mount a case. Meanwhile Profumo's lies to the Commons had been rumbled and he resigned both as Minister and MP.

Ward's trial opened at the Old Bailey on 22 July 1963. There were five counts against him: the first three of living on the immoral earnings of (1) Christine Keeler, (2) Mandy Rice-Davies and (3) two common prostitutes called Ronna Ricardo and Vickie Barrett, and two charges of procuring.

Because of the rich and diverse characters that the case had spewed up and because also my instincts told me that this was going to be another miscarriage of justice though of

278

*a rather different kind, I attended the trial throughout, and
six months later published my book on it.*

There were crowds outside the Old Bailey ten deep. They
were there because Christine Keeler was expected to give
evidence and they wanted to see her and Dr Ward for themselves. They were prepared to wait long hours in the sun for
this, just as people at funfairs are prepared to queue for freaks;
only here the freaks were sexually not physically deviant.
Round the corner nearly a hundred people were queuing
for the tiny public gallery. Some had been there all night.
One of them said: 'I got here at one. It was a lovely night. I
had a nice four hours' kip on the pavement. Bar accidents
I'm in.' Beyond the crowd and the marshalling policemen
was a space of open road and beyond that, lining either side
of the main entrance like a guard of honour at a wedding,
were the cameramen. I never saw so many cameramen, not
even at the American elections. They were fearful of missing
anybody important and snapped promiscuously at every
likely arrival.

As I went up the marble steps, I heard a great hum and
clatter of conversation from above. Normally the hall outside
the main courts is empty, but now it was alive with people:
journalists mostly, alert tumbledown fellows with weather
nostrils cocked to the prevailing wind; lawyers wigged
and robed, modestly expressing in their dress the national
obsession for charades; a sprinkling of beefy policemen to
prevent unseemly behaviour; and the rude mechanicals
themselves, soberly dressed and with stolid anonymous
faces, from whom the jury would be chosen.

At the Public Office they were issuing Press tickets. There
was a crowd in there too, all jostling impatiently behind
a long wooden counter. It was a small Dickensian sort of
place. I saw Wayland Young and Rebecca West, pioneers in
the tangled byways of, respectively, sex and treason; Sybille
Bedford too, whose title for her brilliant book on the trial of
John Bodkin Adams – *The Best We Can Do* – is as succinct
a comment as one could find on this or any other country's
system of justice. A woman from New York was clamouring
for a ticket without success. A man from one of the agencies

smiled at me: I smiled back: later I found out he had a nervous tic and smiled at everybody. Beyond the counter a tall, sober man in spectacles and morning coat did his best to create calm. He explained that there were only twelve tickets for the Commonwealth Press and nobody had told him how to allocate them. I asked for my ticket and was informed, after much routling, that it wasn't there: it came to light eventually marked Victor Gollancz. Beside me, in pepper and salt trousers, were three small black barristers from some steamy clime. They asked diffidently if they could have some tickets, and were told firmly there were none left. What were they thinking of our wicked white society?

Court No. 1 at the Old Bailey is a famous court. Thompson and Bywaters, Hatry and Bottomley, Evans and Christie, Birkett, Hastings, and Marshall Hall are among its many ghosts. Yet it is a court which, it would seem, is expressly designed to prevent all laymen except the merely curious from hearing or seeing what is going on. From the stage where he sits in pomp under the coat of arms of Edward VII and the symbolic sword of justice, the judge can chat easily to those in the witness-box, a few feet to his right; to the jury, a few more feet beyond the witness-box; to counsel in the well of the court to his left; and to the prisoner in the dock in front of him. Because judge, witnesses, counsel and prisoner are all part of this tight concentric circle, they do not have to raise their voices much to hear one another. This is as things should be: a conversational tone of voice helps to keep down the temperature; but it does mean that the only non-participants who are assured of hearing and seeing all are people who have least need to, those sitting on the benches of the City Lands Committee, and those in the Public Gallery. The first, who are directly behind counsel and thus almost part of the inner circle, are the friends and relations of the city aldermen and senior members of the bar. Today, as on all days of the trial, they were mostly women; and they sported a variety of fetching, and less fetching, hats. Above them, slung beneath the arches of the ceiling in a sort of oaken container, were the seats of the Public Gallery. Here twenty-five assorted citizens, some of whom had been on the pavement all night (and looked it), had already gathered to watch the proceedings. There were two policemen to watch them. Below privilege, above democracy: thus by a few justice would be seen to be done.

But not by the Press (or, as Mr Justice Marshall was later inevitably to call it, 'the fourth estate'). Or heard either. It is true that a few were lucky enough to find seats in a small area on either side of the dock but the majority of journalists were placed on benches *behind* the dock. Now the dock in Court No. 1 is huge. It is the size of a small room. It is as big as it is in order to hold up to a dozen prisoners simultaneously (before shipping them off to Botany Bay, said Wayland Young) and it is as high as it is to prevent any prisoner from jumping out (if, as Mr Griffith-Jones would put it, he be so minded). The result is that those on the top bench behind the dock can see the judge, the bobbing heads of counsel when they are standing up, and part of the jury; those on the bottom bench can see nothing but the back wall of the dock; and *nobody* can hear *anything* for certain. The solution to this grotesque situation would be to lower the dock several feet so that it is more on a level with the well of the court. But the occasions when there are a hundred journalists to cope with are so rare that I daresay it has never occurred to them.

One had heard so much, one had read so much, it was difficult to remember where or when one had first read or heard it. Profumo, Keeler, Rachman, Rice-Davies, Astor, Edgecombe, Gordon, Ward – they were like stopping places on a London bus. Other names too had been bandied about, those of peers and cabinet ministers lurking on the periphery. There had been tales of unspeakable orgies, of a sort of General Post of unbuttoning of trousers and lifting of skirts. Tremendous whipping parties were said to go on at a house in Mayfair; at one, I was told, a small grocer had had a heart attack and died. A certain senile delinquent was understood to derive exquisite pleasure from waiting on tarts with nothing on but a little gingham apron; another's private joy was believed to be urinating on a piece of plate glass which some supine whore held obligingly above her head. Still others were said to find difficulty in getting off the mark without the aid of manual, oral or electrical stimulation. No-one, it seemed, was interested in, or indeed capable of, doing or having it straight. The players were new but the play was as old as civilization. Would we be hearing from some of these players, and if not from them, then about them? It had been said for some time that if the good doctor's ship was going to go down, he would make a point of taking all the first-class passengers with him. (As events turned out it was the first-class passengers who abandoned ship first, quicker even than the proverbial rats.) Rumour abounded, and none knew where fact began and fiction ended.

One thing, though, was certain and that was that the events leading to this trial were almost unique of their kind. In most criminal cases a crime is committed, the police are informed of it and then, working backwards from it, they seek to discover the criminal. But in this case police action had been stimulated not from below but from above. They had started their investigations not after but before they were aware that any crime had been committed. They did not seek to discover the criminal because there was no criminal to discover; and their efforts were directed to finding out not whether Dr Ward had done it, but what Dr Ward had done.

But now surmise was at an end, and we were, we believed, about to hear the truth for ourselves. We were here, judge and jury, learned counsel and solicitors, police, witnesses and a hundred journalists – to discover one thing and one thing only: whether Stephen Thomas Ward, the prisoner at the bar, as well as being a deviationist, which we knew, was also a criminal. Sooner or later and it would probably be sooner, some wigged figure would tell the jury to dismiss from their minds everything they had ever read about the case and concern themselves only with the facts and the law as it was presented to them. It was something that we on the Press benches could share too, for what the jury were about to hear, we would hear ourselves. And at the end of it all we could, as it were, compare notes and see whether or not our verdict tallied with theirs. None of us on that first day, I am sure, had any idea how disparate the results would be.

And now there was a stirring in court and we all struggled to our feet, and a door at one end of the judge's bench opened, and a tall sheriff and a lean alderman came in, followed by a tiny, tubby judge. He came billowing in like a small Dutch *schuyt* under a full spread of canvas, grey and black and scarlet, and he came to anchor just beyond the sword of justice, slightly left of centre. And when he had settled himself in and sniffed the air around him, he looked, I thought, like nothing so much as a keen determined mole, all set for a good day's burrowing, a mole moreover whose beady eye signified that he was not going to brook any nonsense from anybody. This was Sir Archie Pellow Marshall, sixty-four years old, Cornwall Congregationalist and non-Conformist Liberal, reared and nurtured in the great English Puritan tradition. On a recent visit to Washington he was reported to have said, 'Christian virtues, abstinence, discipline, unselfishness, patience and humility are at a discount in England now.' (Abstinence and discipline, I reflected, were not exactly Ward's strong points.) He had been President of the Cambridge Union and a Liberal candidate three times. Most of his career had been spent as a criminal lawyer on the Midlands Circuit. Some of his colleagues referred to him endearingly as the Hen: I was told of one occasion when he returned to counsel's bench after the lunch interval to find, sitting among his nest of papers, a single boiled egg.

And facing him now, alone in the vast dock which until a moment ago was quite empty, was the accused himself; a man also born in the Puritan tradition, the son of a parson, but who from an early age had abandoned tradition and shaped his own course. There was no mistaking the now familiar figure, the roué of fifty who looked thirty-five, perceptive eyes set in a face rather too full to carry them, boyish hair swept back along the sides of the head to meet at the back like the wings of a partridge. Ageing men who look half their years are often fairies; and one wondered whether within this screaming hetero, a homo was not struggling wildly to be let out. But this was an afterthought. He was dressed in a sober heather-mixture suit, and one's first and most striking impression was that he was a man of intelligence and dignity.

And so, for a moment, the Puritan and the Libertine faced each other; and as one's thoughts were dwelling on this, a man in a black gown suddenly shouted out, as though his life depended on it: 'All persons who have anything to do before my Lady the Queen's Justices of Oyer and Terminer and General Gaol Delivery for the Jurisdiction of the Central Criminal Court draw near and give your attention God Save the Queen.' A French woman journalist next to me said, 'It is strange that so gallant an affair should begin by asking God to save the Queen.' And so we were off.

Mr Mervyn Griffith-Jones was educated at Eton and served in the Brigade of Guards. During the trial his dapper figure was often to be seen entering and leaving the building, wearing a neat double-breasted suit and bowler, and carrying a rolled umbrella. He is a good-looking man in a chiselled, square sort of way. Square is a word that suits him. He is so ultra orthodox that some aspects of modern life have escaped him altogether. The most famous example of this occurred during the *Lady Chatterley's Lover* trial when, as prosecuting counsel, he solemnly asked the jury whether it was a book they would wish their servants to read. It simply had not occurred to him that the members of the jury might not have servants; or, if they did, that they might have minds of their own. His colleagues find this sort of naïvety quite endearing. As an advocate he has a reputation for perseverance and ruthlessness. 'If, during a trial, a relevant document suddenly turns up in the Shetland Islands,' one of his contemporaries said to me, 'Mervyn will send a police officer there by special aeroplane to fetch it.'

Mr Griffith-Jones's opening speech lasted an hour and a half, but reading it afterwards gives one no idea of what it sounded like at the time. It reads moderately sensibly, but it sounded totally unreal. Somehow or other Mr Griffith-Jones managed to make everything seem so very much worse than it could have been. I was reminded of what Ward's defence counsel, James Burge, had said at the Magistrates' Court, that his learned friend would make even a honeymoon sound obscene. I did not doubt it. He gave the strong impression that he thought that sexual intercourse was shocking.

The outraged tone of voice in which he delivered his strictures did nothing to increase their appeal. He seemed to be assuming a part, not merely as the state prosecutor of public criminals but as the state guardian of private morals, to be acting as a sort of Establishment front man for an ethos which few people besides himself any longer believed in. Nor was he helped by a use of language which at times wandered perilously near to Wonderland. Instead of 'although' he said 'albeit', a word which I didn't think anyone wrote any more, let alone said. For 'it doesn't matter' he said 'it matters not'; for 'with each other' he said 'the one with the other'; for 'if in a mind to' he said 'if so minded'. When he wanted to tell the jury that Christine Keeler left home to look for work and found it as a dancer at Murray's Club, he said: 'She then left home in search of employment, and she obtained employment at a club called Murray's Club as an *artiste.*' When he wanted to tell us that Mandy Rice-Davies had gone off with a young Persian he said that she 'went to live with a Persian boy friend whose acquaintance she had made'. He over-reached himself in describing how Ward had seen a pretty girl in a shop. 'The defendant,' he said, '*cast his eye* through the window of the shop.' One had a mental picture of Ward letting his one glass eye fall into his hand, and then as it were hurling it through the shop window. It was this weird mixture of the colloquial with the archaic that at certain moments made Mr Griffith-Jones, to us on the Press benches, seem such a figure of fun. But how were the jury, new to court procedure and with the burden of responsibility heavy upon them, reacting to him? To them, were not these very small pebbles indeed, and would they even see them in the flowing tide?

The first three counts, said Mr Griffith-Jones, concerned living on the earnings of prostitution: of Christine Keeler at Wimpole Mews during a fifteen-month period between June 1961 and August 1962; of Mandy Rice-Davies at Wimpole Mews during a four-month period between September and December 1962; and of 'two women certainly' (though he did not at this juncture name them) at Bryanston Mews during a five-month period between January and the beginning of June 1963. The prosecution's case, said Mr Griffith-Jones, was that these women were prostitutes, not street walkers admittedly, but women who sold their bodies for money none the less; and the law was that if the jury were satisfied that they were prostitutes and that Ward was living with them or habitually in their company or exercising influence over them in any way, then it was up to him to prove that he was not living on their immoral earnings, either wholly or in part. When I heard this I thought that Mr Griffith-Jones was going to have an uphill job: even if he did satisfy the jury that the women were prostitutes rather than good-time girls, surely Ward, with his earnings from his osteopathy and drawings, would have little difficulty in proving that he was not living on immoral earnings. That very morning an exhibition of his drawings had opened at a Bloomsbury gallery, and prices were being asked up to five hundred guineas.

'Miss Christine Keeler,' called the usher, and one heard the cry echoing in the hall outside. There was, among Press, public and bar alike, a sense of keen and pleasurable anticipation. For this was the nymph who had started it all: nearly everything we had read and heard about the affair could in the last analysis be traced back to her. Was it more than coincidence that so many of the people she had been in contact with had come to ruin? It was because of her, indirectly, that the two West Indians, Edgecombe and Gordon, had gone to prison; that the Russian naval attaché, Ivanov, had been banished to some dismal post in Siberia; that the British War Minister, Profumo, had had to resign and the Government itself been on the point of toppling; that Ward was now in the dock. Without her we would not have heard about Lord Astor and his friends, Peter Rachman and his slums, Mariella and her parties, Ivanov, Lord Normanbrook and MI5. One way and another she was responsible for quite a lot. The photographs of her which had filled the newspapers during the past few weeks showed her to be uncommonly attractive, and on her own admission she had a prodigious sexual appetite. The anticipation was understandable.

She came into court wearing an odd sort of mustard-coloured cloak, shaped like a small tent, which reached to within a few inches of her skirt, which was made of the same material. It was the sort of dress that aims at being chic and looks rather vulgar. This was the first thing I noticed. The second was how small she was. In her photographs she had seemed quite tall, but in effect, and despite the tarty high-heeled shoes, she was tiny, a real little doll of a girl, and here of course was half the attraction. She walked superbly on long slender legs, her carriage was remarkable; one was struck too by the mass of copper hair that reached to her shoulders and framed within it the small oval face with the high cheekbones and hint of Red Indian blood. She was in short like an animal, and one could see at once her appeal to the animal instincts of men.

But that was all; and even that was not for long. For two things happened to dispel any illusions. The first was a close-up view of her. While she was walking to the witness-box and even while she was in it, I could not see her features properly. But when she walked out at the lunch interval a quarter of an hour later, she passed within a foot of me. It was a terrifying little face, vacant yet knowing, and it belonged not to a girl of twenty-one but to an already ageing woman. The eyes were dead, like those of fish on a slab: the face itself was painted an inch thick, but round the chin one could detect the lunar blemishes, the ravages of the years. What would she look like at thirty?

And then there was her voice, which in itself was enough to kill any romantic notions that anyone might have of her. For it was not just that it was the voice of any little shop girl, lacking style and distinction, but that she – or perhaps Dr Ward – had tried to do something with it, to lift it out of the rut. The result – when one could hear it, which was seldom – was both bizarre and pathetic. It was perhaps unfortunate for her that almost the first words we heard her utter – in reply to a question about her early life – was that she had lived at Staines until she had gone to Slough: there are no two towns in Britain less happily named.

This attempt at improvement also showed in certain gestures she made when speaking. When in a tight corner or embarrassed she would shrug her shoulders uneasily and rotate her right hand, movements aimed at conveying a sense of poise and composure but which merely revealed how unsophisticated she really was: indeed in the crass mistiming of her gestures she was only ever equalled, in my experience, by Sir Anthony Eden. Occasionally, out of nervousness, she would turn her head to one side, raise her hand to her mouth, and give a little genteel cough. For here she was in an alien world, where her charms meant nothing. She might have had her little moment in the street, with the jealous women booing and the randy men pressing their faces against the window of her taxi and the photographers asking her to pull the edge of her skirt a little higher still, but here the air was clinical, the women detached and superior, the men immune. Even Mr Griffith-Jones who was, so to speak, on the same side as herself, clearly made her ill at ease. Probably no man had ever spoken to her before with such lofty detachment, and she had no idea how to cope with it. Sometimes she made a feeble attempt at a joke, hoping to strike some spark of warmth and recognition from Mr Griffith-Jones's flinty exterior. She would have been wiser not to have attempted it: the jokes died on the wind: Mr Griffith-Jones was not amused.

Although in her evidence in chief Christine Keeler admitted to sleeping with numbers of men, some for money, others not, she denied that Ward was living on her immoral earnings. Asked what proportion of money she had received from men while living with Ward and which she had given to him, *she replied that she usually owed him more than she ever made and had only repaid half of it*. If that was so, how could the prosecution say that Ward was living on her immoral earnings?

It was now the turn of Ward's defence counsel, Mr James Burge. Mr James Burge was not a QC, as might have been expected in a case of this importance, but I understood that Ward had been so pleased with his handling of the case at the Magistrates' Court that he had decided to retain him for the trial. On the other hand, Mr Burge is of the same seniority as many QCs and considered to be the leading junior criminal counsel at the Bar. He is a jovial, sunshiney, Pickwickian sort of man, who always seems to be smiling. It was not entirely coincidence, I thought, that some of his practice was devoted to licensing cases. Beer and Burgundy seemed to blend with his beaming face.

In short, Mr Burge was a very nice man; indeed, as the trial went on, I began to think that alongside Mr Griffith-Jones, he was almost *too* nice a man. He was a civilized being, a person of wit and humour. I had been told by one of his colleagues that he was one of the few men at the Bar who could laugh a case out of court. The atmosphere here, as I think he realized, was not conducive to this sort of approach, but I was told he had tried it once or twice at the Magistrates' Court with some success. In addition to his quip about Mr Griffith-Jones making a honeymoon sound obscene, he had also said that he had no objection to some of Mr Griffith-Jones's leading questions, as they were not leading very far. Mr Griffith-Jones himself would have been incapable of either of these two remarks. But equally Mr Burge could not match Mr Griffith-Jones's cold relentless *plodding*, his battering away at the walls until, by sheer persistence, they began to crack. It was this, in the last analysis, that made one admire Mr Griffith-Jones as much as one deplored him. Because his own attitude to the case was committed, one became committed in one's attitude towards him. It was this outward lack of commitment, not in matter but in manner, that at times led one to feel that Mr Burge was doing himself literally less than justice. They say that the days of the committed lawyer are over: yet one would have liked to see Ward's defence accompanied by some passion, with his counsel as contemptuous of the charges laid against him as the prosecution were contemptuous of Ward himself. As it was, while I had no doubts which of the two counsel was the more intelligent, urbane and congenial, equally I had no doubts, where the jury was concerned, which was the more effective advocate.

To be fair to Mr Burge he was labouring under certain handicaps. The first was that the judge did not appear as sympathetic to the presentation of the case for the defence as he was to the case for the prosecution. He had an odd little trick, when addressing Mr Burge, of allowing a noticeable pause between 'Mr' and 'Burge'. There were other instances, and they increased as the trial went on, when various remarks he made and the moment at which he made them had the effect of taking the edge off what Mr Burge was saying.

He did not do this, or he did not do it so often, with Mr Griffith-Jones.

Mr Burge's other great handicap was his inability to hear much of what the witnesses were saying. Miss Christine Keeler was only the first of many female witnesses who gave their evidence in a whisper. Again and again Mr Burge found himself saying: 'You went where?' – 'What do you say he was doing?' – 'You said what?' Often he repeated the witnesses' answers so as to be sure that he had heard right: often he heard wrong, so that the witnesses had to repeat themselves. But sometimes, while they were drawing breath to repeat themselves, the judge, who was halfway between Mr Burge and the witness-box, saved them the trouble by relaying their answers for them. He did this, I thought, in a most unfortunate manner, raising his voice and enunciating each syllable, as though talking to a backward child. Psychologically, all of this combined to put Mr Burge at a slight disadvantage. Nor was he helped by Ward's blow-by-blow comments on the trial which came tumbling over the dock wall in a seemingly endless stream of little pieces of paper.

Asked by Mr Burge to confirm her saying to Mr Griffith-Jones that she had never given Ward as much as she had received from him, she replied categorically, 'No.' She also at one point gave perjured evidence to Mr Burge which was not revealed until later that year when she was sentenced to nine months' imprisonment for perjury. Had the perjury been known at the time, it would have totally discredited her as a prosecution witness.

The next witness was Miss R, who was an Austrian. She was extremely pretty and extremely well built: one could understand Ward casting his eye at her ample bosoms through the window of the shop. She had a wealth of light auburn hair, and she was accompanied into court by another woman with light auburn hair whom I took to be her sister but who turned out to be her mother. She was dressed in a blue jacket and skirt with white sweater, and she had pink fingernails. She was allowed to remain anonymous because, according to Mr Griffith-Jones, she was 'respectable' and 'of no public interest'.

Mr Griffith-Jones asked her how old she was, and in a voice which had only the suggestion of an Austrian accent she said she had been born in May 1941 (which made her twenty-two). Mr Griffith-Jones then asked:

'What is your father's occupation?'

It was an odd sort of question and it deserved, and got, an odd sort of answer.

'My father,' said Miss R, 'lives in Berlin.'

Mr Burge was on his feet. 'I really do not see the point of that question,' he said.

Mr Griffith-Jones's reply threw little light on the trial but was revealing of himself. 'I simply wanted to find out,' he said, '*the type of family she came from*' – and the inference here presumably was that if her dad was an architect or doctor or perhaps even a barrister, she would be less likely to succumb to Dr Ward's charms than if he were a plumber or a dustman. We were back once more in the Is-this-a-book-you-would-want-your-servants-to-read country.

'Miss X!' called the assistant clerk of the court. We waited what seemed a very long time and nothing happened. 'What has happened to your witnesses, Mr Griffith-Jones?' said the judge at the very moment that Mr Griffith-Jones must have been asking himself the same question. Miss X swam into our ken and out of it. 'Miss Marilyn Rice-Davies,' shouted the assistant clerk.

Until the proceedings at the lower court Miss Rice-Davies had been just a name. Rather a grand name, it is true, and one – like others in the case – which conjured up visions of informal weekends in comfortable country houses. ('Cynthia and I are popping down to the Rice-Davies's on Saturday. John and Paula Hamilton-Marshall are going to be there. Why don't you come too?') I wondered at what moment in history the house of Rice had decided to merge with the family of Davies, and why? Her family lived in Birmingham, in what she later called the 'exclusive suburb of Solihull'; and her father worked in a local factory. She was clearly a cut above Christine socially, and indeed her object from the beginning seemed to have been to outshine her at every stage of the game. A mixture of demureness and sauciness had marked her appearance at the Magistrates' Court. When asked by counsel if she was aware that Lord Astor had denied her statement that she had been to bed with him she said: 'Well he would, wouldn't he?'

It was the same here. Unlike Christine, who photographed better than she looked, Mandy Rice-Davies looked much better than her photographs. She was still only eighteen and had not yet lost, as Christine had, the bloom of youth. It was a hard, cat-like little face, but a very pretty one. After two years as Rachman's mistress she still looked fresh as a milkmaid, and that was quite a feat. Astride her golden head sat a little rose-petalled hat, such as débutantes wear at garden parties. Her shoes, unlike Christine's, were quite lady-like. Her simple grey sleeveless dress accentuated the impression of modesty – until one looked at it closely. Then one saw that the slit down the front was only held together by a loose knot at the middle. When she walked one could see quite a long way up her leg.

As with her appearance, so with her performance in the witness-box. It was a marriage of the brazen and the bashful. She was in turns pert, cool, innocent, tearful, giggly. Unlike Christine she was never pathetic; unlike her too she was not in the least abashed either by the company or her surroundings. She was one of the very few female witnesses one was able to hear. She smiled at Ward, at Mr Griffith-Jones, at the judge. When counsel was thinking out the next question she pouted at friends in court, gazed at the ceiling, fingered the pearl bracelet on her left wrist, or stroked one fleshy arm with the other. At one moment she was calling counsel 'Sir' from behind lowered lids, the next she was trying to split a joke with the judge. She was in short wholly unpredictable, and what made most of her evidence a matinée of suspense was that no-one, not even she, had any idea what new revelations she was about to spring on us.

Mandy too admitted to sleeping with large numbers of men while living with Ward, some as with Christine for money, others not. She also agreed with Mr Burge that the police had put considerable pressure on her to give evidence against Ward. To what extent they had done this she revealed in her memoirs published after the trial. Having twice refused police requests to make a statement about her relations with Ward, she was arrested on a motoring charge when about to leave London airport for Majorca and sent to Holloway on remand. Roused at 6 a.m. and sent to bed at 9 p.m., she described the conditions there as 'absolutely vile'.

> After a day or two of this I was ready to do anything to get out. The police came to see me and asked if I would like to reconsider my refusal to make a statement about Dr Ward. The prospect of having to spend a further spell in Holloway over the motoring offence was enough to convince me that I had better keep on the right side of the police . . .

Having been fined £42 for the motoring offence, Mandy flew to Majorca, but was met by the police on her return who wanted a further statement about Ward. She refused to give it, but they called her in a few days later and grilled her for more than four hours. About to leave for Majorca again, she was again arrested at London airport, this time on a dubious charge of stealing a television set. Released on bail of £1,000, she had her passport confiscated so as to ensure her presence at Ward's committal proceedings at Marylebone Court.

Of the trial itself Mandy said she found it a farce:

> No-one would deny that Stephen was a depraved and immoral man. But to suggest that he made a living out of it is nonsense . . . He most certainly never influenced me to sleep with anyone, nor ever asked me to.

And finally she let fall that while living with Ward, she was still receiving £100 a week from her former lover, the slum landlord Peter Rachman. Had Mr Burge had this information at the trial, the charge against Ward of living on Mandy's immoral earnings must have collapsed.

What made the evidence of the prosecution at Ward's trial of such unflagging interest was the variety of the women who had been associated with him. The four on the bench could hardly have been more different: now a new star came to grace this milky cluster in the night sky. Her name was Margaret (Ronna) Ricardo and unlike Christine and Mandy she made no pretensions about not being a tart. It would be untrue to say she was not ashamed to admit it, for clearly she was ashamed or at least unhappy about it, but admit it she did. This honesty made a welcome change. She had red hair and a pink jumper and a total lack of any sort of finesse; but after the genteel caperings of Christine and Mandy and the deadly respectability of Miss R, this also was welcome.

We had heard of Miss Ricardo before. She had given evidence at the Magistrates' Court proceedings three weeks earlier. There, among other things, she had said that she had visited Ward two or three times at his Bryanston Mews flat and on each occasion she was asked to stay behind to meet somebody. Men had arrived and she had gone to bed with them. Since then, however, she had gone to Scotland Yard to make a statement denying this. At the moment nobody knew for certain what she was going to say.

She took the oath and in answer to Mr Griffith-Jones said that she had visited Ward at his flat in Bryanston Mews with two other people, a man and a girl.

'Did you have intercourse with anybody on that occasion?'

There was suddenly a hush in the courtroom, as if we knew, as a pointer knows when he sniffs the wind, that something interesting lay ahead.

'Yes, I did.'

'Who did you have intercourse with?'

'With my boy friend.'

Miss Ricardo took a long time to answer each question and when she did, it was very quietly.

The judge said: 'What did your girl friend do?'

There was another pause, and then she said: 'She was with Stephen.'

This time it was Mr Griffith-Jones's turn to pause. Perhaps he knew what was coming. He said: 'In the other bedroom?'

Now there was a very long pause indeed. Miss Ricardo looked miserable. She tried to speak, but nothing came out. Eventually she shook her head.

'In the same room?'

No answer.

'All four of you together?'

She nodded.

'Were you all taking part together?'

Another pause while Miss Ricardo screwed up her face and bit her lip. She nodded again.

So that was it. A foursome. Who had done what to whom? A hundred imaginations ran riot. The permutations were endless. One looked at Ricardo standing so miserably in the witness-box, and at Ward sitting with dignity in the dock, and saw them naked and unashamed, like animals.

The judge said: 'I want to hear what happened in that room, the four of you together?' Good God, were we not going to be spared the awesome details? Perhaps the judge realized what he was asking, for he said quickly: 'Was there anything beyond sexual intercourse?' What did he mean *beyond* sexual intercourse? What is there beyond sexual intercourse except more sexual intercourse and variations on sexual intercourse? But Miss Ricardo shook her head.

'How many times', asked Mr Griffith-Jones, 'did you go to the Bryanston Mews flat?'

At the Magistrates' Court Miss Ricardo had said two or three times, but now she said, 'Once.'

'Miss Ricardo,' said the judge, 'I want to be quite certain about this. How many times did you go to Ward's flat?'

'Once,' she said, 'never more than once.'

Mr Griffith-Jones turned to the judge and said: 'I desire to draw your attention to statements this witness has made on her deposition and my application is for permission to treat her as hostile.'

As with Mandy's memoirs, it wasn't until after the trial that I had the full story of how and why Ronna Ricardo had given evidence incriminating Ward at the committal proceedings and yet had gone back on it at the trial. Having discovered that Ronna knew Ward, the police seized the opportunity of persuading her into making a statement against him. The bait for this was the future of her two sisters, Gwen, aged sixteen, and Dorothy, aged thirteen, who lived with her. She said that the police threatened that unless she gave evidence which they would provide, they would send Gwen, who was on probation for CND offences, to a remand home, and they would take Dorothy away, as being in need of care and protection. Prostitutes are notoriously vulnerable to police pressure and faced with these, Ronna signed a statement that she had pimped for Ward, slept with men in his flat and given him part of the proceeds. She had confirmed this at the committal proceedings, but knowing it was beyond her to repeat such lies in the full glare of Old Bailey publicity, she had publicly reneged on them before Ward's trial. She was given a rough time by Mr Griffith-Jones but refused to go back on her word, and one couldn't help but admire her courage in doing so.

Up to this moment in the trial the general feeling in court had been that although there could be little doubt that Ward was a habitual associate of prostitutes there had been nothing in the way of evidence to justify the charges of living on their immoral earnings, which, when all was said and done, was why we were here; and the impression on the Press benches that this was really a political trial, an instrument of revenge by the Establishment for the scandal caused by the exposure of Profumo, was growing all the time.

But with the calling of the name of Vickie Barrett this changed. For she was the witness for whom we had been waiting, the girl whom Mr Griffith-Jones had said in his opening speech had visited Ward's flat for a period of over two months to give sexual comfort and stimulation to a variety of men for money which she had never received. Would her performance in the witness-box bear out the promises that Mr Griffith-Jones had made of her? If it did, then as surely as the coming of night the jury would find, and rightly find, Ward guilty.

She came into the witness-box, a little whey-faced blonde, wearing a sort of green raincoat with a white scarf round her neck; and when she turned to face the court and while she was giving the oath, one's impression was one of shock: shock that Ward, whom one had believed to be a man of some fastidiousness in his tastes, had sunk so low. For of all the whores the prosecution had paraded or were still to parade before us this one was the bottom of the barrel. Christine and Mandy and even Ronna Ricardo had had a certain style, a kind of robustness, which compensated for their other deficiencies, but this little waif had nothing. She was like a little sad, sick elf, a photograph, as Rebecca West later put it, from a famine relief fund appeal. Clearly no improving influences had come to grace her life, no Professor Higgins had taken her under his wing: she was, in officers' mess parlance, a ten bob knock in the Bayswater Road. I looked at her standing so awkwardly in the witness-box, and then I looked at Ward, intelligent and sophisticated, in the dock, and I found it difficult to reconcile the two.

Vickie's evidence was electrifying. It was that at some time previously Ward had picked her up in Oxford Street, taken her back to his flat, given her a contraceptive and told her to do business with a man who was waiting in his bedroom. This she had done, and afterwards Ward told her that the man had already paid him the money for her services. During the next two and a half months she had visited Ward's flat two or three times a week to have intercourse with some men and to cane and whip others. On each occasion Ward told her that the men had given him money for her services, and he was saving it up for her; but she was never paid. Although such a story seemed entirely out of character from all one knew about Ward, Vickie gave her evidence with such quiet certainty that for a time disbelief was suspended.

For what we had just heard had fully confirmed what Mr Griffith-Jones had said in his opening speech. There had been flaws in Vickie Barrett's evidence certainly, inconsistencies and contradictions, but against the solid oak of most of it, they were quickly forgotten. She had seemed, in her soft pathetic little way, so certain: she had rarely hesitated. Somewhere deep down perhaps one felt that such a relationship as she had described was utterly out of keeping with all one had ever heard or read about Ward, that her story was a tissue of lies, a total invention. Then one dismissed such thoughts as wishful thinking. One did not like to face the truth about Ward because that meant one had been wrong in one's judgement of him. Yet one had to face it. Ward was a ponce, a pimp, a professional brothel-keeper. And by far the nastiest thing of all about him was the bit about taking the money from the men and not giving any of it to Vickie: this was meanness of an order that made one want to vomit. Surely something so detailed, so huge as this could not have been contrived. And if it was true, then the sooner he was sent down the better.

As the trial progressed it became clear from other witnesses that Vickie's story was a fabrication, but it wasn't until after the trial and Ward's suicide that we learned the reasons for it. A Daily Telegraph *journalist called Barry O'Brien visited Vickie in her lodgings, taking a copy of Ward's farewell letter to her in which he asked why she had told such lies. At first she denied having told lies but then broke down and admitted that she had been to Ward's flat but only to do business with him. Asked why she had told lies about him, she said that on the evening of the day that he was committed to trial, she had been arrested for soliciting and the police had found Ward's name and telephone number in her diary. Asked by an officer the nature of her business with Ward she said that she had whipped him. The officer then said,*

> 'Wouldn't it be better if you said that you whipped other men at the flat?' I said, 'Why should I say that?' He told me that if I didn't say that, I will never be able to show my face in Notting Hill again. He said that girls could get very heavy sentences for soliciting. He said I could get nine months or more.

The last witness of the day was a man of whom we had already heard much, whose spirit had seemed to hover, as it were, over many witnesses, yet who so far had not graced us in the flesh. This was Detective Chief Inspector Samuel Herbert. He looked like so many of his kind that it is difficult in retrospect to describe him. He was clean shaven, square built, wearing a greeny suit, and aged, I should say, between forty and fifty: in short a good family man. He looked the sort it would be useful to have in a tight corner. He did not need and was not offered any assistance in taking the oath. He picked up the Bible with the ease and familiarity of a country parson and rattled off the tautological absurdities in a voice which wearily told us that he had been this way before. He gave his evidence in the flat text-book tones in which all police officers are encouraged to give, and do give their evidence, venturing and gaining nothing, revealing nothing either. He had not grasped the first principles of spoken communication: he preferred the abstract to the concrete, the passive to the active, circumlocution to directness. Long before he lumbered into sight one knew the questions or sort of questions he would be asked and the answers or sort of answers he would give: they were as predictable as Mandy's had been unpredictable; and it was this that made his occupation of the witness-box seem like a fragment from eternity.

The next witness was Mr Herbert's henchman, Detective-Sergeant John Burrows, a spruce but melancholy blood-hound. He had a long, firm, sad face and his hair was thinning on top. He wore a natty blue pin-stripe suit with blue shirt, red tie and tie-link, and I suppose he was about thirty-five years old. I had seen him once or twice outside, puffing at an enormous pipe, a minuscule, embryonic Sherlock Holmes. Mr Griffith-Jones did not keep him long, for his first question was whether his notes were the same as Mr Herbert's. He said, a little cautiously, that they had made the notes together, whereupon the judge, who was now indulging in quite a few quips as and when the mood took him, said: 'I shall be surprised if they are *not* the same,' and we all had a good giggle.

Mr Burge asked whether Sergeant Burrows had inter-viewed Ward on certain dates, and we expected a short affirmative answer. But Sergeant Burrows was not a man to be rushed, to say mad, wild things without first checking them. He pulled a notebook from one of his pockets, but it was the wrong one. He pulled another notebook from another pocket and it was still the wrong one. He tried a third pocket and drew out a third notebook with the same result. Soon the edge of the witness-box was supporting a small monument of notebooks. It was like watching a conjuring trick that has failed to come off. Sergeant Burrows smiled a little in embarrassment and a ripple of sympathy ran round the court.

Then, from his vest, I think, he extracted another notebook. He studied it closely. 'Yes, sir,' he said.

Two more police officers followed Sergeant Burrows into the witness-box. Their names were Eustace and Glass, which seemed unlikely. They were the officers who had been detailed to keep an eye on Ward when he had been put in a room by himself after his arrival at Marylebone Lane police station. They had come to confirm what Herbert and Burrows had said about Ward sending a message that he wanted to see Herbert, rather than Ward's version of Herbert sending for him. I was sorry to see Ward dispute this, as not only did it make no difference to his case, but Herbert and Burrows' version was more believable. To put a man alone in a room immediately after his arrest is common police practice. The object of it is to quicken his desire to talk to someone as an alleviation from his loneliness and fear, and so get at the truth. Ward was gregarious by nature, and loquacious too; and I did not doubt that he wanted to speak to Mr Herbert very badly. In a way it seemed that both versions of the story could be true, i.e. that after some time Ward had sent word to Mr Herbert that he wanted to see him, and that after some more time Mr Herbert sent for him.

But Ward had disputed the matter, and as he had disputed it, here were Eustace and Glass (they sounded like a firm of estate agents) to back up Herbert and Burrows. They took their time over this, so that I was able to take stock of what was going on around me.

The central figure in the court was still Ward: yet in a curious way he seemed remote from it all, as though he, like us, was listening to the story of another person: somehow there seemed as little connection between him and the man we were hearing about as there is between the photographs of one's youth and the person one is today. He sat in the front of the dock on a hard, wooden chair, with one policeman behind and the other beside him. His eyes were focused downwards most of the time, but this was not due to shame or embarrassment, but because, to give himself something to do, he was drawing pictures of Mr Griffith-Jones and Mr Burge. Even in comparative repose he looked a very lively person.

Opposite him the judge scratched away with his pen in what looked like a vast ledger. It was odd, I thought, that modern recording techniques had not yet found a way of supplying judge and counsel with transcripts of each day's hearing. But lawyers are conservative people and innovations of this sort are anathema to them: was it not Mr Griffith-Jones earlier who had contemptuously referred to the microphone in the witness-box as 'that machine'? As it was, the scribbling often could not keep pace with the speaking, and counsel were obliged to interrupt with weird admonishments like: 'Not so fast, Miss Barrett, please, my Lord is taking a note,' which sounded like a negro spiritual. Yet old-fashioned though the note-taking may have been, it was highly effective. Hardly ever was the judge at a loss for a name, a number, a date, the smallest detail of what some witness had said perhaps two days before. With his pen and ledger and spectacles he was mole-sharp, accountant-quick. And every other day or so he would take off his spectacles for two or three minutes; and then he looked like an *old* mole, a mole gone to grass, heavy and tired and wise, full of understanding and compassion.

Immediately below the judge sat the Clerk of the Court at a little desk of his own. He also wore a wig but a yellow wig, I noticed, in contrast to the grey wigs of most other barristers, and I wondered if this denoted some peculiar hierarchical significance. There was a telephone on his desk and every now and again he used it. But where to and what for? It was remarkable how discreetly he used it. I sometimes saw his lips moving but, even when the court was at its most silent, I never heard him utter a word. In the chair on the judge's right sat a long, gangling man, who, I was told, was the judge's clerk. He pottered in and out, never staying for long, and using the opposite door to that used by the sheriff and aldermen. The sheriff himself came in occasionally and sat in the centre chair. The bench behind Mr Burge and Mr Griffith-Jones was packed with barristers, sardine-tight, some pink, some brown, all grey, the best advertisement for integration I ever saw. There was one woman among them, pink and pretty. Her hair was done in a beehive so that her wig lay vertically instead of horizontally. It made a bizarre sight.

Later Mr Griffith-Jones said to the judge: 'There is a matter on which I desire your Lordship's ruling. Might I do so in the absence of the jury?' I wondered what this was about. The judge said 'Certainly' and the jury, like prisoners in a chain-gang, shuffled out. When they had gone Mr Griffith-Jones said he wanted to talk about pornographic books, and although we were at the end of a very long morning, there was a quickening of interest everywhere. It seemed, according to Mr Griffith-Jones, that some seventeen pornographic books or pamphlets had been found. It was not at all clear where they had been found, or when, or even who had found them. I thought I heard Mr Griffith-Jones say that at one time they had been in Ward's flat, but that later he had got rid of them. Whatever the background picture Mr Griffith-Jones wanted the books to be admitted as evidence and Mr Burge didn't: they were, he said, quite irrelevant to any of the charges and would undoubtedly prejudice the jury.

After listening to both sides the judge said: 'I suppose I'd better have a look at them.' The thought that the books were close at hand and could actually be *seen* had not, I think, occurred to many of us. The atmosphere in court suddenly heightened. *The judge was going to look at some dirty pictures.* What would his reaction to them be?

A very grubby brown paper parcel was produced from what looked like the lower portion of the Clerk of the Court's desk. It was handed over to Mr Griffith-Jones who opened it and with suitable gravity picked out a book or two at random. There was not a sound in court. Mr Griffith-Jones chose three books altogether and handed them up to the judge. A hundred pairs of eyes watched the judge receive them. A hundred pairs of eyes watched him put two of the books aside and open the pages of the third. And a hundred pairs of eyes strained every optical nerve they possessed to see if they could catch a glimpse of the exhibits within. Needless to say none could. The judge's behaviour was a model of impeccability. He flipped through the pages of each book at a pace which was fast enough to avoid any accusations of indulgence and yet slow enough to obtain a general idea of the sort of stuff they contained. His face remained inscrutable. Then he made up his mind. 'I think,' he said, turning to counsel, 'that strictly speaking these books are admissible as evidence. On the other hand their effect on the jury is in my view likely to be so prejudicial that I intend to exercise my discretion and not allow them – that is, unless a particular witness is concerned with them.'

This ruling – the inadmissibility of evidence which is more prejudicial than probative – has been built into English law as a safeguard for the accused – in much the same way as Crown counsel's licence in his opening speech of making allegations against the accused which are not subsequently substantiated seems to be a sort of insurance for the prosecution. It was, in this instance, a sensible enough ruling. Although few dirty-book collectors in the land are likely also to be living on immoral earnings, Mr Burge might have had a hard job convincing the jury of it. Their experience of *erotica* (apart from the woman, who would obviously have been appalled) was likely to have been restricted to the bedside tables of tarts; and I could hear Mr Griffith-Jones's voice awakening youthful memories for them. 'For what purpose, members of the jury, was the defendant keeping these filthy books? Was it for satisfying his own depraved desires, or was it, do you think, for something far more sinister? Are not these just the sort of books that ponces supply to prostitutes as part of the goods and services of their trade, and was that not exactly what the defendant was doing?'

Later, after the trial was over, I was told that the books did not originally belong to Ward, but had been left with him by a friend who had gone abroad. But if the books had been allowed as evidence, would Mr Burge have been able to convince the jury of that? It seemed unlikely. On such hairs does justice sometimes turn.

Then it was Ward's turn. He was ushered out of the huge dock, along the well of the court and into the witness-box. He walked there with grace and a certain sort of dignity which even in his most extreme moments, he was never to lose. He took the oath firmly, resonantly; and he faced us.

Anyone who visits the criminal courts regularly knows that the man in the dock is usually the least interesting, most inarticulate of those present. Here the opposite was true. This was not simply because of the facts of the case, that such a person should be involved in such charges, but rather because of something in the man himself. One had heard of his charm and personality, and now one was experiencing them. It was difficult to pinpoint where they lay, for his features were not attractive. Mostly I think it was in the voice, a voice of quite extraordinary power, richness and resonance. When he was silent one hardly noticed him; when he was speaking, his voice transformed him, gave him life and magnetism. It was a voice which had been used to win friends and influence people – friends like Lord Astor and people like Christine Keeler. It was a voice which one could hear exhorting, persuading, demanding, and in the end having its way. It was undoubtedly his most precious asset. Now it was to be used – and no-one was more aware of this than he – in defence of his life and career.

He started off quietly enough, answering in monosyllables Mr Burge's inquiries as to his credentials as osteopath and artist. Some people can say more in monosyllables than others in whole sentences. Stephen Ward was one of them. All the time one had the impression of dammed water, banked fires. As his tenure of the witness-box went on, one realized that behind this bland exterior was a man of daemonic energy: indeed to have lived a life as full, if not as rich, as he did, to have run a successful practice, been a successful artist, and at the age of fifty to have put such frequent and unusual sexual strains on himself, called for more than ordinary endurance.

Sometimes the temptation to unbank the fires, open the floodgates, became irresistible. One felt that he had been warned beforehand that loquaciousness was his besetting sin, that if he said more in reply than the questions demanded, the jury would hold it against him. Yet clearly his whole being was crying out to speak, to explain, to justify, to see the old magic working on all of us. It was this struggle within himself to hold himself in check, to put a rein on his emotions, that made his evidence so fascinating to watch. When he did go overboard it was for one of two reasons: either he had become over-confident and felt he could afford a little levity, or else something was said which went to the very roots of his being. The first was as harmful to his case as the second was favourable. For instance he described with obvious enjoyment how Mandy had fallen down in a faint when he told her of Rachman's death: 'When she had recovered, she opened her eyes and said "Did he leave a will?"' He told the story well, but the stony faces of the jury indicated that he was not the man, and this was not the time or place, to tell it. Similarly, when asked if he had said to the police, 'Mandy is not a prostitute, she is a nice girl,' he was unwise to answer with a smile: 'I hate to think I used those words, but I may have done.' There are occasions in the witness-box when it does not pay a man to be himself, and this was one of them. Yet once when he felt goaded beyond endurance, he banged the side of the witness-box and shouted out: 'Any little tart from the streets can come forward in this court and say I am lying. Apart from this case I am considered to be a truthful person.' It was an impressive, because spontaneous, rejoinder.

On the whole he was a good witness, a little too plausible sometimes but clear and precise in most of his replies. His manners were impeccable. He addressed counsel as 'sir' and the judge as 'your lordship'. His hands were seldom idle. Often while thinking out an answer he would turn his palms upwards and look down at them, as though inspiration lay there. Sometimes while counsel was addressing him, he would brush the fingers of his left hand across the top of the witness-box, gathering invisible dust. And when he wanted to emphasize a point in his reply, he would tap the wooden surface in front of him lightly with his fingernails. But then hands had always played an important part in his life. With them he had healed the sick, sketched the famous, excited women.

When Vickie Barrett had mentioned the name of Vasco Lazzolo as a client, I wondered whether we would see him in the flesh. I thought probably not, unless he wanted to clear his name. So that when he took Ward's place in the witness-box, one had a fair idea what he was going to say. He was a square, burly man, wearing a double-breasted blue suit with a blue tie and a blue handkerchief sticking out of his breast pocket like a tent. He had greyish hair and smallish eyes for so large a face, and he looked about fifty.

He said he was a painter and sculptor and lived at Edwardes Square, Kensington. Vickie Barrett was brought into the court and Mr Burge asked Mr Lazzolo if he knew her. Mr Lazzolo glanced at her as though she had just crept out from under a stone, and then looked quickly away. 'I believe,' he said, 'that I met her once, three or four months ago.' He said this in the pained tones of one admitting to having recently had an accident in his trousers. 'I was coming out of a bar in Soho,' he went on, 'and there were two girls looking at my car. There were some drawings on the back seat of the car and they were looking at them. I had a conversation with one of them and she said that she wanted to do some modelling.' He had given her his telephone number and asked her to ring him. Later she did ring him and came along to his studio. He had intended to do some drawings of her, but he did not do so, and that was the end of the story. It was an improbable story, and it was not improved by the telling of it.

'Did you ever have intercourse with her?'

'Definitely not.'

Mr Burge then asked him about lying naked in bed in Ward's flat, and not surprisingly he said that was quite untrue. 'I have only been in Ward's flat on one occasion, at about 9.30 in the morning, and that was for less than five minutes. He was treating me as a patient. I had a twisted hip, and I came round to his flat in my car to pick him up and take him to his surgery.' (Earlier Ward had said that Lazzolo was an old friend.)

Mr Griffith-Jones asked the only relevant question which in the circumstances he could ask.

'Is there anything you have done to this girl which causes her to be spiteful towards you?'

'No, I am sure there isn't.'

'Your telephone number is in her diary next to Stephen Ward and in front of others who I gather were clients?'

'I gave her my number and she obviously put it in her book.' What did he mean *obviously*? Did he not see her write it down? And if he didn't, was he expecting us to believe that she carried the number in her head?

'You cannot help us as to why this girl should make these gross allegations against you?'

'I have no idea why she should make these gross allegations.'

Just before he left the witness-box Mr Lazzolo said, without being asked: 'May I say I would hardly have been mad enough to go round to Ward's flat at this time and behave in this manner, knowing there was a case pending against him.'

He said this with emphasis and conviction. It was the most convincing thing he said.

The defence were taking Vickie Barrett's charges seriously, as indeed they had to. For the rest of the afternoon a succession of witnesses took the stand to refute her evidence, to testify that she couldn't have been in Ward's flat at the times she said she was, because they were there themselves.

The first was an elderly author called Mr Edward Warwick, who had a green suit, a sad tortured face and a bald head. He was a loquacious man but stubborn, and not to be deflected by anyone from what he wanted to say. He and his wife had been to Wimpole Mews frequently, mainly in the evenings, and they had met other men and women there: they would not have continued going if they thought there was anything improper. He himself had often been to see Ward at Bryanston Mews. From January until the end of March he visited the flat four or five nights a week some weeks, and once or twice a week other weeks. There were often pressmen there, and he had also seen a girl called Sylvia Parker. Vickie Barrett was led into court for him to examine like a prize ewe. He said he had never seen her.

'Is it right to say,' said Mr Burge, 'there would not be people there after 12.30 in the morning?'

'Not really, because one went to the flat intending to stay half an hour, and one went on talking, talking, talking (*I could just hear him and Ward at it like a pair of old crows*). I went there intending to stay half an hour one night and stayed all night waiting to see the papers come out. Whenever one saw a light in the place one went in. There was no lock on the door.'

Then came Vickie Barrett again to be confronted with Mr Burge's accusations of some of her lies, and after her the long awaited Sylvia Parker. She was a tall willowy girl with a mass of red hair parted in the middle and wearing a smart biscuit-coloured outfit. She leaned on one of the pillars of the witness-box in a languid sort of way and thought herself very *blasé* and sophisticated. Despite a tendency to give much of her evidence down her nose, she was easily the most audible of all the female witnesses. She chattered away about boy friends and girl friends and Mayfair, and Stephen being very well known 'around town'. Her own life had been plagued with disasters: her father had been sick, her boy friend had been shot, she herself had had problems and bad publicity. She struck so many attitudes that at one moment the judge told her not to pose. In loud forthright tones she told us that she had never wanted to be brought into the case, and the only reason she had consented to appear was because 'things have been written down which are completely and utterly untrue'. She had stayed at Bryanston Mews for five or six weeks 'at about March' as a guest: she had slept on the living-room sofa and gone to bed each night at about eleven – 'a perfectly respectable time'; and she had not had any 'illicit association' with Ward. She seemed particularly anxious to defend any imputations on her virtue. She said that if Vickie Barrett's story of being brought in for sexual intercourse after 12.30 a.m. were true, she would have known of it; and she described her evidence as 'a complete load of rubbish'. All this was very convincing, but it would have been even more convincing if, as Mr Griffith-Jones was quick to point out, Mr Warwick had not just said that he was in the living room four or five nights a week into the small hours of the morning. I wondered whether Sylvia Parker had not perhaps slept chastely in Ward's room, yet for fear of misinterpretation had not liked to admit it.

It was now after four o'clock, and soon the court would rise for the day, not to meet again until Monday. The name 'Frances Brown' was called. It was an ordinary enough name and it did not make any impact. A small bird-like woman with a pale face and a fringe teetered down the court and into the witness-box. She was wearing a dark blue dress with a white bow, and I had a feeling, which turned out to be correct, that we were back in Vickie Barrett land. Yet that was all one could have foreseen.

She gave her address as Great Western Road, Paddington, and said that she had come to court because she had read the evidence of Vickie Barrett in the newspapers.

'Did you,' said Mr Burge, 'know her?'

'Yes.'

'For how long?'

'Since January this year.'

'Where were you living at that time?'

'St Stephen's Avenue.'

She was not all that easy to hear but quite definite in her answers, quite sure.

'Would you recognize Vickie Barrett if you saw her?'

'Yes.'

The prosecution's prize exhibit was led into the court for the third time that day.

'Is that the girl you are talking about?'

'Yes.'

Vickie Barrett was led out.

'Did you ever see her at an address in Leighton Road, Kentish Town?'

'Yes, a few times.'

'Did she ever come to St Stephen's Avenue?'

'I got her a place above me in St Stephen's Avenue.'

As on one or two other occasions during the trial, there was now almost complete silence in court. Everyone felt that we were on the brink of further startling revelations; and we were.

'What were you both doing during that time?'

'Soliciting.'

'Were you aware of her activities, whether they were small or great, and what she was earning?'

'She was earning about £9 to £15 a night.'

That worked out at fifty to eighty pounds a week: yet according to her own evidence she had been content to go round to Ward's flat three nights a week for two and a half months for nothing.

Mr Griffith-Jones got up and said: 'In the course of soliciting with Vickie Barrett, did you ever meet a Mr Vasco Lazzolo?'

'Yes.'

'Where did you meet him?'

'In Shaftesbury Avenue.'

'Yes, go on.'

'Well, he asked us if we'd like to go back to his flat with him, and we said we would.'

'And did you go back to his flat?'

'Yes.'

'And what happened there?'

Now there was dead silence everywhere.

'Well, he gave us a few drinks, and then Vickie Barrett did business with him.'

A long pause.

'Were you present in the room together?'

'Yes.'

Another pause.

'You saw it?'

'Yes.'

'What, if anything, did you do?'

A small pause this time, but it seemed like eternity.

'I helped.'

God, what a multitude of things those two words covered! *I helped.* It should be engraved on her tombstone. She also served who only stood and helped.

Yet even that was not all.

'Were you soliciting with Vickie Barrett regularly before the incident you have just described?'

'Yes.'

'Did you ever see her picked up in Oxford Street by Dr Ward?'

'Yes, I was with her.'

With her? There seemed no end to the coincidences.

'How many times did you see her picked up?'

'Twice.'

'Not more?'

'No.'

Well, that tied in with what Ward had said.

'Did you yourself ever visit Dr Ward's flat?'

I felt it was a question asked more as a gesture than anything else.

'Yes. With Vickie Barrett.'

The suspense was almost too much to bear. What new revelations were we going to hear now?

'How many times did you both go there?'

'Twice.'

'When was that?'

'Between the middle of March and the week the Pope died.'

It was as good a way of pinpointing it as any.

'And what happened when you were there?'

'Well, the first time Vickie did business with Dr Ward.'

'And what did you do?'

Oh, God, I thought, not helped again. But she said: 'I looked on.'

'And the second time?'

'We just had coffee.'

To sum up so far, two of the prosecution's four main witnesses, Mandy and Ronna Ricardo, admitted that the police had put pressure on them to say what they wanted, while the other two, Christine and Vickie Barrett, had been placed in positions where they were very susceptible to pressure (and one of these admitted pressure later). Ronna Ricardo agreed she had lied at the Magistrates' Court, Mandy Rice-Davies was proved to have lied, Vickie Barrett's evidence was a series of lies and Christine Keeler had also lied. The evidence of the police officers involved had been very much less than frank. Indeed, the more one looked at the prosecution's case, the more dubious a thing it appeared. I hoped the judge would open wide the windows and throw the whole mess out.

But the judge had other ideas. Until now he had been, as it were, the stage director, flitting busily about the wings, occasionally seen, sometimes heard, always felt; restraining some players, giving others their head, guiding, encouraging, admonishing, warning, impressing with his own stamp everything that was said or done. But now the principals and chorus had departed, leaving the epilogue to him alone. It was a moment, one felt, for which he had been waiting; an occasion, a personal challenge perhaps, a footnote or even a paragraph in history. He was nervous as he came out from the wings, washing his hands with invisible soap, an hygienic Heeplike mole. He knew, as we all did, that the spotlight of the world was on him. He addressed the rude mechanicals casually, conversationally; but his opening words were for other breeds than them. 'There have been, as we all know,' he said, 'repercussions arising out of what we have to investigate which have widely spread their tentacles across the public life of this country and have aroused great interest in foreign countries. One would have thought from what we have all been faced with in the national newspapers that this country has become a sort of sink of iniquity. But you and I know that the even tenor of family life over the overwhelming majority of our population goes quietly and decently on.' As he said the words one could see in his mind's eye a million telegraph wires zinging them across the world to far-away places like Cork and Alice and Dusseldorf; and, in one's own mind's eye, their arrival there with all the impact of stale and soggy bread.

His was an elfin, workaday mind: even his clichés lacked the distinction and originality of those of Mr Griffith-Jones. 'The heart of this great metropolis': 'One crowded hour of glorious life': 'a great power sometimes known as the fourth estate': 'justice is not a cloistered virtue'. And yet one could not but marvel, as in our courts I have always marvelled, at the spontaneous combustion of English prose, the creation of sentences and paragraphs, the placing of colons and commas, the effortless jam session of an English judge in the groove. He looked at the jury and his notes, rarely elsewhere; and the jury, desperate for portents to let them do the right thing (whatever that might be), looked at him. He had few mannerisms. Sometimes at the beginning, when he was still nervous, he gave his left hand, almost lost in the huge sleeve of his robe, a little shake, as a woman does to free a bracelet. His diction was orthodox: only a soft 'a' in 'example' and a long 'e' in 'period' hinted at the incubator in which he had first been hatched.

'One of the great tasks of a tribunal,' he said, 'is to seek to keep the atmosphere down as we consider the facts dispassionately,' and for an hour or so it really seemed as though this were happening. The bitter taste in the mouth left by Mr Griffith-Jones's words was slowly dispelled. The judge praised those attributes ('artistic talents of no mean quality' – 'job is to heal and make whole') he believed the defendant had; he praised too Mr Burge and Mr Griffith-Jones for their professional skills; he praised the jury for their patience. Suddenly all was summer and singing, as though we loved one another, so that it seemed almost a shame that we could not now call it a day and go home, hand in hand, to Pimm's and Shepherd's Pie. But already the judge had turned to those things to which every judge turns – the jury were the sole arbiters of the facts, they must disregard his views if they conflicted with theirs, reasonable doubts were not fanciful doubts, etc. This routine was familiar to most of us, and to the judge more than any of us; yet he made the words sound fresh and alive, as though he was saying them for the first time.

It is difficult in retrospect to say at which moment one became aware that the sun had dipped behind the hill, that the air had an evening chill to it. There is no clear dividing line in the text. Indeed the more one reads the Press accounts of the judge's summing up, the more fair and reasonable it seems. But this was yet another example of the difference between how things sounded at the time and how they read afterwards. Mr Burge read far more effectively than he sounded: Mr Griffith-Jones sounded much more hostile than he read. And now here was the judge who at the time sounded totally unsympathetic to the accused, yet who read so sweetly afterwards. When I first saw the summing up I could hardly believe I had an accurate report of it, so great was the gulf between the words and my memory of them. Yet I was certain my memory was not playing me false. I puzzled over the discrepancy for a long time, and it was not until after the trial, when I came across an account of it in – of all places – *France-Soir*, that I found the explanation. This extract is from the issue of 2 August 1963:

If Ward had not attempted suicide, we would have heard yesterday evening what he had been sentenced to by Judge Marshall who – it has to be said – despite

313

trying to appear impartial, was betrayed time and again by his tone of voice.

Mr Marshall is a puritan and Ward, who is debauched, licentious and cynical, horrified him. Undoubtedly, the final summing up of the judge was utterly impartial if one limits oneself to reading it; the arguments for the defence feature more prominently than those for the prosecution.

But every time Mr Justice Marshall explained to the jury the questions which they were going to have to answer, his voice betrayed him: Mr Marshall disliked Ward who had brought scandal to England.

When I read this and applied it to my memories of the summing up it fitted into place. It was not that the judge had omitted what was favourable to Ward – the record belied that. It was, simply, a question of emphasis. When the judge was pointing out to the jury those things in Ward's favour, he often did so in a flat matter-of-fact voice. He appeared so uninterested in what he was saying that one could not be interested oneself: the mind automatically shut off from him. Yet when he came to matters which told against Ward, his tone changed: his voice and bearing became brighter, livelier; he held the attention where elsewhere he had lost it. It was this that made the summing up sound so one-sided. Now I do not say that the judge was conscious of what he was doing, he probably wasn't; but with his puritan background, it would have been surprising if some of his own attitudes had not trickled through. Impartiality and objectivity are at best relative terms; we are all prisoners of our pasts more than we like to think.

There were two other things the judge said which, while not directly relevant to the issues before us, were immensely revealing of the judge himself. Referring to Mr Eylan as a witness who had had the courage to come forward and publicly admit to having paid Christine for her favours, the judge said: 'and in doing so, you may think, he regained his self-respect.' It was an illuminating remark and pinpointed not only the huge gulf separating Ward's world from that of the judge, but the judge's world from that of many of the rest of us. The other

remark occurred at the end of a long day, when no doubt
the judge was tired and his powers of concentration waning.
Instead of 'Marilyn Rice-Davies' he said 'Marilyn Monroe'.
The slip was interesting; for one would normally expect the
mention of such a sex-symbol in court to arouse the judicial
comment, 'And who, pray, is Marilyn Monroe?' Yet this
latter-day Harlow, this Anglo-Saxon Bardot was so far to
the front of the judge's unconscious mind that she actually
spilled over into speech. He corrected himself with a little
moley smile. 'I am going back,' he said, 'to my youth.' And
that was interesting too. For the judge was sixty-four. Marilyn
Monroe did not become a household word in England until
about 1949, at which time the judge was fifty, the same age
as Ward now. Was this what he considered his youth? (One
would have liked to hear Mr Griffith-Jones on the subject.
'Members of the jury, you have heard evidence that the
accused, Sir Archie Marshall, considered himself still in his
youth when he was fifty. And you have also heard evidence,
members of the jury, that when he was fifty, he was having
thoughts about a beautiful young film actress called Miss
Marilyn Monroe. He a man of fifty, members of the jury,
and she a young girl, lately arrived in Hollywood from the
country, and only just out of her teens. Members of the jury,
what was this man of fifty *doing* thinking about this young
girl in Hollywood? I suggest that the evil of this – and it is
evil, you may think – goes very deep . . .')

The court rose as usual at half past four. As usual Ward
was smiling, hiding from the world whatever he was feeling
inside. I never saw a man put such a brave face on things. He
chatted briefly to Mr Burge and his solicitor and when his
bail had been renewed for the last time, he left as usual by
taxi. By then his mind must have been already half made-up.
The rest of us drifted out into the street, uneasy, depressed.
Some of us were going home to work, some to dinner or the
theatre, others to books and an early bed. But Ward, already
halfway to Chelsea in his taxi, had had his fill of all these
things. Ward was going home to die.

When I went through the swing doors of No. 1 Court the
next morning, the policeman on duty said to me: 'And what

flowers will you be sending along?' I have always believed in life that when someone says something incomprehensible, it usually saves time and energy to pretend one understands. 'Oh, roses, I expect,' I said and went towards my seat. It was not until I had been there five or ten minutes that I heard the news: during the night Ward had taken an overdose of sleeping tablets and been rushed to the aptly named St Stephen's Hospital, where his condition was said to be serious but not critical. Mr Burge entered and left. The time for the sitting of the court came and went. It was rumoured that Mr Griffith-Jones was in the library, busily looking up precedents. The journalists huddled together, exchanging gossip like flies. Would the trial go on? What would happen if Ward died? Why had he been given bail last night when it was always possible that something like this would happen? Was it true that he wouldn't have been given bail if the Clerk of the Court had not gone on holiday? Did anyone know what sort of pills he had taken? Just before eleven Mr Griffith-Jones came back into court, and the two duty policemen took their places in the dock. The rude mechanicals filed in and sat down, and soon after them the judge, looking pale and nervous.

Mr Griffith-Jones outlined what had happened and said (and God knows one believed him) that there were few precedents to go by. He said that latest reports indicated that with the Bank Holiday ahead, Tuesday of the following week (it was now Wednesday) would be the earliest date on which Ward might be expected to be fit enough to appear. The judge asked Mr Burge for his views, and Mr Burge said that without Ward in court, it would be impossible for him to take instructions. The judge, looking very unhappy, said that the time for taking instructions was now past, and he therefore proposed to continue the trial until the point where the jury reached a verdict but not beyond. The fact that the case was a misdemeanour and not a felony entitled him to do this, and that when you came to think of it, was a nice little paradox in itself. The judge added: 'I give instructions that the defendant shall immediately be put under surveillance. I shall give instructions for bail to be withdrawn from now on and normal steps to be taken for greater security.' No expression of sympathy for the plight of an, as yet, innocent man, no regret: simply a bolting of the stable door after the horse had gone.

The decision to continue the trial was one which some lawyers have since contested. It seemed to them yet another example of the haste which had characterized the proceedings ever since they had started, the reflection of an official wish to get the thing over as soon as possible, to bring on a verdict which promised catharsis all round. Certainly the atmosphere in court had changed dramatically. There was a sense of anti-climax, the knowledge that Ward now had no interest in the result of the contest, not even an interest in life itself. There was talk then of his recovery, but the general consensus was that by contracting out as he had done, Ward had immeasurably lessened his chances with the jury. For over a week we had watched with admiration the way he bore his huge burden, the strength and vigour with which he met his enemies. His dynamic and lively presence in the dock was a constant reminder to the jury that it was to *this* man, to *this* fellow human before them, that they were there to do justice. But now only his ghost was there, and perhaps the jury could relax a little, as people do when the man one is talking about goes out of the room, feeling the responsibility lift from them a little, knowing that when the time came for him to hear their verdict, they would not have to endure his searching eyes. They could even ease their consciences a little – and who knows, perhaps they did? – by telling themselves that the attempt at self-destruction was in itself evidence of a guilty mind. Whether the fault was Ward's or not, his absence put him at a disadvantage. It would have been fairer, I think, to have postponed the trial until such time as he could return.

Continuing his summing up, the judge was full of implication. He referred to Ward's income of £5,500 or so a year, and after reading out some of his outgoings, suggested that the net figure must have been fairly substantially less. If the object of saying this was not to suggest that the net figure was so much less than the gross that Ward had need to supplement his income by living on immoral earnings, then I do not know what the object was. And if that *was* the object, then why not say so? He told the jury that they must disregard Ronna

Ricardo's evidence altogether, but he did ask them if 'events such as happened in the foursome would have occurred if the relationship had not been a close one'. Probably not; but the fact that the relationship was a close one did not mean that Ward was living on Ronna Ricardo's earnings. I do believe that the judge found it impossible to imagine any sort of social non-professional relationship existing between two people so superficially disparate as Stephen Ward and Ronna Ricardo. Then he came to Vickie Barrett and instead of saying to the jury that she had lied in her teeth over and over again, he asked them: 'Am I misrepresenting Barrett when I say she answered her questions quietly and straightforwardly?' Of course not: it was this that had fooled us in the first place. But not to add that she had told one whopping lie after another, not to say that the crucial parts of her evidence were wholly unsupported by other evidence, this surely was a deficiency in the summing up.

We went to lunch just after one o'clock. After lunch the judge quickened his pace a little, as though he were running behind time and had received orders to have everyone out by nightfall. Unbelievably the two policemen who had been guarding their non-existent prisoner in the dock all morning were still stoically sitting there in the afternoon. I suppose it had not occurred to anybody to remove them.

The judge dealt with Counts 4 and 5 and told the jury that they must only convict on Count 4 if they were thoroughly satisfied with the evidence. Miss X, he said, 'never fell to the sexual blandishments of Stephen Ward', which brought Mr Burge to his feet to say that she had never said that Ward had made any blandishments. Well, said the judge, the jury would decide whether there had been blandishments or not. At 2.34 his marathon solo came to an end. His closing words were in character. 'The ball,' he said to the jury, 'is in your court.'

The ball remained in their court all afternoon and early evening. When they had gone, the Press benches emptied reluctantly, as though hostile to this break in the customary routine. I went downstairs to the canteen for a cup of coffee and sat at a table next to Mr Herbert and half a dozen other officers. Mr Herbert said to one of them: 'You've got to take the dirty books to Lord Denning.' The afternoon passed slowly. In the hall outside No. 1 Court we formed into little groups like strands of seaweed in the tide, drifted apart, came together again. The lawyers said they had never known such a hum of conversation while awaiting a verdict and that if Ward had been in court, it would have been much quieter. We talked, walked, sat down, got up, telephoned, yawned, made notes. A man from one of the dailies organized a sweepstake on the time the jury would return. The tickets were a shilling each and I bought two, at 4.17 and 5.17.

But it was at five o'clock exactly that we heard they were on their way back. As we scampered for the doors I became aware that my heart was pounding: this was the moment for which we had been waiting for eight long days. I looked closely at the jury while they were taking their seats. Two of the younger members were talking together and smiling, and the woman was smiling too. Did this mean that they had cleared Ward on all counts? The judge came in, and was handed a note. Now there was a cold silence not a sound anywhere. The judge said: 'I have received a note from the jury. I haven't read it. I will just read it and pass it to both of you.' It was a very long note covering two pages, and it took the judge about three minutes to read. There was no sound, no movement, all the time he was reading. I looked at the jury to see what their faces were saying: they said nothing. At last the judge finished the note and handed it down to Mr Griffith-Jones. He put it on the little table in front of him and he and Mr Corkrey read the note together, standing up. Then he passed it on to Mr Burge and he read it too, and during all this time, which must have been about seven or eight minutes, the silence was unbroken.

Yet when it was broken, it was something of an anti-climax. For it turned out that the jury did not fully understand the position about establishing the fact of prostitution and the shifting of the burden of proof. With great care the judge explained it to them. Then he said that he understood that the jury wanted some refreshment. He would give orders for this, *but they would have to pay for it themselves to avoid any suspicion of favours.* When I heard this I was sorry Ward was not with us. He liked a good joke and this, I think, would have delighted him.

So we all went away for another two hours, and paced up and down outside and smoked and gossiped and generally tried to forget the deep depression that was stealing over many of us. And then, soon after seven o'clock, we heard that the jury were coming back for the second time. Inside the court I looked at their faces as they filed into their seats, and from the suitable solemnity on all of them – quite different to when they had reappeared for the first time – I knew that on at least one count they had found Ward guilty.

'Members of the jury, are you agreed upon your verdict?'

'We are.' This was said by a little man with pink cheeks, rimless glasses and (so far as one could see) no eyes.

'And how say you on Count 1?' (Living on the immoral earnings of Christine Keeler.)

'Guilty.'

'Count 2?' (Living on the immoral earnings of Mandy Rice-Davies.)

'Guilty.'

'Count 3?' (Living on the immoral earnings of Vickie Barrett and Ronna Ricardo.)

'Not guilty.'

'Count 4?' (Procuring.)

'Not guilty.'

'Count 5?' (Procuring.)

'Not guilty.'

The guilty verdicts came as a shock. In the light of the whole course and conduct of the trial, they were, I suppose, inevitable, but they were not the verdicts I or the people around me would have given, and the saying of them was quite numbing. The judge, business-like as ever, said he would wait until Ward was physically ready to appear in court, and he would then come back and deal with him. The two charges concerning abortion would stand over until the next session ('I feel we have all had enough'). He thanked the jury for their attendance and excused them further service for twenty years ('That may let some of you out altogether'). And then, almost before one was aware of it, he was on his feet and through the door and gone.

Slowly, wearily, the court emptied. Papers were shuffled into pockets, pipes and cigarette packets fondled, ties adjusted, glasses put on and taken off. We pushed open the swinging glass doors for the last time and spilled out into the hallway. High up on the wall I read: 'Right lives by law, and law subsists by power.' You could certainly say some of that again. We pushed on along the hallway like a sort of ragged army, separate but together, each alone with his thoughts yet driven, I think, by a common purpose, which was to get away from that place as quickly and decently as possible. We went down the great marble staircase and out into the evening street. As I remember it, nobody said anything. It wasn't surprising. There wasn't, then, anything more to say.

The trial ended on Wednesday 31 July, and for the next three days Ward lay in St Stephen's Hospital, hovering between life and death, unaware of the verdict against him. He must have had a strong constitution, for he did not die until the Saturday afternoon. His death was not a great tragedy, for he had brought too much on himself; yet there were many people in Britain who, on hearing the news, felt a little ashamed, a little diminished. For a man who loved life as much as he did, it was a miserable end; but an end to agony too, peace from a persecution which would have broken many people earlier. His had not been a morally good life, nor a fulfilled one, but I do not think even in the loosest sense of the word that he was a criminal. He surrounded himself with girls for pleasure, not profit; some were already profligate, others not; but there is no evidence that he ever forced anybody to do anything against their will. If John Profumo had not lied to the House of Commons it is unlikely we would ever have heard of him.

Since the trial many people have asked who it was who was responsible for Ward's persecution. I think the answer lies not in the specific orders of any one person but in the spontaneous actions of many. When the establishment closes its ranks, when authority takes arms against what it mistakenly believes to be a sea of corruption, there is no need for the posting of battalion orders. Within the hierarchy each

321

member knows what is required of him, what he must do; and during the long investigation and trial each man did it. The proceedings against Ward had a certain inevitability. Once put into motion, they gained a momentum of their own which it subsequently became impossible to stop.

In September Lord Denning's Report on the affair was published as a White Paper, and turned out to be a racy, readable and in parts rather nasty document. It was nasty in a number of ways. There were several occasions when Lord Denning could not resist the temptation to regale his readers with gossipy titbits of the women's magazine variety which had no bearing on his brief at all. For instance, he informed us in detail of how and where Mr Profumo had told his wife that he had been lying. It was in Venice. ' . . . they had a quiet dinner first. After dinner Mr Profumo told his wife the truth – for the first time – that he had had an illicit association with Christine Keeler. He told her all the details. They talked over it most of the night. Mrs Profumo said, "Oh darling, we must go home now just as soon as we can and face up to it".' It is difficult to read those words without acute embarrassment; one would have thought that Lord Denning might have spared the Profumos the revelation of personal intimacies which were the concern of them and nobody else, and did not help the inquiry at all. It was also unnecessary, one would have thought, to publish the detailed account that Christine Keeler gave of the inside of Profumo's house. ('The stairs bend to the left and on the wall is a picture, of all the things that Valerie likes and dislikes including pigeons and jewellery' . . . 'there were a lot of mirrors in the bathroom,' etc.) Lord Denning's excuse for publishing this tittle-tattle and embarrassing the Profumos further is that 'she described the house so exactly that one would think it was not likely to have been invented.' But no responsible person publicly suggested that the incident was invented. It was not in public controversy, and even if it had been, it had nothing to do with the matters to which Lord Denning had been asked to apply himself. It was gossip and nothing more. A last example of the somewhat curious quality of Lord Denning's mind occurred in paragraph 58 of the Report where he referred to a photograph of Christine Keeler in the *News of the World* of 3 February and said that most people seeing it 'would really infer the avocation of Christine Keeler'. The photograph showed Christine posing in a swimsuit, but it was presumably not that avocation that Lord Denning had in mind. What he had in mind, one imagines, was the avocation of being a whore. But there are many girls who earn a living by posing in swimsuits, and to assume that all of them, or even most of them, are also necessarily whores, seems to me to be assuming rather too much. This was another indication, if any were needed, of how remote from the rest of us are the worlds in which some judges live.

But the nastiest part of the Report concerned Lord Denning's assessment of the characters in the story. In a high-falutin' introduction he announced the high principles by which he would be guided. Where the facts were beyond controversy, he said, he would state them as objectively as he could, irrespective of the consequences to individuals; but when the facts were in issue, he would always remember the cardinal principle of justice – that no man was to be condemned on suspicion. 'The interest of justice to the individual,' he wrote, 'overrides all other.' As far as the living were concerned Lord Denning carried out this noble precept faithfully. He went to some pains to tell us that Profumo was loyal to his country, which few had ever seriously doubted. He told us that Lord Astor had done sterling work for hospitals, refugees and charities, which was no doubt true, but irrelevant to the matter in hand. Even Christine Keeler was not to be judged too harshly because of her youth: at the time she had not been sent to prison for perjury.

But with the dead it was a different matter. When it came to discussing Ward, Lord Denning's flowery phrases about justice to the individual and not condemning on suspicion flew smartly out of the window. Ward, he said, 'procured girls of 16 or 17 to be mistresses for his influential friends'. Did Lord Denning not know that despite interviewing nearly 140 witnesses, the police had only found enough evidence to bring two charges of procuring against Ward, and on both of these the jury had found him not guilty? 'Ward,' he went on, 'also catered for those of his friends who had perverted tastes. There is evidence that he was ready to arrange for whipping and other sadistic performances.' The only evidence that had been produced at his trial to support this allegation had been that of Vickie Barrett, and on that charge also the jury had found him not guilty. Finally Lord Denning stated that Ward 'was known to be involved in a call-girl racket' – known, that is, by the Security Service. They must have known something that other people did not know, for no evidence of a 'call-girl racket' as such was produced at Ward's trial.

When I read these allegations of Lord Denning's about Ward, I was astonished. I assumed that the only possible explanation of them was that Lord Denning had heard fresh evidence for which there had been corroboration, and that if only this fresh evidence had been produced at the trial, Ward would have been found guilty of several more charges. So I telephoned one of the officials who had assisted Lord Denning in his inquiry. To my further astonishment he told me that in fact there had been no fresh evidence (in the sense of evidence from witnesses whom the police had not already seen) and that most of the allegations about Ward *had been supplied by Christine, Mandy and other prosecution witnesses.* I asked for the source of the allegation about Ward arranging whipping parties, and I could hardly believe my ears when he said, 'Vickie Barrett.' I pointed out that these and other allegations had not been proved at Ward's trial, to which he said, 'Well, I daresay we were a bit unfair to Ward there. We were under a lot of pressure, as I expect you know, and we didn't really have time to read the report of the trial in detail.' We have reached an odd state of affairs in England when a judge with the reputation of Lord Denning can state hearsay as fact, and in the same breath as it were, say that he would never do any such thing. The Denning Report was criticized for whitewashing the living: a less attractive feature of it was that it also defamed the dead.

In 1966 the family moved to Scotland, and it was there, a few years later, that another miscarriage of justice came my way. After I had spoken in Lord McLeod of Fuinary's Rectorial debate at Glasgow University, I travelled back to Edinburgh in the train with another of the speakers, the advocate Nicholas Fairbairn. Knowing of my interest in miscarriages of justice, he said, 'Tomorrow morning I have to make my closing speech in defence of a man who is on a murder charge and whom I know for certain to be innocent.'

The man was Patrick Meehan, and after he was convicted and sentenced to life imprisonment, clearing his name became the subject of my next book, A Presumption of Innocence. I have told his story and my involvement in it at some length in my autobiography, On My Way to the Club. After seven years' imprisonment he was granted a free pardon and subsequently compensation of £50,000.

Although at this time I had decided that I did not want to look into any further miscarriages of justice, another one landed in my lap that I found impossible to refuse. One morning I received a letter from my literary agent enclosing a handwritten manuscript of some 100,000 words written by a prisoner named David Cooper, then completing ten years of a life sentence for murder, and passionately declaring his innocence in any part of it. On making further enquiries I found that Cooper's alleged partner in the murder, one Michael McMahon, had also written a manuscript of similar length (though fortunately typed), and equally vehement in his protestations of innocence.

These were the facts of the case. A four-man gang had descended on the manager of a Luton sub-post office after he had locked up, and demanded his keys. A shotgun held by one of the gang had accidentally gone off and killed him. One of the gang, an ageing villain named Mathews, was subsequently apprehended but refused to name his accomplices. The officer in charge of the case, a Commander Drury of Scotland Yard, then put a proposition to Mathews: to turn Queen's evidence by giving the names of three innocent men supplied to him by Drury (all petty thieves) as his accomplices, in return for which he himself would not be prosecuted and would share with Drury £2,000 of the reward money offered by the Postmaster General, John Stonehouse (later to be imprisoned himself). And this is exactly what happened. It was by far the most shocking of all the cases I have ever looked into, for whereas most miscarriages are the result of police officers deluding themselves into thinking that they have found the right man, Commander Drury knew from the beginning that Cooper and McMahon were innocent.

What made the story so very much worse was that the case of Cooper and McMahon was considered by the Appeal Court no less than a record five times, twice on referral back by the Home Secretary: the judges, of whom the worst offenders were Lord Justices Lawton and Roskill, simply could not see that the evidence of the villain Mathews was a tissue of lies.

In the end but not before time, justice was done. My book on the case, Wicked Beyond Belief, to which Lord Devlin (who had some harsh things to say about the conclusions of Lawton and Roskill) and Bryan Magee (Cooper's MP) also contributed, was first seen by the Permanent Secretary to Lord Hailsham, the Lord Chancellor, to whom I had sent a copy. The Secretary was so disturbed by it that he passed it on to the Registrar of Criminal Appeals. From there it went to the Under Secretary for Crime in the Home Office with the result that within three weeks of publication Willie Whitelaw, the Home Secretary, announced that after discussions with Lord Lane, the Lord Chief Justice, he had ordered Cooper and McMahon to be released unconditionally from prison. He added that this was not a case for a free pardon, as there was no proof that the two were innocent. This was nonsense, but it wasn't until I met Willie on holiday that I learned the true reason. 'I wanted to recommend a free pardon,' he said, 'but the Lord Chief Justice was against it.' And so, because Lord Lane had interfered (no doubt to protect the wretched Lawton and Roskill) in a matter in which he had no business, and Willie Whitelaw had lacked the strength to stand up to him, Cooper and McMahon, without a pardon or any monetary compensation for eleven wrongful years in prison, were released into the world to be branded ever afterwards as convicted murderers.

THE AIRMAN AND THE CARPENTER

*IN SEPTEMBER 1981 I was in New York on a BBC assignment.
One morning early while awaiting the arrival of orange juice
and coffee, I was flicking through the various television
channels when my attention was held by an item on the
NBC Today show: an elderly woman with a German accent
declaring with passion to her interviewer that her husband
was innocent of the crime for which he had been executed
forty-five years before. Before long I realized that the woman
was Anna Hauptmann, widow of the man whose haggard,
anguished face, filling the front page of British newspapers
on the day after his arrest, had been one of my earliest and
most vivid childhood memories.*

*The more I listened to Anna Hauptmann the more con-
vinced I was that she was telling the truth. It was clear
that she and her husband had been very close and had
she known him to have been the kidnapper and murderer
of the Lindbergh baby that a New Jersey jury had claimed
him to be, it was inconceivable that nearly fifty years later
she would have wanted to appear before the public to assert
so vehemently and persuasively his innocence.*

*Although (as I have said before!) I had not intended to
write any more books about miscarriages of justice, I was
immediately fired to look into the case; and in 1982 my
documentary film on it,* Who killed the Lindbergh baby?, *was
broadcast in Britain and the United States, and in 1985 my
book on it,* The Airman and the Carpenter, *was published.*

*The story opens on the eve of Lindbergh's epic solo flight
across the Atlantic in 1927.*

On the evening of 20 May 1927 Charles Lindbergh, then aged
twenty-five, was on his way to Broadway with some publicity
people to see a musical. Before entering the theatre, one of

the party telephoned the weather bureau and was told that conditions over the Atlantic, which had been thick for the last few days, were now clearing. At once Lindbergh returned to the field to make preparations for a dawn departure.

When dawn came it was still drizzling. The runway was sodden, the plane was carrying a thousand pounds more than ever before, the moisture on the fuselage made it even heavier, the engine was running below maximum revolutions because of the damp, and as he reached the start of the runway the wind changed direction from ahead to behind. It was going to be touch and go but, as he said, nothing could be accomplished without taking a chance. He signalled the chocks away and started off down the runway, the wheels sluggish on the waterlogged ground. Halfway along, the wheels became airborne briefly, dropped back into the wet, lifted again, dropped again, lifted a third time, rose a little higher and a little more and cleared the telephone wires at the end of the runway by twenty feet. It would be 3,500 miles and thirty-three hours later when they touched land again, in the heart of the French capital.

No need to retell the story of the flight, for no-one has done it better than he.[1] It was an epic on many levels. First the boldness of it, the sheer effrontery of this boy of twenty-five who looked eighteen, relying on his skills and the endurance of his frail craft to take him where no-one had been before. It was an odyssey like that of the heroes of antiquity, a voyage into the uncharted – into a tunnel of darkness and storm, cold and turbulence, hallucinations and exhaustion – all of which he overcame to emerge into a daylight that was both real and metaphorical, purified and strengthened by the ordeal.

Of course he wasn't the first to fly the Atlantic. The British airmen Alcock and Brown had done it in their twin-engined bomber eight years earlier. But they could prod each other into wakefulness, and in any case had travelled only half Lindbergh's distance, taking off from St John's, Newfoundland and crash-landing in a bog in Ireland. When Lindbergh passed over Newfoundland he had already been airborne *ten hours*.

[1] *The Spirit of St Louis* by Charles A Lindbergh.

To win the Orteig Prize Lindbergh didn't have to fly to Paris. The rules said the shores of France, and nobody would have thought any the less of him if, after two days and a night in the air, he had put his plane down before dark in some convenient field in Normandy or Brittany.

But he knew it had to be Paris. It was where the crowds were, and where he was expected; a night landing at Le Bourget among cheering crowds would be – and in the event was – a dramatic end to the most dramatic of journeys. Psychologically it was right too that an emissary of the New World should make his touchdown in the capital of the Old, the continent from whose loins America was formed, the matrix of her people. So the journey was as much into the past as the future; home-leaving and home-coming at one and the same time.

It was right too that it should have been an American and not a European to blaze this particular trail. Europe had had its fair share of pioneering explorers: Stanley and Burton, Scott and Amundsen, Nobile and Andrée, Eckener and Blériot. Now an American could join their company. And the craft in which he had done it symbolized, more than any other, the new technology with which America was soon to lead the world.

And finally there was the realization, by only a handful then, but later by increasing numbers, that the flight had altered irrevocably the way people looked at the map. Abroad, at one stroke, seemed no longer unattainable and mysterious, the province of sailors and adventurers, artists and the rich. Abroad was at hand, or soon would be: soon, it was said, no place on earth would be further from any other by more than a matter of hours.

No wonder America, and Europe too, took Lindbergh to their hearts. In an age of hedonistic materialism he had shown courage and self-denial of a high order; in an age of corporations and committees he had acted alone. From afar people worshipped him for having done and been what they would have liked to do and be and never would, and so made of him a kind of god. The gangling mechanic from the backwoods of Minnesota had gone for ever. Henceforth he would walk in glory and sup with presidents and kings.

*

The world in which Anne Morrow grew up could hardly have been more different to that of Charles Lindbergh. Although Dwight Morrow had come from modest beginnings, he had since prospered, especially as senior partner in J.P. Morgan, the international bankers. He kept a house and staff at Englewood, New Jersey, just across the river from New York; he had a summer home, Deacon Brown's Point, on North Haven Island off the coast of Maine, and an apartment in New York.

In the year that Lindbergh flew the Atlantic Anne was twenty-one, though she looked younger. She was, according to one biographer, 'a tiny brunette with an elfin figure and an air of shy fragility which was apt to bring out the protective instincts of everyone who met her, men and women alike . . . It was a joke in the family that though she presented herself as a timid mouse to the outside world, in fact she had the courage of a tigress, plus a dogged determination that was not prepared to let anything or anyone stand in her way when she wanted something badly enough.' She had oval features, a high forehead and a warm, generous mouth that was not without a hint of self-mockery.

She was then in her third year at university, having followed in her mother's footsteps to Smith College at Northampton, Massachusetts. The historic date of 21 May does not appear in her diary, and absorbed as she was in books and music and college life generally, it is clear that the flight made little impact. She spent the summer vacation at North Haven, swimming, sailing, reading, writing observations on flowers, birds, the weather. She read Chekhov, Proust, Plato, and visited her neighbour Helen Choate to hear her play Brahms and César Franck. And yet she was dissatisfied. 'I want to write – I want to write – I want to write, and I never, never will. I know it and I am so unhappy and it seems as though nothing else mattered . . . I wish someone would tell me brutally, "You can *never* write *anything*. Take up home gardening."'

On his return to America Lindbergh met many of the leading public figures of the day, among them the million- aire Harry Guggenheim who gave Lindbergh the use of a suite in his mansion on Long Island to complete his first book on the flight, *We*; and it was here that Lindbergh and Dwight Morrow met for the first time. Morrow had just been appointed American ambassador to Mexico City, and because relations between the US and Mexico were then at a low ebb, Morrow invited Lindbergh to make a goodwill flight there, and stay with him and his family over Christmas. Lindbergh accepted.

Anne's first diary entry in Mexico is a preparation for what is to come. 'This was to be an objective diary. It stops here! I don't care how much I rave, if only I could get down to keep a little the feeling of what has happened in the last week. I wish to heavens I had written it down as it happened, but I was too moved – and too ashamed of my emotion.' Still in a state of turmoil a week later, she tried to recreate her reactions as they occurred.

The train had reached Mexico City in the evening, and she and her sister Elisabeth were met by their father and other sister Constance. He told them of Lindbergh's arrival. Anne was a little annoyed – 'all this public hero stuff breaking into our family party . . . a nice man, perhaps, but not at all "intellectual" and not of my world at all, so I wouldn't be interested. I certainly was *not* going to worship "Lindy" (that *odious* name) anyway.'

At the embassy a red carpet had been rolled out, with officers at attention lining the steps and her mother and a group of people at the top. She heard her mother say, 'Colonel Lindbergh, this is my eldest daughter Elisabeth,' and looked, and saw 'a tall, slim boy in evening dress – so much slimmer, so much taller, so much more poised than I expected. A very refined face, not at all like those grinning "Lindy" pictures – a firm mouth, clear, straight blue eyes, fair hair and nice colour. Then I went down the line, very confused and overwhelmed by it all. He did not smile – just bowed and shook hands.'

She was in love already. 'He is very, very young and was terribly shy – looked straight ahead and talked in short direct sentences which came out abruptly and clipped. You could not meet his sentences – they were statements of fact, presented with such honest directness; not trying to please, just bare simple answers and statements, not trying to help a conversation along. It was amazing – breathtaking. I could not speak. What kind of boy was this?'

In the New Year Lindbergh took Anne on a visit to the Guggenheims. He left for Roosevelt Field to fetch the plane while the Guggenheims horrified her with tales of 'Slim's' practical jokes. Presently a silver-winged biplane skimmed over the trees and landed in a field. He showed her how to operate the controls, and then they were up, and she tried to fly a little and couldn't and loved every moment of it. And on the way home she found what she had found that morning, that she could now be quite natural with him, that she didn't feel afraid of him or worship him any more, that he was no longer a Norse god but a dear, gentle, considerate man.

After that it was a question of time. There were more flights and more visits to Englewood, and exchanges of views on a thousand things, some of which she confided to her diary or in letters to Constance. 'He was very cautious,' she told an interviewer years later, 'and sometimes it was very irritating. Even in a car he'd check all the instruments and the tyres. You felt he was over-careful, but then I remembered that in the air he had to be.' And then the press (who had earlier reported the Colonel engaged to Elisabeth) found out, and the family had to be more secretive than ever, referring to him in their letters as Boyd (a character in a magazine short story based on him). There were also moments of doubt. 'He never opens a book, does he?' she wrote to Constance. 'How that separates him from our world. Oh, I am afraid, terribly afraid. I do not want to see him again. It is terribly upsetting, liking someone so utterly opposed to you.' In fact it was the wish of each to explore and understand each other's world that became the core of their relationship.

He joined her in Mexico in November. They flew only once, but for Anne it was an unforgettable experience; a journey far into the interior, over pine forests and green gorges and rivers, meeting the snows on the western side of Popocatepetl and spiralling up to 17,000 feet to peer down at the smoking crater on top. This was what flying gave you, a passport to the secret places of the earth, to a world as far removed from the pages of Proust and T.S. Eliot and Virginia Woolf as you could imagine. She was aware too of what cross-country train travellers experience on a lesser scale, 'the immeasurable chasm between *us* and *it* . . . the contrast of being so perilously near and so impossibly far away at the same time.'

And doubts were melting day by day. In a letter to the frail Elisabeth, convalescing on Long Island from the heart condition from which she would never fully recover, she wrote: 'He is much more like us than you could imagine . . . amazingly understanding, sees far outside of his world, even into ours.' And she admitted frankly, 'As you can see, I am completely upset. He is the biggest, most absorbing person I've ever met . . .'

She was home for Christmas and for the huge New Year party for nearly a thousand guests to celebrate the move into Next Day Hill, their new fifty-acre Englewood home, with its pine panelling, pile carpets, Hoppners and Raeburns. And early in the New Year she was writing to her old friend Corliss Lamont, son of her father's partner in J.P. Morgan, Thomas Lamont, 'Apparently I am going to marry Colonel Lindbergh . . .'

They were married in May 1929 at the house in Englewood where their son was born on 22 June 1930, his mother's twenty-fourth birthday. In the American fashion, he was named Charles Augustus after his father and grandfather. 'When I first saw it,' Anne told Mrs Lindbergh, 'I thought, "Oh dear, it's going to look like me – dark hair and a nose all over its face." But then I discovered what I think is Charles's mouth, *and the unmistakable cleft in his chin.'* A month later she was writing to Elisabeth of her great happiness and of how Charles had been 'understanding, patient, dear beyond words'. The baby was 'such fun now' and gaining weight. 'Every day I hold him once or twice and talk to him, his eyes – very big and blue – look at me and then he smiles and opens up his face as Charles does.' In August she was reading baby-care books which advised against over-fondling. 'I don't want to "fondle" him at all,' she told her mother, 'so perhaps there's something wrong with me . . . And he doesn't like "fondling" but kicks and knocks his fists about, so perhaps there's something wrong with him! But he enjoys being talked to and he is curious and attentive.'

By the end of September, after much searching, she and Charles bought a piece of land on which to build a house. It lay on a hill a few miles from Hopewell in the Sourland Mountains of New Jersey, twenty minutes by car from Princeton and two hours from New York. It was surrounded by woods – oak and sassifras and dogwood – had a fine rolling view, and there was a field in front on which to land a plane. Meanwhile they rented a small farmhouse with white palings five minutes from Princeton from which they could supervise the building of the house and Charles could commute to New York by train. Anne was thrilled. 'Our own home – imagine it!' she wrote to her mother-in-law, and asked advice on how to run a house.

Thoughts of the baby were paramount. 'It almost breaks my heart,' she wrote to Constance, 'when I get back from the city late, after six, and from the far corner of the main road I have watched for the light in his window to see if he is still awake, and I see that it is dark, and I know he has been put to bed and I will not get one of those eyes-squeezed-up-smiles until ten o'clock.' And she finished another letter to her sister, 'I must go and get my fat lamb, who is sleeping in the barn . . . He has a blue sweater suit on and lifts his arms for you to pick up, and laughs when C takes him ceiling flying.'

The next year Charles and Anne Lindbergh made a proving flight to China via Hudson's Bay, Alaska, Siberia and Japan, leaving the baby and his Scottish nanny, Betty Gow, at North Haven. In October these last two moved to Englewood and it was there that parents and son were reunited after their trip had been cut short by the news of Dwight Morrow's death. Anne found him what contemporary photographs confirm: 'a strong, independent boy swaggering around on his little firm legs', not recognizing his parents after so long an absence, yet not afraid of them either. She sometimes took to referring to him as Charlie to avoid confusion with his father. His father adored him, gave him titbits of cornflakes and jam from the breakfast table, tossed him playfully in the air which the boy enjoyed so much he came running to his father with outstretched arms, crying 'Den!' (Again!) Every night he took his grandmother Lindbergh's toy lamb or pussycat to bed with him, hid it under the bedclothes, then like some artful conjuror pulled it out with shouts of glee. He was less certain about a duck which quacked when pulled: he laughed at the noise but shied away from pulling it himself.

The house at Hopewell was almost complete and Anne took her mother, Elisabeth and Charlie to spend a night there. Inviting Mrs Lindbergh to stay, she wrote, 'We're not going to make much of Christmas, except for the boy.' The doctor had said he needed a haircut – 'but I don't want to cut his curls off till you see him'. She added: 'He has great fun with his father. C says, "Hi, Buster!" to him whenever he sees him, so the other day when Charles came into the room, the baby looked up and said, "Hi! Hi!" and . . . when C left the room, the baby said, "Hi all gone!"' And he could now say 'P'ease' for 'Please' and 'Da-da' for 'Thank you'.

Early in the New Year of 1932 they began to use Hopewell regularly for weekend visiting, although some of the furniture was borrowed and temporary, and there were no curtains to the windows. This meant that at night, until the shutters were drawn, anyone could approach the house through the woods and observe what was happening inside; and the location and development of 'the eagle's eyrie' had been well publicized in the press.

Set in 500 acres of woodland and meadow, the house was approached from a narrow country road by a half-mile winding drive. It was a modest establishment, one oblong central section flanked by two small wings and made of fieldstone with a whitewash finish; from it there was a pleasant view across open country to the south.

The interior was fussy and a little gloomy; many small rooms and a plethora of doors and closets. The nursery, situated above Lindbergh's study, had three windows: a long one facing south and two smaller ones with square panes facing east. The wallpaper was of toy trees, a church, a man with a dog, while between the two east windows was a fireplace with Dutch tiles (still there today) of a fisherman, a windmill, an elephant and a boy with a hoop. On the mantelpiece and beneath the two sconces (also there today) stood a large ornamental clock. Against the wall opposite was Charlie's crib with its tapered wooden bars – what they called a fourposter cot; beside it, to keep out draughts, was a pink and green screen with pictures of farmyard animals.

On the last weekend of February the Lindberghs were at Hopewell again. They were due to return to Englewood on the Monday (Anne knew how much her mother dreaded Mondays, the day her father had died), but as Charlie had a nasty cold, Anne chose to stay over at Hopewell until Tuesday, 1 March. By the Tuesday Charlie's cold was no better, so she decided to stay that night too, and rang Englewood for Betty Gow to be sent over by car to help her look after him. This decision was taken on the spur of the moment. Charlie had never spent a Tuesday night at Hopewell before.

Tuesday was bleak and cold, and for most of the day the rain swept steadily across the Sourland Mountains. Beyond the house the dogwood trees in winter white looked like an army of dripping, ragged ghosts. It cleared a little in the afternoon, and Anne went for a walk. On return she stood outside Charlie's nursery window and threw a pebble against it to attract his attention. Betty Gow came to the window holding Charlie, and when he saw his mother he waved and she waved back.

In the evening the rain stopped altogether, but then the wind rose and it blew most of the night. Betty took Charlie down to the living room to play with his mother, while she went to the staff sitting room for tea. Later Anne would write how glad she was that she had spoiled him that weekend when he was sick, had taken him on her lap and had rocked and sung to him.

Shortly before six Betty took him upstairs. She read to him, then gave him his supper, a plate of cereal which he ate at a little maple table, surrounded by his toys. When Anne came in, the two women prepared him for bed. Betty put drops in his nose and Vick's ointment on his chest, and wrapped him in a little flannel shirt stitched with blue Silko thread that she had run up specially to keep out the cold. On top of this was put a sleeveless wool shirt, diapers and rubber pants and, to cover everything, a Dr Denton's one-piece sleeping suit. It seems a lot of clothing for so small a child, but they were anxious to protect him from further cold.

For the same reason, having put him in the crib, they fastened two large safety pins through the sheets, blankets and mattress at the head of the bed, to prevent him kicking off his bedclothes during the night. They placed the pink and green draught screen at the head of the bed, but opened the south window a little to let in fresh air. They closed the two east windows, also two of the three green lattice shutters – but the shutters outside the window to the right of the fireplace had become so warped they would not shut. They were the only warped shutters in the house, and had been that way for at least three weeks; no-one had thought to have them fixed.

As Charlie dozed off, Anne went down to the living room to write while Betty moved to the bathroom next door to wash some of his clothes. At eight she returned to the nursery and satisfied herself that Charlie was sleeping peacefully; then she went to the staff sitting room for supper. At about 8.35 the Colonel arrived from New York and, after hearing from Betty as he passed through the house that his son was better, joined his wife in the living room.

Between 8.35 and 9.20, said Anne, she and Charles were having dinner in the dining room. They then went into the living room for five or ten minutes, and while there Charles heard, above the moaning of the wind, a sharp crack, like (as he described it later) 'the top slats of an orange-box falling off a chair' and which he presumed came from the kitchen. Then they went upstairs to run baths. By this time Betty Gow and the housekeeper, Elsie Whately, were also upstairs in Elsie's room, looking at her new dress.

At ten Betty broke off her discussion with Elsie to take Charlie on his final visit to the bathroom. On entering the nursery she did not switch on the light, so as not to startle him, but she closed the south window and turned on a heater to take the chill from the room. Standing in the dark and warming her hands, she began to sense that something was amiss. She could no longer hear Charlie's regular breathing. 'I thought that something had happened to him, that perhaps the clothes had got over his head. In the half-light I saw he wasn't there, and felt all over the bed for him.'

Puzzled and concerned, Betty knocked at the bedroom next

door to ask Anne Lindbergh, then preparing for bed, if the baby was with her. No, said Anne, surprised. 'Perhaps the Colonel has him,' said Betty, praying yet doubting he had, and ran down to the study to ask. No, he said in even greater surprise, he didn't have the baby; and he ran upstairs to join Anne in the nursery.

With the light on they saw that the two big safety pins were in their place, and that the bedclothes and pillow still bore the imprint of Charlie's small body. Husband and wife stared at the empty crib with incredulity, having to think the unthinkable, to register an event of such hideous and shocking enormity that the mind instinctively recoiled from it.

The Colonel was the first to accept it.

'Anne,' he said, 'they've stolen our baby.'

Outside in the darkness the wind howled like a dog, as if to articulate their anguish.

'Oh, my God!' said Anne.

Bruno Richard Hauptmann was born in the town of Kamenz in Germany, not too far from Dresden and the Czechoslovak border, in 1899: he was therefore two years older than Lindbergh. He was the youngest of four boys and a girl, children of a stonemason. He seems to have had a happy childhood, spending much time with his brothers and schoolmates exploring the neighbouring woods and fields. At the age of fourteen he was apprenticed to a local carpenter which was to stand him in good stead later. Four years later, in 1917, he was called up, served on the western front and was slightly wounded.

Returning home in 1919 he found that Kamenz, like other places, had been badly affected by the war: few families had not lost a father or son in the fighting (his three brothers had all been killed), necessities were scarce and work almost impossible to obtain. In desperation for food and clothing Hauptmann and a friend took part in three burglaries in the course of six days in March 1919, stealing cash and watches from private houses, and foodstuffs and ration cards from a pram being wheeled by two women. They were arrested, tried and convicted, and served three years in prison before being released. In the prison garden they went on walks together, 'but we never talked about our past, we were too ashamed of it'.

Back in Kamenz, Hauptmann tried to find work again, even travelling as a tinker as far south as Bayreuth and Nürnberg, but without success. Finally he decided that there was no future for him in Germany and to emigrate to America. In Hamburg he stowed away in the liner *York*, but was apprehended and sent back to Germany. He and a Kamenz friend made their way to Bremen to try again. They suffered extreme poverty and hunger, sharing a bed in a small room, selling their watches and Hauptmann's good shirt to survive: his weight was down to 126 pounds. 'But,' he claimed, 'I remembered my promise to my mother not to transgress again, and no-one could say I even stole an apple.' A second attempt to reach America, this time from Bremerhaven in the *York*'s sister ship *Derflinger*, also failed when he was recognized by the same officer who had apprehended him in the *York*; and once again he was returned to Germany.

It says much for Hauptmann's determination to make something of his life that, despite these two unsuccessful attempts, his first thought was to try from Bremerhaven again. But he had learnt some lessons: not to mix with the passengers, and thus avoid contact with the officers; and to choose an American ship rather than a German one. So he travelled to Hamburg where the American Line's *Washington* was taking passengers on board, and after a thorough inspection below decks, made his way to the coal bunkers, put on overalls and dug himself a hiding-place in the coal.

Twelve hours out and feeling cramped and hungry, he heard a noise, looked up and saw a man approaching. At first he thought the man was looking for stowaways, then to his astonishment he saw him crawl over the coal towards him and, on reaching his hole, hold out a chicken and a bottle of coffee. Gratefully Hauptmann took them, even more gratefully ate them. But who was his benefactor? The answer came as he prepared to sleep, when a noise close by revealed the intended recipients of the food, a nest of three stowaways. Apologizing, he offered them his bread and water; but far from feeling resentment they invited him to move over and share their nest and further supplies of food which, said Hauptmann, came down with extreme regularity.

Here they passed the time companionably enough, being able, despite the discomfort, to appreciate the absurdity of their situation. 'We were all so black with coal dust that we could only see the whites of our eyes.' On the third day out they found a nest of three more stowaways, making seven in all. They took it in turn to keep an eye on the hatchway, and one day two men came down with flashlights; but by closing their eyes and remaining quite still, they avoided detection. There were no further alarms after this, although as more and more coal was used up, they had to keep digging nests further along the bunkers.

They were still in the bunkers when the ship docked at Hoboken.

'Now we made our way to the bathroom, just like the crew, and gave ourselves a thorough cleaning. The passengers had already left the boat while I was still shaving.

'Now I too walked down the gangplank without being stopped. I reached the pier and from there went into the street. "God, I thank you." These were my first words as I trod the pavements of the New World.'

It was the state of New Jersey (in which Hoboken lies) that welcomed Hauptmann to his new life. Twelve years later it would help to usher him out of it.

Alone in a strange land, knowing no more than a word or two of English, understanding even less, and with only a few cents in his pocket, Hauptmann might have been excused for feeling disoriented and apprehensive; the more so when, having crossed in the ferry to Manhattan and walked from 23rd Street to 86th Street to see his only contact in New York, a friend called Albert Diebig, he found that Albert had moved to an unknown address. But to be alive and free, with the prospect of work and of earning and saving money, was exhilarating. 'I was so happy I wanted to sing. I was in the best of health and had recovered my inner peace.'

Although he had failed to find Albert, a young German who had overheard his enquiries invited Hauptmann to stay at his parents' home until he could find work and a place of his own. His name was Fred Aldinger and his mother, Lena, was a washerwoman. From this base Hauptmann set out on foot and by subway in search of the magic sesame sign, 'Dishwasher wanted': within a few days he spotted it in the window of a lunchroom in Greenwich Village.

'My heart beat somewhat faster as I walked up and down past the window. I rehearsed my English several times. At first softly and then louder and louder I said to myself, "I am a dishwasher."'

At last he took his courage in both hands and, as he put it, 'stormed into the lunchroom'. As the owner approached and was about to say something, Hauptmann almost shouted at him, 'I am a dishwasher.' The owner looked startled and attempted to reply. 'To everything he said to me,' declared Hauptmann, 'I answered "Yes" and sometimes by way of variety, "All right." Naturally I had not the slightest idea of what he was saying.' The cook, who had overheard what was going on and understood German, came to the rescue. 'The boss says you can start work right away and he will give you $15 a week.' Hauptmann was overjoyed. 'Oh, God, what a surprise. I had no idea it would happen so quickly.'

He worked in the lunchroom from eight to four, and in the evenings and at weekends, and with the help of the Aldingers improved his English and learnt American customs and idiosyncrasies. Mistakes were inevitable, and one that Hauptmann always remembered was seeing a car negotiating a street corner and a man in the passenger seat looking at him with outstretched arm. Thinking this was some acquaintance from the *York* or *Derflinger* he went over and warmly shook his hand. The man looked astonished. He had put out his hand to indicate a turn to the right.

After a few weeks' dishwashing, he had saved enough money to buy a set of machine tools: with these he obtained work as a repair locksmith at a wire factory on the East River, and later as a lathe operator in Brooklyn. He was then taken on as a carpenter by a firm on 44th Street which specialized in repair work.

Among those for whom Lena Aldinger did washing was a well-to-do Jewish couple called Rosenbaum who lived on Riverside Drive. They employed a German maid called Anna Schoeffler, and when Lena was at the Rosenbaums she often spoke to Anna of Richard, whom she described as 'the quiet young man who is like another son to me'. Lena, who came from the same part of Germany as Anna, often invited her home in the evenings, but Anna was shy and took some time to accept. On her first visit she met Richard. 'We talked and listened to the radio. Richard and another friend sang. It was like our home in Germany. I enjoyed myself very much.' At the end of the evening Richard walked her to the subway.

One Sunday Lena and Anna visited Coney Island, then a popular New York seaside resort. 'All my life I had heard of Coney Island,' said Anna, 'and was anxious to go.' When they arrived, they saw Hauptmann sitting on the sand. 'He joined us,' she said, 'we made the round of all the amusements and had a fine time.' They began seeing each other regularly, so that later Hauptmann could write, 'During that summer of 1924 I knew I had found my dear wife.'

Anna was then twenty-six, a year older than her future husband, red-haired, handsome rather than pretty, with a charming smile and the same moral principles as those of her future mother-in-law. 'An upright Christian woman,' Hauptmann once called her, 'to whom truth is sacred'; and all those who have known her would agree.

Richard and Anna went for walks in the evening when he picked her up after work on Riverside Drive. During those long summer nights they might stroll along the Hudson watching the river traffic, count the cars as the freight trains rolled by, feed the squirrels in the park. 'He loved nature,' she said, 'and all kinds of animals and birds.' They talked of their homes and families in Germany (Anna noted with what love he spoke of his mother), and of their hopes for the future. And, painful though it was, Richard told her about his past. 'I must say,' he declared with honesty, 'that I passed over everything as superficially as I could, for I was afraid that I might lose her love.' But Anna accepted it. 'It was not hard to understand,' she wrote, 'if you were in Germany after the war. Food was scarce and there was no money. It was hard to live.' She told him, 'That is all behind you now, and will not affect our happiness and love.'

In the spring and summer of 1925 Richard and Anna continued to save, so that by the time they were married on 10 October 1925 at the home of a cousin of Anna in

Brooklyn, they had put by some $1,600; in addition, and without telling Anna, Richard had set aside a further $1,000 to go towards the purchase of a house.

During the next four years Richard and Anna prospered. They lived at first in a furnished room, then moved to an apartment on Park Avenue near 118th Street, which they furnished themselves. Hauptmann had regular work with a Swedish contractor named Herman Olsen in the well-to-do Riverdale area of the Bronx, and also took on contract work of his own for the construction of houses. By 1926 he had become so skilled at his trade that he applied for and was granted membership of the Carpenters' Union.

Anna too was making money, as an assistant in a bakery; first an Italian one on 183rd Street and later at Fredericksen's Bakery and Café in Dyre Avenue. Here, in addition to free meals during working hours, she was given food from the kitchen to take home at night. Between them they were often earning more than $100 a week and saving most of it.

So, by hard work and thrift, the impoverished ex-soldier of Kamenz now found himself with money to spare. To several friends he lent it at 6 per cent interest. He bought a lunchroom for $800 with Albert Diebig and sold his share in it at a profit of $400 a month later. On the Monday after the Wall Street crash of 24 October 1929, he withdrew $2,800 from his savings account and began buying stocks. Initially this was a smart move as the market had nowhere to go but up. There is also evidence, with the banks crashing all over the country, that he was putting a fair proportion of his assets into a trunk at his home. By 1931 he and Anna were telling their friends that they were worth $10,000–12,000 and he had advanced a friend a $3,750 mortgage for a house, on which he was receiving $224 a year interest. In 1931 they bought a Dodge car and with their closest friend, Hans Kloppenburg, made a three-week trip to California.

On 15 October 1931 the Hauptmanns moved into a new apartment, the upper floor of a two-storey house at 1279 East 222nd Street in the Bronx. It consisted of a sitting room, two small bedrooms, kitchen and bath and was reached by a door and staircase leading from the front hallway of the house. The rent was $50 a month (or $48 a month for every two months they guaranteed to stay) and the landlord, a Mr Rauch, lived with his mother on the ground floor. There was no garage for the Dodge, but room for it on an adjoining plot. Mr Rauch said that if Hauptmann was prepared to build a garage, he would supply the wood for it and let him have it rent-free. Hauptmann, who also wanted the garage for a workbench and to store tools, agreed.

To save money for a trip to Germany she was planning for her mother's seventieth birthday, Anna returned to her old job at Fredericksen's Bakery. Richard would take her there in the Dodge each morning, and on Tuesdays and Fridays, when she worked until nine, come to fetch her. Mr Fredericksen would give him supper and afterwards, waiting for Anna to finish, he would sometimes take the Fredericksens' German Shepherd dog for a walk. On some Saturdays he and Hans Kloppenburg had musical evenings at home, playing on mandolin and guitar, and on Sundays when the weather was fine the Hauptmanns and their friends met for games and picnics on Hunter's Island where Richard kept a canoe.

One morning in mid February 1932, soon after the Lindberghs began to visit Hopewell regularly, Hauptmann met a customer in the bakery to whom Anna served breakfast every day, and who worked at the Reliant Employment Agency on 6th Avenue. Hauptmann asked him about prospects for work, and the man suggested he go down to the agency and enquire. There a Mr E.V. Pescia told him there was a likelihood of steady employment for a skilled carpenter in the near future. 'In order not to miss an opportunity,' said Hauptmann, 'I went to the agency every day from then on, either in the morning or afternoon.' In America as in Germany, no-one could accuse Hauptmann of not exerting himself to find work whenever there was the least chance of it.

Pescia's records show that towards the end of February he informed Hauptmann that there would soon be a vacancy for a skilled carpenter at the Majestic Apartments – a big block on 72nd Street and Central Park West then in the course of completion; and that having received from Hauptmann a $10 booking fee, he instructed him and another carpenter called Gus Kassens to report to the construction supervisor at the Majestic, one Joseph M. Furcht. Hauptmann reported on Saturday, 27 February and was told to start work on Tuesday, 1 March (the day of the Lindbergh kidnapping) at $100 a month.

'On 1 March 1932, at 8 a.m.,' declared Mr Furcht, 'Bruno Richard Hauptmann and Gus Kassens reported for work at the Majestic Apartments and worked throughout that entire day until five o'clock . . . Hauptmann was a skilled carpenter who much against my wishes I was forced to put on maintenance work which is ordinary work instead of skilled carpenter work.' Kassens later recalled having met Hauptmann that day.

After work, it being a Tuesday and Anna's late night at the bakery, Hauptmann drove there at around 8 p.m. to fetch her, so that she would not have to come home through deserted streets alone.

The news of the Lindbergh baby's kidnapping that night, like the news of the assassination of President Kennedy thirty-one years later, was an event so shocking and traumatic that long afterwards people could remember where they were when they heard it. Later, as will be shown, this enabled two people to recall that they had seen Hauptmann that evening, and in circumstances in which one encounter independently confirmed the other.

Anna first heard the news at the bakery next morning, after Richard had dropped her there at 7 a.m. 'I went inside, put on my uniform, and went behind the counter. There was a customer there having his breakfast. A steady customer. And he got up to pay me and went to the counter and he held up a *Times* and said, Honey, did you see that? And I looked at it, and I see a baby and I read "Kidnapping". And I said, what is that, does that mean somebody *stole a baby*? And he said Yes. I said, Oh my God!' It was what Anne Lindbergh had said the night before. Hauptmann heard the news when buying a paper at the 225th Street subway on White Plains Avenue, on his way to work at the Majestic Apartments. That evening he and Anna talked about it; there was no-one in America who didn't.

Mr Furcht said that for the rest of that week Hauptmann worked at the Majestic Apartments from eight to five every day.

345

The kidnappers had gained access to the nursery by a ram-shackle ladder which they left behind and a rung of which had broken as the baby was taken down. Searching the nursery for clues, Lindbergh found a ransom note on the window sill demanding $50,000. In the following days and weeks more ransom notes were sent, and a garrulous and sycophantic septuagenarian schoolmaster named Dr John F. Condon volunteered to act as go-between between Lindbergh and the kidnappers. The kidnappers having accepted him, Lindbergh followed suit. Condon had two meetings with a member of the kidnap gang in Bronx cemeteries at night, and on the second he took with him the $50,000 demanded in marked gold certificate dollar bills of varying denominations. At first in the dark Condon was unable to locate the gang member, and Lindbergh, sitting in his car a hundred yards away, heard his voice say the two syllables, 'Hey, Doc!' Condon handed over the money. Six weeks later the baby's decomposing body was found in the woods near Hopewell.

All America was outraged by this news, for Lindbergh was their foremost hero, and he and Anne thought of as a golden couple. Right across the country there was a burning and sustained desire for the perpetrators of the crime to be brought to justice. But although a few of the ransom bills surfaced intermittently in New York banks, and despite intensive and prolonged investigations for two years by the New Jersey police, the New York police and the FBI, the kidnappers had vanished as though they had never been.

Hauptmann meanwhile continued to prosper, though spending less time now in carpentry and more at the offices of Steiner, Rouse, on stock-market transactions. In the summer of 1933, in the German group with which he associated, he was introduced to a little Polish Jew from Leipzig, Isidor Fisch. Fisch, who suffered badly from tuberculosis, claimed to be a successful fur dealer, and hearing of Hauptmann's profits in the stock-market, proposed that they go into a fifty-fifty partnership. Hauptmann, who was quite simple about money matters, agreed. What he did not know was that Fisch was a crook who had persuaded many of their joint friends to invest money to the tune of some $15,000 in his non-existent Knickerbocker Pie Company, none of which they ever saw again.

In the summer of 1933 Hauptmann and Fisch entered into a formal business arrangement in furs and stocks, of which the basis on paper was an investment of $17,500 by Hauptmann and $17,000 by Fisch. But the details of it were never spelt out, and Richard's nephew chided his uncle for such unprofessional ways. Why did Fisch have no place of business? he asked. Why had they not employed a notary public to draw up a proper agreement between them? Why had they not opened a partnership bank account? And where did Fisch keep his furs?

'I ask him one time, I said, "Richard, if you go in storage business and you buy so much furs, don't you have to have storage or loft?" He said, No, that is not done in business like this . . .'

The absence of these facilities gave Fisch the conditions he needed to fleece the naïve Hauptmann. In June, Fisch's brother, Pinkus, in Germany sent him a shipment of cat skins worth $84. Fisch sold these to a firm called Fishbein and Klar and the proceeds, which he should have sent to Pinkus, he pocketed. The name gave Fisch the idea of inventing a bogus firm which he called Klar and Millar, ordering up stationery with the name printed on it, and arranging for a stenographer he knew, Louisa Helfert, to type out a list of non-existent furs which he then valued at two to three times their actual worth. It was because Fisch had invested so heavily in these furs, Hauptmann believed, that he was unable to pay into the stock account the balance of $5,000 which he owed to it. Hauptmann was left with the impression that the partnership owned more than $20,000 worth of furs, and that this $5,000 would be realized when the furs were sold.

Whether it was at this time or earlier that Fisch, in addition to all his other crooked activities, began acquiring 'hot' money is not certain. But evidence that hot money, including Lindbergh ransom money, was being offered for sale at discount and that Fisch had a part in it, comes from several sources. Early in 1936 a man called Oscar J. Bruchman told his lawyer and the *New York Times* that Fisch had asked his help in disposing of hot money; and Fisch's friend Henry Uhlig was informed by a private detective that Fisch had been seen exchanging money in a pool room at 86th Street and 3rd Avenue. Also in 1936 a convict named Stephen Spitz produced $1,000 of Lindbergh ransom money and said he had bought it in New York at forty cents in the dollar. And in a deposition quoted in Anthony Scaduto's book *Scapegoat*, a friend of Fisch by the name of Arthur H. Trost tells of meeting Fisch frequently in the same pool room at 86th and 3rd from the summer of 1931 onwards. After February 1932 (just before the kidnapping) he did not see him there again until the summer. His deposition ends:

> I have been acquainted since March or April 1931 with a man who is also a painter and who I know only by the name of Fritz . . . In June or July 1932 I met Fritz at a restaurant at 1603 2nd Avenue at which time he asked me if I wished to buy some 'hot money' for fifty cents on the dollar from a friend of his. I told him that I would go with him to see the people who had it for sale and he then took me to the same billiard parlor, and when we arrived there he started to introduce me to Isidor Fisch. I then told Fritz that I was already acquainted with Isidor Fisch and needed no introduction to him. I also told Fritz that Fisch was already indebted to me for borrowed money, and that I could not believe any of Fisch's stories. I was led to believe that this 'hot money' was in the possession of Fisch and that Fisch had it for sale.

On 3 November 1933 Anna gave birth to her only child, a boy whom they called Manfred. Fisch meanwhile was planning to return to Leipzig to set up with his brother Pinkus the German end of an import–export business, and on 14 November he visited the steamship ticket office of a Mr Steinweg to buy tickets for himself and his friend Henry Uhlig who was returning home for Christmas. There are two accounts of this visit[1] and both agree that (1) Steinweg was

[1] *The Lindbergh Crime* by Sidney Whipple and *Scapegoat* by Anthony Scaduto.

surprised to see so much cash come out of the pockets of an impoverished-looking fur cutter, (2) the bills were in gold certificates which had been taken out of bulk circulation when America had come off the gold standard earlier in the year, and (3) bank officials subsequently identified the bills as Lindbergh ransom money.

Never willing to pay for anything himself that he could persuade others to pay for him, Fisch approached Hauptmann later that day and (without telling him he had already paid for his tickets and traveller's cheques) asked if he would advance him $2,000 from their joint stock account for his fare and living expenses in Germany: he said he did not want to have to sell any of the investments tied up in their joint fur account. Hauptmann, unaware that the fur account existed only on paper and believing it would produce more profits, agreed and wrote Fisch a cheque. The two of them then hurried to Hauptmann's bank where Fisch managed to cash the cheque just before the bank closed.

During this period Fisch seems to have continued to lead an extraordinary double life. To his friends he seemed as penniless as ever. One, observing his general condition and how scantily he was dressed, gave him a sweater to keep him warm. Others slipped him the odd dollar; and when he met Charlie Schleser, his former partner in the Knickerbocker Pie Company, and told him he wanted to go home to Germany for Christmas but couldn't afford it, Schleser and another friend gave him $34 towards the fare. One way and another Fisch's steamship ticket was proving quite profitable.

On 2 December 1933 the Hauptmanns gave a farewell party for Fisch who, flush with the $2,000 he had recently conned from his host, very sportingly provided the drinks. When Fisch came he brought a package wrapped in paper and tied with string which Hans Kloppenburg, who was standing by the door, described as a shoebox. Fisch asked if Hauptmann would look after the package while he was away (he had already left two valises and some furs) and Hauptmann readily agreed. Fisch said to keep it in a dry place. 'I asked if it had papers in it . . . but I no longer remember his reply . . . I stuck the package on the top shelf of the kitchen closet and soon forgot about it.' It seems to have been a good party, with much music-making and drinking and conversation, and didn't break up until after one. At 9 a.m. the next day Hauptmann collected Fisch and Henry Uhlig in the Dodge and took them to the boat. But Fisch would never return to America to claim the belongings he had left with Hauptmann. In the New Year of 1934 his tuberculosis worsened and on 29 March he died.

Let Hauptmann now describe the event on which turns the central nub of this story:

> It was about the middle of August 1934 on a rainy Sunday, when we did not go out because the weather was too bad for the child. Late in the afternoon I had transplanted some flowers, and some soil had fallen on the floor. I went to the kitchen closet to get the broom. In taking out the broom I touched the things on the top shelf with it. As I looked up to see if I had knocked anything over, I saw the little package which Mr Fisch had given me to keep for him when he left. I had broken through the wrapping which was soaked with water, and . . . I saw the yellow shine of money.

When Fisch had given him the package six months earlier Hauptmann hadn't attached any importance to it, and since then had forgotten it. Had he remembered it and, after Fisch's death, had the slightest suspicion that it contained money, there can be little doubt he would have opened it. (Indeed, had he discovered the money earlier it is unlikely he would have written to Pinkus on 4 May saying that Isidor owed him $5,500.)

He put the package in a bucket and took the bucket to the garage. Here he opened the package and found it crammed full of $10 and $20 gold certificate bills. The notes were so wet and glued together that when he tried to separate them, they tore. So he put them in a basket to dry and when they had dried he counted them. They came to $14,600.

What was he to do? What would any of us have done? There can be little argument as to what he *ought* to have done, which was write to Pinkus Fisch in Leipzig, tell him what he had found and ask for instructions. That is what a truly honest man would have done and what Anna, with her high standards of morality, would have insisted he do. But truly honest men are rare in this world, and Richard Hauptmann was not one of them. For months past he had been searching unsuccessfully for Fisch's assets in order to repay himself the $5,500 plus $2,000 travelling expenses that Fisch owed him: now here it was for the asking. If he disclosed what he had found to Pinkus, he would be in danger of losing it, for (apart from a note in his ledger) he had no documentary proof to back his claim. What about helping to reimburse all the other friends whom Fisch had swindled? He could hardly do that without telling them what he had found and making them accessories. And what about the balance of around $7,000 after he had appropriated the $7,500 he was owed? Well, he may have said, I'll cross that bridge when I come to it.

But where to put it? Had the money been in regular green-backs, he could have (and surely would have) put it on deposit account at his bank or credited his stock account at Steiner, Rouse. It being in gold certificates which it was now illegal to hold in bulk, he could do neither. So if he was going to keep it, he had to hide it. If he hid it in the apartment there was always the risk that Anna might find it and tell him he had no business to keep it. But it should be safe in the garage: no-one went there except himself. So he hid the money in various parts of the garage, in a shellac tin stuffed with rags, in holes drilled for bits beside his pistol, on a boarded-in shelf wrapped in June and September copies of the *New York Daily News* and *Daily Mirror*.

He drew out a dozen or so notes for himself, however, and late in August and at the beginning of September he began to spend them in the stores: at Boccanfuso's fruit and vegetable store, at the Exquisite Shoe Corporation, and then on Saturday, 15 September at the Warner-Quinlan gas station on Lexington and 27th. When the attendant there was handed a $10 gold certificate bill by Hauptmann, he said, 'You don't see these around much any more', and Hauptmann replied, 'I have only about a hundred of them left.' Quite an under-statement; but hardly the remark of a man who knows he is passing much-publicized ransom money. As Hauptmann drove away, the attendant, not knowing if the banks were still accepting gold certificate bills, jotted down on the back of the bill Hauptmann's car licence number: 4U13.41. When the bill turned up at the Corn Exchange Bank on 125th Street, the manager called the police.

Lieutenant James J. Finn was in a state of high excitement. He was, he believed, about to arrest the Lindbergh kidnapper. From the Bureau of Motor Vehicles he had obtained not only his name and address but two facts about him which seemed to clinch the matter: first that he was a German – it was now generally agreed that a German had written the ransom notes; second that he was a carpenter, which provided a powerful link to the ladder. That there were thousands of other Germans living in the Bronx who could equally well have penned the ransom notes, and that no professional carpenter would have fashioned the ramshackle affair that had been used to kidnap little Charlie were not thoughts that occurred to him. A German carpenter in possession of ransom money was enough.

Finn's first instincts were to collect a posse of men and go straight to Hauptmann's house to apprehend him. He rejected the idea because he wanted the arrest to be as unobtrusive as possible, and if, as seemed likely, Hauptmann had turned his apartment into a sort of mini-fortress, there might have to be a shoot-out; also, if taken in his house, Hauptmann might not have any ransom notes on him. If they were to follow him when he left the house he might lead the way to confederates or to the cache where the ransom money was hidden.

So Finn made arrangements for three plain police cars to wait discreetly near Hauptmann's house. As his own car travelled down 222nd Street Finn observed the houses – 'wood and stucco with shingled roofs and with neat bits of lawn and beds of flowers – homes apparently of simple, hard-working, God-fearing people.' But when he came to No. 1279, which was no different from the rest, his reflections were rather different. Here, he said, 'lived a creature who had not hesitated to go into the house of another man . . . and had so destroyed the happiness of that home that its owner and his young wife had been forced to abandon the house of their dreams and flee to scenes that had not been blighted by this filthy creature's foot.' One can assume that those with him felt the same.

The cars assembled near No. 1279 in the late afternoon of 18 September. In the early evening the officers held a conference in a nearby German tavern (whose owner was later to find himself doing brisk business) where it was agreed that Finn should make the arrest, that a gunfight was to be avoided unless Hauptmann tried to shoot his way out, and that he should be allowed to travel some distance from the house before being halted. They saw the Hauptmanns leave the house in the car at 8 p.m. and return at about 2 a.m. on the 19th (they had been to the *Europa* to see a cousin of Anna who was sailing for Europe). Then the lights were turned off in the apartment and they took it in turns to keep watch and doze during the night.

At 8.55 a.m. the front door of No. 1279 opened and Hauptmann came out. He was dressed in a double-breasted blue suit with brown shoes and a soft hat. Finn recalled the details of his motor vehicle application form – thirty-four, 180 pounds, 5 feet 10 inches, blue eyes, blond hair. This was the man all right. He watched Hauptmann walk briskly across the lane to his garage, unlock the doors and back out the Dodge. The numberplate read: 4U13.41.

Hauptmann closed and relocked the garage doors, climbed into the Dodge, and set off south. For him the day was little different from any other. After breakfast he had kissed goodbye to Anna and Manfred and was now on his way to Steiner, Rouse.

From Fordham Road he turned down Washington Avenue to 189th Street, then west to Park Avenue. He drove fast and well, said Finn, so that the three police cars had difficulty in keeping pace with him. When they had travelled some five miles and were approaching Tremont Avenue, Finn realized that if Hauptmann got through on the last of the green, they might lose him. So he gave the signal to close in. The first car overtook the Dodge and edged it into the curb, the second drew alongside it, the third pulled up behind.

With guns at the ready, the detectives surrounded the car. Finn opened the driving door and looked into Hauptmann's bewildered face. 'What is happening? What is this?' Hauptmann asked. His first reaction was that he had been stopped for speeding. But why so many men to apprehend him, why the hostility and the guns?

'Get out,' said Finn.

He got out. Detective Wallace slipped the handcuffs on him. Then he was frisked. He had no weapon, but in his wallet they found a $20 gold certificate bill. They checked it against the list of ransom money serial numbers and found it matched. But Finn didn't yet want Hauptmann to know what he knew.

'Where did you get this counterfeit money?' he asked.

Counterfeit money, thought Hauptmann. So this is what Fisch had landed him with. He wasn't altogether surprised.

'I have been collecting gold certificate money against inflation,' he said. 'At one time I had three hundred dollars' worth.'

'Don't you know the President has said that all gold money has to be turned in to the Federal Reserve Bank?'

'Yes.'

'How much more gold money do you have at home?'

He thought of the $14,600 hidden in the garage, and knew that if a charge of hoarding (let alone stealing) was not to be preferred against him, he had to lie. 'About a hundred and twenty dollars' worth,' he said.

'We'll check on that,' said Finn; then, weighing up Hauptmann, he allowed his fantasies to run away with him. 'He was the bird we were looking for all right . . . I could defy any man who was a man to like him . . . I felt that he would kill a baby in a crib and never turn a hair.'

He went off to telephone his Inspector about the arrest and to arrange for one of the officers to drive the Dodge back to 222nd Street. While waiting for the Inspector to join them, Finn ordered Detective Wallace to sit with Hauptmann on the back seat of his car.

Wallace looked at the stupefied Hauptmann with the same sort of distaste as Finn had shown, seeing only what he wanted to see.

'So you're the Lindbergh kidnapper?' he said.

The what? The *what*? Hauptmann felt himself tossed about in a whirlwind of increasingly nightmarish dimensions, a world where normal expectations and reactions were in abeyance. First it was speeding, then passing counterfeit money, now this. It must be all a joke, a farce, some horrible mistake. When would it end?

Another detective smiled, with venom. 'You're going to burn, baby,' he said.

With the arrest of Hauptmann, there was not a soul in America who did not believe that at least one of the kidnap gang had been caught; and the hatred towards him and desire that he should meet his just deserts as soon as possible were almost universal.

Expecting him to confess, the police were baffled by his repeated assertions that he was innocent, a claim at first supported by the opinions of two of the best-known handwriting experts in the country, Albert D. and Albert S. Osborn, that there was no resemblance between Hauptmann's writing and that of the author of the ransom notes. Nor was there a scrap of evidence to connect him with the kidnapping or murder.

The police however had no doubts about his guilt and dismissed his story of how Fisch had left the money in the shoebox and then inconveniently died as 'a fishy story'. When, a day or two later, they found the $14,600 hidden in the garage, their beliefs were more than confirmed; and when the experts were told this they thought that after all there was *some* similarity between Hauptmann's writing and that of the author of the ransom notes.

Having no evidence on which to extradite Hauptmann to New Jersey, yet as convinced of Hauptmann's guilt as their colleagues in New York, the New Jersey police approached an impoverished woodcutter and well-known local liar called Millard Whited and for a fee of $150, expenses of $35 a day and a promise of a slice of the reward money, persuaded him to travel to the Bronx and testify that he had seen Hauptmann twice near Hopewell on or about the day of the kidnapping (interviewed after the kidnapping two years earlier he said he had seen nobody). This was sufficient evidence for Hauptmann to be extradited to the little New Jersey town of Flemington, the nearest court house and prison to the scene of the crime.

Hauptmann's trial for murder opened at Flemington on 2 January 1935, and 500 press and spectators crammed into the tiny courtroom which rarely ever saw more than a handful of people. Among those on the press benches were Damon Runyon, Ford Madox Ford, Edna Ferber, Walter Winchell; among the spectators Ginger Rogers, Jack Dempsey, Moss Hart, Lynn Fontanne, Lowell Thomas, Jack Benny and the haut monde of New York brought down in limousines with liveried chauffeurs and accompanying Pekinese. Forty-five telegraph lines were set up for direct filing to Paris, London, Berlin, Buenos Aires and Sydney. H.L. Mencken called it the greatest story since the Resurrection, others The Trial of the Century.

Hauptmann's savings being now exhausted, he accepted an offer from the Hearst Press to pay for his defence lawyers. Heading the team was a fat, flamboyant, alcoholic clown named Edward Reilly, nicknamed Death House Reilly because of the many capital cases he had lost. Among the others was a much respected Flemington man, C. Lloyd Fisher, who unlike Reilly believed in Hauptmann's innocence from the outset. Chief counsel for the prosecution was New Jersey's newly appointed Attorney General, the dapper David Wilentz.

So utterly convinced were the prosecution that Hauptmann was guilty that, lacking evidence to prove it, they had no compunction in inventing it. In addition to Millard Whited's false evidence, they dredged up another local man, the half-blind, eighty-seven-year-old Prussian war veteran Amandus Hochmuth whom they bribed to say that he too had glimpsed Hauptmann on the day of the kidnapping, driving a car with a ladder in the back! A taxi driver named Perrone testified that a man who gave him a ransom note in the dark to take to Dr Condon's house in the Bronx was Hauptmann, although when first asked by police, he said he would not be able to recognize the man again. Dr Condon, who had failed to pick out Hauptmann at a police line-up as the man he had met in the two cemeteries and to whom he had given the $50,000 ransom money, was told that if he didn't change his mind at the trial, he would be arrested himself, so obligingly did so.

But the worst perjuries came from those who should have known better. After his arrest in New York, Hauptmann had been asked to write out the ransom notes, first as dictated to him, correctly, and then with their peculiar mis-spellings ('ouer' for 'our', 'bee' for 'be', 'note' for 'not', etc.). It was these latter that the state proffered in evidence to show that Hauptmann must have written the ransom notes, as the chances of anyone else making such a similar combination of mistakes were inconceivable.

What must have been the final nail in Hauptmann's coffin was the evidence of Colonel Lindbergh. Before his extradition from New York, Hauptmann had been made to shout 'Hey, Doc' in the District Attorney's office in a variety of voices while a disguised Lindbergh listened – the words that Lindbergh had heard the man in the cemetery shout to Dr Condon when about to hand over the ransom money. Having told the DA that he could not possibly be certain that this was the voice he had heard (it was dark and he was 100 yards away) he was then approached by Colonel Norman Schwarzkopf, head of the New Jersey State Police[1], assured that there was no doubt at all that Hauptmann was the murderer of his son, and as a result agreed to testify that the voice he had heard in the DA's office was the same as the voice in the cemetery. For the jury this evidence, coming from the national hero, must have been conclusive.

What might have saved Hauptmann were the time-sheets that showed he was at work from nine to five or six on the day of the kidnapping and so would not have been able to go home, pick up a ladder and any accomplices and reach Hopewell in time for the kidnapping. Both Wilentz and Foley, the Bronx District Attorney, saw these time-sheets but declared that there was evidence (there was none) that on that day Hauptmann quit work early. These time-sheets were then given to the New York police, and were never seen

[1] Father of General Norman Schwarzkopf, Commander of United States forces in the 1991 Gulf War.

again. Other time-sheets and payroll records were doctored to show that Hauptmann did not start work at the Majestic Apartments until after the day of the kidnapping and that he quit work the day before the ransom money was handed over.

Finally, and in order to clinch Hauptmann's presence at Hopewell, the prosecution sought to show that one rail of the kidnap ladder had come from a floorboard in his attic. This evidence had been fabricated by two detectives. Aside from the ludicrousness of Hauptmann, a skilled carpenter who always kept lengths of timber in his garage, climbing up the cleats of the linen cupboard to reach the trap door to the attic, and there chopping up bits of his landlord's flooring, two woods experts testified categorically for the defence that the rail from the ladder did not match the board from which it was said to have come. By this time in the trial, however, the mountain of false evidence that had piled up against Hauptmann was too great to be dislodged.

At 11.14 on the morning of 13 February 1934 the jury retired to consider their verdict. Ford Madox Ford in his seat in the balcony of the courtroom wrote that if he had been a member of the jury, he would, despite all the evidence against Hauptmann, have voted for an acquittal ('the fox was not given enough grace . . . there must remain some doubt'). But when the jury returned eleven hours later, they had come to a different conclusion: guilty of murder in the first degree. It was a verdict which eight months later the New Jersey Court of Errors and Appeals confirmed. The sentence was to be death by electrocution in the state prison at Trenton.

For Hauptmann the decision of the Court was shattering. Lloyd Fisher was leaving the prison after seeing him at around 1 p.m. when his secretary brought him the news; he at once retraced his steps. Hauptmann took it well, he said, his only comment being, 'What a terrible wedding anniversary present for my Anny.' Anna said she would do all she could to carry on, adding, 'I hope and pray the true facts will come out before they can do anything to my poor man.'

All that afternoon, his guards noticed, Hauptmann sat motionless on his bed, staring at the floor. Now he knew that everything that had gone before was not the empty formality, the shadow-boxing he had imagined. They really did mean to kill him.

Was there nothing or nobody that could help him now? He had been told that the new warden of the prison, Colonel Mark O. Kimberling, owed his appointment to his friendship with the Governor of New Jersey, Harold Hoffman; and that the Governor was not only the chief executive of the state whose servants were mainly responsible for his present plight, but also the *ex-officio* chairman of the Court of Pardons, the only body that had the power to commute his sentence to life imprisonment. Several times recently Hauptmann had mentioned to Colonel Kimberling that he would like the Governor to come and see him. Now, more urgently, he repeated the request.

At this stage of his career Harold Hoffman had two claims to fame: at thirty-nine he was the youngest Governor in the country, and in 1934, when he was elected, he was one of the few Republican Governors to take office.

He was at this time a stocky, chubby-faced man, married with three daughters, a Methodist and member of numerous charitable organizations such as the Shriners, the Elks, the Masons and the Rotarians. His secretary Andrew Dutch said he had an enormous capacity for work, an astonishing memory and an independent mind. Told by a friend that some action he proposed to take would lose him political support, he answered vigorously, 'I know what I'm doing is right. The votes can take care of themselves.'

Although he had not taken office until Hauptmann's trial was under way, he was as Governor and Chairman of the Court of Pardons more interested in it than most. He had been perturbed by what he saw as the rail-roading of the defendant. 'I have never in my life,' he told Andrew Dutch, 'seen more hatred shown to a man than at that trial.' His interest grew when an old friend and brilliant investigator, Ellis Parker, chief of Burlington County detectives and asked by Hoffman's predecessor Governor Moore to look into the case, had assured him that Hauptmann was not guilty. Then came a call from a friend of Capitol Hill days, Charles Curtis, a former Vice President of the United States. 'Governor,' he said, 'there are a lot of funny things about that case. I've read some of the testimony, and it doesn't seem to me that Hauptmann was adequately represented or had a fair deal. I think you ought to look into it.' And now here was Colonel Kimberling in his suite at the Hildebrecht hotel with Hauptmann's request to come and see him.

But what did Hauptmann want to see him *about*? Was he now ready to confess, to 'thaw', as Wilentz had crudely promised he would when faced with the certainty of the electric chair. If so, then as the state's chief executive, he would be lacking in duty not to comply. In any case the temptation to talk with the man who for months past had gripped the attention of the world must have been well nigh irresistible. So, five days after the judgement of the Court of Errors and Appeals, and when an evening appointment was suddenly cancelled, he decided to visit Hauptmann on the spur of the moment. 'As to the propriety of my going, one of the highest judicial officers in the state had assured me that such a visit would not conflict with any existing statute. Not only that: governors before me had visited the Death House.' Nevertheless he was anxious to avoid publicity; a visit in darkness and under the personal supervision of the warden would ensure that it went unreported.

Concerned that he might not understand everything that Hauptmann said, Hoffman telephoned Ellis Parker's secretary Anna Bading, a fluent German speaker and professional stenographer, to ask her to accompany him. She lived at Mount Holly, fifteen miles away, and was at a function being given the accolade of Worthy Matron of the Chapter by the *Eastern Star*. She had no time to change before answering the Governor's call, and joined him at Kimberling's residence in full evening dress. Kimberling lent her a big overcoat and they drove round to the 3rd Street entrance which gave access to Death Row. There they were let in by the deputy warden, Colonel Selby. They walked through the darkened death house, a flashlight picking out the electric chair, 'covered in white muslin', said Hoffman, 'like a seated ghost'. Hoffman asked Mrs Bading to sit on a bench near the chair and said he would call her if needed. Then he was taken through the iron door on the other side of which lay Hauptmann's cell.

Hoffman's account of his visit to Hauptmann is taken from a series of articles he wrote in *Liberty Magazine* (and in which he spelt Hauptmann's words phonetically so that readers might catch the flavour of his voice). Noticing that Hauptmann was dressed in a blue-grey open shirt and dark blue trousers, that there was a Bible and the paper-bound volumes of the trial record on the table and photographs of Anna and Manfred on the wall, Hoffman sat down on Hauptmann's bed, bracing himself to hear a plea of mercy to be conveyed to the Court of Pardons. Instead he found himself facing an angry and frustrated man. 'Vy does your state do to me all this, Governor?' Hoffman records as Hauptmann's opening remark. 'Vy do they want my life for something somebody else have done?' Hoffman interjected to say he had been found guilty. 'Lies, lies, lies!' Hauptmann almost shouted back. 'All lies. Vould I kill a baby? I am a man. Vould I build that ladder? I am a carpenter.'

Ironically Hauptmann found that Hoffman was prepared to give more time listening to him than had his own counsel, Edward Reilly; Reilly had talked with Hauptmann for a total of thirty-eight minutes in four months; Hoffman now gave him an hour. This was the first opportunity Hauptmann had had of putting his case to a New Jersey official, uninterrupted; and all the manifold weaknesses in the prosecution's case which Reilly had failed to stress or even state came tumbling out in a flood.

Why (he asked) hadn't it been emphasized at the trial that the police, despite taking numerous sets of his fingerprints, hadn't found a single one on the ladder or in the nursery, and that the two footprints found on the Hopewell lawn and in St Raymond's Cemetery didn't match his own? Why did they infer that the chisel found on the lawn was his chisel, when the chisel he used and which they had taken away was a quite different type? Why had they suppressed all the letters Fisch had written him from Germany? Would he as a carpenter build a ladder that would not bear his own weight? Why would he go up to the attic to tear up a floorboard to make the ladder when he had plenty of boards in the garage? How could the nicks in the ladder have been made by his plane unless he had not sharpened it once in two and a half years? Would he have told the gas station attendant who took his car number that he had a hundred more gold certificate bills at home if he knew they were Lindbergh bills?

All this and much more; and he finished bitterly: 'The poor child haf been kidnapped and murdered, so somebody must die for it. For is the parent not the great flyer? And if somebody does not die for the death of the child, then always the police will be monkeys. So I am the one who is picked out to die.'

As Hoffman rose to go, Hauptmann asked to be given the lie-detector test. 'Vy won't they use on me that?' he asked. 'And on Dr Condon also use it?' He added, 'If he vill tell the truth, I vill be a free man.'

The Governor collected Anna Bading from her gruesome vigil beside the chair, left her at Kimberling's residence, then returned to his suite at the Hildebrecht and wrote all he could remember far into the night. He had been deeply disturbed by what had occurred because it was so different from what he had expected. 'Here was no cringing criminal pitifully begging for mercy but a man making a vehement claim of innocence, bitter in his denunciation of the police and the prosecution and their methods . . . and bitter too in his excoriation of his former chief counsel, Reilly.'

If Hauptmann had not asked for mercy, he had asked for further investigations, and in the interests of justice the Governor determined he should have them. 'His story and his unanswered questions put new doubts in my mind and aided in fashioning a firm resolution to search out, within the limits of my resources and my ability, the truth and the whole truth in this mysterious and challenging case . . . My duty,' he concluded, 'seemed clear.'

And next day he motored over to Flemington to buy the eleven volumes of the trial transcript.

In mid January 1936 the Court of Pardons, with Hoffman in the chair, met to decide whether there were any grounds for the exercise of clemency. One impressive submission, because its author had no axe to grind, came from the Reverend James Matthiesen, Pastor of Trinity Lutheran Church and one of Hauptmann's two spiritual advisers:

I have had fifteen very intimate and soul-searching interviews with Bruno Richard Hauptmann, and am convinced that he tells the truth. If Hauptmann had had a reliable defense lawyer at the outstart, and if he had asked for an interpreter during the trial, the very evidence used against him would have spoken in his favor. Hauptmann felt no need for them until it was too late. After careful study of that case I have come to that conclusion.

First, know Hauptmann as he really is, and his wife Anna, and then study the evidence; and you will arrive at the same conclusion. Hauptmann does not fit into the frame of circumstantial evidence. I bring these findings to your honorable members of the Court of Pardons not because of sympathy for Hauptmann, although I claim to know him better than anyone with the exception of his wife, but I want to see justice prevail.

I would ask for the supreme penalty if Hauptmann were guilty. My creed has no objections to that. There is nothing else in my mind than this: that I may serve the State of New Jersey with my findings. I feel it is a sacred duty I have to discharge.

For having the courage to discharge this sacred duty the Reverend Matthiesen was rebuked by his parish council, so angry were they at his having questioned the received wisdom.

Nor did his plea have any effect on the Court of Pardons who, like his parishioners, did not want to have their conclusions disturbed. When the vote was taken at the end of the day, Hoffman declared in favour of commutation to life imprisonment, the others against. Fisher went to the prison and with Kimberling broke the news to Hauptmann. Fisher told Hauptmann that no other channel of clemency now remained, and that if he had anything to say he had not said before, he should reveal it. Like a music box which repeats its tune *ad infinitum,* Hauptmann said once again he was innocent; he had never changed his story and never could. Outside the prison Kimberling and Fisher met reporters. 'As we were leaving,' said Kimberling, 'Hauptmann asked Mr

Fisher to see his wife and tell her he was all right. His eyes were filled with tears as he said that.' And Fisher told them, 'You might add that I believe that Hauptmann is innocent and nothing has happened in any shape, form or manner to change that. He is as guiltless as any of you.'

Now there were only five clear days before Friday, 17 January, when Hauptmann was to die. When Anna visited him on the Monday, she found him calm but despondent. Hadn't eleven months' prison been enough suffering for something he hadn't done? he asked her. Did they really have to kill him as well? And why didn't the real perpetrators of the crime come forward? One day the truth would come out, but they couldn't bring him back then. Anna was distraught. 'I cannot sit here and watch this terrible thing happen to Richard,' she wrote in the *Mirror*, 'but I do not know what to do. I know he is not guilty and yet I can do nothing to save him.' On Tuesday she moved into the Stacy-Trent Hotel in Trenton so as to be near him up to the end, and on Wednesday morning was allowed a special visit. During it, on the other side of the wall, John Bloom tested the electric chair.

Meanwhile the defence team of Fisher, Rosecrans and Pope, temporarily strengthened by two young Washington lawyers, were pulling out all the stops they could. On the Monday they petitioned the US Circuit Court of Appeals for a writ of habeas corpus on the grounds of a mis-trial, but this was rejected by Judge Warren Davis. Then in a last desperate attempt to stave off the inevitable, they again petitioned the US Supreme Court, also for habeas corpus, and this was denied just thirty-six hours before Hauptmann was due to mount the chair.

But there was still the Governor. On the evening of Wednesday, 15 January (before the Supreme Court had reached its latest decision) Hoffman was travelling to New York to stay the night. He was a deeply worried man, for more and more information had been arriving on his desk to cast doubts on Hauptmann's guilt. He had also learnt that Hauptmann had turned down an offer from Sid Boehm of the *New York Evening Journal* to pay Anna Hauptmann $75,000 (later increased to $90,000) if he would give them a full, confidential confession to the crime, only to be published after his execution. Hoffman knew how devoted Hauptmann was to his wife and son, and how concerned he was about their future. How could he possibly refuse such an offer unless he really did have nothing further to say?

At the New Yorker Hotel, Hoffman learnt that David Wilentz was dining with friends in the Terrace Room. This was too good an opportunity to miss and after dinner Wilentz came to Hoffman's suite for what Hoffman called 'a long, earnest and important talk'. Having known Wilentz since schooldays, said Hoffman, he didn't have to pull his punches. 'We have disagreed in politics; we certainly disagreed, without any personal feeling, on the Hauptmann case.' Hoffman told Wilentz his doubts about Hauptmann's involvement, and in the end they agreed it was more important to get the complete story – 'just how a man could conceive and execute such a ghastly plan single-handed' – than it was to take his life. And they made a solemn pact: that in the morning the Governor would see Mrs Hauptmann and ask her to tell her husband that if he made a full statement of his involvement – however great or small – he and Wilentz would jointly recommend to the Court of Pardons that the death sentence be commuted to life imprisonment.

After three hours' sleep, Hoffman left on the 7 a.m. train for Trenton. He knew that Mrs Hauptmann was staying at the Stacy-Trent Hotel, and made arrangements to see her in the manager's suite. As the hotel lobby was swarming with pressmen and photographers, Hoffman arrived by the back entrance and reached the suite by way of the freight lift. Fatigued and red-eyed by worry and lack of sleep, Anna Hauptmann was waiting for him.

'Mrs Hauptmann,' he said, 'tomorrow, as you know, your husband is to die. I wanted to help him, but he has not been telling me, or anyone else, the truth.'

Anna became galvanized into life.

'*No, no, no!*' she shouted. 'That isn't so. Richard *did* tell the truth. He *is* telling the truth.'

He waited for her to calm down, then told her of the pact he had made with the Attorney General.

'You must go to the prison this morning and see your husband. You must tell him that he can save his life. You must tell him that you want him to tell the truth.'

Anna exploded. *'No, no, no!'* Hoffman reported her as saying. 'My husband has only a few hours to live. Could I do that to him – make him think that I, too, believe that he would kill a baby? Would I make Richard think I too have believed those lying witnesses who, for money, would send a good man to die? No, no! Never would I do that. Not even to save my Richard's life would I do that.'

Hoffman made one last attempt, but realized it was useless. 'The truth he *has* told,' said Anna. 'What more can he say? Yes, maybe he could make up lies to say he did it and save his life. But soon it would be found they were not the truth. No! Always I – and some day Bubi – would be sorry that he would say he had done such a thing even to save his life.'

Hoffman, seeing Anna for the first time, had expected a run-of-the-mill housewife, not this outraged woman of courage and principle. Listening to her, he asked himself whether she was telling truths that burned deeply in her heart or staging a scene that would rival those of the great actresses of America. 'It was hard to think of Anna Hauptmann as an actress.'

Well, he said, if she wouldn't do what he had asked, would she ask her husband if he would talk further to Hoffman and someone from the Attorney General's office, and answer any questions? Yes, she said, she would gladly do that, she would do anything except tell her husband that she doubted he was telling the truth.

Hoffman gave her his telephone number at the Hildebrecht, and an hour later she rang from the prison. 'Richard says he will be glad to see you and Mr Wilentz. He will be glad to see anybody. But, Governor, his story is just the same. He has told everything he knows – nothing more he can tell.'

Hoffman rang Wilentz and told him what had happened. 'The hell with it, Harold,' was Wilentz's reply. 'If that's still his attitude, I'm damned if I'm going to do anything to help him.'

But the Governor was now ready to act on his own: there were still too many unanswered questions which, if

Hauptmann were to die the following night, might never be answered. He did not have the power, as some Governors did, of commuting the death sentence to life imprisonment; but he was entitled to grant a reprieve of up to ninety days. As an execution had to take place not less than four and not more than eight weeks from the date it was determined, this meant that Hauptmann could expect at least another two months of life. Announcing his decision, the Governor said there would be only this one reprieve – unless some event occurred which led him and the Attorney General to consider a further stay.

Hauptmann took the news of his reprieve calmly, Anna said, 'God be thanked,' and in Kamenz old Paulina Hauptmann, woken from sleep, said, 'This is the happiest day of my life. Now everything will be all right.' But the effect on others was extraordinary. Although, as Hoffmann said, Governors' reprieves were customary and justification for granting one had never before been demanded, this time there was a burst of popular indignation: solid citizens for whom the death of Hauptmann would be catharsis and expiation feared the experience was to be denied them. Death threats began arriving at Hoffman's home at South Amboy and guards were posted. The newspapers too condemned him. An hysterical editorial in the *Trenton Times* declared that the Governor had 'flaunted *(sic)* the highest courts of state and nation . . . dishonored himself, disgraced the state and converted New Jersey into an international laughing-stock . . . sacrificed all legal and moral right to serve as Chief Executive of New Jersey', and called for the House of Assembly to institute immediate proceedings for impeachment. Even the staid *New York Times* called his action 'a desperate gamble' and 'indefensible'.

But, said Hoffman, the letters he was receiving applauding his action far outnumbered those criticizing it, and in answer to his critics he issued a long and reasoned statement: if impeachment was the price he had to pay for following his own conscience, he was ready to pay it. He had never expressed a view as to Hauptmann's guilt or innocence and did not do so now:

I do however share with hundreds and thousands of our people the doubt as to the value of the evidence that placed him in the Lindbergh nursery on the night of the crime. I do wonder what part passion and prejudice played in the conviction of a man who was previously tried and convicted in the columns of many of our newspapers. I do, on the basis of evidence which is in my hands, question the truthfulness and mental competency of some of the chief witnesses for the state. I do doubt that this crime could have been committed by any one man, and I am worried about the eagerness of some of our law-enforcement agencies to bring about the death of this one man so that the books may be closed in the thought that another great crime mystery has been successfully solved . . .

He made no apology for the reprieve. It would provide time for investigating some of the most baffling aspects of the case and, in particular, Hauptmann's continued refusal to admit to any part of the crime, even though he knew that an admission to the Court of Pardons would spare his life and an admission to the *New York Evening Journal* would guarantee his family financial security after his execution. Nor, said Hoffman, as the father of three children himself, was he motivated by maudlin sentiment. What he was interested in was 'that thing we have rather proudly called "Jersey Justice" ', and he concluded, 'I hope that real and full justice will finally be done in this case.'

Hoffman now appointed a small team of detectives to look into every aspect of the case, including the files of the New Jersey state police. Here they found Whited's statement made only five weeks after the kidnapping that he had seen nobody suspicious in the neighbourhood and a statement by a state trooper holding out to Whited a share of the $25,000 reward money; a statement by the half-blind Hochmuth that at the time of the kidnapping he had not seen anyone suspicious near his house; and the record of Condon being told by the police that if he did not identify Hauptmann as the man in the cemetery, he would be indicted as an accessory. And the manager of the agency that had employed Hauptmann for work at the Majestic apartments on the day of the kidnapping confirmed that he had worked that day. Further confirmation, he said, would be found in the firm's time-sheets, but when Hoffman applied for these, he was told they were missing. Finally Hoffman paid a visit to the Hauptmanns' attic and found, as he thought, that the evidence about a rail of the kidnap ladder having been part of a floorboard was a fabrication.

By now Hoffman had formed the view that the execution of Hauptmann would be a gross miscarriage of justice, and in a long statement released only three days before the day set for the execution, he declared that the case reeked with passion, prejudice and unfairness. He revealed that he had been to see the trial judge to enquire whether the new information would permit the judge to set aside the conviction and order a new trial, but that the judge had said that the time limit for this (within six months after the conviction) had expired. There was no loophole left.

The day before, however, every member of the Court of Pardons had received a confession from a nutter named Paul Wendel that it was he who had kidnapped and murdered the Lindbergh baby; and in the light of this and at Lloyd Fisher's request the Court of Pardons was convened for a second time, just thirty-six hours before the time set for the execution. The night before, an agitated Samuel Small, a handwriting expert, had come to Hoffman's suite at the Hildebrecht to ask if he could testify before it. Hoffman replied it was impossible, the rules didn't permit. 'But,' said Small, breaking down and crying, 'do you mean to say that your state will send to the chair a man who *couldn't possibly* have written those notes?' He paused, momentarily too distressed to continue. 'Listen,' he said, 'it isn't a question of *if* Hauptmann wrote those letters. It is a question of whether he *could* write them. I tell you, Governor, that if you went to the prison and said to Hauptmann, "I will let you free if you can write a single sentence the way it is written in the ransom letters", Hauptmann would have to stay in prison the rest of his life. A person cannot change his handwriting from one known system to another.'

At 11 a.m. the court met in the State House annex and was still in session when Anna Hauptmann went to see Richard for the last time. The prison band was practising and the sound of the music reduced her to tears. But, said *The New York Times,* she controlled herself quickly, 'and with the aid of a little face powder, put on her best appearance before meeting her husband'. It was what she had always done, whatever her feelings, whatever the state of her purse. They talked of little Manfred whom his father had not seen for more than a year because, as he had said then, 'I do not belong here', and the idea of Manfred in later life remembering such a visit was abhorrent to him. 'You must have faith,' Anna told him; 'something may still happen.' But she could see from his face that there was little faith left. They were allowed to hold hands through the bars, and they cried together, aghast and incredulous that nine years of married happiness had to end like this. Then she left.

By mid afternoon a huge crowd had gathered outside the State House annex to hear the decision of the Court of Pardons. At 5 p.m. the clerk of the court, Albert Hermann, fought his way through the mob to the State House and there, holding aloft a piece of typewritten paper, announced that the appeal had been denied. Fisher told the press that the judgement was incomprehensible. 'We are very bitterly disappointed,' he said.

He took the news to the prison. Hauptmann had been half expecting it. After Fisher had left Hauptmann called to one of the guards for pencil and paper. Now that all hope had gone and his death was a certainty, he wanted to write a farewell letter.

It was addressed (in German) to Governor Hoffman and was a kind of last testament. 'My writing', he began, 'is not for fear of losing my life, this is in the hands of God. It is His will. I will go gladly, it means the end of my tremendous suffering. Only in thinking of my dear wife and little boy, that is breaking my heart. I know until this terrible crime is solved, they will have to suffer under the weight of my unfair conviction.'

Once again he emphasized his innocence and lack of knowledge about the case ('I passed the money without knowing it was Lindbergh money . . . up to the present day I have no idea where the Lindbergh house in Hopewell is located'); railed against Dr Condon ('Why did Dr Condon say in my cell he cannot testify against me? My God, Dr Condon, did you ever realize what you did?'); attacked Reilly ('Why did my chief lawyer send important witnesses home without even bringing them on the stand? My God, my God, I can't hardly believe all what happened at my trial'); but kept his bitterest comments for the state's prosecutor:

> Mr Wilentz, with my dying breath, I swear by God that you convicted an innocent man. Once you will stand before the same judge to whom I go in a few hours. You know you have done wrong on me, you will not only take my life but also all the happiness of my family. God will be judge between me and you.
>
> I beg you, Attorney General, believe at least a dying man. Please investigate, because this case is not solved, it only adds another dead to the Lindbergh case.

He concluded with a message for the Governor. 'I see this as my duty, before this state takes my life, to thank you for what you have done for me. I write this with tears in my eyes. If ever prayers will reach you, they will come from me, from my dear wife and my little boy.'

When his supper came that night, he didn't touch it. After it had been taken away, unable to reconcile God's will with the workings of so malevolent a fate, he wept.

Next morning he didn't eat his breakfast or his lunch either. After the lunch hour, as was customary with condemned men, he was moved from his own cell to Cell 8 on the other side of the death chamber: this was in case he had hidden some weapon in his own cell by which he could cheat the executioner, and also to be made ready for death. Apart from a chair and a table the cell was empty of furniture. Hauptmann was allowed to bring his Bible there, but nothing else, not even the photographs of Manfred and Anna. Fisher, visiting him, found him deeply distressed. 'I have been a good prisoner,' he said, 'I have never made anybody any trouble. Why should they do this to me? Why should I be pushed around when this is my last day to live?' Later the prison barber arrived to shave the crown of his head: this was where the executioner would fix one of the electrodes. Then a fresh suit of clothes was brought in, a blue shirt and dark-striped khaki trousers. Hauptmann noticed a long slit in one of the trouser legs and was told this was for placing the second electrode.

Alone again in the bare cell, Hauptmann broke into another fit of weeping, less perhaps at the thought of his extinction or the wrongfulness of it, but because of the pitiful, degraded figure they had now reduced him to. He was still weeping when the Warden came to see him, and asked for time to recover his composure. Kimberling said he'd heard Hauptmann had had nothing to eat for nearly twenty-four hours and encouraged him to eat now (though with death only hours away it is difficult to see why); the Warden said he could order a special meal of anything he liked. Hauptmann suggested he send it to Condon, then made one last impassioned assertion of innocence. Could not the Warden arrange for him to make a radio broadcast to the American people, beg anyone who knew the truth about the kidnapping and murder to come forward before it was too late? Colonel Kimberling shook his head.

After Kimberling came the defence attorneys, Fisher and Rosecrans and Pope, who did their best not to show their distress at seeing this man whom they had grown to admire and like appear before them like some grotesque clown, ashen-faced, hair shaved like a monk's tonsure, one trouser leg obscenely different from the other. He shook hands with them and thanked them for what they had done, and then the two pastors, Werner and Matthiesen, who had already visited him once or twice that day, came again to comfort him. The Reverend Werner asked if there was anything he wanted to say about the case, and for about the millionth time he said no, he had nothing to add to the truth. They asked if he would like to pray, and when he said his mind was too full to concentrate, they reminded him of the solace St Francis of Assisi had derived from murmuring to himself the single word 'God'. Then, together, they read the Bible.

From around 6 p.m. crowds began gathering outside the main gate of the prison: they saw, beneath the floodlit walls, two fire trucks and ninety fully armed policemen and state troopers, for Kimberling was taking no chances. An hour later the first of the forty-five guests arrived and walked down the aisle formed by some of the troopers, beneath the frieze of rams and serpents above the entrance gate, and into the prison. Thirty of the forty-five were press, the others New Jersey officials. At the top of the entrance steps the guests were frisked for cameras and weapons, and the state police officers had their pistols removed. A more detailed search was made in a small office and carried to almost ludicrous lengths. 'The guards', said *The New York Times*, 'examined everyone's hatband, coat and trouser linings and cuffs, buttons, pencils, fountain pens, matchboxes, watches, wallets, keyholders, envelopes, notebooks, papers, and the soles and heels of shoes.' They were then taken to another office and asked to wait.

They had been told they would be taken to the death chamber soon after 7.30, but the hour came and went and the clock moved on towards 7.45. There had been some muted chatter to begin with and the lighting of cigarettes, but now, thinking they would be summoned almost any moment, they fell silent, extinguished cigarettes. Meanwhile, in Cell 8 at the other end of the prison, Hauptmann was waiting too, using up the last minutes of his life in prayer with the Reverends Werner and Matthiesen. 'The Lord is my shepherd . . . he shall feed me in green pastures . . . yea, though I walk through the valley of the shadow of death, I will fear no evil; for thou art with me; thy rod and thy staff comfort me.' Soon he would be in Paradise, his sufferings over.

As the voices droned on, Hauptmann heard the sound of footsteps on the stone floor. They were not what he expected, the slow, heavy footsteps of the guards come to summon him next door, but quicker, lighter steps. The ministers stopped praying. Hauptmann looked up. Fisher was standing outside the bars. He was smiling. 'They've postponed it for at least two days,' he said.

Anna heard of the decision in her room at the Stacy-Trent. She had seen her husband for the last time the day before, and today she could do nothing but think of him, wondering how he was coping with the hours of waiting, knowing that he too was thinking of her. She had been out once, to buy herself a black dress, hat and veil, in recognition that the state was about to make her a widow. Now she lay on the bed wearing the dress, still thick with cold, drowsy from the sedative the doctor had given her. The telephone rang; it was Fisher with the news. Anna leapt from the bed, crying, 'I knew it! I told you so!' and went to change into a blue print dress with red and white flowers in readiness for the waiting photographers. She was overjoyed, interpreting the decision more as a cancellation than postponement. There must be some overwhelmingly strong reason for it taking place at the eleventh hour, she decided; and the state, having taken them all to the brink once, surely could not do so again.

The forty-five witnesses were led back to the main gate, half relieved, half disappointed. They mingled with the crowd, now nearly ten thousand strong, and disappeared into the night. The crowd itself refused to believe repeated announcements of the postponement, thinking the troopers wanted to get rid of them, and stayed around until after ten when the newsboys came round with the extras' banner headlines, HAUPTMANN REPRIEVED.

And the reason for the postponement: the Mercer County Grand Jury had taken it upon themselves to consider a possible bill of indictment against Paul Wendel for the murder of Charles Lindbergh Junior. They had sat all day and, not having reached a conclusion by evening, instructed their foreman, Alleyne Freeman, to telephone the Warden to ask that the execution be postponed. Kimberling, having discretionary powers to carry it out on any day within the same week, now ordered it to take place on the evening of Friday, 3 April.

Public reaction to the news of the postponement was as divided as had been the response to Hoffman's thirty-day reprieve. Many read into it a further sly attempt by the Governor to pervert the course of justice. A front-page editorial in the *Trenton Times* made a fresh call for Hoffman's impeachment, and a Professor of Astronomy and thirty-four other members of Princeton University faculty staff petitioned the state legislature to enquire whether grounds existed for removing Hoffman from office. Also, in a fit of pique, the Church of Seventh Day Adventists, Christians to a man, were so incensed by the Reverend Werner having publicly voiced his belief in Hauptmann's innocence that, despite his having been a pastor for thirty years and not now in the best of health, they declared him unfrocked and deprived of his pension.

Against this the Governor received many letters and telegrams applauding the postponement, including one from Clarence Darrow who had himself received numerous letters 'from all classes of persons including countless mothers of children'. Many of these letters condemned Condon, 'heretofore so eager to occupy the limelight, but now prevented by Wilentz from shedding further light on the situation'. To Darrow the immediate death of Hauptmann seemed unprofessional. 'In the face of such widespread public disapproval, he should be granted a new trial.'

But it was a foreigner, not an American, whose comments on the postponement caused the greatest stir. Writing in *Le Figaro,* the distinguished French man of letters André Maurois expressed the views of many Europeans who deplored the cruelty which condemned men were often obliged to suffer in the long-drawn-out American judicial process. Three times, he said, Hauptmann had awaited death on a date known to him:

> He has counted days, hours and minutes. Three times during these fearful days his mind has turned, supposedly for the final time, to the dreadful scene in that room, to the signal, the final shock and convulsions to follow. The last time his imagination was further stirred by the gruesome preparations in the death chamber, and by the shaving of his head for contact with the electrode.
>
> This is not all. This man has a mother and a wife. For them as well, these three frightful rehearsals have taken place. Three times the wife said her last farewell, and on Monday, while leaving the prison, she saw the workmen hastily installing telegraph equipment for

newspaper reporters. Nobody can picture such things without feeling pity.

Whether Hauptmann is guilty or not is no longer the question. The death of a guilty man may be necessary for the good of society. But all civilized people ought to admit that a man who has had the order of his execution countermanded at the last moment, should not then be forced to die.

The condemned man however had managed to recover some of his composure and appetite. On being taken back to the familiar surroundings of Cell 9 after the postponement, he had changed back into regular prison clothes, eaten a good dinner and then fallen into a sound sleep from which he didn't wake until ten the next morning. Anna Hauptmann was allowed a two-hour visit and reported him cheerful and hopeful of another reprieve.

Next day, after confessing to Anna transient doubts about God, he wrote, 'He has put it into my heart that I should live and that I should see you and Manfred again. God forgive me and help me in my lack of faith. From now on I shall leave everything in His hands . . . He will stay with me whatever will become.'

The Mercer County Grand Jury sat all Tuesday and Wednesday and then decided to discontinue their deliberations without a finding. If they had returned a true bill or a no-bill, Kimberling would have known what to do. But without either and yet with Wendel's arraignment for murder still on the file, he was in a dilemma. Should he make a further postponement to the end of the week or go ahead as planned? He asked Wilentz for a ruling and Wilentz was quite definite. The execution must be carried out as ordered unless (a) there was another reprieve from the Governor, (b) a direction from the Hunterdon County Court or some other competent court, or (c) commutation by the Court of Pardons. So Kimberling had all the witnesses telephoned to confirm that the execution would take place on the night of Friday, 3 April.

So now there was no going back; the demand for a burnt offering was irresistible, the public thirst for expiation could only be assuaged by Hauptmann's death. On 3 April he was moved back to Cell 8 where in the course of the day Fisher had a long talk with him, found him more composed. 'You don't know, Lloyd,' he said, 'what I went through three days ago. Even now I don't know what I do. If I cry like often I want to do when I think of Anni and Bubi, everybody will say I am guilty. If I fight with my heart and soul they will say I am cold-blooded fellow like one who would commit such a crime.' He asked Fisher to let Anna know he was all right, and not to mention about being moved to another cell.

Once again, this time at a little before seven that evening, the first of the fifty-odd witnesses made their way towards the main gate of the prison. It was a cold, grey, blustery evening, unlike the picnic weather of three days before, and although the fire trucks and police and troopers were again in position, it looked as though there would be no need for them; for tonight the crowd, half expecting another reprieve, numbered no more than five hundred. As before, the witnesses were first thoroughly searched by prison guards, then taken to Kimberling's office where they signed affidavits that they were not carrying cameras, weapons, drugs or other contraband. Then the deputy warden, Colonel Selby, took them to the prison centre, a circular space from which corridors radiated to the various cell blocks. He told them he would return presently and they could smoke. A clock on the wall showed close to 7.30.

Hauptmann meanwhile, back again in execution clothes – grey shirt, trousers with one leg split, slippers – and with a re-shaved scalp, was praying with Matthiesen and the loyal Werner. Earlier, in an article which would be published after his death, Hauptmann had written of his feelings sitting within ten feet of the chair and preparing to walk 'that last mile'. He imagined that the witnesses would include some who had helped prepare the case for the prosecution. 'It is my belief that their suffering, their agony, will be greater than mine. Mine will be over in a moment. Theirs will last as long as life itself.' (True, if they could ever have brought themselves to admit they had made a mistake, which they naturally never did.)

Fisher, still half hopeful of another last-minute reprieve, came to say goodbye. Matthiesen handed him a piece of paper on which Hauptmann had written a statement in German; it would, said the minister, be his final statement. He translated:

> I am glad that my life in a world which has not understood me has ended. Soon I will be at home with my Lord. And as I love my Lord, so I am dying an innocent man.
>
> Should however my death serve for the purpose of abolishing capital punishment . . . I feel that my death has not been in vain.
>
> I am at peace with God. I repeat, I protest my innocence of the crime for which I was convicted. However, I die with no malice or hatred in my heart. The love of Christ has filled my soul, and I am happy in him.

Hauptmann stood up, shook Fisher by the hand and thanked him again for all he had done ('You have been very kind to me, Lloyd'). Fisher looked at the shaven crown, the putty-like face on which for eighteen months the sun had never shone, reluctant to admit that everything he had done for him (and it was considerable) had been in vain. He had given Hauptmann a part of his life; until his own death things would never be the same again.

Fisher went along to the Warden's office, where Kimberling told him the Governor had sent word there would be no further reprieve. Fisher reminded Kimberling that his discretion in ordering the time of the execution lasted until midnight on Sunday. Would he defer it until then? The Warden shook his head. But in case there was a last-minute change of heart somewhere, he would postpone it by forty minutes.

And so the witnesses left standing in the draughty prison centre smoked more cigarettes and grumbled among themselves and asked what the delay was; it wasn't until just before 8 p.m. that Colonel Selby arrived to form them into two rows and not until 8.15 that Kimberling arrived to address them. They would watch the execution in silence; anyone who cried out or spoke would be removed by the guards; if Hauptmann spoke, if he indicated he wanted to confess, the Warden and no-one else would give whatever response he deemed necessary. Finally, because there had been persistent rumours that there would be an attempt to photograph the execution, there would be another search, beginning with himself, before they entered the chamber.

They set off two abreast in a file a hundred feet long, through the middle cell block, the dimly lit mess hall and kitchen corridors and out into the prison yard. The clouds had cleared, the stars were out, there was a pale moon. Ahead of them lay the squat shape of the death house, two guards with rifles and fixed bayonets patrolling its floodlit roof. A sound as of the murmur of the sea came to them: the voices of the crowd on the other side of the walls, now some two thousand strong.

They went through folding doors to the death-house court-yard and after being searched were allowed one by one into the execution chamber. It was a bare, square, brightly lit room with poorly whitewashed walls and a skylight in the roof. Resting against the centre of the far wall was the chair, like some tawdry throne awaiting the crowning of a new occupant. Between it and the ten rows of plain, wooden chairs had been draped a three-foot-high white canvas strip, to separate, as it were, the spectators from the performers.

Behind the chair was a cabinet enclosing an instrument panel and a large wheel, and standing beside it Robert Elliott, the executioner, and his assistant John Bloom. Elliott, in a grey suit, was grey-haired and had a deeply lined face, not unconnected with the nature of his job. 'I dreaded this assignment more than any other,' he wrote later. He had read the trial testimony, spoken to friends who had attended it, and was much concerned about the rightness of the sentence. 'I wondered whether justice would best be served by the snuffing out of the life of this man.' His not to reason why: killing people was his job.

The witnesses took their seats. The Warden, still wearing hat and topcoat, moved in front of the chair and asked everybody to button their coats and keep their hands out of their pockets. Reporters who wanted to make notes could do so as long as pads and pencils could be clearly seen. He motioned to a guard who held up a large clock: this was to fix the exact time of the execution. It read 8.36 p.m. He said to another guard, 'Before we call Hauptmann, I think it would be wise to telephone the central office and see if there is any message.'

The guard nodded and left. Elliott placed a wooden bar with light bulbs on the electric chair, then turned a switch on the instrument panel: the bulbs lit up. He removed the bar, and now everyone waited. They were waiting outside the prison walls too; in New York's Times Square a huge, silent crowd was waiting to see the announcement go up on the big illuminated ticker-tape; all over America and the world families and individuals waited by their radios to hear the words that would at last write *Finis* to this terrible story. So long overdue was the news that many thought there had been yet another postponement. Only those in the death house knew the event was imminent.

The guard who had gone away returned. There were no messages. Kimberling looked at Elliott who signified all was ready. Kimberling still hesitated, as though reluctant to assume responsibility for the final, irrevocable act. Then he turned and told the guards to bring in Hauptmann. Lieutenant Robert Hicks looked at Kimberling's face. 'I could read there', he said, 'an immense distaste for his task.'

The guards went through the steel door and closed it behind them. Now there was dead silence, for they were about to see a pornographic live show and live shows, whether of copulation or killing, instil a certain awe: both are about the mystery of life, its renewal and its ending; both are acts normally performed in private. A minute later the doors opened again. First came the guards and behind them Werner and Matthiesen, chanting a prayer in German; after them the semi-bald Hauptmann, pale and expressionless, one trouser leg flapping, shuffling to his doom in brown carpet slippers. He walked past the chair and would have collided with one of the attendant doctors had not a guard guided him back. He sat down heavily, laying his arms on the armrests as in the famous Abraham Lincoln statue. For a fleeting moment he glanced at the witnesses, and there were those who thought they caught the flicker of a smile. Some of the press still had pencils poised for a confession. 'Here was Hauptmann's chance to talk,' said Edward Folliard of the *Washington Post,* and seemed surprised he didn't take it.

The guards strapped Hauptmann's arms, chest and legs firmly to the chair. Elliott took one of the two cup-shaped electrodes dipped in brine, placed it on his head like a sort of coronet and secured it with a strap under the lower lip, as with the busby of a Coldstream guardsman. It took but a moment to fix the second electrode through the slit in the right trouser leg. Then a mask was placed over his face, so that the spectators might be spared the horrific contortions that two thousand volts do to a man's features, forcing his eyes almost out of his head.

Elliott walked to the control panel, looked at Kimberling. The guard held up the clock: it said 8.44. Kimberling nodded. Elliott turned the wheel, there was a drawn-out mournful whine from the dynamos like the wind in the Hopewell treetops, the bulbs in the control panel lit up as if on a Christmas tree, and the full charge drove into Hauptmann's body. He went rigid, strained against the straps, dropped back as the whine of the dynamos fell. One rookie spectator, unable to contain himself, cried out, 'Christ, it's terrible!' The process was repeated a second and third time. Against it could be heard the chanting of the defrocked Reverend Werner, continuing to give comfort to one already far beyond it, at 8.44 a sentient being, at 8.45 a corpse. '"I am the Resurrection and the Life," saith the Lord. "Whosoever liveth and believeth in me shall never die."' The spectators noticed a wisp of smoke above Hauptmann's head.

Elliott switched off the current, the three attendant doctors put their stethoscopes against Hauptmann's chest. Dr Wiesler, the prison doctor, spoke for all three. 'This man is dead,' he said, and again, 'This man is dead.'

The guards unstrapped the body and carried it into the autopsy room next door. The spectators, stunned and silent, rose from their chairs. Kimberling went outside to give the news to the press. Under the arc lights movie cameras and microphones had been positioned; some reporters had set up typewriters on little makeshift tables, others stood poised with pads and pencils at the ready; nearly all wore hats and many were smoking cigarettes.

There was only one question they wanted to ask. 'Did he make a statement before he went? Did he confess?'

'No,' said Kimberling, 'he made no statement after he left the cell.'

Why not? Expecting it, they felt puzzled, cheated, let down. But then the whole case had been a puzzle from the beginning, and as yet no-one had been able to figure out why.

Presently, in New York, a sub-editor of *The Times* roughed out a Page One headline for the next day's paper: 'HAUPTMANN SILENT TO THE END'.

Silent? It was a travesty of the truth, as great a lie as the headline that had told the world of his arrest back in September 1934 – 'LINDBERGH KIDNAPER JAILED'. Far from remaining silent he had from the outset, and with every breath in his body, unceasingly asserted his innocence to anyone who would listen. But to this the American press and people remained deaf: it was not, and never had been, what they wanted to hear.

As I write this, at Easter 1991, Mrs Hauptmann is still alive, now in her ninety-third year.

In 1988 the Independent Magazine *asked me to contribute to their series, 'My Hero', and I chose Anna Hauptmann. This is part of what I wrote (published on 3 December 1988):*

During the three years it took to make the film and write the book, I saw much of Anna Hauptmann; and I do not know of any woman whose integrity and strength of character I have admired more. During our many meetings she was calm, constant, resolute; sad and uncomprehending but never bitter: qualities, I was interested to see, that reporters had already found in her at the time of her husband's ordeal.

As she spoke, I came to understand something of the nightmare days she had lived through after his arrest, when he was savaged by the entire American press and beaten up by police desperate to obtain a confession to a crime which both he and Anna, themselves the parents of a much loved baby, found as abhorrent as anyone.

Then came the farce of the trial. 'Oh, Mr Kennedy, those lies they told. I couldn't believe people could stand there and tell such lies, and for two months my poor Richard and I had to sit and listen to them and say nothing.' She spoke with disdain of Edward Reilly, Richard's chief counsel, partly paid for by the anti-Hauptmann Hearst Press. 'He wanted me to say I had seen a box on the kitchen shelf when I had told him I hadn't. I said to him, "Mr Reilly, you want me to tell a lie, too." I can't do it, I said. Not even to save Richard.'

Then the year in Trenton prison's Death Row; a year in which, among others, New Jersey's governor and the prison chaplains also came to believe in his innocence. And, finally, the terrible day when they brought her the news that the law had taken its course. In her hotel room in Trenton she fell weeping and prostrate on the bed.

Their hunger for retribution assuaged, the American people turned their backs on the case, and on Anna too. But she had to live with it and the memory of how her life with Richard had been so brutally ended. Forgotten as though she had never existed, and with almost no money, she struggled to survive, often having to share a bed with her young son. For many years she supported the two of them with casual employment in bakeries and laundries.

For forty years Anna remained in limbo. Then in 1976, when Anthony Scaduto's book *Scapegoat* first questioned the correctness of the verdict, interest in the case was renewed. Articles were published, the FBI and the New Jersey police opened their archives, my film and book appeared. Anna came out of the shadows. She received hundreds of letters as a result of all the publicity, and drew comfort from the knowledge that now many others believed in Richard's innocence too.

You would have thought that all this would have led the New Jersey authorities to re-open the case, even declare that the verdict against Hauptmann was no longer safe. But that would have been asking too much of them. Only Anna remains optimistic. When newspapermen ask her how she has lived so long after all she has gone through, the blue eyes in the craggy face meet theirs unflinchingly. 'I am waiting for Richard's name to be cleared,' she says. 'When that is done I shall die. And I shall die happy.'

*

At the time of writing, a film script based on my book has been completed by playwright Bill Nicholson, author of the award-winning play Shadowlands. *With luck it should be in production within a year or so. My prayer is that Anna Hauptmann lives long enough to see it. Then the American people will know – and she will know they know – of the terrible thing that was done to her husband in their name, and which she has had to live with alone for the past fifty-five years.*

REFORMING THE ENGLISH CRIMINAL JUSTICE SYSTEM

HAVING WRITTEN FIVE books about miscarriages of justice, I began to ask myself whether, as regards the causes of the miscarriages, there was any common denominator between them; and it did not take me long to find out what it was: firstly the fabrication of evidence by a small but perennial hard core of corrupt police officers, and secondly the blindness of the judiciary in failing to recognize it. When I discussed this with my friend Jeremy Hutchinson, QC, he invited me to read a paper on the subject to the first-ever annual meeting of the English Bar Conference in 1986. This in turn led to an invitation to the International Bar Conference in New Zealand (1987), and later to give the Howard League of Penal Reform's annual lecture (1990). The piece that follows is a blend of all three.

When I was a boy it used to be said that British criminal justice was the finest in the world, a view held most strongly by those who had never studied any other system. Nobody says it today; and the release of the Guildford Four after fifteen years and of the Maguire seven after ten years of wrongful imprisonment, which are only the latest in a long line of miscarriages of justice – both the conviction of the innocent and the acquittal of the guilty – emphasizes what many of us have felt for some time – the urgent need for reform.

In cases which I have studied in depth and others which I have known about, the principal cause of miscarriages has been the same: the arranging and presentation of false evidence by the police, rarely to frame a man whom they know to be innocent (though this has happened) but rather to secure a conviction against those who, because of the pressures to obtain results, they have deluded themselves into thinking are guilty; and in this crude way to ensure, as they see it, that justice is done.

Consider some of these cases. In that of Timothy Evans, hanged for a murder he did not commit, the police first browbeat a confession out of him in the middle of the night, and then persuaded some workmen to retract a statement they had made which would have gone a long way to clearing him. In the case of Patrick Meehan, also granted a free pardon for a murder he did not commit and £50,000 compensation, they rigged an identification parade and planted incriminating evidence in the pocket of Meehan's accomplice James Griffiths. In the Luton Post Office murder case they bribed the one member of the gang they caught to name three totally innocent men as his accomplices. In the Confait case they bullied confessions out of three young men which resulted in their conviction for murder, and there are reasons to suppose that something similar happened in the Margaret Livesey case. And today there languishes in Long Lartin prison at Evesham a young man called George Long who has been in prison now for eleven years, convicted of a murder as a result of another so-called 'confession' to the police and which, having seen him and read the papers on his case, I am as certain as he is that he did not commit. In addition to these cases there are now serious doubts about the conviction of Judith Ward, the defendants in the Carl Bridgewater case and the Broadwater Farm case and the cases of the Darvell brothers, Ernie Clarke, Stephen Spencer, Robert Brown, Anthony Steel, Robert Campbell and Sammy Davis.

How many are there in our prisons at any one time who have been wrongly convicted? David Jessel of the *Rough Justice* programme has pointed out that even if 99 per cent of all convictions are correct, that still leaves in a prison population of 40,000 convicted persons some 400 people who shouldn't be there. Asked his view, the late Secretary of JUSTICE, Tom Sargant, estimated that at any one time between 200 and 300 of the prison population had been wrongly convicted, and from the correspondence I have received from prisoners or their families over the years, I would think that a fair figure.

This of course is something that judges and others are apt to pooh-pooh. 'Oh, we all know about those fellows,' they say, 'trying it on in the hope that someone will believe them. And why not? They've got nothing to lose.' This has not been my experience. On the whole, as any prison governor will tell you, guilty men come to accept their conviction and sentence. They do not have the motivation, the evidence or indeed the acting skills necessary to assert their innocence and go on asserting it year after year after year. Yet this is what innocent men do. They never let up, always searching for fresh evidence, always writing to those who they think might help them, always seeking to have their cases reviewed. I have no hesitation at all in saying that those cases which year after year, decade after decade, go on demanding to be reassessed, cases like those of Timothy Evans, James Hanratty, Patrick Meehan, the Confait case, the Luton case, the cases of the Guildford Four, the Maguire Seven and the Birmingham Six, are all cases about innocent people. For in the end truth will out, and even though the Home Office will try to fight a rearguard action about the safety of the convictions of the Birmingham Six for a little while longer, they cannot do it indefinitely.

When cases like these have dragged on for years there inevitably emerges another litmus test of innocence which, though it can have no place as evidence in a Court of Appeal, might well be regarded favourably by a Court of Last Resort, especially if such a court included lay assessors. I am thinking not just of the unadorned declarations of innocence by those convicted, but of the nature and quality of those declarations, especially as they emerge in letters to their families or solicitors.

Here is Gerard Conlon, one of the Guildford Four, describing in a letter home how he came to sign his confession. After relating how the police had spent some time calling him an effing, murdering Irish bastard, squeezing his testicles, hitting him in the kidneys and slapping his face, he wrote:

> I was crying and frightened. Simmons said if I didn't make a statement, he would ring Belfast first thing in the morning and I would never see my mother or sister

again. The last of my resistance shattered when he said that. I was crying and shaking uncontrollably. I said my family hadn't done anything. I fell apart. Simmons said what happened to my family was up to me. I said I would make a statement like they wanted, but it wouldn't be true as I really didn't do it . . .

And he ended, 'Mum, we was fitted up something rotten.' Does anyone seriously think that a guilty man, one who had blown up a pub, killed five people and wounded many more, would have had the acting skills to write something as seemingly spontaneous and convincing as this?

Or again, take what David Cooper and Michael McMahon wrote in their diaries nine years after being convicted of the Luton Post Office murder and, at this time, without any news of when they would be released. Cooper first:

I shall be vindicated, I am more certain of that than I am of anything in my life, and although it is at times a slow and agonizing road I tread, the time will come when I shall be heard and cleared of the indictment held against me.

And now McMahon:

For the past ten years I have been keeping vigil in a nocturnal maze, and will continue to do so until daybreak. I am sometimes weary, sometimes depressed . . . but the driving force created by the injustice never deserts me. In and out of prison I will relentlessly fight my case until my conviction for murder is finally quashed.

Once again one has to ask, are those the words of guilty men, brilliant dissimulators? Could guilty men writing only for themselves manage to express themselves like that? A year later, after I had published a book on the case to which Lord Devlin had contributed, they were quietly let out of prison.

If police malpractices which lead to miscarriages of justice are in themselves deplorable, then even more so surely must be the inability of the Court of Appeal on so many occasions to correct them. In the Luton case it failed to do so, in the Guildford case, after two IRA men had admitted to the bombing, it failed to do so, in the 1987–8 rehearing of the case of the Birmingham Six, it failed to do so. Why is this? It is, I suggest, because of a deep-seated reluctance of the Court to disturb the verdicts of juries, especially when those verdicts have depended primarily on police evidence.

The judiciary and the police, that is the administrators and guardians of the law are, and to a great degree must be, seen to be in partnership. The police, when all is said and done, are the thin blue line that stands between us and anarchy, and if they did not believe that their word would be given greater credibility in a court than that of any other witness, their morale would sink even lower than it has already – though paradoxically it is because their position gives them this credibility that enables them to go on committing malpractices. In the last analysis though, and until the police are seen to have cleaned up their act, the judiciary should treat police evidence, especially where it is challenged, with as much caution as any other evidence. When the judiciary do not do this, then they, no less than the police, have allowed the system to corrupt them.

But where judicial reluctance to overturn a verdict or admit to a miscarriage is most marked is in the findings of those inquiries set up by the Home Office and conducted by a judge or senior QC. As I have already said, in the first inquiry into the Timothy Evans case, Mr John Scott Henderson, QC, concluded that there had been no miscarriage of justice; while in the second a few years later Mr Justice Brabin concluded that while Evans was probably not guilty of the murder of his child on which he had been convicted and hanged, he probably was guilty of the murder of his wife on which charge he had never been tried. In the Hanratty case Mr Lewis Hawser, QC, concluded that his conviction had been perfectly safe and satisfactory despite a whole body of evidence to suggest otherwise. In the Confait case the three youths had the convictions quashed by the Court of Appeal, but a subsequent inquiry by Sir Henry Fisher concluded that two of the three youths were guilty of murder and that all three were guilty of arson. Later fresh evidence emerged which led the Attorney-General in the House of Commons to announce that none of the three youths had been involved at all.

And lastly in the Meehan case the Scottish judge, Lord Hunter, after a four-year inquiry concluded that while Meehan and his friend Griffiths probably had not committed the murder for which Meehan was convicted, those who had committed it had probably taken them along as a sort of back-up team – a preposterous suggestion which helped to sustain the false evidence of the police that they had found incriminating evidence in Griffiths's coat pocket.

What emerges from all this is that judges and senior QCs are, as Mr Michael Mansfield, QC, has suggested, somewhat unreliable when it comes to interpreting the facts. Perhaps it is not so surprising. 'I will explain to you the law,' they tell juries, 'but it is for you to reach a verdict on the facts.' I would feel a lot happier about the appointment of Sir John May to conduct an inquiry into the Guildford and Maguire cases if I knew that he would have a couple of lay assessors to help him.[1] Lay assessors with open minds, who would give to disputed police evidence no more or less weight than to any other evidence, were what the House of Commons committee on Miscarriages of Justice advocated for Courts of Last Resort; and it was deplorable that the Home Office should have turned down the whole concept of a Court of Last Resort.

So what are the most urgent needs for reform, first to prevent miscarriages of justice as a result of police manipulation of the evidence, and secondly to ensure that the Court of Appeal reassesses evidence in a less restricted and cavalier way than it does at present? I think there is room for short-term and long-term improvements.

In the short term the remedy is quite simple. It is that in all cases of serious crime, murder, manslaughter, rape, armed robbery, offences for which the penalty is likely to be many years of imprisonment, the questioning of suspects be taken out of the hands of the police and given instead to

[1] My plea was successful! Lay assessors were appointed.

an examining magistrate, analagous to the *juge d'instruction* in France, and who will direct the police in their inquiries. It has been suggested recently that confessions obtained by the police should not be admitted as evidence unless strongly supported by other independent evidence, as happens under Scottish law. I would go further and, because of the whole, long, dreadful history of false confessions, would like to see as inadmissible any alleged confession obtained by the police at any time. Video tape recordings of interviews will provide only limited safeguards, for if a policeman goes to arrest a suspect and reports the suspect as saying 'Who grassed me, gov?' or whatever is its modern equivalent,[1] even though the suspect didn't say it, then there is nothing to stop it being admitted as evidence, and another miscarriage of justice is given a push from behind.

The appointment of an examining magistrate, which incidentally is supported by that wise man Lord Scarman, would do three things. It would prevent innocent people being convicted as the result of bogus confessions to the police. Secondly, in cases where juries are suspicious of police evidence (and I'm told that an increasing number are), it would prevent the acquittal of the guilty. And thirdly, if the questioning is fair and non-partisan, there can no longer be any reason for retaining the suspect's right to silence. Indeed I would extend the abolition of the right to silence to the court of trial; with the proviso that if the defendant chose not to answer the questions put to him, either by the examining magistrate or at trial, the court would be entitled, as it is not entitled at present, to view this as indicative of guilt.

Next, how to improve Appeal Court procedure, ensure that in future the Courts arrive at more realistic judgements? If I say that justice is too important to be left to the judiciary, I shall not be popular in certain quarters, but I believe that their record in recent cases, both in Court of Appeal judgements and in the findings of post-Appeal Inquiries, shows this to be so. British criminal trials are based on the lay element.

[1] In December 1990 evidence emerged of officers in the since disbanded West Midlands Serious Crimes Squad fabricating bogus confessions from suspects in the backs of police cars.

It is the jury, not the judge, who are interpreters of the facts, the jury, not the judge, who determine the fate of the defendant. Why therefore exclude this lay element from the Court of Appeal? Why discourage the judge at the court of trial from extrapolating from the facts, yet allow the judges of the Appeal Court to do so? As Lord Devlin has forcibly said, there is a lack of consistency in the matter.

The advantage of a lay element – I am thinking of a single judge with two lay assessors – would be considerable. First, as I have said, the lay assessors would not have the same inhibitions as the judges about assessing police evidence. Secondly, it would obviate the need to send a case back for retrial with all the problems of tracing witnesses, some maybe abroad or ill or even dead. Thirdly, while the judges of the Appeal Court are not forbidden from reassessing old evidence as well as considering fresh, they are always reluctant to do so, and in disputed cases the assessors would no doubt insist that they did. Fourthly, it would free two of the three judges who normally hear appeals to sit with other assessors and so help to ease the perennial backlog of cases waiting to be heard. There would of course be no need for lay assessors in appeals which depended solely on point of law. Nor, with assessors sitting with judges in the Appeal Courts, would there be so pressing a need for a Court of Last Resort.

I would hope however that there would be scope for the calling of new (and where feasible former) witnesses; also that the court be not bound by the strict rules of evidence which apply in courts of trial and which so often impede the discovery of the truth. I would also advocate a lay element in the decision whether or not to grant leave of appeal; this would reduce the risk of the judiciary refusing an appeal which a more open-minded lay person might feel had merit.

What I have suggested so far – the appointment of examining magistrates to interrogate suspects in all serious cases, and the appointment of lay assessors to join the judges in the Appeal Court – is in my view not only desirable but also practicable. It would require no more than an extension of existing legislation. And yet it is only tinkering with the problem, and what I propose now is altogether more radical.

It is that the adversary system of criminal justice which we employ in this country and which we have exported to the United States and Commonwealth and which is essentially one of conflict, is not only extremely childish, but a most unsatisfactory way of attempting to dispense justice. In a situation where one side is doing its best to vanquish the other, truth is apt to fall by the wayside.

The adversary system was a comparative late development in English law. Until well into the eighteenth century cases were heard without benefit of counsel so that the trial judge was both examiner and cross-examiner, as he is in France today. This, said Hawkins, in his *Pleas of the Crown* in 1721, was just as it should be. 'The very speech, gesture and countenance of those who are guilty, when they speak for themselves,' he wrote, 'may often help to disclose the truth which would probably not be so well discovered from the artificial defence of those speaking for them.' This, in essence, is the inquisitorial system as practised on the continent.

By this time, in France they had already established the system of the examining magistrate sifting out prosecution witnesses and preparing a dossier on the case for the trial judge. In England, having no such sifting process, all sorts of vagabonds – reward seekers, those with a score to settle, accomplices turning King's evidence – would appear for the prosecution; and it was to protect the accused against the likes of these, at a time when you could be hanged for petty theft, that defence counsel first began to emerge. Often, having demolished the prosecution witnesses, they found that there was no case for their clients to answer and no need for their clients to speak; and from there it was a succession of steps, first to the accused earning the right not to speak, then to his being forbidden to speak, and finally under the Criminal Evidence Act at the turn of the last century, to him being permitted to speak if he wanted to. Next it was decided that an accused could not be convicted on the word of an accomplice alone, and that was the start of the tortuous path leading to the Rules of Evidence with which we are plagued today and which seem to many even more complicated than the Rules of Golf. And gradually over the years counsel became what they are today, the dominant figures in court.

Thus the adversary system came about, in the words of Charles Langbein, Professor of Law at Chicago University, 'slowly, incrementally, without plan or theory,' until it became the top-heavy, wholly artificial creature that it is today. It is a system in which the accused, the most important person present in the sense that he has more to gain or lose than anyone else, is somehow seen to be the least important, an object rather than a subject; in which a spurious sense of drama is created which encourages counsel to strike postures and attitudes, and even indulge in sarcasm; in which counsel see it as one of their tasks to destroy the credibility of the other side's witnesses, whether the issue be pertinent to the verdict or not; in which some questions that could provide a shortcut to the truth are not allowed to be asked and others which are asked are not allowed to be answered; in which the evidence of witnesses is shaped by what the prosecution and defence want them to say or what they think prosecution and defence want them to say; in which other witnesses whose evidence might help to shape the jury's verdict are not called for fear of saying the wrong thing; in which police evidence given or suppressed can convict an innocent man and the skills of counsel can – and in many cases have – set free a guilty one. Is that really the best we can do? If we were devising a system of justice today from scratch, would it ever occur to us to dream up something so patently idiotic and inefficient as this?

Let us therefore consider an alternative system, and in particular the one that is nearest to us and when the Channel Tunnel is completed, will be nearer still, the inquisitorial system as practised in France and elsewhere.

Now among the members of the English Bench and Bar there is a strong feeling of antagonism towards the inquisitorial system. To many the word has overtones of the Spanish Inquisition, of torture employed to obtain confessions, of the third degree once practised by the police in America. Also being French, it is automatically suspect. I have heard English barristers refer to French judges as faceless bureaucrats – though as they do not wear wigs, you see rather more of their faces than you do in Britain. I have heard others speak scathingly of the 'so-called' inquisitorial system, which is so called because an inquiry is what it is.

How does it work? I have already explained the role of the examining magistrate or *juge d'instruction*. Initially the *juge* will interview a suspect alone, but once he has been charged the accused is entitled to have a lawyer present. Some French lawyers have told me that a man reluctant to answer questions from a hostile policeman is often more ready to unburden himself to a neutral *juge* who He keeps a running dossier on the case which can be inspected at any time by prosecution and defence. When his inquiries are complete, he forwards the dossier to the Public Prosecutor who himself will forward it – if the case merits it – to the court in which it will be tried. This will either be the *Tribunal Correctionel* in which three judges sit without a jury or the highest criminal court of all, the *Cour d'Assise*, in which three judges and nine jurors sit together and agree together, under the direction of the presiding judge, on both verdict and sentence. Some, I know, think that the proximity of judges and jurors makes the jurors susceptible to judicial influence, but it is also said that they are made to feel less the detached observers they are under the adversary system and more a responsible and integral part of the trial process. In the *Tribunal Correctionel* the verdict of the three judges must be unanimous. In the *Cour d'Assise* of the twelve votes cast there must be a majority of 8 to 4 for verdict and a simple majority of 7 to 5 for sentence.

The inquisitorial approach which began with the investigations of the *juge* is continued in the court of trial; which means that the questioning of witnesses is not done by partisan counsel but by the presiding judge, counsel's role being limited to opening and closing speeches, though at any time they may ask the presiding judge to put questions they think he has omitted to put.

This method has several advantages. Firstly it avoids the pseudodramatic atmosphere of the adversary-system trial. One reason why you see so few third-rate courtroom dramas emanating from countries with the inquisitorial system is that the system, being essentially low key, simply does not lend itself to that kind of thing. Secondly, the questioning of witnesses in a quiet, firm but non-partisan way is often more productive of a fruitful response than by the employment of a more aggressive approach. Thirdly, the system saves time for it obviates the need for prosecution and defence to cover, often at tedious length, the same ground; and this also can be less confusing for the jury. And lastly the trial itself does not come grinding to a halt, as so often happens in Britain, when the jury are shuffled out of court so that the judge can decide what is or is not admissible evidence. In a system whose object is to find the truth, there is very little evidence – so long as it is thought relevant – that is not admissible.

Another attractive feature of the French system is the way in which expert witnesses are treated. In Britain prosecution and defence each produce their own tame psychiatrist or pathologist and, by skilful questioning along narrow lines, invariably make them seem to contradict each other. In France it is the custom of the court to call as many expert witnesses as the court or counsel may require and by painstaking eliciting of information try, wherever possible, to reach a consensus. This is surely a more effective method of reaching the truth than the adversary approach, which can be both humiliating for the expert witnesses as well as puzzling for the jury.

How does the inquisitorial system fare as regards results? In the *Tribunal Correctionel* the conviction rate is around 90 per cent, in the *Cour d'Assise* 95 per cent, which compares poorly with our conviction rate of some 50 per cent of contested pleas. It is sometimes said that this high conviction rate comes about because in France you are presumed guilty until proved innocent. That old cliché is untrue. What is true is that the investigations of the *juge* are so thorough that by the time the case goes to trial, the likelihood is that the accused *is* guilty. If after his inquiries the *juge* is unable to make a charge for lack of evidence, then no name will go forward. Unlike the police here, the *juge* will not chuck a name into the ring in the hope that it will stick.

Are there fewer miscarriages of justice in cases of serious crime in France? Certainly there are fewer reports of them in the papers, though that could be a reluctance of officialdom to admit to them. My own impression is that in the *Tribunal Correctionel* and the *Cour d'Assise,* fewer guilty men go free and fewer innocent are convicted, though under an inquisitorial system that is what you would expect; for the elimination of police malpractices combined with the rigorous investigations of the *juge* and the accused having to give an account of himself at all stages are factors built into the system to bring about a correct verdict. I think it probable that if there had been an examining magistrate investigating the cases of Timothy Evans, James Hanratty, Patrick Meehan, the two in the Luton case, Margaret Livesey, George Long, the Guildford Four, the Maguire Seven and the Birmingham Six, not one of those unfortunates – in addition to scores of others – would have come to trial, let alone have been convicted.

Despite all this, I do not see our deeply conservative Bar and Bench responding warmly to these proposals; I do not see our barristers accepting passively a role in court where they can no longer shine. I do not see our judges of first instance changing willingly from being boxing-match referees to seekers after truth. Yet surely the time has come, indeed is long past, to persuade our law makers and our law dispensers to look at our system of criminal justice, for so long taken for granted, with fresh eyes.

In praising the French system I am not unaware of its defects or of the adverse comments that the French people consistently make of it in practice. They say that many of the *juges d'instruction* are too young and inexperienced to be allotted such power; that suspects are kept in prison for far too long while awaiting trial (though the same charge can be levelled here); and that the whole investigative process is too laborious and time consuming. There are other criticisms too but I still maintain that the *principle* of trial by discovery is a fairer and more effective one than of trial by conflict. If we were to adopt the former, with perhaps the sort of modifications they have in German criminal courts, I am certain that we could exercise it more efficiently and justly than do the French.

There are two other reforms I would like to see. First, the establishment of a Ministry of Justice, responsible for all matters relating to justice and, unlike the Home Office, to nothing else; and with a Minister answerable to Parliament. And secondly, the modernization of court dress and court language, both of which help to sustain those who sit on the Bench in a kind of fairy-tale world of their own inventing, and give them an inflated importance which is bad for them, bad for society and bad for justice. Maybe there was a time when paternalism was all the rage and judges felt it necessary to dress up in outlandish gear both to emphasize their authority and to distance themselves from the rest of us. But not, surely, today. Gentlemen gave up wigs in the eighteenth century, bishops in the nineteenth, and it was a nineteenth-century Lord Chief Justice, Lord Denman, who called them the silliest things in England. Yet today's judges continue to parade before us as so many Mrs Tiggiwinkles. If judges can abandon their wigs to talk to children in child abuse cases, lest the very sight of them give the children either the giggles or the jim-jams, then they can dispose of them when talking to adults too; for fear must always be a bar to understanding. For Bar and Bench alike surely no more is required than a gown and white bands.

And while at it, why not make an effort to modernize court language. Why *albeit* instead of *although,* why *avocation* instead of *job*, why *resiling* and *ex parte* and *res ipsa loquitur*? And why refer to judges as 'my lord' and 'your lordship' when they are no more than knights? Why not address them as 'Sir James' or 'Sir John' when first addressed and simply 'Sir' in between whiles? Judges are human like the rest of us, and to try to dehumanize them by the use of fancy clothes and fancy language can, in my view, only be counter-productive. To those who believe that fancy clothes and language help to enhance the dignity of the law, I would reply that they tend to diminish it.

But within the legal profession itself there are, I think, signs of a movement for change; and one of the most hopeful has been the recent report of a Bar working party recommending in principle the televising of certain trials. There will be problems in this of course, but there seems no reason why what the public gallery sees should not, thanks to modern technology, be seen by other members of the public – a view which the House of Commons, rather late in the day, also came to accept. Edited versions of the trials of, say, John Christie, Stephen Ward, Jeremy Thorpe and more recently of the Birmingham Six and of the Guinness defendants, also of the libel actions of Jeffrey Archer against the *Star* and of Lord Aldington against Count Tolstoy would, I believe, have been for a public who have never been inside a court of law nor are ever likely to be, a revealing and informative experience.

Let me conclude by repeating what I wrote in 1965 at the end of my book on the trial of Stephen Ward, and not a word of which would I wish to withdraw today:

> The antique ritual of our courts is positively harmful, for it drives a wedge between the citizen and the law, outlawing him as a stranger in his own land, making him hostage to customs which he has had no share in framing.
>
> There is need for flexibility instead of fossilization, for all the diverse elements in a courtroom to be brought nearer together, not driven further apart, a need for communication and understanding. It is time not only for the rules of the game to be revised; but also, if people like Stephen Ward are to have a just trial in future, to ask ourselves whether the game we have chosen is the one that we wish to go on playing.

THE BIRMINGHAM SIX

MEANWHILE THE TWO *cases which have become known as the Guildford Four and the Birmingham Six were beginning to raise their heads. In 1974 as part of a terrorist bombing campaign in England the IRA planted bombs in two public houses in Guildford and two in Birmingham with horrific casualties. In the two Guildford pubs five people were killed and fifty wounded, and in the two Birmingham pubs twenty-one were killed and 162 wounded, mostly young people. Outrage and anger made themselves felt throughout the country, and there was tremendous pressure on the police to bring the perpetrators to book. As a result the Guildford police picked up three young Irishmen and an English girl, and by a process of prolonged beatings and threats, terrorized them into signing 'confessions' which led to their trials, convictions and sentencing to life imprisonment.*

Two years after their trial I was approached by the BBC to look at the papers in the case and on a cursory reading came to the conclusion that there were grave doubts about their guilt: apart from the 'confessions' there was not a single piece of evidence against them. However, the BBC decided at that time not to pursue the case further. During the next ten years doubts about the verdicts increasingly surfaced and then in 1986 my friend Robert Kee wrote the first book on the case, Trial and Error, *a devastating indictment of both the trial and the appeal. True to form the authorities ignored it; but two years later another book on the case,* Time Bomb *by Grant McKee and Ros Franey, was published, for which I wrote a foreword.*

Eventually and as a result of continued public unease and the relentless efforts of the Four's solicitors, the Home Secretary ordered an inquiry by the Avon and Somerset Police into the circumstances of their arrests and convictions. On receipt of their first report the Home Secretary, Douglas Hurd, let it be known that he was not of a mind to pursue the allegations of a miscarriage of justice further; but faced with the prospect of a continued campaign by Cardinal Hume, two former Home Secretaries (Jenkins and Rees) and two Law Lords (Devlin and Scarman), he instructed the police to continue their inquiries. They then found enough evidence of perjury by the Surrey police to confirm the Four's claims that the 'confessions' were unreliable, and when the case came up for appeal, the Director of Public Prosecutions offered no evidence to sustain the convictions. The Lord Chief Justice ordered their release and after a total of fifteen years' imprisonment and amid scenes of great jubilation, they were let out into the street to rebuild their lives and rejoin society. Each was awarded £50,000 compensation with a promise of more to come.

Meanwhile campaigners for the Birmingham Six were being equally active in the efforts to have their cases reviewed, and in late 1987 as the result of an inquiry conducted by the Devon and Cornwall police it went back to the Appeal Court. All six appeals were rejected. Although assured by those whose judgements I respected that here was another gross miscarriage of justice, I knew little of the details of the case; but at the invitation of The Sunday Times, I undertook a thorough survey of it in the winter of 1989–1990 and formed my own conclusions. Because of restrictions of space The Sunday Times had to trim my article (published on 25 February 1990) by about a fifth. Here is the original article as I wrote it.

Just over two years ago the Court of Appeal in the shape of Lord Lane the Lord Chief Justice, Lord Justice O'Connor and Lord Justice Stephen Brown heard fresh evidence in the case of the six Irish drinking companions, convicted in 1975 for the murder of those killed in the IRA bombing of two Birmingham pubs. Evidence was led on the two heads that had resulted in the men's convictions: firstly that it could no longer be concluded that any of them had been in contact with explosives, and secondly that their alleged 'confessions' had been obtained by threats and violence (as in the case of the Guildford Four). The court rejected both submissions. 'The longer this case has gone on', they said, 'the more convinced this court has become that the verdict of the jury was correct'. The appeals would be dismissed.

Yet the case refuses to die . . . which in itself and like so many other cases, indicates that whatever the opinions of judges may be, there are others no less worthy of belief who continue to assert that justice has miscarried. So were the judges in the recent appeal of the Birmingham Six right in their judgement or wrong?

Whenever in the past I have looked into a case of an alleged miscarriage of justice, I have always gone first to the convicted men's solicitors because they are least likely to be conned by the guilty proclaiming innocence. Ivan Geffen has been solicitor of two of the six for twelve years and Gareth Peirce of the other four for nine years. Neither has the slightest doubt about their innocence. Peirce has called the findings of the Court 'disgraceful', Geffen says, 'It's only what one has come to expect from this Court of Appeal.'

The three counsel for the men take a broadly similar view. Lord Gifford, QC, told me, 'The judges had no business dismissing the evidence of police malpractice and violence. To come to the conclusions they did on evidence which was 90 per cent written and only 5 per cent oral is to assume powers of divination which no-one should arrogate to themselves.' Richard Ferguson, QC, said the findings had sickened him. 'The whole demeanour of the judges was not to find the truth but how to counter the good arguments of our side. They were also gratuitously offensive. Coming as I do from Northern Ireland, I find it particularly distressing when justice fails to live up to the high standards we were brought up to believe in.' And Michael Mansfield, QC, who thinks there should have been a retrial, most of the participants being still alive, said that the judgement had left him angry and upset. 'I think it did incomparable damage to people's concept of justice.'

It was the same with the three distinguished scientists whose evidence clashed with that of Dr Frank Skuse, the forensic scientist who had appeared for the prosecution and was later dismissed on the grounds of limited efficiency. David Baldock, a former senior scientific officer at the Home

Office Laboratories, told me, 'When I turned up at the Old Bailey to give evidence, Michael Mansfield said, "We're wasting our time. They're not listening. I think the judges quite failed to grasp the nettle of the scientific evidence."' Dr Brian Caddy, head of the University of Strathclyde's Forensic Science Unit agreed, and Dr Hugh Black, former Chief Inspector of Explosives at the Home Office, went further. 'Their decision,' he wrote to me, 'was an outrage.'

Having myself read the Court's judgement and the evidence presented to it; having spoken personally to some of the new witnesses; having visited Birmingham's Queens Road Police Station where the alleged beatings of the prisoners and the 'confessions' that followed took place; and having also read Chris Mullin MP's well-documented book on the case, I am led inexorably to the same conclusions. So if we are all right in our views, how was it that the Court's findings came to be so at variance with the evidence presented?

In many murder cases where justice is later found to have miscarried, it often happens that quite early in their investigations the police light on some small but seemingly convincing piece of evidence that leads them to draw the wrong conclusions; and which, if pursued tenaciously, leads in turn to wrongful prosecution, conviction and sentence. In the 10 Rillington Place case they assumed that Timothy Evans would not have sold his furniture and fled to Wales had he not murdered his wife and child whose bodies they had discovered in the ground-floor wash-house; and from there it was a short step to their manufacturing a false confession which led to his conviction and hanging. In the Ayr murder case Patrick Meehan's life sentence originated from his admission to the police that he and his friend Jim Griffiths had been engaged on a criminal enterprise near the scene of the crime when the only firm evidence the police then had was that the two intruders had called each other 'Pat' and 'Jim'; and to make certain of a conviction the police planted false evidence in Jim Griffiths's coat pocket. Similarly in the Lindbergh baby kidnapping case the discovery of $14,000 of marked ransom money under the floorboards of Hauptmann's garage in the Bronx was enough to convince New York and New Jersey police of his guilt, and with a wealth of fabricated evidence to railroad him to the electric chair.

In the case of the Birmingham Six their undoing was their association with an IRA bomber named James McDade who on 14 November 1974 blew himself up while planting a bomb in the Coventry Telephone Exchange. Five of the six (Gerry Hunter, Paddy Hill, Richard McIlkenny, Billy Power and Hughie Callaghan) had grown up with McDade in the small Roman Catholic enclave of the Ardoyne in West Belfast, where as children they had suffered abuse and discrimination from the surrounding Protestant majority. All had come to Birmingham to seek work, mostly in the 1960s, and it was there that the sixth member of the group, Johnny Walker from Londonderry, came to know McDade and the others. Until McDade blew himself up, only one of the six, Walker, suspected that McDade was an IRA activist. They themselves were not members of the IRA, or even of Sinn Fein. But they were staunch supporters of the Republican cause and its belief in a United Ireland, and they all helped to raise money to send to dependants of Ulster fellow Catholics who had been imprisoned or interned.

On 21 November 1974 the body of James McDade was to be flown from Birmingham to Belfast, and to show Ardoyne solidarity five of the six agreed to combine attendance at his funeral with a visit to their families. Their friend Hughie Callaghan saw them off at Birmingham's New Street Station on the 7.55 p.m. train which would connect with the night boat from Heysham. At 8.17 p.m. the first bomb went off in the Mulberry Bush pub and a few minutes later the second in the Tavern in the Town, both near to the station, and resulting in the horrific casualties of twenty-one dead and 162 injured. Ports and airports were immediately alerted, and when the booking clerk at New Street reported that he had sold consecutive numbered tickets to a group of Irishmen travelling to Belfast, the Lancashire Police were asked to interview them at Heysham.

The five reached Heysham at 10.45, having spent most of the journey smoking and playing cards and having been observed by a British Rail guard as being in good humour. Paddy Hill was out first, and after showing the contents of his luggage to the waiting police and told them he was going to see his grandmother and aunt in Belfast, he was allowed through to the boat where he settled himself in the bar to wait for the others. They also were interrogated and had their luggage examined. If they were innocent, they knew nothing of the explosions in the two Birmingham pubs; but because of the IRA bombs that had gone off in the Birmingham area in recent months, they said nothing about going to McDade's funeral. Then their clothing was searched, and in Walker's coat were found Roman Catholic mass cards for the funeral of McDade. The local police called up the head of Lancashire CID who ordered the men to be taken to Morecambe police station for further interrogation, and for Dr Frank Skuse to be there with his equipment for detecting traces of explosive. As the four men were being taken away, they asked what had happened to their mate. They were asked what mate, and when they said Paddy Hill, he was taken off the ferry to join them.

If the six were guilty, there are already two things wrong with this scenario. Firstly, as Lord Scarman has pointed out to me, as trained IRA men they would hardly have been so foolish as to set the bombs to explode at a time which they knew would give the police two and a half hours to alert the Lancashire Police to their arrival at Heysham. And secondly, they would not have called the police's attention to the missing Paddy Hill; they would have been glad that at least one of their number looked like getting away.

There is evidence that on the journey to Morecambe all five of the group appeared relaxed which, if innocent, they had every reason to be. On arrival they were put in different cells. In the small hours of the morning Dr Skuse arrived, also Superintendent George Reade from Birmingham and detectives from the West Midland Serious Crime Squad, now disbanded because of misconduct of many of its officers. One by one the five men were escorted in to Dr Skuse to have their hands swabbed in what was called the Griess test, then regarded as a reliable method of detecting nitro-glycerine but now, like Dr Skuse himself, considered un-reliable. McIlkenny's, Hunter's and Walker's hands proved negative, as did the left hands of Power and Hill. But the right hands of Power and Hill proved positive. This, said Frank Skuse, made him 99 per cent certain that both Power and Hill had recently been in contact with explosives.

Before considering the 'confessions' that followed, let us follow the forensic evidence which began with Dr Skuse's findings at Morecambe right through to the final verdict on them at the 1987–8 Court of Appeal. At the trial of the six in Lancaster, Mr Justice Bridge said that the forensic test was one of two 'absolutely critical' chapters in the prosecution's case. Yet Skuse in evidence had to admit that when he subjected the traces of Power's and Hill's right hands to two further tests, one of which, the GCMS at Aldermaston, was said to be a hundred times more sensitive than Griess, both registered negative. But he stuck to his 99 per cent certainty of the tests at Morecambe, and added that in the GCMS test a trace from Hill's *left* hand (which was found negative at Morecambe) had also proved positive. However, Dr Hugh Black for the defence said he had seen a print-out of this GCMS test and that it had *not* proved positive.

Nor was that all. In May 1985 the Granada television programme, *World In Action,* invited Mr David Baldock and Dr Brian Caddy, the two forensic scientists referred to earlier, to carry out the Griess test on a variety of common substances. Between them they found that items containing nitro-cellulose, such as lacquer, aerosol spray, cigarette packets and old playing cards, all gave Griess positive. It will be remembered that the men were smoking and playing cards on their journey to Heysham. Asked later if he was surprised that Dr Skuse had been so certain of his findings at Morecambe, Mr Baldock said he was amazed. Also asked to comment on Skuse's findings of nitro-glycerine on the GCMS on Hill's left hand, both he and Dr Black said that the test had not been properly carried out. 'What Skuse should have told the Court,' said Baldock, 'was that it did *not* confirm the presence of nitro-glycerine.' This was also the view of Mr R.A. Hall, Director of the Northern Ireland Forensic Laboratory and vastly experienced in the science of detecting explosives.

In the appeal of the Birmingham Six, the evidence of Mr Baldock and Drs Black and Caddy again clashed head on with that of Dr Skuse; with the result that the judges found themselves obliged to admit that 'in our judgement the Griess test at Morecambe *should not be regarded as specific for nitro-glycerine.*' One would have thought that that left all of Dr Skuse's evidence in ruins. But like shipwrecked sailors on a spar, the judges clung to Dr Skuse's positive finding on Hill's left hand in the GCMS test, and indeed found another spar in the evidence of a Dr Janet Drayton who had conducted the GCMS test with Skuse. But she would go no further than to say of Hill's left hand, '*possible* ng present, very small increase'.

So on this flimsy edifice and disregarding the evidence of Mr Baldock and Dr Black that the test had not been properly carried out, and of Dr Black that when he had seen the GCMS print-out thirteen years before it had not registered positive, the Court came up with this:

> So far from creating any doubt the fresh evidence on this topic [Dr Drayton's] makes us sure that Hill's left hand is proven to have nitro-glycerine upon it, for which there is, and can be no innocent explanation. That conclusion is fatal to the appellants.

Some conclusion!

I should say here that some months after this article was published, I succeeded in tracking down Dr Janet Drayton at her home in Woking with the help of Heather Mills, home affairs correspondent of the Independent. *I showed her the above extract from the Court's judgement which she had not seen before. She told us that the Court had no business in saying that Hill's left hand was* proved *to have nitro-glycerine on it when she had gone no further than to say it was* possible. *(She even thought her findings could have been 'a rogue result'.) She also said that she could not see how any findings about Hill could have any bearing on the guilt or innocence of the other five. Nor could we. But that is the sort of perverse reasoning we have come to expect from senior judges in recent times.*

Let us now turn to the 'confessions', the first of which (that of Billy Power) was obtained at Morecambe at about lunchtime on the Friday, and a further three (those of McIlkenny, Walker and Callaghan) on the Saturday after the return of the prisoners to Birmingham. But first it is necessary to look at the background circumstances in which the 'confessions' were obtained.

When the news of the pub bombings with their appalling casualties became known, there was hardly a man in Birmingham who would not have been ready and willing, such was their anger, personally to lynch any of those responsible. When the six arrived at Winson Green Prison on remand only three days later, they were beaten up mercilessly both by prison staff and inmates. Even the wives suffered. Sandra Hunter experienced paint and beer glasses being thrown at her house, bangings on the door in the middle of the night, nooses left hanging on the front gate and daubed on the walls the words HANG IRA BASTARDS. And after Theresa Walker had taken her children to Londonderry, their house was broken into and vandalized, the television set and coins from the gas meter stolen.

It would have been extraordinary if the Birmingham police at Morecambe, once the Griess test had shown positive on Power and Hill, had not also felt, and to some degree shown, their sense of outrage and anger. It is well known that when routinely interrogating suspects police invariably simulate belief in their guilt so that, if guilty, the suspects will be encouraged to admit to it. 'They have to be certain,' Lord Devlin once wrote of police attitudes, 'they are no use if they aren't.' On this occasion they did not have to simulate certainty: they *were* certain. The scum of the earth, those who had killed and mutilated nearly two hundred people, many of them young girls and boys, had been delivered into their hands; and they had the power to do to them what they wanted.

Yet if we are to believe those who interrogated the Birmingham Six, they did not so much as lay a finger on them. Reading their evidence, one would be entitled to assume that they never even raised their voices, and that all the 'confessions' were given freely and voluntarily.

But those arrested told a different story. This is part of Power's, taken from evidence at his trial and after his right hand was proved Griess positive. Two officers called Watson and French led him to an upstairs room.

As I walked through the door French punched me on the back of the head. I stumbled forward and they both set about me. I was pushed into a chair. They were shouting, 'You dirty, murdering IRA bastard. You got gelly on your hands.'

They and another officer, said Power, beat him up again, and then French said they would throw him out of the car on the way back to Birmingham, and explain it by saying he was trying to escape.

Then they started telling me there was a mob outside my home ready to lynch my wife and children. All that was saving them was the police who were searching it. The only way to save my wife and children was to tell them what they wanted to know.

He was taken to another room where, he said, several more officers set on him:

From all sides I was punched, hit and kicked. When I slid down the wall, I was dragged up by the hair. This was repeated three or four times.

It was at this stage, said Power, that he fouled his trousers. Then one officer said, 'Stretch his balls', and another bellowed into his ear, 'You'll never have sex with your wife again.' 'I screamed "OK OK." I had to say something to stop them. I couldn't take any more.'

Yet even then they hadn't done with him. When he stalled over answering a question, someone shouted, 'Throw him out of the fucking window.' Power was not to know that the window was sealed. They dragged him over to it, and another officer said, 'If the fall doesn't kill him, the crowd will.'

Power screamed, 'I'll tell you anything you want me to say,' and they prepared to write his confession.

The others told broadly similar stories: of being slapped and punched and kicked, and hearing the screams of their friends as they were punched and kicked in other rooms. Hill said he was dragged round the room by his hair, told he would be shot and his body dumped on the motorway, but that if he signed a statement saying he'd planted the bombs, they would stop beating him. Walker said he was punched repeatedly on an operation scar on his stomach, was also told he would be shot and had a gun pressed against his head and the trigger pulled, had a cigarette stubbed out on a blister on his toe. 'In the end I became completely deranged.'

In the late afternoon the five men, without shoes and socks, were bundled into police cars. Hunter said that as soon as he got in Superintendent Reade, who was smelling of drink, started slapping and punching him. In another car, Walker said that an officer called Kelly who also smelt of drink, head-butted him. In a third car, Hill complained that a Sergeant Bennett whipped his testicles with the leather thong of his truncheon. Later, he said, an Inspector Moore put a revolver into his mouth, 'said he was going to blow my fucking head off', pulled the trigger so that it clicked, then laughed.

Although the prisoners were all kept segregated from each other the police maintained that all these stories, so similar in what they claimed, were total inventions; that they did not assault any of them.

Yet worse was to come. Late that Friday night the five were taken to Birmingham's Queens Road police station where they were joined by Hugh Callaghan, and kept there until the Sunday afternoon. During this time they claimed that they were further savagely assaulted, that they were kept awake all Friday night by the bangings of the cell-door hatches and by an Alsatian dog that was made repeatedly to bark at them, that they were continually made to stand up or sit down and that they were continually abused; and that it was this sustained intimidation and violence that led all but Hill and Hunter to sign written 'confessions'. (These two allegedly gave oral ones.)

The 'confessions' themselves were a mass of contradictions and untruths. Three of the four referred to the bombs being carried in plastic bags (in which, only the police knew, previous unexploded bombs had been found). In fact they had no plastic bags with them, and forensic examination of the remains showed that the bombs had been carried in holdalls or briefcases. Callaghan said he put his bomb *outside* the Mulberry Bush on one side and that Hunter had put his *outside* on the other. Forensic evidence showed that the bomb or bombs had been placed *inside* the pub. Despite Callaghan's claim that he and Hunter had bombed the Mulberry Bush, Walker claimed that Hunter had been with him bombing the Tavern. Callaghan said there were six bombs, Walker and McIlkenny said three.

Subsequently all six denied the voluntariness of the confessions. Callaghan said, 'I was in a state of shock. I do not know what I said. They said things to me. I agreed. At the end one of the officers put a pen in my right hand, placed it over the paper and guided my hand as I signed.' Similar assertions were made by the Guildford Four.

At their trial neither judge nor jury believed the allegations of beatings or disbelieved the 'confessions'. With amazing naïvety Mr Justice Bridge spoke of the allegations against the police as being 'of the most bizarre and grotesque character'. If the defendants were telling the truth, he said, 'I would have to suppose that a team of fifteen officers had conspired among themselves to use violence on the prisoners and to fabricate evidence.' Poor innocent, he did not seem the least aware that when the police feel sure they have the right man or men, this sort of conduct is not unusual: there was no need for a conspiracy because everyone reacted spontaneously. He concluded, 'All the police officers who gave their evidence of the circumstances in which the statements were taken, impressed me as being straightforward and honest witnesses.' But this is how they are trained to appear; that is how they were with the Guildford Four; that is why they lie and lie and know they will be believed.

In November 1977 the six men brought a civil action against the police and the Home Office for injuries they had received while in police custody; for fresh evidence they were relying on the findings of a Dr David Paul, a former police surgeon and City of London coroner, and a specialist in the interpretation of injuries from photographs. Shown enlarged photographs of the six taken while they were in custody at Queens Road, he found signs of injuries on all.

The action was allowed and application made for legal aid. But the police appealed and in an uncharacteristically depraved judgement Lord Denning upheld them. If the action were to succeed, he said, it would show evidence of police perjury and violence, and the six might have to be pardoned; this was such an appalling vista that the action could not be allowed to proceed; i.e. better that the six rot in jail than to find there had been police wrongdoing.

But the supporters of the six, including some of the media, continued to press their case; and in December 1986 a retired police officer by the name of Tom Clarke, who had been at Queens Road at the material time, appeared on Granada Television to say what he had seen and heard there. Seven weeks later the Home Secretary announced that he was sending the case back to the Court of Appeal and was ordering an inquiry into it by the Devon and Cornwall Police.

At the Appeal hearing Clarke confirmed the prisoners' claims of police intimidation and ill-treatment, even admitting that he himself had joined in verbal abuse of the prisoners ('I was thrilled to know we had got the right people'). He supported what they had said about being kept awake all night, the dog barking at them, the cell-door hatches being banged up and down, their being made to stand up or sit down. He described one prisoner, whose blanket had slipped from him, as having on his stomach a red weal turning bluish and measuring about six inches by four. 'He had been hit so badly that, although I wanted to see him dead, I was worried about him. He had had the hell of a hefty thump.' When he went off duty at 5.30 a.m. on the Saturday morning he said, the prisoners were 'scared out of their wits'; and when he came back on duty that night, he observed puffiness over and under their eyes and red faces. 'They had', he told the Court, 'been hammered.' By the time he left on the Sunday morning, the prisoners were 'all in a petrified state, all physical wrecks' . . . an observation which the photographs of them taken at Queens Road tend to confirm.

Tom Clarke knew when he came to give evidence that he would be discredited as a witness for having been dismissed from the police force for having stolen £5 from a prisoner. He contests that verdict, and having read his papers on the case and spoken to him, I would say there could be a doubt in the matter (it was his word against another's). But he was supported in his Appeal Court evidence by a former member of his first-aid team, a Sergeant Brierley, who said that Clarke had told him within weeks or months of the bombings that cell doors had been banged, the prisoners had been kept standing up and that police dogs had been let into the cell block to bark at them. Another former policeman, Paul Berry, also told the Court of having called in at Queens Road at this time on a routine matter and seeing in the cell block a prisoner 'whose left eye and lip were puffed and swollen'.

Yet the most impressive witness for the appellants was Joyce Lynas, who was on duty at Queens Road as a police cadet. She gave evidence to the Court on two occasions. On the first she said that on arrival the prisoners were pushed through her office to the cells fairly roughly and had been called 'fucking bastards' and 'murdering bastards'. She also remembered the dog inside the cell block and the cell-door hatches being banged up and down. But she denied having witnessed any prisoners being assaulted.

But a few days later she was back in court to say that she *had* witnessed a prisoner being assaulted. Asked why she had not said so at her first appearance, she said that she had been frightened off by two telephone conversations: the first in the summer when she rang Queens Road to enquire about the bona fides of the Devon and Cornwall inquiry and was told by an officer to whom she was put through, 'You know what you saw and heard, but remember we have families', and the second, an anonymous call to her home before the hearing began, 'Don't forget that you have children.' However on the Saturday after her first appearance, she had seen a television programme about bullying in the army and people not reporting it, and after talking to her husband and her minister, she volunteered to return to court, even though it meant having to admit to perjury. This required the same sort of courage as I had witnessed at the trial of Stephen Ward when Ronna Ricardo, having been blackmailed by the police into saying at the Magistrates' Court that Ward had procured clients for her, refused to substantiate it at his trial.

And what new evidence did Joyce Lynas have to offer? Quite simply that when she took tea to officers who were interviewing the prisoners in a room upstairs, she saw two officers holding one by the arms while a third kneed him in the groin. As she entered she heard the third man say, 'This is what we do to fucking, murdering bastards,' and what she called 'other vile words'. In court she declined to say what these were, but when I asked her, she told me: 'You won't be having sex with your wife again because I'm going to put your balls where your brains are.' I asked if she was certain about this, and she said that it was not the kind of thing you could forget.

There was other confirmatory evidence of the prisoners having been beaten up. Prison officer Brian Sharp of Winson Green was on duty when they arrived at the prison on the Monday morning. He said that when Walker undressed, 'his torso from the neck to the middle had numerous amounts of bruising, purple, blackish, some had tinges of yellow', which he thought were a day or two old. At the trial of the six, another officer called Murtagh confirmed this, speaking of 'a long yellowing bruise' running from Walker's waist up across the front of his ribs, and which he thought was two or three days old. Sharp thought the injuries so bad that he telephoned for a hospital officer to come down and examine them.

And then the former Superintendent Reade appeared, the man who had arrested the six at Morecambe and claimed never to have touched them, and had to admit that later in his career he had led a party of officers on a raid in a house at Walsall at which a Mr Buckley had, in Reade's presence, been punched, kicked and thrown down the stairs; and Mr Reade had to admit that later Mr Buckley had sued the police and been awarded £800. Mr Reade was also found to have altered a document relating to interviews with the six; and Dr Skuse, too, admitted to altering certain timings at the police's request.

*

And how did the three Appeal Court judges respond to the overwhelming evidence that over a period of three days the appellants had been assaulted and intimidated by the police and that their 'confessions' were therefore no longer tenable?

Until 1966 it was obligatory on the Court of Appeal when reaching a decision about new evidence, to put themselves in the minds of the original trial jury and say what verdict they might have given in the light of the totality of all the evidence, old and new. This is the course which Lord Devlin thinks should have been taken; and had the three judges done so, they must surely have said that doubts in the minds of the jury would have led to acquittals for all six. But the judges, as they are now entitled to, took it on themselves to decide the truth of the facts – an unfortunate decision for, as lawyers and others have pointed out, judges are notoriously shaky when it comes to assessing the facts.

Those who attended the court, and in particular the appellants' counsel, said it was clear from the start that the judges had made up their minds that the appeals were not going to succeed, although even they had not bargained for the manner in which their witnesses would be rubbished. This is what the judges said of them:

Tom Clarke: 'a most unconvincing witness and an embittered man. His motive was . . . at first at least to make money and secondly to blacken the reputation of the West Midlands Police Force.' (A year later the reputation of the West Midlands Serious Crime Squad had become so blackened that it had to be disbanded.) Whatever Mr Clarke's motives, the judges did not seem to have asked themselves the only question that mattered: were his observations, corroborated by the appellants, true?

Paul Berry who had glimpsed a prisoner with a puffed and swollen face, was 'mistaken'. But how could he have been mistaken? All the cells in the cell blocks were occupied by the appellants: there were no other prisoners there.

Brian Sharp who had said that Walker's body was covered with bruises on his arrival at Winson Green, was, the judges said, trying to conceal or minimize the violence that prison staff and inmates had inflicted on the prisoners and so 'forfeited any credibility that he might otherwise have had'. But Sharp had no motive to conceal anything: he had been tried for assaulting the appellants and been acquitted. And again, was his evidence true? If the bruises he and Murtagh saw were coloured yellow, purple and black, they must have been a day or two old and therefore incurred at Queens Road rather than Winson Green.

Joyce Lynas: the writer Robert Kee was in court on the day of her second appearance. He wrote in *The Times* that the way in which she gave her evidence 'was so totally convincing that had I been a member of a jury asked to judge her credibility there would have been no question in my mind that she was speaking anything but the truth, or that in consequence very considerable doubt attached to the validity of the men's confessions.' Richard Ferguson, QC, agreed: 'Anyone who heard her give evidence must have known she was speaking the truth.' But the judges described her as 'a witness not worthy of belief' and her reasons for changing her story 'not acceptable'. Mrs Lynas is a committed Christian whose character while in the police force was assessed as 'Exemplary' and she was upset and angered by these attacks on her integrity. 'I did not have to go back,' she told me. 'I went because I felt I ought to, and I told the absolute truth.'

For the judges to declare, in the light of all they had heard, that the original verdicts were *safe* and *satisfactory* seems to me both an abuse of the English language and an insult to anyone's intelligence. So why did they do it? The harsh truth is that just as the CID have corrupted themselves by their readiness to fabricate evidence against those who they have wrongly convinced themselves are guilty, so the judges, otherwise honourable men, have also corrupted themselves by refusing to recognize police fabrication, even when it is staring them in the face.

All that is new about this is that cases like the Guildford Four and the Maguire Seven and the disbandment of the West Midlands Serious Crimes Squad have brought the corruption to the surface. But it is an old story. 'British justice is in ruins,' said Lord Denning after the release of the Guildford

Four. But it had been in ruins for a long time. Judges at trials of first instance, as well as judges in the Appeal Court, have consistently refused to entertain the idea of police fabrication unless it is so clear cut that they have no alternative. And every judicial inquiry into miscarriages of justice in recent years – Scott Henderson and Brabin in the two Evans inquiries, Fisher in the Confait inquiry, Hawser in the Hanratty inquiry, Hunter in the Meehan inquiry, as well as Lawton and Roskill in the fourth Luton appeal, Roskill at the appeal of the Guildford Four and again of the Maguire Seven – all have preferred to accept dubious police evidence rather than give the people concerned a clean bill of health; and in so doing they have done both themselves and British justice a grave disservice. Lord Hunter spoke for them all when he wrote, 'Reliance is rightly placed on the integrity and competence of police officers.' He could not bring himself to believe that the police in question had planted incriminating evidence in a dead man's pocket.

It can, I think, only be a matter of time before the Home Secretary decides that it is time for the ordeal of the Birmingham Six to end and for them to receive proper compensation for all their years inside. And when that has happened, the three judges who had the evidence and power to open the prison gates for them and yet failed to do so, and in whose judgement not only the public but some members of their own profession have lost faith, might care, as honourable men, to consider their position. For collectively they have gravely undermined confidence in British justice.

Towards the end of 1990 and as a result of fresh evidence obtained by the Devon and Cornwall Police, the case was once again referred back to the Court of Appeal. As with the appeal of the Guildford Four, the Director of Public Prosecutions announced that he would not contest the case, but unlike that of the Guildford Four, the three judges appointed to hear the case decided that they wished to hear the new evidence which, according to the DPP, made the convictions unsafe.

The appeal was heard at the Old Bailey between 4 and 14 March 1991, and was based on two grounds, both forensic.

The first was the final discrediting of Dr Skuse's Griess test which expert evidence said was not and never had been specific for nitro-glycerine. When writing my Sunday Times *piece I had omitted to say that Dr Hugh Black, the former Chief Explosives officer for the Home Office had in fact said this for the defence at the trial. But Mr Justice Bridge had clung to Dr Skuse's findings as though they were holy writ and told Dr Black in no uncertain terms that his opinions were worthless and he was wasting the court's time. Further expert evidence at the appeal supported Dr Black's trial evidence that Dr Drayton's findings on the GCMS test had not proved positive, and in the witness-box she herself confirmed what she had said to me about her findings possibly being 'a rogue result'.*

The second piece of new forensic evidence concerned what has been called the Electrostatic Document Analysis test, or ESDA, which showed that some police officers' statements of interviews with the accused were not contemporaneous as they had claimed at the trial but had been written at different times on different pads with different pens, and that some parts had been added to or altered afterwards; and an interview which the police claimed to have had with McIlkenny was denied by McIlkenny as ever having taken place. Faced with both these heads of new evidence, the judges concluded that had they been available to the trial jury, they must have made a considerable impact. The convictions therefore were unsafe and unsatisfactory, and the appeals would be allowed.

For me one of the most refreshing aspects of the appeal was that, with the Crown having conceded defeat, this was the nearest I had seen in a British court to the inquisitorial system as practised on the continent. In contrast to the impatience and hostility displayed by Lord Lane at the previous appeal, the three judges here (Lloyd, Mustill, Farquharson) really did want to understand what was being put to them, and for the appellants Mr Michael Mansfield, QC, guided them most skilfully through the maze of highly technical forensic evidence. The only sour note came at the end of the submissions when Mr Graham Boal, QC for the Crown, powerless to challenge the new forensic evidence, solemnly told the judges that circumstantial evidence alone *would have been sufficient to secure convictions against all six. This was not only dotty and untrue but, said in the presence of six men who he knew had just endured sixteen years of wrongful imprisonment, extremely distasteful. But that is the adversarial system for you: in an inquisitorial system such a submission would not be made.*

I was sorry that Mr Mansfield did not raise the matter of the Six's allegations that their 'confessions' had been beaten out of them by the police, as this partly enabled the judges to belittle the claim by saying there was no evidence that they had suffered any injuries before their first appearance in court, and then to join with Lord Lane's rubbishing of the witnesses at the 1987 appeal who said they had seen evidence of injuries inflicted on the Six when they were at Birmingham's Queens Road police station. The new evidence had shown that the Six were not guilty as charged, and if they were not guilty as charged, what other explanation could there be of their 'confessions' – which were detailed, varied and contradictory – than that they were beaten out of them by the police?

Afterwards the judgement of Lord Lane and his colleagues in the 1987 appeal was seen to have been so crass and to have so undermined public confidence in the administration of criminal justice that there were many calls for his resignation. The Times urged him to take early retirement and more than 140 MPs signed a motion calling on the Queen to remove him from office; but he gave not the slightest indication that he intended to do other than remain where he was; and he would presumably have considered any sort of apology for his ineptitude, infra dig. Yet one cannot think of any other profession or business where had the managing director been guilty of similar incompetence (in this instance a further three years incarceration for six innocent men) he would not have been faced with a call for his immediate resignation or dismissal.

Predictably the legal establishment closed ranks. The Lord Chancellor, who had earlier described my Sunday Times article as 'clamour', made soothing noises about judicial integrity. The Attorney-General said that all judges do is to see that the rules are kept, while former judges such as Sir Frederick Lawton were quick to point out that it is not they but juries who reach verdicts and judges can only be as good as the evidence put before them – conveniently forgetting that judges do not hesitate to discount good evidence they don't agree with, as Bridge did at the trial of the Birmingham Six, as Lane did at their appeal, and as Lawton himself did at one of the Luton appeals. The Independent summed it up:

> Instead of taking a hard look at its own failings, the Court of Appeal has sought to exculpate itself. There could be no clearer evidence that judges are temperamentally inclined to protect the legal system rather than the lives of those with whom it deals. To them the dignity of the law too often seems to be more important than justice itself.

Thankfully the Home Secretary realized that after the cases of the Guildford Four, the Maguire Seven and the Birmingham Six, things could not be allowed to continue as before and announced the appointment of a Royal Commission under Lord Runciman to inquire into the whole criminal justice system; and to make every effort to report within two years.

I cannot think of any public pronouncement in recent times which has given me so much satisfaction. Indeed, with the real possibility it brings of change, I see it as a justification of part of my life's work.

TAILPIECE

To conclude this section, two short tailpieces: one on the popular novelist Jeffrey Archer, the other on the less popular Austrian President, Kurt Waldheim. One of the most talked about libel cases of the 1980s was that in which the former MP Jeffrey Archer sued the Star newspaper for alleging that he had been consorting with a prostitute named Monica Coghlan, and was awarded damages of half a million pounds. There were many who thought that on the evidence offered Mr Archer was fortunate to have been so successful in his suit, there being no dispute that he had arranged payment to Monica Coghlan of £2,000 so that she could go abroad until things had died down and he could avoid the likelihood of scandal. During the course of the trial Mr Justice Caulfield was so clearly bowled over by Archer's wife, Mary, an attractive brunette who sat with him in court each day, that in his summing-up to the jury, he went clean over the top. 'Remember Mary Archer in the witness-box', he told them. 'Your vision of her will probably never disappear. Has she elegance? Has she fragrance? Would she have, without the strain of this trial, radiance?' As for Archer himself, 'his history is worthy and healthy and sporting – President of the Oxford University Athletic Club and ran for this country.' That being so, 'was he in need of cold, unloving, rubber-insulated sex in a seedy hotel?' The jury thought not, though it was the view of many people that they were really more interested in clobbering the gutter press for their attempts to frame Archer than in the libel itself. Notwithstanding Archer's victory, Caulfield's view showed such an abysmal ignorance of the world and its ways, in particular that it is often the very elegance, fragrance, radiance, etc., of some men's wives that lead them by way of a change to seek rough trade, that I wrote this letter to The Times:

Sir, There are three former Tory ministers alive today whose wives were, and I am sure still are, no less fragrant than the wife of Mr Archer; yet this did not prevent them from consorting with prostitutes, in consequence of which they were all obliged to resign.

Why then did Mr Justice Caulfield consider Mrs Archer's fragrance to be so special as to be likely to dissuade her husband from following the same trail? It is also worth noting that none of the three mentioned above became the social lepers that Mr Justice Caulfield said would be the fate of Mr Archer if the jury found against him.

If there has been a more eccentric summing-up in any libel case in the past 50 years, I have not read of it.

Yours etc,

LUDOVIC KENNEDY

To my surprise I got fifty-five letters supporting me; and only two against.

Another topic of the 1980s was the guilt or otherwise of war crimes of the Austrian president and former Secretary General of the United Nations, Kurt Waldheim. The Independent *newspaper invited me to review a long programme put on by Channel 4, which had been set up to examine the case against him. Because I find that there are still those today who are uncertain about Waldheim's participation in Nazi war crimes, I reprint the review below. I understand that Sir Frederick Lawton's summing-up was not dissimilar.*

Last night, Channel 4 showed the hearing of a Commission of Inquiry into the wartime activities of the Austrian president, Kurt Waldheim. Presumably it called itself a commission of inquiry to avoid parrot cries of 'trial by television!', and for the same reason, decided not to pronounce on Waldheim's guilt or innocence, only whether he had a case to answer. It was a trial just the same and a most exhaustive and exhausting one.

The commission consisted of judges from Germany, Sweden, the United States, Canada and England. The benign president was the English representative, Sir Frederick Lawton, a former Lord Justice of Appeal who might have thought of a happier phrase than 'you may be excused' to elderly witnesses who had come to the inquiry of their own volition: it sounded like Nanny giving Master Thomas permission to get down from table.

I am writing this without knowing the conclusions of the commission, as they were not added to the programme until just before transmission. I have therefore imagined what might have been said had I been in Sir Frederick's place.

Members of the court and public, Before telling you of our conclusions, let me first give you the reasons that persuaded me and my fellow judges, all of high repute in their own countries, to agree to take part. Had the proposals put to us indicated a superficial, half-hearted sort of investigation I doubt if any of us would have accepted. But the inquiries made by Thames Television into Mr Waldheim's wartime activities could hardly have been more thorough. For over a year, they employed two dozen researchers who interviewed more than 250 witnesses and trawled through twenty-nine separate archives. We ourselves deliberated for six days before coming to our conclusions: you have been watching us for four hours. But we all felt that it was worth it, because for the first and, let us hope, last time everything that could have been discovered about Mr Waldheim's wartime service has been discovered and brought into the light of day.

Let me also say how well we have been served by our two counsel – the bearded Mr Allan Ryan for the prosecution, a former director of Special Investigations from the US Department of Justice, and whose quiet, low-key approach has been in interesting contrast to that of counsel for the defence and former English Attorney-General, the urbane and more outgoing Lord Rawlinson. We were all greatly impressed by their clarity of presentation.

And what did you make of their witnesses? Were you not deeply moved, as we were, by the Jewish lady who spoke of her terrible journey to Auschwitz; by the Yugoslav villager who returned home to find that among those killed by the German army were his father, four sisters and three brothers; by the captured British commando, Captain Bluett, who spoke of being put in an empty cell, deprived of food and water for days, and being beaten so badly he could no longer stand? And what did you think of those elderly former members of the Wehrmacht who served alongside Mr Waldheim, and said they knew nothing about atrocities – until Mr Ryan confronted them with documents that showed that, so far as knowledge was concerned, they were up to their necks in it? Their reluctant admissions were not a pretty sight.

Now in summing up, the first thing to say is that not a scrap of evidence was presented to us, either from a document or a witness, to show that Mr Waldheim participated in any of the criminal acts then being perpetrated by the German army in the areas in which he was serving: no reports of him beating up a prisoner, ill-treating a Jew, shooting a hostage, setting fire to a village.

The second thing is that there has been massive and, you may think, conclusive evidence to show that as a staff officer, he knew full well of the existence of these criminal acts. His awareness of what was going on is not even a matter of dispute between Mr Ryan and Lord Rawlinson. They both acknowledge it.

So what is the conflict between them? It is this. Mr Ryan is saying that even if Mr Waldheim did not personally take part in any war crime, his work on the staffs of various Army Groups must have contributed considerably to what was being done in the field, that without the preparatory work, intelligence, etc., that he and his fellow staff officers provided, the atrocities could not have taken place, and therefore he is no less guilty than those on the spot.

And what does Lord Rawlinson say? That while accomplices in war crimes may be culpable in law, in practice they are not prosecuted. And he supports his arguments with the evidence of the expert on the international laws of war, Mr Christopher Greenwood, who stated that in the last war those who had knowledge of war crimes but did not take part in them could not be held to be guilty. And he cited what had happened to the senior officers of the two Army Groups in which Mr Waldheim was serving – the commanders-in-chief were convicted of war crimes but the two generals who were their Chiefs of Staff were acquitted on the grounds that they were not in a position to 'palliate or rescind' the orders handed down to them.

We have no hesitation in saying that we think that Lord Rawlinson is right and Mr Ryan wrong. If Mr Ryan's argument is taken to its logical conclusion, then every dispatch rider, every batman, every cook, must also be guilty, which is plainly ridiculous. And if the Chiefs of Staff who ordered these criminal acts are in the clear, how can a junior staff officer like Mr Waldheim be said to be guilty? It should not be forgotten what very small beer Mr Waldheim was then, an ordinary lieutenant in no position to influence events or give criminal orders to anybody.

Lord Rawlinson said in his closing speech that he does not care a fig about Mr Waldheim. Nor may you. We understand that he has told lies about his past, and coming from a past secretary general of the United Nations and now president of his country, that is contemptible. But we are not concerned with lies, only justice. And we are all agreed that as a matter of law, Kurt Waldheim has no case to answer.

VERY LOVELY
PEOPLE

VERY LOVELY PEOPLE

IN 1963 SOME of us who were working for the BBC current affairs programme Panorama *formed a group to set up an independent television production company of our own and called it, portentously, Television Reporters International. We signed a year's contract with Lew Grade's ATV company and made some interesting, even unusual documentary films which were well received by the critics. Sadly it was an idea before its time, for when the contract had expired, Lew Grade, for whom it had been something of a novelty, decided not to renew it: and the doors of the BBC, whose mandarins were still sore at our having left them, remained closed to us.*

So, having completed my book on the trial of Stephen Ward, what to do? It was then that an idea came to me for another book as the result of my travels abroad with Panorama *and TRI. The British Empire was then on its last legs, and in country after country, I had observed two things: the hauling down of the Union Jack and the departure of the Governor and the British administration; and the swelling numbers of incoming Americans, as AID administrators, Peace Corps volunteers, agriculturists, technical advisers, servicemen and tourists. Was there a book to be written about them, the mid twentieth century's new global colonialists? Peter Schwed of Simon and Schuster in New York and Jamie Hamilton of Hamish Hamilton in London thought so; and with a satisfactory advance from each and helpful concessions from Pan American Airways and Intercontinental Hotels, I set out on a year's journey round the world: first New York and Washington, then Latin America, Africa, Europe, the Middle East, the Far East and back to America. I called the book* Very Lovely People, *a phrase Americans use to denote people they approve of ('Oh, you should meet her.*

She's a very lovely person.'). Sorting through material for inclusion in this anthology, I was surprised to see how well, after more than twenty years, parts of Very Lovely People *stood up. I hope that a new readership may find so too.*

THE AMERICAS

It was Saturday morning in New York and Saturday afternoon in London; Saturday, 30 January 1965. I sat alone in the huge empty dining-room of the Yale Club, among the rows of bare wooden tables and chairs. The members had gone off for the weekend to Long Island and New Jersey, Texas and California, even Paris and Hawaii, leaving me the place to myself. Actually there were two of us there, myself in substance and, in the little box in the corner, David Brinkley in shadow. I was in his country and he in mine; but while I was alone, he had half the world with him. For he was describing to his fellow Americans direct from London the last splendid journey of Sir Winston Churchill. He stood on a kind of raised platform in Fleet Street, and beneath him in the cold winter air, the soldiers and sailors, statesmen and politicians rolled self-consciously by. I could see the steam from the horses' nostrils and hear the gravelled bite of the moving feet; and it was still strange to think that one was seeing and hearing these things at the moment of their happening. The world had shrunk to a pin-head.

It had not been like that in Churchill's early days. Then there was no television or radio, and the telephone and motor car were still in their infancy. People apart could communicate only by letter, and they often did so at prodigious length. Official letters were not only written by hand but sometimes copied by hand too, for the typewriter was not yet in common use; and a reply to a letter sent to Australia in January would be lucky to reach London by May. To be sure, the train and steamship had speeded things up a bit, but in a hundred years the tempo of British daily life had hardly changed. On the throne there sat a lady of unmajestic proportions, whose regal manner and middle-class mind symbolized for her subjects the affluence and propriety of the age. Most, if not all Britons, had got the Queen they deserved. This spry and opinionated little matriarch was residual legatee of the largest property-grab organization the world had ever seen. The British Empire then encompassed a quarter of the globe, which not only made the feats of Alexander and Xerxes shrivel in comparison, but enabled its possessors to boast, to the intense irritation of foreigners, that there was always some part of it on which the sun shone.

Every year thousands of dedicated young Englishmen, Scotsmen, Welshmen and Irishmen exchanged the comforts of home for a lifetime of service in faraway, romantic sounding but often uncongenial places, to act as the Empire's protectors, administrators, bankers and developers. They went with a keen sense of adventure and mission, sure in their belief that the Queen and the Almighty together wanted them to bring enlightenment and salvation to those whom Rudyard Kipling, the Beowulf of the times, called lesser breeds without the law. They lived, many of them, in conditions that we would regard today as intolerable; and they and their wives and children suffered unflinchingly the scourges of sunstroke, typhus, cholera, yellow fever, gangrene, violence and, often, unexpected death. But it was suffering in, they believed, a good cause. They did what they came to do, and on the whole they did it well. To many areas of darkness they brought order where there had been chaos, justice where there had been injustice, hygiene where there had been filth, hope where there had been despair. They put a brake on widow burning in India, cannibalism in Borneo, infanticide in Polynesia. They brought with them the idea of a loving God; they built roads and railways and hospitals and schools.

And yet, in many ways, their lives were a paradox. They extolled the virtues of Parliamentary democracy but practised instead a benevolent dictatorship. They told the natives they were there for their own good, but whenever the natives showed they thought otherwise, they stamped on them with a quite surprising severity. Local leaders who propagated autonomy in their own affairs were known as 'trouble-makers', and regarded as tiresome irrelevancies.

431

'Those damned trouble-makers are at it again. They're up-setting the natives, and it can't do any good.' But in the end the trouble-makers won through, as they had to, so that the political prisoners of the Empire became the political leaders of the Commonwealth: men like Nehru and Jinnah, Makarios, Kenyatta, Banda. The empire-builders preached fair play, but exploited native labour ruthlessly; it was not to the indigenous that the first fruits of each newly developed country went, but to the hungry English manufacturers; and on these fruits England grew richer still. Native education, mostly the work of devoted missionaries, was encouraged so far but no further: too much learning would have been a dangerous thing. The colonists would have been incredulous and appalled had they been told, as the United Nations was recently told, that in terms of human potential they and the natives were equal; the edge they had over them, and it was a big one, was two thousand years of western civilization. 'Johnny Native's a good enough fellow,' they liked to say, 'so long as you treat him right and see that he doesn't get too uppity. But you've got to tell him what to do. Leave him to his own devices and the poor chap doesn't know where he is.' They genuinely believed that the native not only did not have, but was innately incapable of ever having, the ability for any post involving responsibility and decision. Any other belief would have threatened the entire fabric of the system to which they had devoted their lives.

Their social life was, as near as they could make it, a copy of the social life they had left in England. People who today criticize Americans abroad for living in enclaves and keeping up the American way of life, either do not know or have forgotten that the old British imperialists practised apartheid on a far grander and more elaborate scale. In many areas of administration isolation was complete: there was the native quarter, the garrison quarter and the British residents' quarter; and between the first and the other two there was almost no communion at all. This was done less for reasons of security than snobbery; in Victorian England one did not mix with those whom one regarded as one's social inferiors. Conversely, the Governors and Proconsuls had no objection to hob-nobbing with the Princes and Nabobs, whom many of them recognized as being socially a cut above them.

Within the British compounds the British way of life was faithfully carried on. In the bungalows that had been allotted to them the wives of majors and magistrates tried to provide their husbands with the familiar comforts of home. No matter what the heat or humidity, there was bacon and eggs for breakfast and roast beef on Sundays. Native dishes were shunned, less on grounds of taste than that no-one knew where they had been, or who or what had gone into them. When the men were away the wives visited each other for tea and gossip, performed errands of mercy, did crochet work and petit-point, read wholesome books, and sweated long hours in the sun with little packets of seeds, pansy and hollyhock and sweet william, to win from the stubborn soil the fragrance of an English garden. The men, as soon as they had a quorum, set up clubs, manned by native servants but banned to native members, and here in the cool of the evening they sipped their Scotch and sodas, played billiards and snooker, and browsed through *Blackwood's Magazine* and old copies of *The Times*. Out of arid patches of scrub and rock they fashioned fields for golf and polo and cricket; and when they went out in the evening, they put on dinner-jackets, as they might have done at home. The wig, the mace, the bat, the putter and porridge were some of the stranger legacies that Imperial Britain gave to an innocent and credulous world. In many places they are still to be found. In blazing India, for instance, as much porridge is eaten as in the whole of the British Isles.

At the top of this social pyramid was the Viceroy or Governor, regent of the Queen, and thus in the eyes of those set under him, aglow a little with the magical mystique of monarchy. These latter-day proconsuls lived in style in miniature palaces, their paths eased by myrmidons of servants capped in turban or fez. When the Governor of Bombay drove from Government House to open the Poona races, he was escorted by two hundred Sikh outriders, all over six feet tall and caparisoned in scarlet and black. Many Governors came from the great English country houses, and they simply carried on, if rather more formally, the sort of life they had lived at home. They made, and received, official calls innumerable; they shot and hunted and fished; they gave luncheon parties and dinner parties and balls; and on balmy tropical afternoons there would be china tea and cucumber sandwiches on the lawn. To be summoned to hospitality at Government House was the greatest treat that any colonial family could have. Many a young subaltern and district officer's wife waited anxiously for the rich, gilt-embossed invitation card; and, oh, the heartache when it failed to come or one's neighbour was asked to a more exclusive function than oneself.

The lower down the colonial social scale, the less satisfactory the relationships between rulers and ruled. Little men whose authority over others in England had amounted to perhaps one ill-paid tweeny, suddenly found themselves men of power. Often, out of ignorance and insecurity, they abused this power abominably and, as the saying went, treated the natives like dirt. But the Governors set an example which those who wanted could follow. They wore their authority lightly, with practised ease; there was after all not much to choose between the tenants and servants of an Empire and the tenants and servants of one's estate. They radiated self-confidence and well-being. As gentlemen they had been brought up always to keep their tempers and never show their feelings about anything; and they did this so successfully that many foreigners wondered, and still do wonder, whether they *had* any feelings about anything. They never deliberately gave offence, and so it was difficult for anyone, even those who wanted to, to take offence against them. They were not perplexed, as some Americans are, by self-doubt: it never occurred to them to question the morality of the system which they served; had they done so, they would have been little use in their jobs. 'Wider still and wider', they sang on ceremonial occasions, 'shall thy bounds be set.' They not only thought that British Imperial rule was the best system of government in the world, but that the world would be a much happier and more efficient place if it were run entirely by Englishmen. Then things would get done.

With some modifications, this Empire had remained in being for most of Churchill's adult life. Indeed, as late as 1940, in one of his most famous speeches he could refer to the possibility of the Empire and Commonwealth lasting a thousand years. Then even he could hardly have foreseen that the Empire would be dead within his lifetime, and the Commonwealth a thin shadow of it, soon to wither too. The manner of its going had been typically British: like all the social revolutions with which we have had anything to do, it had been for the most part bloodless. We had seen the wind change direction early enough to set in motion the apparatus for relinquishing power. In one country after another elderly men in knee-breeches and plumed hats watched the Union Jack come down, heard 'God Save the King' played for the last time, and sadly packed their bags. They had gone out in state, in slow and stately ships; now, in the twinkling of an eye, among film directors and advertising men and tourists, they were jet propelled rudely home. Those who had given their lives to what they believed to be a great cause came back from the warm plains of India and Africa to the chill shires and windy towns of Britain, to an alien world of TV personalities and pop music and the credit squeeze, to a country that had already turned its back on them and their problems. The ease with which they absorbed themselves into modern British society says much for their adaptability and courage; but then it might be said that these were the qualities which had made them good colonists in the first place. Thus, the twilight of the Empire coincided with the twilight of the life of its greatest leader. Through a glass darkly the old boy saw it all, and understood it all, even if he didn't approve of it; for he, more than most, knew that the current of history is never still.

With our going we had created a vacuum, of men and money and skills. Had anyone come forward to fill this vacuum? Yes, the Americans had, those who had once been part of the British Empire themselves but had long since contracted out; who, when the Empire had been at its zenith, had stayed inside Fortress America and preached the virtues of sturdy isolationism. Imperceptibly, almost apologetically at first, later with increasing enthusiasm and sense of purpose, they had begun to spread themselves across the globe. Today, as any seasoned traveller knows, there is no corner of a foreign field that is not in part American; no mountain however high, jungle however deep, desert however wide, that there is not a GI, Peace Corps volunteer or missionary at the end of it. The world, often against its will, is going American, shopping in shiny supermarkets, wearing sweat-shirts and jeans, eating hamburgers and ice-creams, drinking Coca-Cola. These are the new gentleman-adventurers of the day, imperialists without an Empire, colonists without a colony, the self-appointed, sometimes reluctant, often abused, servants and masters of half the world. How were they making out? What were they doing? What did other people think of what they were doing? Soon I would see for myself.

The funeral cortège rumbled eastwards, and the camera tilted up to show the great west front of St Paul's, the sanctuary of Nelson, Wellington, and other English heroes. The gun-carriage neared the steps, and at the top the Queen waited the arrival of her dead leader. David Brinkley said: 'And so the body of Sir Winston Churchill is taken to St Paul's Cathedral, whose one-time Dean, the poet John Donne, wrote these words:

'No man is an island, entire of itself. Any man's death diminishes me, because I am involved in mankind. Therefore never send to know for whom the bell tolls. It tolls for thee.'

The coffin was borne up the steps, the picture faded. It was an epitaph and, I hoped, an augury.

Up Riverside Drive, on the west side of Manhattan, stands a large, austere, stone building which in another country might be mistaken for a hotel or hospital or even police headquarters. In fact it is the Inter-Church Center, the clearing house and co-ordinating body for the work of America's many religious organizations. It employs 2,200 people, and much of their work is concerned with foreign missions. I had been told that there were some thirty-five thousand American missionaries living and working abroad, sponsored by nearly five hundred different agencies. In addition to the more orthodox agencies, these included the Air Mail from God Mission, Back to the Bible Mission, Door to Life Mission, Go-Ye Fellowship Inc., Harvesters International, Pillar of Fire Mission, Pocket Testament League, Self-Help Inc., and

Things to Come Inc. I was making enquiries about missionary work in South America, the first area I was visiting; and a helpful man told me that an interdenominational meeting on that very subject was just starting, and I would be welcome if I cared to come.

There were about a dozen people at the meeting, half a dozen in dog collars. One young minister with ginger hair was puffing at a huge cigar which, to British eyes, gave him an air of slight rakishness. Another had a small Bible in front of him which he glanced at occasionally as though to quell rising doubts. There were two women, one a large middle-aged lady in a green hat, the other a secretary. They were all very friendly and relaxed and quipped ecclesiastical jokes. When the meeting was ready to begin, the secretary put a tape recorder on a spare chair, and switched it on. She picked up the microphone and said: 'Testing. One, two, three, four, five,' and played it back. Then, in turn, we were asked to say who we were. Some people found this very shy-making, and tried to overcome their embarrassment by being funny: they weren't funny at all, but the others, especially those whose turn was to come, gave little forced laughs to put them at their ease.

The object of the meeting was to allow the assorted Baptists, Presbyterians, etc., present to hear a report from Father Vermilion, a Roman Catholic priest, on an interdenominational conference on Latin-American missions that had just taken place in Chicago. Father Vermilion was a dark, smooth, energetic man with lots of black fur on his hands, especially the backs of his fingers. Aware that he was a stranger in a foreign land, that the route to God of his audience was not his route, he determined to impress by the power of his personality. 'First,' he said, 'I know you would all like to join with me in an expression of regret that Mr Kantor, that fine young preacher, cannot be with us today. I was visiting with him last week, and he was telling me he was looking forward to this little gathering and meeting with you. Unfortunately we heard only yesterday that he had been stricken down with hepatitis.' Somehow Father Vermilion made this sound like the plague, and there were murmurs of sympathy all round. 'As many of you know,'

437

Father Vermilion went on, 'Mr Kantor, or Harry as his friends know him, is a true witness in Christ (pause), a man respected by his Church (pause), by his family (pause), and by his community (pause), —the kind of man who in his own humble way, has helped to make America great. I'm sure we all wish him a speedy recovery.' The audience nodded approval, and Father Vermilion passed to the Chicago conference. 'At Chicago,' he said, 'we set the guide lines (pause), guide lines for the future (pause), guide lines for what I believe will be exciting and challenging work for Christ in the mission fields of Latin America.' He raised one hairy hand upwards. 'At Chicago one of the first things we did was to establish joint workshops (pause), workshops on almost every aspect of Latin-American field work. I am happy to tell you that those workshops are in session right now (pause), and I don't doubt that they're having some real, down-to-earth discussions.'

I didn't doubt it either. I could see them all at it, crowds of earnest and dedicated young men, pontificating away at each other for hours, grabbing hold of some minor point and worrying it to death, spending weeks and perhaps months reaching conclusions which a few informed, intelligent men could arrive at in a matter of days. The growth of the workshop in American life has always seemed to me an extension of Parkinson's Law; that work expands not only according to the number of people available to do it, but in relation to the amount of money available to support it. In America there are many political, cultural and religious organizations which have more money than they know what to do with; for them, workshops and people to put into workshops are the answer.

Some of Father Vermilion's more histrionic moments were punctured by late arrivals. When Father Hooter showed up, the only chair left was the one supporting the tape recorder. The recorder was put on the table, Father Hooter sat down, and someone said gravely: 'Man has taken the place of the machine.' The meeting was full of jokes like that, and the machine recorded them all. When Father Vermilion was through, which took him quite a time, the meeting was open for comments. Most people rang tinkling variations on the theme of Church unity. One minister spoke of the difficulties for missionaries of what he called 'professional orientation', and Father Vermilion said that one of the workshops was taking care of that. The lady in the green hat said: 'What we have to teach the people of Latin America is citizenship responsibility. We have to help them to strive towards a better life.' She said this more than once. No-one seemed inclined to question whether the Latin Americans *wanted* citizenship responsibility or a better life, or indeed, what was meant by 'better'. Father Vermilion, as you might expect, had the last word. 'What we have to do,' he said, clenching two hairy fists to the sides of his head, as though he had earache, 'is open the minds of these people to Christ (pause). That is the task before us.'

The tape recorder was switched off, the meeting ended. Now some secretary would have to spend a day transcribing it all, including the jokes, and then another day typing, copying and circulating it. But who was going to wade through it all, and what possible benefit would they gain from it? It had been a jolly, friendly meeting, nice ecumenically too, at which not a memorable word had been said. Lucky Mr Kantor, I thought, to be stricken down with hepatitis.

When it was time to leave for Washington, it was snowing hard, and the airport had closed down. So I took the train. Penn Station was rebuilding, and the redcap who took my bags along with those of a lady from Buffalo said that we would have quite a walk. We had a half-mile marathon; up ramps, down ramps, into elevators, out of elevators, round pillars (sometimes *into* pillars), through tunnels, out of tunnels, all over. Sometimes the redcap told us to go one way while he went another; he said we would meet up, and we did, though *how* we did was a mystery. When we reached the train, the lady from Buffalo asked how much she should give the redcap. My feeling, in view of all the exercise we'd had, was that he ought to give us something; but I said, how about a dollar? The redcap said, 'Five pieces at a quarter a piece is one dollar and twenty-five cents. Thank you, ma'am.' I had three cases and gave him a dollar; he didn't give me any change.

The train to Washington was pretty crowded. I went along to the club car and found myself next to a delightfully tight man of about fifty with sandy hair and a Hitler moustache. 'My name's Pitman,' he said, 'and I'm in adult education. I arrange workshops and seminars and things all over the country. Christ, how I hate it. This is Mother.' Mrs Pitman was a large spreading blonde. She was holding a newspaper and pencil, and she said, 'Barnyard fowl. Eight letters.' Mr Pitman said, 'Mother's produced three daughters. They're all married and have children. Christ, are they prolific!' He sipped at his drink. 'Mother and I are on our way home. We went to New York last night to see *Hello Dolly.* Isn't that a great show? Isn't that something?' I said I had found it so boring I had come out halfway through. 'Oh, we didn't find it boring at *all,*' said Mr Pitman, 'did we, Mother?' Mrs Pitman said, without looking up, 'It was lovely, just perfectly lovely.' Mr Pitman said, 'Oh, we both thought it was just *great.*'

Mr Pitman looked around and noticed a man in a blue suit who had sat down beside us. 'This man looks like Faulkner,' said Mr Pitman. The man looked embarrassed. 'My *God,*' said Mr Pitman, 'he *is* Faulkner.'

Mrs Pitman said, 'Honey, Mr Faulkner's dead; you know that,' and to me, 'What's "Alcoholic refreshment" in five letters?' I said, 'Scotch?' and Mrs Pitman said, 'No, that's six.'

Mr Pitman said, 'Do you know where this man's going? He's going to Hickory, North Carolina, to get better. Do you know how many people there are in Hickory? Forty-eight. That's right, forty-eight. Christ, there's nothing else to *do* in Hickory but get better. He can't miss.' His mind went off at a tangent, and he said, 'Our eldest girl married a young Jewish boy. He hasn't got a thing. But he's a real doll.'

Mrs Pitman said, 'E, F, blank. Salamander.'

'What do you mean, E, F, blank, salamander?' said Mr Pitman, and the man who looked like Faulkner said, 'I think it's *eft,* which is a kind of newt.'

'Well, my, aren't you clever?' said Mrs Pitman. Mr Pitman said, 'Noot? Who said anything about a noot? You're crazy. I'm going to wee-wee.'

He got up and lumbered off down the corridor. Mrs Pitman put down her pencil and said, 'I love Gordon, though his mother was a nut. We have three beautiful children. My second daughter's blind – did he tell you? She's just the loveliest creature in the world. Both her sisters are pregnant right now, and boy, are they jealous of her figure! My youngest is a joy, too. She's been borrowing the car Tuesday nights. She wouldn't say where she was going for a long time, and then last week we finally got it out of her. She's been going to give extra coaching to some of the backward coloured kids. Now that the schools are integrated, the backward ones can't keep up unless they have extra coaching. Isn't that just wonderful?'

Mr Pitman came back, and Mrs Pitman said, 'Honey, that was a real good idea you had there,' and she got up and teetered down the train. Mr Pitman yawned and said, 'Oh, boy!' He looked as though he had sobered up a bit. He said to me, 'You know, you were right about that *Hello Dolly* thing. I thought it was a load of horseshit.' I said, 'Why didn't you say so?' He said, 'Well you can't, can you? Not in public. Not about a big hit like that. Besides, it would have upset Mother.'

I had asked a tour operator, Mr Charles A. Cabell III, if any tours of his were in Rio, and he said only one, the Association of New York Cattlemen. They were leaving for home the next afternoon, but in the morning they were going up the Sugar Loaf mountain to look at the view and the statue of Christ the Redeemer. I would be welcome to join them if I cared.

They were staying at the Copacabana, and we assembled in the lobby at 8.30 in the morning. There were about thirty or forty cattlemen, and they wore little badges which said 'GOODWILL AMBASSADOR U.S.A. PEOPLE TO PEOPLE.' I wondered whose benefit this was for, and what kind of reaction was expected, and whether a real goodwill ambassador would ever wish to emphasize that he was one. The cattlemen were all shapes and sizes. They mostly wore shirts and slacks: some had golfing caps and some straw hats and some no hats at all. A few had brought their wives and most their cameras. The party's guide was a handsome young man of nineteen called Byron, and I remembered what Mr Cabell had said about him. 'I found him up the Amazon. He speaks nine languages, and I give him the cream of the tours. It's a hell of a responsibility for a kid of his age, but I pay him well and he's up to it.' Byron introduced me to the cattlemen's leader, a Professor Vazey, who shook me warmly by the hand and said he was real glad to have me go along with them. 'We represent all types of cattle-breeders,' he said, 'big ones, little ones, pedigree, regular. We think that's pretty nice.'

We all got into a bus to go to the cable-car station. When everyone had taken their seats, Byron got up at the front and said: 'Was the service any better for breakfast this morning?' They chorused that it was, and the man next to me whispered: 'Yesterday it was just lousy.' As we drove through Rio the cattlemen kept peering out of the windows, as though fearful of missing something important.

At the cable-car station there was a train already waiting. It had a roof but no windows. The compartments consisted of simple wooden benches facing each other. Some of these were already occupied by local people who lived up the mountain and had been down in Rio shopping at the market. We all piled in and sat down seven or eight to a bench. It was a bit of a squeeze. Presently a little bell rang and the train moved off, or rather up. One of the wives said, a bit late, 'Let's go!', and another, 'Where are the life preservers?' They were all determined to enjoy themselves. Opposite me a dark Carioca combed wet hair flamboyantly.

We stopped at two stations, and then, at the third, which was quite large and called 'Silvestre', we waited for the train coming down the mountain. Most of the locals got off here, which gave us rather more room. We climbed slowly through cool jungly trees and admired at the side of the track a profusion of pretty pink flowers, shaped like four-leaf clover. Then, suddenly, we were above the tree line, suspended in space, clinging to the mountainside like flies to a curtain, all Rio beneath us. 'Hold your hat!' shouted one of the cattlemen, 'here we go!' They were great jokers, these cattlemen, and never tired of wisecracks about the precariousness of our position. 'Glad I checked up on my life assurance before I took this trip,' said another man ponderously, and those round him giggled. Some leaned over the edge of the compartment and peered down. Beyond the track the ground fell sheer away, so that we looked down on treetops a hundred feet high. 'Long ways down there,' murmured one man, and his friend said, 'I never saw such tall trees.' They all snapped away with their cameras, and another man took out a huge map and said to his wife, 'Honey, do you want to orient yourself?'

Presently we reached the station at the top. Byron told us that it was a five-minute walk to the platform at the summit, and that we must be back at the station in twenty minutes. The cattlemen piled out of the train and set off up the steps like a ragged army. As they went they exchanged questions like 'How ya coming?' and 'How's tricks, Charlie?' and answers like 'OK, Ed' and 'Pretty good, I guess'. It was a long pull up the steps and when we reached the top some joker said, 'Twenty minutes up. Time to go back.'

It was misty on the platform but the view was impressive. You could see the whole biscuity coastline, Leblon, Ipanema, Copacabana, Botafago, Flamengo, and the local airport beyond. Nearer, on the green hills beneath us, which looked like so many ant-heaps, sprawled the cancerous favelas. And behind us stood the reason for our visit, the monstrous white Christ, feet together and arms outstretched, weighing 1,450 tons, and with an arm span of over 90 feet. From below it had looked quite attractive, even moving, but here, close to, it was gross and overpowering, like Battersea Power Station or the Eiffel Tower, a feat not of art but engineering. The cattlemen didn't pay much attention either to Christ or the view. Tourists everywhere have a knack of diminishing everything they see, and these were no exception. They bought postcards and drank Coca-Cola, photographed each other, and generally milled around. I heard one man say, 'That was a pretty good breakfast this morning,' and another, 'We took the radiator cap off, and the water just poured out everywhere.' Two wives ate fresh pineapple at a stall, and one said, 'Why can't we get fresh pineapple in the States?' After ten minutes we drifted down the steps again and met a sad-looking cattleman sitting on a bench at the bottom. 'I never made it,' he said, 'I'm glad I didn't. What was it like up there?' A voice in the crowd said, 'Oh, you didn't miss a thing.'

Back at the station Byron told us that the bus which had collected us at the hotel that morning had also been climbing the mountain, and would pick us up at another station a little way down the line. I think the party was glad of this, finding going downhill in the cable-car a good deal more unnerving than going up.

When we were all in the bus and Byron had counted us like sheep, Professor Vazey came and sat beside me. I asked him what he was Professor of, and he said Animal Husbandry at Cornell. He added that altogether there were thirty-five professors of Animal Husbandry at Cornell. I looked at him sharply to see if he was drunk or joking, not believing there were that many professors of Animal Husbandry in the world. I said I had never thought of New York as being a cattle state. 'And you'd be right,' said Professor Vazey, 'because it's not *primarily* a cattle state, not numbers-wise, not percentage-wise. It's more a *dairy* state.' I wondered whether to tell Professor Vazey that he had missed the point and that I hadn't thought of it as a dairy state either.

'Let me wise you up on our little group,' said Professor Vazey. He pointed down the bus. 'That man is an undertaker but he keeps a few cattle on the side. That one in the check shirt is a poultry keeper, and he also keeps some cattle on the side. This man just in front of us is one of the biggest cattle-owners in America. That guy over there in the golfing cap . . .' Locust-like, Professor Vazey left no cattleman untouched, and by the time he had finished, we had reached the bottom of the mountain.

'You seem a very varied group,' I said.

'We're what you might call a selected group,' said Professor Vazey. 'We're pretty choosy who we have. We don't just put an ad in the papers. Basically this is not a sightseeing holiday. We tell people, if you just want to go sightseeing, you've picked the wrong trip.'

'What kind of trip is it?'

'Basically it is to get to know our counterparts and their families in Latin America, visit their ranches and see how they're doing. Of course we do a little sightseeing as well, it would be silly not to, but that's not the object of the trip.'

'How much time have you spent in Brazil getting to know your counterparts?'

'Well now, I should think one day or maybe two. Of course we would like to have had more, but we have only three weeks for the whole tour, and that takes in three other countries besides Brazil, so with the sightseeing and all we can't spend as much time with everyone as we would like. Now yesterday we had a very interesting day. We went visiting at a ranch in the morning and the University in the afternoon. That was a *delightful* day.'

'You don't find it too rushed?'

'Oh no, we don't find it rushed at all. We just love to meet people and for them to see what we're like, and it's nice for us too because everybody has been so friendly. We wear these little goodwill people to people badges, as you see, and everybody thinks that's pretty nice.'

'Does this goodwill people to people idea work in reverse?'

'How do you mean?'

'Well, do Latin American cattlemen and their families go on goodwill trips to the States?'

Professor Vazey thought deeply. 'Well now,' he said, 'if they have done, I don't recall it. I don't recall any Latin American cattlemen doing a thing of that kind.' He was struck by the novelty of the idea. 'Now you mention it,' he said, 'I sure do hope they will, because I sure would like them to come and visit with us.'

Professor Vazey then told me about the various strains in cattle, which he said he knew would interest me, and when he was through with that, we arrived back at the hotel. I went up to my room to make a couple of telephone calls, and when I came down, the cattlemen were getting ready to leave for the airport. Near the cashier's desk there was a bit of a commotion going on. I edged round towards it, and saw one of the cattlemen waving his arms about and shouting. 'How do you get out of this place?' he bawled. 'You ask these people to give you a bill and they won't *give* it you.' He lowered his head like one of his own bulls and glared around him. 'I'm going to forget about the whole thing and get out of this goddam place. I wish I was back in the United States.'

The desk staff of the Copacabana stood silent, appalled. Even among the cattlemen and their wives I detected a certain simmering unease. Two American ladies staying in the hotel appeared beside me, and one said, 'Excuse us, but who is that gentleman?'

I couldn't resist it. 'That, madam,' I said, 'is a goodwill ambassador USA.'

The Pan Am jet to New York screamed skywards. There was only a handful of us in the plane, and I had three seats to myself. The hostesses, with time on their hands, gave us special attention, and one, a beautiful young English girl called Tessa, told me she had been with the company two months. When I asked why, she said, 'To see the world and have a good time.' I said, 'Are you?' She smiled and said, 'You bet!'

At Caracas a new lot of passengers came aboard, and I gained a neighbour. She was a small, dark, pert and pretty girl in her early twenties, and although she must have sat down only seconds ahead of me, she was already busy scribbling in a large exercise book. Going down the runway most of the passengers looked out of the window for reassurance, but she went on scribbling. The plane climbed through the clouds and levelled out, Tessa and her friends offered us coffee or a drink, but my companion never took her pencil from the page.

In the end curiosity got the better of me. Over her elbow I read: 'Education viewed as very important. People will work together and feel pride. Nearest school may be far away – too far for little children to walk – too expensive for parents to pay transport.'

'You seem busy?' I said.

I regretted it almost as soon as I spoke, for she was a girl who gave her undivided attention to what she was doing. Up to now it had been the exercise book, from now on it was to be me. She shut the book, smiled a friendly, sexless smile, and said, 'Oh, I am. I have *so* much to do.'

She told me what it was without prompting. Her mouth was like a bath-tap which someone had forgotten to turn off, the words poured out in a continuous flow. 'So all these business companies got together and formed this organization called *Accion en Venezuela,* that means Action in Venezuela, it's a kind of private Peace Corps really, the object is to do Community Development Work in the *barrios,* those are the slums, and when I got the opportunity to join them I jumped at it. I've been living in a *barrio* these last few months, studying the conditions and needs of the people, and now I'm going home for a month to prepare a report on how things in the *barrios* can be improved, you know, adult education, and transportation and proper sewerage and so on. Oh, those *barrio* people are sweet. You know eighteen of them came to the airport to say goodbye. Wasn't that wonderful? And my fiancé is going to meet me at Idlewild, he hasn't seen me for three months, this is the ring he gave me. You know, I'm twenty-two and I've been travelling since I was nineteen. My name's Sally Kroger, what's yours? How do you do? Well, I've been to Africa and Asia and I've stayed with native missionaries and other wonderful people. I started travelling because I wanted to see what other people were like, I knew Americans were different, but I wanted to see just *how* they were different, and after a bit I realized the important thing wasn't just that Americans are different from the rest of the world, but the rest of the world are different from *each other.* You've got to experience this to realize it, but when you do, it's a big help, I mean it's a big help to know that, say, Venezuelans are different from Filipinos.'

It went on like that all the way to New York. After a time I stopped listening; the mind shut off, unable to take any more. But the gale of words blew on, over the canapés and cocktails brought by Tessa and her friends, over the veal from Maxims (the Paris restaurant), over the coffee and ice-cream. It only began to ease when the lights of Manhattan showed ahead.

In the silence before landing I said, 'What are you looking forward to most in New York?' 'Making a plan for the *barrio,*' she said. Not a word about seeing her fiancé.

Tessa came by with a heap of trays, and I caught her arm and said, 'What are *you* looking forward to in New York?' 'Oh,' she said, 'going on the town, I suppose. Having a ball.' She smiled across at the other girl, and for a moment their eyes met: Swinging Britain, you might say, and the Great Society.[1]

At dinner in New York's Gotham Hotel I had been aware of three men dining at an adjoining table, but had paid little attention to them. But when coffee arrived, and the room began to empty I could not help overhearing their conversation. All three were employed at the United Nations, all three were Americans. But what was interesting was this: two of the three were in the process of sacking the third.

The chief sacker, and the eldest of the three, was a clean-shaven, rather red-faced man of about forty-five, with crew-cut hair and a pair of steel-rimmed glasses. His name was George. His assistant, a few years younger, was a smaller, darkish individual with a pointed chin, a bow tie, and thick eyebrows. He was called Bob. The third member of the group was about thirty, a lean rather weak-faced man with freckles on his cheeks and already thinning on top. He too wore spectacles, heavy and horn rimmed. He had longish fingers, nicotine stained, and on the fourth finger of his left hand was a marriage ring. His name was Pete.

George said, 'I'm sorry Pete, but that's how it is. That's the way things go.'

Pete said, 'You mean I'm not up to the job?'

Bob said, 'Hell, no, Pete, it isn't like that at all. It's just that the particular talents you have – and both George and I think you have one hell of a lot of talents – don't we, George?—'

'—You bet—'

'—aren't best suited to this kind of work. Isn't that right, George?'

'Sure.'

'You mean,' said Pete, 'that I'm a kind of a square peg in a round hole?'

'*Exactly,*' said George, grasping this unexpected hostage to fortune, 'that's just it. I couldn't have put it better myself. And what we have to do now, Pete, is find you a *square* hole.'

Pete said, 'When did you decide on this?'

[1] Descriptions of the UK and the USA much in vogue then.

George said, 'Don't ask me to put a date on it, Pete. I couldn't if I tried. It's one of those things that's evolved, if you know what I mean.'

Pete said nothing, and Bob said, 'Listen, Pete. We've all been together a long time now, eh? We know each other pretty well, eh? Now I don't mind saying that I have the *greatest,* but the *very* greatest admiration for you as a person. I haven't said this before because I didn't want to embarrass you. But I can tell you this, that everyone back at the office, the stenographers and everybody, Judy and Anne and so on, feel just the same way. I've heard them say it. "Isn't that Pete just something?" I've heard them say. No kidding. You have real talent, you have qualities which I certainly don't have, and which I daresay George, if he's honest, would admit he doesn't have either—'. He smiled at George for approval, and George, looking solemnly at his plate, said, 'Dead right, Bob.' '—But the fact is that these talents of yours are wasted in this particular job. Now we don't want to see your talents wasted any more than you do.'

Pete said, 'Do you have a new job in mind?'

George was expecting this, and said, rather too quickly, 'Well, now, Pete, we don't have anything in mind *right now.* But you know how it is in the organization. There's things coming up all the time, and if you don't find something soon that really suits, you know that's really tailor-made for you, I'll eat my hat. And let me say this. If there's anything I can do in the way of a letter or anything, why, you only have to say the word.'

Pete puffed at a cigarette and said, 'What am I going to tell Mary?'

Bob said, 'Hell, Pete, you can manage Mary. She's an understanding kid. Tell her what we're telling you. Say we think you're too good for this job, because that's what it amounts to.'

George said, 'Sure does,' but even he didn't sound convinced.

There was a bit of a pause then, and George said, 'Hey, you don't have a drink, Pete! Why don't we all take some brandy?'

Bob said, 'Great idea.'

I thought, this is not really happening: this sort of conversation happens only in the movies. The brandy came, and cigars. Pete handled his cigar as though it was the first in his life. George and Bob drank Pete's health. After this Pete rallied a little, smiled at his executioners and said, 'You know, it's a kind of a shock.'

George said, '*Of course* it's a shock, Pete. We understand that. It's bound to be. But you'll look at it all in a different light when you've had time to think it over. And one day, you know, you'll look back and be glad it happened.'

Pete looked at his brandy glass and said, quietly, 'I guess you're right, George.' It was the first time he had used George's name since the conversation began. George said, 'Good boy! That's what I like to hear.'

The talk was rather desultory after this while everyone changed gear, tried to get back to pre-execution relations.

After a bit Pete said, 'George, there's something I'd like to ask you, get your opinion on. You too, Bob.'

George said, 'Sure Pete. Anything you want. Be glad to help.'

Bob said, 'Go ahead.'

'Well, I've been thinking recently about a lot of things, you know, life and the role of the intellect and all that, and there's one thing that's been puzzling me.'

George and Bob nodded sympathetically.

'It's this. In the kind of society we live in today, and where true evaluations are increasingly harder to make, we have these two great intellectual pillars, on the one hand Politics and on the other, Art. Right?' He made them sound like two boxers, Art in the red corner and Politics in the blue, about to slug it out for the heavyweight title of the world.

'Right,' said George.

'Now then,' said Pete, 'which in your view, and in Bob's too, is the more important, the more significant for our times. Politics? Or Art?'

There was a slight pause, and then George said, rather slowly, 'That's a hell of a good question. Politics or Art, eh? That's a real teaser.' He looked at Bob for help, and Bob just smiled and said to Pete, 'You're quite a pitcher.'

But I didn't stay to hear the answer. I had heard more than any self-respecting eavesdropper should. So I never did find out whether Art had KO'ed Politics or Politics Art.

AFRICA

Five miles above the darkened Atlantic, in the black void between America and Africa and one day and another, the Pan Am stewardess switched off the cabin lights. We wrapped rugs round our knees, tilted back our seats, and attempted sleep. All except six young Nigerians in the two rows opposite: you could tell they were Nigerians because there were also American Negroes in the plane, and these were blacker by far. Ever since take-off they had giggled among themselves, commenting on the food and drink, passing remarks on the pretty stewardesses. 'Man, those girls certainly work.' 'Yes, but they go travel lots of nice places.' 'Yes, but what a life though!' The one in the front seat, nearest the aisle, found a switch which turned on a little red light on the back of his seat: I think it was for summoning the stewardesses. When the man behind first saw it, he said to the others in his row, 'Man, look at this! What is this?' The one in front leaned back, and said, 'That's the devil, man, come to remind you of your sins.' He turned off the light and the one at the back peered forward suspiciously; but the switch was on the arm rest and he didn't see it. Soon the light came on again, and the man at the back jumped in his seat. His friends, who had been let in on the joke, said, 'There's that devil again, man. Man, you must be a *great* sinner.' It was a game that afforded them endless amusement. I think the man at the back knew quite well what was going on, but pretended he didn't to keep the party going. They were still at it when I fell asleep.

In the morning I was woken by a stewardess with orange juice. Of the Nigerians, the man at the back was still asleep, but his companions were all awake, gently ticking over, waiting for something to happen. The stewardess teetered down the aisle with hot towels. The Nigerians had not seen such things before, and the stewardess had to explain their purpose. They laughed till I thought they would be sick.

Instead of wiping their own hands and faces, they wiped each other's. Their bodies shook with laughter and the tears rolled from their eyes.

The Nigerian at the back woke up and stretched himself. The one next to him said, 'Man, you sleep like a dog.' Another said, 'You don't know what you just missed. You missed a hot towel.' The man yawned and looked about him with unseeing eyes. 'What you mean?' he said, dully. The other said, 'Man I'm telling you God's truth. This beautiful girl came by with hot towels to clean your dirty, black face.' The man stared and said nothing, utterly uncomprehending. 'He doesn't believe us,' said the other, 'we are telling him the truth about this fine Pan American service, and he doesn't believe us.' Another said, 'We have all had our hot towels. We are clean and he is dirty.' The man said, 'Why you wasting my time with that silly talk?' A stewardess went by, and one of them said to her, 'Excuse me, miss, but our friend here did not receive one of those hot towels, would you be so kind as to fetch him one?' The girl said, 'Certainly, sir' and went off to get one. The man looked at his companions suspiciously. When the towel arrived, he accepted it disbelievingly, holding it in his hand loosely, staring at it like a child with a comforter. He didn't alter his expression or position, but sat there incredulously. The others laughed fit to bust.

We came down at Dakar in the hot dawn, and went to the airport building for free drinks. There was a strong smell of fish about the place. A zany American woman said in excruciating French, '*Donnez-moi un specialité de Dakar!*' The waiter said, 'All I got is bottled pop. Take your choice.' He produced Coca-Cola, Seven Up, pineapple juice, orange juice, and Fanta. She chose Fanta, thinking it was a Dakar brew, unaware it was a stepchild of Coca-Cola. We climbed aboard with one new passenger, a vast African in green robes and a little red nightcap. The Nigerians giggled all the way from Dakar to Lagos. A white American in front of me tried to join in their jokes, become one of the party, but his mind worked on quite a different wavelength: they didn't so much ignore him as show themselves totally unaware he was there: after a bit he gave up and started reading a book. At ten we landed at Lagos.

*

To pursue the question of the American Negro[1] in Africa, I went to see one of the top coloured American administrators in Lagos, Mr Jim Jackson, Associate Director of Management for the Peace Corps. Mr and Mrs Jackson lived in a trim little house along Awolowo Road and when I arrived were having supper on table-trays and watching a western on television. Mr Jackson was a huge man with flaring nostrils like a dragon, and big red gums and a lovely smile. He wore a white shirt and black woollen tie, black socks, slacks and slippers. Mrs Jackson was on the big side too, with a solid gentle face, and hair bunched up on top and kept at anchor by a ribbon. She sat me down and gave me a cup of coffee; Mr Jackson turned down the sound on the television but the pictures, cowboys and Indians, flickered on.

Mr Jackson said he had been born and raised in Texas. He was now forty-eight, and had spent most of his career in the Pentagon. 'At the Pentagon they looked on me as a kind of invisible man. I did my work and I kept quiet. I didn't cause any difficulties for them or have any chips on my shoulder about hating the white man. But when they said, "We can't promote this man", I used to smile and say, "Why not? Just tell me why not?" Always with a smile. My mother told me you can best catch flies with sugar. So they promoted me. And I kept on at night school, and at the end of ten years I qualified as an accountant. There's not many Negroes who are on the economic level that I am.'

'How did you get from the Pentagon into the Peace Corps?'

Mr Jackson took out a pair of spectacles and started to polish them. On the television screen another redskin bit the dust. 'One day I took my wife to watch the Peace Corps playing a baseball game at the back of the White House. At that time my wife was working in the Talent Search Office in the Peace Corps. During the game, the head of the Talent Office came up and talked to my wife, and after she'd introduced us he asked me what I did. So I told him, and a few days later he gave me a call, and said would I be interested in doing a spell in the Peace Corps? My wife and

[1] The word 'black' did not gain common currency until later.

I talked it over, and though I'd never been out of the States before, curiosity got the better of me and I said Yes.'

'Why do you think they asked you?'

'Well, as I say, I've never hated the white man. I've always been free of prejudice. We've always had all the social freedom we ever wanted. All I've ever fought for is economic freedom.'

Mrs Jackson said: 'We've never felt trodden down or abused.'

Mr Jackson said: 'I went along to the Peace Corps office, and I was interviewed by about twenty people, and finally by Shriver himself. I liked that. It was a real challenge all the way. Shriver wanted me to go to Latin America, but the African bureau wanted me to come here. In the end Shriver yielded. At that time I didn't know too much about Africa. I'd been brainwashed by all those Tarzan pictures. When they asked me about getting my car shipped over, I didn't appreciate there were any roads for it to run on. I thought it was all bush. My friends thought I ought to get the Distinguished Service Cross for coming to Africa at all. A neighbour wrote the other day and said, would we come home with bones in our noses? They think we see elephants all day, and eat elephant meat.'

Mrs Jackson said: 'I've never had some of the wild thoughts about Africa that some people have because I've always been internationally minded. I studied international relations as a girl.'

Mr Jackson said: 'I think the biggest shock when we came here was the African's ignorance about the American Negro. One day I decided not to give any dash to those little boys who open the car door for you, and they said to me, Negroes in the States don't get dash, they get beaten. So I told them the truth, but they didn't believe me. Another time at a cocktail party I met the Premier of Eastern Nigeria. He thought I was a Nigerian and gave me a handshake like a wet fish. Then he heard my voice and gave me a double handshake. He didn't expect to find an American Negro at a diplomatic cocktail party. He asked what I did, and when he learned I had authority over white men, he could hardly believe it.'

'What about this question of affinity?' I said.

'Many white men ask me, do I feel kindred with these people? And the answer is No. I've noticed there are some occasions, like getting someone quickly through the Customs, that I can get things done more quickly than a white American. But when I'm with an African, I don't feel, this man is my brother. The fact is I'm a Negro with a white man's tongue and a white man's thoughts.'

Mr and Mrs Jackson finished their supper, and Mrs Jackson put the trays on the side. On the television screen a stagecoach started out on a journey which, I assumed, would not be without incident.

'Do you have children?' I said.

'We have a daughter here in Nigeria,' said Mr Jackson. 'In Lagos we found there was only one school suitable for her, a Nigerian school for 9th grade. But she was the only American girl there, and they discriminated against her, they wouldn't accept her. So I ribbed the schoolteacher. I said, "You sold my foreparents so you ought to take my daughter." He laughed. 'So I sent her to a mission boarding school at Enugu. The pupils there are sons and daughters of diplomats and missionaries and business people. She's the only Negro there, and her best friend is an American girl from the South. She lives in a hostel with other boys and girls, and she's having a ball.'

I asked Mr Jackson if being an American Negro in Africa caused any friction between himself and his white colleagues, and he said he didn't think so. 'Some white Americans', he said, 'keep their distance. You know, they say they're going on a trip and why don't we go too, and when I tell them we're ready, they find some excuse. But that's no different from the States.' He added, 'But you have to watch out. People here mix so free and easy you sometimes forget their prejudices. I know a lot of Negro stories, and one time I used to tell them at parties. But I had to be very careful who I told them *to*. You know the story about the Negro father who dropped a pot of white paint all over his son. Three relatives tried to scrape it off, but they couldn't. And the son said: "I've been a white man five minutes and already I hate three niggers."' He chuckled. 'I told that story at a party where there were some white Americans, and they were really shocked.'

Mrs Jackson said: 'You should have *seen* their *faces*. They were quite *disgusted.*'

'But on the whole', I said, 'you like it here?'

'Oh, we like it fine,' said Mr Jackson, 'we have a social status here that we would never have in the States. We know people like the ambassador and the head of Lufthansa and members of the cabinet, people we'd never meet back home. We're on a higher plateau.'

Mrs Jackson said: 'And I would think when we get back, the sort of people who would otherwise say "Hi!" and pass us by, would ask us to cocktails and all that.'

I looked out of the window at bare-footed Nigerians slogging along Awolowo Road, and began to understand the Jacksons' lack of affinity with them.

'The only thing we've tried to be here', said Mr Jackson, 'is ourselves. We haven't put on any airs and graces. We haven't tried to hold a cup of tea with two fingers.'

'What will you do when you get home?' I said. 'Go back to the Pentagon?'

'I don't know,' said Mr Jackson, 'it depends on the visibility I have. So many avenues have been opened to us.'

Mrs Jackson said: 'Jim's been such a success here that I think he feels anything is possible.'

On the television screen the stage-coach had been ambushed by Indians. But the sheriff's men were coming down fast from the top of the hill. Mr Jackson leaned forward and turned up the sound, and suddenly the room was filled with war-whoops and rifle shots. Mr Jackson said, 'They get some pretty good programmes here.' Now the sheriff's men had joined battle and Indians were crashing to the ground. I looked at the Jacksons' faces alight with enthusiasm. There was no doubt whose side *they* were on; two brownskins watching with joy the whiteskins knocking off the redskins; two Americans approving the triumph of law and order over savagery and disorder. It helped to confirm a lot.

A day or two later I met the white wife of the white American ambassador, and told her I had talked with Mr Jackson, and how interesting he had been.

'In what way?'

'As an American Negro,' I said, 'coming back to the land of his fathers. What he feels about it all.'

'Oh, I see, well, of course, that's *not* the sort of thing *I* would *ever* talk to him about.'

I thought, but didn't say: why not?

Liberia is the African Headquarters of the Voice of America, and its Director was a man called Hank Miller, about six and a half feet high. He sent me in a car down to Careysburg, twenty miles from Monrovia, the transmitting station which picks up VOA's signals from Washington, and beams them all over Africa. It was a big, dull building, tucked away in the hills and surrounded by groves of antennae, two hundred feet high, like something out of science fiction.

Here I met a VOA man called Sarkisian who was compiling a library of tribal music from all over Africa. He was leaving shortly to record what he called 'a town meeting' between the AID man and some tribal chiefs in a place called Foya about a hundred and fifty miles into the interior, near the Sierra Leone border. If that interested me, why didn't I go with him?

Mr Sarkisian was an Americanized Armenian, and looked the image of Britain's Mr Punch, a short, stubby man, with bald head, hook nose, and thin moustache. He was surrounded by tape-recorders, microphones, and yards of cable and tape. He said he had learned music originally from his father, who had emigrated to Massachusetts from Armenia after the Turkish massacres in which his father's parents were killed. 'Ever since a child I have played Turkish and Arabian instruments. I can play the Egyptian harp and the Arabic lute and the Persian dulcimer, and pretty well all types of flute and clarinet and drums. When I go to record in a new village, I start off by sitting down in the middle and playing the drums myself. They all crowd round and listen and say, well, that's fine, now we'll *really* show you how it's done. Which, of course, is just what I want.'

Two days later Mr Sarkisian and his wife left for Foya by car and I arranged to meet them there by charter plane. The charter firm had a small office at the airport, but when I arrived at 7.30 a.m., it was closed. So I went to the airport café, and presently this young Greek God came in, with blue eyes and fair hair, a slim figure in khaki shirt and trousers. Greek God, hell! He was the all-American boy.

'You Mr Kennedy?'

'Yes.'

'I'm McTeague. How are you, sir? I'm going to take you to Foya.'

We walked out to the plane. It looked like a clapped-out dragonfly. There were patches of tape on the windows, and McTeague said that a big battery he had been ferrying a few days before had got loose and gone partly through the window. I seized a strap to pull myself into the plane, and it came away in my hand. McTeague hauled me up and started the single motor. It wheezed and spluttered into life. We trundled on to the runway and turned down it, and took off.

We circled once, over the sea, climbed to a thousand feet and headed east. Monrovia dropped away, and soon there were no roads beneath us or anything, just little clearings in the trees and groups of native huts clustered like autumn mushrooms.

After half an hour a group of mountains appeared ahead, and McTeague said that Foya lay beyond them. Now there was nothing beneath us but thick forest, not a trail or a clearing or a hut in sight, nothing but this huge carpet of trees. I wondered what McTeague would do if the engine packed up.

'McTeague!' I shouted.

'Yes.'

'What do you do if the engine packs up?'

'Try and land.'

'Where?'

'On the tree-tops.'

'You're joking?'

'No I'm not. I'd rather try and land on the tree-tops than on water or in a swamp. When you land in a swamp with a fixed wheel aircraft, the first thing that happens is the aircraft turns on its back. But the tree-tops should give a nice cushion.'

'How do you get from the tree-tops to the ground?'

McTeague pointed a thumb behind him. I turned and saw at the back a huge coil of yellow rope, like a sleeping snake.

'Have you ever had to do it?'

'No, but I heard of a guy who did – and he got away with it.'

We cleared the mountains and McTeague lost height. In about five minutes a road appeared, and we flew along it until we came to a village. We circled the village and saw a landing strip, like a swath of bandage, in a field of sugar-cane. 'I think that's Foya,' said McTeague, 'but we'll go down and find out.' It was.

The 'town meeting' took place in a little village called Karwohun, in the local hall. There were a lot of people there: Mr Hutton, the AID[1] man, who had a face like an old moon and fur on his chest like a bed of watercress; Mr Sarkisian, now wearing a black and white striped, tasselled hat, Mrs Sarkisian who had red hair scraped back in a bun, a Mr Moore who was Mr Sarkisian's Liberian assistant, and a whole lot of Chiefs and villagers. The chief Chief was a fine-looking old man called Thomas Kollie, who wore an old pair of khaki trousers and a loose khaki shift, buttoned up to the neck. Mr Sarkisian said he reminded him of Jeff Chandler, the movie actor. He had seventy wives and most of the villagers were his relations.

Mr Sarkisian set himself up behind a battery of tape re- corders, microphones, and boxes marked 'Virgin Tape', and we were ready to begin. Mr Hutton walked over to the micro- phones and beamed. I had a feeling he was going to make a real meal of the occasion, and I was right. 'Chief Kollie,' said Mr Hutton ponderously, 'it is *so gracious* of you to welcome us here today, and give us your hospitality, and make this town meeting possible. And I want to say right away how grateful and pleased we all are.' He beamed again. One of the Chief's relations translated this, and everybody nodded and clapped. 'And now,' said Mr Hutton, 'I would like to intro- duce ourselves to you.' At length he introduced Mr Sarkisian,

[1] Agency for International Development.

Mr Moore, myself ('Mr Kennedy is an English writer, and we are so honoured to have him with us today') and his wife. All this had to be translated and told a second time. 'And now . . . ' said Mr Hutton, and stopped. 'Oh, my goodness,' he said, 'I made a terrible mistake. I forgot to introduce *Mrs* Sarkisian.' Sarkisian, from behind his tape-recorders, said: 'She's the one who carries the boxes.' Mr Hutton said, 'She's his head wife, and his *only* wife.'

We all laughed to please Mr Hutton, who then said: 'And now, Chief Kollie, we would be happy if you would introduce your people to us. We know you are the Paramount Chief, and therefore the greatest of the Chiefs, but we would like to meet your town chiefs.' There were a dozen town chiefs, and Chief Kollie started wading through them. At one point the translator got so muddled that Chief Kollie pushed him away and took over translating himself. Mr Hutton said, 'This is one of the problems we have brought you, I fear. We wish we could talk with you in your language, and we are so sorry we can't.' After what seemed a lifetime, the introduction of the town chiefs came to an end. Mr Hutton said, 'Chief Kollie, it is most gracious of you to let us meet all these people, because we want to get to know them by name. And now let's talk a little about the school.'

It seemed that AID had a plan, or Mr Hutton wanted AID to have a plan, to build a school. But at the moment it appeared to be no more than a germ in Mr Hutton's mind. 'I can't say when the school will be built,' he said, 'but I can say it will be built, and I know that's the thing in most of your minds today. Now let's see how many boys and girls would be likely to go to school to read books.'

Everyone was asked how many children he had, and one or two chiefs said they had lost count. One old chief, who was Kollie's uncle, said he would like to read book himself.

'Ask him,' said Mr Hutton to Chief Kollie, 'why he would like to read book?'

The old man muttered something, and Chief Kollie said, 'He would like to read book to tell more English.'

'Chief Kollie,' said Mr Hutton, 'do the chiefs think that reading book is going to cause all the boys and girls to leave family and go to Monrovia?'

'No,' said Chief Kollie, 'that is not in their minds at all.'

'Well,' said Mr Hutton, 'we've talked about the school, what's the next most important thing?'

'The next thing is roads,' said Chief Kollie.

Mr Hutton looked round the chiefs as though they were a class of five year olds, and said: 'Now why do you need roads?'

'We need roads', said Chief Kollie, 'to send our goods to market and the children to school.'

Mr Hutton nodded, as though to say, good boy, go to the top of the class.

'I can't say when you will have roads,' said Mr Hutton, 'but I know you will have them. I know that roads are very much in the front of your President's mind.' A chief in a peacock-blue robe said: 'We know what the President has done for us, and we pray God to grant him a long and healthy life. Before we had no money. Now we have thirty dollars.'

Mr Hutton said: 'That certainly is a great tribute to your great leader, and I'm sure he'll hear of that one way or the other, and it is certainly a fine tribute for all the great things the President has done for you.'

Chief Kollie said: 'Our love for President Tubman is in every Liberian heart. He is showing the way we must follow.'

'Well, now,' said Mr Hutton, 'we're going to have to close this meeting soon, because I know that some of us have to go in not too many minutes. Let me say this to you. I am not a big man. I am just an adviser. I will pass on your message to my people and to your government. I understand your first need is for the school, and the second is for roads.'

Chief Kollie said: 'And we also need a clinic.'

Mr Hutton paused, and looked at Chief Kollie with his moon face as though to say, *that* isn't on the programme *at all.*

'Now why do you need a clinic?' he said.

Oh, Christ, Hutton, I thought, do take a pull on yourself.

'Many children sick,' said Chief Kollie.

Mr Hutton nodded again. 'Well, thank you for interrupting me, Chief Kollie,' he said, 'I'm very glad to know that. All I can say is that with your drive and your determination (half of them, by this time, were asleep) you will get the things

461

you want. I can't say when you will get them, but I know you will get them for certain. To talk with men like you makes one very encouraged. So let me thank you, Chief Kollie, and all these other fine, gracious people, for this very wonderful town meeting.'

Chief Kollie said: 'Thank you. Now we are happy. We are thankful to the President and the American people for all the interest they have shown in us.'

Mr Sarkisian sat behind his recorders with earphones on his head, adjusting levels. I felt as I had done at Father Vermilion's meeting in New York. What had been said was wind and warm air. Who was going to *listen* to it all, and what would they gain if they did?

Three villagers came forward to sing to us. One wore a brown astrakhan hat, a pair of khaki shorts with half the flies undone, and a striped shirt; the second wore khaki shorts and a red fez with a gold star in the front, and was carrying a huge fly-whisk; and the third had on a yellow satin cap, of the kind used by goalkeepers in England, a black and white striped robe, and bathing trunks. Each was holding a hollowed-out piece of tin and a stick which they used for accompaniment. The noise was awful. The man doing most of the singing, the one with the fly-whisk, was on the left and Mr Sarkisian had to stop everything and shift him to the centre, to be nearer the microphone. ('I guess the lead singer turned out not to be the lead singer,' said Mr Hutton). They started up again, and Mr Sarkisian bounced up and down shouting, 'That's great.' It went on for ten minutes that seemed like a hundred. Then Mr Sarkisian rewound the tape and played it back. They loved that: it was real white man's magic. They crowded round and laughed and listened, and listened and laughed. 'The playback is always a cinch,' said Mr Sarkisian. Afterwards Mr Hutton said to the room at large: 'I'm going to make a copy of the tape of this whole meeting, and send it to our director in Washington.' Did he mean the Director of AID, I wondered, and did he seriously think that busy man was going to give up an afternoon listening to it?

Later I asked Mr Hutton this, and he said, 'Well, that was a Public Relations gimmick. The real reason I'm recording this meeting is for my doctoral dissertation.'

'Your what?'

'My Ph.D. I'm working for a Doctorate in Education, and I shall send this in as part of my field work.'

He beamed and looked around the room, and said loudly: 'Now it is time for us to go, but we shall be back, I promise you. I don't know when we shall be back, but I know that we will.' He took a five-dollar bill from his wallet. 'We all know how generous Chief Kollie is with his white heart, and we'd like to conclude by giving him some of our white heart too.'

He handed Chief Kollie the bill, and the chief looked embarrassed. He tried to refuse it, but Mr Hutton pressed it on him. To me he said: 'That's the common practice here.'

'I thought he seemed rather offended,' I said.

'Oh, no,' said Mr Hutton, 'they all do it. When President Tubman was here the other day, he gave him 1,000 dollars. It's not payment, but a recognition of what's been done.'

'Wouldn't it have been better to have given him a bottle of whisky?'

Mr Hutton thought. 'I guess it might,' he said, 'but I didn't have a bottle of whisky with me.'

There were six of us in the plane from Robertsfield to Lisbon, and six Pan Am stewardesses, so it looked like a nice flight. I had three seats to myself, and another man took the three seats on the opposite side of the aisle. He was a small middle-aged man with a balding head and spectacles and a sharp foxy little face. He looked as if he might have a bit of a temper.

They gave us lunch after take-off, and then I read for an hour. Yet all the time I was aware of Foxy's presence. He hardly touched his lunch, and I lost count of the number of cans of beer and menthol cigarettes he had since the bar opened. Although he had been given a glass for his beer he seemed to prefer drinking it from the can. He just sat by the window, swilling down the beer and puffing at the cigarettes. He looked as though he had something on his mind.

I put down my book and glanced in his direction at the very moment he was doing the same to me.

'Care to have a drink with me?' he said.

I moved to the seat beside him, and the stewardess brought another can of beer and a glass of brandy. Foxy took the cigarette packet from the tray and flicked a cigarette towards me. I said I didn't smoke. He took one himself and said, 'Been in Liberia long?'

'Two weeks,' I said. 'And you?'

'Five months. Boy, am I glad to be getting out!'

'What were you doing?'

'United States Seabees. You heard of them?'

'They're the naval construction corps, aren't they?'

'Right. I'm a Petty Officer Instructor. There was a group of us sent there to teach Liberians about mechanics. Or I should say to *try* to teach Liberians about mechanics. They're unteachable.'

'Really?'

'Sure. We were stationed way out in the boondocks, about a hundred miles from Monrovia, near a place called Foya.'

'I know it.'

'Yeah? Well, there were thirteen of us, and we lived in these Quonset huts, and gave these guys lessons. I'd say to them: "In an internal combustion engine there are four strokes to make up the cycle. The first is the intake stroke, the second is the compression stroke, the third is the power stroke, and the fourth is the exhaust stroke." Well, I'd go through it all with these guys and then I'd say to the first man, "What is the first stroke?", and you know what he'd say? *The crank shaft!* Christ! I must have gone over that routine at least twenty-eight times.' He took a pull of his cigarette and said, 'I don't know how I'd *describe* Liberians if anyone asked me. It would take a week. They gave us some books to read about the place before we went there. One of them was by this fellow John Gunther. I don't recall the name of it, but I thought he was exaggerating. Turned out he was *under*-exaggerating. That's a fact.'

'In what way?'

'Liberians are about one remove from the monkeys. I'm telling you. I've seen things no white person has ever seen. One night I saw of boy of nine initiated into manhood. He came into this hut, all wet and with nothing on, and this old man who was sitting there picked him up and put him over his knee and cut his shoulders and chest with this sharp steel knife. You should have seen the blood that came out.

Christ, the blood! And when he was through with that, he turned him over and circumcised him. The boy didn't make a sound. I don't think he had anything to deaden it, but he didn't make a sound.

'Then they used to get drunk regular on this cane-juice. God, does that stuff drive them out of their minds! Cane-juice is a kind of ruin. I'd say it was around 180 per cent proof. You can put a match to cane-juice. You won't see it burn, but you can't put your hand over the top of it. The area gets smaller and smaller and then it's all burnt up and there's nothing there.'

'Did you ever try it?'

'God, no! I don't drink nothing that don't come out of a can or bottle or hasn't got a label on it that I can read. I don't believe in that home-made stuff.'

'Did you ever get down to Monrovia?'

'Not too often. About once a month we'd make a trip there and walk around and do the night-clubs. The women there are dead though. They're like logs.'

'So I've heard.'

'I used to spend my leisure time on the Ham Radio. I'm a great Ham enthusiast. There was a guy in some AID educational outfit at Foya, and he didn't live too far from the camp. He was a Ham enthusiast too. I'd go over there weekends, and we'd have a great time. We used to call up people all over the world . . . Japan, Korea, Australia. That was great.'

He looked out of the window and said, 'Christ, we're a long ways up.' Then he stubbed out his cigarette and said, 'You on a business trip?'

'No, I'm a writer,' I said.

He looked at me with sudden interest, as if I was a new arrival at the zoo. He pulled out another cigarette and said, 'Anyone tell you about Careysburg?'

'You mean the Voice of America place?' I said.

'No, I don't mean the Voice of America place. I mean the area around.'

'No,' I said. 'I don't think anyone mentioned that.'

'It would interest you, being a writer. Boy, that's quite a place! You don't want to break down there at night.'

'Why?'

'People just disappear.'

'White people?'

'No, blacks.'

'What happens to them?'

'Nobody knows. But ask any Liberian about Careysburg, and he'll tell you the same thing.'

'What do *you* think happens to them?'

He took a puff at his cigarette, looked me hard in the face and said, 'I think they get eaten.'

I ordered another round of drinks, and when they had come, Foxy said: 'I haven't told you why I'm going back to the States.'

'No.'

'As a writer it might interest you. I'm in disgrace. I'm being *sent* back.'

'What for?'

He took a long pull and said, 'You don't know my name and I don't know yours, and we're not ever likely to meet again, so I'll tell you.

'I got up this training programme for the Liberians I was telling you about, and the shop steward liked it and I liked it and everybody liked it. It was a good programme. But after a few months, living up there in the jungle got to be quite a strain. There was the heat and the insects and the general lack of utilities. And to add to that, there was this balls-up about our papers, so for two months we didn't get paid. And that wasn't any good, because we had to pay for our food and there were other expenses.

'It was all the fault of this new officer. He was twenty-three years old and about the most prejudiced and obstinate man I've ever met. He insulted at least ten Liberians within a week of getting there. He just didn't know how to talk to people. One of the Liberians said to me, "I went to the States for my education. I got kicked around there because I was a black man. But I don't expect to get kicked around here. This is a black country."

'So at the end of the week, when we hadn't been paid for two months, I went to this officer and I said, "Will you fix up these papers over the weekend and send them off to base?" And he said he would, and I went over to Foya and spent the weekend on the Ham radio with this guy I was telling you about. I came back on the Monday and went into the office and the first thing I saw was the papers, which were still lying on the desk and hadn't been touched. So I went into the little cubicle this officer had, and I said to him, "You haven't done the papers?", and he just sat there on his ass and said, "No, I haven't gotten around to it yet".

'So then I blew my top. That's all there was to it. I called him about every name in the book. I know I shouldn't have done it, but I guess I couldn't help myself. A man can only take so much. So he waited until I'd finished and then he said, "OK, pack your bags, you're going home". Well that really loused me up, because I'd worked out a good training programme, and the only reason I'd volunteered for Liberia was to do a good job and help people.'

'What happens now?' I said.

'Right now I have to go to Providence, Rhode Island, which is where my base is. The plane I'm booked on goes to Boston, which is only thirty-eight miles away, but this officer has routed my luggage through New York, so I guess I'll have to go there first, and then back to Providence. He fouled that up like he fouled everything else.'

'What happens when you get to Providence?'

'I'm going to ask for a court martial because I want the whole situation looked into. I want them to hear my side of the story, not being paid and everything, and what sort of a guy this officer is. I've been seventeen years in the Navy, and I've only got another three to go, so I don't want this to mess me up. I'm afraid it may mess me up a little. I know I shouldn't have said what I did. But I guess I was mad at the time. If I'd been a dog I'd have bitten that officer.'

'Do you think you will get a court martial?'

'Yeah, I guess so,' said Foxy. He pulled out another cigarette, and said, 'See, one of the commanders at the base is a very good friend of mine. He's a fellow that knows me well, and that I wouldn't do anything stupid unless I had good reason to. I've already told him what happened.'

'You've written to him?'

'No, I haven't written to him. I called him up on the Ham radio.'

'Is he a Ham enthusiast too?'

'No, but there's a friend of mine in Providence who is, and I called him up and said I'd like to speak to this commander, and so he got hold of him and I spoke to him the following night.'

I mulled it over for a bit, and the more I did, the more curious it seemed. 'In the British Navy', I said, 'it would be very unusual for a petty officer to call up a commander in this sort of way.'

Foxy said, 'Yeah, I guess it is kind of unusual.' He paused for a moment and said, 'See, this commander and I are very close. We have a special kind of relationship.' He glanced at me in an odd way and the thought flashed through my mind they might be a couple of poofs. Foxy said, 'I don't know why I'm telling you this, but this commander is a very good friend of my wife's. He sees a lot of her while I'm away, takes her out in my automobile and things like that, which is very nice for her and OK by me.' He gave me another quick glance and said, 'They're real intimate, if you understand what I mean.'

I nodded. 'He's a good friend,' said Foxy, 'and he'll want to help me all he can.'

'Yes,' I said, 'I can see that.'

Foxy turned towards the window and looked down. 'Christ!' he said, 'that must be the Sahaira down there.'

EUROPE

There are half a million American soldiers stationed in Europe, and I went to see some at Frummingen, near Stuttgart, the headquarters of the Eighth Cavalry Division. At Stuttgart Airport in the evening, I was met by a tiny, neat colonel with a round face and spectacles and the general appearance of a sparrow. He took me downstairs to wait for my luggage, and after we had waited fifteen minutes and no luggage had come, we found we should have been waiting upstairs. During the next few days things like that were to happen with the colonel all the time.

We got into a big army station-wagon driven by a very silent young soldier from California. The colonel said Frummingen was in Baden-Württemberg, an area originally inhabited by the Swabians. It was a town of about 50,000 people, famous for making pins. 'But I'll be giving you a full press information kit tomorrow.' We cleared the airport and swung on to the autobahn: it was dark, but on either side you could see trees.

'This is real nice country,' said the colonel. 'To me Germany is just one big beautiful park. The Germans are real clean people. They're cleaner than we are.'

We passed through Frummingen without seeing a soul ('the Germans', said the colonel, 'are real early-bedders') and went up the hill the other side. The colonel said the base was in two parts; the kaserne or main compound where the offices were and most of the soldiers lived, and the area outside. I was staying outside, in what the colonel called the VIP suite of the Bachelor Officers' Quarters.

We drew up outside a barrack-like building, and went into a darkened hall where the colonel shouted for the janitor. Nobody came. The colonel went down to the basement, and the Californian driver and I stood uneasily in the dark, not seeing each other or saying anything. Then the colonel and the janitor appeared and led us to the VIP suite. This consisted of a bedroom, sitting room and bathroom, and was a pretty modest affair. The Californian soldier put down my luggage, and the colonel said he'd send his car for me at 9.30 in the morning.

The VIP suite was stifling, like Death Valley in midsummer. I tried to open a window but they were sealed. There was an ice-box in the bedroom, but the ice compartment had seized up. I undressed and went to the bathroom to wash; but there was no soap or towels and no means of getting any. All that was left was to lie down, hot and unwashed, on the bed and read; which I would have done if there had been a bulb in the table light.

The colonel's car which had been promised for 9.30 didn't come. I waited an hour and then a huge man, all of seven feet high, arrived. He said he was Sergeant Cogswell and worked in the colonel's office. His uniform was bright with crazy insignia. He was sorry the arrangements had broken down, but an emergency field exercise had been ordered at 5 a.m., and the colonel had had to take part in it.

Hardly had Sergeant Cogswell left when the colonel arrived. For a moment I didn't recognize him. He looked like a bit player in *The Longest Day*. He was wearing battledress and a tin hat and a pack which was practically crushing him. He seemed tinier than ever. 'When they blow this god-damn whistle,' he said, 'you have to scramble. It would happen the day you arrive. Gee, I'm sorry.' I was beginning to like the colonel.

The colonel said he had arranged for me to take tea that afternoon with a typical Frummingen family. He couldn't come himself, but would fetch me later. Sergeant Cogswell would drive me there and Sergeant Day, who also worked in his office, would do the interpreting. Sergeant Day had just married a Frummingen girl and later in the evening had invited us to a drink at their apartment in the town. 'Sergeant Day speaks German like a real native,' said the colonel. I was really touched by the thought he had given to my programme.

Sergeant Cogswell lumbered into the VIP suite at four o'clock and said he had orders to pick up a lady called Frau Stauss and take her to the tea-party with us. I asked who she was and Sergeant Cogswell said a local writer. We must have spent an hour looking for Frau Stauss's house, with Sergeant Cogswell bellowing instructions from the back and the Californian driver silently obeying them. That driver was the most taciturn man I've met: even when Cogswell's instructions landed us in a cul-de-sac or one-way street, as frequently they did, he made no comment but shifted into neutral and waited for Cogswell to take another look at the map. When we found Frau Stauss's house, a neighbour told us she had left half an hour before.

We had more difficulties finding the place for tea, and arrived there at a quarter to six instead of half past four. This was the apartment of a government official called Herr Mäder. He wasn't there but we were welcomed by Frau Mäder, a large, comfortable woman in her fifties who, far from being annoyed at our lateness, seemed overjoyed we had come at all. With her were two doe-eyed daughters, Stella and Andrea in their teens; also sitting hungrily round the table were Frau Stauss and Sergeant Day. He had buck teeth and looked about sixteen. The table itself was heavy with plum cake and marmalade cake and apfelstrudel and bowls of cream. I murmured to Sergeant Day that they had really put themselves óut to entertain me, and he said in Germany a writer was held in high esteem.

I asked about the Americans, and Andrea said, 'It is so sad we cannot fraternize more with them. They are so lonely, these boys, and very good-looking, some of them. But my parents are very strict and won't let me go to the base for dances. It is unfair.' Andrea spoke excellent English but had to repeat this in German for her mother. Her mother said prostitutes went to the base, all soldiers drank, and what was wrong with German boys anyway? Frau Stauss nodded heavily. Andrea said, 'Mother is so old fashioned. She thinks all soldiers are fiends who want to rape and murder. There's nothing wrong with German boys, but most of those I know are so *dull.*' Sergeant Day said, rather boldly, 'If you got to know the GIs up at the base I think you'd find them pretty dull too.' Andrea, not to be outsmarted, said: 'Well, I'm sure they are dull in a different way.'

By six-forty there was still no sign of the colonel, so, heavy with apfelstrudel and cream, we tottered down to the street. We found the colonel about fifty yards away, peering up an alleyway in search of the apartment: he said he'd been looking for it for half an hour.

The colonel and I got into his Volkswagen. 'How did you make out there?' said the colonel. I said Day's interpreting had been a great help. 'He's an interesting boy, that,' said the colonel. 'When he first came I didn't know what to do with him. He just didn't fit into anything, and I was thinking of transferring him. But he slogged away with his German, and then he got married to this girl we're going to see, which incidentally is a story in itself, and the two things completely transformed him.'

The colonel said he had fixed for us to drop by for five minutes at the house of the Chief of Staff. This was like about a million other American houses, with the drapes drawn and the coffee table bare and not a hair out of place or a book or magazine in sight. The Chief of Staff gave us two massive whiskies and we stayed with him forty minutes. We had intended to have something to eat after this but the colonel said the Days were now expecting us, and we had better go straight there. I asked where the Days lived, and the colonel said he didn't know, we would go to where Sergeant Cogswell lived and he would tell us. We went to where the colonel *thought* Sergeant Cogswell lived, but that was a different matter. We drew up outside a gloomy barracks in which there wasn't a light showing, and the colonel disappeared inside. Presently a light came on which lit up the central staircase and four landings. From the Volkswagen I watched the colonel climb from floor to floor, stopping on each landing to check from a list that Cogswell wasn't there. Unfortunately the colonel hadn't realized the light was automatic, and when he reached the top landing it went out, leaving him in the dark. Alone in the Volkswagen I laughed out loud. It was quite a time before he got back.

We tried one or two more barracks and then the colonel said we should go to the officers' club and telephone somebody who would tell us where Sergeant Day lived. We passed the VIP suite on the way, and parked outside it was Sergeant Day's car containing himself and Mrs Day and Sergeant Cogswell. They had been waiting there some time, they said, this being the rendezvous the colonel had agreed. The colonel strenuously denied having ever made such a rendezvous and Sergeant Cogswell didn't seem disposed to argue with him. I said how-do-you-do to Mrs Day, Sergeant Cogswell got into the back of the Volkswagen where his head touched the roof, and we set off in convoy for the town.

'Now you've said hullo to Mrs Day,' said the colonel, 'I might as well tell you how John met her. When he'd been learning German for a while, he started walking down to the town every night – down this very road – to see if he could find someone to practise on. It wasn't easy for him because by nature he's shy. See, he had this very puritanical upbringing – he did a year in a seminary in Chicago – and he didn't carouse around like the others. Well, this girl used to take her dog for a walk every evening, so eventually John plucked up courage and spoke to her, and they got on fine and he arranged to speak to her again the following night.

'After this they met regularly and the boys used to tease poor John mercilessly. They'd say to him, "Well, haven't you laid her yet?", and this really embarrassed him. See, he'd never laid *anyone*. When I saw the way things were going, I called him into my office and said, "Listen, I can transfer you to Nuremberg if you like" – see, I wanted to give him an out. But he said, no, he wanted to stay, and go on with the girl. I told him he was young and there were millions of women in the world to meet. But he wouldn't listen, he went ahead and got married and we all went to the wedding and reception in the Paradise Gasthaus. The parents weren't too keen to begin with, but they came round to it. I guess Papa was glad to get daughter off his hands.'

The car ahead turned into a sort of compound and stopped beside a building in the middle. Sergeant Cogswell said this was where Day's in-laws lived, and he thought it would be roomier than his apartment. We went upstairs to a long, rather bare room and were introduced to Day's father-in-law who was old and fat and had fought in both world wars, and a cousin called Ralf in his middle forties, and Ralf's wife. There was no sign of Day's mother-in-law, and when I mentioned this to the colonel he said, 'You haven't missed a thing. She's a real old cow. She weighs over two hundred pounds and measures five by five.' Day's wife produced a couple of bottles of Swabian wine and some cocktail biscuits and we all sat down. I thought, whatever else one's views on the American army, it was wonderfully democratic, with the colonel and Cogswell and Day and Day's family, all mucking in together.

I didn't do more than sip the wine, for we hadn't eaten and I was still feeling the effects of the whiskies of the Chief of Staff. The colonel had no such inhibitions and swigged away. The party was a little sticky to begin with, for Day's wife and Ralf's wife and Cogswell were born listeners rather than talkers. But Day made up for them, chattering away in German and English, interpreting for one and all, showing much affection to his father-in-law, pouring out wine and handing round biscuits. He agreed with Frau Fahle about many GIs being too tired at the end of the day to start learning German: his own walks downtown to practise it had been very tiring. 'There and back is all of three miles, and not too many GIs are prepared to consider it. The average soldier takes a taxi to the town till his money runs out and then sits in the barracks and vegetates.' Ralf said the same barriers to fraternization applied to the Germans. They too worked a long day, often until after 7 p.m., and didn't have energy left to start learning English or entertaining Americans.

Around eleven we got up to go. The colonel could hardly stand, and Sergeant Cogswell and I had to help him to the car. 'I'm going to drive you home,' I said. He was too far gone to argue and got into the front offside seat. Sergeant Cogswell got into the back, where again his head touched the roof.

'Do you know the way home, Sergeant Cogswell?' I said.

'Yes, sir.'

'Good,' I said, 'because I don't.'

I drove across the compound and out at the gate. There was a T-junction at the end of the road, and Sergeant Cogswell said, 'You make a left here, sir.'

'A left?' I said.

'Right,' said Sergeant Cogswell.

'What?' I said.

'You make a left,' said Sergeant Cogswell, 'and you go all the way.'

So I made a left and drove for what seemed about ten miles and the country got wilder and lonelier and it felt as if we were nearing Berlin.

'Sergeant Cogswell,' I said, 'I don't believe this is the right road.'

'Sir,' said Sergeant Cogswell, 'I don't believe it is either.'

So I slowed the car and when I saw there was nothing behind, made a U turn across the road; and as I did, I became aware of the offside door opening a little, and a draught coming in, and then I heard, like a blow with a damp towel, the quick, wet slap on the German road of the American colonel's vomit. He himself didn't make a sound; a modest self-effacing retcher. Six times he threw up over Baden-Württemberg; then he shut the door, wiped his mouth and fell asleep.

We got back into Frummingen, took another wrong road, went two miles the other side of the town, came back again, and finally found the barracks. As we approached the Bachelor Officers' Quarters, Sergeant Cogswell said to the colonel, 'Sir, you may recall that you and Mr Kennedy were coming to the NCOs' club as my guests, but if you feel you'd like to get some sleep, why, I'd be very happy to look after Mr Kennedy myself.' The colonel opened his eyes, and with as much authority as he could muster, said, 'OK Sergeant Cogswell, I guess that's a pretty good idea.' Then he got out.

At the club Sergeant Cogswell and I had one for the road and I said I hoped the colonel was all right. 'Oh, the colonel's OK,' said Cogswell. 'My colonel sometimes gets a little sick when he goes to a party. I have to look after him times like he was a little baby. And tomorrow morning, you can bet your life, he'll call me up and bawl me out for something I have or haven't done.'

In the morning the destroyer *Dewey* came close alongside the aircraft-carrier *Shangri-La* and steamed on a parallel course. I was put into a big chair, like a throne, which was fixed to one of the ship's derricks, and slung out into space. The sea looked a long way below. I felt rather foolish sitting there in my old raincoat, holding a rope with one hand and my Panama hat in the other. They lowered me on to the *Dewey*'s deck, and then the chair went back and my luggage came over the same way.

A young officer who said his name was Lieutenant Smith took me to the bridge. It was an enclosed bridge with plenty of glass windows and central heating, not like the open-air boxes that I served in during the war. Here I met Captain Tazewell, commodore of the destroyer division, and the ship's captain, Commander Bradley. Captain Tazewell was a neat, small man with monkey-like features and the build of Eddie Cantor. Commander Bradley had a lean and handsome look. He introduced me to Lieutenant-Commander Vishenski, the supply officer, who looked like the Michelin man, round as a rubber ball: he had been in the ship three years and was going to leave at Rhodes.

We were due to enter the Dardanelles at two o'clock, so after lunch I went up to the bridge and saw the squadron had formed single line ahead, with the *Shangri-La* leading, the cruiser *Little Rock* next, ourselves in the middle and two destroyers astern. The entrance to the Dardanelles was about five miles ahead. It was a grey, misty afternoon, but through the drizzle and haze you could see the land coming up on either side. It was green near the water's edge, but higher up it was blotted out by low cloud, like on the west coast of Scotland.

Captain Tazewell sat in a little chair on the left of the bridge and the captain and officer on duty stood in the middle. Now and then the officer on duty said things like 'Two-thirds speed, one four two rpm, right ten rudder, steer zero three nine,' which the helmsman repeated. On the other side of the bridge Lieutenant-Commander Vishenski had taken up position beside a microphone which fed into the ship's public address system. The *Encyclopaedia Americana* was in front of him, and as we approached the narrows, he began reading the entry marked 'Dardanelles'. It wasn't terrific prose in the first place, but Vishenski's monotonous, bored delivery killed it dead.

The Dardanelles! The name had been stamped on my mind ever since I could remember. The bloody campaign which the allies had fought there against the Turks might, if it had turned out differently, have changed the course not only of the First World War, but of subsequent European history. It was one of the crucial battlefields of the twentieth century. And the names associated with it were ones to remember: Winston Churchill above all, Asquith, Fisher, Kitchener, Hamilton, de Robeck, Roger Keyes, Dunbar Nasmith, Rupert Brooke, Compton Mackenzie. And the place that was at the centre of it all, that symbolized the whole bloody futile conflict was Gallipoli. Where along this drab green coastline was it? Where were the beaches where our men had swarmed ashore in such hope, and down which in anger and despair they had retreated, less than a year later?

Aloud, and to no-one in particular, I said, 'Where's Gallipoli, I wonder?'

No-one responded. At length, out of politeness, Captain

Tazewell said, 'What was that place?' I said it again, I even spelt it, but it was clear they were all hearing it for the first time (it is possible that Vishenski might have mentioned it but everyone had stopped listening to him long ago). I thought, this is astonishing, surely everyone has heard of Gallipoli; then I thought, well is it? Have they? What is equivalent to Gallipoli in American history? Say the *Maine* at Havana and the subsequent Spanish–American war. How many British naval officers know about that?

It was the navigating officer who finally found it on the chart. But it was spelt Gelibolu, and when it came into sight a little later, it turned out to be a small dull town of white and yellow houses with red-tiled roofs. I looked at it long and hard, searching for some point of recognition, trying to make a connection between it and the dreams of my youth. But there was no connection. Gelibolu, Gelibolu, I thought: what have you to do with my Gallipoli? Nothing at all. The false had become real and the real false: it was a surprise and a disappointment.

We went on up the straits, following in the wake of the *Little Rock* and *Shangri-La,* obeying orders from the admiral as to course and speed. Along the green coastline white minarets began to show up, pencil thin. Two Russian merchant-ships passed us going south, and dipped their flags: I knew that would please some of the boys. Then we overtook a Greek steamer called *Hermes*, carrying German tourists. Vishenski, who had finished his running commentary, looked in the encyclopaedia and said: 'Hermes is the Greek name for Mercury, that's the messenger of the gods.'

THE MIDDLE EAST

It was Easter Sunday when I landed at Jerusalem airport. The taxi-driver said, 'Merry Christmas, sir', and drove me to the top of the Mount of Olives, to the Intercontinental Hotel.

This was before the time of the last Arab–Israeli war, and this part of Jerusalem was then Jordanian territory. The doorman at the Intercontinental was dressed like no Arab I had seen, in a robe of many colours, and with a headdress like Lawrence of Arabia or one of the Hashemite kings. 'Welcome!' he said. All the staff at the Intercontinental said 'Welcome!', sometimes when they meant 'Goodnight'.

They took me to my room, and there, out of my window, was Jerusalem in three colours, the milky blue of the sky, the green of the cypresses, and the biscuity beige of the buildings. It was late afternoon and the sun was already setting over the city, lighting up the golden cupola of the Dome of the Rock. Below me was the Garden of Gethsemane, the Pool of Siloam, the brook Kedron; and away on the hilltop the spire of the Church of the Holy Sepulchre, scene of Christ's burial and resurrection.

I came to Jerusalem in search of American tourists, to join up with some for a day and see what they made of the sights. I did not have to look far. The corridors of the Intercontinental were thronged with elderly men wearing broad-brimmed hats and string ties. 'Please take me to your leader,' I said to one, and he went away and came back with Miss Harriet-Louise Patterson.

Miss Harriet-Louise Patterson was around sixty, a spry, chirpy bird, with gingery hair and spectacles and much energy and humour. She invited me to join her group the next day; it would have to be the next day because they were leaving the day after; they would be visiting the Dome of the Rock, the Wailing Wall, the Stations of the Cross, the Church of the Holy Sepulchre, and the Garden of Gethsemane.

'But, oh, Mr Kennedy,' said Miss Patterson, 'do, do be kind. I feel so ashamed about us Americans, we're so stupid, some of us. We go around the world and show our stupidity to everybody. Some of my group now, they say things like, "I didn't know there was any trouble between Israel and the Arab world!", and then we expect people to love us.'

Suddenly she jumped up and said, 'But you must come and meet the group.' This took time, as there were twenty-five of them and they were scattered about the hotel. There were more women than men, and they all looked pretty old. But they were friendly and welcoming and said things like, 'Real glad to have you come along with us.' At the end, when we were in a group of four, Miss Patterson said, 'Oh, how silly of me! I quite forgot to introduce Mrs Hemby!' I shook hands with Mrs Hemby, and an ancient among ancients in the group said, 'Till you've met Mrs Hemby, you haven't lived.'

Next morning we all assembled in the sunshine to wait for the limousines to take us to the Dome of the Rock. The men shuffled about in these old-fashioned hats and string ties, and the women had too much make-up and elaborate hair-styles. They had enough cameras between them to put *Life* and *Paris-Match* out of business.

A ramshackle bus approached and drew up beside us. Then Miss Patterson appeared with a wodge of cotton wool over her ear: she had an infection and was full of anti-biotics, and couldn't come. Everyone clucked around and sympathized. She said that the limousines weren't available and we would have to go in the bus; an Arab guide called Ali would come with us. Everyone laughed and we got in. One man said, 'I think it's appropriate we're going to the Wailing Wall in this bus,' and another: 'We got up at three this morning, and took communion from Dr Pauling in the Garden of Gethsemane.'

The mosque of the Dome of the Rock is in the form of an octagon, with the dome rising from the centre. Ali said it was here that Abraham had made his sacrifice, David had raised an altar, Solomon and Herod had built their temples, Christ had overturned the tables of the money changers, Omar and later Saladin had built their mosques. At the entrance we took off our shoes and put on slippers. 'You don't know who's been wearing these slippers,' said one old lady cautiously, 'but I guess the stone floor would be too cold on the stockinged feet.' It was cool inside and rather dim. In the area beneath the Dome Arabs on mats prostrated themselves towards the east or read the Koran. One lady of our party plonked herself down on one of these mats and started praying too; a nice, ecumenical gesture, though the Arabs seemed a little startled.

On the way to the Wailing Wall we passed a group of Arab workmen chipping some stones. One of our ladies said, 'Such wonderful things they make, without any of the tools we have in our country. But I guess they're happy. Look, there's a lady with her face covered! And there's a man drawing water from a well! Look at that! He drinks from the jug. I guess they all

479

drink from the same jug!' A small, mild-mannered man in the party said, 'This Moslem religion makes me mad. No religion's any good unless it results in right action, and what right action does it have for them? Just look at those people! Look at the poverty! Look how far they are behind us! They want lifting up but they won't help themselves. They make an excuse for not helping themselves by saying, "Oh, it's God's will", and that lets them get away with anything.'

We passed some brilliant yellow acacias and entered a long narrow passage that led to the Wailing Wall. Everyone took photographs of the Wall, and then we walked up the Via Dolorosa to the Stations of the Cross, the landmarks along Christ's journey to his crucifixion. It is a narrow, old, rather pretty street, full of children and citizens about their business. Ali gave a running commentary as we went along, delivered in a brisk shorthand. 'Here is the first Station of the Cross where the Lord Jesus was condemned to death by Pontius Pilate. Why was Pontius Pilate coming to the Temple Area? Because Pontius Pilate was afraid the Jews would revolt against him.' We moved to the next station. 'Here is the Second Station of the Cross, where the Lord Jesus received the Cross.' At most stations there was a little plaque in the wall, and everyone took out their cameras and clicked. 'Here is the Third Station of the Cross where the Lord Jesus fell for the first time under the weight of the Cross.' One saw it as if for the first time; the courage of this extraordinary man bearing to his execution the instrument of his own death. 'Here is the Fourth Station of the Cross where the Lord Jesus met his Mother.' More cameras clicked, but the group was unusually quiet. I remembered what Miss Patterson had said about the trip starting off as a tour and ending as a pilgrimage. I think we all felt the drama of following Christ's footsteps; not *exactly* here, perhaps, but certainly hereabouts; there was an unusual sense of occasion. 'Here is the Fifth Station of the Cross where St Simon of Cyrene helped the Lord Jesus to carry the Cross.'

One woman leaned towards another.

'St Simon of Cyrene was a Negro, did you know that?'

'*No?*'

'Yeah. An *African* Negro.'

Pause.

'There weren't any *other* Negroes at that time, were there?'

'I guess not.' Another pause. 'He certainly didn't come from Alabama.'

'Here is the Sixth Station of the Cross, where the woman wiped the face of the Lord Jesus with a veil.'

'What a beautiful, beautiful day.'

'Isn't it? My, aren't we lucky to be here?'

'Here is the Seventh Station of the Cross, where the Lord Jesus fell for the second time.'

Here too the Via Dolorosa passed through the Souk, a long, covered-in bazaar, with shops of all kinds on either side. Here people pushed and jostled their way along; beefy Jordanian policemen, Greek Orthodox priests, tiny, round nuns, gaping fellow tourists; a boy with a sheep's head, a man holding a live fowl by its legs, another boy with hollow bread rolls like rubber rings round each arm, a man in a cookshop frying strange, exotic dishes. The shops sold just about everything: rosaries and lavatory brushes and grapefruit and plastic mugs; dried fish, rubber balls, Kodak films, dark glasses, bags of grain and bottles of spice, fish from Beirut and Aqaba, bowls of olives black and green, coloured eggs and feather dusters. Everywhere people shouted and chattered, and a hundred transistor radios blared out local music. One of our ladies pointed to a counter brimming with sweetmeats and said, 'Is that their candy?' Ali, anxious to help, said, 'Yes, you like some? I buy.' Quickly the lady said, 'No, *thank you*,' and, to the others, 'I'd rather die!' The ancient among ancients said, 'If you ate that, you surely would die.' An importunate Arab said, 'Two dollars for colour slides of the Stations of the Cross. OK then, lady, a dollar seventy-five.'

We came out of the Souk and arrived at the Church of the Holy Sepulchre, built on the alleged site of Christ's crucifixion and burial. There was not one church here but several: Catholic, Greek Orthodox, Armenian; and the entrance gate was owned by a local Moslem.

We went through a great, rococo door, and up steep stairs to Calvary. One old lady said to her husband, 'I'm gonna have to go first, and you're gonna have to hold on to me.' At the top were two chapels, one Greek Orthodox, one Franciscan. The Greek Orthodox one was full of oil-burning lamps and incense and icons. The Franciscan had six plain candles with a crucifix in the middle. There was a Church of England parson there, sitting by the altar, reading the Bible. I thought of the Arabs I had seen reading the Koran in the Dome of the Rock, not an hour before, not a mile away.

We went to the far end of the church to the place where Jesus was believed to have been buried. A heavy, stone mausoleum had been built over the top of the tomb, with an entrance so low and narrow that it could only take one person, stooped, at a time. On the walls twelve oil lamps were burning, and beneath them were portraits of the twelve apostles. Here a great press of people was waiting to get inside. Mostly they were women, and we, mostly women, joined them.

An hour later we were still waiting to enter the tomb. Suddenly, they had had enough: lunch and a rest for tired feet were more important. A tomb which had gone by default for sixty or seventy years could wait another day, perhaps even another life. As they drifted away, I heard one woman consoling another: 'Anyway, there's nothing to see. He's not there. He's *risen*.'

I came out into the sunshine, and went back through the Souk to the Damascus gate. I thought of all the places we had visited that morning, where Christ's presence had seemed so real, and felt the need to check up in a Bible. Just outside the Damascus gate, as if in answer to my thoughts, was a big bookstall with papers and magazines and second-hand books.

I strolled over and picked up some books at random. *Cravings* by Jack Woodford. 'Riper than love, deeper than lust, her strange needs drove Erica to the brink.' *Maureen* by Burton St John. 'Beautiful, dark and sultry, she kept nothing back from her wealthy white lover.' *The Twisted Ones*. 'A story of strange love between beautiful women, so frankly told you will completely understand their desperate hungers.' *Sin Doll*. 'The only way Cherry could get places was by going bad – and Cherry wanted to get places.'

But they hadn't got a Bible, no not anywhere there.

After lunch we assembled again outside. Two men in our party crossed the road and looked down at the brown rocky fields that stretched away south of Jerusalem. One said: 'I can't think why the Jews and Arabs want to fight over this. You couldn't do a thing with it. It's too rocky for crops and there's not enough grass for grazing. I guess they just like fighting each other.'

Presently we walked down the Mount of Olives to the Garden of Gethsemane at the bottom. I have never really thought of Gethsemane as a garden in the formal sense so much as a place where wild flowers grow. But whatever its character in former days, there's no disputing it's a garden now. There are criss-cross gravel paths, and neat, trim borders with rows of pansies and daisies and roses and pinks. Except for eight ancient olives, you might be in Surrey or Massachusetts.

Of all the tourist attractions in Jerusalem, the Garden of Gethsemane was the only one to fail to convey to me the presence of Christ. Loud with the chatter of visitors, it was impossible, surveying those trim ranks of domesticated flowers, to imagine the long night of the agony, the lonely figure wrestling with his conscience on the hill, the disciples sleeping below. So I gave it up, and went and sat in the sunshine on a low wall, and eavesdropped on the pilgrims passing by.

'Hi.'

'Well, hi!'

'American Express this way.'

'Did you get a shot of the Blessed Virgin's tomb? Oh, it's fabulous. I liked it better than Bethlehem.'

'Hi.'

'Carol was sick yesterday, so we've had to stay over a day.'

'Honey, how can I ever thank you for bringing us here. It's been the most wonderful, beautiful, moving experience.'

'I want you to know that that Bufferin did wonders.'

'Say, I believe you have the same camera as I have. Can you tell me how to set the flash?'

'My first daughter's name is Charlene. I shouldn't say this, but she has just the sweetest disposition in the world.'

'That's real olive wood. If you can't smell it, lick it.'
'Hi.'
'She's with her niece and sister, so she's all right.'
'Have you tried their butterscotch? It's real good.'
'If you don't come now, Mr Johnson, we're going to lose you. There's a whole lot of people coming up the hill.'

Of all the American ghettos I visited, the strangest was the headquarters at Dhahran in Saudi-Arabia of Aramco – the Arabian–American Oil Company. Around the township the lone and level sands stretch far away, the great desert where only wandering Bedouin live in black tents and only black vultures fly. But behind the palisades lies a world more American than America, ordered, hygienic, secure. In the big, cool administration building Americans and Saudis work together behind shuttered panes and pad down corridors as bare and antiseptic as those of any stateside hospital. And in the evening when the Saudis go home in the company's buses, the American executives and secretaries walk home along trim, American-style streets and avenues to trim, one-storey American-style houses: here, behind dainty formal hedges, bougainvillaea and oleander, tamarisk and acacia bloom, and sprinklers dampen the burnt lawns. For visitors there is a company guest house with foam-rubber mattresses in air-conditioned bedrooms, drinking fountains in the corridors and prints on the walls. Here there are no old people, no young adults and, except in holiday time, no teenagers above the age of fourteen.

Out at Half-Moon Bay on Sunday, I sat in the sea on a deck chair and watched the pale grey and milk-white jellyfish come and go, and let the water slop over me. Next to me was a man with two bluebirds tattooed on his chest and 'USS California'. He pulled at a Coca-Cola and said: 'Aramco does everything for you. I would say too much. It's like going back to mother's womb. You get out of the habit of taking decisions. But I like the life. With all its disadvantages I'd rather have it than life back home. Of course you have to be temperamentally suited. It's no good coming just for the money. We all do that, but you have to come for something else as well.' Jack said: 'I'd like to know what.'

Mrs Zinola, cool in green trousers and a green flowered blouse behind the blinds of her cool tidy house, said, 'It's certainly an easy life. If the window doesn't open, you call Housing on the phone and they come and fix it. You get on the bus and the bus is free. You go to the store and buy what's there. You don't start haggling over it because there's only one place to buy it. And with a standard fee for utilities you don't bother to go around switching off the lights.'

At a wedding-party (the wedding, forbidden in Dhahran, had taken place in nearby Bahrein), I met three wives. One was married to a Saudi, and wore glasses which made her eyes the size of billiard balls. She said, 'I don't know where I belong any more. I'd like to get into some group but I can't. We have a son of six, and he *really* doesn't know where he belongs. I feel so uneasy with people, and it makes me behave like I was a little girl of fifteen.' Another, recently arrived in Dhahran, sighed and said: 'We want to go and live in al-Khobar. This place is strictly for the birds.' And a third, who had just completed two years, said: 'You get kind of sponge-like here. There's nothing to stimulate you. Have you noticed how *quiet* everything is?'

And one day I went to a lunch-party and was given a drink and put on a sofa near a pretty woman who was talking on the telephone. When she rang off she looked sad, so I said sympathetically, 'Problems?' She forced a little smile and said, 'Well, kind of. Our little kiddie has just had an operation.' I thought, how strong-willed of you not to be at the hospital, how admirable to come out to lunch. She said: 'He just came round from the anaesthetic, and he's still a little unsteady on his feet.' I looked at her sharply and thought, well, Christ, I should think he is, and what kind of a hospital is it that lets him try, and why aren't you over there anyway? I said, trying to keep calm, 'What's been the matter with him?' She said, quietly, 'My husband and I decided to have him castrated.' I'm not well, I thought, I'm hearing things, women like this don't exist. Trembling, I said, 'You decided to have *who* castrated?' The woman said, 'Why, our little kitty, like I told you. To stop him from becoming a great, big tom.'

*

And then I visited the bachelor girls who lived like birds in the wilderness, in neat little houses with never a hair out of place. They were all ages between twenty-five and fifty, and some lived singly and some together. A few had come to Aramco a long while ago looking for husbands, and not found them; now they had settled for the long-term benefits, sunshine and travel and a cushioned retirement, with perhaps the bottle or the Church or the occasional affair to help them along the road. I asked young and old alike why they had come and how they liked it. Most answered briefly enough. But Miranda Bugatti of the olive skin and raven hair and extravagant gesture, Miranda Bugatti who was twenty-five years old and had been at Aramco six months, Miranda Bugatti drew a deep breath and said:

'I had this very, how do you say, cosmopolitan upbringing in San Francisco with, you know, Negroes and Mexicans and others. My brother had this, you know, creative eye for photography, and I was helping him. That's why I didn't join the Peace Corps because they only give you about fifty dollars a month. But I never lost my interest in what you might call foreign people. I was very good friends with a Japanese housemaid in Connecticut, and this interest kept growing. And when I went to work in New York, I belonged to the Tagore Society which helps to promote, how do you say, culture exchange like Indian dinners and music programmes. And I participated in the Asia Society and I belonged to the Friends of the Middle East and I came across this Japanese poetry called Haiku which describes natural things, you know, blossom and whatnot, and then it also has, how do you say, philosophy, philosophical ideas. I also helped with eastern people, you know, broadening them out. It was a kind of volunteer-type thing, and I had a Persian student and I helped him apply for college. And I was in touch with a chaplain who associated with the Young Men's Christian Association, you know, the Y, and they looked after people in the Belgian lines, and you went to small parties, it was person to person like, and you taught them, you know, that cop meant policeman.

'So it all added up. I had this, how do you say, sensitivity to different peoples, and I wanted to travel and see them all, and then I met this man at a party, and he happened to say that Aramco had this, you know, opening. Oh, I had such great ideas of Arabic, Rubaiyat of Omar Khayyam and all that, and when I came here, everyone thought I was Persian or Lebanese or something, even the Saudis did. I never knew I looked like that. Last Sunday I went to a wedding at Qatif, and that was just wonderful, you know, the colour and the ceremony. A lot of people, you know, Americans, don't realize what they've got here. It's like, how would you say, a personal matter. But everyone here at Aramco is so gracious and friendly. The money's wonderful. You can meet with the local people and associate with them. I feel I have a, you know, affinity with them, and they have with me.

'I don't date steady. It could be either coffee or dinner, or down to the airport or a drive to Ras Tanura or the pool café, or sometimes I go to the library and carry on my correspondence. I write to about thirty people from India to, you know, Greece. I write to a German oceanographer, a Japanese law student, a Greek officer. Once a week I go to the hospital. I buy balloons, I take about thirty balloons down there for the children. I meet a lot of nurses there, Indian nurses mostly. Now that's a whole new world. That hospital is like a, how do you say, like a channel into the people. But when you visit, you ought not to be too, how shall I say, artificial. If you're visiting, say, a Jamaican, then you should be a little, you know, Jamaican.

'I remember Eleanor Roosevelt writing in a magazine and saying, "I believe in all my travels that the American youth have the greatest opportunity to use their vision and reach for the stars and fulfil themselves. Then there'd be no excuse for them saying they'd love to travel but they couldn't." There was some wonderful thinking in this article. It was just a little before she passed away that she wrote it. In *Woman's Day*, I think it was. And my brother wrote this wonderful poem:

> *Not that you did, but you didn't*
> *Not that she did, but she didn't.*

and in the end he just said, "*You are the losers*". It was really very good.

'I would have liked to work in an orphanage in India but they have, you know, local people and can't afford Americans. I'd have liked Catholic relief too, but I didn't want to get too, how do you say, dedicated. I want to be both worldly and have something of myself. If I went full time in the charity work, I wouldn't accumulate enough money to, you know, live on. Like as I say, I think the Peace Corps is wonderful if you have a livelihood already.

'But I do love certain, you know, constants. I love the sea. I love natives. I love Manhattan. It's good for the arts and all that. I love children very much and, you know, people. At fourteen I could like the Rubaiyat, now it might be something else. It's not in my nature to like, how do you say, authority things. I pick up periods rather than the whole epic from A to Z. I'm the poet and peasant type, not the tower type. I don't like anything for too long. I'm not the, you know, intellectual or aesthetic type either.'

Suddenly there was silence, as when a street excavator outside one's window abruptly ceases, or one closes a door against a gale of wind. Miranda Bugatti smoothed her raven hair.

'Is that the kind of thing you want?' she said.

'That's it,' I said. '*That's it exactly!*'

The train pulled out of Teheran at one o'clock. I was going to Tabriz, 400 miles away on the Russian border. I shared a compartment with a Persian who wore a black coat and pepper and salt trousers. His hair was parted in the middle and he had a thin moustache. He looked like a bank clerk.

We rattled through the Teheran suburbs, and the waiter brought lunch. First there was tomato soup with an egg in it, then grilled chicken and rice. I had already eaten the Persian rice and found it the best in the world, soft and dry and very sweet. We were out in the country now, and on either side was flat, sandy desert and, in the distance, a range of mountains capped with snow. It was a beautiful day with sun and blue sky, and an amazing purity of light. Twice we stopped at tiny brick-built stations. The first was in the middle of nowhere, with no roads leading to or from it, and no reason at all for its existence. The second was equally small, but about three miles beyond it, across the sand, lay a walled village with a squat, gleaming mosque. Here quite a lot of people got out.

After lunch I slept and woke to see my companion in the act of waxing his moustache. Our eyes met, and we both looked away, embarrassed. He went into the corridor to gossip with another Persian, a man who hadn't shaved for days, and whose teeth were mostly gold. Then he went down the corridor and this other man poked his head round the door.

'Hullo', he said. 'How are you?'

'Fine,' I said. 'And you?'

'Very well, thank you.'

I could see he wanted to improve his English, so I asked him in and he came and sat down.

'Is this your first visit to Azerbaijan?'

'Yes.'

'You are a businessman, yes? You are going on business?'

'No, I'm a writer.'

'A writer? You are a writer?'

'Yes. What are you?'

'I teach. I am a teacher.'

'What do you teach?'

'Persian literature. My wife is a teacher too.'

'Is she? What does she teach?'

'Gymnastics.'

'This other gentleman,' I said, indicating the empty seat. 'You know him?'

'Yes.'

'What does he do?'

'He is a railway official. He works for the railway.'

'Ah.'

He gave a little smile and said, 'You are American, yes?'

'No,' I said, 'I'm British. But I'm writing a book about the Americans. That is why I'm going to Tabriz. To see the American consul.'

His eyes lit up. 'You are writing a book about the Americans? That is very interesting. They are a fine people, yes? I have a son and a daughter who are studying in the United States.'

Now it was my turn to look surprised.

'Have you?'

'Yes. My son is studying engineering and my daughter business.'

'That must cost you a lot of money,' I said.

'Yes, that is so. That is why my wife and I both work. So we can send our children away to have a good education. That is what my country needs, to send more and more people away to the United States. To learn things, to teach us what to do.'

I was hoping to find out more of how he had managed to send his children to America, but suddenly he got up. 'Please sir', he said, 'I am taking up your time. I will go.' And he went.

At 7.30 when it was growing dark, the waiter announced dinner at the other end of the train. I made my way through several wooden carriages where women in *chadors* were nursing babies, and soldiers sat gossiping or playing cards. It was a bright, modern dining-car, already full. They gave us the same soup as at lunch and a *chello-kebab* and a pot of yoghurt, and masses more rice with about two ounces of butter laid on top. Opposite was a family in which were two small girls in identical dresses, red with green spots. One looked quite normal, but the other had huge cheeks and great bushy eyebrows and an unusually dark skin. She shovelled her food into her mouth with both hands, like a demented old woman. Next to me was a policeman with his cap on, and then the railway official came in wearing a green felt hat. Headgear in Persian dining-cars seemed to be *à la mode*.

When I returned to the compartment, I found the door locked. The teacher was standing outside.

'The railway official', he said, 'has locked the door. Against robbers, yes?' He took out his wallet and showed me photographs of his son and daughter, an enchantingly pretty girl of twenty-one. I showed him photographs of my wife and children.

'Your wife is beautiful,' he said.

'Yes,' I said. 'She used to be a ballet-dancer.'

He seemed surprised.

'She made a film called *The Red Shoes*. It was very famous. Did you see it?'

'No. I do not often see the films.'

We chatted some more, and then the railway official came and opened the door. But he didn't stay long. An inspector arrived and bundled him out. He was followed by a man in blue dungarees who made up three beds. An army officer came in wearing dark glasses, and a charming Persian of about thirty who said he had been four years at college in Denver, Colorado. 'My friend and I,' he said, 'are travelling second-class, but we have paid the difference to get a good night's rest.'

Before turning in I went down the corridor to the wash-room. On the way I passed the teacher and the railway official chatting together. The teacher said: 'I am telling my friend here what you are telling me, that your wife is a belly-dancer. Like me, he finds it interesting, yes?'

INDIA

Two hundred miles north of New Delhi, 22 miles north of Dehra Dun, and 6,000 feet up in the Himalayas stands the fairy-tale township of Mussoorie, a hill station built by the British to escape the heat of the plains, and now a popular spa for middle-class Indians; here cars are banned, and the only wheeled transport is the rickshaw.

Mussoorie is built on a long, thin fertile ridge and the cliffside immediately below it. The views are tremendous. To the north, across a great, empty cavernous valley, are gigantic purple peaks, riding like ships of war the pale Himalayan sky; to the south, 5,000 feet below and stretching for perhaps 50 or 60 miles, the burning northern plains.

Along the centre of the ridge runs Mussoorie's main artery, the Mall with houses above and below it: there is a handrail on the southern side to prevent people tumbling over. Here ply the rickshaws. Each has a crew of four boys or, to be accurate, middle-aged men. They go everywhere at the trot, spindle-legged, barefoot, their soles strips of leather, ringing little bells and chanting strange cries to shoo people out of the way.

There is a castle-in-the-clouds, story-book atmosphere about Mussoorie which lends it total enchantment. It is not merely that the things that distress one elsewhere in India – the filth, the poverty, the hopelessness – are much less evident here; it is that it is unlike anywhere one has been. The height has much to do with it, and the setting, and the absence of the motor car. One goes backward in time in Mussoorie as well as upward in space; people take on a new dimension, like characters in a costume play, rather than toilers from the plains.

Toilers or actors, they are, as they stroll along the Mall, a pageant in themselves: teenage, teddy-boy Indians in white sharkskin suits and pointed shoes with turned-up toes like Chinese mandarins; very old Indians with beards and button-up jackets, carrying posies of flowers; small Sikh boys on roller skates, their hair in nets like girls; hygienic Boy Scout policemen in khaki shirts and shorts. Non-conformists too: women in veils and Punjabi dress, tiny, tough Gurkhas from Nepal, and Tibetans of all kinds – red-robed monks with shaven heads, men in felt hats and woolly stockings, women in pigtails and shawls. Two things only spoil a walk along the Mall: the Indian habits of spitting and flushing the nose with the hand.

There is much greenery about, and after the brown of the plains it soothes the eye. Here are chestnuts and planes and pines, millions of pink and white daisies lighting the cliff-face, stocks and pansies in the gardens. At night invisible small birds nest in the foliage of the trees, rustling and twittering like starlings. Apart from the cuckoo and the rickshaw drivers they are almost the only sounds you ever hear. Mussoorie is magically still.

And then there are the advertisements peeping from the trees, Indian copy-writers murdering the English tongue. 'Get a Latest Suit for Your Quick Selection and Increment' proclaim the Sewak Tailors, while the Zammar Institute urges 'Controlled Emaciation' [sic] a course in slimming. Here, straight from the shires of England, is a local school: 'Bramleigh Towers, Cambridge Academy, formerly Rock-cliff', and at Professor Banerji's dancing establishment Rock 'n' Roll and Cha-Cha-Cha are dispensed to ladies, children and mixed ('Maximum learning in Minimum Time'). Here is the roller-skating hall, where by the window you can watch the skaters in front of you and fifty miles of India beyond. At the Savoy Hotel the crowning of the May Queen is soon to take place. And at Hakman's Hotel today there is to be a jam session, noon to 2 p.m. Here I stop the rickshaw and go in.

I had come to Mussoorie to catch the last two days of a three-week seminar on American Institutions and Culture arranged by a body called the US Educational Foundation in India. It was being attended by thirty-five graduates from colleges and universities all over India, and five American professors. The syllabus included American politics, law, agriculture, industry, and education. The 'Culture' lectures were confined to literature, with such titles as 'Melville's Uneasy Quest', and 'Thoreau at Walden Pond'. I wondered what the Indians were making of these.

The seminar was taking place in the YWCA building not far from the hotel. On the front was written: 'Mussoorie YWCA Home, 1902. Patroness Lady Digges LaTouche', a name no novelist would dare invent. Mrs Jacobs, the Indian housekeeper, took me to the lecture hall, and opened the door. Thirty-five youngish Indian faces looked up, and the lecture stopped. A middle-aged American in a bow tie and spectacles rose from the front and said he was Dr Dawes, in charge of the seminar, and why didn't I take a seat? He said the lecturer was called Dr Garth. At first I thought Dr Garth was Indian, then realized he was a Negro in his thirties.

Dr Garth was lecturing on 'America in the Sixties'. Beside him was a blackboard showing a circle with six segments: Political, Economic, Religious, Social, Artistic, Intellectual. He was working his way through these. Dr Garth went in for a good deal of mouthing and frowning, and said earnest, obvious things. 'The American family is a small nuclear affair. There is evidence that the American family consists of two parents and children, and it is only rarely that other members of the family live with them.' I thought, if they've only got as far as that, they haven't got anywhere at all. Dr Garth spoke in a sing-song dirge, as though conducting a service. 'In the United States,' he said, 'we are 66 per cent Protestant, 26 per cent Catholic, and 2–3 per cent Jewish. The remainder have little or no religious faith.' I wanted to know how much faith the 66 per cent Protestants had but Dr

Garth had gone on to civil rights and Vietnam. 'Sometimes it is necessary,' he said, screwing his face into a ball, 'to make the State a shield as well as a sword, to protect us from each other's evil ways. We have been criticized for not being sufficiently dynamic in internal affairs, and now we are accused of being too dynamic in external affairs.' An anonymous Indian in the audience yawned loudly, and quick as anything Dr Garth said, 'In the United States we would regard that as a gross insult, but I suppose things here are different.' Everybody laughed, glad to know Dr Garth had a sense of the ridiculous.

Then it was Dr Dawes' turn. He was wearing a grey suit and small black boots with buckles. Dr Dawes was a real performer: he gave of himself every time he opened his mouth. He had the American academic's supreme self-confidence, the intellectual arrogance that says, as it were, to the American businessman: we may not be making a million bucks like you, but we're cleverer than you'll ever be, and don't you forget it.

'But I must hasten on,' said Dr Dawes, a phrase with which he signalled each change of subject, 'I must hasten on to our foreign policy. Our foreign policy is the containment of China, and it is for that reason alone that we are pursuing our present policy in Vietnam. We believe that if we pull out of Vietnam, Laos will go and Cambodia will go and Thailand will go, and then China will be on India's flank. So don't kid yourselves, gentlemen, don't kid yourselves, my friends, this country is in mortal peril.' He let the words sink in, straightened himself and changed key. 'Of course I know what many of you are thinking. You are thinking that America has no right to be in Asia at all, and it's good for Americans to come here and find what you think of them, find out that they're not the great people they thought. But there's a big debate going on in the States just now, a debate that concerns both our countries very deeply. And that debate is how much we should continue with foreign aid to countries which are hostile to American policy in Asia and which resent the American presence.' He left the words dangling in mid-air, and you could see the audience pondering their implications.

Dr Dawes sat down, and a long, slender Indian got up. He was wearing a buttoned-up jacket and his face was sad and beautiful.

'Yes, Mr Pori?' said Dr Dawes.

'I want to make a comment,' said Mr Pori.

'How long will the comment take?' said Dr Dawes, who had evidently been this way before.

'It is a long comment,' said Mr Pori.

'OK,' said Dr Dawes, 'so you won't mind if we take the questions first.'

So Dr Garth and Dr Dawes took some questions, and then Mr Pori made his long comment.

'Countries like ours and yours', he said, 'which are democratic, and countries like China, which are not, have two entirely different philosophies. Now we believe that when there are differences, they must be negotiated and best place to negotiate is United Nations. No doubt at all that China is a great nation and therefore ought to have seat in United Nations.' He sat down to a murmur of agreement and one or two claps. I wondered how Dr Dawes would cope. He coped brilliantly.

'There are millions of people in the United States,' he said, 'who would agree with every word you say. And because they live in a democracy, like India but unlike China, they have perfect freedom to say it.'

The session ended. Dr Dawes introduced me to his wife and Drs Oliver and Garth. Dr Garth, a bachelor, was Professor of Sociology at a women's college at Greensboro, North Carolina where the students were 95 per cent negro and the faculty 40 per cent white. He'd been in India for a year on an exchange programme at a women's college at Bangalore. Dr Oliver was a real academic, smooth and dry, an erect, rigid sort of man with a dry clipped voice, like the storekeeper in a western.

Some of the Indians introduced themselves, showing that blend of curiosity and enthusiasm which are among the most endearing of Indian characteristics: Mr Singh, head of the department of English at Agra Rural Institute ('you must understand, Mr Kennedy, that not all Singhs are Sikhs'), Mr Suresan from Andhra Loyola College, Professor Siddhanta from

Serampore, Mr Sengupta who looked Chinese from Calcutta, Mr Behl from Chandigarh, Mr Sanganker, Mr Borgohain, Mr Pori. They all looked so young and giggled so much it was hard to realize they were not students but graduates. They asked me what I was doing and when I told them, Mr Singh said: 'So you are a globe-trotter, eh?' and laughed loudly.

I walked back to Hakman's for lunch and fell in with another of the graduates, a Miss Bhatt, going shopping. Miss Bhatt was a serious young lady, with a caste-mark on her forehead and a very sober sari, and with her I had one of those dotty conversations one seems to have in India all the time.

'How has the course been?' I said.

'So-so,' said Miss Bhatt.

'How's that?'

'Well, I will say this. Professors have done level best. Nobody can say they have not. But it all depends on outlook. My outlook is make seminar a much more international affair, have Pakistanis and British and Chinese and everyone. What is your university?'

'My university?'

'Yes.'

'Well, I was at Oxford.'

'Why is Oxford sponsoring your visit here?'

'It's not. I used to be at Oxford a long time ago.'

'Then who is sponsoring your visit?'

'No-one really. I'm here on my own. I'm a writer.'

Miss Bhatt looked surprised. 'What are you writing?'

'A book about Americans.'

'You have written chapters?'

'No, not yet. I've made a lot of notes, though.'

'You are writing about professors?'

'I will do.'

'How many chapters have you written?'

'Miss Bhatt, I haven't written *any* chapters *yet*.'

We came to the Mall.

'So,' said Miss Bhatt. 'Now I go to shops, and we meet at the Nehru ceremony after lunch. Bye-bye.'

In the dining-room of Hakman's hotel, the jam session was in full swing. Trumpet, piano and drums were bashing out

'It's Been a Hard Day's Night' and 'Let's Twist Again' in the style of the fifties. I ate curry and rice pudding, and between mouthfuls and earfuls, wondered what the Nehru ceremony might be: there was nothing about it on the schedule.

Dr Dawes told me about it when I returned. This was the anniversary of Nehru's death and there was to be a special, commemorative ceremony. Miss Bhatt had rigged up a kind of altar consisting of a table with a white cloth, on which was a photograph of Nehru flanked by white lilies. At the foot of the altar incense was burning in a brass pot.

We took our places, the graduates, the professors, and an elderly, light-coloured Indian called Dr Naik, Principal of Gujarat College and guest speaker. Miss Bhatt sang a wailing song at the piano, and this was followed by Dr Naik's address. Dr Naik wore a grey achkan and tinted glasses, and spoke of 'walleys' and 'wastnesses'. After Dr Naik a man in a brown achkan got up and read extracts from Nehru's will. Then Dr Oliver spoke about Nehru's writings and as if that wasn't enough, we had Mr Pori. Mr Pori fluttered his eyelids and rubbed his hands and talked nonsense. 'Nehru's great achievement was that he immortalized rationality,' he said. I wanted to get up and shout, 'You're talking nonsense!', but everyone was taking it quite seriously. Some Indians and Americans seem to have a need for this sort of windy thing.

The ceremony had now lasted an hour, and I thought this must be the end. But it seemed the graduates wanted to add their widow's mites. A bore in a *dhoti* spent five minutes telling us Nehru's death had left the world grief-stricken, and a man in a green jersey compared him to Ashoka and the Gautama Buddha. Another man told us Nehru's bank account at his death was half what it had been, but without saying what it had been or where he got the information. 'That shows a great wirtue and honesty,' he said, 'which is wery rare in politics.'

It was left to a rather weary Dr Dawes to conclude on a note of realism. 'One of our great difficulties in assessing Mr Nehru,' he said, 'is that our vision is blurred, and not as sharp as it will be one day. I also think it would be a disservice to Mr Nehru to regard him as a god or matchless perfectionist.

He didn't like people doing this when he was alive, and we shouldn't do it now.'

Everyone clapped very loudly. Conformists themselves, Indians admire the non-conformist view in others. I heard one graduate say to another: 'What Dawes is saying is true. Wision is blurred now, but will not be later.'

Later I asked Dr Garth how an American Negro regarded the Indian scene, and he said he had been surprised to find Indians were what he called 'dark-skinned white supremacists'. He said, 'I have had some warm personal relationships while I have been here, but this has not blinded me to the fact that Indians as a whole look down on Negroes. You might think a people who had been subjected to racial prejudice themselves, as the Indians were under the British, might be less inclined towards it. But this is not so. In their conversations they make no distinction between African Negroes and American Negroes. To them we are both equally inferior. They think the American Negro is far more downtrodden than he is, and the more insecure of them feel this is how things should be. One chap said to me, "In America they lynch Negroes" — not condemning the whites, but approving of what he thought was a fact.' Dr Garth told me all this with an air of cool detachment, as though he, a trained sociologist, was somehow above the fray; yet I got the impression this was a mask for feelings gravely shocked by the unexpected prejudices he had found.

Dr Dawes, an historian, had spent most of his career at the Carnegie Institute of Technology. He had taught history at Allahabad and Lucknow, and then went to Delhi to help administer the Fulbright scheme. 'I came because the Fulbright people asked me to. It wasn't a question of mission or dedication or the white man's burden or anything. I'd been too long in one pulpit, and I knew it.'

'How has the seminar been?'

'It's the third I've organized and the best so far. We had one hundred applications for thirty-five vacancies from colleges all over the country. They were very suspicious when they arrived. They thought they were going to have American propaganda thrown at them all the time. I think we've cleared their minds of that. Our object has not been to praise or condemn the United States but to be as honest and self-critical as we can. Sometimes I think we've been too self-critical.'

'Any disappointments?'

'Only that they didn't use the library. We brought along a library of six hundred books and they haven't touched them. The other major disappointment has been the lack of intelligent discussion. The lecture system which the British introduced has been the *mortmain* – the dead hand – of Indian education. These people haven't been taught to think critically at all.'

'How much is that due to the system, and how much to their own temperament?'

'I'd say a bit of both. There is one major difference between these people and ourselves, which in my view is completely unbridgeable. It's this. They are primarily interested in a state of Being, in what life has to offer them now. We are more interested in a state of Becoming, in what we can make of our lives in the future. We're ambitious and conscious of material rewards, and on the whole they're not.'

In Hakman's hotel that night, I asked to be called at 8 a.m. with tea. I was called at 6.30 a.m. with a banana. In India this sort of thing is the rule rather than the exception. The lady at the desk said: 'I am very, very sorry about it. I cannot think how a thing like this came to happen. But I will do the needful and look into it. I will definitely do the needful.'

The last lecture was called 'America in the Future', and was another symposium by all three lecturers. Dr Oliver started by telling us about population explosion and automation and living underground and farming the sea. He said he didn't know how the human mind was going to stand the incredible increase in information. The implications of automation were also staggering. 'Banks and courts and places are already using automation. I think some teaching will be done by automation too.' A graduate interrupted to say automation would cause unemployment, and in India where there was mass unemployment already, this would be disastrous.

Dr Garth said he supposed he ought to talk about the Negro problem, and he did so with a great deal of mouthing and face making and opening and closing his eyes. 'We cannot expect Negroes to be more angelic than their white neighbours,' he concluded. 'While there are disgusting whites who bomb churches and kill civil rights workers and all that, then there will be nasty Negroes.' He turned to Dr Dawes. 'We are all', he said, 'disgustingly equal.'

Dr Dawes glanced at Dr Garth and then at the audience. 'I don't know why you look at me when you say that!' he said, and everyone laughed and clapped.

There was an hour to fill in before lunch, so I took some of the graduates into the garden. They clustered round with grinning, cheerful faces, like urchins at an accident, all wanting to talk at once, intoning in that curious semi-Welsh lilt which in India passes for the English tongue. They looked so very young and childlike, and again I had to remind myself that these were not students but graduates, qualified teachers at Indian universities.

'What is your opinion of the seminar?' I said.

'I would say without fear of contradiction', said Mr Singh, 'that many notions have been changed.'

They chorused assent. 'Agreed.' 'Definitely.' 'That is what I am thinking.'

'What sort of notions?'

Mr M. N. Borgohain, whose ancestors came from Thailand, said: 'Well, before, I had notion that America was flowing with milk and honey. I think we were all having this notion. But now we find it is not so. America has poverty too.'

'That is true', someone broke in, 'but American poverty is not Indian poverty. Mrs Barnett was telling us that in some places American children were not having enough to eat, and no shoes to go to school. Well, I agree that is bad social evil, but in India there are thousands who die every year from starvation. Now you must agree, Mr Kennedy, that is a worse social evil, there is really no comparison between the two?'

Mr Singh said: 'This is true. We get depressed by the poverty here. There are times when we think it can never end. But what they have done in America with natural resources gives us hope. Take that film they showed on the

Tennessee Valley Authority, and what they have done with natural resources. I must say I was impressed by this. It gave encouragement. It showed what we can do.'

'Agreed,' said a voice from the back, 'but tell me this, who is going to do the needful?'

No-one answered. Perhaps there was no answer. Mr Singh said: 'Another notion changed is idea that life in the United States is easy, and no need to work hard. We saw this isn't so, how hard people do work. This made me think of Untouchables. Here Untouchables are 25 per cent of population. It is outlawed but still goes on. You see, we feel it is dignity here to own land, but beneath dignity to work on it. This is all wrong. Americans have showed us dignity of physical labour.'

Mr Behl from Chandigar, plump with a thin moustache, said: 'I agree. I was frankly amazed to see Dr Dawes carrying a heavy burden of books, which we would never carry. We would be offended if we were asked to carry a burden like that. We would not say anything but we would be offended. The gospel of Dirty Hands is what Nehru called it.'

Mr Sanganker, who had a black beard and a wild eye, said: 'My candid opinion is that Americans don't have firm convictions of life, and this makes men have no faith in their promises. I was thinking they were frank, but now I am thinking they are not so frank. They say they are democratic but it is not so. They outlaw the Communist party in some states. Why? Why not let people have a free choice?'

'My opinion,' said Mr Sengupta, with the Chinese eyes, 'was that President was main thing. I thought President was almost dictator. But now they have explained about checks and balances and all that, so this notion is changed. Another thing. I thought Negroes were like Untouchables, just servants of the whites. But they sent this Negro lecturer who is clearly a very educated man, and it seems they have other Negroes now in key positions, so this notion is changed too.'

Mr Pori appeared from nowhere and said: 'Dr Garth thinks all Indians have an impression that Negro is an ape. Well, I talked to him very strongly about this, and I said, "You have got this all wrong."'

'What about the professors?' I said. 'What do you think of them?'

'They have impressed us very much,' said Mr Sengupta. 'They were very self-critical. They were very candid too.'

Professor Siddhanta said: 'We are finding them very friendly people. When British visit our college they have a stiff-necked superiority. They are not friendly. But these Americans are friendly and informal. I am stating this as a fact. No, I am sorry, I am stating this as a fact. Another thing that surprised me was that they knew anything about India. They are knowing more about India than many of us here. Now that is very much to their credit.'

'Agreed,' said several voices. But Mr Sengupta said: 'We must not form a judgement of the American people from that because, you see, these are only a handful of intellectuals.'

This started an argument among themselves, and while it was going on I noticed a very old man walking down the garden path, carrying a basket. He was dressed in rags and had a tangle of wild white hair and looked about a hundred and ten. He sat down on the grass beneath a tree, opened the basket, pulled out a pipe and started playing. The graduates paid no attention: snake charmers in India are two a penny. As the snake's head came out of the basket Mrs Jacobs's houseboy ran past to tell the old man to go away. Before the boy reached him he started putting away his pipe, then closed the basket, rose wearily and moved slowly towards the gate. His legs were stork-like, long and brittle. I wondered how old he was and where he would sleep and if he had enough to eat. Then he passed through the gate and was gone.

THE FAR EAST

Going from India to Thailand is like going from South to North America. It is a journey from a state of Being to Becoming, from poverty to affluence, darkness to light. Bangkok, like Tokyo, is a western-style city inhabited by easterners. Here the taps work, buses run, streets are cleaned, people know the way. English is spoken almost as widely as in

India and a good deal more comprehensibly. Foreigners, once shunned, now have their needs catered for. 'Skin and Breast Rejuvenation' says a sign on the road to the airport, and a grocer in central Bangkok advertises: 'Just arrived: Smoked Salmon, kippers and liver sausage.' *The Bangkok World* is a better English language newspaper than anything in India because it syndicates features from the British and American qualities. In India the peasants are bent double under crippling burdens: in Thailand they have burdens too, but also sense enough to sling them between poles.

So many people had said to me, if you're going to Bangkok and want to meet an American businessman who's different, go and see Jim Thompson: he's unlike any American businessman you've met. Who is Jim Thompson? I said. He's a kind of a legend, they said, he runs the Thai Silk Company which employs 3,000 people: he built it up from scratch. He's a genius with colours, they said. He designed the fabrics for *The King and I* and he lives in this fantastic house: it's a composite of six houses assembled from all over Thailand, and he's filled it with his own unique collection of Thai antiques. He's a man you shouldn't miss.

So I called up Jim Thompson and he asked me to dine with him at his house on the edge of one of Bangkok's many canals or *klongs*. From the outside it was unremarkable, little different to other Thai houses I had seen. But the inside was a cool, rich world of marble and old teak and limestone Buddhas and paintings of astonishing beauty.

Jim Thompson was a surprisingly small man, in his fifties I guessed, and there was something about his firm, rather elongated face that reminded me of two very dissimilar characters – James Bond's creator Ian Fleming, and Lawrence of Arabia. He spoke in a recognizably east coast, Ivy League accent and was dressed simply in a white silk shirt and trousers, both, I assumed, the products of his own firm.

A Thai manservant brought cold soup, and a beautiful white cockatoo which he placed on Jim Thompson's chair. 'I got him two days after he landed from Singapore,' said Jim Thompson. 'I went down to the docks to get a red parrot, and I found him.' I said, 'He's a very handsome bird,' and Jim Thompson said, 'He's forty-five years old.'

I wondered how he knew. 'He loves Beethoven', said Jim Thompson, 'and sometimes he gets carried away like we all do and starts conducting.' The cockatoo sat there patiently all through dinner, sometimes cooing like a dove and sometimes leaning over Jim Thompson's shoulder to kiss his cheek. 'I have a black lorikeet too', said Jim Thompson, 'who's just like the blackamoor in *Petrouchka*. He spends most of his time lying on his back banging his head with corn-on-the-cob.'

Jim Thompson said he'd been born and brought up in Delaware, in a well-to-do family with a butler and servants and a French nanny. Later he went to Princeton, studied architecture, and became an architect in New York. In 1939 war broke out in Europe and in 1940, when America was still neutral, he enlisted as a private in the US Army.

I said, pointing to the things all round me, 'It's difficult to imagine you as a soldier!'

'Oh, I was quite a good soldier, it's in the blood. I had a grandfather who was a general in the Civil War at the age of twenty-seven. He led the charge at Selma. He commanded the largest body of troops for a man of his age since Napoleon. His name was James H. Wilson. When he got out of the army he built the Third Avenue Elevated. Then he got sent to the war in Cuba where his wife was burnt up in a carriage, and from there he went to Peking to deal with the Boxers. He stayed a long time in China, and when he was an old man he used to tell me about it. It was he who first got me interested in the east.'

The cockatoo made a sort of croaking noise, leant forward and nodded its head vigorously up and down. I thought it was going to have a fit.

'I was in the army six years,' said Jim Thompson. 'I got married, was made an officer, and then posted as aide to a general. I liked the general but not the job, and I persuaded him to let me join the OSS.

'Well, then the European war ended, and they wanted to post me to Florence. But I didn't much care for that and I found I could get out of it by volunteering for special service in the east. So it was all fixed, but the day I was due to be parachuted in here, the Japanese war ended. So we flew in from Rangoon a week later. I was a major by this time, and we were billeted in the Prime Minister's Palace and lived like kings.

'By now', he said, 'my marriage was through and I'd got a divorce. I had no responsibilities, and I decided that rather than go back to the States and take up the architect practice, I'd see what I could find here. The Prime Minister knew about this and one day he said to me, "Thompson, the tourists are coming back here, have a look at all the hotels in Bangkok, see which looks the best and fix it up." So I decided to fix up the Oriental and make it the most beautiful hotel in Asia. I went to the States to redesign it and Pan American were interested in putting up the money. But when I got back I found there'd been a *coup d'état*. The old regime was out, and the new one said they didn't want any foreign capital. So then I decided to concentrate on silk.'

'Why silk?'

'I was in the habit of looking for silk. My wife was very fond of silk, and I used to send her silk from wherever I happened to be. The day we liberated Lyons I ran across Duchèsne *père et fils*, who were both in the Resistance, and I managed to buy some silk which they'd kept hidden during the war. I was sort of silk-oriented.

'Well, when I got back from that trip to the States, I found that nobody was wearing silk any more, and therefore nobody was weaving it. They all said it was too expensive. It was never a huge trade, but people used to weave it for their own use, and for the Royal Family. I knew there were looms in many houses. The Chams who settled here – they're Moslems from Cambodia – were all great weavers.

'When I decided to go ahead with the silk, I went back to the States to settle up my affairs and sell the family estate and find agents for the weavers. I was in the States the whole of 1947. Then when I got back here I had a stroke of luck. There was a letter from my sister's husband who's a lawyer saying I was concerned in Kate Osgood's will, and did I want him to handle it? She was a rich old cousin who had just died. She'd made a very curious will, leaving a fortune to be divided between fifteen people with the proviso that if any died, I was to have something. Well, most of them were younger than me, but almost immediately one of them did die, and that's how I got the money.

'It wasn't a great deal, but it was enough to get started on. I think the original stock was around 25,000 dollars. I got the weavers weaving again, and I sold the silk for them on consignment. I'd send around four to five thousand dollars' worth to New York. New York paid me and I paid the weavers. To start with I picked out things I knew would be saleable, and after that I told them what I believed would sell. Up to the time of *The King and I*, I was using traditional patterns, but after that I did my own designing. Colour is something that has always fascinated me. When I was studying painting for my architectural examinations I used to forget about the drawing because I wanted to get on with the colouring. I had to *discipline* myself to draw.'

The manservant came in with an insecticide gun. He got down on the floor and started spraying my ankles. 'The insects get pretty bad here in the evening,' said Jim Thompson. When the manservant was through with my ankles, he did my arms and neck. Then he handed me fruit salad.

'The business just grew and grew. We've never advertised, but every time there's been publicity about us, the mail order business has boomed. There was an article about me in *Reader's Digest*, and we had a flood of letters after that: a Finnish firm wrote and we appointed agents in Venezuela and South Africa.' He smiled. 'Back in the days when I was an architect, one had to learn to hide one's light under a bushel. Now I've learnt that in the business world publicity is good.

'And what about the house?' I said.

We'd finished dinner by now, and Jim Thompson said: 'Before I tell you about how the house was built, let me show you round.'

So we walked round the house which, considering it consisted of six houses, was smaller than I expected. There was the dining-room and a lovely, big, oblong drawing-room, and Jim Thompson's study and bedroom, and a guest room and the kitchen and staff quarters, and that was about it. But in all the rooms and passages were these fantastically beautiful things: serene, smiling Buddhas of every period from AD

500, fragile paintings of scenes from the Vessantara Jataka, Burmese mats and tapestries, Chinese porcelain, painted tables, lacquer chests, glass mosaics, heads of stone and terracotta, torsoes of stucco, figures and animals in bronze. And everywhere, all round, were these glowing walls of polished golden teak, each slightly inclined inwards after the Thai fashion, enveloping the treasures in a warm, protective cocoon. It was like being in a rich, exotic and brilliantly alive museum, a monument to one quiet American's stupendous, individual good taste.

We sat down in the drawing-room, on a sofa between two windowless windows, and the manservant brought coffee and the white cockatoo.

'I wanted to start building in August, 1958,' said Jim Thompson, 'but the Brahmin astrologers wouldn't let me, and here you're wise to do what the Brahmin astrologers say. They looked at my horoscope and said I couldn't start till mid-September. So we started at twenty minutes to nine on the morning of 15 September.

'Of course we weren't engaged in building in the strict sense of the word so much as assembling these various houses that I'd seen and bought in various parts of Siam. The room we're sitting in now was part of a beautiful old house belonging to one of my weavers in the village across the canal. When I heard he was going to pull it down, I offered to buy it. The second house, which consists of the hall and dining-room and stairs, came from Pak Hai in the north-west, and the connecting passages came from another house there too. They belonged to the aunt of one of my weavers, and he told me she had gambled all her money away and was heavily in debt. So I took a trip up there. The old lady was eighty-three, four feet eight inches high, and still playing cards furiously. She said if I bought all her houses for 10,000 tics, that would clear her debts. That's what I did. The third house is my bedroom and guest room, the pantry and kitchen come from a weaver's house across the canal, and the cook's house which belonged to a cousin of another weaver, came from the other side of Bangkok. The old lady's houses came here by river and water, a hundred miles across Siam, and the cook's house arrived by truck at three in the morning. We had to get special police permission for it.

'The workmen assembled the houses during that winter, and the Brahmin astrologers said I could move in at 9 a.m. on 3 April 1959. We had a little trouble there because the priest was basing his calculations on the assumption I'd been born in Bangkok, and when I told him no, I was born in the States, he had to readjust because of the twelve-hour time difference. However I moved in when he said, even though the house wasn't ready. There were twenty-eight carpenters here when I moved in. Some of them liked it so much they stayed on after they'd finished.'

'And the antiques,' I said, 'how did you get them?'

'Well, I told you I started collecting when I had that other house. It began accidentally really. I used to go off into the country looking for looms, and sometimes I'd see or hear of something that was for sale, and I'd go and see it, and if I liked it I'd buy it. After a time people got to know I was collecting, and when they heard I was in the area they'd come and see me and show me things. My biggest buy was a collection of Buddha heads which a villager up north found in a cave in the hills. They must have been there hundreds of years. It wasn't until I got them all back here that I realized how valuable they were. Later I heard the government were interested, so I sent them along a catalogue of everything I'd got. Then I went away on a trip, and the government sent a whole lot of people here who made notes on the heads and interviewed the servants and actually took one or two things away. Well, I was very angry when I heard this, and when I got back I changed my will, in which I'd left the house and everything in it to the Siam Society, and I made it over to a distant relative instead. Meanwhile, I open the house twice a week, on Monday and Thursday mornings. I charge visitors twenty-five tics a time, and that makes a hell of a lot of money for the blind.'

'Since you've been a success,' I said, 'do you get a lot of people pestering you?'

'They never stop. Every week I get scores of letters from friends, and often not even friends, saying old so and so is

508

about to hit Bangkok and will I look after him. In the old days I used to ask them to dinner because I wanted them to buy my silks.' He smiled. 'Now I'm a success I have a different routine. When they call up, I ask them along to the office to see what they look like. If I like them, I ask them to dinner. If I like them a little bit, I ask them to cocktails. If I don't like them at all, I say: "Do come and visit the house. It's open Mondays and Thursdays." Oh, I get the most *horrible* people coming to see me. You wouldn't believe how horrible some of them are.'

That was the last time I saw Jim Thompson. For he disappeared. In 1968 he stayed with a friend in the Cameron Highlands of Malaysia, and one day went for a walk and never came back. No-one knows what happened: some say he was eaten by a tiger, others that he was killed by Communists. Either way, it was a very shocking death. For so brave and talented and debonair a man it was the wrong kind of death altogether.

From a thousand feet up the houses and streets seemed like houses and streets in any Asian country, the fields like those in Thailand or Cambodia. Yet one looked at them with a new eye, expecting them somehow to be different. For this was Vietnam, where for a long time now a bloody war was being waged.

At the airport, opposite the rows of helicopters and parked military planes, were trim lawns and bushes, a gay green awning, and tiny exquisite air hostesses in white and peacock blue. One hadn't expected that. A taxi took me into the town and on the way we passed a sign that said 'General Pershing Sports Ground. For Recreation and Athletics'. We drove down a wide avenue, shaded by tall trees as in Provence and with Provençal villas behind them, and came to the main square, all still and sleepy in the Sunday sun. Here was the Caravelle hotel with its melon-cold lobby and concealed amplifiers relaying the Emperor Concerto. Sitting alone beside the big plate window in the lobby was a figure that looked familiar. It was Emlyn Williams the actor, come to Saigon to give his rendering of Dickens's reading from his own works. I hadn't expected that either.

I registered at the desk and was given my key and a booklet called 'Saigon Round-Up'. Then I was shown upstairs to an airy room with a vast double bed and mirrors. I took off my coat, lay down and opened 'Saigon Round-Up'. The opening article was called 'How Good is Your English?' and was a review of the Gowers edition of Fowler's *English Usage*. The next article was called 'Vietnamese Politeness and Impoliteness', and said: 'When people refer to you as *ong ay* or *ong do*, then you may be really proud of yourself. The equivalent for a female would be *ba do* or *ba ay*.' There was a section on where to eat in Saigon and another on where to shop, and then came: 'Racing Programme. Probable Runners at Phu Tho', and a list of horses with names like Ngoc Xuan, Dam Do and Thanh Phung. Finally there was the sightseeing section. 'At Bien-Hoa, only twenty miles from Saigon, is the pottery where visitors can also observe rural life, rubber plantations, etc.' I reflected that if they'd been there three weeks ago they could also have observed a brilliant attack by the Vietcong on the airfield, in which many military planes were destroyed and several American servicemen killed and wounded. 'At Thu-Dau-Mot, also only twenty miles from the capital, lacquerwork will be under way in many painstaking stages.' I put down the booklet, concluding the man who wrote it must be either mad or a practical joker, and went to sleep.

In the evening Emlyn Williams and I dined in the hotel's roof-top restaurant, which looked out over the surrounding country. There was a clean, white cloth and a bowl of fresh flowers on every table. I asked the waiter where the Vietcong were, and he pointed at the country and said: 'There. All round. Everywhere.' I had crabmeat soup and a *filet mignon*, Emlyn *consommé* and a *sole Colbert*, and we shared a bottle of *rosé*. There were sounds of merriment coming from an adjoining room: the waiter said the German ambassador was giving a large dinner-party.

In the middle of dinner a large bald middle-aged American came into the dining-room with a little Vietnamese boy of about seven. He wanted to introduce himself because he was the father of the actor Rip Torn, who had worked with Emlyn in New York; he was also called Rip Torn and he was working with AID. 'I'm hoping to get this little fellow rehabilitated,' he said, pointing to the little boy. 'I found him on the street. He has no father or mother and I'm hoping to get him into a Catholic orphanage.' I said would the boy care for a Coca-Cola or something, and Rip Torn senior said, 'No, we just had a soda downstairs.' Then they went.

After dinner Emlyn and I went for a walk along Tu Do Street, the main street of Saigon. The bars had opened up and some of the shops too, and the streets were full of people strolling and laughing as though they hadn't a care in the world. Beside the tiny, delicate Vietnamese, the American soldiery, in slouch hats and waterproof knickerbockers, looked huge and repellent, pink giants from beyond the seas. A man approached us with a big folio, which I thought must be views of Saigon. But they turned out to be dirty pictures, jumbo-sized. A sign in a car salesroom said 'DRIVE AWAY YOUR OWN CADILLAC', and another in a travel agent's office: 'A HOLIDAY IN EUROPE FOR YOU. FIVE DIFFERENT WAYS OF GETTING THERE'.

At the end of Tu Do Street was the river. It was very still there and very beautiful. The lights from the big ships flickered on the water. On the quayside a couple were sitting on a rushmat holding hands and drinking a bottle of red wine: below on the rocks a man was urinating. Then I heard Emlyn say, 'Look at this!' I turned and saw him standing by one of those artificial golf-putting courses, complete with slopes and curves and little tunnels. We might have been in Bognor Regis or Margate, Atlantic City or Disneyland.

We walked home. The Americans were beginning to spill out of the bars, and the little, barefoot orphaned boys were doing a brisk trade selling the drunker ones toy hats. I was told later this was a nightly occurrence. I slept well that night in my air-conditioned room, and when I came down in the morning, there was a note from Emlyn at the desk, together with a clipping. The note said: 'More hot news from war-scarred city' and the clipping, from the *Saigon Daily Times*, said 'Peter Rabbit Author dies in Massachusetts aged 91'.

A little later a contact at the American embassy telephoned. 'Sorry I didn't call you yesterday,' he said. 'How are you making out in Saigon?'

'Fine,' I said, 'but it's not quite what I expected.'

The flight to Da Nang went from the military side of Saigon airport. The Embarkation Room was full of people, American troops mostly, some waiting to go to other parts of the country, others to Japan or the States. There were one or two civilians like myself, three Vietnamese nuns, and a dozen South Vietnamese soldiers dressed in spotted black and green camouflage, like muddy leopards. The Americans had on a variety of hats: forage caps, about four inches high, which made the smaller soldiers ridiculous, peaked caps, red and green berets, slouch hats with struts like in ancient biplanes. They wore dark glasses, smoked cigars, drank Coca-Cola, read the *Stars and Stripes*, pornographic paperbacks and the fantasies of Ian Fleming. On their tunics were their names: 'RAKEBRANK, MAIDAN, COLON, TRUSCOTT, CORTEZ, HUFF, WALTOS, KRASS, CLINGBEIL'.

The Press quarters at Da Nang were the Riverside Hotel, put up by the French for tourism, a one-storey, three-sided affair built on the banks of the river. There were about twenty rooms, and they opened on to a central courtyard, like looseboxes for horses: some were marked 'AP', 'UP', 'CBS News', etc., to indicate permanent residence. Most rooms had big double beds and mosquito netting and austerity French furniture. I asked where everyone was and was told up at the base or out on assignment: they usually got back around five.

Across the road from the main gate, I had observed a kind of miniature park, a big mound dotted with small trees, with a low stone wall all round and a long, shallow flight of steps in the middle. Where did they lead to? I crossed the road and walked up the steps. At the top more steps fell away to a little hollow in which was a courtyard fringed by frangipani. Beyond the courtyard was a low, three-sided building without doors or windows. As I approached, I saw it was a museum, full of stone statues cemented to their plinths to stop people taking them away. But it was no ordinary museum. It harboured the cream of Vietnam's sculptural past, treasures that even Jim Thompson in Bangkok might have envied. There were things from the 7th century and 10th century and 13th century, from the Cham period and the Chinese period and the period of the Chinese wars. There were statues of Vishnu and Lakshmi and Shiva dancing, of fantastic Chinese elephants and lions, of giant lingams reaching for the sky, and circular rows of exquisite disembodied breasts. To add to this windfall, I seemed to have the place to myself. I wandered from object to object in a kind of dream, stunned by the unexpectedness of it all. I had come to Vietnam because of its savage war; and yet in the heart of it I had found this harbour of beauty and peace.

Indeed so bemused was I that on entering the second of the museum's two wings, I didn't see there was someone there until almost on him. He was a civilian, a quiet American by the name of Carrier, working for the Rand Corporation. We looked at the remaining statues together, and a bond grew between us, like birds in the wilderness. He was an interesting man, and I was intrigued as to what he did.

'My job', he said, 'is to interview Vietcong prisoners and try and evaluate their motivation in fighting.'

'What would you say their motivation is?'

'Basically to get a better deal for themselves. The history of the Vietnamese villager is a history of neglect, and the history of every Saigon government is a history of corruption.'

'I've heard it said that the villagers don't really care which side wins, all they want is a quiet life.'

'At the moment they want a quiet life in that they want to be sure the protection they're getting, whether it's South Vietnamese or Vietcong, is strong enough. But if by a quiet life is meant going on living as they always have done, it's simply not true. These people have been disillusioned by broken promises, first by the French, then by their own people. They believe the Vietcong represent a regime that really will do something to improve their standard of living.'

'What do they think of the Americans?'

'They think we're here for our own good, and that's true whatever way you care to interpret it. They think we're here to prop up a corrupt regime, and that's true too. No-one has any idea of the extent of the corruption of South Vietnamese officials. They say we have no business here and they want us out. And they're terrified of our Negroes.'

'Why?'

'Because when the French foreign legion were here, they had these huge Senegalese native troops who frequently used to rape their tiny women.'

'What do you say to the prisoners when you first see them?'

'I have a girl interpreter and she sees them first, softens them up, you know, the old theory. Then I come in and tell them I'm a long hair, I'm making a study of revolutions. The prisoners say: "I am like a fish on a cutting board. I don't care what you do with me." They expect to be killed and are surprised when they're not.'

'Are you staying at the press hotel?'

'No. I always stay in Vietnamese hotels with my interpreters.'

'What's that like?'

'It's noisy. They stay up till all hours. The one I'm staying in now has bedroom walls which don't reach the ceiling – they're kind of partitioned. Next to me is a room shared by three Chinamen and a girl. They have the girl in turn. It's quite a racket. By the time they're through it's damn near morning.'

I said: 'You're an American, but you don't seem to me to be part of what one might call the American effort here, the American establishment . . .'

'I'm not.'

'Well, what do you think of it?'

He thought a bit and said: 'Forgive me if I don't say anything too obvious. But there are two things I ought to say. First, how many Americans here or at home know anything about Vietnamese history? And if you don't know Vietnamese history, you don't know anything about this country or the people who live in it. The Vietnamese have a very strong sense of their own identity. They were occupied by the Chinese for a thousand years – how many Americans know that? – and they still kept their identity. Whether they're from the north or south, they loathe the Chinese and always have done. But most Americans think the Chinese are only waiting to come and help them.'

'And the other thing?'

'You hear a lot of criticism about the American soldiers here, how ignorant they are and so on. It's perfectly true, but what people don't realize is they're peasants. Peasants are traditionally thought of as being rural. Well, we live in an urban society, so we have urban peasants. But they're peasants just the same.'

We walked through the courtyard, past the sweet-smelling frangipani trees, and down the steps to the road. At the bottom Mr Carrier went on towards the town, and I crossed over to the hotel. Most of the correspondents had returned and were sitting drinking on a terrace outside the bar. I intro-duced myself. They represented the world's press: UP, AP, *Life*, NBC, *Paris-Match*, CBS, Reuters: they were all experts in their field, men trained to enquire, to observe, to record: some had been in Da Nang for months. Yet when there was a lull in the conversation and I mentioned the museum across the road and the treasures in it, they all looked blank. None of them had been there: none had even heard of it.

Formosa or Taiwan is an attractive island, with its many lakes and hills, and you would never guess that except for Holland it has the highest population density in the world. Taipei, the capital, is less agreeable. For the first fifty years of this century it was occupied by the industrious Japanese, who made of it a grey, drab, industrial city.

In a big gloomy building I found the American Medical Research Unit. Its staff was 12 medical officers of the US Navy, 12 enlisted men and 300 Chinese civilians. Its head was a doctor called Captain Phillips, who was fifty-nine, and wore khaki trousers and an open shirt, and had cropped grey hair, like a field of fertilized stubble. Captain Phillips smoked sixty cigarettes a day, and when I taxed him on this, he justified it on the grounds that Taiwan was free of the smog which they had in London and Los Angeles.

'What kind of research are you doing?' I said.

'Our mission', said Captain Phillips, 'is acute infectious diseases of the Far East. Trachoma, cholera, etc.'

'But why is the US Navy doing this? They don't suffer from these diseases. They're inoculated against them.'

'No, but they sail the seven seas and go to countries which do suffer from them.'

'So it's for humanitarian reasons?'

'It's like this,' said Captain Phillips. 'There are approximately five million people in the world suffering from trachoma. They live in countries which don't have the know-how to provide a cure. We do have the know-how, and therefore we have a duty, a conscience if you like, to utilize it. In addition a man who has trachoma can maybe see enough to till a paddy-field, but not enough to work on an assembly line. So some developing nations are being held back from becoming industrialized. Trying to find a cure for trachoma is one of the ways they can be helped to help themselves, and in the long run that's good for all of us.'

Captain Phillips handed me over to a warrant officer called Chief Pancratz, who said he would take me to the zoo: the whole of the top floor was occupied by animals, which they used for experiments, and the man in charge was Captain Favero. So we went upstairs and met Captain Favero who was an army, not a navy captain, and when I asked why, he said the navy didn't have a veterinary corps. In Captain Favero's office was a stuffed white rabbit in a glass case. I asked what it was doing there, and Captain Favero said: 'That was a rabbit we were trying to artificially inseminate, but it didn't take so we stuffed her.'

Captain Favero led us to the experimental section. We saw rabbits with red eyes munching carrots, guinea pigs, hamsters and mice. We saw a swan, a pig, and a goose. We saw a cat in a very small cage, looking miserable. 'Right now that cat is undergoing experimentation,' said Captain Favero. 'That's why he's in that small cage.' We saw a rabbit in an even smaller cage, with his head sticking out and eating a carrot. 'This rabbit', said Captain Favero, 'has had part of his bowel removed and the two ends joined up. He has a tube inside him to analyse the secretions there, and eventually he'll be infected with cholera to see how the secretions change. We'll be able to study the formation of the various anti-bodies on the wall of his stomach.'

'Why's he in such a small cage?' I said. 'He can't even move.'

'We don't want him to move,' said Captain Favero. 'If he moved the tube would fall out, and that would ruin the experiment.'

Then we visited the operating theatre. There was a coloured man there whom Chief Pancratz introduced as Chief Grant, and a Chinese girl whom Chief Grant introduced as Miss Lucy Jean. When I said that wasn't a very Chinese name, she said her real name was Chien, but Jean was easier for the Americans. Chief Pancratz asked Chief Grant what was cooking, and Chief Grant said only the routine monkey tests and gestured to the other side of the room.

I followed his arm and saw something I would have preferred not to see. Lying on his back on a small table was an ordinary grey monkey with a big bushy tail and closed eyes. His arms were stretched behind his head and his legs were similarly splayed, each at right angles to the other; hands and feet were tied to posts at each corner of the table so that he looked about to be stretched on the rack; Chief Grant said this was to keep him from moving. There was a black teat wedged in the corner of his mouth to make an airway for his breathing. The monkey lay on a long white cushion which Chief Pancratz said was a heated pad to keep him warm, and a loose sheet of plastic covered his body.

At one side of the table was a glass container half full of a blue liquid. This emptied into a tube which ran under the plastic sheet and into a hole in the monkey's stomach. A few inches away another tube had been inserted into another hole, and this carried the blue liquid out of the stomach and into a glass container at the other side of the table. Lying across the monkey's stomach was a long, thin pair of forceps or similar instrument, which held together the monkey's skin where the cuts had been made for the holes; I assumed these were handier than stitches. At the foot of the table lay a kidney-shaped dish containing rubber gloves and surgical instruments, and beneath it a bucket full of used bandages.

'We'll continue with this experiment,' said Chief Grant, 'until the blue ceases. The blue is the means of telling us when to stop. They call it Evans blue. It's a very simple sort of dye.'

'What is it all for?' I asked.

'This monkey', said Chief Grant, 'is being given a mixture of sodium 22 and sodium 24 with potassium 42, which is made in a reactor and is therefore radioactive. What we're trying to find out is how much radioactive sodium is absorbed by the monkey as the solution passes through the small intestine. We give different doses to different monkeys. When we've discovered the correct dosage, we aim to try it out on humans and see if it helps give a cure for cholera.'

'Do you use a lot of monkeys?'

'We try and keep a good supply on hand. I would say we were using around two a week. We have used as many as six a week, but two or three is average.'

I looked at the monkey on his heated pad, unaware of what had been done to him, and I said to Chief Pancratz: 'What happens to the monkeys when the experiment is over?'

'Oh,' said Chief Pancratz, 'we sacrifice them. We give them an overdose of magnesium sulphate which is a saturated solution.'

Going back to Captain Phillips' office I couldn't get this monkey from my mind. He was the apex of everything I had seen, the epitome of all those helpless creatures in their cages, tubes in their stomachs, bandages on their wounds, infected with cholera and trachoma. I had been taught, and believed it, that the cardinal sin was exploitation of others for one's own ends, of using people as things. This admirable precept applied to some sections of the animal world as well: domestic and farm animals were treated with consideration, there was a limit to what could be asked of circus animals, even in the pursuit of wild animals there existed some kind of relationship. The less their freedom of action was interfered with, the more they kept their dignity: the more they kept their dignity, the more we gave them our respect.

But these pathetic creatures, monkeys and rabbits and hamsters and mice, and millions like them in laboratories all over the world, had been exploited mercilessly. They had been deprived of their freedom wholly and therefore also of their dignity; they were being used as things. The justification, it would be said, was the benefits they had brought to humankind: by their deaths they had saved, and would continue to save, millions of human lives. Was might then right, and did the end justify the means? It would seem so. But let no-one then pretend otherwise. Let no-one engaged in this work kid himself that his job is not one of exploitation and expediency, nor deny that what he is doing is – however important to man – a deeply shameful thing.

JAPAN

Today I have been lunching with little Mrs Yuasa whom I met with her husband, a Tokyo banker, while waiting at Teheran Airport for the flight to New Delhi. Mrs Yuasa said then, 'Come and see us in Tokyo', and gave me a card, like any American. Actually Mrs Yuasa is more English than American, having been to Sherborne, a leading English girls' school, and now she talks like any witty English dowager.

Mr Yuasa was busy banking, but Mrs Yuasa took me to the International Centre, where we had a nasty western lunch looking at a pretty Japanese garden. After lunch we went to the Meiji gardens, first to the shrine where people clap hands and pray and toss coins into a box for ancestor worship, and then for a walk in the park. I was much stared at. Here were white and purple irises growing as thickly as buttercups, and a big pond of carp with mouths like teacups, and people feeding them with popcorn from a nearby stall. The stall also sold hot dogs and hamburgers and doughnuts and cookies. 'Hot dogs!' said Mrs Yuasa, laughing, 'I can remember the time when one had to ask what a hot dog was. Such a ridiculous name, don't you think? And all that chewing the Americans go in for. We were taught as children never to chew, but their grown-ups chew all the time.' I asked Mrs Yuasa, an English-educated upper-class Japanese, what she thought of Americans, and she said she would tell me a story. Once when she and Mr Yuasa were touring the States, they came to Las Vegas. During the floor-show they sat next to an ageing American husband and wife, both a little drunk. When the nudes came on, the wife, still looking at them, said to the husband: 'Shut your eyes, honey, shut your eyes!', and the husband, looking at them too, said to her, 'It's OK, sweetheart, you're more beautiful than any of them.' What made this so funny, Mrs Yuasa said, was that during the exchange neither husband nor wife looked at each other: they'd paid good money and didn't want to lose a second of the show. The memory of it all set Mrs Yuasa chortling again, and because laughter is so infectious, I started chortling too: Mrs Yuasa and I chortled together, there in front of everyone, in the middle of the Meiji Gardens.

THE PACIFIC

From Honolulu we had a lovely trip to the States, free pineapple juice at the airport with the compliments of Hawaii, free champagne in the Boeing with the compliments of Pan Am. Across the aisle from me were three handsome teenagers, two brothers and a sister in their late teens, on the way home from vacation; Mum and Dad sat several rows ahead. The elder brother by the window wrote letters, but the other two had a gay time, playing cards, teasing each other, lapping up all the free champagne they could get. She was a lovely, fleshy girl with honey-coloured hair and white teeth and plump breasts, like an ad for bras or camping. Sometimes her brother got so mad with her teasing, he put his arms on hers and shook her, like a child, and then they both giggled. It was odd to see two such attractive people being so intimate and happy with each other without any sexual awareness. Once Mum came clucking down the aisle to see they weren't having too much of the champagne. 'Mum, we just had the one glass, I swear,' the boy said. He pointed to me. 'I gave my second glass to this gentleman here, didn't I, sir?' I smiled. 'And Shirley, she gave her second glass to Tom, didn't you, Shirl? Honest Mum, cross my heart I'm not lying.' Later Mum brought a scrabble board and said, 'Why don't you play an interesting game instead of those stupid cards?' The boy took the scrabble board politely, and when Mum had gone, put it under the seat.

There was one person on the plane I wanted to talk to before journey's end. This was the air hostess who had served me drinks, a pretty, English-looking girl with deep-set brown eyes and a wide, generous mouth, who looked about thirty and said she had been with Pan Am seven years. Many times on my travels I had wondered about the lives of these American stewardesses abroad. What sort of existence did they have? What did they think of the passengers, how did passengers behave towards them? I made a date with her while the plane was sleeping and after lunch went down the aisle and joined her at the back.

Her name was Blanche, and she was a senior stewardess. Her family came from Czechoslovakia, her widowed mother lived in Chicago, and she had a flat in San Francisco, which was her present base. She spoke with more of an English than an American accent, and was very feminine in a European way, gentle and passive.

'What about the passengers?' I said. 'How do they look from your end?'

'The Japs are the quietest,' she said. 'They never ask for anything. They wouldn't complain if you didn't give them a meal for two days. One time I had a Jap faint in the aisle, and his two friends just sat there and looked at him and did nothing. So I said, "Aren't you his friends?" and they said yes, but they never moved. You can't tell whether they're angry or happy or depressed or what. The Americans on the other hand make themselves heard. If they don't like something, boy, you soon hear about it. The English are that way too.'

'Are they?'

'I know you're English, and I hope you don't mind my saying this, but I believe I've had more bitter complaints from the English than the Americans. I've been really surprised how short and snappy the English can be. I've had English people on the flight write out letters of complaint to the President of Pan Am, and then give them to me. Some of these have been so unreasonable I don't think my bosses would pay much attention to them.'

'What are they about?'

'Well, one Englishman got really mad because we were having lifeboat drill at a time when he wanted to wave goodbye out of the window. That kind of thing. On the other hand we have many English stewardesses, and I haven't met one I didn't like. They have a tremendous sense of humour and say the funniest things with a straight face. They keep me in stitches. I don't believe they're typically British. We have some German stewardesses but they're apt to be bossy and aggressive and the pursers don't like them, and then we have a few Scandinavian girls and they're very reserved and quiet. I like the British the best.'

'I've heard some Americans say they make better stewardesses than American girls.'

'Well, Americans don't make naturally good servants anywhere – in restaurants or hotels it's the same. But it's not true about all of them. I know one American stewardess who just loves looking after passengers. She says that so long as she can make one passenger happy, that is all she wants.'

'Do you ever get really rude passengers?'

'Sometimes we get passengers who are rude without meaning to be, like the Latin-Americans who go "Psssssst!" when they want service instead of ringing the bell. When I was on that run we used to make a joke about it and say, "We've got another snake on board."

'But there are others who are deliberately rude, and you can meet them on any trip. Mostly they jump at us for reasons which have nothing to do with ourselves. They've been charged excess baggage, they haven't been able to get a window seat, they've had a row with their wives, or a bad day at the office. So they take it out on us. They use anything from sarcasm to profanity. This worried me terribly when I first joined, and I often used to end up in tears, but now I take no notice. There was a new girl in tears the other day. She said a sailor had deliberately put out his foot to trip her up. I said, "Do you think he did it *deliberately*?" I'm sure he didn't, but I couldn't convince her. I used to be like that in the beginning.'

'Do passengers make passes?'

'Not nearly as much as most men seem to think. I've been asked that question more times than I've had passes made at me.'

'Do they date you?'

'Sometimes. Sometimes a stewardess will go out to dinner with a passenger or a group of passengers, and I do know two girls who are notorious for making a play with passengers.

A few girls have married passengers, but very few. I dated a courier steadily for a year, but I would say that 90 per cent of the girls who are dating steady, aren't dating with passengers.'

'How about the crew?'

'There's been quite a lot of affairs between stewardesses and crew. Some of the young stewardesses idolize the captains, make father figures out of them. There've been a few cases recently of captains who've been married for twenty years divorcing their wives and marrying twenty-one-year-old stewardesses. Some of the foreign girls come over looking for an American husband, and will latch on to any eligible crew member. They have a real edge on the American girls.'

She went away to get a passenger a couple of aspirins, and when she came back, she said: 'I'll tell you a funny thing about the passengers. I go up and down the aisle perhaps thirty times on a long flight, so the passengers get far more opportunity to see what I look like than I do with 120 of them. And yet when my chores are over and I go into town, I find I recognize their faces more often than they remember mine. Walking down the main street in Honolulu, I'll pass people who've been my passengers and smile at them, and I can see them thinking, who the hell is that?'

The voice of the captain came over the intercom, telling us the weather at Los Angeles was good, and we'd be there in just under an hour.

I said, 'You say you've been with Pan Am seven years. Do you enjoy it now as much as when you started?'

'Not so much. It used to have glamour, but now it's just a job. Now I go through the routine mechanically. In some ways it's a satisfying job, and well paid too. But it's not *for* anybody. It doesn't have a point any more.'

'How about your apartment in San Francisco?'

'I quite enjoy that, but it can be a let-down when you've been with people for days. The place is empty and there's no-one to greet you, you feel very much alone.'

'You sound as though you'd had enough.'

'I think I've had enough flying. I really do.'

'What would you like instead?'

She smiled and said, 'What every woman wants, I suppose. Someone to come back to. Children. Staying put.'

The coast came up, brown and hazy, and the plane skimmed over the lime-green sea and landed. As we came to a stop, the younger brother across the aisle took his sister's hands in his, looked in her eyes and said, 'Darling, you know this means goodbye,' and they both had a last giggle.

Next morning I was to fly over the Pole to London, so I went to a nearby motel. A boy showed me to my room, put down my bags and turned on the television. Sound and picture came through, and a man in close-up said: 'Have you got bad breath? *Most* people have bad breath.'

Had I? Did they? There was no other country in the world that could greet you quite like that. Truly I was back at first base.

EXTRACTS, ARTICLES
AND SPEECHES

ONE MAN'S MEAT

On coming down from Oxford in the summer of 1948,
I became Librarian of Ashridge Adult Education College
in Hertfordshire. As well as writing my book on Nelson's
captains there, I kept a diary; and when Moira and I were
living in Santa Monica the following year, I wrote it up, taking
Evelyn Waugh's advice to me that even when a writer has no
theme that he wishes to develop, he should write a little every
day in the way a professional pianist practises scales. In due
course it was published as One Man's Meat. *This fragment is*
all I wish to preserve from it.

6 August. London
In a clearing at one end of Wimbledon Common there stands
a peculiar sign. It is a little wooden sign, close to the ground,
and it has been badly battered by the elements. It looks as
though the purpose for which it was erected had ceased to
exist and that someone had forgotten to remove it. This
is quite true, though few people know the story behind it. I
know the story because it concerned my great-uncle Archibald.

Uncle Archibald was a remarkable character. His passion
in life was shooting. It would not be an exaggeration to say
that he lived for shooting. He was born in the middle of the
Victorian era, a time when English gentlemen could, at small
expense to themselves, obtain all the shooting they wanted.
Later he went into the Army, a profession which, on and off
duty, enabled him to gratify his desires to the full. In England
he shot partridges, in Egypt ducks, in Canada caribou, in
Kenya hippopotami. In India he shot Indians and on the
veldt of South Africa, Boers; all with conspicuous success.
It was one of the greatest disappointments of my uncle's life
when, at the outbreak of the First World War, he was told
he was too old to shoot Germans.

Some time at the beginning of the present century my uncle married. At the request of my aunt, a genteel person who did not take to camp-following in outlandish places, he retired from the Army and bought a house on Wimbledon Hill. At that time the suburbs of London had not stretched their tentacles into this part of Surrey, and in the fields and woods were many pheasants and partridges. For several years my uncle enjoyed what he called capital sport. Then, slowly, the houses grew up around him. The woods were cut down and the fields levelled. The game flew away. Soon my uncle's activities became confined to stalking a colony – or, as he used to say, 'wisp' – of snipe, which had made their home near the Wimbledon Sewage Works. Eventually the snipe, either because of my uncle or the disagreeable nature of their surroundings, went away too; and there was nothing left to shoot.

I suppose the most sensible thing for my uncle would have been to sell his house and buy another in the country where he could have continued his life's work. But by this time he was getting old and, like most old people, could not bear the thought of moving. However he was determined, so long as he could walk and hold a gun, to go on shooting; and there being no game left to shoot, he started shooting rubbish.

I know this sounds rather peculiar; but it was, after all, the logical thing for my uncle to do. He would naturally have preferred to shoot game, but game were no longer obtainable: rubbish was, and its supply practically inexhaustible. Yet it must not be thought that my uncle shot rubbish in a haphazard or sloppy manner. He did not, for instance, empty the contents of the dustbin on the ground, walk a dozen yards, and fire blindly into them. He planned a rubbish shoot as carefully as if it were an ordinary shoot. Between tea and dinner of the evening beforehand, he collected crates, boxes, tin cans, bottles, discarded clothing and old books. When it was dark he went out to the Common with his manservant Briggs and scattered these things at random in the bushes. The next day he rose early, put on his tweed knickerbockers, and after a hearty breakfast at which he discussed the prospect of the day's sport with my aunt, set out with Briggs for the Common.

My uncle had divided the Common into various sections or beats, and it was the custom for him and Briggs to line up at the first beat about fifteen yards apart. When all was ready my uncle blew a whistle. This was the signal for them to march forward together, and for Briggs to start banging at the bushes with a stick and to utter strange noises. Moving through the undergrowth my uncle would suddenly spy an old sock hanging from the branch of a tree where he had tossed it the night before, or a copy of *Paradise Lost* nestling in a clump of nettles. (If Briggs saw the object first he would cry 'Mark right' or 'Mark left', as the case might be.) Up flew my uncle's gun and the target was peppered with shot. Briggs immediately retrieved it and stowed it in the game-bag for use another day.

My uncle was always careful to observe proper shooting etiquette. On Mondays and Tuesdays there was usually a good deal of rubbish left behind by Sunday picnickers. My uncle never would shoot this. He called it poaching. He had an extraordinary knack of being able to distinguish, almost in a flash, between his own rubbish and other people's. Occasionally he did unwittingly shoot strange rubbish, but he would not allow Briggs to put it in the game-bag. 'No, Briggs,' he would say, coming up to a splintered ginger-beer bottle, 'that's not our bird.'

These rubbish-shoots kept my uncle happily occupied for many years. They ended finally when my uncle was ninety-two. His eyesight was not what it was, and there was a succession of unpleasant incidents. On one occasion he fired at the wheels of a perambulator thinking that they were gramophone records; and on another he discharged two barrels at an ostrich plume which he imagined was my aunt's, but was in fact the head-piece of a hat being worn by a Mrs Ethel Jubb, partaking of a picnic tea with her grandchildren. Mrs Jubb and the owner of the pram were annoyed about this, and persuaded the local people to sign a round robin demanding that my uncle be restrained from his activities, which they forwarded to the borough council for action. This created an awkward situation for the borough council, as my uncle was their chairman and they were very fond of him. However they convened an

Extraordinary General Meeting (one member said afterwards that that was the only adjective to describe it) at which they agreed to put up a clay-pigeon machine in my uncle's garden, and to grant Briggs a small annual salary to work it. My uncle was somewhat put out at this offer, for the whole point of the rubbish-shoots had been the variety of scenery they afforded; but eventually, at my aunt's urgent request, he accepted.

Just to be on the safe side the borough council erected a small sign on the edge of the Common opposite to my uncle's house. It read 'SHOOTING RUBBISH IS PROHIBITED'. This sign, as any traveller in the Green Line bus will tell you, still stands today. It is situated about four hundred yards from the Kingston by-pass, on the left-hand side of the road.

The only true thing about that story is the fact of the sign, SHOOTING RUBBISH IS PROHIBITED. It was where I said it was, and of course SHOOTING meant TIPPING. In 1988 the writer Byron Rogers picked up a second-hand copy of One Man's Meat, *read the Uncle Archibald story and devoted the whole of his* Sunday Express *column to it. This is how he ended it:*

I was entranced by the story, read it out to my wife, repeated it to many people, and last week, being in London with time on my hands, rang various departments of Morden borough council which has annexed Wimbledon.

After many startled exchanges, I was put through to a group known mysteriously as the Conservators of the Common. The man who answered said: 'What?', then 'WHAT?' and, in a little while: 'Not in living memory it hasn't.'

There was a pause after which a new note came into his voice. 'There is no rubbish on Wimbledon Common. D'you understand? If there is no rubbish you can't shoot it.'

I rang Mr Ludovic Kennedy, resting after his memoirs. He sounded even more startled than Morden borough council and wanted to know what I had been up to, poking around in that old book. I did not tell him about the sale.

The sign, he insisted, had been there, and he had seen it, but the rest, Archibald and all, he had made up. He thought that would have been obvious.

My mother always said I would have difficulty, growing up.

THE WORLD IS TOO MUCH WITH US

The Standard Telephones and Cables
Communication Lecture for 1982

THE GREAT ORGANIZATION which has sponsored this lecture tonight, Standard Telephones and Cables plc, and the great organization for which I work, the BBC, may be said to have had their genesis in a saying of the American writer Ralph Waldo Emerson, some 120 years ago. 'We are in great haste,' he declared, 'to construct a telegraph between Maine and Texas.' Then he added these significant words, 'But it may be that Maine has nothing to say to Texas'. In our time the British writer Eric Partridge went further, 'Most people', he wrote, 'have nothing to say and go on saying it', and anyone who has listened to a Radio 1 disc-jockey or to a crossed line on the telephone will know just what he meant. And if in 1807 in the tranquillity and isolation of the Lake District the poet Wordsworth could write that the world was too much with him, how much more so do we find it in the general hubbub of today?

This is not to say that the inventions of the past century – the telegraph, the telephone, the radio, television, the jet engine, the computer, the rocket, the satellite, the silicon chip, (whatever that may be) – have not been of inestimable value in the service of mankind. Because of them lives have been saved, projects established, businesses of all kinds speeded up, information of all kinds exchanged, so that one may say that the world, which for so many centuries lay mysterious and uncharted beyond the horizon, has now shrunk to an imaginable size; there are no longer any far away countries of which we know little, or if there are (and there are) we must not say so. I deny none of those benefits. All I would claim is that with the good has come the bad, and that the bad is in some danger of being ignored.

Let us look at the good first. Two things in particular seem to have resulted from the communications explosion of the past hundred years. The first is that we have become a much more egalitarian society, in which undue deference to authority has disappeared and where respect has to be earned and not assumed. 'God Bless the Squire and his Relations/And keep us in our proper stations', went the old Victorian jingle. The stations were thought to be permanent. The rich and powerful moved exclusively in a world of their own. It was an age of genuflection.

But slowly things began to change. The squire and the vicar moved to stations further down the track; and as lines of human communication improved, so those to the Almighty rusted. The coming of television dramatically hastened the change. Prime Ministers, Archimandrites and so on, were faced with the unpalatable thought that unless they ventured to dip a toe in the waters of this new medium, they would become even more removed from the lives of most people than they were already. So gradually, and graciously, they came down from Olympus in twos and threes, and chairmen and managing directors and interviewers were at first so unnerved that they called them Your Grace and Your Eminence and said what an honour it was to welcome them to humble studio. Happily that didn't last long. When they were seen to be as human and as fallible as the rest of us – and all the nicer for it – the sycophancy had to go too; so that at a BBC Current Affairs meeting in the early 60s, my friend Sir Robin Day was able to say to those present, 'When I interview a king, I am on a level with the king, and when I interview a dustman I am on a level with the dustman.' A voice from the back of the hall called out, 'Hear, hear'. I am sorry to say it was mine.

There has also been a healthy change in the language used, both in what is said and how it is said. Politicians who used to get away at garden fêtes with exploring avenues and not leaving stones unturned dare not do so on television; even those most conservative of all our fellow countrymen, the Trades Union leaders, are at last beginning to appreciate the soggy impact of phrases about having exhausted existing negotiating machinery. Many of what used to be called the lower classes now attempt to talk posh, and many of what are still called the upper classes have developed a tendency to talk Cockney. That kind of levelling is, I am sure, all to the good. It is in the written word addressed to a few rather than in the spoken word addressed to many that some regression has taken place; that growth industry of gobbledegook spawned mostly by sociologists, psychologists and analysts and which the magazine *Private Eye* has satirized under the general heading of 'Meaningful and Viable Scenarios at This Moment in Time'.

There has been external levelling too, so that in foreign affairs English has become, as it were, the *lingua franca* of the world; and now that the British Empire has gone to join all the rest of history's Empires in the dusty attics of the past, the fact that the inhabitants of a small island on the periphery of Europe gave to the world its principal international language will surely stand as our most lasting legacy to mankind.

In many places, I'm told, English is often the only language in which non-English can communicate; and I'm also told that the results are such that any Englishman who happens to be present cannot for the life of him understand what is being said. But it is now commonplace, and indeed gratifying, to find former enemies like Chancellor Schmidt of West Germany and present enemies like Senor Costa Mendez of the Argentine conversing publicly in fluent English. Nor is there that wide gulf in speech patterns that used to exist between those of English origin but different nationalities. Britishers who today visit the United States are no longer taxed, as I was when I first went there forty years ago, with having cute Limey accents. Today in each others' countries the accents of Canadians, New Zealanders, Britishers, Americans and Australians may be noticed but go largely unremarked. Thanks to jet aircraft and satellites and *Kojak* and *Upstairs Downstairs* and *Picnic at Hanging Rock*, there are fewer variations in the English we share than at any time since around 200 years ago when the chicks vacated the nest. Let us admit however that it is mostly we who have adopted Americanisms rather than the other way round. Those of us who until twenty years ago had never heard of task forces or guidelines now trot out such phrases as though we'd been using them all our lives.

There is one other benison which one hopes that the spread and universal use of English may one day bring; the lessening of conflicts brought about through misunderstandings or a sense of alienation. For the moment however wars of all kinds continue to flourish in almost every quarter of the globe, and because of television we can now watch them from the comfort of sitting room or bedroom while sipping gins and tonic. It was this armchair viewing of the Vietnam war that led Mr Edward Heath in a previous STC Lecture to suggest that it was the televised pictures of the fighting there that had so demoralized American viewers as to lead to eventual American withdrawal. But with respect to Mr Heath it was not just pictures of the fighting that demoralized American people, it was the gradual realization, after years of conflict, that it was a war they could no longer win, and which it was morally questionable whether they should be fighting anyway. Let us not forget that throughout the Second World War there were nightly newsreel showings in American picture houses of Americans fighting and dying in the Pacific; but these strengthened rather than weakened the resolve of the Americans to continue, knowing as they did that this was a just war, on the outcome of which depended their survival.

One other effect of the communications explosion has been to make autocratic societies more secretive and rigid, and democratic societies less so. In dictatorships aids like bugging machines, tape recorders and data banks have enabled those in power to keep a sharp eye on their enemies and nip resistance in the bud. But in democracies that have shed paternalism it has had the effect of making our dealings more open. Reasons now have to be given for courses of action where previously reasons were thought unnecessary. The staffs of some organizations – the BBC is one – now have a right to see what is written in their annual reports. In military affairs it is now accepted that those who have to obey orders should be given some inkling of what the purpose of those orders are. And doctors who used to baffle us by writing prescriptions in hieroglyphics now feel obliged to give the hieroglyphics names – which are of course no less baffling. The greatest advance in this field, I suppose, is the United States Freedom of Information Act, by which the follies and wisdoms of what was done under previous administrations are laid bare. Has not the time come for us to have a similar act here?

By the same token television has given us access to institutions and organizations which were denied to us, and which, on the grounds of both security and taste, we always thought would be denied to us. *Sailor*, *Hospital*, *Strangeways*, *Police*; one by one the citadels have fallen. Twenty-five years ago who would have thought that cameras would have been allowed inside the inner sanctums of Buckingham Palace, that the Thames Valley Police Force and the Manchester Prison Service should have opened their doors to BBC teams for three months and given them carte blanche to film what they wanted? It required courage of those in authority to give permission for these films to be made, and in the main without conditions, because they feared, understandably, that in some way their public image would be distorted; but in every case, I think, their fears proved unfounded.

There are however two institutions which have so far held out against allowing television to visit them. One is the law, in particular the criminal law. If the only object of a court of law is the pursuit of justice, would the presence of cameras militate against this? For many years, I confess, I thought it would, that witnesses who are often nervous anyway, would be made even more so by the knowledge that their evidence and with it perhaps intimate details of their private lives, wrested out of them by a tenacious counsel, would be exposed to the gaze of millions: and that in this way justice would be defeated.

Today I take a modified view. If justice has not only to be done but needs to be seen to be done, what other medium but television will enable us to see it? And if it can be done in other countries without detriment to justice, as for instance in some German trials and in the recent von Bulow trial in Boston, why not also here? And finally if the royal family and the prison service and the police can open their doors to cameras, then surely the guardians of the law can at least consider the matter too? For them it would not be an opening of the floodgates, for there are only a few trials, perhaps not more than one a year, that the public would be sufficiently interested in seeing. They should also know that the electronic cameras of today require no extra lighting and are therefore quite unobtrusive.

The other great institution where cameras are still forbidden is of course the House of Commons.[1] In a lecture I gave in 1973 I said that historians of the future would look back at this omission and find it extraordinary. When they look back to 1982, nine years further on and find the situation unchanged, they will, I am sure, find it bizarre. In recent weeks at a time of international crisis, with the country drifting towards war, we have been able partially to hear but quite unable to see what our legislators in their place of business have been doing. I say partially because too often their voices have been drowned either by the baying of their colleagues or by the commentator trying to tell us who the owners of the voices are. If I were an MP – a fate I once narrowly avoided – I would say to my colleagues, 'What is there about us that is so special, so sacred, so unique that we cannot allow a pictorial record of our activities to be made? What larger lunacy forbids us to be seen but permits us to be – with difficulty – heard?'

One knows the answer. They fear that the semi-private, semi-mystical nature of their proceedings will somehow be beyond the common understanding. Who can persuade them that once the cameras had been there a few months, they would soon forget there was a time when they were not there – just as we have all forgotten now that there was once a fourteen-day rule that prevented public discussion of any issue within fourteen days of it being debated in Parliament? Who can persuade those who fear that a member will use the cameras to address his constituents that it is impossible to address more than one audience at a time and that anyone who tried would soon make himself a laughing-stock? It is a sad comment on our elected representatives, is it not, that they

[1] Television was finally allowed to cover Parliament in 1990. Afterwards, people wondered what all the fuss had been about.

should have so little faith in either themselves or in us.

And while I am on the subject of television, may I once again put in a plea for the final despatch of that universal cliché of our times, that television is the most powerful and influential medium of communication there is. It is nothing of the kind and never has been. That it can have a certain imitative effect, that if you constantly show scenes of the heroic it will encourage some to strive for the heroic, and that if you constantly show scenes of mindless violence or loveless sex, it will encourage others to strive in that direction, I would not deny. It has also, I think we are agreed, widened our horizons.

But in the field of opinions and ideas, I do not know of anybody, and I doubt if you do either, whose views have been radically altered by anything he or she has seen or heard on television. To think otherwise is to confuse influence with size, to imagine that a thing said simultaneously to twenty million people is somehow more influential than the same thing read in a book or a newspaper or said privately by a friend on the telephone or in a pub. Those who hold that view do not seem to realize that among people of all ages and classes the readiness to reject a given opinion is as great as the readiness to accept it – as anyone knows who has listened to a party political broadcast. What opinions expressed on television do is to reinforce existing prejudices. 'Listeners,' wrote Gerald Priestland recently, and after thirty years in broadcasting, 'only want to hear what they agree with.' 'Everyone now recognizes', said Brian Walden in his recent IBA Lecture, 'that television has no magic powers.'

Indeed I would go further and say that because of its inherent ephemerality, television is probably the least influential of all the media. Watching television is like watching the passing countryside from an express train. The scenes, the images, die as you observe them, others take their place, they also die, so that by the time you reach journey's end and provided you haven't fallen asleep – an occupational hazard both with trains and television – you are hard put to remember anything you saw. One hears people complaining of the rubbish that is shown on television. In my view, and taken overall, there is far less rubbish in British television than any other, and certainly far less than in British newspapers and books. My complaint is the opposite, that so much of it is so good, so well written, photographed, directed, dressed, performed, edited, dubbed, that night after night work of the highest quality goes out on both the BBC and ITV, and yet so little of it stays in the mind.

Well, that is the nature of the beast. Seeing a film on a big screen in a darkened cinema as a member of a paying and expectant audience is an altogether different experience from seeing it in a semi-lighted room on a screen no larger than the back of a chair, where the children and the dog, the evening paper and the telephone, are also competing for attention. Even those breakthrough programmes I mentioned earlier, like *Hospital*, *Prison Service*, *Police*, have not radically changed our attitude towards those institutions. To learn that they are inhabited by human beings like ourselves is not perhaps to learn very much. If you want to know what institutional life is really like, then you must be a member of the institution – though in the case of the royal family that is perhaps rather easier said than done. The fact is that however much insight we think we are being given when we look at these films, however privileged we may feel by doors being unlocked, we are less viewers than voyeurs. One watches on television, but one rarely sees.

The advance in communications in general then, and television in particular, have given us much to be thankful for; a more egalitarian society, a more open society, a more informed one. But there is the other side of the coin. We are also, and I do not think this can be denied, a more fragmented society, a more uncertain society, a more troubled one. This must be true if you compare the world we live in today with the one our great-grandfathers lived in, but it is, I think, also true if you compare it with the period between the wars, the one I grew up in and which was known as the jazz age. There is today more organized crime, more assaults against the person, especially the old and helpless, more drug-taking – I'm told that the cannabis explosion is about to give way to the heroin explosion – more sexual promiscuity, more divorce – one marriage in four[1] now ends before death – more fiddling and cheating, more cruelty, more sick jokes, more contempt for established values than ever before – all the signs of a society in the process of disintegration.

What the reasons are for this phenomenal change in our values is not within the scope of this lecture to inquire. But it could well be that what happened in the Nevada desert back in 1945 has at least something to do with it. Before that time men and women had some idea of where life was leading them; and most of them believed that some sort of progress was being made towards a better, juster and happier world. There are not many who believe that today. Also before 1945 people at home – I except of course the fighting services – had every expectation of living out a normal life span. Today, and especially among young people, that expectation is less. Not only have we all lived the last thirty-five years in a state of tension between east and west previously unparalleled in history, but today, outside the existing club, nuclear weapons are beginning to proliferate like mushrooms – even the Argentine, I understand, now has the capacity for making bombs – and the more there are, the greater the chances of one and then others going off. And today this proliferation has only just started.

We learn of all this of course through the media; and you may say, well, what has the media got to do with it, why blame the messenger for bringing the message? But I do say that the media bears some responsibility in the amount of time and effort it devotes to bringing to our attention not only this message but thousands of others, and whether in the process of doing so the media itself is not adding to the general tension and malaise.

Let me take you back a little in time. The date is Good Friday of 1929, the place Savoy Hill. The duty newsreader, wearing no doubt the dinner jacket on which the great Lord Reith insisted, comes to the microphone to read the 8.45 evening news. And this is what he says, 'Good evening, ladies and gentlemen. There is absolutely no news tonight. We will have some piano music instead.' With what a sense

[1] That was ten years ago. Today it is one in three.

of envy, ladies and gentlemen, one reads those words. But of course the newsreader was right. There was no news. Yet this didn't prevent many newspapers from taking the BBC to task and the *Sunday Chronicle* to say, 'There was that night a considerable amount of news. The BBC could have announced the death of Lady Glanely, the fire at Lord Haddo's mansion, the mountaineering accident to Professor Huxley and the motor collision involving Lady Diana Cooper' - news for the *Sunday Chronicle* being death and disaster among the upper classes.

Absolutely no news on Good Friday 1929, and news every hour on the hour in 1982! Even allowing that the car radio and tranny were not in existence then, has the nature of news and the demand for news really changed that much in fifty years? Or has the whole thing got out of control? When I joined ITN as a newscaster in 1956, the main bulletin lasted fifteen minutes. Over the years it swelled until today at half an hour it is double. In America now there are two television stations broadcasting news for twenty-four hours a day, and you can't get much more news than that. And soon, we're told, we're to have breakfast news dished out to us over the cornflakes – rather rich fare, you may think, for delicate early morning stomachs. That this venture will be a modest success, I have few doubts, but why did it come into being? And why did all those news bulletins on the hour and the half-hour also come into being? Was it because of popular demand?

Far from it. They came about because they were imposed on us bit by bit, almost without our being aware of it, so that now we are conditioned to them, we are hooked on them like so many junkies. We could abstain of course, but we won't because we feel we might be missing something that others will have heard. It was Somerset Maugham, you will recall, who could never walk along the north side of Piccadilly without wondering what he was missing on the south side. And yet when we do manage to kick the habit for a couple of weeks in the summer, when we find ourselves in some remote and shady spot which the British media have not yet penetrated, what a release from tension that is; and when we return home, we find that whatever happened when we were away was of really no import at all.

There are other distractions too like the video revolution which means that if we miss a television programme or two by going out in the evening, we can see them on the machine when we return, which will help to fill in the time nicely before the breakfast news at 6 a.m. Soon after the papers will arrive. And later if we enter a restaurant for lunch, the chances are that the management will have laid on some gluey Muzak to knock all conversation on the head.

'The isle is full of noises.' So said Caliban in *The Tempest*, and I'm sure he wouldn't want to trade the sweetness of his noises for the cacophony of ours. The messages and statements and warnings and threats – and Muzak – that make up our noises are now an integral part of our lives; and if we cannot divest ourselves of them, we can at least be aware of how unnecessarily caught up in them we are.

I began the evening with Wordsworth:

> The world is too much with us, late and soon,
> Getting and spending we lay waste our powers.

Let me end with Wordsworth too, his discovery of, and entry into, what he called:

> That blessed mood,
> In which the burden of the mystery,
> In which the heavy and the weary weight
> Of all this unintelligible world
> Is lightened . . .

'And', he concluded, 'with an eye made quiet by harmony, and the deep power of joy, we see into the life of things.'

In the hurly-burly of a world that is too much with us, that may not be all that easy. But it is surely worth a try.

SCHLOCKWATCH

THE TELEVISION AND radio weekly magazine The Listener invited me to contribute to a series they were running entitled Schlockwatch where writers could give free rein to their feelings about a particular television show. Readers who have ever seen the ITV early morning breakfast show, TV-am, whose object, its founder Peter Jay once said, was to be 'a mission to explain', may have sometimes wondered where it lost its way.

Hello, good morning and welcome to the Mission to Explain Show.

This is Mike. Mike's nice. Mike has ginger hair and a ginger moustache and looks like the rugger master at a boys' prep school. Mike used to have a colleague called Nick who looked like a Wimbledon ticket tout, but he hasn't been around for a while.

This is Anne. Anne's pretty. Anne used to have lovely black hair, but it's mostly ginger now to match Mike's moustache. She scratches it a lot (everything OK there, Anne?). Anne looks like a super-cool, super-efficient chairman's right-hand girl. Sometimes Kathy takes Anne's place. Kathy has lovely dark hair like Anne used to have and is just as pretty and doesn't make so many faces.

You can't help but admire the relaxed, spontaneous way Mike and Anne interview people, even the thickest, though they do have an odd trick of glancing at the camera from time to time, as if to make quite sure we're still there.

Mike and Anne use a language which is all their own. The other day Anne asked a man called Hank whether Rock and Roll wasn't a 'faded art form', while on National Courtesy Day Mike told us, 'Politeness is our birthright.' Over on *Breakfast Time* they tell different things in the same tone of voice, but on the Mission to Explain Show when something solemn comes up they have to stop giggling and start being po-faced.

And they say things to match. The day after the Greek cruise liner had sunk Anne said, 'Of course, all our thoughts are very much with the families of those that are still missing.' Well, mine weren't, Anne, and I doubt if yours were either, but that's the kind of yuk the feeble-minded like to hear, right? 'Of course' is one of Anne's favourite phrases. Joan Collins would be there next day, she said, to tell us why she had dedicated her book to her father 'who, of course, died last year'. For Christ's sake, Anne, some of us didn't even know that Joan Collins *had* a father. I shall miss Anne, now she's gone. Hurry back.

Mike's euphemisms are modelled on those of Charlie Chester. The other day he told us he wanted to 'pay tribute' to someone who had 'passed over at age sixty-four'. Mike, he didn't pass over or through or up or anywhere. He *died*. Mike also spoke recently of 'a hero of considerable proportions' as if he were a Michelin man.

This is Carol, who does the weather and looks like a small, plump blackbird. Standing by a map that must have been drawn by a five-year-old, she gabbles away at such a rate that you are lucky to pick up more than about one word in ten. Fewer teeth might help. Sometimes Carol says, 'Hello, and nice to see you,' but as all she is looking at is a piece of hardware, she probably means 'Hello, and nice for you to see me.'

This is Gyles, who gives the impression he's wandered on to the wrong channel, is wearing a yellow golf ball on his sweater and looks quite demented. Gyles tell us of a boy who can hold 272 marbles in his trouser pocket and that a rat can go longer without water than a camel. He also brings us a knock, knock story. 'Dishwater.' 'Dishwater what?' 'Dishwater way I used to speak before I got false teeth.' That's the fun of the Mission to Explain Show – you never know what's going to turn up.

This is Greavsie, who used to be a footballer and looks a little like Alf Garnett. He is wearing a dreadful-looking woolly shirt which I wouldn't have commented on had Greavsie not told us that he found it in a tea-chest and that it smells of tea. I can well believe it. Greavsie told us he had been living in a van in Cornwall, but he hoped to get a wardrobe together soon. Good.

A regular feature of the Mission to Explain Show is the appearance of pop stars. Recently we had Hazel and Cheryl. Hazel told Mike that she had too much calcium in her blood and came out in blotches. Cheryl got stuck in the traffic so to fill in we had a film about pot-bellied pet pigs in America. When she did arrive, she was got up as if for a garden party. Mike said her dress had 'a Spanish motif'. We then saw a video of Cheryl and others singing in a garden: also there were a black boy in a sailor suit and an old man pushing a wheelbarrow.

And lastly here is Jayne. Jayne has mostly very blonde hair and very wet, red lips and looks like one of the classy ladies who tend the perfume counter in swish stores. Jayne's speciality is bodily functions. The other day she warned us that too much exercise could stop menstruation. Thanks for the tip, Jayne. She also said that we were all 'dying to know' what the Queen has for breakfast and what sort of paper they have in royal loos. An expert called Ingrid said bacon and eggs and toast in answer to the first question, but I missed the second (Andrex with embossed coronets, perhaps?). 'Do the royals eat lavishly?' asked Jayne, and Ingrid said the Duke of Edinburgh used to like tripe but was now into health foods.

Well, folks, that's it for today. Back at the same time tomorrow. You have been watching the Mission to Explain Show.

THE RIGHT TO A GOOD DEATH

OFTEN A WRITER first becomes interested in a subject about which he knew next to nothing as the result of some personal experience. So it was with me and voluntary euthanasia, a topic which until a few years ago had never crossed my mind. Yet if it was my mother's senility that had first awakened me to the desirability of it, it is now my own declining years coupled with an awareness of how wretchedly some old people are permitted to die, that persuades me more than ever of the need for, and the right to, a good death. This is an extract, published in the Observer *of my Chatto and Windus* Counterblast *booklet,* Euthanasia: The Good Death.

When my mother was eighty she went to live in a private nursing home where I visited her regularly. She was not terminally ill in the sense of having cancer or some other fell disease, but her whole system had run down. Chronic arthritis and moments of giddiness kept her mostly in bed, and failing eyesight meant that she could no longer read or watch the television with any degree of enjoyment. In short, life had become a burden to her.

When she was eighty-three, and I asked her on one of my visits how she was, her answer surprised me: 'Oh, how I long to be gathered!' – the Scottish euphemism for death. On my subsequent visits, she repeated this wish, adding that she had had a wonderful life, but the time had now come for it to end. But there was no means of ending it, and she survived for another year in increasing discomfort before I received a telephone call in the middle of the night that her wish had at last been granted.

Whether my mother would have been ready to embrace voluntary euthanasia, had it been available, I cannot say. (Throughout this article the term 'voluntary euthanasia' is used to denote medical assistance in terminating life at the request of the patient and no other. Because deformed infants and those in a persistent vegetative state such as the advanced stages of Alzheimer's Disease are not in a position to volunteer anything, their cases have not been considered.) But what I learned from her was something I had not realized before, that while today's world supports plenty of sprightly ninety-year-olds, there are many other old people whose wish to die is no less strong than the wish of young people to live. Robert Louis Stevenson had the words to express it:

> It is not so much that death approaches as life withdraws and withers up from round about him. He has outlived his own usefulness and almost his own enjoyment; and if there is to be no recovery, if never again will he be young and strong and passionate . . . if in fact this be veritably nightfall, he will not wish for the continuance of a twilight that only strains and disappoints the eyes, but steadfastly await the perfect darkness.

Yet every year there are an increasing number of increasingly old and sick people for whom the twilight continues unbearably and whose steadfastness in awaiting the perfect darkness often falls short of what they would wish; for the prolongation of living which has been brought about by advances in medical science has also meant the prolongation of dying.

For millions of people whose span of life has been extended, its quality has been diminished. Some are in pain from cancer or have a wasting muscular disease; some are in acute discomfort from vomiting, diarrhoea, insomnia, bed sores, flatulence and general exhaustion, being fed by drips in the vein or tubes up the nose and into the stomach. The law at present does not allow doctors to grant them their pleas for merciful release. The compassion we show to sick animals by putting them out of their misery, we deny to our fellow human beings.

In the old days when most people died at home, the family doctor often felt no compunction in administering a lethal drug to help a dying patient on his or her way; but now that most people die in hospitals, doctors cannot do it without the knowledge of the nursing staff and thus, because it is a criminal offence, they endanger their professional careers.

The most we can expect of doctors at present is the exercise of what is called passive euthanasia, that is the withholding of some life-sustaining drug or giving sufficient analgesics to alleviate pain yet which can also shorten life; but the effect of opiates such as morphine and heroin is by no means certain, and death can take a dismayingly long time. In the old days too pneumonia often came to give a terminally ill patient a quiet and comparatively speedy death; but today, when pneumonia sets in it is quelled with antibiotics which will keep the patient's heart beating for a few more miserable weeks or months.

Nor is it only the patient who suffers. In hospitals there are paid staff to look after the terminally ill. But at home the job often falls on the wife or daughter or husband, having to feed and wash and nurse, often for months on end, a loved one who no longer wishes to live and whose relentless deterioration they can only helplessly watch.

There is another factor to be considered. Prolonged and painful dying, the gradual transformation of a much-loved parent or spouse or sibling from a familiar upright figure to that of a semi-corpse, can mean, when death finally comes, that they are not mourned. 'I had an excellent relationship with both my parents,' a woman wrote to me, 'but after watching the deterioration of their personalities and minds, caused by years of pain-killing and life-saving drugs, watching their suffering and coping with their irrational behaviour, I was glad when they died.' Sorting through their letters, she remembered how close they had once been and felt guilty about not mourning them. 'Parents should go when they are remembered as their true selves. Parents should be mourned. That is the healthy, natural way.'

In recent years there have been distressing tales of how terminally ill people, unable to obtain deliverance from their doctors, have brought it about themselves. One was the writer and philosopher Arthur Koestler who only a couple of years earlier had written the preface to the Voluntary Euthanasia Society's Guide to Self-Deliverance. In this he said:

Animals appear to give birth painlessly or with a minimum of discomfort. But owing to some quirk of evolution, the human foetus is too large for the birth canal, and its hazardous passage can entail protracted agony for the mother ... Hence we need midwives to aid us to be born.

A similar situation prevails at the exit gate. Animals in the wild, unless killed by a predator, seem to die peacefully and without fuss from old age ... I cannot remember a single description to the contrary by a naturalist, ethologist or explorer. The conclusion is inescapable: we need midwives to aid us to be un-born ... or at least the assurance that such aid is available. Euthanasia, like obstetrics, is the natural corrective to a biological handicap.

But the midwife for whom Koestler had pleaded was not at hand for him when his own time came. On 3 March 1983, suffering from Parkinson's disease and advanced leukaemia which he knew could only become worse, he took an overdose of barbiturates which he had hoarded over a period of time; and he left a note saying he wanted his friends to know he was leaving their company in a peaceful frame of mind.

Others have been less fortunate. The painter Rory McEwen, suffering from an inoperable brain tumour, threw himself under a train. Some have jumped from heights, shot or gassed themselves, and one young paraplegic, unable to contemplate further useless existence, set fire to himself fatally in the bungalow that had been specially equipped to house him.

These at least succeeded; but many more have failed. Here is what one correspondent recently wrote to me:

'I myself went through a harrowing experience with my beloved mother's final years. To see somebody you love suffering and daily getting worse is torture. She had very bad and very painful rheumatoid arthritis for several years before finally coming to live with us.

'The cortisone she was prescribed effectively destroyed her body, but death seemed as far off as ever. At last she said: "Tonight I'm going to do it, I'm going to cut my arteries in my room."

'I never felt more helpless, more grief-stricken. I lay in bed in the next room, while she tried to kill herself with a pair of scissors. The horror of that night thirty years ago will be with me for ever.

'In the morning she was still alive, though she had lost a lot of blood. We sent for the doctor and, thank God – well, no, I don't thank God – we managed to get him to give her a quick release. But all that tragedy was so unnecessary: she could so easily have been spared that final agony.

'This problem of the chronic sick and chronic pain-ridden is the greatest social evil of the day and it's getting worse as the population ages. I am nearly seventy now, so meet a lot of old people, and their views on euthanasia are almost unanimous. No-one wants to linger on, blind, crippled, in pain. All those in poor health want the option of deliverance, but lack the means, the know-how, the courage, to do it themselves.'

A famous couplet by the poet Arthur Clough says, 'Thou shalt not kill but needst not strive/Officiously to keep alive.' But officiously keeping alive patients who wish to be dead is common hospital practice. Dr Christiaan Barnard, who pioneered transplant heart surgery, is a fervent supporter of voluntary euthanasia. 'I have never practised it, but that is not something I am proud of; for, as a doctor, I have often seen the need for it.' He has however practised passive euthanasia, and on his own mother. 'After years of illness during which she often used to say, "Oh, why doesn't God take me?" she suffered a severe stroke. Her age was now ninety-five and she had suffered enough.'

> . . . at that stage she could not swallow, and the hospital doctors had decided to pass a tube through her nose into her stomach to force-feed her. She also had pneumonia and they were going to give her antibiotics for that. Can you imagine greater madness? I said to my brother that the doctors must not be allowed to do these things to our mother. And she died two days later.

In all the industrialized countries of the world stories like those can be multiplied almost indefinitely. Here is a letter from a fifty-six-year-old retired Metropolitan Police Sergeant:

I suffer from Buerger's Disease. I have had twelve general anaesthetic operations in University College Hospital ... I have had just one amputation, half of my left foot. I had gangrene in all four limbs so the medical profession said it would be safer not to work. In winter my limbs are ice. In summer I perspire buckets.

And now to plain talking. It is just a matter of time before another amputation is necessary due to the normal process of ageing. I will eventually become limbless. There is nothing the doctors can do. Therefore I shall just have to stay in a hospital bed suffering from the hellish pain of gangrene, waiting for another part of my body to be taken from me.

The inability of this man and others like him to be granted the deliverance they seek has also resulted in recent years in an increasing number of mercy-killings. In a less understanding age those who carried out mercy-killings were often sentenced to imprisonment, but now a more compassionate attitude prevails. Here are one or two cases out of many submitted to the Royal Commission on Criminal Procedure by the Voluntary Euthanasia Society:

A twenty-six-year-old gardener was tried for murder at Nottingham Crown Court. He had put weed-killer in his mother's drink, as she was incurably ill and begged him to do so. The judge said, 'No-one can have anything but sympathy for you,' and gave him an absolute discharge.

Mrs Eva Lyons of Wanstead was charged with the murder of her mother-in-law who had several times tried to commit suicide, and finally begged her daughter-in-law to end her life. Mrs Lyons pleaded guilty to manslaughter with diminished responsibility and was given two years probation.

Mr Walter Saunders of Liverpool was due to appear in court charged with the murder of his wife. She had been suffering from a slowly worsening brain disorder and Mr Saunders was totally devoted to her. He ended her life with an overdose of drugs. On the day he was due to stand trial, Mr Saunders committed suicide.

While we can be thankful that those who carry out mercy-killings rarely now have to endure imprisonment in addition to the other agonies they have been through, it seems dreadful, indeed shameful, that those they have helped to die were not permitted to call on professional help to enable them to do so.

In recent years the number of mercy-killings has, as you might expect, risen considerably, both here and in America, where of the 134 cases recorded since 1921 *no less than 70 per cent* took place between 1980 and 1985. In other words, the more that modern medicine has prolonged life, the more mercy-killings there have been. And parallel with these mercy-killings, parallel with the number of successful and attempted suicides, has been a growing recognition, all over the world, of the need for voluntary euthanasia.

In Britain a Mass Observation poll conducted in 1969 showed that 51 per cent of the population was in favour of it. Only seven years later an NOP poll showed that this had risen to 69 per cent and by 1985 to 72 per cent. Recent polls in France and Canada have shown figures of more than 80 per cent, while in 1988 on the BBC television programme *Reportage*, targetted at those aged between sixteen and twenty-six, 7,402 answered Yes and 692 No to the question: 'Should those who are terminally ill be allowed when to choose to die?' The British Voluntary Euthanasia Society, formed in 1935 with a handful of members, now has 10,000. In the United States membership of the Euthanasia Educational Council grew from 600 in 1969 to 300,000 in 1975. In several states bills to make euthanasia legal have been introduced but rejected. However, the concept of Living Wills (the early declaration by an adult that he or she does not wish to be kept artificially alive in certain circumstances) has been accepted by thirty-six state legislatures. In 1980 the World Right to Die Society was formed and now has thirty-one groups in eighteen countries; while in America, England, Scotland and Holland, manuals have been published on methods of committing suicide. No less interesting have been the changing views of British doctors. An NOP poll conducted in 1987 indicated that 35 per cent of doctors would be prepared to practise active euthanasia on request if it was made legal, and a further 10 per cent said they might possibly do so. Younger doctors were more in favour than older ones.

Yet, despite the progressive views of so many people, to the Churches suicide still remains a mortal sin, and in Britain until as late as 1961 it was also, unbelievably, a crime. Even today the Roman Catholic Church maintains an entrenched view on the matter, as was made clear in the Vatican's Declaration on Euthanasia of 1980. After declaring suicide to be as wrong as murder, the Pope went on:

> It is necessary to state firmly once more that nothing and no-one can in any way permit the killing of an innocent human being, whether . . . an old person or one suffering from an incurable disease or a person who is dying. Furthermore no-one is permitted to ask for this act of killing, either for himself or herself . . . nor can he or she consent to it, either explicitly or implicitly. For it is a question of the violation of the divine law, a crime against life and an attack on humanity.

This cruel pronouncement was then compounded by a statement of sheer ignorance:

> The pleas of gravely ill people who sometimes ask for death are not to be understood as implying a true desire for euthanasia; in fact it is almost always a case of an anguished plea for help and love.

One would like to hear the Pope repeat that to someone suffering from terminal cancer of the bowel, doubly incontinent and being fed through a tube in the nose. But the Pope is incorrigible; he even has a word of cheer about suffering:

> According to Christian teaching, suffering, especially suffering during the last moments of life, has a special place in God's saving plan; it is in fact a sharing in Christ's Passion and a union with the redeeming sacrifice which He offered in obedience to the Father's will.

I imagine that to most people today those views will be regarded as tosh and, what is more, pernicious tosh; for there will always be those wanting others to do their thinking for them. Indeed, in a 1987 NOP poll of general practitioners only 22 per cent of Roman Catholic doctors agreed with the concept of voluntary euthanasia while 66 per cent disagreed; a figure bound to have been reflected in the 54 per cent of all GPs who would be unwilling to practise voluntary euthanasia even if it were made legal.

Yet religious opponents to euthanasia and suicide must be an ever-diminishing band for, as Mary Rose Barrington says, 'people are ever more detached from dogmas and revelationary teachings about right and wrong'; ever more detached too from the concept of immortal life. In this connection it is interesting to note that a religious breakdown of the 1985 NOP poll showed that 89 per cent of atheists were in favour of euthanasia, 84 per cent of Jews, 75 per cent of Church of England, while of Roman Catholics, who might have been expected not to want to delay their passage to Elysium, only 54 per cent . . . a majority nevertheless.

Indeed, after the Roman Catholic Church, the greatest opposition to euthanasia comes from the medical profession and, in particular, the British Medical Association. In 1988 the BMA published a booklet setting out the reasons for their opposition and, choosing my words carefully, I have to say that it is one of the most prejudiced, irresponsible and cowardly documents to emanate from a professional body that I have ever read. But when you remember what a deeply reactionary institution the BMA has always been, for years setting its face against the introduction first of contraception and then of abortion, it is perhaps not all that surprising.

The reason the booklet is all I have said is that the profession refuses to recognize the consequence of its own technological progress, and while this has resulted in prolonged and satisfactory living for some, it has also led to prolonged and miserable dying for others. Grudgingly admitting that patients now have a right to have a voice in what is to be done to them, the authors query whether this right is absolute; and from there it is an easy step to assume the old paternalism, pretend that it is the doctors who are being asked to decide when euthanasia should be administered, when every pro-euthanasia group in the world insists that it is the patient and only the patient who shall be entitled to make that decision.

Like their fellow countrymen, the doctors of the Netherlands have a reputation for fierce independence, a quality which gained them much praise during the war when, despite threats and the withdrawal of their licences, they refused to play any part in the Nazi programme of sterilization and of medical experiments on Jews, gypsies and mental defectives; and it was this assertion of independence combined with great moral courage that resulted in a case that was to herald the advent of active euthanasia.

In October 1971 the mother of Dr Gertrude Postma, a general practitioner, was a patient in a nursing home where she had been severely ill for some time. She had had a cerebral haemorrhage, was partly paralysed, had difficulty in speaking and was deaf. She had tried and failed to commit suicide, and on several occasions had begged her daughter to bring her misery to an end.

For some time Dr Postma felt unable to comply, but one day when she went to the nursing home she found her mother propped up in a chair, tied to its arms to prevent her falling over. It was the last straw. 'When I saw my mother hanging in that chair, a human wreck,' she said, 'I couldn't stand it any more.' The next day she met her mother's wishes by injecting into her veins a lethal dose of morphine.

In due course, Dr Postma was indicted for mercy-killing, which then carried a maximum penalty of twelve years' imprisonment. Asked at her trial if her mother's suffering was unbearable, she replied candidly, 'No, it was not unbearable, though it was serious. But her mental suffering was unbearable.'

Asked if she had any regrets, she said, 'On the contrary, I am convinced I should have done it much earlier.' Instead of the prison term she might have expected, she was given a week's suspended sentence and a year's probation. Not only did this win the approval of the general public, but a number of fellow doctors wrote to the Minister of Justice to say they had done the same thing themselves.

This landmark case opened the way for the formation, in Dr Postma's village, of a Society for Voluntary Euthanasia, from which tiny beginnings it soon expanded to become what it still is today, the largest voluntary euthanasia society in Europe with a membership of 35,000.

Since its inception it has had two objects. First, to act as an information centre for those mostly elderly and often lonely people who, while not actively seeking euthanasia, want to know more about it; and second, to give guidance to those seeking euthanasia because of an incurable disease or infirmity. All members are advised to make Living Wills to indicate to the doctors that, should they ever deteriorate into a vegetative state where they can no longer make rational decisions, they do not wish to be kept artificially alive.

In 1976, the society began recruiting volunteers, mostly over fifty years of age, to act as counsellors to those expressing a wish to die. These counsellors (there are now some forty of them) visit the members concerned, assess the extent of their suffering and whether they think everything possible is still being done for them, what sort of family support they have, whether their wish for death is strongly held and entirely their own, and their relationship with their general practitioner.

Often the volunteers find that those who want death are reluctant to broach the subject with their doctors, either because they have grown fond of them over many years, or because they fear the doctor may be anti-euthanasia. In such cases the society, with the member's permission, tells the doctor what has been said to them, so that he may then approach the patient himself. This has proved very beneficial, as many doctors are themselves reluctant to discuss with their patients the question of their deaths.

Most applicants are cancer sufferers, some suffer from multiple sclerosis, rheumatism or emphysema, others simply feel they have lived long enough. If the applicant's own doctor is unwilling to help him or her in bringing on death, the society will endeavour to make contact with a doctor who is willing, provided there is sufficient time for the doctor to get to know and care for the patient.

In 1981, in response to the growing demand and practice of euthanasia by the medical profession, the Rotterdam criminal court set out guidelines for euthanasia which, if followed, would be unlikely to render the doctor concerned liable for prosecution:

1. There must be physical or mental suffering which the patient finds unbearable.

2. The wish to die must be sustained.

3. The decision to die must be the voluntary act, given in writing, of the patient.

4. The patient must have a clear understanding of his condition and of any other possibilities in the way of treatment open to him.

5. No other solution is acceptable to the patient.

6. The time and manner of death must not cause avoidable misery to the patient's family, who should be kept informed of the situation at all stages.

7. The decision to give aid in dying must not be that of one doctor alone. Another doctor, who has no professional or social relationship with the first, must be consulted and give his approval.

8. Only a fully-qualified doctor will prescribe the correct drugs and administer them.

9. The decision to give aid in dying and the actual administering of it must be done with the utmost care.

10. The patient need not be terminally ill (i.e. the decision could be that of a paraplegic).

*

557

Soon after the issuing of these rules, another case arose which was to further advance the cause of euthanasia. A ninety-four-year-old woman, a patient in a nursing home, in poor health for some time and who had repeatedly asked her doctor for euthanasia, fractured her hip in a fall. As a result she became totally bedridden, had to be catheterized and was wholly dependent on the nursing staff for washing and all bodily functions: in time her sight and hearing declined, she was unable to drink or take solid food and had difficulty in speaking; and once again, but even more urgently, she begged her doctor for release.

As she had signed a Living Will several years previously, the doctor consulted with another doctor and after a conference with him, the patient and the patient's son, he agreed to act. 'This doctor,' she told her son, 'deserves great respect.'

After she had said goodbye to her son and his wife, the two doctors entered her room and asked if her wish was still the same, to which she replied, 'Straightaway, doctor, if it is possible. Please, not another night.' Her doctor then gave her three injections, the first of barbiturates to send her to sleep, another of barbiturates to induce a coma, and the last of curare to bring about respiratory arrest.

Having written 'Unnatural death' on the death certificate, the doctor was brought to trial in the district of Alkmaar and acquitted. The public prosecutor however appealed against the verdict, submitting that what the doctor had done was a violation of Section 293 of the Dutch Criminal Code ('Any person who takes the life of another at his or her explicit request shall be sentenced to a term of imprisonment not exceeding twelve years'), and the Court of Appeal agreed.

The case then went to the Netherlands Supreme Court and their opinion was that the doctor was justified in what he did, in that he believed and his patient believed that there was no satisfactory alternative. In referring the case back to the Court of Appeal for reconsideration, the Supreme Court broke new ground in declaring that the primary judgement in cases of medical euthanasia should be the responsibility of the medical profession, and so should not be considered as a violation of the Criminal Code.

Since then voluntary euthanasia in Holland has become commonplace, although there are many doctors who refuse to practise it while it is still illegal. It is believed that between 2,000 and 5,000 patients are helped to die each year, but as many doctors, to spare grieving relatives from intrusive and distressing police questioning and the removal of the corpse for post-mortem, continue to write 'Natural causes' on the death certificate, no accurate figure can be given. Although in such cases there is no room for abuse in that the doctor has followed the rules laid down by the Rotterdam Court, the Royal Dutch Medical Association has instructed its members to comply with the legal requirements ('not filling in forms truthfully is unbefitting a physician') while making recommendations that in future questioning is less intrusive. This has already borne fruit with the result that many more cases of euthanasia are now being reported.

As of today, the whole euthanasia debate can be summed up as a conflict between two very powerful and conflicting emotions: on the one hand the fear that if voluntary euthanasia is legalized, it will in time slide imperceptibly into compulsory euthanasia, and we shall all be in danger of being snuffed out before our time; and on the other the fear that if euthanasia is not legalized, we may have to face a future of degraded senility, our last days passed wired to machines, unable to control our bodily functions, all love of living gone.

It seems to me that the first fear is an irrational one, being speculative and based on ignorance, but that the second fear is well-founded, being based on what we know is happening in every hospital and in many homes in the land.

Because of that I am of the opinion that whereas, say, twenty years ago the first fear would have had precedence in most people's minds, today it is increasingly the second.

When people heard I was writing this *Counterblast* pamphlet, they asked if I did not find the subject a gloomy one. Far from it. What I do find gloomy is the thought of the needless miseries now being endured by millions because societies have lacked the courage to seek to bring about a change in the law.

Yet it is not only the law that has to change, but our attitudes. What is needed is a totally new view of death, so that it is no longer a taboo subject, so that we are no longer afraid of it – of dying, yes, but not of death itself (though paradoxically this will be easier for those who have come to accept the idea of their own mortality). It is time we listened to the poets, Shelley's 'unacknowledged legislators', who for centuries have been urging us to treat death not as an enemy but as a friend. Here is Shakespeare echoing the Robert Louis Stevenson passage which I quoted at the beginning:

If I must die, I will encounter darkness as a bride,
And hug it in my arms.

Yes. And for those for whom the light is already draining from the sky, let it be sooner rather than later.

TRUTH WITHHELD

LIKE MANY TELEVISION presenters, I have often been called on to make after-dinner speeches, sometimes for a fee, sometimes because I have felt it an honour to have been asked. Among the latter was this one, given at the 1990 annual dinner of the Campaign for Freedom of Information.

It is a pleasure, Mr Chairman, to be once again sharing a platform with Des Wilson. He and I have shared many platforms in the past, though there have been times when I have been uncertain as to exactly what cause it was that we happened to be espousing. Yet this I can say, that it was always a good cause, and none better than the one that brings us here this evening; for as Daniel Webster once said, 'Knowledge is the fountain of all true liberty.'

When I look back today from the vantage point of three-score years and ten to the days before the war, I look back on a time in this country of lingering paternalism. Prime Ministers and other senior members of the government did not give interviews to journalists unless the journalist was the editor of *The Times*, and then only every now and then. The Royal Family remained inviolate behind the gates of whatever palace or castle they happened to be in, preserving that mystery and mystique which Walter Bagehot said was essential to their well-being: a view to which, half a century later, neither Fergie nor Princess Michael of Kent have felt much able to subscribe. York and Canterbury, the Governor of the Bank of England, the Chief of the Imperial General Staff, the Lord Chancellor and others of elevated office were equally inaccessible.

Forelock tugging was still very much in vogue, members of the Automobile Association being instructed to reprimand any AA patrolman who in his motor-bike and side-car failed to salute the AA sign on one's car radiator as he whizzed by. Depending on who you were, it was, as was said of an earlier period, the best of times and the worst of times.

Family life too was still somewhat authoritarian; and if the sons of upper-middle-class parents did not call their fathers 'Sir' as they did in Edwardian days, they still knew their place. But the seeds of rebellion against despotic parents and guardians were already stirring, as the writer Saki illustrated so well in his short stories about them: in particular 'Sredni Vashtar' where a much put-upon small boy persuades his pet ferret to gobble up his hated aunt; also in the story 'The Lumber Room' about another small boy:

The children were to be driven as a special treat to the sands at Jagborough. Nicholas was not to be of the party: he was in disgrace. Only that morning he had refused to eat his wholesome bread and milk on the seemingly frivolous ground that there was a frog in it. Older and wiser and better people had told him there could not possibly be a frog in his bread and milk, and he was not to talk nonsense; he continued nevertheless to talk what seemed the veriest nonsense, and described with much detail the coloration and markings of the alleged frog.

The dramatic part of the incident was that there really was a frog in Nicholas's basin of bread and milk: he had put it there himself, so he felt entitled to know something about it. The sin of taking a frog from the garden and putting it in a bowl of wholesome bread and milk was enlarged on at great length, but the fact that stood out clearest in the whole affair, as it presented itself to the mind of Nicholas, was that older, wiser and better people had proved profoundly to be in error on matters about which they had expressed the utmost assurance.

But that was perhaps an exception, and it wasn't until after the war that the old order, which for so long had kept us in our proper stations, began to crumble. And there were, you may agree with me, two principal reasons for it. The first was the gradual rise in the general standard of living so that for a time anyway, the rich became less rich and the poor less poor, and there was a boom in the sale of fridges and washing machines and spin dryers, a first car for some households and a second for others.

And the other influential factor was of course television which has been, I think, the greatest leveller of our time. Of course this didn't happen overnight. I remember the appearance of Sir Anthony Eden, then Foreign Secretary, in what must have been his first filmed interview. The opening exchange went something like this:

Interviewer: 'So good of you to spare the time, Sir Anthony, and I wonder if I might put to you one or two questions about foreign policy.'
Sir Anthony: 'By all means, but first let me say how delighted I am to be here.'

Robin Day and others helped us to move away from that, so that today there is almost no public figure who does not feel obliged from time to time to appear on the box to give an often unconvincing account of what it is that he or she has been up to. Indeed you may think that some public figures, especially in the field of politics, are now rather overdoing it. And the levelling process has extended also to television's presenters and interviewers. Gone are the plummy, avuncular tones of Grisewood and Snagge, Philips and Hibberd, and in have come a whole variety of national, regional and ethnic voices from Jimmy Young to Trevor MacDonald, from Derek Jameson (whom God preserve) to Gloria Hunniford.

Yet despite the levelling, it cannot be denied that in recent years, and under this present government, there has been a marked backsliding, a return to the old outworn paternalistic attitudes. Deep in many of our fellow countrymen there is, I believe, a masochistic streak which yearns for domination by both male and female. In what other mainline railway stations in the world will you find in the public telephone booths little cards giving telephone numbers and saying things like 'Ring Miss Whiplash for Corrective Training' and 'Strict governess to satisfy all your needs'. Nor do I think it entirely accidental that we have in Mrs Thatcher the Prime Minister we do have, have had for the past ten years and look like continuing to have until the end of time.[1] For those who crave domination, who feel all the safer for a strict Nanny figure in their lives, she is, as it were, tailor-made. And such a figure is not and by its nature cannot be an egalitarian one, nor one that is prepared to reveal its own humanity, at least publicly. It must by its nature be the opposite, its slogan must be Nanny knows best, and Nanny will not share with you things she feels you have no need to know. Hence, instead of a Freedom of Information Act, we have a new Official Secrets Act, with no defence allowed for public interest and, despite the farce of the Spycatcher Affair, no defence of prior publication.

We have all had our own experience of being denied access to information that could harm nobody, Mr Chairman, so let me add mine to the growing pile. The most ludicrous I can recall was when I came to write a book about the trial of Stephen Ward. I had attended every day of the trial, and indeed must be one of the very few people still alive to have actually seen and heard Miss Mandy Rice-Davies utter the words she immortalized, 'Well, he would, wouldn't he?' on being informed that Lord Astor had denied that he had been to bed with her. After the trial I wrote to the Registrar of the Central Criminal Court to ask for a copy of the trial transcript. He told me it would cost £300. I said I would pay it. He then wrote to say I couldn't have it. I asked why, as all I was asking for was confirmation of what I had already heard in open court; and I added that other authors had been permitted to buy transcripts of other trials. He said no reasons had to be given. Finally I asked who had made this momentous decision and he said the Lord Chief Justice, Lord Parker. I imagine that Lord Parker feared that I was going to write a book about yet another miscarriage of justice which, with my notes and the help of the Press Association transcript, I duly did.

[1] Mercifully not.

On the same tack I was asked the other day to write a foreword to a book[1] which is coming out later this year on the Craig–Bentley Croydon rooftop murder, and where the author believes that the execution of the nineteen-year-old Bentley was not only a denial of natural justice but a miscarriage of justice on the facts too. He made application, as any self-respecting historical writer would, to be given sight of the official papers on the case, now nearly forty years old. He was told that they would not be available for public scrutiny until the year 2047 by which time he would be ninety-eight.

I came across the same problem recently when asked to write a foreword to another book, this one on the search on the seabed of the German battleship *Bismarck* whose sinking I witnessed some forty-nine years ago. When I wrote my own book on the *Bismarck* in 1973 I had no difficulty in obtaining from the Admiralty the report of the interrogation of survivors which showed that the crew had hastened the ship's end by scuttling her – an assertion hotly disputed by certain patriotic gentlemen in the correspondence columns of the *Daily Telegraph* not so long ago. But since 1973 some Nanny figure has been at work, for when I applied for another look at the report, I was told it was under wraps for seventy-five years. In the end I was allowed to see it, having explained that my own copy was with all my other *Bismarck* papers in the archives of a public library. But why was the report under wraps for seventy-five years? The survivors were not beaten or tortured, nothing had been done to them of which we could be ashamed. This was a good example of what I can only call mindless secrecy, first cousin of mindless violence, secrecy for secrecy's sake. There can surely be no justification for withholding information on any matter which is not inimical to the country's defences or the prevention of crime.

Allow me, Sir, to congratulate you and your colleagues on your campaign to promote an all-party bill in the House of Commons for patients' access to their medical records, if for no other reason than to prevent some patients' records being wrongly filed with those of other patients, with dire results.

[1] *Let him have it Chris* by M.J.Trow (Constable 1990).

You report one woman being described on her notes as having emotional problems since the death of her husband, who was in fact very much alive, and a man described as having a drink problem who was a teetotaller. 'You must face up to your problem,' his doctor solemnly told him. Access would also stop doctors writing witty derogatory remarks on patients' records, such as 'This man is a crashing bore', though I suppose it could be said that if he knew he was thought to be a bore, he might make an effort to stop being one.

But at least in the medical profession the old paternalism which we all experience and which Richard Gordon used to write about in his various doctor books is now fading fast, especially among the younger doctors. They all accept that every patient has the right to know about the state of his body and to have some say in what is to be done about it. Furthermore, if you are told the truth, whatever it may be, you can adjust to it. One doctor told me recently how important he thought it to tell a patient what his prospects were and how wrong it was of some doctors, as they did in the old days, to tell the relatives but not the patient, so that the patient, deprived of the truth, imagined and fretted over the worst. 'There is all the difference in the world,' he said to me, 'between the attitude of the patient who knows and can adjust to the fact that he may have only a year or less to live, and one who has been kept in the dark.'

All around us, Mr Chairman, we see under this government an erosion of hard-won liberties: the 1986 Public Order Act which puts unnecessary restrictions on public assemblies and demonstrations; the 1988 Education Bill which squeezes university financings and threatens academic freedoms; the undignified attacks on Church leaders for speaking their minds; a whole series of attacks by Norman Tebbit and other undesirables on the integrity of those in broadcasting; the forbidding of interviews on television with Sinn Fein leaders with whom, since there can be no military solution, we shall have to talk one day; and the appointment of Lord Rees-Mogg, the man who banned the *Real Lives* programme, as television's first censor-in-chief, to tell us what in his view would and would not be wholesome viewing.

As Professor Hugo Stephenson of the City University has pointed out, no other country in Western Europe has put such clamps on its citizens' liberties, especially as regards freedom of the press. In those countries, he says, 'Their written constitutions, their press laws and their courts are attuned to the idea that freedom of the press, warts and all, is more important to a healthy society than the preservation of state and commercial secrecy. We have no constitution and no positive press law, and the courts take the opposite view.' And he concludes with this sombre thought: 'Unless British journalists, editors and proprietors rapidly develop a strategy to contest this galloping erosion of press freedom, the game is up.' So, my dear Des, continue in the great work that you and your colleagues are doing. Be like Nicholas in Saki's story, continue to talk what looks to older, wiser, better people like the veriest nonsense, and show that the older, wiser, and better people are often profoundly in error on matters about which they have expressed the utmost assurance.

One last thought. When we talk about the suppression of information, what I think we really have in mind is the suppression of truth. In public affairs as in private ones, unless we can know what the truth of any matter is, then we cannot come to grips with it, it slips like quicksilver through our grasp. One of the reasons I am so against our lousy system of criminal justice is that it is not aimed, as the courts on the continent are, at seeking the truth, and because of that it often hides it; because of that, evidence which should be admitted is often disallowed; because of that, corrupt policemen can secure the conviction of the innocent and skilled counsel the acquittal of the guilty.

So let me conclude with three truths about truth by three English poets. The first is by Cowper. '*He is the freeman whom the truth makes free.*' The second is by Shakespeare. '*O while you live, tell truth and shame the devil*' which, nicely framed, could I think be hung with advantage over the beds of Margaret Thatcher and Bernard Ingham.[1] And lastly the concluding lines of Keats's 'Ode on a Grecian Urn':

[1] Her press secretary.

When old age shall this generation waste,
Thou shalt remain in midst of other woe
Than ours, a friend to man to whom thou sayest,
'Beauty is truth, Truth beauty – that is all
Ye know on earth and all ye need to know'.

SCOTTISH INTERLUDE I:

HOME THOUGHTS FROM ABROAD

THERE IS MUCH windy talk nowadays, a legacy of the little Englander Margaret Thatcher and her long regime, of Britain being 'great' again. It is not a view I have ever been able to subscribe to, and it is in fact uniquely held by English people who think that Britain and England are synonymous. 'Britain' is a soggy word, traditionally and wisely ignored by poets, admirals and lyricists alike. 'O, to be in Britain now that April's here', 'Britain expects that every man will do his duty', 'There'll always be a Britain' are hardly inspirational. But 'England' 'Scotland' and 'Wales' are all words that can stir the blood, create feelings of pride and love for those who belong to them. Ever since visiting Culloden battlefield as a child and being told by my mother that our family was Scots not English, I have cherished a love of that rugged country and its once proud people that I have never been able to give to anywhere or anyone else; and this from the London Evening Standard *attests to that affection. It was written the week after Jim Sillars' stunning 1988 victory for the SNP in the Govan by-election.*

The English, who mostly think of Scotland as an appendage to England, do not know what to make of Scottish national-ism. Nor, come to that, do the Scots. From time to time, as at Govan last week, it bobs to the surface like some long-submerged submarine, then disappears as quickly. For how long is it destined to stay afloat this time?

If past performance is anything to go by, not long. The last renaissance took place twenty-two years ago when Winnie Ewing stood for the SNP at the Hamilton by-election. I spoke for her there because as a Scot it seemed to me that Scotland deserved at least as much autonomy as that being currently dished out to the Cook Islands, the Faeroe Islands, and the Cameroons. Winnie won.

Within a few years, the SNP had gained eleven seats in Parliament, Edinburgh's old Royal High School was converted into a Scottish Assembly Hall, and it seemed that Home Rule was on its way.

Then came the Scottish national referendum, and while there was a clear majority for Home Rule, it was less than the 40 per cent that Parliament had decreed. In the light of it you might have expected protests, marches in the streets, riots, even as in that other Celtic country across the water.

Instead a great sigh of relief could be heard all over Scotland: we had reached the brink but pulled back just in time. Support for the SNP fell off as rapidly as it had mounted, and soon their parliamentary strength was reduced to two.

And it stayed like that for years. In 1984 BBC Television mounted a St Andrew's Day debate in Edinburgh on the motion that devolution was dead. Given the choice of speaking for or against, I chose for, because it seemed to me beyond argument then that devolution *was* dead. But I could lament it.

'Stands Scotland where it did?' I said quoting *Macbeth*, 'Alas, poor country, almost afraid to know itself,' and concluded by asking the House to accept that we had become a nation of political eunuchs, which it duly did.

It is strange when you come to think of it, but Scots have always had a deep sense of inferiority in their relations with the English.

Strange because of what they have achieved: writers of the calibre of Burns and Scott and Stevenson; architects like the Adam brothers; philosophers like Hume and Adam Smith; inventors like Stevenson and Bell, Dunlop and Macadam, Baird, and Fleming; great financiers, administrators, merchants; engineers and teachers and sea captains who, like the Jews, have helped to people the world.

But with the English, they have tended to be on the defensive, a defensiveness exemplified by the jingle, 'Here's tae us/Wha's like us?/Damn few/All deid', with its blend of bravado, and self-pity. It stemmed originally from the Act of Union in 1707, which was intended to be a marriage of equals but in fact was the absorption of a poorer country by a richer.

And the favour the English believed they had granted Scotland by the union received a rude shock when in 1745 an army of rampaging, rebellious Scots came to within 100 miles of overthrowing the government in London.

From this time on, and despite the burgeoning culture of eighteenth-century Edinburgh, the English regarded the Scots as a race of barbarians who wore outlandish clothes, lived in a vile climate, ate strange food and spoke an incomprehensible tongue. (It is an attitude that has not entirely disappeared today.)

Scots who came south were often vilified. When Boswell attended a London theatre at which fellow Scots were present, he was shocked when the audience turned on them with cries of 'Out, Scots, out!'

Such insults the Scots accepted because they needed the English more than the English needed them: the union meant jobs in the south, and in the expanding empire, and improved outlets for trade.

Recognizing, as the historian Smout says, that beside the English they felt themselves to be 'backward, boorish and uncouth', they hired English tutors to come north and teach them couthy manners, how to drink tea, and speak so as to be understood.

And so a type of Scot grew up who still exists today: the genteel, bourgeois Scot typified by Glasgow's Kelvinside and Edinburgh's Morningside, whose table talk in unfamiliar company is inhibited for fear of saying the wrong thing, who takes things English as his model.

One example of this attitude used to be seen in the leadership of the Scottish Rugby Union, which, until recently at Murrayfield, made the band play the British national anthem for the Scottish team, rather than 'Scotland the Brave' or 'Flower of Scotland', despite every other team in the Five Nations tournament having its own tune.

They thought that 'Scotland the Brave' would offend the Queen. In fact the relevant national anthem, with its line about crushing rebellious Scots, greatly offended Scottish spectators who booed and whistled during the playing of it until a changeover to 'Flower of Scotland' was made.

If these sorts of Scots are now on the wane, as I believe, the political allegiance they hold – that of union with England – is, among thousands of their compatriots, still widely held, particularly by professional and business people who view the SNP's extreme left-wing policies with some alarm.

Despite this, Jim Sillars' carrot of an independent Scotland operating within the EEC, along with other small countries like Greece and Denmark, may well have supporters: disillusioned Labour voters who have come to recognize and resent the impotence of their forty-nine MPs, middle of the roaders like myself who have long shared Compton MacKenzie's dream of people loving their countrymen through loving their country and, by recreating themselves, recreating their nation.

As a Scot I would dearly like to see it come about. As a writer I doubt whether we could ever bring ourselves to cut the umbilical cord.

SCOTTISH INTERLUDE II:

THE SIR WALTER SCOTT CLUB DINNER

THE ANNUAL SIR Walter Scott dinner in Edinburgh is an event of some social importance, the invitations (at least in my day) demanding a white tie. The President, who is elected for one year, takes the chair at the dinner and calls on the other speakers to make the toasts to the judiciary, the Armed Forces, etc., to which a judge of the Court of Session and the Officer Commanding the Army, Navy or Air Force in Scotland usually respond. When I was President, I used the occasion to say a few things about Scotland that had been simmering in my mind for some time.

Some of you may have been wondering, as indeed I did when I first heard it, why I should have been graced with the honour of presiding over you this evening. My immediate predecessors have all, I think, had more obvious claims on your attention. Lord Polwarth, who took the chair last year, is the head of Sir Walter's branch of the Scott family, and you will all remember how affectingly he spoke of him. Sir Alec Douglas-Home, the year before, had much in common with Scott, notably possession of a most desirable gentleman's Tweedside residence as well as paid-up membership of the local Conservative Party. Lord Cameron, who preceded him, is a distinguished member of that profession to which Scott himself brought such credit. Professor David Daiches, who lives in England, is a leading literary authority on Scott, and must not be confused with his brother, Mr Lionel Daiches, who lives and works in Scotland. And then of course there was Mr Malcolm Muggeridge, one of the last lay minstrels of our time.

Now, ladies and gentlemen, I do not have those sort of

claims, but I do have a few, and with your permission I will put them before you. Like Sir Walter, I was born in this noble city, in the house in Belgrave Crescent of my grandfather, Sir Ludovic Grant, for many years Professor of International Law at Edinburgh University and also sometime Captain of the Royal and Ancient Golf Club. He and I were great friends. When he was seventy and I ten, we used to play golf together level, and it was always a toss-up who'd win; and many a canty tram ride we'd have together, down to the Leith docks and back, or round the Marchmont Circle. But the reason I mention his name tonight is that just sixty-three years ago this week, he presided over the annual dinner of the Edinburgh Sir Walter Scott Club, just as I am doing now. I understand from the secretary that this constitutes some kind of record, and I hope you won't mind my adding that it gives me particular pleasure that a living link with my grandfather in the person of his only daughter, and my only mother, should be with us tonight.

Now, ladies and gentlemen, if you think that brief reference to my family history is all you are going to hear on the subject, you are in for a rude shock. Prepare for further gems in what Queen Caroline in *Heart of Midlothian* called 'the terrible chapter of Scottish genealogy'. In the dining-room of my house in the Borders are portraits of two forebears. One is of Professor John Wilson of Edinburgh University, alias Christopher North, a frequent contributor to Blackwood's Magazine, author of *Noctes Ambrosianae* and a great friend of Scott. The other is of his brother-in-law, John Ferrier, WS, married to Christopher North's sister, Margaret, and whose own sister, the novelist Susan Ferrier, was also a friend of Scott. Christopher North was a rumbustious sort of character, and I am indebted to his friend William Maguire for this description of him: 'A sixteen stoner, a cocker, a racer, a six-bottler, a twenty-four tumblerer, an out and outer, a true, upright, knocking-down, poetical, prosaic, moral, professorial, hard-drinking, fierce-eating, good-looking, honourable and straightforward Tory.' It might be Mr Quintin Hogg himself.

A little while ago, keen to know the precise relationship between Christopher North and myself, I consulted

Sir Ludovic's sister, great aunt Susan, now alas no longer with us – she died last year at the age of ninety-four – but until then she was the recognized family authority on all matters genealogical. Well, she did a great job. She produced a family tree – I think bush would be a more accurate description – which not only clearly showed that I was Christopher North's great-great-great grandson, but equally clearly showed that I was the fifteen times great grandson of James II of Scotland. Well, friends, it's not every day we learn we are of the Blood Royal, so happening soon after this to find myself at dinner next to the Albany Herald, Sir Iain Moncrieffe of that ilk, an even hotter authority on genealogy than great aunt Susan, I asked for his comments on this somewhat surprising piece of news. It was, he confirmed, most probably true, but, he added, it was a privilege, if indeed I cared to call it a privilege, which I shared with several thousand – I'm not sure if he didn't say million – other Scots.

So much for past links with Scott. Coming to the present, my house in the Borders lies under the lee of Smailholm Tower and the farm at Sandyknowe where his grandparents lived, and where he was sent as a small boy to be cured, as it was hoped, of the infantile paralysis from which he ever afterwards suffered. It's a curious place, set on a high ridge, rocks and green turf intermingled, the tower at the top rising a hundred feet sheer into the sky, a little lochan below it, and below that the farmhouse nestling snugly into the side of the hill, and then this incredible view across the wide valley to the Cheviots and England. To understand Scott at all, I think one must go there, for this for him was the genesis of it all, the place where his poetic imagination was first fired. In the introductory epistle to the third canto of *Marmion*, he writes of '*those crags, that mountain tower/Which charmed my fancy's wakening hour*'. The tower – still wonderfully preserved – fascinated him. In his mind's eye he saw the garrison shut up there with their cattle during a long siege, waiting for the English to go away, then at last venturing out. '*Forayers*', he wrote, '*who with headlong force,*

Down from that strength had spurred their horse
Their southern rapine to renew,
Far in the distant Cheviot's blue.
And home returning filled the hall,
With revel, wassel-rout and brawl'.

There, in six lines, is the essence of Scott. All through his life he was deeply conscious of the debt he owed Sandyknowe, not only poetically but physically too, for there, despite his withered leg, he learned to walk and run in a way that he felt would have been impossible in Edinburgh; and every year he made a pilgrimage from Abbotsford, and once more climbed the hill and looked at the tower and across the valley to England whose king had become his friend, and remembered with a grateful heart where it had all started. One other small thing about the young Scott's visits to Sandyknowe should be noted. It was here that he first showed signs of that loquacity which, when transformed into poetry and prose in later life, made him both rich and famous. Dr Duncan, the Smailholm minister, sometimes visited Scott's grandparents at the farm for a quiet chat. But Scott, spouting Border ballads all over the house, made talk difficult. 'One might as well speak in the mouth of a cannon', commented Dr Duncan, 'as where that boy is.'

Let me now clear up two misconceptions about Scott which seem to follow him wherever he goes. The first, which has even been perpetuated by past presidents of this club who ought to know better, is that his works, which once excited universal acclaim, now lie on the shelves forotten, that the Great Unknown has become the Great Unread. Now it is perfectly true that no nineteenth-century author has the same wide public as he used to have. That age had a leisure which is denied to us: we have other stimuli besides books – the radio, the cinema and the telly, all bombarding us for attention. *No* nineteenth-century author is read as he was, but to single out Scott as the one who is not read at all is a travesty of the truth. In the London Library these last ten years the borrowings of Scott have only been fractionally less than those of Dickens; Trollope, as a matter of interest, beats them both. In Edinburgh City Library Dickens is top of the pops, Trollope and Thackeray are equal second, and Scott is a close fourth. Incidentally there are nine copies of *Heart of Midlothian* in Edinburgh City Library, and at the time I made my enquiry, all were out: Mr Minto, the librarian, estimates that there are between 180 and 200 borrowings of this book each year.

On a slightly different front, the 1969 Annual Register of Scottish Studies tells us that at this moment studies on various aspects of Scott's work are in course of preparation at no less than nineteen universities throughout the world, among them St Andrews and Stirling, Heidelberg and Los Angeles, Belfast and Illinois, Bergen and New Brunswick. My neighbour, Dr James Corson, of Lilliesleaf, who I imagine knows more about Scott than anyone alive, tells me that he receives between two and three hundred letters a year on various enquiries about Scott. These sort of statistics, I think you'll agree, hardly indicate an author whose works are forgotten, whose novels are unread.

And the other great misconception about Scott, especially south of the border, where they get so muddled about so many things, is that Scott was a gloomy sort of man who lived in a gloomy, Gothic house, writing gloomy, Gothic novels. I hardly have to remind you how far that is from the truth. He had a tremendous zest for life, whether riding over the border hills, spearing salmon in the Tweed by torchlight, buttonholing all manner of people, entertaining constantly old friends and sometimes total strangers, eating a sheep's head for breakfast, drinking claret – when he removed from Castle Street, you remember, 360 dozen of claret went with him – collecting mementoes of the past, doing a full day's work at the Court of Session, and with all this managing to write one and often two books a year. 'People have said to me, "Do only one thing at a time",' he said, 'and all my life I've done a dozen.'

I often think you can judge a man by what amuses him, and both Scott's work and life are shot through with humour. The dialogue of characters like old Mause and Alison Wilson in *Old Mortality* are as richly comic as anything in Dickens. And what splendid earthy stories he used to enjoy. One of his favourites concerned an old lady living in Carlisle in 1745 when the Highlanders were approaching the city. Hearing reports of their savage ways with women, she retired to her bedroom and bolted the door. Several hours later, nothing having happened – the Highlanders, I think, were in the pubs – she leaned out of the window and said to a passer-by, 'Pray, sir, when does the ravishing begin?' Another story he liked was about a farmer who asked the minister to put up the banns for a second marriage only a month after his first wife had died. 'It's no possible, John,' said the minister, deeply shocked, 'why, your wife's *no cauld* in her grave.' To which the farmer replied, 'Aweel, sir, never heed ye that. Put up the banns and she'll be aye cooling the while.' He once likened the fatuity of a certain Scottish politician to a man in a sinking ship who relieves himself over the side in order to lighten the load – we can all think of one or two Scottish politicians like that today, can we not? But of all his stories I like best the one of the only meeting between Adam Smith, the economist, and Dr Johnson. The doctor's religious beliefs, it seems, had been gravely offended by Adam Smith's account of the death of David Hume, where he wrote that Hume had died without any belief in a god or afterlife, yet with perfect composure. Adam Smith confirmed that this is what had happened, which drew from the outraged doctor the rejoinder, 'Sir, you lie.' 'And what did you say to that?' Smith was asked. 'I said,' said Smith, 'And you are the son of a bitch.' 'On such terms,' wrote Scott, 'did these two great moralists meet and part, and such was the classic dialogue between them.'

Scott could also laugh at himself. He was, he tells us, incredibly absent-minded. He once corrected a set of proofs of a book he'd been writing, and a little later, finding a second set, corrected that too. His publisher took the best of both. He was always losing things. He lost the manuscript of *Waverley* for several years and then found it looking for some fishing-tackle. He had no sense of smell and not much of sounds. 'He could not tell,' says one biographer, 'when venison was high, when wine was corked, whether sherry was madeira, whether music was noise or the other way about.' He admitted overtipping waiters in order to make them smile and look genial – a tip I happily pass on to all those of you who haven't yet settled your wine bills.

But all this is Scott of the past, and what I think we should be concerned with this evening is what, if anything, he still has to say to us today. Is he no more than a ghost flitting about the crags of Sandyknowe, the library at Abbotsford, the streets of Edinburgh, a great entertainer who once breathed life into the chronicles of his country's past, and now sits down there in Princes Street, a fossilized passenger in a frozen space-rocket, waiting for a countdown that will never come?

I think he *has* got something to say to us, and let me say what I think it is. We are living today in a time of profound change, not only in the world at large but in these islands as well. This old country of ours – and standing as I am within a stone's throw of the Heart of Midlothian, I do not have to explain what country I mean – this old country is beginning to waken again after a long sleep, to flex its muscles, to question its identity, to seek for itself a new purpose and sense of direction, to rediscover that organic unity without which, Edwin Muir says in his brilliant essay on Scott, no nation can live.

Now what is it, ladies and gentlemen, that makes a nation, that makes it unique and different to other nations? Three things, I think. Language, culture, history. We all of us now in these islands speak (more or less) the same language, but in history and culture we are different. The history of England is an admirable history, but it is not the history of Scotland. There, out of those windows, lies Scotland's history: Malcolm Canmore at the castle, Mary at Holyrood, Prince Charles Edward marching to Prestonpans, John Knox in St Giles, Montrose and Argyll on their execution carts, Captain Porteous, Major Weir and a thousand others. And all round us lies evidence of our culture too: the Adam Brothers at Register House, Burns at Adam Fergussons, Raeburn at Stockbridge, Stevenson and Scott everywhere. To Scott indeed we owe a double debt, both of culture and history. For in the *content* of what he wrote he explained to his fellow countrymen, and the world, what Scotland's history had been; and in *the way* he did it, in his descriptions of events and characters, he became one of the world's acknowledged story-tellers. 'I can think of no other instance in history', said Sir Robert Horne at the centenary celebrations at Galashiels, 'in which one man has become the personification of his country.'

And even that was not all. In life, as in art, Scott strove mightily for Scotland. In his journal he wrote of the efforts he had made to preserve the peculiar features of the manners and characters of Scotland, which, he said, 'are daily dissolving into those of her sister and ally'. It is to him and his friend and patron George IV that we owe the return to the castle from London of the famous cannon Mons Meg. It is to them again that we owe the restoration of the Scottish peerages, forfeited after the Forty-Five. It is Scott we have to thank for the survival of the one-pound note Scots which the British Parliament were about to abolish. And, perhaps his greatest contribution of all was to rediscover in a locked box in the castle the ancient regalia of Scotland, the crown and sceptre and sword of State with which the kings of Scotland had once been crowned, and which had last been used 160 years earlier at the coronation of Charles II at Scone. Today the sovereign of the United Kingdom is crowned in Westminster by an English Archbishop in an English coronation service ordered by the English Earl Marshal whose authority, like that of the Archbishop, stops at the Scottish border. Am I alone in this room, I wonder, in hoping that at the next accession there may also be a coronation in Scotland, that the regalia of Scotland be bestowed on the person of the sovereign by the Ministers of the Church of Scotland, according to the usage of the Scottish coronation service, long ratified by Scottish law?

Ladies and gentlemen, the world today faces many problems, problems of race and religion and population and territory. But one of the greatest problems it faces, I suggest to you, is the problem of reconciling the big unit with the small, nationalism with internationalism, centralization with devolution. Every day the world diminishes before our very eyes, every day it gets nearer to what Marshall McLuhan, in a celebrated phrase, called a global village. When the crew of Apollo 8 were approaching the moon, they were simultaneously seen and heard by over a billion people. More and more big businesses are swallowing up more and more little ones, so that soon all our earthly needs will be catered for exclusively by just a few vast international combines. Already sinks in Mallaig and Melbourne, Marseilles and Madras are being cleaned with the same brand of detergent. Armies on either side of the Iron Curtain have standardized their weapons. Travel the world and you can plug in your electric razor almost anywhere. Audiences in Bournemouth and Bangkok gape at the same internationally tailored films, and in a hundred developed and underdeveloped countries James Bond has become the folk-hero of our times. We are entering the age of common culture, where uniformity is all.

Now uniformity has many desirable economic advantages. But it has one great drawback and that is this. Human beings are conservative by nature and have not yet learnt to give their love and loyalty to anything much bigger than the patch of earth on which they were born, and to the friends and neighbours with whom they share it – what Shakespeare called 'a local habitation and a name'. And therefore the *bigger* the unit *becomes*, the more *remote* that political power *gets*, the more *standardized* the common culture *is*, the greater will be the revolt against them, and the more will each man and each country proclaim their own uniqueness. This is what is happening in Scotland today, but it is happening in many other places in the world as well.

In this peculiar dilemma Scott has something to tell us too. Not so much Scott the patriot, to whom we owe so much of our history and culture, but Scott the philosopher, the liberator, the reconciler. He was, says John Buchan, Scotland's *great* reconciler. In his works he reconciled opposites, rich and poor, good and evil, young and old, the valiant and the faint heart, as all great artists must. And in his life he did the same. He was both a romantic and a realist, a Jacobite who was a Hanoverian, a man who dealt openly and in secret, a famous writer who wished he'd been a man of action. By the greatness of his heart and his love of humanity he succeeded in integrating not only the contradictions and conflicts in himself, but those in the world outside. More than any other contemporary he helped to heal the differences between the warring factions of his time, first Highlander and Lowlander, then English and Scot.

My friends, in the coming months and years we are each of us going to have to face the contradictions and conflicts of our own time, the conflicts of bigness and smallness, of individuality and anonymity, of the common and uncommon culture, and we are going to have to do our best, both privately and publicly, to resolve them. It will not, I think, be easy. Yet, even if few of us have Scott's own genius for reconciliation, we all have his example to guide us. For that reason, let us now stand and drink together to his immortal name.

When I sat down the wife of the secretary of the club leaned over to complain about the Kennedy tartan smoking jacket I was wearing in preference to white tie which I last wore in 1939 and consider to be an invention of the Devil. 'I enjoyed your peroration', she boomed, 'as much as I deplore your jacket.' Only an Edinburghian could put it quite like that.

582

SCOTTISH INTERLUDE III: THE ROBERT LOUIS STEVENSON CLUB LUNCH

I hate the bustling citizen,
The eager and hurrying man of affairs I hate,
Because he bears his intolerance writ on his face,
And every movement and word of him tells me how
  much he hates me.

There is, I feel sure you will agree, a certain irony in the fact that the descendants of those respectable Edinburgh folk who were such a thorn in RLS's flesh when he lived among them should have gathered here to honour him today. Like many of you I was partly brought up in this east windy, west endy, smoky city on a diet of both Scott and Stevenson, and I was as clear in my mind then as I am now that while one was the man to admire, the other was the one to love. And it will always be a matter of pride to me that the first literary prize I ever won was for a holiday task essay on *The Black Arrow*.

My mother read to me from an early age, as I daresay your mothers read to you and you in turn have read to your children and perhaps grandchildren, *A Child's Garden of Verses*. And as I sat in the library of my grandfather's house in Belgrave Crescent, as I often did on winter evenings, the lamplighter would come down the street with his long pole to light the lamps. And I knew something about him that I didn't think my grandfather or grandmother knew. I knew his name was Leerie.

As a writer myself I have always felt that if I had been given the gift of writing fiction, I would not only have liked to write like RLS, but to have looked like him too. With his high forehead, big eyes, droopy moustache, long, sensitive face and even longer body, we would, if suddenly he was to walk through that door there, with or without the famous velveteen jacket, recognize him in an instant. And what are the characteristics of his writings that set him apart from other writers and which we all so admire? First, I think, the sheer gusto of his prose, the love of life, of people and places, that make one feel that he enjoyed setting the words down as much as we enjoy reading them. And combined with that an acute vividness of description, so that the words not only delight the ear by their sound but leap out at one from the page and in just a few sentences manage to convey a whole atmosphere, whether it be the docks at Bristol, the streets of London, the hills of France or the Forth at Queensferry. In only a few sentences he could bring some passing stranger memorably to life. In a waiting room in Pittsburgh railroad station he meets his first black man:

He did me the honour to wait upon me after a fashion, while I was eating; and with every word, look and gesture, marched me farther into the country of surprise. Imagine a gentleman, certainly somewhat dark but of a pleasant warm hue, speaking English with a slight and rather odd foreign accent, every inch a man of the world, and armed with manners so patronisingly superior that I am at a loss to name their parallel in England. A butler perhaps rides as high over the unbutlered, but then he sets you right with a reserve and a sort of sighing patience which one is often moved to admire. And again the abstract butler never moves to familiarity. But the coloured butler will pass you a wink at a time; he is familiar like an upper form boy to a fag; he unbends to you like Prince Hal with Poins and Falstaff. Indeed I may say, this waiter behaved himself to me throughout that supper much as a young, free and not very self-respecting master might behave to a good-looking chamber-maid. I had come prepared to pity the poor negro, to put him at his ease, to prove in a thousand condescensions that I was no sharer in the prejudice of race; but I assure you I put my patronage away for another occasion, and had the grace to be pleased with the result.

He also had to a high degree the novelist's gift of suspense, of making one aware that there were always dark deeds and new surprises waiting round the corner. Listen to this, from *Doctor Jekyll and Mr Hyde*:

Some two months before the murder of Sir Danvers, I had been out for one of my adventures, had returned at a late hour, and woke the next day in bed with somewhat odd sensations. It was in vain I looked about me; in vain I saw the decent furniture and tall proportions of my room in the square; in vain that I recognized the pattern of the bed curtains and the design of the mahogany frame; something still kept insisting that I was not where I was, that I had not wakened where I seemed to be, but in the little room in Soho where I was accustomed to sleep in the body of Edward Hyde. I smiled to myself, and, in my psychological way, began lazily to inquire into the elements of this illusion, occasionally, even as I did so, dropping back into a comfortable morning doze. I was still so engaged when, on one of my more wakeful moments, my eye fell upon my hand. Now, the hand of Henry Jekyll (as you have often remarked) was professional in shape and size; it was large, firm, white, and comely. But the hand which I now saw, clearly enough in the yellow light of a mid-London morning, lying half shut on the bedclothes, was lean, corded, knuckly, of a dusky pallor, and thickly shaded with a swart growth of hair. It was the hand of Edward Hyde.

Who, reading that, could forbear to read on?

All his books too are shot through with the sort of humorous assessment of the human condition which is really a sense of perspective, common to all English novelists as different as Jane Austen and Dickens, and without which any novelist tends to become a prig and a bore. And he was never funnier than when observing and recounting the odd things that happened to himself. Here he is aboard ship, en route from the Clyde to America:

To such of the officers as knew about me – the doctor,

the purser and the stewards – I appeared in the light of a broad joke. The fact that I spent the better part of my day in writing had gone abroad over the ship and tickled them prodigiously. Whenever they met me they referred to my absurd occupation with familiarity and breadth of humorous intention. Their manner was well calculated to remind me of my fallen fortunes. You may be sincerely amused by the amateur literary efforts of a literary gentleman, but you scarce publish the feeling to his face. 'Well!' they would say, 'still writing?' And the smile would widen into a laugh. The purser came one day into the cabin, and touched to the heart by my misguided industry, offered me some other kind of writing, 'for which' he added pointedly, 'you will be paid'. This was nothing else than to copy out the list of passengers.

As for the contents of his novels, they are full of what David Daiches calls 'moral embiguities', so that *Treasure Island* is not just a boy's adventure story – though it is first and foremost that – but also a story about greed. And if Long John Silver is the first great anti-hero of our times, so too *Doctor Jekyll and Mr Hyde* is also the first essay in modern times on schizophrenia. Incidentally, you'll remember that at Bournemouth Stevenson tore up the first version of *Doctor Jekyll and Mr Hyde* because Fanny didn't like it, and threw it into the fire, and I've often wondered how far it differed from the revised version. But the reason *Doctor Jekyll and Mr Hyde* has always been a bestseller and always will be is that there are Jekylls and Hydes in all of us; and how much we each have of the one and of the other is something we can only discover for ourselves. *Doctor Jekyll and Mr Hyde* then is not only about good and evil, hero and villain, it is also an invitation to self-analysis.

As a novelist RLS was not without flaws. His characters, especially in the early novels, were mostly black and white creatures and not of much depth; and as others have pointed out, his Highlanders were not so much genuine Highlanders as Edinburgh men transported to the Highlands.

He also asks us to accept some of the grossest improbabilities. Take *Kidnapped*, for instance. Firstly, in the ruined castle of the House of Shaws over towards the Forth there, Old Uncle Ebenezer tries to murder David Balfour by sending him up an old stairway that ends in space in the night sky. Any other boy to whom this happened would go shrieking out of the house as fast as his legs could carry him. But what does Davie do when he reaches the ground and finds his uncle shivering and trembling in the corner, but pulls out his blue phial of medicine to help him recover.

Presently they go to Queensferry to see Captain Hoseason of the brig *Dysart*. Now although Davie knows that his uncle wants to murder him, although he's just seen the cabin-boy with a great gaping wound in his leg inflicted on him by the mate, although he says that nothing would induce him to board the brig, and although he knows that Ebenezer and Hoseason have been as thick as thieves in the Hawes Inn, what do we find him doing a little later but allowing himself to be taken on board?

Later in the story I find it almost inconceivable that the fifteen men in the brig were unable to overpower Alan Breck and Davie after they had come out of the roundhouse, and *quite* inconceivable that after Alan was shipwrecked, he managed to escape from the seven men who were shipwrecked with him. Having swallowed that, we come to the most implausible situation of all – the two mind-boggling coincidences, the first, that at the very moment when Davie stops Campbell of Glenure on his way to Appin, there should happen to be an assassin lurking in the heather to pot him (which he does unsuccessfully) and then, glory be!, that Alan Breck, whom Davie hadn't seen since the shipwreck ten days before, should also happen to be lurking in the heather a few yards away. All this of course was necessary to make Alan and Davie fugitives from the law and thus allow RLS to describe their great journey back across the Highlands to Queensferry. It says much for Stevenson's gifts as a story-teller that on a first reading at least one is prepared to suspend disbelief totally, so skilfully has he persuaded us to follow his narrative to the end.

And finally, there is what I regard as RLS's supreme gift which is that in nearly all his books you have this tremendous sense of movement, of travelling ever further onwards, an obsession which he encapsulated in a memorable phrase, that it is better to travel hopefully than to arrive; and when he did arrive, he at once set about thinking of when and in what direction he would move again. 'Travel is of two kinds,' he wrote, 'out of my country and out of myself.' From Edinburgh to the Highlands to France to America to Braemar to Hampshire to London to America again and finally to the South Seas, he was always on the move, and it could be said that in his travels he found his books and in his books he found himself. In *Travels with a Donkey in the Cevennes*, *Inland Voyage*, *Treasure Island*, *Kidnapped*, *Catriona*, *The Master of Ballantrae*, even *Doctor Jekyll and Mr Hyde* there is always a feeling of a sense of departure, of setting off into the unknown.

I have left his verse until the end. Yet it seems to me that much of his verse exemplifies that sense of movement. It comes in *A Child's Garden of Verses*, in Leerie the lamplighter as he goes from post to post, it comes in the view from the railway carriage window:

> *Faster than fairies, faster than witches,*
> *Bridges and houses, hedges and ditches,*
> *And charging along like troops in a battle,*
> *All through the meadows the horses and cattle,*
> *All the sights of the hill and the plain*
> *Fly as thick as driving rain,*
> *And ever again in the twink of an eye,*
> *Painted stations whistle by.*

And I think it finds its apogee in that poem called 'Where go the boats?'

> *Dark brown is the river,*
> *Golden is the sand,*
> *It flows along for ever,*
> *With trees on either hand.*
>
> *Green leaves afloating,*
> *Castles of the foam,*
> *Boats of mine aboating,*
> *Where will all come home?*

> *On goes the river*
> *And out past the mill,*
> *Away down the valley,*
> *Away down the hill.*
>
> *Away down the river,*
> *A hundred miles or more,*
> *Other little children*
> *Shall bring my boats ashore.*

There surely in movement and mystery, in language a child can understand and with a wonderful lightness of touch, lies the genesis of all his books. And there's another later poem where he looks back to his own childhood and sees the same thing; yet aware that in the end all must come to dust.

> *Sing me a song of a lad that is gone,*
> *Say, could that lad be I?*
> *Merry of soul, he sailed on a day*
> *Over the sea to Skye,*
> *Mull was astern, Rum on the port,*
> *Eigg on the starboard bow,*
> *Glory of youth gleamed in his soul,*
> *Where is that glory now?*

There is Stevenson as he was in the earlier poems of childhood, playing at soldiers and Indians, the embryonic Davie Balfour and Jim Hawkins. And then as you all know, a few years before his death, he stopped travelling and settled down as a laird at Samoa just as Scott settled down as the laird of Abbotsford. And he stopped travelling in his writings too. *Weir of Hermiston*, that unfinished masterpiece, is in a different mould from the others; it is not a novel of movement but a study of relationships as most great novels are. Intellectually and emotionally he had reached journey's end: the boat which had been so long aboating had at last come home.

In his poetry he had stopped moving too. He recollected in tranquillity but with undisguised affection the bystreets and buildings of the Auld Reekie of his boyhood, and he dedicated *Weir of Hermiston* to his wife with a sonnet whose opening five lines are among the most beautiful he ever wrote:

TO MY WIFE

I saw rain falling and the rainbow drawn
On Lammermuir. Hearkening I heard again
In my precipitous city beaten bells
Winnow the keen sea wind. And here afar,
Intent on my own race and place, I wrote.
  Take thou the writing: thine it is. For who
Burnished the sword, blew on the drowsy coal,
Held still the target higher, chary of praise
And prodigal of censure – who but thou?
So now, in the end, if this the least be good,
If any deed be done, if any fire
Burn in the imperfect page, the praise be thine.

And not long after that, he was dead.

SPEECHDAY AT PUMPHREYS

HEADMASTER, BOYS, MUMS and Dads,

As I rise to my feet, my mind goes back to those occasions of some sixty years ago when I used to find myself in the position that you boys find yourselves today. And as the speaker – in those days he was generally a bishop or a general – rose to *his* feet, the thought used to pass through my mind as it must be going through yours now, how long is this old geyser going to keep us here? That he might have something interesting or useful to say to us never crossed our minds; and quite rightly too, for with one or two rare exceptions, successive speechdays showed up the wide gulf that existed between our world and that of the bishops and generals. They were apt to talk down to us which is something I promise I shall not do to you. And the answer to the question, how long will I keep you here? is, or should be if the timing of the run-through can be relied on, about twelve minutes. So at any moment, if you begin to feel restless, you can refer to your watches and see that there are only x more minutes to go.

In sixty years of course prep schools have changed a lot. Like the abolition of caning, for instance. A good thing too, for I have never thought that a man asking a boy to stand still while he repeatedly hit him was anything other than a form of child abuse. Another civilizing influence in schools today has been the introduction of girl pupils. Recently I went back to my own prep school, happily now under new management, and sitting next to the headmaster at the school lunch, I spotted a very pretty little girl standing by a window. 'Does she not want lunch?' I asked the headmaster. 'That's Rebecca,' said he. 'She's in disgrace. She's been throwing bread rolls again.' At least she wasn't caned.

For those of you who are leaving this term, this is a great day. Five years of hard labour have come to fruition, you have reached the top and cannot, at least here, go further. Next term, at Eton or Marlborough or wherever you're bound, you'll have to start again at the bottom; and then in a further five years, which is further ahead than any of you can see, you will reach the top again, only to find yourself at university or in business or the services, once again at the bottom. And that's how it will be throughout your life until you reach what Shakespeare calls 'the sere and yellow' which is where I am, and there thankfully you'll find there's nowhere else to go except, to quote the Bard again, 'that bourne from which no traveller returns', and I cannot tell you what a blissful prospect that is.

Now as you move ever onwards and upwards, there's just a couple of bits of advice I'd like to give you, advice which I wish, when I was your age, someone had given to me. And the first is this, and if the masters who are here today think it subversive, they will have to lump it. *Never take on trust, wherever it may come from, anything that you yourself suspect may not be true*. The memoirs of famous men often speak of the nonsense told them as children by their so-called elders and betters. My own mother, I remember, always instructed me to put down sheets of lavatory paper on the seats of public loos in order to avoid catching some dire disease left behind by another. I don't know if any of you have ever tried that, but I found it almost impossible to complete the oval without at least half the sheets of paper falling off or in. When I asked my mother what disease I was hoping to avoid, she could not tell me. So then I asked the family doctor and he didn't know of one either, and after that I took a chance, without any dire results, of totally ignoring the instructions.

But I could give you more weighty examples than that. I remember my American publisher once telling me that he was about to publish a book in which opposite pages would contain separate accounts of historical events such as battles viewed by historians for the two main protagonists involved. He said that the English account of the battle of Waterloo was so different from the French account that you would not think they were describing the same event. For what to the English was a clear-cut victory was to the French historian, if not a victory, at least an honourable draw. Religion is another field, I submit, where, if you want to reach the truth of the matter, you must also cast a critical eye. The Bible as a work of literature is of its kind unsurpassed – I am talking now of the old King James's version – and no-one who wishes to be called educated can be without a working knowledge of it. And yet the Bible, especially the New Testament, does contain some strange assertions, tales of virgin births and miracles and resurrections which are presented as historical facts. A time will come for you, if it has not come already, when you will have to ask yourselves, are these claims true as historical fact, and if they are, how strong is the evidence for thinking so?

What I am asking you to do is to develop a critical eye, to make up your own minds about a subject, not slavishly follow the opinions of others. For a long time that won't be easy, for you are still at an age when you lack the breadth of information which only age and experience can bring to form a proper judgement. But there's no reason why you shouldn't make a start; and when somebody tells you something with which instinctively you know you disagree, cling on to that instinct, cherish it in your heart, even if you feel you are not yet in a position to express it publicly. The advice I am giving you here is the advice that Shakespeare's Polonius gave in one of the most famous passages in all English literature. 'This above all:' he said, 'to thine own self be true, And it must follow, as the night the day, Thou canst not then be false to any man.' If you can take that thought with you through life, and also have the courage to act on it, then you won't go far wrong.

Let me pass on to you something else which I wish I'd known when I was young. Often in life, when you've decided on some course of action, you may begin to have doubts about it. The temptation is, as I know from bitter experience, to dismiss the doubts, for reasons of pride or obstinacy or ambition, and go ahead with whatever it was you had planned. Let me say to you bluntly, *never* disregard doubts, listen to them carefully, analyse whatever it is they have to say. The more you do that, the more you will realize that doubts are the unconscious forces working within you to say that your initial and perhaps not fully considered decision was not so brilliant after all. So, boys, if in doubt, don't.

And lastly a piece of advice which my father passed on to me and for which I have always been grateful. In three words it was this: 'Try everything once.' Because until you've tried everything, or at least most things, you'll never know the sort of things that may be waiting to enrich your life. Things like all types of games and sports, outdoor and in, languages, music, natural history, poetry – indeed all the rich varieties of human activity there are. Some may not attract you in the first place, others you may soon discard. But a few, I guess, will be with you all your lives.

For me the most lasting pleasure of all that I have experienced has been poetry, so let me conclude with two poems by a fellow countryman of mine, Robert Louis Stevenson. One for Youth and one for Age, one for You and one for Me. Here is the one for you.

I will make you brooches and toys for your delight
Of bird-song at morning and star-shine at night.
I will make a palace fit for you and me
Of green days in forests and blue days at sea.

I will make my kitchen, and you shall keep your room,
Where white flows the river and bright blows the broom,
And you shall wash your linen and keep your body white
*   In rainfall at morning and dewfall at night.*

And this shall be for music when no-one else is near,
The fine song for singing, the rare song to hear!
That only I remember, that only you admire,
Of the broad road that stretches and the roadside fire.

And here is the one for me.

Under the wide and starry sky
Dig the grave and let me lie.
Glad did I live and gladly die,
*   And I laid me down with a will.*

This be the verse you grave for me:
'Here he lies where he longed to be;
Home is the sailor home from sea,
   And the hunter home from the hill.'

Good luck, boys.

AN END TO BELIEF?

ANOTHER OF MY interests – I might say (and some have said) obsessions – has been the Christian religion, stemming from ten years' indoctrination at prep and public school which took me half a lifetime to abandon. I have never ceased to feel resentment at the time wasted (some 1,300 hours, I reckon) on being fed as historical truths such instances of magic as the virginity of Christ's mother, his so-called miracles and physical resurrection, etc., claims which those who taught me must have known, had they ever paused to consider it, were nonsense. People ask what harm there is in learning these things, and my answer is that it is always harmful to peddle falsehoods as truths. In time I joined and became an Associate of the British Humanist Association and was very pleased when in 1984 they invited me to give that year's Voltaire Memorial Lecture.

The Voltaire lecturer, whoever he or she happens to be, is doubly fortunate: firstly in the honour done to him, or her, in being invited; secondly in the knowledge that the great man's spirit of toleration gives the lecturer a fairly free hand. Although himself a Deist, Voltaire would not, I think, have objected to a talk entitled 'An End to Belief' with a question-mark; for he not only had a lively and enquiring mind, but was far ahead of his time in recognizing that a person's religious views or lack of them, while often of interest to others, were of ultimate concern only to himself. Nor do I think that many of the present bishops of the Church of England would object to the title. If that surprises you, I shall give my reasons later.

Let me begin by setting a few guide-lines. With the Ayatollah Khomeini preaching, and indeed practising, fire and brimstone in Iran, the Ayatollah Paisley conducting a now more muted anti-Popery campaign in Northern Ireland, and with the various sects in the Lebanon continually at each other's throats, you may think this a strange time to be delivering a talk entitled 'An End to Belief' even if it does carry a question-mark. But the conflicts in the Lebanon and Northern Ireland, it seems to me, are less about religious disagreements as such than about opposing cultures of which the religious element is only a part, and the resentment of those who object strongly to having what they regard as an alien culture thrust upon them. Likewise, the rise in Iran of the Mullahs, so chillingly reminiscent of the Spanish Inquisition, is not, I think, because the people there have suddenly discovered that Allah is the only true god and Mohammed his prophet, but because Islam has been found to be a useful tool for harnessing the national will and re-establishing the national identity.

In any case it is not the beliefs of infidels and heretics, as Christians once called them, that I am concerned with this evening, but those of our own countrymen and countrywomen here at home; the beliefs or anti-beliefs of the people of one of the oldest and most tested democracies in the world; a country which, insulated by the sea and undisturbed by European-style revolution, has created for its people a climate in which traditionally they have been encouraged to reason and debate, so that in the process they have become, as Voltaire discovered for himself when he came here, one of the most civilized and tolerant societies in the world. In a way we have seen it all, and one of the things we have seen, perhaps ahead of other countries, is the continuing decline of the Christian religion. It may be helpful therefore, both for ourselves and for those who may be heading in the same direction, to ask why and how this has come about.

Before doing so, however, a word about my own position. For me Christianity has not been a light that failed but one that never managed even to splutter. At an early age I was fed the usual clichés about this character called 'God' who made the world, lived in the sky and demanded to be prayed to. 'God Bless Mummy and Daddy,' I said each evening, 'sisters and cousins, Aunt Mab and Uncle Tom, Dorothy the nursemaid and Ponting the dog, and make me a good boy Amen' – though I never observed this brought results for any of us. When I first visited the local church, which I thought was a strange place, my mother told me it was 'God's' house, the place where he lived; and I was amazed that 'God' managed to get along without kitchen, bathroom or lavatory. As a result the image he presented to me then was that of an emaciated tramp. When I taxed my mother about the lack of these facilities, she said in an airy way that 'God' didn't need any of these things, and then I realized what a truly remarkable character he must be. At school, having stubbed my toe or bruised my funny-bone, I gained some relief by calling down blasphemies on the Holy Ghost – whom I saw as a kind of elderly church-warden – and was mildly surprised not to be struck by lightning or a thunderbolt, as threatened in Mark 3:29. When I was fifteen, I agreed to be prepared for 'confirmation' in the hope that this might somehow put a rein on my almost continual sexual longings. Happily it didn't. Although from early childhood I suspected that the tales my mother and the headmaster and the local parson told me were at best speculation and at worst moonshine, it was many years before I found the courage even privately to reject them. When I did, I experienced, as Julian Huxley did before me, a heady sense of spiritual liberation, knowing that I would no longer have to pay lip-service to a lie. Even then it was several years more – because in those days it did not do to question the received wisdom – before I felt able to state what I felt publicly.

Belief in the continuance of the Christian ascendancy dies hard. If one were to take the correspondence columns of *The Times* and *Telegraph* as one's guide, one would doubt that Christianity had suffered any kind of setback at all. Hardly a day goes by without letters in one or other of those two influential and widely read papers assuring us that we are living in a Christian country which is upholding Christian values – though where Christian values differ from human values their authors never pause to explain. Recently in *The Times*, Professor Hanson of Manchester University declared that Christianity was neither decaying nor collapsing; the Reverend D. M. Stanesby called it a rational faith – unaware perhaps of Hume's dictum about reason being the slave of the passions – and a group of scientists wrote a letter saying they believed the Virgin Birth and the Resurrection to be historical facts. Coming from scientists, this was obviously meant to impress. What impressed rather more came from a theologian, Don Cupitt, Dean of Emmanuel College, Cambridge: 'Whether chromosomally haploid or diploid,' he wrote in *The Listener* in July, 'a virgin-born human being would have to be female, having only X chromosomes.'

Also earlier this year, *The Times* published a mind-boggling correspondence as to whether or not the Christian god had deliberately struck York Minster with lightning; and last year, I seem to recall, there was an even madder correspondence as to whether this same god was a woman. Nobody – and I found this surprising – put forward the notion that the devil also might be a woman, which (speaking as a man) I would have thought rather more likely.

It is, understandably, two thousand years of the Christian experience – two thousand years of Christian art much of it of superb quality, two thousand years of Christian wars and massacres and tortures – that allows the authors of letters like those I have mentioned to delude themselves into thinking that this is still a Christian country, that their beliefs are widely shared. The facts are otherwise.

Statistics since the turn of the century show a continually dwindling number of baptisms, confirmations, communicants and clergy, and one has only to use one's eyes to observe the number of city churches that have been turned into warehouses or dwelling-places or bingo halls, and the number of country churches where services have either ceased or are held but occasionally. Practising Christians in this country are in a minority, and a decreasing minority at that. Non-Christians therefore need not be on the defensive as they sometimes are.

Unlike Judaism and Islam, Christianity has not one but two separate yet linked supernatural strands – the life of Jesus Christ on the one hand, and on the other the alleged existence of the god whose son he is uniquely claimed to be. It is the astonishing claims made for certain events in the life of Jesus – events said to be historical facts – that the modern generation finds so hard to accept. And who can blame them? If tonight a messenger were to arrive here in the Conway Hall with the news that around fifty years ago in, say, Sumatra or Timbuctoo a man whose mother was a virgin had performed a variety of miracles which included transferring an evil spirit from a man into a herd of pigs who then rushed down a hill and drowned in the sea, had walked on water, had raised people from the dead, and was himself seen to be walking and talking three days after his own death, we would probably send, would we not, for the men from the funny farm? His story would hardly be one that any newspaper, even *The Times*, would dare to print.

If it is impossible to believe in such things happening today, what conceivable reason warrants a belief that they took place two thousand years ago – a time when a Messiah was expected, when superstition was rife, and when people everywhere were on the look-out for signs and portents? Christians will say, well that is the rock on which the Church was founded, that is what millions of people have believed for hundreds of years. But for hundreds of years people also believed that the world was flat, and later that the sun went round it, until Copernicus and others lifted the veil from their eyes.

The incontrovertible fact remains that not a single eye-witness account of the supernatural events claimed for Jesus survives, the epistles of Paul make no mention of them, the gospel accounts which do were written between thirty and a hundred years after Jesus's death, and the authors of the later ones had access to the material of the earlier ones. On that lack of contemporary evidence, you would doubt the accuracy of any reporting of natural events, let alone supernatural ones.

That Jesus Christ, or Joshua as he was known to his contemporaries in Palestine, was an exceptional man, a brilliant if dogmatic teacher and healer, with profound insights into human nature and a moral sense and stance unique in those times, we can, I think, accept. We can also accept that the story of his life, rendered into impeccable and memorable prose, is one of the great books of literature. The rest is surely story-telling. Was not the personal impact that Jesus made on people so great, were they not so concerned that what he said and did should not be forgotten, that the story grew, as stories are apt to grow when passed from person to person, so that what began as a tale of the extraordinary slid, almost without anyone being aware of it, into a tale of the miraculous? Did not accounts of his successes as a healer become exaggerated? Did not his disciples feel his presence after his death so vividly that they imagined he had returned to them? None of it was he, being dead, able to refute, and none of it did his followers wish to refute. And so in his name a legend was born and a Church founded; and no-one, I think, would have been more surprised to hear of it than he.

Other claims followed. People said he was divine, thinking they were uttering some mystical truth, unaware that there is nothing divine or sacred or holy but that some group of people, somewhere, at some time, have decided to call divine or sacred or holy. Holiness and divinity are not states or characteristics, but labels. In the same way, the extraordinary ideas of the Holy Trinity and of the Incarnation barely existed until 300 years after Jesus's death, when a group of churchmen decided to make them official; and from that day to this they have been central tenets of Christian doctrine. And so with the Annunciation and Ascension and Assumption and so on and so forth – layer upon layer was added to the Christian superstructure, making it increasingly complex, artificial and top-heavy.

Now when you ask committed Christians why they accept the miracles, the Resurrection, and so on, they say, as though it somehow explained everything, that it is a matter of faith. Knowing the powerful associations that the word 'faith' has ('Oh, ye of little faith', 'the faith that moves mountains', etc.), this is usually the conversation-stopper they hope it will be. But what is faith but belief, and to say you believe because you believe is hardly an adequate explanation. To believe the unbelievable is surely less a question of faith than of need. You and I could say we believed in mermaids and unicorns, but if pressed we would have to admit that they existed only in our imaginations. We do not need to believe the unbelievable. The committed Christian does.

*

But it is when we turn to the whole question of gods, and in particular the Christian god, that we encounter even greater difficulties.

It is common knowledge that gods first swam into man's consciousness at an early stage of his development. He did not know what fearful creatures lurked in the forests that lay beyond the horizon and might one day come after him: the god who lived in the forest might, if appealed to, stop them. When there was thunder and floods drowned the harvest, that was a god voicing displeasure; when the sun remained behind clouds and the harvest failed to ripen, that was another. But when a full harvest had been gathered in, when enemies had been defeated in battle, why that was a time for rejoicing and giving thanks for deliverance, a sure sign that prayers had been answered, that the gods were taking care of him.

And so the need for gods to propitiate and gods to give comfort was born; and as history ran its course and human societies developed, gods and goddesses multiplied. Before long there were thousands of them: Nut and Geb in ancient Egypt, Thor and Odin in Northern Europe, Hermes and Aphrodite, Apollo and Poseidon in Greece, Mars and Bacchus and Diana in Rome, Shiva and Vishnu in India, Xipe and Quetzalcoatl in Mexico; Eskimo gods, Aztec gods, African gods, gods of the Pacific islanders; benign gods and cruel gods, gods of every shape and nature. And then as man's development continued, he no longer felt the need – or perhaps it was too inconvenient – to continue with compartmentalized gods, one for war, another for love and so on, but rather to embrace one all-purpose god who could embody and reflect all human attributes. And so the world's monotheistic religions came into being, that of the Jews with their god Yahweh or Jehovah, and later that of the Moslems with their god Allah. Between the two came the Christians with their god 'God' – a name not only strikingly unoriginal but one which, you may think (and I will return to it in a moment) begs the whole question.

The rise and spread of Christianity, with its mixture of promises and threats for the future, is not within the scope of this talk. But its decline is. If I were to put a date on it,

I would say the end of the nineteenth and beginning of the twentieth century, when there were two striking but separate developments in human knowledge which together changed man's view both of the natural world and of himself.

Until this time or thereabouts, there had always been some part of the globe unknown to western man, there had always been new frontiers to cross, new lands to discover. But now, as European explorers made their way across the continents and found no King-Kongs living in island vastnesses, the world was becoming increasingly knowable, increasingly tameable. Hand-in-hand with this mapping of desert and jungle, science was beginning to peel back many of the mysteries of the natural world: to explain things formerly inexplicable, to cure diseases hitherto thought incurable, to make discoveries in the fields of evolution, communication, transportation and consumer goods as to make for less hazardous living; and the more all this happened, the less hostile the outside world seemed, and the less hostile the outside world, the less reason for gods. Gods inhabit the unknown. Where there be dragons, there also be gods.

And the other great advance of course was not in the external world but in the world of the mind. Religion as a legislator of morality, as a check on man's licentiousness and cunning, is a strong element of most religions and of Christianity more than most. If you sinned, the Church taught, without redemption or atonement, you were in for hell-fire and damnation. But the radical ideas of the school of Viennese psychiatrists who were active at the turn of the century persuaded man to look at his own nature in a rather different way. They taught that good and evil should be seen less in terms of black and white than in varying shades of grey, that our pasts condition our futures more than we know, that our motivations are often other than what they seem, and that while it might be wrong to sin against the Holy Ghost, it was a worse sin to act against one's own nature, to accept any orthodoxy whether temporal or spiritual which the heart rejected as false. And so the psychoanalyst came into his own as a new-style confessor, not like the old to absolve venial sins but to resolve psychological problems; not to forgive or redeem but to help people discover their own natures.

One result of this was that the word 'sin' gradually fell into disuse. Today it has a curiously old-fashioned ring to it, so that the idea of abasing oneself in public by declaring, as for many years we had to, that we were miserable sinners who had erred and strayed in our ways like lost sheep and had no health in us, is seen to be not only demeaning but fatuous. If one is going to sin, one at least ought to do it with conviction.

A further cause of the erosion of Christian belief has been the opening up of the world to western man as a result of the coming of mass air travel. And western man (if himself not a Christian, then born in the Christian tradition) has for the first time come into direct contact with other religions than his own: the disciplines of Islam, the complexities of Hinduism, the tranquillity of Buddhism. He has met people of those faiths, and of no faiths at all, who seem to be leading useful and contented lives, people who have never heard of John the Baptist or Mary Magdalene or Simon Stylites, and seem none the worse for it. And many have come to realize that the claim of Christianity to be the one true faith is at least questionable; that other faiths and dogmas are for their followers equally true. Indeed, some westerners have found eastern religions so appealing that they have journeyed to Japan and other places to study them. How many easterners, one would like to know, disillusioned with their own religions, have made a similar journey west in search of Christendom?

And then there is the vexed question of the after-life. From earliest times man has believed that there is something beyond this vale of tears. In ancient times kings and chieftains were buried with little picnics of food and drink to sustain them on their journeys across the nether regions. In later times the Christian Church offered a choice between Hell, if you had sinned, and Heaven if you had repented, and this concentrated the mind wonderfully. Latterly, when heaven and hell were found not to be places but states of mind, belief in the after-life began to lose some of its hold. Ask most people who say they believe in life after death whether they also believe in life before birth, and – apart from the reincarnation brigade – they look at you baffled; for people are less interested in where they may have been than in where they hope they may be going.

I now want to return to what I touched on earlier, the matter of the Christian god having no other name but 'God'. The word 'god' began life as a common noun and is still used in that sense today. But somewhere along the line it also began to be used as a proper noun, God with a capital G, to indicate the god of Christianity. This was understandable in an age when the assumption of a single Supreme Being was universal, but it has left us in a confused situation today. For to spell god with a capital G is halfway to accepting his independent existence. It is like calling the Atlantic 'Ocean' or Everest 'Mountain', as though there were not and never had been other mountains and oceans worthy of consideration; and every time writers and publishers and printers spell god with a capital G, they are making themselves and their readers party to the assumption of this god's existence, whether they actually assume it or not. Christians and non-Christians alike, we are all locked into the system and cannot escape from it. 'God Almighty', we say, 'Good God' – 'Thank God' – 'God knows' – 'God willing' – 'God forbid' – thus helping unintentionally to perpetuate the idea of his existence.

For surely the only true and safe thing you can say about the concept of a god is that it is an idea that exists in the mind, and that our interpretations of it will be as different as there are minds to consider it; for the concept that lurks in my mind may be quite different to the concept in yours, where indeed there may be no concept at all. Is it the need for self-protection that causes people to extrapolate from this the idea of the existence of an external being, beyond and independent of its existence in the mind? Is it a desire for collective security that creates the idea of a collective god – one whom the present Archbishop of York in his enthronement said he wanted to see more collectively worshipped? This is the god whom the Church calls The Lord God of Hosts, the Most High, Mighty in Battle, characteristics which many modern minds find repugnant and which may well be another reason for the empty pews. Conversely, could the reason that poets such as Donne and Herbert and Vaughan are now enjoying a quiet revival be the intensely personal, almost private nature of their metaphysical musings? Their concept of 'God' was unique to each of them; and instead of making extravagant claims for some lofty, impersonal figure, they more often spoke of what they were experiencing in their minds. In many poems they expressed those experiences obliquely. Donne, on his death-bed: 'Since I am coming to that holy room.' Herbert: 'Love bade me welcome, but my soul drew back.' And Vaughan: 'I saw Eternity the other night/Like a great ring of pure and endless light.' We can understand those kind of experiences, can we not, even if we do not share them?

But still the proponents of the external god bang on. If 'God' didn't create the world, they say, who did? I have no idea, I say, and I doubt if you have either; and even if we allow that it was 'created' in any meaningful sense, as we ourselves are a part of that process, we are not in the best position to say what happened. To suggest that 'God' made it does not really take things much further. For that matter, who made 'God'? In pulpits and pamphlets up and down the country, ministers and others tell us that 'God' wants us to do this or that, when they cannot have the faintest notion what this god, even if he existed outside the confines of their own minds, does want. That is why the sermon has become such a dead art form. When I hear some of the claims made both *for* 'God' and *to* 'God', I recall Sir John Squire's quatrain about the First World War:

> God heard the embattled nations sing and shout
> 'Gott strafe England!' and 'God Save the King!'
> God this, God that, and God the other thing.
> 'Good God,' said God, 'I've got my work cut out'.

What have the Christian Churches done to arrest the decline of Christianity in the west? Several things, many of which their followers think misguided. The biggest, I suppose, is what is called the ecumenical movement, in which the various denominations share each other's facilities and sometimes take part in joint services, both to save expense (it should really be called the economical movement) and to

606

show that there is really not all that much to choose between them. This is a far cry from the days, not so long ago, when members of each sect or denomination – strong in numbers, finances, and convictions – sniped at one another from a distance and would as soon have been seen in the town brothel as in one another's churches. Some, in Scotland at the turn of the century, did their sniping closer to. On Sunday mornings the little Presbyterian boys would wait for the Episcopalian churches to empty, then shout at the emerging congregation: 'Piscie, Piscie, Amen, down on your knees and up again.' And when the Presbyterian congregation came out an hour later, there the Piscie boys would be waiting for them. 'Presby, Presby, never bend,' they chanted, 'Sit on your seat on man's own end.' Is the present new-found unity, one has to ask, anything deeper than a marriage of convenience?

Individual Churches have devised their own schemes to meet the spiritual needs of twentieth-century man, but not, I think, successfully, and certainly not in the radical way they might have done. It is astonishing to me, in an age of female emancipation, that both in the Roman Catholic Church and the Church of England women are still barred from taking the cloth, that in an age of sexual emancipation the Roman Catholic Church still requires its priests to be celibate, that the Church of England has not moved faster towards disestablishment – all omissions which show the Churches' deep conservatism.

The modernizations they have brought in have been mostly emollients. In the Roman Catholic Church the Mass is no longer generally said in Latin but in the language of the country where it is being celebrated. This has been a disappointment to many Catholics, for not only has it broken a link that runs back to the days of the early Church in Rome, but it removes much of the mystery and gloss – as when secular man hears a much loved but incomprehensible Italian opera rendered into stage English.

Similarly the new versions of the Bible which have been produced by the Churches of England and Scotland are in no way an improvement on the King James version, which for us is unique in literature; for there is surely little to be gained and much to be lost by changing phrasing that was obscure yet beautiful to that which is crystal clear but utterly banal; and the same sort of criticism can be made of the Alternative Prayer Book. In the 1662 Prayer Book one was enjoined to undertake marriage 'in the fear of the Lord'. This has been changed to 'with serious thought'. The former was sonorous bombast; but is the latter any kind of improvement?

I am sometimes asked, as a non-Christian, do I wish to see a Britain in which Christian institutions and Christian worship have disappeared altogether; a Britain in which the now half-empty churches are completely empty and the church bells silent; a Britain where baptisms and weddings and funerals are entirely secular affairs; a Britain without priests and parsons, bishops and archbishops, not only to minister but also to prick our consciences in a disinterested way and add their contributions to the consideration of public affairs? Is that the sort of Britain I am after? Does it not make for a bleakish prospect? Whatever our religious views, will we not have lost something worth having?

Let me take these points in order. First, the idea that any of the principal Churches are likely to go out of business in the foreseeable future is simply not credible. One reason, of course, is their immense wealth – the legacy of bygone supremacy, tithes and direct debits wisely invested – which gives a totally false impression of their standing in Britain today. Without it, the Church of England would not be able to play the part it does in the national life; indeed, would make little more impact than that of any other minority activity. In addition, and despite continued contraction, there will always be a hard core of the faithful.

As regards baptisms, weddings and funerals, these also are on the wane. Many parents now regard baptism as an empty ceremony – though some make use of it so as not to deprive their offspring of the material benefits, if not the spiritual guidance, of godparents. Many young people now prefer to be married – if at all – in register offices; and many old people at the end of their days opt for disposal in crematoria. Of those who do go for a church wedding I would guess that few do it on religious grounds, more because such an important event in their lives demands a formal ceremony, and the ceremony the Church offers is the only one available. It is interesting to note that in the Soviet Union, where so many churches have been closed, they have recognized people's need for ceremony by setting up marriage parlours where you can rent an organ, music, flowers and, for all I know, best man and bridesmaids.

As for morality, it is surely a long time now since we relied on the Church to tell us how to behave. Do to others as you would be done by is a maxim that has been posited by almost every civilized society since the earliest days, and while we may often fall short of it, it remains as good a rule of thumb as any. In addition, every society has what one might call its collective conscience – a lodestar which from time to time and place to place is in a continual state of flux, but which, embodied in the country's laws, reflects at any given time its general moral stance, what it will permit and what it will refuse. Certain truths about human conduct are constant and self-evident and no longer need the blessings or *imprimatur* of gods to reinforce them.

There are others who say, well, if you are going to take away our religion, what are you going to put in its place? But why the need to put anything in its place? If the limb on a tree dies, you lop it off; you do not try to graft a fresh limb on to it.

Then, they say, where are we going to find spiritual refreshment? To assume that the Bible affords the only fount of spiritual refreshment available is, I think, mistaken. In addition to Religion there is Nature; and in addition to Nature there is Art, many-splendoured and multi-faceted, offering spiritual refreshment almost without end; not only religious art – Titian and Tintoretto, Bach and Handel, Milton and Blake – but secular art too: a Turner sunset, an ode of Keats, a sonata of Mozart. Here and elsewhere is rich sustenance for the spirit. Listen to Wordsworth on London:

> *Earth has not anything to show more fair;*
> *Dull would he be of soul who could pass by*
> *A sight so touching in its majesty:*
> *This City now doth, like a garment, wear*
> *The beauty of the morning. . .*

And to this, by the American poet, Robert Frost:

> *The woods are lovely, dark and deep.*
> *But I have promises to keep,*
> *And miles to go before I sleep.*
> *And miles to go before I sleep.*

And this, by Walter Savage Landor:

> *I strove with none; for none was worth my strife;*
> *Nature I loved, and, next to Nature, Art;*
> *I warmed both hands before the fire of life;*
> *It sinks, and I am ready to depart.*

Is there not as much food for the spirit in poetry or music as in any Christian hymn, whether ancient or modern?

Let me conclude on a more positive note. In the course of this talk I have suggested some of the reasons for the present decline of Christian belief, and related some of the measures, largely ineffective, that the Church has introduced in order to check it. But recently, it seems to me, two new ideas in Christian thinking have been trying to break surface, radical in their conception and far-reaching in their implications, for Christians and non-Christians alike. The first arises from the fundamental difficulties experienced by so many today in imagining and accepting an external transcendent god who, like Big Brother, watches over us individually from afar; and the replacement of him by a god within, not even a god really but a sense of otherness, a presence, a pinpoint of light at the end of a long tunnel. St Francis of Assisi experienced this sense of internal numinousness, so, as I have shown, did the metaphysical poets. In our own time it was developed by the theologian Paul Tillich when he described the Christian god as the ground of our being, re-stated by Pastor Dietrich Bonhoeffer when he declared that 'God' had been elbowed out of every sphere except the last secret haunt of the individual's needs, and then, not so long ago, given wider coverage by Bishop John Robinson in his book *Honest to God*. It is not something which Humanists have experienced, but it is equally, I think, not something to which they can object.

The other idea is even more radical and revolutionary, for it is concerned with the claim, to which Humanists have always objected, of supernaturalism – or, as I prefer to call it, antinaturalism – in the birth, life and death of Christ. Some twenty-five years ago I interviewed on television the then Archbishop of York, Dr Michael Ramsey, and asked him afterwards what, above all else, one had to believe to be a Christian. His answer was immediate and unequivocal. 'The Resurrection,' he said. 'As an historical fact?' I asked. 'Most certainly as an historical fact,' he replied. 'That is the core of Christian belief.'

'That is the core of Christian belief.' Well, it may have been then, but there are indications today that it is no longer. Two and a half decades later, in the summer of 1984, Professor David Jenkins, on the eve of his consecration as Bishop of Durham, flatly contradicted Archbishop Ramsey. On a television programme called *Credo* he declared, equally un-equivocally, that he did not believe in the Virgin Birth or the Resurrection or the miracles as historical facts, and in his view one could be a Christian (assuming one still wanted to be!) without believing them. And not only this: of thirty-one Diocesan bishops canvassed after the interview, two out of three agreed that it was not necessary to believe in the divin-ity of Christ to be a Christian (which seems to me like saying one doesn't have to be a soldier to go into the army), half agreed that they had similar doubts about the miracles, and one out of three also denied a belief in the Virgin Birth and the physical Resurrection. In addition, Bishop Jenkins con-firmed in a Radio 4 interview what non-Christians have been saying for years: 'Historical facts are a matter of probability and doubt and uncertainty . . . *there is absolutely no certainty in the New Testament about anything of importance.*'

Fifty years ago, perhaps less, this sort of talk would have been regarded as the grossest heresy; five hundred years ago it would have meant breaking on the wheel or burning at the stake. And if, in so short a time, between one-third and two-thirds of the current crop of bishops can doubt the supernatural elements of the Christian faith (and for

611

what else in Christianity does one require faith?), then how much longer before they all do? How much longer before they come to regard Christ in the same way – no more and no less – as they regard Socrates and Shakespeare and others of the world's original thinkers? And what happens then to Christian sacraments, Christian worship, Christian prayer? What, precisely, is left?

I do not see how on this evidence anyone can deny that among the hierarchy of the Church of England we are now witnessing, if not the end, then the beginnings of the end, of Christian belief. Hence the title of this talk.

The Church's rank and file, for whom the supernatural elements of Christianity are everything, have greeted this shift of attitude with a sense of shock and disillusionment and betrayal – indeed, some of them tried to stop Bishop Jenkins's enthronement. Others have tried to make the best of a bad job by declaring that we should really look on the supernatural events as myths – not realizing perhaps that the essence of myth is that it is fiction, and that to regard Christianity as a mythology is to put it on a par with the mythologies of Greece and Rome – today's mythologies being yesterday's religions. We do not believe today in the gods the Greeks and Romans worshipped, but they did. What reason is there to suppose that the people of five hundred or a thousand years hence – assuming there still are people – will think any differently about the Christian god of today?

The implications of this minor earthquake that is now gently rocking the Church of England – I used the word gently because so far they seem hardly aware of it – are too far-reaching and fundamental to go into here in depth. But Humanists should welcome them; for do they not herald for the first time a closing of the gap between Humanists and Christians – perhaps (who knows?) the first faint stirrings of our own ecumenical movement? It is a heady prospect, and worth further exploring. And who better to explore it than Bishop Jenkins, and – dare I suggest it – what better occasion for the exploring than the next Voltaire Memorial Lecture?

HERE'S TO THE NEXT WORLD

I HAD MORE to say on the subject of the after-life when, in 1989, I was resident columnist of a magazine for the elderly called Trust.

I suppose that the concept of the after-life first gained credence hundreds of years ago when life for most people was nasty, brutish and short, and religions, to hold their grip on people, promised by way of compensation a marvellous future after death. The idea caught on generally and became one of the pillars of the Christian faith. Indeed, I remember at school that a large proportion of the hymns we sang were about the joys of the after-life, sitting on God's right hand with Cherubim and Seraphim (whoever they might be) in attendance, angels twanging harps and heavenly Muzak being broadcast twenty-four hours a day. We didn't believe a word of it of course and on the whole felt sorry for those, mostly older people, who did.

I mention all this because, being now an older person myself, I have recently found myself asking the same question: Is there an after-life?

I know, or think I know, what actuates the question. Firstly, if death is nothing but oblivion, what has my life's work, such as it is, been for? Would I not have done better, if there is nothing to come, to have led a more lotus-like existence, so that now I could look back with satisfaction on all the multifarious pleasures the world had given me? And secondly, if death really is the end, that must mean that I am never going to see again or have any sort of contact with those I have known and loved, my wife and sisters, children and grandchildren, friends from school, shipmates in the war, colleagues in radio and television. I find the prospect of not seeing them again bleak; and if I allow myself to believe that

I *may* see them, I am filled with what the poet Wordsworth called 'that blessed mood in which the heavy and the weary weight of all this unintelligible world is lightened'.

Yet when one stops to consider the matter a little further, one realizes one is indulging in wishful thinking. Because I want my consciousness in some form to continue, I convince myself that it will continue. The wish is father to the thought – who ever believed in an after-life against their better judgement? Analyse what one means by life after death, apply reason to it, and the concept begins to crumble. Asked for his view on the matter, the great English philosopher and non-believer Bertrand Russell said that he could not imagine a future state without a mind to comprehend it. And when one looks, as some of us have done, at the handful of yellow ashes which is all that remains of a human being after cremation, one has to ask oneself where the mind is to be found in all of that. Believers say that it is the spirit or soul that will provide perception, but that is a fancy that seems to me to be wholly unconvincing.

There is another factor which I think militates towards a belief in survival, and that is that we do not want to think that we are so insignificant that there is not some part of ourselves thought to be worth preserving. The fact of the matter is that in the general scheme of things we are insignificant. Asked what he thought the meaning of life was, the writer Somerset Maugham said that life had no meaning. Had he been less of a cynic, he might have added, except whatever meaning we choose to give it ourselves. What is left of us when we depart is, if we are lucky, our children, perhaps also some small thing we have created like a book or a garden, also whatever memory of ourselves lives on in the minds of others.

The more I considered the matter, the more I knew that I was letting my emotions outrun my reason; and so I turned, as I have done before, to the account given in 1776 by James Boswell, the biographer of Dr Johnson, of the last hours of his fellow Scot, the great philosopher David Hume.

'I found him alone, a-dying, in a reclining posture in his drawing-room. He was lean, ghastly and quite of an earthy appearance. He was drest in a suit of grey cloth with white metal buttons and a scratch wig.

'I asked him if it was not possible that there might be a future state. He answered that it was a most unreasonable fancy that he should exist for ever. The immortality, if it were at all, must be general; that a great proportion of the human race has hardly any intellectual qualities; that a great proportion dies in infancy before being possessed of reason, yet all these must be immortal; that a porter who gets drunk by ten o'clock with gin must be immortal; that the trash of every age must be preserved and that a new universe must be created to contain such infinite numbers.

'I asked him if the thought of Annihilation gave him any uneasiness. He said, not the least. "Well," said I, "Mr Hume, I hope to triumph over you when I meet you in a future state; and remember you are not to pretend that you was joking with all this infidelity." "No, no," said he, "but I shall have been there so long before you come that it will be nothing new".'

Hume's good humour and levity was such, said Boswell, that there was no solemnity in the scene; and death for the time did not seem dismal.

Nor, any longer, does it seem so to me.

SHORT STORIES

SHORT STORIES

I ONCE TRIED my hand at a novel, but it was unpublishable. However, while at Oxford after the war, and for a year or two afterwards, I did publish a number of short stories. What follows is a selection of them plus a couple I have written more recently.

ANNE AMONG THE BULRUSHES

CHARLES' DECISION TO put his sister Anne among the lilies in the lily-pond had been inspired by the second chapter of the Book of Exodus, and was to be the means of regaining his parents' affection.

Charles was seven, Anne three months. Ever since her birth Charles had felt that the attention of his parents, once exclusively his, was being more and more transferred to her. Many little incidents combined to make him feel that he was being pushed slowly into the background. He had been used to climbing into his mother's bed each morning to discuss plans for the day; this had been vetoed for some obscure adult reason connected with Anne's feeding arrangements. He had been forbidden the use of the schoolroom where he kept his railway engines and Kliptiko set because Anne required it for a day nursery. When people came to tea it was Anne, not he, who was brought forward for their entertainment. Worst of all – and for this he could find no plausible reason – his mother had handed over the task of after-lunch reading to Nanny.

She was the second of Charles' Nannies and he did not like her. Old Nanny had recently been dispatched to her sister-in-law at Stoke Poges, it having been feared that her frail arms might not support Anne's weight. Charles missed her. She had been like some vast and ever-open bosom into which he might at any time fly. She did not scold, lecture or lose her temper.

New Nanny was of sterner stuff. She was young and smart and thought she knew all the answers. Whenever an opportunity offered (and they were frequent) she moralized on the wickedness of the world in general and Charles' ways in particular. The wickedness of the world, she said, was due to people not heeding the Word of God, and Charles' wickedness could be attributed to the same reason. What Charles' wickedness was he did not know, nor were its character and extent told to him. But the Word of God was.

Charles was immensely bored by the Word of God. With his mother he had voyaged to the fairy lands of Lilliput and Brobdignag, defended the stockade on Treasure Island, walked the golden sands in search of Friday. The Word of God kept him on *terra firma*. It did more than that. It undermined his faith in God's goodness.

Nanny opened the book and Charles, lying on the sofa by the window, let his eyes roam into the garden. Copley the gardener was trimming the yew hedge. Seeing Copley reminded Charles of The Game, another of his activities kyboshed by the insatiable Anne. In The Game the garden was the territory of the Blackface Indians with whom Charles, who was a Cherokee, was at mortal enmity. The Blackface were few in number and usually turned out to be Copley, whom Charles would stalk with great care and then attack, shrieking the Cherokee war-cry. Now The Game had been forbidden on the grounds that it might wake Anne, who spent each afternoon in a pram at the bottom of the garden.

'And there went a man of the House of Levi and took to wife a daughter of Levi.'

Oh, dear, thought Charles, the same old stuff. He turned back to the window. Copley was nearing the end of the yew hedge. A Cherokee posted round the corner would be in a fine position to smash in his skull with a tomahawk.

'And the woman conceived and bore him a son.'

'What's conceived?' said Charles casually. He knew that by asking questions at decent intervals he was not so likely to be pulled up for inattention.

'Never you mind!' said Nanny, and went on quickly, 'and when she saw that he was a goodly child she hid him three months.'

'Why?'

'If you'd been listening to what I read yesterday, you'd know why. Because the king of Egypt was a very cruel man and had ordered all the little Israelite boys to be killed.'

'Why?'

'Because he was afraid that when they grew up, they'd kill him.'

This was an admirable explanation and one that Charles wholly understood. It was what the Blackface and Cherokees felt about each other. He relapsed into a satisfied silence.

'And when she could no longer hide him, she took for him an ark of bulrushes and daubed it with pitch and put the child therein: and she put it in the flags by the river's brink.'

Charles sat up and concentrated all his attention. This seemed a most astonishing thing to do, a most astonishing and romantic thing. Prams and cots were the proper place for babies, not bulrushes in the river. He asked no more questions but kept his eyes steadfastly on the Book until the story was finished.

'Now you must go out and play,' said Nanny, closing the Book.

'That was a lovely story,' said Charles fervently, 'will you read it again tomorrow?'

'We'll see.'

Charles wandered out into the garden, the picture of the baby lying in the rushes still vivid in his mind. Nanny had said that its name was Moses and Charles was aware that Moses was Important – almost as Important as God. For someone like that to have spent their early days lying among the rushes in the river seemed to Charles a very strange and wonderful thing. He concluded that it was a miracle. He was not quite sure what a miracle was but thought it an event that everybody knew had happened but nobody seriously believed.

He wandered past Copley who was putting the finishing touches to the yew-hedge, past the pram where Anne was sleeping off her latest feed and came to the edge of the lily-pond. The lilies were of a larger and more beautiful variety than is usually found in England, having been imported from South America by Charles' grandfather. The cups were as large as fruit bowls and each protected a delicate white flower. Sitting on the bank and looking at them, Charles conceived his idea. If he were to bring the news to his parents that Anne was in the lily-pond, their gratitude to him as her saviour would be immense. His mother would continue her readings of *Treasure Island*; he would be allowed an occasional visit to the schoolroom; he might even be able to resume The Game. Later there might be questions as to how Anne came to be in the lily-pond in the first place: if so he would say it was a miracle.

Charles walked back to the pram and peered in. Anne was asleep, her left thumb wedged firmly in the corner of her mouth. He looked cautiously round. Copley had finished the yew-hedge and gone to the vegetable garden. There was no-one else about. He pushed his hands underneath Anne's clothes and very tenderly lifted her upwards and towards him. It required all the strength of his small arms to raise her clear of the pram without overbalancing. He crooked one arm round her shoulder, the other beneath her legs, and made his way back to the lily-pond.

The biggest and best-formed of the lilies lay a little way out from the bank. The depth of water was not more than two or three feet, but neither was Charles' height. He eventually found a suitable lily a foot or so from the bank. Squatting on the edge and leaning precariously forward he gently lowered Anne into the cup. The lily quivered slightly and took the weight. Anne still slept. Flushed with excitement, Charles ran up to the house.

'Mummy!' he shouted, 'where are you?'

Nanny appeared, ogre-like, at the top of the stairs.

'I thought I told you to go out and play. You're a very bad boy.'

'Where's Mummy?'

'In the sitting-room and not to be disturbed. Now you run along and play. Waking up the household at this time of the afternoon! Disgraceful!'

Charles burst into the sitting-room. His mother was at her desk, his father deep in a chair.

'Baby's in the bulrushes!' said Charles, leaping up and down, 'you must come and see!'

His mother went on writing. After a moment she said, 'Oughtn't you to be out in the garden now?'

'But *baby's in the bulrushes*!'

'What is the child talking about?'

'Lord knows,' said his father.

'You must come and see,' said Charles, 'quickly!'

'We'd better,' said his father, 'there'll be no peace till we do.'

Charles led the way out of the house, prancing about in an ecstasy of joy. His parents followed more leisurely, their talk already on other things. He made a detour through the rose-garden to avoid passing the pram. His mother stopped to examine the roses.

'Oh, do hurry!' said Charles, now a little anxious as to how Anne was faring, 'do hurry, please!'

'He's very excited about something,' said his mother.

'Something to surprise us, I expect,' said his father, 'some sort of a game!'

Charles went on ahead, turned the corner leading to the lily-pond and stopped dead. Anne had vanished. There was not a sign of her anywhere. He ran up and down the bank searching. He couldn't remember exactly where he had left her. Was it on this lily? No, further up than that. This one? No, too near the bank. This one, then, tilted slightly and with a broken petal. Yes, that was the one, he was certain.

Charles sank down on the grass, his mind numb with fear. He felt himself to be in the presence of some great and terrible disaster, something altogether beyond his understanding. He tried not to think about it. The tears trickled down his cheeks and his body shook with sobs. He clasped his hands and prayed for a miracle, a real miracle, prayed to God to bring Anne back. The tears flowed unchecked and the sobbing became a sort of wailing like that of an old sick dog. The sound brought his parents hurrying from the rose-garden.

'What is it then?' said his mother picking him up.

He had a sudden desperate longing for his mother's protection and threw his arms round her neck.

'Baby's gone!' he shrieked, 'baby's gone!'

'There, there,' said his mother comfortingly.

Charles was already exhausted by the excess of grief and the sobbing gradually dwindled. His mother put him down.

'There now,' she said, kneeling and drying his eyes, 'that's better, isn't it?'

'Baby's gone,' repeated Charles flatly.

'You are an old silly, aren't you?' said his mother. She added brightly, 'I'll tell you what we'll do. We'll go and see a *real* baby. Shall we?'

She took one small hand in hers, his father the other. Together the three of them, Charles silent now, his parents already discussing some new problem of the world outside, turned their backs on the lily-pond and walked slowly towards the empty pram.

New Statesman and Nation (1948)

THE UNCHARTED

THE CRUISER *APOLLO* was beating north-eastwards across the South Atlantic to Bermuda. Her navigating officer, Lieutenant-Commander Kemp, sat in the privacy of his charthouse, pondering on his chances of promotion. His seniority as Lieutenant-Commander was seven and a half years and his last chance of promotion to Commander would come with the publication of the half-yearly lists on 1 July. It was now the beginning of May.

Kemp was regarded by those who knew him as a conscientious officer of high integrity and character; and it was common knowledge in the *Apollo* that ill luck rather than bad management had so far robbed him of his laurels. As captain of a small vessel during the early days of the war, he had ordered the depth charges to be made ready. The order had been misunderstood with the result that an enemy submarine which ought to have been sunk had got clean away. A Court of Inquiry had remarked tartly that Kemp should have satisfied himself that the order had been carried out; and later Their Lordships had expressed Their views in a letter that showed neither charm nor charity. It had been a small blemish on an otherwise chaste record; but not one (as Kemp himself knew) which an officer seeking promotion could afford.

As he lay stretched on the narrow charthouse bunk, tuning his body to the motion of the ship, listening to the waves slapping monotonously against the sides, he let his mind dwell for a moment on the new horizons that the rank of Commander would open to him. The financial aspect was the most appealing. He would be assured of at least another seven years' employment on a higher scale of pay, and (even if he were not promoted to Captain) an increased pension at the end of them. This thought pleased him less for his own sake than for his wife's. He had married Laura, the beautiful daughter of an impecunious Somerset clergyman, ten years previously. She had borne him four sons, Jonathan, Nicholas, Peter and Paul. Peter and Paul were twins and had been mistakes. They were mistakes he could ill afford. It was not easy to support a large family on Lieutenant-Commander's pay. Neither he nor his wife had any private income and the new naval allowances had been largely offset by the risen cost of living. He thought of his home, the upper floors of a gaunt Victorian villa in the back streets of Southsea. On Commander's pay he might be able to exchange it for a cottage at West Meon or a small house at Havant. There were many small luxuries he might afford on Commander's pay: a full-time Nanny for the boys; a new dress for Laura. If only something would happen between now and 1 July whereby he might prove his mettle to Their Lordships. But what?

His thoughts were interrupted by a knock at the door.

'Navigating officer, sir?'

'Yes.'

'Captain would like to see you, sir. And he says to bring a chart of the area.'

Kemp hoisted himself out of his bunk, selected a chart marked East Coast of South America, and went below.

'You sent for me, sir?'

'Ah, Pilot.'

The captain was at his table and motioned Kemp to a chair beside him with a precise authoritative gesture.

'The Chief has just reported an engine-room defect that will take twenty-four hours to repair. We can do the job ourselves but the ship must be stopped. He'd rather not risk waiting till we get to Bermuda. Nor would I. I've suggested that we run in to some sheltered bay along the coast, adjusting course and speed so as to arrive about noon tomorrow. What do you think about that?'

'Sounds all right, sir.'

'Let's have a look at the chart. Now then, where are we?'

They plunged into a technical discussion concerning knots and distances.

'This looks a good place,' said the captain, stubbing the chart with his forefinger. 'Patagan Bay.'

'Or how about Belos Bay, sir, a bit further to the no'thward?'

'There's not much between them. Yes, Belos if you like. We'll pop in there. You might make the necessary arrangements.'

On his way back to the charthouse, Kemp called up to the bridge, 'I haven't had a decent sight for two days. You might see that I'm called for morning stars.'

Three thousand miles away, Laura was saying goodnight to Jonathan and Nicholas.

'Mummy, where's Daddy now?' asked Jonathan.

'Oh, a long way away.'

'Are there pirates where Daddy is?'

'I expect so.'

'Miss Pumpton says that parts of the Chinese coast are infested by pirates.'

'Does she?'

'And Perkins, that's a boy in my class, says he's going to be a pirate.'

'I'm going to be a Chinese pirate now,' said Nicholas, gripping his pillow.

'Oh, no, you're not.' She smoothed the pillow and pushed him gently back into bed. Nicholas giggled. 'Now, you're both to go to sleep.' She tucked in the sheets, kissed them and turned off the light. The telephone began ringing.

'How long has Daddy been away, Mummy?'

'A long time, my darling.'

'As long as a year?'

'Almost. Now no more talking.'

'I wish he'd come back.'

She closed the door.

'Hullo?'

'Laura?'

'Hubert! I wasn't expecting you.'

'I think I can get down tonight.'

'Oh, darling, that's wonderful.'

'By the 7.40. How's the rabbit-warren?'

'Stormy and rather piratical. How's Grub Street?'

'Sordid but fairly profitable. They wanted me to go to the Yemen tomorrow. To cover a war.'

'And you're not going?'

'No, the Arabs or whoever live there have postponed it. I've got the day off so I shall spend it with you instead.'

'That will be nice. I'll go and make up your bed.'

'Will you?'

'*Really*, Hubert . . . '

Dawn came creeping early over the black waters, stamping the waves with streaks of silver, twisting them into huge ingots of molten lead. Boy (2nd Class) Briggs, bridge messenger of the morning watch, did not notice it. This was his first trip at sea and for the last three days he had been continuously and thoroughly sick. He had not thought it possible that anyone could be so sick. He squatted wretchedly in a pool of water at the back of the bridge, his eyes half-closed, his lips opening and shutting in a desperate effort to keep down the rising nausea.

'Messenger!'

The voice of the officer of the watch came to him remotely from out of the pit. He croaked a reply.

'Go down and tell Mr Kemp we've some beautiful stars for him but if he doesn't come soon they'll fly away.'

Briggs could make no sort of sense of this but he was too exhausted to question it. It seemed to be all part of the nightmare existence he was experiencing. The only officer he knew was Kent, the doctor, who had given him some large yellow pills in the mistaken belief they would cure his sea-sickness. He presumed the message was for him. He stumbled down the bridge ladder and set off aft.

The doctor was a heavy sleeper. During the war he had become accustomed to being woken at all hours of the night to unravel obscure and often meaningless ciphers. Three years of peacetime service had not dulled him to the appreciation of eight hours' uninterrupted sleep. He was woken by a noise like a steam-hammer and opened his eyes to see the sodden figure of Boy Briggs beating a vigorous tattoo on his washstand.

'Waddyerwant?'

'Got a message.'

'Wassisay?'

'The officer says the stars are beautiful. They'll fly away soon he says.'

The doctor gripped his blankets angrily and turned over.

'Oh bugger off,' he said, 'bugger off for Christ's sake.'

But Boy Briggs, who knew when the contents of his stomach had reached a point of no return, had already buggered. He reached the quarter-deck rails just in time.

When Kemp arrived on the bridge, it was daylight.

'Oh, well,' he said philosophically, 'we'll have to rely on dead reckoning.'

The ship glided into the narrow channel between the two headlands. The wind had died away and the clouds were separating to reveal patches of blue sky. On the fo'c'sle were the anchor-party. They stood about like so many sheep waiting for a signal, their eyes fastened on the bridge where the captain, shepherd-like, held aloft his absurd little anchor-flag. Kemp, crouched behind the pelorus, was fixing the ship's position by compass bearings. Other officers, attracted to the bridge by the curiosity of a new anchorage, stood quietly at the back of the compass platform and commented on the scenery about them. The coast was rocky and, except for a few bare hillocks near the shore, featureless. There was no sign of human or animal habitation.

'If this is Belos Bay,' said the captain, 'I don't think I like it. Are you ready to anchor, Pilot?'

But Kemp was not ready. Until a few moments ago he had been feeling hugely pleased with himself. Without the help of sun or stars he had brought the ship across 700 miles of ocean to the threshold of her destination; nor in doing so had he had to deviate one degree from his estimated course. It was a feat of which he was justly proud. Now it seemed he was to be beaten on the post. He had taken as landmarks for his bearings the two headlands on either beam and a small bun-like hill at the head of the bay. Instead of the three bearings neatly intersecting, there had appeared on the chart a 'cocked hat' triangle of alarming proportions. Kemp could not make it out.

'If we don't anchor soon, Mr Kemp, we'll be on the bloody beach.'

associates. All afternoon and evening the little party applied themselves to his commands, now taking soundings from the whaler, now measuring angles and distances from the shore. And when the sun had set behind the mountains inland and dusk had come swiftly upon the anchorage, they had not returned to the ship.

'Mummy?'
  'Yes, darling.'
  'Who's that man?'
  'A friend of Mummy's.'
  'Why's he always here?'
  'Because it's nice for Mummy to have someone to talk to when Daddy's away.'
  'But you can talk to me and Nicholas and Peter and Paul.'
  'He's a grown-up, darling. It's different, you see . . . '
  'Do you like him?'
  'Very much.'
  'Does Daddy like him?'
  'Daddy doesn't know him.'
  'Would Daddy like him if he did know him?'
  'I don't know really. Yes, I expect so.'
  'Mummy, where's Daddy now?'
  'Oh, my darling, what a lot of questions.'
  'Where do you think he is? What do you think he's doing? *This minute.*'
  'I think he's in a beautiful town in South America where there are fountains playing in the square, having lots to eat and drink and being looked after by hundreds of lovely ladies.'

They returned to the ship at midnight. One midshipman and two ratings were suffering from sunburn and had to be taken away to the sick-bay; the others were in lesser stages of exhaustion. A relief crew was detailed for duty in the morning. Several officers volunteered to take Kemp's place but he would not hear of it. This was his property and he wanted no trespassers. Also he remembered Drake having said that it was not the beginning but the continuing of the same until it was finished that yielded the true glory.

633

Early in the morning he embarked in the whaler with his new crew. They were away three hours, returned to the ship for breakfast and a fresh midshipman and were out again half an hour later. All morning they struggled in the heat to have the survey completed before the time of sailing. Their efforts were finally successful. Twenty minutes before the sea dutymen were piped to their stations, the last distance had been measured, the last sounding taken.

Late in the afternoon, when the anchorage was a blue smudge astern and the *Apollo* was ploughing northwards through the long easy swell, Kemp emerged from the charthouse and walked briskly to the captain's cabin.

'Well, Pilot, how did it go?'

'Very well, sir. The Admiralty chart is definitely at fault. Would you like to see?'

He spread the survey and the chart side by side on the table.

'Now, sir, you can see that while the shape of the bay is almost identically the same in both, there are several noticeable differences. For instance the two headlands on the Admiralty chart are much longer than on mine – than in fact they really are. Then the Admiralty chart gives the height of the hill at the head of the bay as forty-three feet. I make it only thirty-one. Then again the depths of water vary considerably. Taking it all round, the Admiralty depths are about two feet more than mine.'

'Did you have a good leadsman?'

'Robinson, sir. I'd trust him anywhere.'

'Can you think of any explanation?'

'Yes, sir. I've studied the East Coast of South America Pilot and there's definite evidence of land erosion in these parts. It's my view that owing to the action of the sea, the level of the coast is gradually subsiding. This would account for the shortened length of the headlands and the reduced height of the hill. As the soil is eaten away by the sea, it forms a deposit on the ocean-bed, and that would explain the difference in soundings. I noticed there was mud on the anchor this afternoon.'

'Well, that's very interesting, Pilot. You seem to have done a good job.'

'Thank you, sir.'

'We must whip this in to the Hydrographer. He'll be as pleased as Punch.'

'Yes, sir.'

There was a moment's pause and then the captain said, 'I tell you what. I don't want to submit this in the name of the ship because it's not something I ordered. You did this off your own bat and any credit that's going should be yours. You submit a fair copy of the survey officially to me and I'll send it on to the Hydrographer with a covering letter. How's that?'

'That's very good of you, sir.'

'Good, that's settled, then.' He added, rather shyly, 'I hope it gets to Their Lordships before the July promotions.'

'Hubert?'

'Yes, love.'

'Such a sweet letter from Kempy this morning.'

'What's he say?'

'I can't quite make it out. He's done something frightfully clever in some bay in Brazil. He says it'll make all the difference to his promotion.'

'Good for him!'

'If everything goes all right, he says, we'll be able to move out of this house. That will be a blessing.'

'Yes.'

'He is sweet, you know. He's so tremendously enthusiastic about whatever he's doing. I do love the old boy. It's funny when you think how little we've got in common. But I really do.'

'Well, of course.'

'I love you both, you see. In quite different ways. I want to protect him.'

'And me?'

'You!' she said suddenly. 'I want to eat you.'

Later Nicholas, who had been playing pirates unobserved in the corner, said to Jonathan, 'Mummy wants to eat that man. I heard her say so.'

It was a warm afternoon at the beginning of June. The

Apollo lay at anchor in a large bay on the west coast of Newfoundland. Beneath the awnings, the ship slept. Most of the officers were ashore, some on a fishing expedition up Harry's River, others to visit the papermills at Corner Brook. Kemp was not with them. He lay in a deck-chair on the quarter-deck, his eyes half closed, a novel of Bartimeus lying face downwards on his lap. Nearly a month had elapsed since the fair copy of the survey had been despatched by air from Bermuda, and the Hydrographer's reply was expected daily. In the ship the survey had been much praised. The captain had said, 'That's a fine job of work you've done there, Pilot.' The doctor, who didn't know the difference between El Greco and Van Gogh, had called it a work of art. Even Boy Briggs, who had glimpsed it on a message to the charthouse, had described it to his messmates as smashing. Everyone agreed that it represented Kemp's last bid for promotion and because they liked him and wished him well, they were as keen about its outcome as he. Kemp himself was quietly optimistic. He believed with an inner certainty that his promotion was now secure. He wished that Laura could be with him when the news came through. He thought of all the drudgery and discomfort she had borne with such patience during the past ten years. He was immensely grateful to her. Before taking up his new appointment he would be given two or three weeks' leave. He thought that if he could find someone to look after the boys, he would take Laura away for a holiday. He wondered where she would choose to go and made a mental list of several likely places. He speculated on the nature of his appointment and hoped that it would be to a shore base in England. Which one? Lost in a reverie of pleasing thoughts, Kemp let the volume of Bartimeus fall from his lap and closed his eyes in sleep.

Later he woke to hear the sound of aeroplane engines and a voice saying, 'Tell the officer of the watch that the mail plane's landing now.'

'Hubert?'

'Yes.'

'Something rather awful has happened.'

'What?'

'I don't know quite how to tell you.'

'Well, I won't bite.'

'I'm what's commonly called "in trouble".'

'Oh, dear. Are you quite certain?'

'Yes. I've known it was possible for some time. I hoped it might be a false alarm. I didn't want to worry you.'

'I am sorry.'

'Oh, it's not your fault. It's mine. I'm sometimes rather careless. It happened once before.'

'Well, don't worry. Leave it all to me.'

'I so terribly want to have it. It's yours, you see. Do you think that's awful of me?'

'I think it's very sweet and flattering to me. But practically speaking, it's not possible.'

'No, I suppose so.'

He took her hand and said very gently, 'Promise not to worry and do what I say. I don't know about these things, but there's a man in the office who I think does. Promise to leave it to me.'

'Yes, all right, Hubert. You are sweet. Thank God Kempy's where he is. I think it would kill me if he knew.'

Boy Briggs marched confidently along the upper deck, climbed the two ladders to the lower bridge and knocked at the charthouse door.

'Navigating Officer, sir?'

'Yes.'

'Captain would like to see you right away, sir.'

The captain was standing in the centre of his cabin, holding a sheet of paper in his hand. When Kemp said, 'You sent for me, sir,' he averted his eyes and said nothing. There was a long pause. Kemp felt embarrassed. He did not know what was happening.

The captain said at last, 'I'm afraid I've got some bad news for you.' He added, 'It doesn't do me much good either.'

Kemp waited. There was another pause while the captain cleared his throat. Kemp saw that he was searching for words. He wanted to help but didn't know how to. Then the captain pushed the paper into Kemp's hands and said, 'You'd better read it yourself.'

Kemp took the paper. It was an airgraph despatch from the Admiralty. It said: 'To the Commanding Officer *Apollo* from Admiralty. Reference survey stated to be of Belos Bay prepared by Lieutenant-Commander Kemp and submitted through C.O. to Hydrographer of Navy. This survey is an accurate transcription of Patagan Bay which is nine miles to the southward of Belos Bay. Their Lordships have no option but to conclude that *Apollo* was in Patagan Bay and not Belos Bay as stated. They view a navigational error of such magnitude with the gravest concern. Lieutenant-Commander Kemp is to be relieved of his duties forthwith and returned to the United Kingdom for disposal. An early report is requested.'

Kemp flew home by Clipper from Botwood two days later. The same evening Hubert, on his way to interview the man who knew about things, was told by his editor that the war in the Yemen had started and that he had exactly one hour to pack his bags. That night both men were travelling eastwards at the rate of some 300 miles an hour, Kemp towards England and Laura, Hubert away from them. At a quarter to ten the next morning the situation was as follows. Kemp was in a telephone kiosk in Southampton trying to summon up the courage to break his news to Laura. Laura, after a sleepless night, was sitting by the telephone wondering why she hadn't heard from Hubert. And Hubert, not unmindful of what he had done and left undone, but believing that everything would work out all right in the end, was a remote speck over the blue Mediterranean.

Horizon (1948)

STILL WATERS

THIS STORY IS about murder. The trouble started when Bill Clements began paying regular visits to Ardnalty. Tich Fraser said it would be less lonely for Mary. Trouble does sometimes start that way.

Tich was managing director of a Glasgow shipbuilding firm which his family had controlled for several generations. Ardnalty had been theirs almost as long. It lay on the west coast of Inverness-shire between the South Morar hills and the sea and facing the islands of Rhum and Eigg. It had been built originally as a shooting lodge in the days when the Frasers' main residence had been a Victorian castle on the outskirts of Balloch. Tich had not been able to keep up both establishments. Soon after the Second World War he had sold the Balloch estate to the trustees of a lunatic asylum, acquiring in its place a small flat in Glasgow. Here he lived during the week, motoring to Ardnalty to join Mary and the children each weekend.

Tich had been married thirteen years, and during this time he had been happier than he ever remembered. As a young man he had suffered from a complex about his size. He had stopped growing at seventeen when he was five foot three, and during his childhood he had always been much smaller than his fellows. The insensibility of small boys to each other's defects is a commonplace, and at school Tich had endured agonies. The continued taunts of his classmates had led him to believe that he was a freak. Often he had sobbed himself to sleep, praying to God that he might wake up taller in the morning. When he had left school and gone into the firm he found that his deformity aroused no comment; but this did nothing to straiten the complex. The jibes of his schoolmates had been like knife wounds, but he much preferred them to the restraint of his

639

fellow workers who, too well bred to mock him to his face, undoubtedly made fun of him behind his back. He did not get rid of the complex until he met Mary. He had confided his fears in her and she, sympathetic and protective, had teased him out of them. Because he loved and trusted her, he had not resented it. She had insisted on calling him by his school nickname and in time this became as natural as if he had been Peter or John. In time the complex left him.

Bill Clements was a distant cousin of Mary and by profession a writer. He had already published one successful novel and had proposed himself to Ardnalty to complete a second. When Tich first saw him, he was astonished. He had never met a writer before and had an old-fashioned notion that as a race they were poor-looking creatures with too much hair and possibly a touch of TB. Bill Clements looked like a Rugger blue, and Tich learned later that he had been one. He was a huge man with a brow like a bull; and when in motion he lumbered rather than walked. In contrast to this, his voice, which Tich had expected to be full and rough, was gentle, almost womanly. Tich was afraid that Bill would embarrass him by discussing art and was delighted to find that he could talk on a wide range of subjects with a freshness and enthusiasm that was disarming. Another curious trait was his passion for fishing. Tich had supposed that an artistic man would despise so masculine a pastime. But whatever the weather and however far the fishing ground, Bill was always ready to accompany him. Once when they were caught in a storm on Loch Morar Bill confessed, quite casually, that he couldn't swim: his father had had some queer views about it when he was a boy and he hadn't learned since. Tich was appalled at having exposed him to such danger and suggested that in future he should fish from the bank. Bill laughed and said it would take more than that to keep him away from the fish. Altogether Tich found him an intriguing and complex character, and when it was time for him to go he pressed him to come again.

Bill came again. His first visit had been for ten days, but the next time he stayed a month. During the week he worked at his novel and at weekends went fishing with Tich. He and Tich became close friends. To Tich the world of art had always been a closed door, and because he had not had entrance, he had been apt to belittle it. The presence of a flesh-and-blood writer brought it within hailing distance. He told his colleagues in the shipyard with casual pride that he was entertaining 'a writer chap'; but he would not have admitted even to Mary that he considered Bill's friendship a privilege.

After this second visit Bill came to Ardnalty at intervals of two to three months, usually staying several weeks. It was not until the summer of the following year (that is about thirteen months after Bill had first come to Ardnalty) that Tich discovered that he and Mary were lovers.

It was a Sunday evening and Tich was shaving in the bathroom that separated his room from Mary's. There were no guests in the house, Bill having gone south a few weeks earlier to visit his publishers. Pressing a little too hard, Tich cut his chin. He opened the medicine chest for some cotton-wool, but there was none. He remembered that Mary often used it at her dressing-table, and went into her bedroom. The roll was not on the table and he supposed it was in the drawer. To prevent the blood spilling on the carpet he held his head upright and felt for the drawer handle with his free hand. In this unnatural position he misjudged the pressure and nearly pulled the drawer from its socket. He felt about for the cotton-wool. It did not seem to be there. He was about to take away his hand when his fingers touched a packet of papers. They were a bundle of letters and the top one began, 'My beautiful darling'. Tich recognized the handwriting immediately as Bill Clements'.

At first he was too shocked to do anything but stare incredulously at what he had found. His first reaction was that he had stumbled on something that did not concern him and he should replace the letters immediately. On reflection he decided that it concerned him very much and however unpleasant it was his duty to look further.

He did not have to look at more than two or three letters to confirm what he had feared. This discovery was horrifying enough, but even worse was the violence with which Bill had expressed himself. Tich did not know that men felt such things, far less revealed them. He was appalled. He could not believe what he read. He felt as if he wanted to be sick.

There was a step on the stair. Tich put back the letters and quickly closed the drawer. Mary came in.

'I've cut myself shaving,' he said.

'Oh, my poor lamb. I'll get you some cotton-wool.'

She opened the right-hand drawer, plucked a piece from the roll and gently dabbed the cut. Looking at her, Tich could not believe what his eyes had just told him.

Nor, sitting beside her at the dinner table, was he able to convince himself that he was not experiencing some frightful nightmare. He could not believe that this good gentle woman with whom he had lived for thirteen years, the mother of his children, was an adulteress. He was not a demonstrative man, but when during the past year he had taken occasion to consummate his union, Mary had not seemed to deny herself or him any pleasure. He could not reconcile this with what he knew. No decent woman could make love to more than one man: those who did were prostitutes.

At first his mood was of silent bewilderment – of half-believing his imagination was playing him false. Later, when he was alone in the smoking-room and could reject the truth no longer, he began to get angry. He felt the bile rising inside him and the blood surging in his head. He became consumed with anger. The rough seas of his emotions stayed at this pitch for some time and then, because he could not sustain them, they subsided, leaving behind an island of loneliness and self-pity. He had no secrets between Bill and Mary, yet they shared something that was denied to him. For the first time in ten years he became conscious again of his size. All the tortured fears and imaginings of his schooldays came crowding back. He was small and puny and insignificant. Bill was big and strong and manly, and that was why Mary had taken him as her lover. He was an outcast, a freak, and behind his back they were laughing at him.

He walked to the open window and stubbed his cigarette viciously on the stone sill. Outside on the lawn the rabbits were frisking round the rhododendron bushes. Beyond the lawn was the sea, gun-metal blue except for a narrow pathway of light where the water had caught the last rays of the sun going down behind the shoulder of Rhum. A great stillness had settled on the land. It was a time of sweet and profound melancholy, a part of the day which normally he enjoyed more than any other . . .

'You're very silent tonight, darling. Anything wrong?'

He looked up and saw her beside him.

'No,' he said, 'I was just thinking.'

'You're tired,' she said, 'come to bed.'

Later when he was in the bathroom he heard her say, 'You haven't forgotten that Bill's coming on Thursday?'

'Thursday,' he repeated flatly, 'no, of course.'

'Why don't you take a long weekend and motor him up?'

Tich thought for a moment.

'Yes,' he said, 'I'll do that.'

Tich imagined that once he and Bill and Mary were all together the problem would somehow resolve itself. Something would happen whereby it would be turned face upwards and they could then look at it and decide what was to be done. He did not look forward to this and had no idea how he would behave; but anything was preferable to this subterfuge; he would suffer anything to share the truth.

He met Bill at Central Station and his hand was clasped in the other's friendly grip.

'Nice to see you, Tich. How's everything?'

'Oh, fine,' said Tich, avoiding his eyes. 'How's the book?'

'Almost finished – thanks to Ardnalty. And I've already started on another. But don't let's talk about that. I want to hear about you and Mary and the children. And the fishing? How's that? Are the sea-trout running?'

During the long drive to Ardnalty – along Loch Lomond-side, across the great moor of Rannoch, down Glencoe into Ballachulish and across the ferry to Fort William – Bill kept up an incessant patter of talk. Tich was hugely disappointed that his manner and bearing were so normal. He had some-how expected that his new-found knowledge would at once enable him to detect peculiarities of behaviour to which ignorance had previously blinded him. Later reasoning told him that this was absurd and if Bill or Mary were to give themselves away, it would be when the three of them were together. But here again he was disappointed. When he went to bed he was forced to admit that the evening's conversation had been normal in every way. They had talked of the fishing, the children, Bill's book, the topics of the times. There had been no sense of strain, no false note. If Bill and Mary had exchanged any private message, Tich had missed it.

The rest of the weekend proved just as fruitless. On Friday the two men fished the river, on Saturday the loch. Mary and the children joined them for a picnic lunch on both days, but the trout were rising and they did not linger over the meal. Between tea and dinner Mary was with the children, and Bill worked at his book. Only in the evenings were they together. Tich kept his eyes open. He even took to leaving the room suddenly and then pressing his ear to the door. Nothing happened to confirm what he knew. He began to wonder whether his imagination had not deceived him and on Sunday evening when Mary was on the beach, he looked again in the drawer. As he had half-feared, the letters had gone. Now he was left with nothing tangible or knowable, nothing but an idea in his own mind. He left Ardnalty early on Monday morning, angry, frustrated, helpless.

The sun had risen high above the South Morar hills and beat down on the white walls of Ardnalty, on the narrow tarmac drive along which Tich had passed on his way to Glasgow two hours before. Mary usually had breakfast downstairs, but this morning it was brought to her in her room. Afterwards she stayed in bed, gazing out reflectively at the islands and the sea, listening to the cries of the seabirds, melancholy and remote, coming in through the open window. There was a group of figures by the water's edge and Mary recognized them as her children and their nurse. She lay looking at them for a long time with a set thoughtful face. Later she dressed and went down to the smoking-room where Bill was working at his novel. He got up as she came near him and leaned forwards to kiss her. Her body tautened and she held him off.

'What's the matter?'

'I don't know,' she said defensively.

'Something's happened?'

She hesitated. 'I think he suspects something.'

'Tich? What makes you think that?'

'He's been very strange this week – sort of detached and remote. I've seen him looking at us sometimes almost as if he were trying to catch us out.'

'You're imagining—'

'No, Bill. I know him too well. Something has happened to upset him. I wish I knew what.'

There was a slight pause, and then Bill said, 'Well, what do you want to do about it?'

She hesitated again. 'I don't know,' she said. 'I haven't thought it out yet.'

'I can think of something.'

'What?'

'Getting married.'

'Oh, Bill—'

'Well, why not? I'm as sick of this secrecy as you are. Why don't we bring it out into the open? Why don't you ask him for a divorce?'

'No, Bill. We've been into all that. Don't ask me again. Please.'

'But you don't love him. You love me.'

She put her hands on his, and said, 'Bill, darling, of course I love you, but that's not the point. I've been with Tich now for thirteen years and I've grown terribly used to him. He does need me, you know – in some ways much more than you – he's less self-sufficient. Then there are the children. They're more important than any of us. For their sake I could never make a final break. Do try and see that, darling.'

It was the old formula and it sounded stale and unconvincing even to her ears. This was the cue for Bill to shrug his shoulders and put away the pieces for another day. She knew, almost before he started to speak, that he had another move to play.

'No,' he said, 'I've seen your way long enough. Now it's time to listen to mine. I believe that when people fall in love like we have, then nothing else matters – *nothing*. If one's going to be happy in the end, one's got to be ruthless. Sooner or later something of this sort had to happen – we couldn't have gone on like that for ever. I'm sorry for Tich and it's bad luck on the children; but he'll get over it in time and children are very quick at adapting themselves to new situations—'

'Bill, you mustn't talk like that, you mustn't.' She was appalled at the enormity of her deception, at the dark web into which her weakness had taken her.

'Mustn't I?' He moved towards her, smiling, triumphant, and she felt herself enveloped in the huge arms.

'You're too violent, Bill.'

'About you, yes. I'd do anything for you. I think I'd do murder.'

Tich did not return to Ardnalty that weekend, excusing himself on the grounds of extra work in the yard. He was unable to concentrate on anything. The canker of jealousy was eating into him and as the days passed its poison slowly spread. During the day the routine of the shipyard kept him from brooding too deeply, but in the evenings, in the silence and loneliness of his flat, he gave himself up to the blackest thoughts. For a long time (and even when reason had cried out against it) he had clung to the straw of doubt; but the memory of the letters always obliged him to reject it. His tortured mind allowed him no sleep. As he lay stretched in the darkness, he imagined Bill and Mary lying at Ardnalty in each other's arms ('at this moment,' he said, each time he thought of it). He could not rid his mind of the image. It played perpetually before him, like a needle in the broken groove of a record. Often it was not until daylight that sleep came to break the hateful vision.

As the days went by the furnace in his brain hardened into a flame of hatred towards Bill Clements. While he had dissipated his emotions they had exhausted him; now that he had found an object in which to canalize them, he became possessed of a new strength. He gloried in his hatred for Clements: the act of hating filled him with a kind of obscene joy. He hated him for his virility of mind and body, his beguiling persuasiveness, his easy self-assurance; for all those attributes of character he wanted most and possessed least himself.

*

She knew that there remained one thing for her to do and that until and unless she did it, she would not be free of the web. It would be easier now, she thought: Tich's silence and the living falsehood of the last few days had determined that. She felt curiously irresponsible, almost as if her course of action was being determined by some force outside herself. She chose a moment towards the end of dinner.

'Bill?'

'Yes.'

'There's something I've got to tell you.'

He looked up, surprised.

'What?'

'I want you to go away.'

His face was a mirror of what she had imagined.

'What do you mean?'

She had come to the last hurdle. One clean swift leap and she would be free. She hesitated a second, then said in a rush of breath, 'You see, I'm not in love with you any more.'

There was a long pause. She knew that there was no answer to this, no counter-stroke: it had a finality it was impossible to dispute. Eventually Bill said, 'How long have you felt like this?'

'I don't know,' she said, 'you mustn't ask me to explain.'

There was another pause, and then Bill said, 'But you don't love *him*!'

'Oh, yes. I don't think I realized how much until this week – until I thought I was going to lose him. I've always loved him, I suppose. It's to do with the children and – the past and – oh, lots of things.'

Bill said nothing. He sat playing with the stem of his glass, his eyes following the movements of his fingers. There was a long silence, broken only by the far-off beat of the waves washing the shore. Once Mary said, 'Can't you say something?' But Bill did not answer. She wanted to go over to him and stroke his hair and ask forgiveness; but she knew that she had made him untouchable, a stranger in a familiar land.

In a little while Bill lifted up his head and looked at her. His eyes seemed to be focused somewhere through and beyond her, and his face was expressionless. She met his gaze, watching him with the caution of an animal, not daring by speech

647

or movement to disturb the atmosphere he had created.

Still he said nothing and as the minutes went by Mary found the tension intolerable. She had been ready for tears, abuse, even blows: caught in this vacuum of silence she was helpless. She held on tight to her chair and tried to strangle the rising hysteria: she knew that unless something happened soon, it must break loose.

Then Bill got up. He was holding the glass in his hand and she thought he was going to throw it at her. She braced herself to meet it. He put the glass carefully on the table, turned and walked slowly towards the door. He turned the handle with his back towards her and then, before he went out, he looked at her once more. When Mary met his eyes she thought she would faint. There was a look on his face she had never seen before – an almost sub-human revelation of anger, frustration, hate, terrifying in its crudity. It only lasted a second and then Bill went out, slamming the door behind him.

Mary heard his footsteps dying away along the passage. There was silence then except for the sea sucking at the shingle. She did not move from her chair.

In the early hours of the next morning, Tich, having finished the half-bottle of whisky with which he now started each night, came to a great decision. He was going to kill Bill Clements.

This decision was the logical outcome of his various stages of thought. He had hated Clements because it had been intolerable not to have some object on which to pinpoint his emotions. He had decided to kill him so as to stop hating him. The pain and exhaustion of hating had also become intolerable. Once he had made up his mind on this, all his frustrated energy was released in a flood of pure destructive thought. To destroy was to create and creation was what his tired mind craved.

At first he was too carried away by the boldness and originality of the idea to consider its practical aspects. Exactly *how* was he going to kill Bill Clements, and *where*? There were plenty of deserted places near Ardnalty where he might strike him down unobserved, but how was he to get rid of his huge body? The problem seemed insoluble until Tich remembered that Clements couldn't swim. Then he thought of the Little Lochan.

The Little Lochan lay fifteen hundred feet up in the South Morar hills. Tich had not been there since he was a boy, but he remembered it well. It was quite small, about the size of a village duck pond, and at one end there was a rowan tree: the memory of the scarlet berries standing out against the dull background of the moor remained vividly in Tich's mind. But the curious thing about the Little Lochan was this. Whereas the depth of water in most of the hill lochs was not more than three or four feet, *the bottom of the Little Lochan had never been plumbed.* Local opinion said it was an extinct volcanic crater which had been flooded by underground springs; but nobody knew its history for certain. Terrible things might happen there to a man who couldn't swim; and the deep waters that witnessed them would bear their secrets well.

Tich left Glasgow on the Friday afternoon. The road was almost empty, and he drove very fast. He felt composed and confident, and for the first time in ten days his brain was clear. He arrived at Ardnalty in time for dinner, and ordered a bottle of champagne; to damp suspicion he said he had just brought off a contract with the Argentine Government.

During the meal, Mary leant across the table, and said: 'Bill's got to go on Monday. Isn't it sad?'

'Oh, don't do that,' said Tich. 'Stay on for a bit. We like having you here.'

'It's very good of you. But I must go.'

'Stuck with the book?'

'Yes, in a way.'

'That's too bad. We shall miss you. But come back soon.'

There was a longish pause, and then Tich said: 'You wouldn't like to take a day off tomorrow?'

'I'd always like to. Why?'

'There's a little loch up in the hills I've been meaning to make an expedition to for some time. There are supposed to be some big fish there. Two- and three-pounders. I haven't been there since I was a boy.'

Bill took his time in answering. 'Yes,' he said, 'I'd like to do that. Very much.'

Later, when Tich had gone to put away the car, Mary said, 'Bill, I wish you'd gone when I asked. It was crazy to stay.'

'Why?'

'It may sound silly, but I've got an awful feeling that something's going to happen tomorrow. I can't explain. It's just something I feel in my bones.'

She had expected him to belittle her fears, but all he said was, 'I think it should be an interesting day.'

They breakfasted early and set out with their rods across the dark, boggy moor that separated the house from the mountain's foot. It was a clear sweet summer morning, cool and windless; between the islands and the coast the sea was a milky mirror. They crossed the railway line and the high wire fence guarding it and began climbing the hill. The way was steep and the ground soft and spongy, and for a long time they did not speak. Three-quarters of the way up the hill they stopped for a rest and water. Below them the contours of the Mallaig peninsula were laid out like a relief map. Beyond the bog they could see the slate roof and chimneys of Ardnalty rising above its ring of protecting pines. To the northwards the ribbon of railway skirted the western shore of Loch Morar before crossing the river close to the famous white sands. The bunch of islands in the loch, amorphous and shapeless from the shore, stood out clearly and separately. The sea islands stood out clearly too, Eigg like some gigantic aircraft-carrier at anchor, Rhum sinister and silent as always. On the horizon was the purple smudge of Barra.

Tich wiped the sweat from his forehead and said, 'Grand view, isn't it?' —and then without waiting for Bill to reply, 'How do you feel?'

'Oh, all right. How much farther is the lochan?'

'We're about halfway.'

They picked up their rods and went on. Tich made slower progress, stopping every few minutes to study the map. He had not been up in these parts for a long time and he wanted to be certain of not missing the way. He was conscious of the burly presence beside him and he found the thought of his own weakness a little frightening. If his plans went wrong, if he made some slip and found himself at Bill's mercy, there would be little hope. Once when he had stopped to look at the map, some instinct made him glance swiftly over his shoulder. Bill was standing on a ledge of rock looking at him, and he thought he caught a look of inexpressible hatred in his eyes. It only lasted a second and when they went on, Tich put it down to a flight of imagination. But from now on, he became increasingly aware of the shadow behind him.

They crested the summit of the plateau and came out upon a great undulating wilderness of bog and moor and hill. Tich consulted the map and struck off inland. Soon they were passing a group of small lochs where the trout were rising freely.

'This looks all right,' called Bill. 'Why don't we stop here?'

'Only tiddlers there,' said Tich, not looking round or stopping, 'three-pounders where we're going.'

He led the way over a bare hump-backed hill, blackened in parts where the heather had been burnt clean, down into a hollow basin where three lochs were linked by a narrow burn and over the shoulder the other side. They had climbed some twelve or thirteen hundred feet and the air was much cooler; and they had penetrated so far inland that the surrounding hills hid them from the edge of the plateau and the country below. They were contained in a little world of their own. Tich was reminded of the days when he had come here as a small boy on solitary fishing expeditions, and how he had imagined that some fearful monster would emerge from its lair to attack him. The same fear of evil persisted now, only now it was different; now the monster was beside him and he was going to attack and destroy it. He looked at the map, and said: 'It ought to be just round that bend.'

He advanced slowly, cautiously, half-fearing that his sense of direction had failed him and he would see nothing but bog and brown heather. The shoulder of the hill drew past and a glint of water caught his eye. Three more steps and the lochan was in view.

Bill came up, and said: 'Is this it?'

'Yes,' said Tich, looking down at the dark peaty water. 'This is it. This is the Little Lochan.'

'It's little enough. You're not going to tell me there are fish in there!'

'There were when I was a boy. That was over twenty years ago, but there's no reason why it should have changed. They were big ones too. It's very deep, you see, and there's plenty—' He broke of involuntarily. 'That's funny.'

'What?'

'Well, there used to be a rowan tree up at that end. I wonder what happened to it.'

'I expect it got blown down in a gale. Anything can happen in twenty years.'

'Yes,' said Tich. He was satisfied with this simple explanation, but disappointed, for the rowan tree had been a sort of symbol. 'Yes, I suppose so.'

They began putting up their rods. Neither spoke, almost as though each was aware of some unnatural tension. When Tich was threading his line through the rings, something made him again glance momentarily at Bill. Again he caught the undisguised look of malice. He became suddenly very frightened. Did Bill know that he knew? He had been too wrapped up in the chrysalis of his own thoughts to have considered it. Had Bill some evil intention towards him? Had he accepted the invitation to do the very thing he intended to do himself? He felt quite weak with fear. There must be no delay. He must act at once.

'What are you going to put on?' said Bill.

'Put on?' His hands were trembling and he found it difficult to concentrate. 'Oh, I don't know. Peter Ross or something.'

They tied on casts and flies and Bill said: 'Where shall we begin?'

'Over there,' said Tich, pointing to a small rocky ledge that fell several feet sheer to the water. 'It's a good deep gut. I'll come and show you.'

They walked round the edge of the lochan and came to the ledge. Tich waited until Bill was standing on the brink and then took up a position close behind him.

'I should cast out right in the middle,' said Tich.

Bill let out his line and cast. Tich took a step or two nearer. He was shaking all over. The great moment for which he had planned had arrived. He looked down on the still black water and thought suddenly, 'How easy! One push and it will all be over. He'll struggle a little, and then when he gets tired he'll go down – deep, deep, down. Perhaps later he'll come up again; but whether he does or not is no matter. I shall say that he slipped off the bank, and everyone in the world will believe me.' He raised his eyes to the great bull-like figure above him and was filled with an inexpressible joy at the thought that he was about to destroy it. Slowly he lifted his arms. At this moment Bill turned round.

Events moved quickly. Bill saw the attitude of Tich's arms and the expression on his face and started moving towards him. At the same moment Tich reached forward and pushed. Bill was caught off his balance and started falling backwards. He grabbed at Tich, but Tich was too quick for him. The rod flew out of Bill's hands and he landed in the water with a gigantic splash.

Tich did not wait to see what happened. Uttering a queer little hysterical laugh, he turned his back on the lochan and began running downhill. The echo of the splash was ringing in his ears and he wanted to get as far away from it as possible. He stumbled clumsily over the rough heather for forty or fifty yards. Then, raising his eyes, he saw something that made his heart stand still and the breath stick in his throat. Two or three hundred yards ahead of and slightly below him was another small lochan. At the far end, vivid and brilliant in the sunlight, a splash of colour against the sombre backcloth of the moor, were the scarlet berries of a rowan tree.

Tich sank down to the ground. For a moment he was too terrified to move. He remained crouched in the frozen attitude of a cornered animal, of a child who imagines a burglar in its room. Then as the seconds went by and nothing occurred to break the terrible silence, he lifted his head uphill.

'No!' he screamed, clawing protectively at the heather; 'no, no, no!'

The monstrous sodden figure of Bill Clements, his hands outstretched, his eyes blazing murder, was wading out of the shallow water and across the heather towards him.

English Story (1949)

GRACE ARROWHEAD

This was based on a true story which I have described in my autobiography.

IT WAS NOT until Nanny came to live with my mother after the war, and at the age of eighty-five broke her leg, that I really found out anything about her as a person.

For longer than I can remember, she had been a part of the background of the Oxfordshire manor house where my family have lived for three hundred years (and where, after my mother dies, they will live no more). As a young girl of twenty-two, she had helped to bring my mother into the world; half a century later she had attended my father on his way out of it. Between these two events, she had been nanny to my sister and me and any number of cousins, and when, as sometimes happened, there was no member of our large and rambling family in need of her attentions, she gave devoted service elsewhere. But it was always understood that we had first call on her, and whenever there was a departure from the normal family routine – when there was a daughter or a niece to be married, a baby to be born, or an invalid to be nursed – whenever there was a domestic crisis and we were left suddenly servantless, then Nanny was sent for and established herself in her old quarters in what had once been the nursery, later became the schoolroom, and at length by common consent was called the sewing room.

Looking back over the years at my attitude towards Nanny when I was a boy, I realize how very little I knew about her. Children have a way of accepting unquestioningly those in whose care they grow up, nor do they picture them as existing in any other environment. All I can clearly remember of Nanny's physical appearance during my childhood is that she had large brown spaniel-like eyes, an expression of almost Christlike mildness, and a pronounced stoop. For a long time, I did not know her real name or where she lived when she was not with us. Other nannies who were inflicted on us from time to time were called according to their surnames, like Nanny Burkett or Nanny Smith, but Nanny unqualified could signify only one person. I might never have known her name during my entire childhood if, one Christmas when Nanny was not with us, my mother had not given me a present to wrap up and mail to her. Nanny's name, Grace Arrowhead, struck me when I first heard it as being somehow unlikely and rather indelicate. However, it could not have much worried me, for I soon forgot it and had to ask my mother again the following Christmas. Nanny's permanent address was care of a sister in Muswell Hill, but as these two words conveyed as little meaning to me then as they do now, I soon forgot them, too.

My childhood memories of Nanny are entirely happy ones. She was, I think, one of the kindest and most generous people I have ever met. Her whole life seemed to be dedicated to my interest and well-being. I have been told that as a small boy I was very troublesome. If so, I did not trouble Nanny, or if I did, she never showed it. She was in this respect quite unlike our other nannies, whom, even at this remove, I cannot recall without a sense of loathing. Because of my troublesomeness (I sometimes bit them while they were bathing me), they never lasted long. Their most hateful fault was a smug superiority. They never tired of moralizing, of bossing, of putting one in the wrong. They said things like, 'Look sharp!' and 'Mark my words!' and when I made a frightful face they said, 'One day the wind will change and your face will stay like that.' Nanny said none of these things, nor – and this is more than I can say of anyone I knew intimately as a child – do I remember a single time when she lost her temper.

Her characteristic phrases were all gentle and affectionate. She always called me 'dear' or 'dear boy'. (Other nannies called me 'Master John'.) If she wanted me to eat something particularly dreary and unappetizing, she would say, 'It's nice and nourishing, dear' or 'It's good for the blood.' I do not think she said this as a ruse but as a genuine statement of faith. Her nearest approach to a show of authority was the phrase 'Make haste,' but this was used only on occasions that would have driven any other nanny demented.

I think I am most grateful to her for the times she took care of me when I was ill, confined to bed with chicken-pox or measles or another of those tiresome children's diseases. 'The boy must lie quiet, Madam, and take plenty of fluids,' she would tell my mother, and then she would carry out her own recommendation faithfully, appearing at the bedside with great muslin-covered jugs of fresh lemonade. Sometimes, to while away the long hours, she helped me with a jigsaw puzzle or a Meccano house, and once, during the mumps, we built a large Spanish ship. While engaged in these tasks, she would hum tunelessly.

In 1939, when I was twenty, I went away to the war. I had not seen Nanny for a year or two before that, and I did not see her again until nine or ten years later, when I came home from London, where I was then living, for a few days before one of my periodic visits abroad and found Nanny back in her old quarters in the sewing room. Although there was no apparent reason for her presence, it did not strike me as the least odd that she should be there; it seemed, in fact, the most natural thing in the world. My mother explained that Nanny's sister in Muswell Hill had died and Nanny was without a home. It would have made no difference to me what the reason was. Nanny was so much a part of my experience that as I had accepted her as a child, so I accepted her now. After her long absence, during which I had reached an age of awareness, I might have been expected to approach her with fresh eyes. But she seemed no different in manner or appearance from what she had been at any other period of my life.

The day before I was due to go abroad was cold and wintry. There had been an early fall of snow, and patches of it still lay here and there. In the afternoon, I went for a long walk, and the sky grew dark as I was returning to the house. My mother was out on one of those numerous errands for the welfare of the community that have filled so much of her life, and I was looking forward to tea and crumpets with

Nanny in the sewing room. As I neared the house, a figure came running down the steps to meet me. It was Mrs Davies, the housekeeper.

'Oh, Mr John, sir, there's been a terrible accident,' she said. 'It's poor Miss Arrowhead, she's fallen downstairs and damaged herself something proper. I've laid her in the drawing room, sir, and the district nurse is with her now.'

I went into the house and met the district nurse coming out of the drawing room. She was a plump, competent-looking woman.

'I'm afraid she's fractured her leg,' she said. 'It doesn't seem to be a bad break, but with these old people you never can tell. She's suffering from very bad shock, too. I've given her an injection to ease the pain, but the sooner we can get her into hospital, the better.'

I showed the district nurse to the telephone, and while she was ringing up the cottage hospital, I went into the drawing room. Nanny was lying on one of the big chintz-covered sofas, her head resting on a pile of red and green silk cushions. I sat down on a chair beside her. She was obviously in great pain. Every now and then, she said 'Oh dear!' or 'Oh, oh, oh!' and moved her right arm to and fro in an instinctive gesture to relieve the pain. Mrs Davies held her other hand and murmured words of sympathy. There did not seem much else to do.

I was profoundly shocked. It is a distressing thing to see anyone in pain, especially when it is somebody old and inarticulate and loved. But in addition to this there was a kind of terrible grotesqueness about Nanny's suffering. For thirty years, I had accepted her not as a being with hopes and desires and emotions of her own but as a source of love and goodness and gentleness; not as one capable of suffering herself but as one who relieved the suffering of others. Now this façade, which unconsciously I had built up over the years, was destroyed in an instant, and behind it was revealed an old, tired, sick woman. Never in all the time I had known her had I been conscious of any social distinction between us. We had never been rich, or Nanny, I think, very poor; but it seemed to me then, looking at her frail body lying on the bright chintz of the sofa and the gaily coloured cushions that emphasized the drabness of her dress, that there was an enormous gulf between us. Nanny's suffering was a monstrous thing, and, as though I was responsible for it, I felt terribly ashamed.

By the time the ambulance arrived, the injection had begun to take effect and Nanny lay on the sofa with her eyes closed. Two men came in carrying a stretcher. The district nurse talked to them for a minute, and then they lifted Nanny on to the stretcher and began strapping her leg up, so that she could not move it. They worked with a cool, unemotional precision. It was easy to tell oneself that their detachment was the result of long experience, but the difference between their attitude towards Nanny and mine troubled me. While they were working, Mrs Davies, who had gone up to Nanny's bedroom on the district nurse's instructions, reappeared with a little bundle of her things – a nightdress, bedroom slippers, a hairbrush, and a washing bag. I had never seen these articles before and I found the sight of them curiously distressing. It was almost as if I had stumbled accidentally on some great friend's love letters.

When the ambulance men had strapped Nanny up, they carried her outside and lifted her into the ambulance. At that moment, I realized that the district nurse was not going to go with her, that her job had finished where the ambulance men's had begun. I could not bear the thought of these cool, efficient men taking Nanny away like a corpse to the undertaker's, and I asked if I might go too.

'Wouldn't it be better if I did, sir?' Mrs Davies asked.

It probably would have been, but I was still obsessed with the idea that I had a personal responsibility in the matter. However ineffectual my presence, I felt that by going with Nanny in this dark hour I would be making some small return for everything she had done for me.

It is about eight miles from the house to the cottage hospital, a journey that normally takes twenty minutes, but the roads were still icy after the snow and we could only drive very slowly. One of the ambulance men was at the wheel; the other sat in the back beside me, on a wooden bench opposite Nanny. There was a full moon shining, so brightly that its rays penetrated the tiny smoked windowpane above Nanny and suffused the knees of the ambulance man and myself with a violet glow. Nanny lay back in the shadows.

We had been driving for a little over half an hour, and were, I suppose, about half a mile from the hospital, when there was a slight stirring opposite me. In the semi-darkness, it was difficult to see anything, but I could tell that Nanny had raised herself up on her elbows. She did not speak or make any sound, but the whole atmosphere of the ambulance suddenly became charged with urgency. The silence lasted for some seconds, and then Nanny said, 'What's this?' In the unnaturalness of this phrase there was something extra-ordinarily foreboding. The ambulance man leaned forward and said, 'It's all right, lady, you just lie back and rest. We're taking you along to the hospital and everything's going to be all right.' Nanny did not move or say anything for several moments, and then she said quietly, 'You can't do anything to me.'

There was another silence then, worse than before. The ambulance man felt it, too; I could tell by the way his body tensed, ready to act at any moment. 'I know what you're after,' said Nanny. 'You want money. Well, you won't get it. I've hidden it, see.' This was followed by a terrible cry, halfway between a laugh and a scream. It died down quickly, and then Nanny said, with the shock of an exploding bomb, 'You buggers!'

The ambulance man leaned forward again. He took hold of Nanny's arm in an effort to coax her to lie back on the stretcher. It was a well-meant but mistaken gesture. The touch of another's hand on her arm gave her mania an external reality. With the quick, instinctive movement of one trapped, she sat upright, so that the top of her head was caught by the rays of the moon and her grey wisps of hair glowed violet, and began thrashing her arms up and down. 'Don't you touch me, you bastard!' she screamed. 'You keep your filthy hands off.' Then the whole ambulance was drenched in a flow of invective and abuse. Oath followed oath, obscenity followed obscenity. Like the steady discharge from a burst sewer pipe the stream gushed: memories from a childhood that froze the imagination; things observed and experienced, remembered and forgotten, in nearly a century of living. It continued unceasing while she was being taken out of the ambulance and carried through the doors of the hospital. In the entrance hall, she caught sight of a group of nurses. 'You're after my money, you whores,' she screamed, 'like those other buggers! I've hidden it and you'll never find it. Never, never, never!' And again there was the awful half-hysterical, half-anguished cry.

I stood in the doorway, appalled, and watched her being carried away down a long corridor and listened to the oaths and obscenities and shouts until they were at last swallowed up in the dark interior of the hospital. A woman standing near me took the little bundle of nightdress and hairbrush and washing things that I had brought in with me and said casually, 'We'll let you know how she is in the morning.'

I left England the next day and was abroad for several months. From time to time, I had news of Nanny in letters from my mother. The doctors were astonished at her rapid progress; they had feared that such a shock at her age would be fatal. In March, my mother told me Nanny had been discharged from the hospital and was back at home. In none of her letters did my mother mention any peculiarity of behaviour.

I arrived back in England in the spring and went down to Oxfordshire one boisterous April afternoon when the daffodils in the park were bending under the gusts of a cold north wind. Mrs Davies met me at the front door and said that my mother had gone to the Women's Institute at Chipping Norton, but Nanny was waiting to give me tea in the sewing room.

At the sewing-room door, I paused. This was a critical moment. If Nanny knew what I knew, if she remembered, or some busybody at the hospital had told her what had happened that night, then our thirty-year relationship would be ended and she would become a stranger to me for ever; but if, as I prayed, she was ignorant of it, then I would be able to accept her as I always had, and she would remain as unchangeable a part of my life as the trees in the park or the mellow stonework of the house.

I turned the door handle and went in. Nanny was sitting by the window, her back towards me, busy with needle and thread. It was an attitude I had seen her in a thousand times. It could have been yesterday, or tomorrow, or a decade ago. The sewing room was the same, familiar, secure, changeless: the white enamelled shelves with their rows of nursery books and groups of toy animals; the tall three-sided fireguard with its gleaming brass top; the Singer sewing machine squatting on the table where it had stood ever since I could remember; the rocking horse, unused for a generation and with paint peeling from its flanks, standing dunce-like in the corner; tea waiting on the table.

'Hallo, Nanny,' I said.

She turned in her chair, took a moment to recognize me, and said, 'Is it you, dear boy? Nice to have you home again.' She got up and came towards me.

'How are you, Nanny? Is your leg really better?'

'Oh, I'm all right, dear. Never better. But how are you? Been abroad, I hear. You are looking well. All that sunshine would do you good.'

I looked into her eyes with a boldness I did not feel, looked for the black shadow of recognition, for the evil thing I prayed I might not see. But there was nothing, only the same kindliness and gentleness and love that I had known and cherished through the years.

'Come and sit down, dear boy,' said Nanny. 'I've got some crumpets for your tea. You always did like crumpets, didn't you?'

The New Yorker (1950)

A LITTLE TOUCH OF HALI

(IN THE NIGHT)

IT WAS THE evening of the day that Diana arrived back from her skiing holiday in Italy.

'Darling,' she said, as we were finishing supper, 'what have you been eating while I have been away?'

'Eating?' I said. 'I don't know. Why?'

'Well,' she said, 'I hate to say this, but you have just a teeny-weeny—'

'Yes.'

'Touch of the hali.'

'Hali?'

' 'tosis.'

'Oh, *no*,' I said, 'how *awful*!'

'It's only a touch. But I thought you ought to know.'

'When did you first notice it?'

'This morning at the airport.'

'Why didn't you say then?'

'I thought it might go. I didn't want to fuss you.'

'Dear God! How long have we been married?'

'Twenty years, isn't it?'

'And is this the first time?'

'Absolutely.'

'I wonder what's caused it.'

'Teeth, do you think?'

'Or tummy. I've heard some people say it can be the tummy.'

'Why don't you check up?'

'Of course,' I said, 'right away.'

Next morning I rang the dentist and asked for an early appointment.

'I'm sorry, Mr Blunt,' the receptionist said, 'but we're fully booked for the next two weeks.'

'Oh, I must see him before then,' I said, 'it's urgent.'

'Are you in pain?'

'Not exactly.'

'Has a filling come out?'

Perhaps it had; perhaps that was the trouble.

'I think so,' I said.

I heard her leafing through the engagement book.

'I've just had a cancellation for four o'clock on Tuesday. Could you come then?'

Tuesday was three days off. 'Is that the earliest?' I said.

'Yes, it is, Mr Blunt.' Did I notice a touch of exasperation in her voice? 'We'll expect you then. Goodbye.'

Next day I was lunching with my wine-merchant, an old friend. I'd have put him off but his office didn't know where he was. Halfway through the meal he said, 'Charles, are you feeling all right?'

'Fine,' I muttered, 'why?'

'Well, generally when we meet, you talk nineteen to the dozen, so that I hardly ever get a word in. Today you've been mumbling monosyllables into that handkerchief as though you'd got lock-jaw, and you've never once looked me in the face.'

'I'm sorry,' I said.

'It's so unlike you. Do you know what I'd say if it was anyone but you. I'd say you'd got a drop of the old hali and were trying to cover it up.'

He gave a huge belly laugh, clearly expecting me to join in. I did my best, but it died a quick death on the handkerchief.

That night I said to Diana, 'Still there?'

'Breathe,' she said.

I did.

'Just a touch.'

At the dentist's I sat in the chair and took a swill of the pink mouth-wash. I really believed my troubles would soon be over. The dentist was wearing his plastic visor, and I wondered whether this was protection against his patient's hali or for them against his own.

'Lost a filling, have you?' he said.

'I'm not sure,' I said, 'but something's happened. My wife tells me I have bad breath.'

663

He didn't seem much interested. 'Open your mouth,' he said, 'and we'll have a good look round.' He made my mouth sound like an art gallery. Presently he said, 'You've got quite a lot of tartar. Maybe that's what's doing it. I'll clean it up.'

He chipped away at the tartar with a miniature spade, then covered a brush with toothpaste, inserted it into the drill and whisked it round. It was ticklish on the gums.

'There,' he said, 'let's hope that will do the trick.'

At home that evening I opened my mouth at Diana. She smiled and said, 'Not a trace. Just dentist's toothpaste. I believe he's done it.'

'Oh, hurray,' I said and hugged her tight. 'We'll go out to dinner to celebrate.'

We went to Vecchio's. The bill was fifty pounds and I didn't grudge a penny. But when we were preparing for bed Diana said,

'Darling?'

'Yes.'

'I'm afraid it's come back.'

Next day I told my troubles to the family doctor.

'Do you suffer at all from flatulence?' he said.

It's not a word I use myself, so I wasn't too sure of his drift.

'Belching and farting, you mean?' I said.

He blanched. 'Yes.'

'No.'

'Get on the couch, will you?' he said, 'and lift up your shirt.' I did, and he went over my tummy like a baker kneading dough.

'Sore anywhere?' he asked.

'No.'

When I had dressed, he said, 'Well, I don't quite know what to make of it. You seem healthy enough and you say your teeth are in good order. It could be some temporary gastric upset, in which case it'll pass. Get yourself some Listerine mouthwash, and if it hasn't cleared up in a month, come and see me again.'

But it didn't clear up, or rather when it did, it was only briefly. As the days passed I became increasingly self-conscious and miserable. Determined not to inflict my infirmity on others (for having been on the receiving end several times in my life I knew how grim it could be), I refused all invitations to lunch or dinner, developed a habit of speaking out of the corner of my mouth, and spent long hours alone, reading or looking at the telly.

My sex-life suffered too. Normally Diana and I would make love once or twice a week, but now the thought of blasting her with the fumes made me totally inhibited. She was wonderfully understanding about it, yet the feeling I was letting her down increased my sense of inadequacy.

'Oh, Charles,' she said, 'don't be silly. As if that really mattered.'

Another worry was that Diana was the only person in a position to tell me the state of play, and when she went away for a day or two to visit her sick mother, I had no-one to turn to. It would have made all the difference if our children had been at home, but Simon was spending a year in Australia before going to university, and Kate was looking after a diplomat's children in Washington. Sometimes in the evenings and early mornings, which Diana said was the worst time, I would blow into my cupped hands and then sniff, as I had once seen a badly afflicted boy at school do; but it told me nothing.

I discovered the cause accidentally. Coming home from the office one evening, I found a note from Diana on the hall table saying her mother had had a stroke and been taken to hospital. She was leaving at once to join her, and would ring me later.

I had a couple of drinks, cooked and ate some scrambled eggs, then wandered into the little room where we keep the television set. There didn't seem to be anything worth watching, and I was looking idly round the room when my eye lit on Diana's pen, lying opened on her desk, and next to it her cheque-book and a neat pile of bills. I assumed she must have been about to write out the cheques when news of her mother came. Then I noticed, half-tucked into one of the pigeon-holes, a letter in her own hand.

Curiosity got the better of me, and I pulled it out and started reading. It began: 'My own darling Guiseppe.' It went on to say how much she had been missing her darling Guiseppe, how he filled her thoughts night and day, how she could not wait until she was in his arms again.

Then I turned the page and read this:

'You ask me, darling, if I have been really faithful to you, as I promised I would, and the answer is, Yes, I have. You say, how is it possible for me to be faithful when I have such a demanding and energetic husband. All I can tell you is *I have*. As to *how*, that must remain my little secret until we next meet. And I hope, my love, that will be very, very soon.'

Later that evening Diana rang up from the hospital.

'Good news,' she said, 'Mummy's on the mend.'

'Splendid,' I said, 'and I've got good news too.'

'Oh?' she said. She sounded genuinely interested. 'What is it?'

'My hali's cured,' I said.

There was a noticeable pause, and then Diana said, 'Oh, I am glad. But, well—'

'How do I know?'

'Yes.'

'Ah,' I said, 'that must remain my little secret. Until we next meet.'

And in the long silence that followed I added, 'And I hope, my love, that will be very, very soon.'

Punch (1980)

THE GREENING OF LORD BILSON

A Political Fantasy of the Thatcher Years

At Victoria station Lord Bilson found himself a seat in a first-class open carriage of an early evening train to the south coast. He was on his way to the Conservative Party's annual seaside conference. As president of the local Conservative Association for the constituency in which he and his forebears had lived for generations, he had attended these annual outings for the past eighteen years. He did not go in order to speak; rather as a social occasion, to entertain his own delegation, meet old friends (some of which, when he first went, included members of the cabinet) and enjoy the sea air.

But this time it was going to be different. This time he was going to speak, and on a motion that was critical of the government's record and policies. When he first decided on it, he was astonished by his temerity; a shy man, he disliked public speaking, and his rare contributions to debates in the Lords were on things he knew about like the rotation of crops and fish farming. He realized that what he was going to say would be construed by some as gross disloyalty. Equally he knew that he had to say it. And when he had said it (and he had told no-one of this) he would announce publicly his resignation as constituency party president.

There were many reasons that had driven him to this step, but the main one (and he had been glad to see in the papers that it was shared by two former party stalwarts, Lords Alport and Rawlinson) was that the philosophy and principles of the Conservative Party and government of today were not those of yesterday. Then, it seemed to him, the men and women running the government were motivated by nothing more ambitious than a desire to serve the public good.

Today's ministers, in contrast, he saw as business managers obsessed by the profit motive. A green light shone for all – and there were many – keen to make a fast buck, but there was little comfort or joy for others. It was this philosophy that had led to the mania for privatization and the upheavals in education, the health service, the law and broadcasting, culminating (as Lord Bilson saw it) in the absurd proposals to denationalize such basic commodities as electricity and water.

But it was the calibre of the people running the show that depressed Bilson most. Whatever else you might say against old-timers like Butler and Macmillan, Home and Hailsham, they were men of recognizable stamp who respected their opponents even when they disagreed with them, who would never have dreamt of saying, as their successors did, that they were out to destroy socialism for ever. They had believed, as Disraeli had, that Britain was one nation: the present lot had succeeded in making it two nations, the haves and the have nots. Bilson had never known the country more divided.

There were a few of the old guard left, like Howe and Younger, but it was the grey men who predominated, the Clarkes and Fowlers and Bakers and Moores who, with their undistinguished looks and nondescript voices, seemed almost interchangeable. There were others to whom Bilson took a more positive dislike, such as the too smooth Parkinson, the polecat Tebbit, the abrasive Mellor.

Yet in the end it was not the acolytes that riled Bilson most, but the high priestess herself. Having suffered from a bossy mother, he had learned to give women with the same attributes a wide berth. Asked his opinion of her when she was elected leader of the opposition, he said, 'One sometimes sees women of that sort bearing down on one at cocktail parties, and that's the moment to head for the door.'

What she was like privately Bilson had no idea, though friends who had met her reported her as being charming and considerate. It was the public image that irritated him. Almost everything about her seemed phoney, from the carefully modulated diction which in ten years had undergone a variety of changes to the *haut monde* wardrobe and hats which latterly had seemed to him more suited to a society wedding than that of a working Prime Minister.

Equally phoney, he thought, were the kites she flew from time to time about her concern for the sick, the poor and the lonely, sentiments all belied by her and her government's policies. However solicitous she might be for the welfare of those she knew, reflected Bilson, it was clear to him that so far as the sick, the poor and the lonely *en masse* were concerned, they were beyond her comprehending; and her efforts to improve on her negative image by visiting the bedsides of survivors from national disasters like that of the Zeebrugge ferry sinking and the M1 air crash, and later in well-advertised mourning attending the memorial services of those who had succumbed, were to Lord Bilson deeply offensive.

After ten years of her premiership Bilson was uncertain which aspect of her he minded most: her condescending arrogance to other European leaders, her hectoring, sergeant-major style of answering at Prime Minister's question time, the pseudo-intimacy with which she tried to seduce television interviewers, her increasing and absurd use of the royal 'we'.

He had heard people say that whatever one might think of her personally, she would go down in history as one of Britain's great Prime Ministers. He believed it to be untrue. What was true, he reflected, was that she was a living embodiment of Lord Acton's dictum that while all power tends to corrupt, absolute power corrupts absolutely.

None of this of course would find a billet in Lord Bilson's forthcoming speech, though it was all part of the motivation that had inspired it. Looking out of the window as the train sped through the outer London suburbs and observing row upon row of dreary, functional houses, Lord Bilson reflected with regret that few of their occupants felt neutral about their Prime Minister: either they worshipped her this side of idolatry or, like himself, they loathed the very sight and sound of her.

He reached up to the luggage rack to bring down the briefcase containing his speech when a strange thing happened: there was the sound of a dull thud a long way off, and in an instant Lord Bilson found himself being propelled through the air and down the length of the carriage. He passed out soon after and when he came to, he found himself lying among the wreckage of the carriage, blood trickling down his cheek and his left foot pinned under the remains of a lavatory door which, he noted, was marked ENGAGED.

For a long time he lay still, fearing that any movement on his part might bring more of the carriage down on top of him, trying to make sense of what had happened, listening to the moans of a woman nearby. Then a face appeared and a rough voice said, 'How are you then, matey? Now don't you fret and we'll soon have you out of here.' Presently another face appeared and a softer voice said, 'Just so you know what's happening, I'm going to give you an injection in your left leg.' Then he passed out again.

When he next opened his eyes he saw he was in bed in a hospital ward and that it was night. A voice said, 'Well, you've had a good long sleep,' and he looked up at a smiling nurse. 'How are you feeling now?'

'Not too bad,' he said, and he was aware that his speech was slurred. 'Wassa damage?'

'Your left foot is broken,' she said, 'which is why you've got this cage at the bottom of the bed. And you've got a nasty bump on your head.'

He raised his hand to feel a turban-like bandage. Then he remembered the crash.

'Everyone else all right?' he asked.

'One or two weren't as lucky as you,' she said.

He spent the rest of that night and the following day drifting in and out of consciousness, being given sips of water and once some thin soup, twice receiving pain-killing injections.

By the following morning he felt much better and was able to sit up and enjoy a light breakfast of a boiled egg and tea and bread and butter. While eating, he remembered the speech he had been going to make at the conference that very afternoon and the gesture of resignation that was to follow it. Now fate had intervened to prevent it: perhaps that was what fate had intended.

About an hour later there was a kind of commotion in the ward with sisters and nurses scurrying to and fro, and food and medicine trolleys being moved hurriedly out of the way. Bilson assumed the arrival of some grand surgeon with a posse of students. Then two young men in dark suits walked the length of the ward, looked out of the window at the end, walked back again. Lord Bilson's nurse said, 'You're going to have a visitor.'

He looked up and saw a little party of people entering the ward. In the lead were the hospital matron and the ward sister and between them was no, it couldn't be, but yes it was, there was no mistaking it, the coiffed head, the dangling handbag and the forward, duck-like waddle of the Prime Minister.

Before his transfixed gaze his worst nightmare was coming true: she was bearing down on him as he had always feared, and there was absolutely no escaping her. With open mouth he watched her inexorable progress towards him. When it seemed she was almost on top of him, she sat down on a chair proffered by the nurse.

'I am much grieved, Lord Bilson,' she said, 'that we should meet for the first time in such unhappy *circumstances*.' (a word she pronounced, he noticed, with a hard 'a'.) 'But I bring you greetings from all your colleagues and many, many friends at our conference. We were all so *very* sorry to hear what had happened, and I myself was *deeply* disappointed to be deprived of hearing the excellent speech that I'm told you had been going to make this afternoon. We all hope and pray that you will get better very, very soon.'

But Lord Bilson was unable to reply. Fate had again intervened. Head on chest and eyes closed, he had fainted clean away.

'I'm afraid,' said the nurse, 'that your visit has been rather too much of a shock for him.'

'I do understand,' said the Prime Minister, already rising and about to move on to the next supine figure. 'But when he comes round, nurse, tell him what I said, won't you? Tell Lord Bilson that in Britain today *we need* people like him.'

Guardian (1989)

A SELECTION OF BIOGRAPHIES AND AUTOBIOGRAPHIES FROM CORGI AND BLACK SWAN

THE PRICES SHOWN BELOW WERE CORRECT AT THE TIME OF GOING TO PRESS. HOWEVER TRANSWORLD PUBLISHERS RESERVE THE RIGHT TO SHOW NEW RETAIL PRICES ON COVERS WHICH MAY DIFFER FROM THOSE PREVIOUSLY ADVERTISED IN THE TEXT OR ELSEWHERE.

☐ 99065 5   **THE PAST IS MYSELF**   *Christabel Bielenberg* £3.95

☐ 99472 3   **THE REIGN AND ABDICATION OF EDWARD VIII**
  Michael Bloch £5.99

☐ 13818 5   **INSIDE THE BRITISH ARMY**   *Antony Beevor* £6.99

☐ 99422 7   **DAPHNE: A PORTRAIT OF DAPHNE DU MAURIER**
  Judith Cook £5.99

☐ 13766 9   **STOLEN YEARS: BEFORE AND AFTER GUILDFORD**   *Paul Hill* £4.99

☐ 13311 6   **MOSSAD**   *Ronald Payne* £4.99

☐ 99353 0   **MAXWELL: A PORTRAIT OF POWER**
  Peter Thompson and Anthony Delano £4.99

☐ 13452 X   **THE DAY THE LAUGHTER STOPPED**
  David Yallop £5.99

All Corgi/Bantam Books are available at your bookshop or newsagent, or can be ordered from the following address:
Corgi/Bantam Books
Cash Sales Department
P.O. Box 11, Falmouth, Cornwall TR10 9EN

UK and B.F.P.O. customers please send a cheque or postal order (no currency) and allow £1.00 for postage and packing for the first book plus 50p for the second book and 30p for each additional book to a maximum charge of £3.00 (7 books plus).

Overseas customers, including Eire, please allow £2.00 for postage and packing for the first book plus £1.00 for the second book and 50p for each subsequent title ordered.

NAME (Block letters) ....

ADDRESS ....

....